To the
POINT

Why Do You Need This New Edition?

The requirements, strategies, and tools for college writing assignments have changed in many ways since the last edition of *To the Point* published, so make sure you're up to date! If you're still wondering why you should buy this new edition, here are a few more great reasons:

❶ A new unit that explores the connections among Americans' passion for SUVs, our dependence on foreign oil, terrorism, environmental impacts, and road safety will give you **information you need to support your opinions with reasons and evidence**.

❷ A new unit on campus violence that asks you to think about guns on campus, institutions' mental health care services, and individuals' responsibilities offers you critical and **relevant arguments to use for response in your own writing**.

❸ A new unit on globalization that discusses the spread of American culture, the comparative weakening of American innovation, and the impacts of globalization on a small Mexican town shows the breadth of **strategies you can use when writing your own arguments**.

❹ New readings on Craig's List, YouTube, illegal music downloading, and Spider-Man 3 offer samples of **how to analyze contemporary culture critically**.

❺ A thoroughly revised Chapter 1 will help you distinguish between fact and opinion, analyze the structure of an argument, **use words that cue or signal different arguments**, and learn multiple argument strategies that work for different purposes.

❻ A brand new chapter on literary analysis offers samples of different types of literary arguments as well as **guidelines that you can use in your own writing for analyzing works of literature and film**.

❼ A new unit on stem cell research raises some issues that aren't often part of the stem cell research debate (such as how cells are used in fertility clinics), showing you **how to find a new and unusual topic within a widely-debated issue**.

❽ A unit on Wal-Mart explores how the store's policies on wages, benefits, and prices have an impact on its employees, customers, and the American economy, showing you how to link causes to effects and **convince your readers of the significance of your argument**.

❾ A new appendix on Avoiding Plagiarism provides concrete suggestions for quoting, summarizing, and paraphrasing to give you **the information you need to avoid unintentionally plagiarizing**.

To the
POINT

Reading
and Writing
Short Arguments

Second Edition

GILBERT H. MULLER
**The City University of New York
LaGuardia**

HARVEY S. WIENER
**The City University of New York
LaGuardia**

PEARSON
Longman

New York   San Francisco   Boston
London   Toronto   Sydney   Tokyo   Singapore   Madrid
Mexico City   Munich   Paris   Cape Town   Hong Kong   Montreal

Acquisitions Editor: Lauren A. Finn
Marketing Manager: Sandra McGuire
Senior Supplements Editor: Donna Campion
Managing Editor: Valerie Zaborski
Production Manager: Ellen MacElree
Project Coordination, and Electronic Page Makeup: Nesbitt Graphics, Inc.
Cover Design Manager/Covr Designer: Nancy Danahy
Cover Image: © Jeffrey Coolidge/Riser/Getty Images, Inc.
Photo Researcher: Anita Dickhuth
Senior Manufacturing Buyer: Roy Pickering
Printer and Binder: Courier Westford
Cover Printer: Coral Graphic Services

For permission to use copyrighted material, grateful acknowledgment is made to the copyright holders on pp. 515–518, which are hereby made part of this copyright page.

Library of Congress Cataloging-in-Publication Data
Muller, Gilbert H., 1941-
  To the point : reading and writing short arguments / Gilbert H. Muller, Harvey S. Wiener.
-- 2nd ed.
    p. cm.
  Rev. ed. of: 2005.
  ISBN 0-321-53371-2 (alk. paper)
  1. English language--Rhetoric--Problems, exercises, etc. 2. Persuasion (Rhetoric)--Problems, exercises, etc. 3. Report writing--Problems, exercises, etc. 4. College readers. I. Wiener, Harvey S. II. Title.
  PE1431.M845 2008
  808'.0427--dc22   2007051104

Please visit us at http://www.ablongman.com

ISBN-13: 978-0-321-53371-5
ISBN-10:   0-321-53371-2

13 14 15 —CRW—14

Brief Contents

Detailed Contents

12 ▶ Work, Money, and Class: Who Benefits?   267

16 ▶ Terrorism: How Should We Meet the Challenge?   371

PART 4 SIX CLASSIC ARGUMENTS   391

PART 6 CONSTRUCTING A BRIEF ARGUMENTATIVE RESEARCH PAPER   467

Preface

In our long history of teaching composition courses, we have come to believe that short is good—and that getting to the point in an essay without fluff and with clear propositions and well-supported arguments is a major objective of academic writing. Hence, this composition textbook wears its heart on its sleeve, so to speak, as it makes its main assertion in its title, *To the Point: Reading and Writing Short Arguments.* In it, we aim to provide essential instruction for college students in college writing courses. By choosing short readings and providing an extensive apparatus, we offer a multitude of selections that cut a wide swath in major contemporary issues. From cell phones to environmentalism, from human rights to love and marriage, from immigration to terrorism—and these are just a few of the explosive issues we address here—we have gathered essays and other short pieces that cut to the chase and provide invaluable models for writing arguments as well as dynamic issues for class discussion.

We realize that "short" is a matter of opinion: what's short to one reader might be too long to another. Most of our selections are three pages or less, and we have tried to keep the essays generally to fewer than seven pages.

WHAT'S NEW IN THE SECOND EDITION

Over one-third of the readings are new. In response to reviewers requesting current essays by established and emerging writers, 28 new selections appear in all major sections of the book. Provocative essays by well-known writers such as Mario Vargas Llosa on immigration and Paul Krugman on Wal-Mart should produce lively class discussion and solid argumentative responses to readings. Other topics presented for the first time include stem cell research and use, globalization, campus violence, and SUVs.

A new Chapter 3 introduces students to literary argument. Guidelines for interpreting and evaluating works of literature, art, and film lead students through the reading and writing process. This highly interactive chapter offers a sample student essay on e.e. cummings as well as a casebook of essays covering types of literary argument, including interpretation and evaluation of poetry, short fiction, and film.

New in-depth guidance on reading arguments has been added to an expanded Chapter 1. This introduction now includes new sections on opinions, facts, and arguments; writers, texts, and readers; reading and understanding arguments; cue words; and types of arguments. The chapter also provides greater coverage of visual arguments.

MLA documentation has been updated in keeping with current guidelines. The section on constructing a brief argumentative research paper now reflects guidelines as they appear in the latest edition of the *MLA Handbook*.

FEATURES

To the Point starts with three introductory chapters that present an overview of reading and writing in general and reading and writing arguments in particular. These chapters introduce (to the point, without question) the basic argumentative paradigms—Aristotelian logic, the Toulmin system, syllogisms, deduction, and logical fallacies, for example—as well as the key elements in the writing process needed to develop a strong argument. We have aimed in these chapters for clarity, accessibility, and contemporary flavor in order to set the tone for the whole textbook and its apparatus. We are passionate about clear instructional language and are certain that we have turned the often-complex explanations of argumentative strategies into unclouded and comprehensible prose. Also, we are keenly aware of the value of visual representations: word charts, columns, boxed information, screen shots, icons, artwork, cartoons, photographs, advertisements, and images of Web pages, for instance. We have integrated several of these features into many sections of the text and provide an important nonverbal dimension to students of argumentation and their teachers.

We highlight critical thinking throughout in our chapter questions and discussions. Chapters 1 and 2 introduce the reading and writing process within the context of learning approaches to argumentation. A new Chapter 3 provides detailed instruction in writing literary arguments. Here we explore works of literature and the arts as the basis for professional argumentative essays and show students how to write their own critiques of books, films, and other artistic endeavors, using essential strategies of argument to advance their positions. Part 1, in toto, sets the framework for the chapters of argumentative essays that follow. Again, short prose essays included in Part 1 demonstrate the various strategies that we introduce to readers in later parts of the book.

In Part 2, we offer a series of paired essays (six chapters in all), pro-con takes on contemporary issues: rap culture, the SUV phenomenon, the megastore Wal-Mart's place in our culture, animal rights, stem cell research, and capital punishment. Although some current argument theory shies away from stark pro-con debates in favor of a "positional" approach, we acknowledge that much of argumentation and persuasion in the public arena, in the media, and not least of all in classrooms and student dorms, adheres to the sharp tone inherent in opposing viewpoints.

With Part 3, however, where we offer seven chapters of several short essays each, we develop a more subtle approach, suggesting that argument and persuasion can serve as mediating strategies when individuals debate issues of significant concern. We organize these chapters around key world perspectives. These are not pro-con selections, but multiple views on major concerns facing citizens today—the prospects of the Internet; work, money, and class; and campus violence, to name just three.

Part 4 presents six longer classic prose arguments by Plato, Jonathan Swift, Virginia Woolf, George Orwell, Rachel Carson, and Martin Luther King Jr. This part addresses the needs of instructors who like to challenge students with more demanding material, thereby preparing them for the more extended modes of argumentation that they might encounter in later courses.

Designed to permit a deep and broad examination of an issue of continuing popular interest, Part 5, "A Casebook of Arguments on Our Diets: Are We What We Eat?" offers varied pieces—including essays, Web sites, and advertisements—on the issue of weight gain and weight control, now so much a part of the American identity. Part 6 shows students how to construct a brief argumentative research paper and provides a model of successful academic research within the reach of today's student.

Apparatus

In Parts 1 through 3 we have divided our questioning strategies after each selection into four major groups, using a variety of subheads that target specific skills.

Prereading

Thinking about the Essay in Advance—The reader considers some of the underlying issues, tapping into prior knowledge and concerns reflected in the piece.

Words to Watch—We highlight and define difficult words, once again *before* the student reads the essay, so as to forestall vocabulary issues that might prevent access to the selection.

In addition, we provide before each selection a *brief author biography*, a thumbnail sketch of the writer to highlight details of the writer's background and accomplishments.

Building Vocabulary

After students read the argumentative selection at hand, we provide vocabulary activities that help students expand their linguistic resources and understand words in context.

Thinking Critically about the Argument

Understanding the Writer's Argument—These questions focus on content issues: Does the student understand the basic elements of the writer's discussion?

Understanding the Writer's Techniques—This category of questions highlights the various rhetorical strategies that define and advance the argument.

Exploring the Writer's Argument—With these questions, readers react to the ideas advanced by the writer. Students consider the terms of the argument within their own worldview.

Ideas for Writing Arguments

Prewriting—Following the principles of the writing process that we have laid out in Chapter 2, we engage students in thinking about and planning an essay before actually writing it. This section leads naturally into the next.

Writing a Guided Argument—A key feature of *To the Point: Reading and Writing Short Arguments,* here we steer students through the writing of an argumentative essay inspired by the reading and the rhetorical strategies used by the writer. Students follow a series of suggested steps to produce an appropriate original essay of their own.

Thinking, Arguing, and Writing Collaboratively—Students work in groups to respond to a major issue that the essay addresses.

Writing about the Text—In this group of questions, we ask students to think about and write a brief critique about features in the text itself.

More Writing Ideas—Here we offer further writing activities that include journal entries, single-paragraph responses, letters, and brief essays.

In short (one of our favorite phrases), with approximately 70 brief, thoughtful essays, fresh but significant topics, integrated visuals and Internet resources, and comprehensive questions and writing assignments, *To the Point* presents concisely and clearly the contemporary world of controversy and persuasion for today's students of argumentative writing. An instructor's manual is also available to adopters of this edition at no extra charge.

SUPPLEMENTS

Instructor's Manual

The instructor's manual for *To the Point* introduces each section with an overview. The authors provide teaching suggestions for starting the discussion regarding each selection as well as possible answers to Understanding the Writer's Argument, Understanding the Writer's Techniques, and Exploring the Writer's Argument.

PEARSON
mycomplab

MyCompLab is a Web application that offers comprehensive and integrated resources for every writer. With MyCompLab, students learn from interactive tutorials and instruction; practice and develop their skills with grammar, writing, and research exercises; share and collaborate their writing with peers; and receive comments on their writing from instructors and tutors. Go to http://www.mycomplab.com <http://www.mycomplab.com/> to register for these premiere resources and much more!

ACKNOWLEDGMENTS

We want to thank Eben Ludlow, vice president at Longman, for his early support of *To the Point*. Calm and collected, droll and experienced, he was the perfect guide for any author embarking on a textbook project. Following him, Lauren Finn provided powerful leadership in helping us develop this second edition of our book. To our friend and agent, John Wright, we offer our gratitude once again. Our assistant Scott Smith has been invaluable in helping us to design apparatus and prepare the instructor's manual. Several reviewers have been most supportive and helpful: Dr. Savitri Ashok, Middle Tennessee State University; Candace Boeck, San Diego State University; Sarah Duerden, Arizona State University; Maureen Phillips, Liberty University; Karyn Smith, Texas A&M University; and Amy Vondrak, Mercer County Community College–Trenton.

Gilbert H. Muller
Harvey S. Wiener

Part One

An Overview:
Critical Thinking
and Argumentation

1 Reading and Understanding Arguments

Contemporary American culture often seems overwhelmed by argument. Television talk show hosts and radio shock jocks battle over countless issues. Hip-hop artists contrive elaborate "beefs" to get under the skin of their rivals. Politicians are in constant attack mode. Advertisements and commercials seduce us into crazed consumption. Internet chat rooms and blogs flame with aggressive language. Deborah Tannen, in *The Argument Culture* (1998), terms this phenomenon the "ethic of aggression." Indeed, the world is awash in what passes for argument, but frequently in its most irritating, insulting, ill-conceived, and illogical forms.

Forget about argument as a quarrel or a beef. Instead, think of argument as *any text—in written, spoken, or visual form—that presents a debatable point of view.* Closely related to argument (and in practice often indistinguishable from it) is *persuasion*, the attempt to get others to act in a way that will advance a cause or position. The kind of argument we deal with in this text involves a carefully reasoned attempt to get people to believe or act according to our own beliefs or points of view. Typically this type of argument requires you to deal with significant issues about which individuals might justifiably disagree. It also requires you to respectfully consider the positions and perspectives of others in an effort to promote civil discourse.

OPINIONS, FACTS, AND ARGUMENTS

Virtually everyone holds **opinions**—beliefs, values, and judgments that are not based on wholly rational or sufficient grounds. Your current opinions, formed by family, experience, institutions, and culture, will probably change over time. Opinions, after all, are not arguments but rather viewpoints that need to be tested, interrogated, and even replaced with better, more logical or inclusive ones.

Of course, your personal views might be consistent, ethical, and based on sound character; in other words, you have informed opinions. Nevertheless, through your interactions with peers and professors, your opinions in all likelihood will evolve and change as you encounter the views of others during your college years.

3

Opinions that are not based on facts are like quarrels devoid of any rational basis. A *fact* is something that exists, is known to have happened, or is known by actual experience or observation. Facts can change our minds and opinions; facts force us to engage in a process whereby we scrutinize the ways we come to our thoughts and beliefs—our opinions. When we think critically about our opinions and seek strong reasons to support them, we are moving from raw opinion to a dialogue with others about the nature of truth. We are, in brief, beginning the process of argumentation.

An *argument*, which offers reasons to support a position on an issue, avoids unverifiable facts and unsubstantiated or irrational opinions. (You cannot argue over a fact because a verifiable fact is beyond dispute.) An argument is not a heated exchange or quarrel. Nor is an argument a statement of personal preferences—for example, that classical music is better than rap—because preferences, which resemble opinions, are matters of taste rather than rational debate.

Thinking Critically

Jot down notes for a class discussion on how you might transform the following opinions into arguments (either pro or con) by developing reasons and providing facts or other types of evidence.

1. Medical marijuana should be legalized.
2. Illegal immigrants should be deported.
3. Stem cell research destroys living human beings.
4. College is a waste of time.
5. The United States should get out of the Middle East.

WHY ARGUE?

You argue in order to influence others to think or believe as you do about an idea or issue, or to act as you would act. Stated differently, you argue to *convince* an audience about your point of view or to *persuade* this audience to adopt a desired course of action or behavior. When you read and write arguments, you enter into a dialogue with this audience. This dialogue or conversation is typically dramatic because your point of view must be defended and usually is open to dispute or debate. Admittedly, much argument—and courtroom dramas in real life or on television provide excellent examples—results in winners and losers.

Argumentation, however, is not always about winning and losing. You can argue for other reasons as well. Sometimes you argue *to explore* why you think or act in a certain way. Exploration enables you *to make decisions*: Should you vote for one candidate or another, attend a private or public college, date a certain person, support abortion, oppose the death penalty, believe in God? You engage constantly in these forms of argument, either on your own or with others, in matters both large and small. You develop options and make decisions through a complex process of internal thinking and even meditation. To be able to arrive at a valid conclusion about an issue or course of action is a powerful aspect of argumentation that involves critical thinking and self-discovery.

Even as you use argument to clarify opinions and beliefs, you can employ argument *to form a consensus* with others about ideas that otherwise might divide or polarize individuals. Rather than constantly battling people and groups, you can advance an argument in order to engage others in a conversation that might produce common ground concerning ideas, policies, and programs. With this approach to argument, you seek a win-win outcome. Looked at this way, argument is integral to free speech and open inquiry and is vital to civil society. Honest and truthful argument (which admittedly is difficult to achieve) is essential to the health of democracy and of nations around the world.

Argument, as you will see, is as old as Aristotle and as new as questions on a standardized writing test that you might have taken when applying for college. Valid argument can produce toleration, consensus, and understanding among people holding diverse points of view. It can be subtle and liberating, encouraging you to examine and perhaps even change what you think or believe about critical ideas and issues.

THE WRITER, THE TEXT, AND THE READER

In order to grasp the nature of the intellectual conversation posed by argumentation, consider the following diagram, which shows certain interacting elements as the writer attempts to *convince* and *persuade* the reader about a debatable topic.

Writer $\longrightarrow$	Text $\longrightarrow$	Reader
intelligent/fair/reasonable/ trustworthy/ethical	debatable topic/claim or main point/supporting reasons/evidence	opinions/beliefs/ feelings/values

We will soon discuss these key concepts; for now, it is important for you to realize that the methods of argument and persuasion involve matters of character (the writer), logic (the text), and intellectual and emotional response (the reader). In practice, these elements are not mutually exclusive but rather are reciprocal activities—for instance, the reader hopefully possesses the same qualities of character as the writer. Nevertheless, writers from the ancient Greeks to the present have highlighted the special interaction among readers, texts, and writers when arguments appear.

Here, for example, is an introductory paragraph from a recent film review by Anthony Lane, who writes for *The New Yorker*:

> The best performance in "Pirates of the Caribbean: At World's End" comes from a monkey. He belongs to the jaunty Captain Barbosa (Geoffrey Rush), and, given that in the course of the film he is required to ignite a rocket, freeze his fur off, dangle from a parachute, and, most ignominiously, take the place of a cannonball, he—or his agent—may well have requested that half his scenes be played by a stunt monkey, or at least a monkey double. On the night I saw the film, he also earned the most laughs, putting more experienced actors to shame. In short, the only person who could derive lasting satisfaction from this movie is Charles Darwin.

Notice how the writer in the very first sentence lures the reader into an amusing conversation or debate over the film. (A complete film review appears in Chapter 3, where we discuss varieties of literary argument.) What do we sense about Lane's character (and his writing ability)? What assumptions does he make about his audience? What tone or attitude does he take? What details does he emphasize? Where does he state his main idea most clearly? And how do we know that Anthony Lane truly dislikes the third installment of *Pirates of the Caribbean*? In generating his argument, Lane offers an entertaining but devastating critique, implying perhaps that we would have to be monkeys ourselves to spend money to see this film.

JUSTIFYING AN ARGUMENT

Argument involves a complex pattern of thought that does not appear in every statement. It is inaccurate to claim that "everything is an argument" because, when thought about carefully, every statement is *not* an argument. You need to determine through a basic *test of justification* whether or not a statement qualifies as an argument.

Imagine what you were thinking about when you woke up this morning. Here are some possibilities:

1. *What a beautiful day—so clear and sunny!*
2. *Did I complete my homework assignment for English composition?*
3. *I'm looking forward to seeing that good-looking classmate in my first-period class.*
4. *I'll wear something light because it is warm outside.*
5. *I need to change my major and get another advisor because I'm not satisfied with either.*

All of these sentences involve varieties of thinking, but not all of them express an argument. Sentence 1 is a simple statement of fact: if indeed the day *is* clear and sunny, who would want to argue with you about its beauty? Sentence 2 is an effort at recall framed as a question, and generally interrogative and imperative (involving commands or prayers) statements do not express claims or propositions. Sentence 3 suggests a bit of pleasant daydreaming; it does not rise to the level of argumentation. Sentence 4 reflects a mental activity that could qualify as an argument if stated differently, but in this form it simply reflects a decision—not essentially debatable—deriving from an observation. The first four sentences suggest a range of thinking largely devoid of argumentation.

Now read again sentence 5, which contains an argument and therefore passes the test of justification. To begin, you see clearly that there is an "argumentative edge" to this statement. Sentence 5 reflects a traditional approach to argument in which a combative or debatable point of view appears. (Greek theorists called this the "agonistic" theory of argument.) This statement, reflecting dissatisfaction with both a major and an advisor, actually has several argumentative and persuasive purposes embedded in it. Reading this statement critically, you sense that the speaker will have to *explore options, inform, convince*, and *make decisions*—four common goals in the construction of an argument. Sentence 5 reflects a process of reasoning and the implicit need to advance reasons or proofs in order *to justify* how an individual thinks and acts, which form the core of argument.

READING AND UNDERSTANDING ARGUMENTS

Effective written arguments reveal common characteristics and rules. Think of such arguments as a special type of game or problem of detection. Just as in any game—whether basketball, poker, or chess—the rules establish and govern the playing field. And argument as a form of discourse relies heavily on rules and regulations.

At the outset, you need to focus on the logical foundation of argumentation—the appeal to reason that distinguishes it from other kinds of writing. This does not mean that arguments lack emotion. In fact, you will see later in this chapter that argument often blends rational, emotional, and ethical elements. Moreover, other forms of writing—for instance, comparison and contrast, definition, classification, and causal analysis—can be used to advance an argumentative purpose. In fact, some teachers suggest that all writing, to the extent that it tries to make a point, is argumentative. Still, the hallmark of effective argument is the premium placed on certain standards of reason—a logical train of thought—applied to a topic that normally can be debated.

Argumentation creates a "court of standards," a formal game of sorts, in which the rules of reason and evidence apply. Here, then, are some of the critical questions that you should ask when reading and ultimately writing arguments:

- What is the writer's *claim*—the key idea, assertion, or conclusion? The writer's claim is a debatable statement that needs to be justified or proved. (Another term for a claim is *major proposition*—the main point of the argument.)
- What *reasons* support the claim or conclusion? Reasons are statements that support a thesis, justify it, or make it more probable. Reasons are also called *minor propositions*—statements offered in support of the major proposition—or *grounds*—rational or factual support for one's position or claim.
- What *evidence* supports the claim and minor propositions? Evidence can be facts, statistics, accepted opinions, expert testimony, examples, or personal experience. Valid evidence will be verifiable and true.
- What *warrants* support the claim? A warrant is the connection, typically assumed and unstated, between a claim and the supporting reasons. It is the rule, belief, or principle underlying the argument—the assumption that makes the claim appear to be acceptable. (The writer assumes that the audience will share this assumption.) A *backing* refers to facts that add substance to the warrant; backings do not always appear in an argument.
- Does the writer qualify his or her claim? *Qualifiers* are words or terms used to limit your claims and warrants. They are ways to control the parameters of your argument and make it more precise. Such words and phrases as *few, for the most part, if it were so, in some cases, in the main, it is possible, it may be, it seems, many, most, often, one might argue, perhaps, possibly, probably, rarely, some, sometimes*, and *under certain conditions* are qualifying terms that refine a writer's claim.
- Where does the writer use *rebuttal*? Rebuttal or *refutation* is the attempt to weaken or invalidate the viewpoints of the opposition. The writer anticipates objections to his or her argument and answers these objections.

Of course, you must determine if a writer's argument is valid and convincing. For instance, the reasons he or she offers might not support the claim or conclusion, or the evidence may be weak or questionable (especially if drawn from the Internet). You must carefully examine a writer's claim, reasons, and evidence before you agree that the argument is valid and makes sense.

CUE WORDS: CLUES TO DETECTING ARGUMENTS

Even as you examine a text for broad signs of its argumentative characteristics, you should look for key words, or cue words, that signal the writer's argumentative purpose. The following list contains some commonly used cue words and phrases.

- *Cue Words Signaling a Claim*: acknowledges that, agrees that, argues that, assumes that, believes that, claims that, concedes that, complains, concedes, demonstrates that, denies, dictates that, emphasizes that, insists that, questions whether, refutes, reports that, suggests, thinks that, urges
- *Cue Words Signaling Reasons*: as shown by, assuming that, because, first (second), for, for the reason that, given that, in the first (second) place, in view of, may be deduced (derived, inferred) from, since
- *Cue Words Signaling Conclusions*: allows us to deduce (imply, infer), as a result, consequently, demonstrates that, hence, implies that, in conclusion, in short, in sum, it follows that, leads one to believe that, points to, so, then, thereby demonstrating, therefore, thus, to sum up, to summarize, which proves (shows) that

Of course, these cue words or "templates," as some call them, do not always appear in professional writing. Nevertheless, when they do appear, cue words and phrases signal an argumentative purpose or objective, and such templates can be useful in constructing your own effective arguments.

TYPES OF ARGUMENTS

As indicated earlier, writers use key rhetorical types or modes to construct their arguments. (*Rhetoric*, in its broadest sense, means the art of writing or using language effectively.) In the Socratic dialogue *Gordias* by Plato (the ancient Greek writer whose work appears in Part 4), philosophers debate the meaning of the art of rhetoric. One of the definitions that they uncover is that rhetoric is the art of "manufacturing persuasion." Among the major rhetorical strategies available to the manufacture of persuasion are comparison and contrast, definition, classification, and causal analysis.

Comparative Arguments

Comparative arguments advance a claim based on the similarities and differences between two subjects. For example, you can strengthen an argument about proper classroom conduct by posing an attentive student against one who is text messaging or plugged into an iPod. In the following paragraph, the noted linguist and feminist Deborah Tannen explores differences between genders:

Getting credit often depends on the way you talk. For example, a woman tells me she has been given a poor evaluation because her supervisor feels she knows less than her male peers. Her boss, it turns out, reached this conclusion because the woman asks more questions: She is seeking information without regard to how her queries will make her look.

—*And Rarely the Twain Shall Meet*

Paragraphs and entire argumentative essays can be organized around the comparative mode.

Arguments of Definition

Arguments of definition deal with the nature of a word, term, or concept. Like most rhetorical modes, definition can serve to structure paragraphs as well as essays. A writer might choose to make a point by exploring the various facets of a term like *race*, for example. Or an extended definition of marriage as, say, a prison can be the basis for examples of henpecked husbands and dissatisfied wives. A Catholic priest, Lorenzo Albacete, offers a definition of celibacy in this selection:

I began to understand the meaning of celibacy, oddly, during a time when I was seriously questioning it. A dear friend of mine in Europe had sent his only son to study in the United States and asked me to watch over him. This friend told me how much he was suffering from this separation. I told him that at least he had a son, whereas I would never experience being a father. This aspect of celibacy, I said to him, was much more difficult than the lack of a sexual companion.

"But you have many sons and daughters," he said. "Look at the way young people follow you. You are a true father to them."

"Yes," I replied, "but let's be honest. They are not really my sons and daughters. Each one of them would have existed even if I had not. They are not mine as J. is your son."

"But Lorenzo," he said, "that is the point. J. is not my son. I do not own him. I must respect his freedom. And I thought that's why priests took a vow of celibacy, to help spouses and parents understand that to love is not to own, but to affirm, to help, to let go. I need this help now that J. has left home."

I understood then that celibacy has more to do with poverty than with sex. It is the radical, outward expression of the poverty of the human heart, the poverty that makes true love possible by preventing it from corrupting into possession or manipulation.

—*The Struggle with Celibacy*

The writer personalizes his perception of celibacy, offering a *stipulative* definition, that is, a particular understanding of the word.

Arguments of Causality

Arguments of cause and effect ask how something came to be, why an event occurred, or what resulted from a particular act or event. Causal analysis investigates the "how" and "why" of an argument. A writer arguing against the death penalty might explain the events or reasoning that led to his or her position. In perhaps the most famous causal argument in American history, Thomas Jefferson gave in the Declaration of Independence the many reasons why the colonies were separating from Great Britain. Jefferson writes, "let Facts be submitted to a candid world" about King George, and then proceeds to list 17 reasons, among them:

> He has refused his Assent to Laws . . .
> He has forbidden his Governors to pass Laws of pressing and immediate importance . . .
> He has dissolved Representative Houses repeatedly . . .
> He has obstructed the Administration of Justice . . .

Jefferson knew—as we do—that we live in a causal world, and analyzing the world from this point of view can enrich one's arguments.

Arguments of Classification

Arguments employing classification break down an issue or subject into its constituent parts, helping readers orient themselves conceptually to the topic. An argument that only movie comedies made before 1950 are any good would benefit from a classification of the different types of comedies made before and since, so that the reader understands the topic and the nature of the claim. In the following paragraph, the Nobel Prize–winning economist Amartya Sen explores the types of overlapping civilizations that require nuanced understanding:

> It is futile to try to understand Indian art, literature, music, food, or politics without seeing the extensive interactions across barriers of religious communities. These include Hindus and Muslims, Buddhists, Jains, Parsees, Christians (who have been in India since at least the fourth century, well before England's conversion to Christianity), Jews (present since the fall of Jerusalem), and even atheists and agnostics. Sanskrit has a larger atheistic literature than exists in any other classical language. Speaking of India as a Hindu civilization may be comforting to the Hindu fundamentalist, but it is an odd reading of India.
> —*A World Not Neatly Divided*

Sen argues in his essay that we should be suspicious of "singular classification." Even as we classify people, societies, and civilizations, we should accept the many ways they overlap.

MIXING MODES

Like civilizations, rhetorical modes are not mutually exclusive. Writers often use several of these modes to advance their arguments, interweaving them as well with other rhetorical strategies such as narration and description, evaluation, proposal, and policy recommendation. The following short essay, "The Harmful Myth of Asian Superiority," by Ronald Takaki, an acclaimed author and professor of ethnic studies at the University of California at Berkeley, illustrates several of the rhetorical modes and argumentative strategies that we have discussed so far.

RONALD TAKAKI
The Harmful Myth of Asian Superiority

1   Asian Americans have increasingly come to be viewed as a "model minority." But are they as successful as claimed? And for whom are they supposed to be a model?

2   Asian Americans have been described in the media as "excessively, even provocatively" successful in gaining admission to universities. Asian American shopkeepers have been congratulated as well as criticized, for their ubiquity and entrepreneurial effectiveness.

3   If Asian Americans can make it, many politicians and pundits ask why can't African Americans? Such comparisons pit minorites against each other and generate African American resentment toward Asian Americans. The victims are blamed for their plight, rather than racism and an economy that has made many young African American workers superfluous.

4   The celebration of Asian Americans has obscured reality. For example, figures on the high earnings of Asian Americans relative to Caucasians are misleading. Most Asian Americans live in California, Hawaii, and New York—states with higher incomes and higher costs of living than the national average.

5   Even Japanese Americans, often touted for their upward mobility, have not reached equality. While Japanese American men in California earned an average income comparable to Caucasian men in 1980, they did so only by acquiring more education and working more hours.

6   Comparing family incomes is even more deceptive. Some Asian American groups do have higher family incomes than Caucasians. But they have more workers per family.

7   The "model minority" image homogenizes Asian Americans and hides their differences. For example, while thousands of Vietnamese American young people attend universities, others are on the streets.

They live in motels and hang out in pool halls in places like East Los Angels; some join gangs.

Twenty-five percent of the people in New York City's Chinatown   8
lived below the poverty level in 1980, compared with 17 percent of the city's population. Some 60 percent of the workers in the Chinatowns of Los Angeles and San Francisco are crowded into low-paying jobs in garment factories and restaurants.

"Most immigrants coming into Chinatown with a language barrier   9
cannot go outside this confined area into the mainstream of American industry," a Chinese immigrant said. "Before, I was a painter in Hong Kong, but I can't do it here. I got no license, no education. I want a living; so it's dishwasher, janitor, or cook."

Hmong and Mien refugees from Laos have unemployment rates   10
that reach as high as 80 percent. A 1987 California study showed that three out of ten Southeast Asian refugee families had been on welfare for four to ten years.

Although college-educated Asian Americans are entering the profes-   11
sions and earning good salaries, many hit the "glass ceiling"—the barrier through which high management positions can be seen but not reached. In 1988, only 8 percent of Asian Americans were "officials" and "managers," compared with 12 percent for all groups.

Finally, the triumph of Korean immigrants has been exaggerated. In   12
1988, Koreans in the New York metropolitan area earned only 68 percent of the median income of non-Asians. More than three-quarters of Korean greengrocers, those so-called paragons of bootstrap entrepreneurialism came to America with a college education. Engineers, teachers, or administrators while in Korea, they became shopkeepers after their arrival. For many of them, the greengrocery represents dashed dreams, a step downward in status.

For all their hard work and long hours, most Korean shopkeepers do   13
not actually earn very much: $17,000 to $35,000 a year, usually representing the income from the labor of an entire family.

But most Korean immigrants do not become shopkeepers. Instead,   14
many find themselves trapped as clerks in grocery stores, service workers in restaurants, seamstresses in garment factories, and janitors in hotels.

Most Asian Americans know their "success" is largely a myth. They   15
also see how the celebration of Asian Americans as a "model minority" perpetuates their inequality and exacerbates relations between them and African Americans.

▶Thinking Critically about the Argument

1. What is the writer's claim or major proposition, and where does he state it?

2. What reasons or minor propositions does Takaki provide to support his claim?
3. Explain the types of evidence that the writer uses to back up his major and minor points.
4. The writer uses several different rhetorical modes in this argumentative essay. What are they? Give examples.
5. Does the writer qualify his claim? Why or why not? Does he use cue words? If so, where? If not, why?
6. Where does Takaki engage in rebuttal?
7. How effective do you find Takaki's argument, and why?

ARISTOTELIAN ARGUMENTS

Arguments must be read critically, based in part on your understanding of concepts, methods, and conventions that follow a long tradition starting with Aristotle (384–322 B.C.). According to Aristotle in his *Rhetoric*, the best arguments contain logical, emotional, and ethical appeals. In other words, reason (which classical commentators termed *logos*), emotion (*pathos*), and moral authority (*ethos*) appear in varying degrees in arguments, working together to change opinions and prompt action. When you read argumentative essays, you see that these three appeals can support a point of view, change attitudes, elicit desired responses, and meet various needs. For now, we will focus on logical appeals—the process of reasoning—and the ways they appear when you read texts.

The ancients emphasized that an argument presupposes a topic, what the Greeks called *topos*. The essays you will read in this book contain a central topic that you should be able to identify. Aristotle claimed that every argument contains this statement of a central topic and proof to support it. For example, Martin Luther King Jr.'s famous speech, "I Have a Dream," which appears in Part 4 of this book, takes as its topic the need for an American society reflecting equality for everyone. His speech contains echoes of many classic documents, among them the Declaration of Independence. It is useful to examine the key idea—or topic—that is the essence of the classic document written by Thomas Jefferson and his collaborators and that influenced King as he prepared his speech.

> We hold these truths to be self-evident, that all men are created equal:
> that they are endowed by their Creator with certain inalienable rights;
> and that among these rights are life, liberty, and the pursuit of happiness.

You will have the opportunity to read, discuss critically, and respond in writing to the text by King, but for now it is only necessary to understand that the topic at the center of these texts is controversial and open to challenge. For example, do you believe that everyone is created equal? Do you think that a Creator endows us with inalienable rights? Do you anticipate, as Martin Luther King Jr. does, that some day all God's children will be free at last? Where is the *proof*? The topics you will be reading about in this book require judgment, evaluation, and confirmation. In essence, you have to test the *assumptions,* or underlying beliefs governing certain statements. Your critical response to these essays will benefit from your understanding of the reasoning or logic supporting the assumptions that are made.

A stated assumption is called a *premise,* and premises are the first elements you must uncover when reading an argumentative essay. You probably have heard about syllogistic reasoning, that type of logic in which a major premise, followed by a minor premise, produces a conclusion. This is the method of *deduction,* the process of reasoning where a conclusion is taken to be true because the statements on which it is based are true. The most famous syllogism, of course, is the one using Socrates as an example.

Major premise: All human beings are mortal.
Minor premise: Socrates is a human being.
Conclusion: Therefore, Socrates is mortal.

This example demonstrates that the validity of any syllogism rests on the "truth" of the premises. In other words, if you accept the truth of the major and minor premises, then you must accept the conclusion.

Of course, there can be false and misleading applications of syllogistic reasoning. For the purposes of this book, we need not go into these errors in syllogistic reasoning in depth, but instead we illustrate the problem with two examples. Here is the first:

Major premise: All cats die.
Minor premise: Socrates died.
Conclusion: Socrates was a cat.

Here the premises are true but the conclusion clearly is false, and thus the argument is not valid.

Consider a second, more subtle (some might say devious) example of syllogistic reasoning:

Major premise: Unwantedness leads to high crime.
Minor premise: Abortion leads to less unwantedness.
Conclusion: Abortion leads to less crime.

Two noted scholars—an economist at the University of Chicago and a professor of law at Stanford—have provoked debate by publishing a paper that can be reduced to this syllogism. They maintain that because of *Roe* v. *Wade,* precisely those women—poor, single, black, or teenage—who might have given birth to unwanted children opted for abortions instead. Thus, the unwanted children who would have committed crimes were never born, and consequently overall crime has declined in the United States. Do you think that the two premises are true? If so, then you must accept the conclusion. If not, you can reject the conclusion because it does not follow from the premises.

The two contemporary professors who base their paper on the relationship between abortion and crime used deduction—what Aristotle termed *artistic appeal*—to construct their argument. In practice, however, as Aristotle asserts, few individuals rigorously apply "artistic" or deductive reasoning to the development of their compositions. More often than not, they use what Aristotle labeled *inartistic appeals*—varieties of *inductive* logic where evidence (in the form of facts, statistics, reports, testimonies, interviews, and other evidentiary modes) support a claim or proposition. When inductive thinking appears in an argumentative essay, the writer gathers and applies evidence in order to make *empirical* (based on observation and experiment) claims. Inductive thinking appears most rigorously in scientific and technical reports, where claims require unassailable evidence or, in Aristotle's words, where statements require proof. But inductive logic is also at the heart of most personal, expository, and argumentative writing. In fact, most of the writing you do in response to the essays in this book will require you to martial evidence to support the propositions or claims that you establish.

You can best appreciate the importance of inductive logic by considering Aristotle's observation that every argument can be reduced to two basic parts: **Statement + Proof.** To use contemporary terms, we would say that an argument requires a claim that is supported by evidence. If you become familiar with this approach to argumentation, you will find it much easier to read and write arguments with a critical eye. Remember that any debatable thesis, claim, or proposition (to get you comfortable with these interchangeable terms) requires evidence to back it up. The varieties of evidence will be considered later in this chapter. For now, examine the way in which evidence supports the claim in the following paragraph by Marian Wright Edelman, a noted attorney, activist, and founding president of the Children's Defense Fund:

> The legacies that parents and church and teachers left to my generation of Black children were priceless and not material: a living faith reflected in daily service, the discipline of hard work and stick-to-it-ness, and a capacity to struggle in the face of adversity. Giving up and "burnout" were not part of the language of my elders—you got up every morning and you did what you had to do and you got up every time you fell down and tried as many times as you had to get it done right. They had grit. They valued family life, family rituals, and tried to be and to expose us to good role models. Role models were of two kinds: those who achieved in the outside world (like Marian Anderson, my namesake) and those who didn't have a whole lot of education or fancy clothes but who taught us by the special grace of their lives the message of Christ and Tolstoy and Gandhi and Heschel and Dorothy Day and Romero

and King that the Kingdom of God was within—in what you are, not what you have. I still hope I can be half as good as Black church and community elders like Miz Lucy McQueen, Miz Tee Kelly, and Miz Kate Winston, extraordinary women who were kind and patient and loving with children and others and who, when I went to Spellman College, sent me shoeboxes with chicken and biscuits and greasy dollar bills.

—*The Measure of Our Success: A Letter to My Children and Yours*

Edelman shapes her message (which is another way to say that she presents a claim or proposition) around evidence drawn from personal experience. She supports her claim—that she grew up in a community where children were valued and where beliefs were transmitted from one generation to the next—with references to numerous role models that molded her values and beliefs. Here we have clear "proof" of the validity of the basic Aristotelian equation: **Argument = Statement + Proof**. Essays based on personal experience offer real intellectual pleasure as well as an accessible way of understanding the arguments they can frame. When you examine the paragraph by Edelman, for example, you see that it is not about "winning" but rather about the strengths of individuals and communities, as well as Edelman's desire to enter into a dialogue with you—the reader—about her complex but nurturing world.

EMOTIONAL AND ETHICAL APPEALS

An argumentative essay has to be rational, reflecting a process of logical thinking. When reading an argumentative essay for its logical or rational appeal, we have to ask these questions:

- Is the claim or proposition presented in a logical way?
- Is the claim presented accurately and fairly?
- What reasons or minor propositions support the claim?
- What evidence supports the minor proposition?
- Is the entire argument logically convincing?

However, we do not read arguments purely for their logical content. The rational basis of an argument typically contains other essential qualities, appealing also to emotion and ethics. Remember that the best arguments, as Aristotle maintained, contain these emotional and ethical appeals.

Many issues—race and ethnicity, sexuality and gender, crime and punishment, to name just three—are complex, emotional, and touch on personal sensitivities. Consequently, it is not surprising that writers would approach such topics not from a strictly logical perspective but also from perspectives touching on emotion and ethics. For example, topics relating to race—as you saw in the paragraph by Marian Wright Edelman—

provoke complex meanings, emotions, and beliefs. Reread Edelman's paragraph to see how emotional and ethical appeals support her argument. Use the following questions, which can be applied to all essays you read, to determine the nature of her emotional appeal.

- Does the writer appeal to basic human emotions such as love, caring, sympathy, rejection, pity, fear?
- Does the writer appeal to the basic senses of sight, smell, hearing, taste, and touch?
- Does the writer appeal to essential physical needs or desires?
- Does the writer appeal to such "higher" emotions or universal truths as patriotism, loyalty, belief in various gods, freedom, and democracy?

Although using claims and evidence to arrive at certain truths is the primary goal of argumentative writing, the appeal to emotion is complementary and perhaps even more powerful than logic in its effect on an audience. Logicians often warn us against the use of emotion in argument, and in fact certain false emotional appeals will be considered in the next chapter. Nevertheless, emotional appeals—especially when they involve the use of humor, satire, and irony—can work effectively in the effort to persuade a reader to accept the writer's point of view.

Consider the emotional impact of these representative paragraphs from an essay titled "Women Are Just Better" by the columnist Anna Quindlen:

> The inherent superiority of women came to mind just the other day when I was reading about sanitation workers. New York City has finally hired women to pick up the garbage, which makes sense to me, since, as I discovered, a good bit of being a woman consists of picking up garbage. There was a story about the hiring of these female sanitation workers, and I was struck by the fact that I could have written that story without ever leaving my living room—a reflection not on the quality of the reporting but the predictability of the male sanitation worker's response. . . .
>
> As a woman who has done dishes, yard work, and tossed a fair number of Hefty bags, I was peeved—more so because I would fight for the right of any laid-off sanitation man to work, for example, at the gift-wrap counter at Macy's, even though any woman knows that men are hormonally incapable of wrapping packages and tying bows.

The emotional *tone* (the writer's attitude toward the topic, self, and audience) of these two paragraphs is evident. The writer, a woman, is angry, provocative, and downright savage in her humor. But the emotional edge is part of the writer's effort to persuade. Of course, her emotional tone might provoke readers—especially those men who know how to wrap packages and tie bows, and even those who don't but believe that those skills have nothing to do with superiority of gender. Nevertheless,

Quindlen does have a point or claim that is suggested by the very title of the essay, and she attempts to stir the reader's feelings as well as opinions through the evocation of emotion. Here, emotion sustains what the writer presents as a debatable proposition: that women are better than men.

Another paragraph, once again by Lorenzo Albacete, the Roman Catholic priest and theologian writing in "The Struggle with Celibacy," raises the role of ethical appeals when considering the overall effectiveness of an argument.

> In the future, the church may decide that particular pastoral situations require a change in the requirement of priestly celibacy. Still, I believe that even if priests marry, they are called to be witnesses of that "celibacy of the heart" that human love requires—namely, the absolute respect for the loved one's freedom. It's time for those of us who treasure priestly celibacy to live in accordance with its intended message or else give it up as an obstacle to what we wish to say.

This paragraph shows the quality of *ethos* that Aristotle mentioned—the presence of the writer offering himself to the reader or audience as an ethical authority worthy of trust and acceptance. Good sense, goodwill, high moral character—these are the three qualities of the writer discussed by Aristotle and the ancients that make the rhetorical situation of any argument complete. Alcabete *claims authority* about his subject based on his personal knowledge and experience of the subject, as well as his background, position, and reputation as a scholar. You thus have to pay attention to this writer, even as his bold and provocative argument in the essay—that celibacy should not be a casualty of the recent scandals involving the priesthood—might raise objections or rebuttals. In fact, when a topic is controversial, readers might understandably be skeptical about the writer's claim to authority. Nevertheless, the sort of thoughtfulness and candor shown in Alcabete's remarks is an excellent way to establish *ethos*, which involves a willingness by the audience to trust the writer's viewpoint.

When considering the impact of ethical appeal in an argumentative essay, pose the following questions:

- What is the tone or *voice* of the writer, and does this tone enhance the logic of the argument?
- What is the writer's training or expertise, and how does this knowledge establish credibility?
- Does the writer have the goodwill of the audience in mind? Why or why not?
- Does the writer have a strong sense of right and wrong in approaching the subject? How strong is this moral sense?
- Does the writer seem honest and trustworthy? How are these qualities revealed?

Building credibility—creating a relationship of trust—is essential to good argument. A writer speaks to readers in many voices, and it is up to you as an active reader to determine if the voice selected is appropriate for the argument the writer presents.

TOULMIN ARGUMENTS

A currently popular way of reading arguments derives from the ideas of British philosopher Stephen Toulmin, who in *The Uses of Argument* (1958) offers a method that updates the argumentative systems of the ancients. According to Toulmin and teachers of writing who have modified his ideas, you do not read or write argumentative essays that follow the demands of formal logic. Instead, writers compose arguments according to the ways they actually think carefully and critically through an issue or debate. As such, Toulmin offers an easy way to understand the dynamics of argumentative and persuasive prose.

Toulmin asserts that all arguments begin with a *claim*—a word that you already are familiar with. Claims, you will recall, are statements of belief or truth that involve positions that others might find controversial or debatable. In other words, a writer's audience must perceive that a statement is open to controversy. There is no sense in arguing that it is not a beautiful day if indeed the sun is out, the temperature is perfect, and the sky is clear. No one would declare that this statement about the weather conditions is ripe for argument.

An essay that contains a claim tends to address readers by taking a stand or arguing a case. Here are some statements that clearly contain claims:

The September 11, 2001, terrorist attacks could have been prevented.

The SATs should be abolished.

There is no such thing as global warming.

Eminem is the greatest rap artist today.

These are debatable points. In themselves, however, they prove nothing. They assuredly do not prove a case. According to Toulmin, a claim is just the first logical and necessary step in a process of reasoning designed to make or prove a case.

Any claim needs *reasons* to support it. Again, you already have learned about the need for reasons drawn from personal experience, facts, authorities, and other sources to create the framework for an argument. Writers often provide readers with *arguments in brief*—a claim appearing early in an essay, perhaps in an introductory or concluding paragraph, and followed by a few reasons. Aristotle called these compressed arguments *enthymemes*. Here is an enthymeme drawn from one of the previous examples:

The SATs should be abolished because they place undue emphasis on certain learning styles, create false impressions of a student's real talents and abilities, and are culturally biased.

Here you see how both the terms and the framework for an argument develop from the enthymeme. Toulmin, however, would say that these reasons are assumptions that need to be tested and supported further. The need for *connections* between the claim and the reasons takes us to the next step in Toulmin argument.

Toulmin calls the connection between the claim and the supporting reasons in an argument the *warrant*. (This word appears in the "Reading and Understanding Arguments" section presented earlier in this chapter, but it requires further explanation.) Often unstated or implied, a warrant establishes the authority underlying a particular claim and its supporting reasons. If the warrant is sound, the evidence assembled to support the claim appears to be justified. On the other hand, if the warrant itself can be challenged or is debatable, then you would expect the writer to defend it.

Based on Toulmin's method, we can diagram the connections among claim, reason(s), and warrant.

This diagram suggests that a warrant is the glue that holds a claim and the reasons supporting the claim together. It is the general principle or underlying assumption that makes the claim plausible or fundamentally acceptable.

Look now at a simple application of the Toulmin diagram to a common situation.

Don't go swimming—there is a strong undertow.

The reason ("there is a strong undertow") is connected to the claim ("Don't go swimming") by the following warrant:

If there is a strong undertow, it is dangerous to go swimming.

Do you see how the warrant is the principle underlying the entire statement consisting of the claim and the reason? Although we could state it in different ways, the warrant for this statement is obvious: you do not want to go swimming in dangerous waters. Diagrammed, the example would look like this:

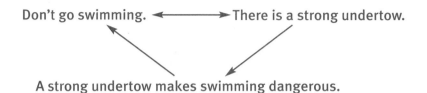

A warrant implying we should avoid a specific dangerous—indeed, life-threatening—situation when deciding whether or not to swim is common-sensical. Such a plausible warrant makes the claim and reason supporting it seem reasonable.

The Importance of Evidence

Claims, warrants, and reasons are the framework of a Toulmin argument, or any argument for that matter, but *evidence* is what makes the case. Evidence—various items of information that support a claim as well as the reasons supporting a claim—is what you look for in any pattern of argument. Toulmin reduces this need for evidence to a question: "What have you got to go on?" Only evidence, carefully selected and clearly presented, permits a writer to present an argument fully and convincingly. If the evidence in an argument is too sparse, it will not convince an audience. If it is too flimsy—based on mere opinion, hearsay, or colorful comparisons or analogies—it will not support an otherwise valid claim or generalization.

You already know that evidence can consist of facts and examples, specific cases and events, statistics and other forms of data, expert opinion, and, if used judiciously and in a representative rather than idiosyncratic way, personal experience. Evidence also can derive from scientific observation, field research, and controlled experimentation—forms of evidence common to technical writing and often appearing in tables, graphs, and other visual documents. In all instances, the most distinctive feature of evidence is that it supports a relevant generalization.

Recall the essay by Ronald Takaki, "The Harmful Myth of Asian Superiority" (pages 12–13). Takaki uses evidence to create authority for his proposition or generalization:

> The "model minority" image homogenizes Asian Americans and hides their differences. For example, while thousands of Vietnamese American young people attend universities, others are on the streets. They live in motels and hang out in pool halls in places like East Los Angeles; some join gangs.
>
> Twenty-five percent of the people in New York City's Chinatown lived below the poverty level in 1980, compared with 17 percent of the

city's population. Some 60 percent of the workers in the Chinatowns of Los Angeles and San Francisco are crowded into low-paying jobs in garment factories and restaurants.

"Most immigrants coming into Chinatown with a language barrier cannot go outside the confined area into the mainstream of American industry," a Chinese immigrant said. "Before, I was a painter in Hong Kong, but I can't do it here. I got no license, no education. I want a living; so it's dishwasher, janitor, or cook."

Takaki, who is an authority on ethnicity in American life, makes his case by fleshing out the claim or generalization that appears in the first sentence with examples, statistics, and interviews. Evidence supports his claim.

The chain of argument is never complete without authoritative and compelling evidence. When you read an essay, ask the following questions about the nature of the evidence that a writer presents:

- Are the examples relevant and convincing? Are they sufficient to make the case?
- Is the evidence presented clearly?
- Is the evidence used to support a warrant (we call such evidence *backing*), a claim, or minor propositions, and in each case is it sufficient?
- If statistics appear, are they relevant, accurate, current, complete, and from a reliable source?
- If the writer offers quotations or expert testimony, is it from a knowledgeable, trustworthy, and authoritative source?

Not all evidence is of the same quality or validity. When reading an argumentative essay, you have to be prepared to think critically about the evidence and even enter into a conversation with the writer in which you ask if the factual information is convincing.

READING VISUAL ARGUMENTS

Visual images are as old as the cave paintings of your Neolithic ancestors and as new as the latest streaming advertisements on your computer screen. In fact, some commentators argue that we are in the process of moving from a print-oriented society toward new forms of literacy in which visual images predominate over written texts. It is probably more useful to appreciate the ways in which visual materials—photographs, cartoons, posters, computer graphics, tables and graphs, various forms of type and other design elements, and more—contribute to written texts. If, as Marshall McLuhan declared more than 40 years ago, "the medium is the message," then you should pay attention to the ways in which visual texts mold your response to ideas, information, and arguments.

Visual texts can convey powerful cultural messages and arguments. Figure 1.1 shows firefighters at the site of the World Trade Center erecting

Figure 1.1   Firefighters at the World Trade Center.

an American flag over the rubble that was once the Twin Towers. How do you "read" this photograph? What does the symbolism of the heap of twisted metal and of the flag convey? In what way does a similar image (see Figure 1.2) of soldiers raising the American flag at Iwo Jima during World War II deepen your interpretation of the message? A photograph is a representation of reality, and here we sense that the photographer has framed a scene in order to convey both the horror of the attack against the heart of America and the heroic resilience of its citizens to respond.

When reading and interpreting visual texts that contain explicit or implicit arguments, you have to be aware of the ways in which the creators or designers "massage" their message in order to influence (and sometimes control) your response. When, for instance, you see a 30-second television commercial for a particular brand of beer in which attractive young people are having a great time, you readily sense the massage and the message. When the blurred, decidedly unappealing image of a political candidate appears in a negative campaign ad, you also know the creators' purpose. Or when great graphics pop up on your

Figure 1.2   Iwo Jima.

screen extolling the virtues of a new snowboard, you know you have been targeted. (How did they know you were a boarder?)

Of course, not all visual arguments sell a product or a person. Ideas—as you see in the photographs from Iwo Jima and the Twin Towers—also can be presented; or complex data can be made manageable while advancing a writer's technical or scientific argument. Again, you might use a PowerPoint presentation to highlight the outlines of a speech you have to give to the class advocating free downloading of music on the Internet. In all of these cases, you see that visual texts present a dialogue or conversation, a struggle of sorts, for your time, money, allegiance, attention, or action.

Visual literacy involves an ability to analyze simple and complex images in terms of their design and content.

Visual arguments, in short, have enormous power to persuade us to think and act in specific ways. Advertisements and commercials can be especially seductive. And computer technology, ubiquitous on campus and dormitory life and increasingly present in our very hands and pockets, transmits a steady stream of visual messages that we "interface" with. Today's electronic tsunami saturates us with images, many having an argumentative edge and using subtle strategies designed to get us to think, feel, and behave in specific ways.

Academic writing (and instruction) in particular makes increasing demands on your visual literacy. Often you have to read and respond not only to written texts but to visual images embedded in them. Both verbal and visual images, especially when used for argumentative purposes, force you to engage in a multifaceted conversation about ideas and their consequences. Often you must not only grasp the textual debate but also the visual argument—whether presented through photo clips, cartoons, charts, tables and graphs, poster reproductions, diagrams, and even design elements such as font types—that reinforce the verbal debate.

It should be clear that carefully selected images can reinforce the strength of a claim and the credibility of the evidence. Imagine, for example, that you read an argumentative essay in which the writer claims that the amount of education an individual completes will correlate with his or her economic status. Assuredly the writer will have to provide verifiable written evidence. But consider the added impact of the following graph that the writer could insert into the essay:

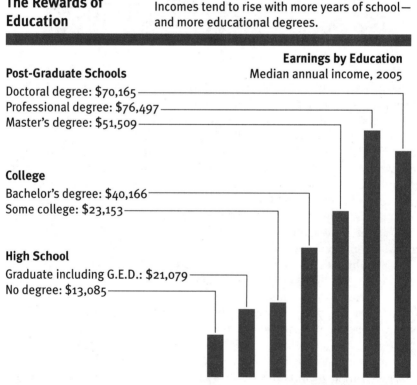

The Rewards of Education   Incomes tend to rise with more years of school— and more educational degrees.

Earnings by Education
Median annual income, 2005

Post-Graduate Schools
Doctoral degree: $70,165
Professional degree: $76,497
Master's degree: $51,509

College
Bachelor's degree: $40,166
Some college: $23,153

High School
Graduate including G.E.D.: $21,079
No degree: $13,085

Source: U.S. Census Bureau

Note how the graph puts the data in visual and verbal form. The vertical bars show readers the comparative relations among the various rewards of education, and the labels connected to the bars spell out the exact median annual income related to educational attainment.

Of course, the images—the visual rhetoric—that are selected must have a clear-cut purpose, reinforce the content, convey authority (note that the source of the above image is the U.S. Census Bureau), and be placed strategically within the paper. And it especially helps if tables and graphs are clear and uncluttered and can be read easily.

Visual elements can also appeal to the emotions, conditioning the way we respond to the development of an argumentative essay. If, for example, you are reading an article defending undocumented immigration into the United States, the following editorial cartoon might very well enhance the writer's claim:

"Well, they look pretty undocumented to me."

The cartoon makes a humorous point about illegal immigration by using contemporary language to identify the arrival of settlers to America when Native Americans ruled the lands. No one on the *Mayflower* was a documented immigrant, certainly. The cartoonist's view of the absurdity of documentation comes across subtly but effectively in the visual representation.

Any visual element, carefully selected and positioned within a paper, has the potential power to clarify and enhance a writer's written argument.

Probably the key virtue of visual elements is that they focus our attention on the writer's argument. Visual elements support the writer's claim. Consequently, you need to think critically about the ways in which the writer uses visual elements to advance an argument and persuade us to accept it. The following questions can help you to analyze visual and multimedia arguments:

Questions about the Content of a Visual Argument

- What is the claim or message the visual conveys? What is its purpose or intended effect? Where do the elements of *logos, ethos,* or *pathos* come into play?
- What media form does the visual utilize: photographs, prints, drawings, graphs, charts, tables, video clips? Is there a multimedia presentation including sound? How carefully have the media been selected? Is the selection successful? Why or why not?
- Who is the audience for the visual? What assumptions about this audience's education, economic status, ethnic or racial background, or cultural values does the visual suggest?
- What is the nature of the evidence provided by the visual, and can it be verified?
- Overall, does the content of the visual seem reasonable, effective, and true?

Questions about the Design of a Visual Argument

- What key details draw your attention immediately? Why?
- What design elements come into play: print, media, photos, video clips, and so on?
- What is the overall design of the visual? What is in the foreground and background? Is the visual perspective from left to right, top to bottom, front to back, and how do the various elements serve to create a coherent image?
- What elements of color and light appear, and to what effect? What is the purpose and effect of any elements of sound?
- What elements are highlighted, and why?
- What elements seem to be deliberately omitted or de-emphasized, and why?
- If words are part of the visual, what is the intended effect? How do image and language interact in the visual?

As with written arguments, you should take nothing for granted when considering visual texts containing arguments, especially when they promote products, personalities, and ideas. When examining visual texts, think critically about their validity and whether or not they are grounded in sound logical, emotional, and ethical appeals.

In the final analysis, reading argumentative texts cannot be reduced to any single system, whether it is Aristotelian, Toulmin, or any other. But you know a good argument when you see that claims are clear, support is good, and evidence is solid. (A sound argumentative essay also typically deals with the opposition and anticipates the possible objections of readers—what Toulmin calls "the conditions of rebuttal.") As you read the five essays appearing next in this chapter, begin to develop a critical perspective on the terms and conditions of argumentation and the various rhetorical and stylistic strategies writers use to bring you around to their point of view.

The Vocabulary of Argument: A Review

- *Argument* is a process of reasoning that presents reasons or proofs to support a position, belief, or conclusion.
- A *claim* is the main idea or conclusion in an argument. It is the statement that needs to be justified or proved. A claim is like a *thesis* or main idea that can be debated, argued, or proved.
- A *proposition* is another term for a claim. The *major proposition* is the main point of the argument. It is what you are trying to prove based on what there is in common in a certain number of acts of knowing, asserting, believing, or doubting. *Minor propositions* are the reasons offered to support the major proposition.
- *Grounds* are like minor propositions. They are the reasons, support, and evidence offered to support a claim. Grounds are any material that serves to prove a claim.
- *Evidence* supports the claim and the minor propositions of an argument. Evidence can be facts, statistics, accepted opinions, expert testimony, examples, or personal experience. Valid evidence will be accurate and true.
- A *fact* is information that can be taken as verifiable. Stated differently, a fact is something believed to have objective reality. Facts differ from *opinions*, which are judgments based on the facts and, if valid, careful reasoning.
- A *warrant* is the connection, typically assumed and unstated, between a claim and the supporting reasons. It is the rule, belief, or principle underlying the argument, the assumption that makes the claim appear to be acceptable. A *backing* is an even larger principle that serves as the foundation for a warrant.
- *Deduction* is a process of reasoning that seeks valid conclusions. Deduction establishes that a conclusion must be true because the *premises*, or statements on which it is based, are also true. As a way of reasoning, deduction proceeds from the general to the particular. By contrast, *induction* is a way of reasoning in which a general

statement is reached on the basis of specific examples. As such, induction moves from the particular to the general.

- A *fallacy* is an error of reasoning based on faulty use of evidence or
  incorrect reasoning from premises or assumptions.
- *Refutation* is the attempt to rebut, weaken, or invalidate the viewpoints of the opposition.

READING AND WRITING ABOUT CURRENT ISSUES

BARBARA EHRENREICH
From Stone Age to Phone Age

*Biologist Barbara Ehrenreich (she got her Ph.D. from Rockefeller University in
1968) became involved in political activism during the Vietnam War and began
writing on topics such as feminism, class in America, and health care. Her books
include* The American Health Empire: Power, Profits, and Politics *(1970)
and* The Hearts of Men: American Dreams, the Flight from Commitment
(1983), and Blood Rites: Origins and History of the Passions of War
(1998). She has written for the Progressive, In These Times, *the* Nation,
Time, *and many other magazines. Her book* Nickel and Dimed: On (Not)
Getting by in America *(2001), recounting her experience working in low-class
jobs, was a best-seller. Her most recent work is* Dancing in the Streets: A History of Collective Joy *(2007). In this selection, which appeared in 1999,
Ehrenreich takes a whimsical look at the ubiquitous phenomenon of cell phones.*

▶ Prereading: Thinking about the Essay in Advance

If you use a cell phone, how is it useful? Why did you want one in the
first place? Could you live without it? Why or why not? If you don't own
a cell phone, do you want one? Explain.

▶ Words to Watch

primal (par. 1) old, instinctive
savanna (par. 2) area of tropical grasslands
hordes (par. 3) large groups
eons (par. 4) millions of years
convivial (par. 12) friendly, social
atomized (par. 12) broken up into small units

1   I was struck by the primal force of my craving for a cell phone. Obviously, others must have felt this, too, since there are now an estimated 100 million people worldwide running around and talking into

the air, with only a small black object nestling against one ear to distinguish them from the deinstitutionalized psychotics. It had become impossible to go anywhere—out on the street, to a shopping mall, or to an airport—without noticing that every other person in earshot was engaged in a vast and urgent ongoing conversation which excluded only myself.

For a stylish explanation of primal urges and even ordinary whims,   2
we turn to evolutionary psychology, which claims that we do what we do because our apelike ancestors once did the same thing. It doesn't matter that our ape-like ancestors did not possess cell phones; they no doubt had cell-phone-related urges. Like most of our primate cousins, humans are social animals. Paleo-anthropologists think we got this way when we left the safety of the forests for the wide open savanna, where we had to band together for defense against a slew of nasty predators. Hence, we are hardwired for wireless telecommunications, or at least for the need to be verbally connected to others of our kind—in case a leopard is lurking nearby. The explosion of cell phone use is simply a reflection of the genetically scripted human inclination to huddle in groups.

There is another interpretation of the evolutionary psychology of cell   3
phones, according to which the cell phone users are seeking not fellowship but isolation from the hordes of fellow humans around them. To a non-cell-phone user, the cell phoners marching through supermarkets and malls project an aura of total inaccessibility. Maybe they are really having meaningful and satisfying conversations. And maybe they are simply trying to repel the advances of any phone-less fellow humans who happen to be physically present.

In their 1992 book, *The Social Cage: Human Nature and the Evolution of*   4
Society (Stanford University Press), Alexandra Maryanski and Jonathan H. Turner argue that for eons before our ancestors were forced to band together in the savanna, they lived contented solitary lives in the trees, much like orangutans today. Our arboreal ancestors were probably pleased to run into others of their own kind only at mating time; otherwise, they regarded each other as competitors for the nicest berries and comfiest nesting spots. If these orangutan-type pre-humans had cell phones, they would have used them to signal each other: "Bug off. Can't you see I have an important call right now?"

Yet another evolutionary-psychological factor probably contributed   5
to cell phone mania. Since the advent of agriculture about 10,000 years ago, and possibly well before then, humans have lived in hierarchical societies where we have been eager to signal our status with accessories such as feather-tufted spears and shrunken-head pendants.

Cell phones serve much the same function, and will continue to do so   6
until they become as common as Walkmen. Thus, the point is not to communicate with distant kin and colleagues, but with all the anonymous others who are around at the moment.

7   If you doubt this, consider when you last heard someone say into a cell phone: "Yes, I am a worthless turd, and if I screw up again, please hasten to fire me." What the person is saying, instead, is invariably, "God damn it, Craig, I told you we need that order by Thursday and no later," or something very similar. It was the opportunity to speak commandingly in public places that tempted me, for several years, to find a fake cell phone designed for playpen use so that I, too, could stride along the sidewalk barking at imaginary brokers and underlings.

8   As soon as I got my own cell phone, I was disappointed to find that, although we may have evolved to be psychologically cell-phone-dependent, our anatomy is still stuck in the era when technology consisted of a sharpened stone.

9   For one thing, our fingertips are too fat for the keypad, so that it takes several tries to dial even "911" with any degree of accuracy.

10   Then there's the tiny size of the phones themselves—more appropriate to a lemur or some other remote primate ancestor than to full-grown Homo sapiens. My own phone's total length is about four-and-a-half inches, so that if I wish to speak and listen at the same time, I have to reduce the distance between mouth and ear by screwing my mouth way over into my right cheek, as if suffering an attack of extreme insecurity. The only hope is that the process of natural selection will soon lead to humans with antenna-like fingers and mouths situated at temple level.

11   Another problem is that my relationships with other humans have not yet evolved to the point that would be truly helpful in the cell phone era. I have the usual quota of friends, relatives, and so-called business associates, but none of them is so underemployed that I can call and ask: "Hey there, you got a few minutes to walk me over to the bank so that I don't look like I, uh, don't have anyone to talk to?" Sometimes there is no alternative but to dial up 1-900-WEATHER and pretend to converse with it, and I suspect that many other cell phone users are doing the same.

12   So here's what I conclude about the evolutionary psychology of cell phones: We are social animals, no question about it, better suited to traveling in convivial bands, hooting and chattering, than to wandering alone in crowds. But few such convivial bands exist within our famously atomized and individualistic capitalist society, where most human relationships now take the sinister form of "deals." So we have regressed to a modified orangutan state: Despairing of true sociality, we settle for faking it. The satisfaction, such as it is, lies in making our equally lonely fellow humans feel jealous.

13   I do have one new friend, though. Everywhere I go now, it comes along, tucked neatly in my pocket or purse. At night I plug it into the wall to recharge, and hear its happy little beep as the nurturing current flows in. Sometimes I take it out during the day, play with its keypad, and confide into its mouthpiece for a moment. Pathetic? Perhaps, but it's not easy striding out into that savanna alone.

▶ Building Vocabulary

Define the following terms from the professional vocabulary of the social sciences:

1. psychotics (par. 1)
2. evolutionary psychology (par. 2)
3. primate cousins (par. 2)
4. paleo-anthropologists (par. 2)
5. hierarchical societies (par. 5)
6. Homo sapiens (par. 10)
7. natural selection (par. 10)
8. capitalist (par. 12)

▶ Thinking Critically about the Argument

Understanding the Writer's Argument

1. What does the writer mean by the "primal force" of her "craving for a cell phone"? (par. 1)
2. What scientific discipline does the writer use to explain her urge for a cell phone? Why does she choose that discipline?
3. What is the paleo-anthropologists' explanation for why humans are "social animals"?
4. What are two other interpretations, from the world of evolutionary psychology, for why people like to talk on cell phones?
5. Why, according to the writer, would people pretend to be on a cell phone?

Understanding the Writer's Techniques

1. Why does the writer admit at the start of her essay that she craved a cell phone? What argumentative purpose does that serve?
2. What are Ehrenreich's implied warrant or warrants in this essay?
3. How does she move from discussing herself and her personal relation to cell phones to discussing humanity as a whole? Why does she do this?
4. Where is the writer's central claim? Write the sentence that best expresses it.
5. Ehrenreich offers several variations on the theme of her claim. List those variations and paraphrase each one.
6. What is the writer's tone? How do you know? Use quotes from the essay to demonstrate your answer.
7. How does the writer's argument change after she says, in paragraph 8, that she got her own cell phone?
8. Near the end of her essay, the writer attempts to reconcile the variations on the theme of her claim and make one central argument. What is that argument, and is her closing effective?

Exploring the Writer's Argument

1. There are two types of arguments here: serious attempts at a critique of cell phone use and flip, jokey attempts at humor. Give an example of each, and analyze the writer's use of humor.
2. After answering question 1, discuss whether you think the jokey quality of the essay is effective or not, and explain your answer.
3. One of the points is that cell phones are status symbols. Explain why you think that is either true or not true.

▶ Ideas for Writing Arguments

Prewriting

Jot down recollections of incidents when you have seen and heard someone talk on a cell phone in an inappropriate place or in an inappropriate way.

Writing a Guided Argument

Write an essay in which you argue that there are some places that should prohibit the use of cell phones. Before writing, make sure that you build evidence, coming up with good examples to back up your minor propositions.

1. Begin by establishing rapport with the reader by making it clear that you too use a cell phone or that you are not against cell phones as a rule.
2. Explain the fact that people can often be rude.
3. Make your claim in a clear, declarative sentence.
4. Offer several examples for cell-phone-free zones, using examples to back up your claims.
5. Anticipate one objection for each of your points.
6. It is important to conclude with a statement of solidarity with cell-phone users, except for the rude ones.

Thinking, Arguing, and Writing Collaboratively

Form into groups of three or four. In these groups, discuss modern technological devices other than cell phones that are used widely or becoming increasingly popular. Each group should choose one device and apply Ehrenreich's method to that device. Come up with at least two or three explanations based in paleo-anthropology. Then each student should write a paragraph on the topic chosen by the group. Exchange paragraphs and peer-critique them.

Writing about the Text

Ehrenreich published this article in 1999, when cell phones were just starting to become popular. Cell phones are much more common now. How is Ehrenreich's essay out of date? How could you update it and still keep her central claim? Is it possible to write an essay such as this without the risk of being out of date several years later? Write an essay responding to one or more of these questions.

More Writing Ideas

1. Many states are passing laws that ban drivers from talking on hand-held cell phones. Many drivers disagree with these laws. In your journal, come up with reasons for both sides of the argument.
2. Write a paragraph or two about the benefits cell phones have brought to humankind.
3. Find a magazine ad for cell-phone service or for a kind of cell phone with special features and analyze the images and text in the advertisement. Write an essay comparing the promises the ad makes to the consumer—both stated and implied—with the realities of owning and using a cell phone.

JAMES TRAUB
All Go Down Together

James Traub is a freelance writer and the author of Too Good to Be True *(1990), a book about a corporate corruption and fraud case in New York in the 1980s, and* City on a Hill *(1994), a history of City College of New York, a public institution in Harlem. He has also written a book about Times Square in New York,* The Devil's Playground *(2004). His most recent book is* Best Intentions: Kofi Annan and the UN in the Era of American World Power *(2006). In this selection, Traub addresses the pitfalls of the country's all-volunteer military and a possible alternative.*

▶ Prereading: Thinking about the Essay in Advance

France and Israel, among other countries, require all citizens of a certain age to serve in the military for a fixed term. Do you think this is a good idea? Why or why not?

▶ **Words to Watch**

beneficiaries (par. 1) those benefiting
deferment (par. 1) putting off until later
conscription (par. 2) military draft
equitable (par. 2) fair
imperative (par. 5) necessity
calculus (par. 6) method of figuring out

1   When Richard Nixon abolished the draft in 1973, I was one of the beneficiaries. I had just become eligible, and in the normal course of things I would have been assigned a lottery number. Of course, it's unlikely that I would have donned a uniform even if I had come up No. 1; there was always a way out if you had access to the right lawyers and doctors. At the time, I knew literally no one who served—no one. Thanks to college deferment, during the Vietnam War, college students served at only half the rate of high-school graduates, and the higher up you went in the socioeconomic scale, the likelier it was that you would keep out of harm's way.

2   But what if conscription were equitable and were used to fill a military that was widely respected rather than scorned? This was the case, after all, in the period between the Korean and Vietnam Wars, when military service was widely accepted as the price of citizenship. Why wouldn't that be true today? Why wouldn't it be just the kind of sacrifice young Americans would agree to make at a time of heightened patriotism? The idea has been in the air since earlier this year, when Representative Charles Rangel of New York introduced a bill to restore conscription. Since Rangel got a grand total of 11 co-sponsors, it is safe to say that conscription is an idea whose time has not come, but it's still one worth thinking seriously about.

3   The most obvious objection to a restoration of the draft is that the all-volunteer force, as it is known, is one of the most successful institutions in the country. The A.V. F. is both the world's most powerful fighting force and a shining example of harmonious race relations and affirmative action. When asked about the draft, Secretary of Defense Donald H. Rumsfeld has essentially said, Why fix what isn't broken? There are several answers to this question. First of all, the war on terrorism is already straining the military and imposing terrible burdens on reservists. Second, we may soon be redefining such civilian tasks as border patrol and airport security as military ones, thus requiring a much larger uniformed force. Charles Moskos, a professor of sociology at Northwestern and an expert on military affairs, has proposed a three-tier draft involving a military, a homeland defense and a civilian component, the last essentially a form of "national service." So a draft would satisfy manpower needs that an all-volunteer force might not. It would also almost certainly be cheaper.

But the ultimate justification for conscription must be moral. Both 4
Rangel and Moskos argue that the A.V. F. recruits working-class young
men and women with bleak job prospects and pays them to put their
lives on the line. "These people should not have to die merely because
they were born to a class of people that lacked the advantages of other
people," as Rangel says. There is also an important issue of political philosophy. Conscription assumes a relationship between citizen and state
that makes most conservatives, and many liberals, uncomfortable. Libertarian conservatives like Milton Friedman object vehemently to any form
of compulsion on the part of the state that's not absolutely unavoidable.
Liberals have traditionally feared the use to which the state puts its soldiers. In 1970, at the height of the Vietnam War, the political philosopher
Michael Walzer wrote that since many citizens are bound to find almost
any use of military power unjust, conscription may be justified only
when the state's very existence is threatened. We owe the state no more
than that.

But is that so? In the age of terrorism, doesn't the imperative of self- 5
defense go well beyond acts of direct territorial threat? What's more, is
the draft really a form of tyranny? We live in a culture in which everyone
has rights and no one has obligations; the social contract has never been
so wan. Perhaps now that our collective safety is jeopardized, the time
has come to rethink that contract. Moskos says that in the Princeton class
of 1956, from which he graduated, 450 of 750 men served in the military.
Last year, Moskos says, 3 of Princeton's approximately 1,000 graduates
served. That can't be a good thing for the country.

Of course, the country was at peace in 1956. A young man or woman 6
drafted today might very well face combat—and might even have to
serve in a war, like Iraq, that he or she considered wrongheaded—the
Walzer problem. Perhaps draftees could be permitted to elect other forms
of national service. But a truly democratic draft might also, as Rangel suggests, alter the strategic calculus: if the children of journalists, legislators
and policy experts were called to military service, we might do a more
thorough, and a more honest, job of deciding exactly what it is that's
worth fighting for.

I have a 12-year-old son. The idea that in six or seven years Alex 7
might be drafted is a little bit comical, but mostly appalling. My wife
thinks I'm crazy even to suggest the idea. Nevertheless, it's true that we
live in a genuinely threatening world; that is, alas, the very reason that
military service, or at least some kind of service, should be mandatory,
rather than a matter of individual conscience or marketplace choice.

▶ Building Vocabulary

1. Traub uses some words that refer to political ideologies and situations. Identify the following and offer examples from history or the present day:
   a. conservatives (par. 4)
   b. liberals (par. 4)
   c. libertarian (par. 4)
   d. tyranny (par. 5)
2. A number of words in this essay refer to social service concepts. Identify the following and use them in a sentence of your own:
   a. socioeconomic scale (par. 1)
   b. bill (par. 2)
   c. co-sponsors (par. 2)
   d. affirmative action (par. 3)
   e. social contract (par. 5)

▶ Thinking Critically about the Argument

Understanding the Writer's Argument

1. Why does the writer start his essay with his experience?
2. Why did Richard Nixon abolish the draft in 1973?
3. During the Vietnam War, why were wealthier young men able to "keep out of harm's way"? (par. 1)
4. Why do Charlie Rangel and other members of Congress want to restore conscription?
5. What is the writer's answer to the objection that the all-volunteer military is working well as it is?
6. The writer gives statistics in paragraph 5 for the number of students in two classes at Princeton who served in the military. Why does he do this?
7. Why does the writer mention his son at the end of his essay?

Understanding the Writer's Techniques

1. What is the tone in this essay? Who is the audience, and how does this affect the tone?
2. Where does his claim appear most clearly? If you don't see the claim, how does the essay succeed without it?
3. What is the argumentative effect of opening this essay with a personal recollection?
4. What, according to the writer, is the main ground for his claim? Where does he express it most clearly?

5. In paragraphs 3 and 5, the writer asks rhetorical questions. Why does he do this, and how effective are they? In the conclusion, what is the rhetorical effect of the writer's mentioning his son and his wife? How effective is the technique?
6. In addition to responding to arguments by the opposition, the writer puts forward his own arguments. What are these, and why are they presented in the order in which they are presented?
7. What is the meaning of the title? How does it reflect Traub's claim?

Exploring the Writer's Argument

1. Traub says in paragraph 2 that the lack of congressional support for the Rangel bill shows that "conscription is an idea whose time has not come, but it's still one worth thinking seriously about." Does this admission weaken the argument or strengthen it? Why?
2. In this essay, the writer is never absolutely specific about what a draft would entail. Is this a problem with the argument? Why or why not? What do you think would be the writer's answer if you asked him what form he preferred the draft came in?
3. Paraphrase the writer's argument in paragraph 6. What is "the Walzer problem"? Are you convinced by the argument in this paragraph? Explain your answer fully.

▶ Ideas for Writing Arguments

Prewriting

Do a focused 10- to 15-minute freewrite about what you think your reaction would be if you were drafted to be in the United States military right now.

Writing a Guided Argument

Pretend that the United States has reinstated the draft, and both men and women are eligible. Write a letter to the draft board either telling them that you will appear as requested, or that you refuse to serve, knowing that the former decision could put you in harm's way and that the latter decision could mean jail time. For either choice, explain yourself fully.

1. Begin, "Dear Draft Board:"
2. Indicate your own particular socioeconomic level, and explain why this has influenced your choice and why it is relevant to your argument.

3. Give at least two grounds for your choice, referring at least once to the arguments over the obligation of the citizen to the state as introduced in paragraph 4 of Traub's essay.
4. Write a rebuttal to a perceived objection to your choice.
5. Include evidence in the form of examples or cause-and-effect analysis for each of your points.
6. Conclude your letter by saying that your choice is one that all young people should make, and reiterate the grounds for your decision.
7. Sign your name (don't worry—it's not official).

Thinking, Arguing, and Writing Collaboratively

Exchange a draft of your Writing a Guided Argument assignment with a classmate. Review your partner's essay for its success in following the steps. Is the major proposition expressed as a choice? Is the major proposition reflected in the minor propositions? Is there sufficient evidence to back up the minor propositions? Write a paragraph evaluating the essay and suggesting revisions.

Writing about the Text

Traub writes several statements in this selection that point to the political spectrum, from conservative to liberal, but he never identifies his own politics. In fact, he seems to avoid the subject explicitly. Try to identify Traub's political bent or ideology, and write an argumentative essay to defend your claim.

More Writing Ideas

1. What does a citizen owe his or her country? What is "the price of citizenship"? Write about this in your journal.
2. Write a paragraph in which you argue in favor of or against Charles Moskos's proposed three-tier draft.
3. In an essay, argue that the situation in the United States today falls under Michael Walzer's criterion for conscription, that "the state's very existence is threatened."

Anna Quindlen
One Nation, Indivisible? Wanna Bet?

Anna Quindlen graduated from Barnard College. She has written extensively, but most visibly as a columnist for the New York Times *from 1981 to 1994. In 1992 she won a Pulitzer Prize for her commentary. A collection of columns,* Thinking Out Loud, *was published in 1993. She is also a novelist.* One True Thing *(1994) was adapted into a movie in 1998. Her latest book is a novel,* Rise and Shine *(2007). Her position as an observer of American life serves her well in this selection from* Newsweek, *which examines the controversy over the words "under God" in the Pledge of Allegiance.*

▶ Prereading: Thinking about the Essay in Advance

The Constitution of the United States calls for a separation of religion and government, more commonly known as "church and state." Do you think this is a good idea? Why or why not? When have you seen a blending of church and state in the United States?

▶ Words to Watch

impermissible (par. 2) not allowed
jingoism (par. 2) excessive patriotism
deplorable (par. 4) morally wrong
machinations (par. 4) workings
spate (par. 6) outburst
eschew (par. 6) avoid

Every year somebody or other finds a way to show that American   1
kids are ignorant of history. The complaint isn't that they don't know the broad strokes, the rationale the South gave for keeping slaves, the ideas behind the New Deal. It's always dates and names, the game-show questions that ask what year the Civil War began and who ordered the bombing of Hiroshima, the stuff of the stand-up history bee. But if American adults want to give American kids a hard time about their dim knowledge of the past and how it's reflected in the present, they might first become reasonable role models on the subject. And the modeling could begin with the members of Congress, who with few exceptions went a little nuts when an appeals court in California ruled that the phrase "under God" in the Pledge of Allegiance was unconstitutional.

2   I don't really know whether that is an impermissible breach of the firewall between church and state. The proper boundaries 'twixt secular and sacred have been argued long and hard by legal minds more steeped in the specific intricacies than my own. But I do know this: attempts to make the pledge sound like a cross between the Ten Commandments and the Constitution are laughable, foolish and evidence of the basest sort of political jingoism.

3   So let's go to the history books, as citizens of this country so seldom do. The Pledge of Allegiance started in 1892 as a set piece in a magazine, nothing more, nothing less. It was written by a man named Francis Bellamy in honor of Columbus Day, a holiday that scarcely exists anymore except in terms of department-store sales and parades. The words "under God" were nowhere in it, hardly surprising since Bellamy had been squeezed out of his own church the year before because of his socialist leanings. His granddaughter said he would have hated the addition of the words "under God" to a statement he envisioned uniting a country divided by race, class and, of course, religion.

4   Those two words went into the pledge nearly 50 years ago, and for the most deplorable reason. It was the height of the Red scare in America, when the lives of those aligned or merely flirting with the Communist Party were destroyed by paranoia, a twisted strain of uber-patriotism and the machinations of Sen. Joseph McCarthy, after whom an entire vein of baseless persecution is now named. Contrary to the current political argument that "under God" is not specifically devout, the push to put it in the pledge was mounted by the Knights of Columbus, a Roman Catholic men's organization, as an attempt to counter "godless communism." President Dwight D. Eisenhower signed a bill making this law, saying that the words would help us to "remain humble."

5   Humility had nothing to do with it. Americans are not a humble people. Instead the pledge had become yet another cold-war litmus test. The words "under God" were a way to indicate that America was better than other nations—we were, after all, under the direct protection of the deity—and adding them to the pledge was another way of excluding, of saying that believers were real Americans and skeptics were not. Would any member of Congress have been brave enough at that moment to say that a Pledge of Allegiance that had been good enough for decades was good enough as it stood?

6   Would any member of Congress, in the face of the current spate of unquestioning flag-waving, have been strong enough to eschew leaping to his feet and pressing his hand over his heart, especially knowing that the percentage of atheist voters is in the low single digits? Well, there were a few, a few who said the decision was likely to be overturned anyhow, a few who said there were surely more pressing matters before the nation, a few who were even willing to agree with the appeals court that

"under God" probably did not belong in the pledge in a country founded on a righteous division between government and religion.

But most of the rest went wild. Even Sen. Hillary Clinton invoked 7 "divine providence," even Sen. Dianne Feinstein called the court decision "embarrassing." What was embarrassing was watching all those people—Republicans, Democrats, liberals, conservatives—shout "under God" on the Senate floor, as though government were a pep rally and they were on the sanctified squad. Sen. Bob Smith of New Hampshire had this to say: "If you don't believe there's a God, that's your privilege, but it is still a nation under God." Huh?

I have a warm personal relationship with God; I often picture her smil- 8 ing wryly and saying, in the words of Shakespeare's Puck, "Lord, what fools these mortals be!" Or perhaps something less fond. Now, as almost 50 years ago, a nation besieged by ideological enemies requires nuanced and judicious statecraft and instead settles for sloganeering, demonizing and politicking. One senator said after the court decision was handed down that the Founding Fathers must be spinning in their graves. The person who must be spinning is poor Francis Bellamy, who wanted to believe in an inclusive utopia and instead became in our time the father of convenient rhetoric.

▶ Building Vocabulary

This selection requires knowledge of some concepts, issues, and people relating to U.S. politics. Check with a dictionary or other reference work and define, identify, and explain the relevance of the following:

1. the New Deal (par. 1)
2. the Red scare (par. 4)
3. Joseph McCarthy (par. 4)
4. cold war (par. 5)
5. litmus test (par. 5)
6. Sen. Hillary Clinton (par. 7)
7. Sen. Dianne Feinstein (par. 7)
8. Sen. Bob Smith (par. 7)

▶ Thinking Critically about the Argument

Understanding the Writer's Argument

1. Why does Quindlen compare the members of Congress to ignorant schoolchildren? What point is she making?
2. What is the "firewall" between church and state? To what is she referring?
3. What are the origins of the Pledge of Allegiance?

4. What would the writer of the Pledge have thought of the addition of the words "under God" inserted in his work? How do you know?
5. Why were the words "under God" finally inserted into the Pledge?
6. Why were members of Congress so against taking out those words? Did any think taking them out was a good idea?

Understanding the Writer's Techniques

1. What tone is set by the title of the essay?
2. The body of the essay includes some strong and combative language that sets a certain tone reflecting how Quindlen feels about the issue. How would you describe that tone, and why? Do you think it is consistent with the title? Why?
3. Where does the major proposition appear most clearly and fully?
4. What argumentative function does the opening serve?
5. Paraphrase the minor proposition in paragraph 2.
6. The writer uses the facts of history to help argue her case. Where in the essay does she do this? Explain why the technique is effective.
7. How do paragraphs 6 and 7 support her position?
8. What is your view of the conclusion? Do you think it is effective? Why or why not?

Exploring the Writer's Argument

1. Quindlen accuses members of Congress of being extreme in their politics. Do you think she is being extreme as well? Why or why not?
2. To help make her case, the author writes in paragraph 5 that "Americans are not a humble people." Do you think this is true? Why or why not?
3. The author says that the Pledge didn't have the words "under God" in it for more than 50 years, so why shouldn't we change it back to how it was? But now the phrase has been in there for almost 50 years. Which tradition should take precedence? Explain your answer fully.

▶ Ideas for Writing Arguments

Prewriting

Read the words to "America the Beautiful," a song that is now sung during the seventh-inning stretch at baseball games in place of "Take Me Out to the Ballgame." What is your reaction to the lyrics of "America the Beautiful" in light of this essay? Why is this a different case?

Writing a Guided Argument

Write an essay arguing that we don't need a Pledge of Allegiance at all.

1. Open your essay with a recollection of reciting or learning the Pledge and of the first time you thought about the words.
2. Refer to the controversy that Quindlen discusses, using a quote from her essay and commenting on it.
3. Use a tone similar to Quindlen's.
4. Clearly state your position and the main ground for your position.
5. Anticipate the main objection to dropping the Pledge in one paragraph, and in a separate paragraph, using proper transitions, rebut the objection.
6. Close the body of your essay with an appeal to the true meaning of America.
7. Conclude by restating your position in light of your supporting points and your rebuttal.

Thinking, Arguing, and Writing Collaboratively

In small groups, examine the concept of jingoism. Where do you see jingoism in your neighborhood? In the media? Write individually on this topic for 10 minutes, and then come together and share your thoughts with your group. Then, as a class, discuss the dangers of jingoism and why it is so tempting.

Writing about the Text

Quindlen uses a sarcastic tone in this selection. Write an essay in which you argue that this tone and use of language is effective here, and explain why. In your essay, be sure to explain exactly which passages you find sarcastic, and explore why you think she uses that language.

More Writing Ideas

1. Do some research on the history of the division between church and state. Quindlen writes that the United States was "founded on a righteous division between government and religion." In which founding document is this division guaranteed, and where? What exactly does the document say? Write a journal entry exploring the quote you find.
2. Use your work on question 1 to add to Quindlen's argument. Write a paragraph in which you develop a minor proposition using the evidence you have gathered.
3. What other rights, privileges, or guarantees from the Constitution do you think are eroding in our times? Write an essay on this question, explaining your answer fully.

Mario Vargas Llosa
The Fence of Lies

Mario Vargas Llosa is a Peruvian novelist, essayist, and political activist. Born in 1936, he is best known for his novels Conversation in the Cathedral *(1969) and* The Storyteller *(1987). He ran, unsuccessfully, for the presidency of Peru in 1990 on a center-right ticket. He is known, most recently, for his pro-market views, views that are reflected in this selection, which was published in the* New Statesman *in 2006. Vargas Llosa questions the logic and efficacy of building the fence the U.S. Congress approved for construction along the southern border of the United States.*

▶ Prereading: Thinking about the Essay in Advance

Do you think that a fence along the Mexican border can effectively keep immigrants from coming into the United States? Is it desirable to stop Mexican immigration? What are the downsides of having Mexicans enter our country illegally? What are the benefits?

▶ Words to Watch

contaminate (par. 1) pollute, make unclean
conjectures (par. 4) guesses
infrastructure (par. 4) large-scale public systems needed for a society to run
constituencies (par. 4) groups of people with common interests
malignant (par. 5) harmful
haemorrhage (par. 5) rapid loss of resources
paraphernalia (par. 6) various objects
manifold (par. 8) many and various
scruples (par. 9) ethical considerations
tariff (par. 11) tax on imported goods
domain (par. 12) scope, area of interest

1   The United States Congress has approved the construction of a 700-mile fence along the border with Mexico, which is expected to cost $6bn in total, to stop illegal immigration, and President Bush has promised to promulgate the law immediately. For someone who, like myself, is fascinated by

the way fiction can contaminate reality, the news could not be more spell-binding. Why? Because this wall will never be built; and if, by some miracle, it is actually built, it will serve for absolutely nothing. Everyone knows this—beginning, of course, with the legislators and the president.

Why then all this theatrical show? Because on 7 November there will 2 be elections in the US to renew the whole of the House of Representatives, part of the Senate and 36 state governorships, and those who are seeking re-election want to have this law in hand as proof that they have begun to do something about the dangerous plague of illegal immigrants, who take jobs away from real Americans and suck the social security system dry (another popular fiction).

The "fence of lies" will run along the southern border of four states— 3 California, Arizona, New Mexico and Texas—and consist of two fences and a futuristic system of reflectors, grilles, sensors and radar, to make it absolutely airtight. But of what use will it be to seal off these 1,200 kilome-tres, if there remain another 1,200 miles (about 2,000 kilometres) of open frontier through which Mexican and central American immigrants can slip into US territory, easily circumventing the fenced, electrified sections?

But these are conjectures with no foundation in the real world, where 4 the construction of this fence faces myriad obstacles, already anticipated in the US media, which I admit to reading and watching every day with real enjoyment. For a start, many mayors and governors in the four states the fence is to cross have already said they will demand that the huge in-vestment be redirected to infrastructure—highways, schools, public serv-ice installations. Several native communities have raised a cry, threatening legal action to prevent the fence from dividing their grazing and farming land; while other constituencies, left to one side along the route the fan-tasy fence will take, threaten legal action to change its discriminatory route. But above all, it is the powerful ecological groups that have come out against it, proclaiming that they will use every political, judicial and civic resource to prevent this predatory, contaminating monstrosity from wreaking havoc on the environment. Interestingly enough, the legislators have taken the precaution of putting an escape clause in the law, empow-ering the government to use part of the budget to build roads.

If the fence project overcomes the variety of judicial obstacles in its 5 way, which will at least delay its construction for many years, it will not serve in the least to stop the flow of illegal immigrants into the United States. There are countless ways of demonstrating this fact, which are vis-ible to anyone of the least intelligence who is not blinded by prejudice, and by the malignant fiction that the immigrants do more harm than good to the host country. As I write this, the press in Washington says that according to an official report, Hispanic immigrants, over the course of this year, will have sent home to their families in Latin America the colossal sum of $45bn, some 60 per cent more than two years ago, when the last survey was made. The bigots deduce from this figure that immigrants are a fearful haemorrhage in the US economy. But the true reading is one of admiration and enthusiasm, since it means that Latin American immigrants have produced for the US an amount of wealth four or five times greater than that figure—wealth which has stayed in the country. And $200bn or $250bn is a considerable contribution to the economy—an economy that, according to all the statistics, is booming, with the highest employment rate of all the developed countries (only about 4.5 per cent unemployment).

6   This imaginary wall will be useless—an arbitrary rambling sculpture running up and down the canyons and mountains of Arizona, scarring the deserts of California and Texas. So, if we are to understand why, rather than cite statistics, which never convince anyone, it is better to tell the story of Emérita (not her real name, but a common one in Guatemala). I met her three years ago when I was spending a semester in Washington, as I am now. Some neighbours recommended her to us to come and clean the house twice a week. We hired her, and she did a fine job; in the two hours she spent in the house with vacuum cleaner, feather duster and other paraphernalia, she left the place as shiny as a butcher's shop in Switzerland. In those days she charged us $60 for the two hours.

7   We have been lucky enough to get her again, and now she charges $90 a visit. In fact, this is a discount price. All our neighbours who have cleaners (the immense majority of them Hispanic) coming to their houses pay $100. Emérita is a central American who has been in the US for ten years, and now gets along fairly well in English. She has a new van filled with all sorts of equipment to sweep, polish, clean, shake, et cetera. On Saturdays—she works six days a week and rests on Sunday—she is helped by her husband, who is a gardener the rest of the time. I don't know how much he makes, but Emérita cleans four houses a day on average, so her monthly income is no less than $8,000. This is why she and her husband have already bought a house here, and another in their country of origin.

        Before they came to the US the couple barely survived. But the worst,
8   says Emérita, was that "there was no hope of improvement in the future. This is the big difference in the United States." Yes, this is the huge difference, and this is why thousands, millions, of Latin Americans, who know the story of Emérita and her husband, are following in their footsteps, escaping from sink-hole countries where there is no hope, and coming here, crossing rivers and mountains, hiding in trucks or paying the manifold, efficient mafias that falsify passports and visas, permits and everything you need to get to the US—where, as everyone knows, they are welcomed with open arms. The proof is that they all find jobs almost immediately.

Low-level jobs

Jobs that US citizens don't want to do, of course. Cleaners, minders for   9
old people, nightwatchmen, lettuce pickers under the burning sun, or
working in factories and shops low-level, precarious jobs. Only they are
prepared to do these jobs which, for the standard of living of the country,
are poorly paid. But not from their point of view: for these immigrant
workers, the low wages are a fortune. This is why US citizens, even those
who talk about the perils of immigration, have no scruples about hiring
them, because thanks to the Eméritas their houses are shining clean, and
their factories and services function.

The only way to stop the immigration is for Mexico and Central and 10
South America to offer better opportunities to their poor masses, and the
same sort of hope for improvement that the Hispanics find in the United
States, which is the incentive that makes them work night and day at
whatever comes to hand. It is good for them, of course, but it is even better for this country—a country of immigrants, let's not forget—which,
thanks to the drive and sacrifice of these 41 million Latin Americans, is
still growing and prospering, in spite of the difficult political and international problems it now faces.

The $6bn that the fence of lies is supposed to cost for a cement mon- 11
strosity that would soon be as full of holes as a Swiss cheese—would be
better spent, as far as illegal immigration is concerned, on factories or
credits aimed at creating jobs on the other side of the border. Or the tariff
barriers could be gradually opened to Latin American products, which
would also benefit consumers in the US.

But all this belongs to the domain of strict reality, and it is well 12
known that human beings—including the grin who pride themselves on
their practicality—often prefer the magic of fiction to the raw reality of
life as it is.

▶ Building Vocabulary

For each the following, write a definition and use the word in a sentence
of your own:

1. promulgate (par. 1)
2. myriad (par. 4)
3. predatory (par. 4)
4. havoc (par. 4)
5. deduce (par. 5)
6. arbitrary (par. 6)
7. precarious (par. 9)

▶ Thinking Critically about the Argument

Understanding the Writer's Argument

1. Why, according to Vargas Llosa, has Congress passed a law approving the construction of a fence along the border of Mexico, and why has the president promised to build it right away?
2. Why does the writer call the fence a "fence of lies"?
3. What are the obstacles the building of the fence will face, according to Vargas Llosa?
4. What is the "escape clause" the author speaks of in paragraph 4?
5. Why would the fence be useless even if it is built, according to the author?
6. Why does the author tell the story of Emérita, the woman who cleans his house?
7. Why do immigrants do low-level jobs in the United States, such as cleaning, taking care of the elderly, and agricultural work?
8. What, according to the writer, is the only way to stop immigration from Mexico and Central and South America?

Understanding the Writer's Techniques

1. What is the effect of Vargas Llosa beginning his essay with a plain sentence stating the situation?
2. What is the tone of this essay? How would you describe the audience for the essay, and how does that affect the tone?
3. How does the author use the title of his essay in the essay itself? Is the title persuasive?
4. What is the central claim of this essay? Where is it stated most clearly?
5. Make an outline of the minor propositions contained in Vargas Llosa's essay. Why does he place them in that order? Would you change the order to make the essay more persuasive? Why or why not?
6. What evidence does Vargas Llosa use to support his idea that the fence would be useless, if it were built?
7. How is the short narrative interlude about Emérita effective? Explain. Analyze the structure of this portion of the essay. What makes it persuasive? How does it connect with the central claim of the essay?
8. What is your opinion of the concluding paragraph of this essay? Does it wrap up the essay persuasively? Why does the author contrast fiction and reality again?

Exploring the Writer's Argument

1. Vargas Llosa seems to think that using narrative rather than other forms of argument is the most persuasive way of getting through to people. Do you agree? Why or why not?
2. Does Vargas Llosa offer an alternative to the fence he ridicules? If so, what is his solution? Do you think it is reasonable? Why or why not? If he doesn't have a solution, what do you think is a possible solution?
3. Do you think Vargas Llosa's language is effective? He seems to use a lot of incendiary language, such as the word "monstrosity" twice, "predatory," and "arbitrary." Why do you think he uses this kind of language?
4. Do you think Vargas Llosa is being critical of Americans who hire immigrants to do the work they don't want to do? What do you think of his discussion of this phenomenon? Is he too matter-of-fact about it? Why or why not?

▶ Ideas for Writing Arguments

Prewriting

Think of any immigrants you may know. What has been their experience coming to this country? If you don't know any immigrants, why is this the case, do you think?

Writing a Guided Argument

Write an essay in which you argue for or against the idea of granting instant citizenship to the 7 million to 20 million illegal immigrants in this country. You might have to do some research to learn about the issues.

1. Begin with a paragraph that introduces your reader to the subject through a simple statement of your position.
2. Establish a tone of authority, using language that leaves no doubt as to your strong feelings about the subject.
3. Explain the opposition's arguments, again using a slight tone of ridicule.
4. Offer two points of evidence based in fact.
5. Inject some interest into your essay by including a narrative about a particular immigrant you learned about during your research.
6. End your essay with a reiteration of your main point, explaining why your narrative example makes your point for you.

Thinking, Arguing, and Writing Collaboratively

In small groups of three or four, exchange your Writing a Guided Argument papers. Offer suggestions in the form of a paragraph or two to help your classmate develop his or her essay. Offer, from your own research, anything that might add to your peer's argument.

Writing about the Text

Look ahead and read Thomas L. Friedman's essay "Globalization, Alive and Well" in Chapter 16. Write an essay arguing how Vargas Llosa and Friedman agree on major issues regarding open borders and globalization.

More Writing Ideas

1. Write in your journal about your own family's origins as immigrants to the United States. How does your family's collective memory change your view of the issue Vargas Llosa discusses?
2. Do some research on Vargas Llosa on the Internet, and in a paragraph or two, write about how his political stance informs this essay.
3. Do some research on the experiences of Mexican immigrants crossing the border into the United States. Many of them have horrendous stories to tell, and each year hundreds are hurt or killed attempting to cross. Write a report on these experiences.

2 Writing Arguments

You probably have noticed already that your instructors across the spectrum of college study are asking you to take a stand on a topic and support it with thoughtful, well-reasoned detail. In the previous chapter we suggested that the world of academic writing has its roots in argumentation. In history, biology, psychology, sociology, computer applications, education, in midterms and finals and research papers, you have to state a position on an issue, propose (or imply) that position in a thesis, and defend that position logically. An important part of argumentation in the disciplines is *persuasion*, that is, effecting some action on the part of your reader—from doing something tangible like buying a battery-driven car or joining a political action group to adopting a point of view, such as acknowledging that global warming is a serious threat to the world. As a writer, you need to persuade readers as a result of your appeals to their intelligence, emotions, and beliefs.

You've already seen that it's important to distinguish written arguments from the heated verbal interchange you have with roommates, friends, or family members. In such an exchange, your position on an issue can stimulate strong emotions on either side of a topic and arouse passionate feelings (and loud voices). We rarely plan our verbal arguments; mostly they just burst open in the course of conversation, and we just as rarely have the luxury to think them out clearly or to marshal convincing support in our own behalf.

Strong written argument, on the other hand, prides itself on its cool logic and substantive details to back up a position. Its purpose is clear. It takes into account its audience. It follows a lucid plan based on careful organization. It builds on appropriate rhetorical strategies—description, narration, comparison and contrast, classification, and definition, to name a few. It draws on reflective research. And through drafting and revision, it develops its thesis through suitable language and style.

THE WRITING PROCESS

As you saw in Chapter 1, we can identify the qualities of well-written arguments when an end product is at hand. As a writer, you need to know how to get to such a place yourself—the production of an effective argumentative paper that is to the point and fulfills the requirements of your assignment. You have to think of writing your argument as the culmination of a process, not simply a one-shot effort but a series of interrelated activities that can help you construct a successful paper.

Within the writing process, most writers identify various stages and activities in creating a piece of writing. Although we can name, more or less, the major elements in this process and encourage you to rely on them as you write, we don't want you to think of them as lockstep procedures where all efforts follow sequentially and require mindless adherence. Many of the steps overlap, some you can take simultaneously, and you may have good reason to skip some steps along the way.

The strategies that follow are essential elements in the writing process. We'll have more to say about many of them later in this chapter as we explore the writing of an argumentative paper.

Stages in the Writing Process

- Discuss your ideas with reliable people who can provide an initial reaction to your proposal.
- Do preliminary research online and in your library.
- Do *prewriting*—warm-up activities before you start to draft your paper.
- Limit your topic.
- Identify your purpose and audience.
- State your claim in a thesis.
- Identify supporting details and evidence.
- Organize your ideas.
- Prepare a first draft.
- Share your draft.
- Revise your draft based on readers' comments and suggestions.
- Produce and edit your final copy.
- Proofread your final draft.

FIRST STEPS

After initial thought and preliminary research, the stages of the writing process usually begin with *prewriting*, a convenient term to identify the limbering-up activities writers produce on paper *before* they start creating a draft. (You know that the prefix *pre* means "prior to" or "before.") This is a very important stage in writing your paper: prewriting helps you thrash out ideas and circle your topic until you can identify clearly what you want to write about. If you begin a draft too soon, you may find that you have to start over and over again, wasting your valuable time and increasing your frustrations as a writer.

Prewriting Options

- *Make a list of ideas that your topic stimulates in your mind.* You can use this list to expand ideas and eliminate others.
- *Keep a journal of thoughts and ideas.* Jot down anything that comes to mind about any topic in an informal notebook that you can return to regularly to help identify a subject that you could develop into an argumentative paper.
- *Freewrite.* Write nonstop for 15 minutes or so. Do not stop to edit or revise. Just let your thoughts fill the page, no matter how disjointed or even silly they seem to you as you write. Free association gets words on the page; if you suffer from writer's block, you know how important it is simply to have something concrete to look at. You can use these words and sentences to zero in on a topic or to eliminate those topics that don't fit your intended task.
- *Use a visual aid.* With a subject map or subject tree, you can write a key word on a blank page and, using lines to indicate roads or branches, follow different elements of the topic by connecting them to lines or shapes that help you track different possibilities.
- *Brainstorm.* Raise unedited questions about the topic. Questions can dislodge answers that might set you on the right track to a strong essay. On a sheet of paper, write the reporter's essential questions, the five W's—*who, what, where, when, why*—and also *how.* Use these to start your own list of questions about your topic.
- *Make a scratch outline.* As ideas take shape in your mind, they can suggest linkages and interrelations, and you can capture them in a scratch outline. Write down an aspect of your topic, and underneath it list the various subtopics that come to mind. A scratch outline is an informal first step in organizing your ideas and can help you later on as you aim for a coherent, unified paper.

Of course, you'll need to pick and choose among these steps. Nobody takes all of them all the time. But if you're attentive to prewriting efforts, you'll discover many possibilities for developing a fruitful topic. As we point out later, once you have a topic, you can proceed to writing a thesis around a debatable issue, finding supporting detail to back up your assertions, organizing your information into a coherent entity, and writing an initial draft and any subsequent drafts that advanced thinking on your topic might require. Editing your manuscript and submitting it for review are important culminating acts in the writing process.

IDENTIFYING ISSUES

A manageable topic is the best way to assure that your essay won't derail as you move through the various stages of the writing process. Where do you begin your efforts to find a topic that you can develop into a thoughtful argument?

If your instructor has made an assignment—the extinction of the dinosaurs, let's say, or the causes of the Boer War, or the psychological manifestations of Alzheimer's disease—some of your work is done for you. (You'll still have to limit the topic, no doubt, in ways that we explain later on.) With an open-ended topic, however, you should let your interests and concerns lead you. Are you worried about global warming? Does the death penalty trouble you? Do the potentials of cyberspace stimulate your thoughts? (*To the Point* presents controversial essays on these topics; if you've read and discussed a selection in class, one of the ideas emerging from the essay may generate a good topic starting point.)

"I'm starting to get concerned about global warming."

The best papers always emerge from a writer's lively interests, and you want to honor your own curiosity and awareness of the world around you. Some global issue may pique your interest—the American military, taxes, famine in Africa—and you'll be able to form an opinion about them. Because of their complexity, you'd have to provide convincing reasons and evidence to support your claim. But topics of more personal and immediate concern also have rich potential as argumentative papers, and you should consider them. Should a strip mall open adjacent to the campus? Is the ban of religious symbols in the town square appropriate? Is the nutritional content of Burger King meals open to serious criticism? Should parents of very young girls allow them to participate in beauty contests?

On reflection, you may find that a topic that interests you is just not arguable or is not worth arguing about. If you believe that children should never be allowed to sample alcohol, for example, who would disagree with you? Almost everyone concurs that alcohol and children are a dangerous mix, and you'd be shouting in the wind—who would listen?—no matter how strongly you made your case.

LIMITING YOUR TOPIC

When you have the germ of a topic in mind, you have to limit it. The best way to begin to limit your topic is, as we've suggested, thinking carefully in advance about it through some of the prewriting strategies presented in the previous section, including, of course, browsing on the Web and in the library. You want to narrow down your topic so that you can accomplish your assigned writing task in a reasonable time. Often, you can narrow your topic in stages so that you can reach a desired level of specificity.

In the following table, look at the way writers have limited the broad topics in the first column into more productive argumentative essay topics. Items in the last column stand the best chance of developing into powerful argumentative essays.

Broad Topic	Limited Topic	Even More Limited
Cell phones	Dangers in using cell phones	The dangers of using cell phones while driving automobiles
Home instruction for children	Teaching children basic skills at home	Teaching reading skills to preschoolers in a home setting
Terrorists	Homegrown terrorists	Conditions in homes and schools that can create terrorists among American teenagers

Writers using the limited topics will have an easier time than those approaching the issues with too broad a scope. For the topic on cell phones, for instance, the writer can rule out any ideas about their use in public places like restaurants and movie theaters. The writer can rule out skyrocketing costs for cell phones and for required monthly service. Though these topics also might make effective papers, for this writer the issue is the dangers of cell phone use while driving automobiles. Any research efforts would concentrate on that dimension of the topic.

KNOWING YOUR PURPOSE AND AUDIENCE

Once you have limited your topic, you have to consider your *purpose* and *audience*. Purpose relates to what you hope to accomplish in your essay. Will your argument about the dangers of cell phones center on a narrative of some dangerous uses you witnessed or read about? Will you explain how to avoid the dangers? Will you show the causes and effects of dangerous use? Will you compare and contrast safe and hazardous cell phone uses? Your argumentative essay will allow you great latitude in addressing your topic through proven rhetorical strategies, and you have to determine which will enhance your topic development. In writing your argument, your purpose might be to propose that some belief or activity is good or bad, moral or immoral, harmful or beneficial. You might wish to push your readers to take some course of action that you deem essential or merely to have them consider a familiar issue in a new light. Being certain of your purpose will help you state your claim forcefully as you continue to think about your essay.

When your purpose is clearly in mind, you need to focus on your intended audience. Just what kind of reader are you aiming for? The glib response here, of course, is "I'm writing for my teacher so I can get a good grade." That's true, certainly, but not to the exclusion of other possible audiences: your classmates, perhaps, or the editor of the school newspaper, or the CEO of some company that treated you badly. When writing, it's always best to imagine specific audiences other than your English professor. In general, your teacher can adapt easily and can assume the personality and characteristics of varied reader audiences. Define a reader, and approach that reader with strategies targeted to her interests.

To take one example, with your cell phone topic, just think about how your approach would differ if you were writing your essay for teachers of driver education in urban high schools, or for applicants for drivers' licenses at the Department of Motor Vehicles, or for high-level executives at AT&T, whose corporate growth over the past several years hinged on increased sales of cellular telephones. Similarly, if you wrote about home teaching, your methods would vary significantly if you wrote for future mothers as opposed to booksellers at a national convention or teachers in your local elementary school. Vocabulary, style, sentence structure, and diction—audience and purpose markedly influence these fundamental elements of writing.

MAKING A CLAIM IN YOUR THESIS

Among the many important steps in the writing process, creating a thesis is high on the ladder of developing an argument. In an argumentative essay, you have to take a position on—that is, make a claim about—a topic. Your thesis must present an arguable topic. So even with a limited subject, you need to restrict your paper's concerns even further: you need to take a position on the topic, and the position on the topic must be debatable.

Note how writers have developed theses from the limited topics you looked at before.

Limited Topic	Possible Thesis
The dangers in using a cell phone while driving an automobile	The dangers to people who use cell phones while operating an automobile are serious, and current laws requiring "hands-free" technology do not adequately address the problems.
Teaching reading skills to preschoolers in a home setting	Teaching reading to preschoolers at home subverts the teacher's role, and parents should avoid the trap of becoming their children's teachers.
Conditions in homes and schools that can create terrorists among American teenagers	Home environments with remote, self-absorbed parents and ready access to weaponry—no matter what the social and financial conditions of the household or the psychological makeup of the child—contribute more than any other factor to developing teenage school terrorists.

Note how one could argue easily *against* any of these claims, which is the best assurance that each has the potential for becoming a successful paper. The topics are arguable; people stand on both sides of the issues. Many writers will produce an antithesis—that is, a thesis sentence opposite to the one they propose—to assure that their own position is arguable.

Possible Thesis	Antithesis
The dangers to people who use cell phones while operating an automobile are serious, and current laws requiring "hands-free" technology do not adequately address the problems.	"Hands-free" technology has reduced dramatically the dangers of cell-phone use by drivers on the road.

Once again, we put in a few words about flexibility here. Your thesis must be flexible. As you write your first and subsequent drafts, you may have to change your thesis as your topic takes shape and your claim undergoes refinement. Don't adhere blindly to the thesis you first developed, no matter how good it seems to you. As you marshal evidence, change your thinking, and delve deeply into evidence from many sources, your thesis may change considerably, usually for the good. Just be sure that you state your topic clearly, that you have identified your position on the topic, and that you make a claim that is debatable.

SUPPORTING YOUR CLAIM

After you have decided on your position and stated it as your claim in a thesis sentence, you have some important work ahead. Because your objective is to convince readers that your claim is valid and worth considering, only strong supporting detail drawn from personal experience or reliable sources will help you win over your audience. As you'll see later on, refutation—that is, acknowledging (and also challenging) viewpoints that oppose your own—is a key element in successful argumentation; not only must you discover information that supports your position, but you must also seek information that tells you what the other side is arguing. As you sift through the potential sources of supporting details, pay close attention to what those who disagree with you say. You'll need to give them due consideration when you write. (We'll say more about refutation later in this chapter.)

If you want to convince readers to accept your claim based on your own observations, you'll need to draw on concrete sensory detail to evoke the moment you are highlighting. Color, sound, and images of smell and touch all can set your reader in the scene as you see it and help make your points. Drawing on personal experience to support an argument doesn't *prove* anything easily, but it can convince readers if the illustration is apt. If you choose to draw on testimony from others—providing proof or evidence—you need to seek out the best possible information to back up your claim about the topic.

For example, arguing that global warming is a serious threat based only on days of high heat and humidity in your hometown during a winter season would not easily convince your readers. Similarly, arguing that your state should lower the driving age to 15 based on your own excellent (if illegal) tractor driving on your aunt's farm would not *prove* anything really, other than that in a single instance a teenager showed responsibility and skill in manipulating a gas-driven vehicle. You'd need to supplement these moments in your personal life with other convincing examples drawn from personal experience or with expert testimony from reliable sources in books and articles and on Web sites.

To prod readers to accept your claim, you often must draw on material that is solid and plentiful, evidence that is plausible, and reasoning that is not faulty. Here, the Internet and library catalogs can point you in the right direction. The World Wide Web has evolved into an invaluable research tool for writers, and you can find list serves and links from which to download abstracts, chapters, articles, and even full books. You already know, no doubt, that amid its many riches, the Web also can lead you on a path to disaster. Misinformation abounds; unreliable sources making wild claims may appear as regular popup windows on your computer or as unsolicited spam e-mail messages. Many chat rooms are notorious hotbeds of hysterical proclamations and assertions that defy logic even on superficial inspection. Also, some assessments on the Web are not current or reliable, or the site may not be open about its biases and objectives.

Therefore, we recommend some serious work at your college or local library, where research librarians can help you appraise Web sites and refer you to appropriate electronic sources. Your librarians, of course, also can put you on the trail to books and periodicals that will supplement your cyberspace ventures with solid resources on the library shelves or on microfilm or microfiche.

Your initial browsing in the library and on the Web helped you find a topic; now, as we have indicated, you need to amass supporting details to back up the topic you've chosen. Read as widely as you can; visit valid Web sites; watch television programs and films; talk with anyone who will listen. Take notes on what you've read and seen and be prepared to present some of your materials as evidence to your argument. Use the three C's as you evaluate your evidence: *currency*, *completeness*, and *credibility*.

Don't be surprised if you find yourself changing the terms of your argument dramatically. The more deeply you explore the topic, the more potential information you have to solidify your position or to alter it dramatically or subtly. With a great deal of resources at hand, you can select those details that seem best to bolster your position.

ORGANIZING YOUR ARGUMENT

The supporting details—the reasons and evidence you garner—make up the *grounds* of your argument, the key elements that establish the validity of your claim. Your claim, stated in your thesis, establishes your general point of view; the grounds provide the reasons and evidence. As you gather information, you should be thinking of how to organize your materials once you're ready to begin. You need to keep in mind the way your grounds will devolve to minor propositions and how you actually will use your evidence to support your claim or to refute an opposing claim.

You might find it helpful even at this stage to consider using one of the following patterns as a guide when writing your essay.

Pattern 1: Refutation First	Pattern 2: Refutation Last	Pattern 3: Refutation Point by Point
Introduce your claim.	Introduce your claim.	Introduce your claim.
State opposing arguments and refute them.	State first minor proposition and supporting information.	State first minor proposition and supporting information and refute opposing arguments.
State first minor proposition and supporting information.	State second minor proposition and supporting information.	State second minor proposition and supporting information and refute opposing arguments.
State second minor proposition and supporting information.	State third minor proposition and supporting information.	State third minor proposition and supporting information and refute opposing arguments.
State third minor proposition and supporting information.	State opposing arguments and refute them.	Conclude the essay.
Conclude the essay.	Conclude the essay.	

We don't propose these patterns as absolutes, and it's probably a bit too early in the writing process for you to map out the full approach your essay will take. Nevertheless, keeping in mind the possibilities for organizing your information and conveying it logically will help you over the hurdles when it comes to drafting your paper.

CHECKING YOUR ASSUMPTIONS (OR WARRANTS)

As you learned in Chapter 1, a warrant is the essential underpinning for your assertion. It establishes the certainty underlying a particular claim and its supporting reasons. A firm warrant justifies the supporting information that you assemble to support your contention. However, if your readers can challenge your warrant, you'll have to defend it.

Why do you have to think about warrants when you write your essays? In many of your argumentative assignments, you can assume that your readers—generally your instructor, other students, family members, or the particular readers that you have defined—are friendly and won't question the warrants supporting your claim. Yet warrants based on certain cultural assumptions, systems of belief, or core values often require their own defense because they too are debatable. When your warrant is controversial, you need to explain or qualify it.

Consider the ongoing debate over abortion rights. Some would use as a warrant the belief that all life from conception is sacred and would build a case from there against all forms of abortion. Others would establish as a warrant that idea that freedom of choice is the principle upon which a woman makes a decision involving abortion. There are numerous additional warrants underlying the abortion debate that often serve as "universal" values that in themselves are controversial. Defending the warrant is as important as providing points to support your assertion. Differing warrants or assumptions underlying debates over abortion, gun control, the death penalty, and other hot-button issues require writers to subject these warrants to the same scrutiny that they bring to their claims and supporting evidence.

REFUTATION: MEETING THE OPPOSITION

Particularly with assertions that you know many people would disagree with, effective arguments always consider the opposition's point of view. As we pointed out briefly before, you have to be aware of what contrasting arguments suggest, and you have to treat them fairly in your essay.

You have some options here. One strategy is to indicate the views that run counter to your own and simply to admit that some parts of these arguments are legitimate—but that your point is more substantial and worthy of greater support. Conceding arguments is an attractive option: this tactic shows your lack of prejudice and your ethical approach to the issue. Essentially, you are saying here, "I know that others disagree with me—and here are some of their reasons, which have some validity. Nevertheless, the points I will make are much more convincing."

Another strategy is to identify opposing arguments and then refute them as part of your own presentation. How can you refute an opposing argument?

- Question the evidence proposed by the opposing camp. Is it valid? Up to date? Sufficient? Accurate?
- Probe the warrants of an opposing argument. What are the underlying assumptions and beliefs for the writer's claim? Has the writer offered a substantive rationale for the warrants on which he builds his argument?

- Identify evidence that challenges the specific elements in the op-posing arguments. Thus, you can extract fundamental points and rebut them one at a time rather than making a sweeping refutation.

With either strategy, concession or refutation, you must treat the op-posing arguments justly and respectfully. True, satirists and ironists often mock opposing views, but in your papers you want to aim for fairness that will establish your credibility and lack of bias as a writer and win over your readers.

AVOIDING TRAPS IN APPEALS AND LOGIC

Argumentative essays often deal with heated topics, but as a fair and thoughtful writer, you want to be aware of excessive appeals to emotion and to a wide range of logic traps that can show fault lines in your think-ing. Be alert to these logic traps and wrongheaded emotional appeals as you write your papers.

- *Ad hominem ("to the man") arguments.* These discredit the person rather than the argument: "Gloria Lee never married. How can she talk about the sacredness of marriage between men and women?" Here, the attack is against the person, not the issue. Avoid *ad hominem* arguments—but do not shrink from challenging someone if the person lacks appropriate credentials to make the claim. You would be right to contest the author of a pro-death penalty Web site put up by a dentist who has no authority in the debate other than his passionate commitment to the issue.
- *Arguments based on longevity.* Avoid proving a point by stating that people always believed it, so why should we change it now? "Women have never competed in professional football in the past, and there's no need to alter common practice." We'd still be talk-ing about an earth-centered universe if we adhered to beliefs based only on their standing through time.
- *Arguments based on transfer.* Here the argument connects the point to a famous person in order to win support. This is an ex-ample of *positive* transfer: "President Bill Clinton is a brilliant scholar and his recent support of the newly nominated federal judge should not be questioned." This is an example of *negative* transfer (or name calling): "President Bill Clinton's personal be-havior challenged family values. Why should we consider as rel-evant his defense of the family support bill?" Neither example makes any logical connection between the person and the issue and, in fact, the transfer distracts the reader from the point to the person.
- *Hasty generalizations.* In this logic trap, you leap to false conclu-sions based on insufficient, untrue, or unrepresentative evidence.

"Cats are disloyal pets. Our cat Phoebe, whom we had for five years, ran off one day and never returned." One example cannot support the generalization. Hasty generalizations at their most pernicious lead to stereotyping, when you use reductive generalizations to characterize an individual or group. "Our South American gardener is sluggish and has no resolve. Newly arrived immigrants in our country are lazy and unambitious."

- *Broad generalizations.* By using words like *never*, *always*, and *all* in an argument, you leave yourself open to accusations of overstatement. "George Washington always knew how to lead a battle"; "All Germans supported the Nazi purge of Jews during World War II"—sweeping statements like these are open easily to challenge. It's best to qualify them: "George Washington almost always knew how to lead a battle"; "Large numbers of Germans supported the Nazi purge of Jews during World War II."

- *Post hoc, ergo propter hoc ("after this, therefore because of this").* This is a logical fallacy built on false cause-and-effect relationships. "The boys ran out of the department store quickly. They must have stolen the woman's purse." Just because their departure was hasty and might seem suspicious, there is no necessary cause-and-effect relationship between the boys' rapid disappearance and the purse snatching. Our most ingrained superstitions— bad luck following a black cat's crossing our path, for example— assume that one event in time causes another soon after. Be sure that any cause-and-effect relationships that you establish are valid.

- *Argumentum ad populum ("to the people").* Arguments that draw on highly charged language can manipulate readers' responses by arousing strong emotions. Words that appeal to virtuous elements, such as patriotism, motherhood, and America, can produce "glittering generalities" that distort meaning so that readers must accept a premise through illogical association. Negative words similarly can make illogical connections: "The dictatorial president of the Student Association has made another bad choice."

- *Bandwagon arguments.* In these arguments the writer falsely generalizes that the voice of the people is always right. "The citizens of this city are voting to renew Proposition 13, and you should too." Just because everyone's doing it doesn't make it desirable.

- *Begging the question.* Here, the writer takes a conclusion for granted before she proves it. "Teenagers are by nature reckless and will benefit greatly from required counseling prior to any voluntary abortion." The writer can go on to indicate the benefits of this counseling; but she has not offered any proof for her conclusion that teenagers are irresponsible. Another dimension of begging the question is assuming in your premise what your conclusion should prove. Thus, if you argue that elected officials' greed is unavoidable because they put personal gain above service to constituents, you are not proving your premise and hence are begging the question.

- *Oversimplified arguments.* Oversimplification is a major impediment to logical argumentation and can take many forms.
  - *One solution.* Complicated issues usually have more than one resolution, and you don't want to argue for just one solution to a sticky problem. "Censoring violence on television will reduce violence in our communities." Surely other possible solutions warrant consideration in the serious issue of violent behavior.
  - *Either-or reasoning.* You shouldn't assume that only two sides exist on an issue—yes or no, good or bad, right or wrong. "He failed so many courses because he works after school and on weekends. Either you work or go to school; you can't do both."
  - *No cost or harm.* If you project a benefit for some course of action, don't assume automatically that no problems, costs, or penalties will follow. "Prohibit all pagers and cell-phone use in public places." The benefits are clear: no interruptions, annoying rings or music, or loud talking in indoor spaces. But what about consequences: preventable emergencies, parents needing to be in touch with children, doctors on call. No-harm generalizations often overlook precarious repercussions.
- *Non sequitur ("It does not follow").* This logical fallacy draws conclusions when no logical connection exists between ideas. "Arnold Schwarzenegger will be a good governor for California because he is a very popular actor." He may be popular, and people might have voted for him because he's popular, but that doesn't guarantee that he will be a good governor. The argument's conclusions do not stem from its premise. The writer might see a logical connection between popularity and leadership, but he should make it explicit. Otherwise, he has generated a non sequitur—that is, disconnected ideas.
- *Weak or untrue analogies.* A familiar tool of argument is the analogy, a type of comparison that relates one object or idea to a basically dissimilar idea so that readers can see the point in a new light. Alfred Posamentier, a professor of education, made this comment about the anxiety at the start of a new school year awash with new policies and procedures: "It's akin to an engineering firm that develops this new machine and doesn't know if all the parts are going to behave the way they are supposed to behave when they flip the switch on a certain day." Analogies enliven writing and help illustrate a point but never serve as evidence. Posamentier, after all, hasn't proved that the system is untested and risks uncoordination. But his analogy helps us see how he views the problem.

- *The straw man*. An argument sets up a straw man when it asserts a weak or invented argument attributed to an opponent for the exclusive purpose of disproving it. "The television commentator would no doubt approve of music that glorifies drugs and indifferent sex. Only an extremist libertine who doesn't believe in family values would question the censorship of any material aimed at teenagers." The statement asserts that the commentator would endorse music that praises drugs and sex—but the operative words here are "no doubt." The phrase suggests an invented argument, one that the writer can attack along with the person who made the argument.

Strong written arguments reflect logical thinking, and we've tried to point out ways in which you can produce thoughtful topics; carefully stated assertions; well-defined claims, grounds, and evidence; and objective data and testimony. These elements in your writing will mark you as a fair analyst with a lively, inquiring mind, and they will help you to produce strong argumentative papers.

PERSPECTIVES ON LOVE AND MARRIAGE: READING AND WRITING ABOUT A CRITICAL ISSUE

JUDY BRADY
I Want a Wife

Judy Brady was born in 1937 and went to college at the University of Iowa. A breast cancer survivor, she is an activist with the Women's Cancer Resource Center and a cofounder of the Toxic Links Coalition, which works to prevent cancer by reducing pollution. In this funny but bitter satire, which appeared in Ms. *magazine in 1971, Brady, a wife and mother, argues that she, too, would like someone to take care of her.*

▶ Prereading: Thinking about the Essay in Advance

Think about the traditional roles that men and women have played in their relationships. What is expected of a husband? Of a wife? Do you think things are the same now as in 1971 when Brady wrote the piece? Why or why not?

▶ Words to Watch

nurturant (par. 3) giving attention and affection
hors d'oeuvres (par. 6) appetizers
adherence (par. 8) faithful attachment

1   I belong to that classification of people known as wives. I am A Wife. And, not altogether incidentally, I am a mother.

2   Not too long ago a male friend of mine appeared on the scene fresh from a recent divorce. He had one child, who is, of course, with his ex-wife. He is obviously looking for another wife. As I thought about him while I was ironing one evening, it suddenly occurred to me that I, too, would like to have a wife. Why do I want a wife?

3   I would like to go back to school so that I can become economically independent, support myself, and, if need be, support those dependent upon me. I want a wife who will work and send me to school. And while I am going to school, I want a wife to keep track of the children's doctor and dentist appointments. And to keep track of mine, too. I want a wife to make sure my children eat properly and are kept clean. I want a wife who will wash the children's clothes and keep them mended. I want a wife who is a good nurturant attendant to my children, who arranges for their schooling, makes sure that they have an adequate social life with their peers, takes them to the park, the zoo, etc. I want a wife who takes care of the children when they are sick, a wife who arranges to be around when the children need special care, because, of course, I cannot miss classes at school. My wife must arrange to lose time at work and not lose the job. It may mean a small cut in my wife's income from time to time, but I guess I can tolerate that. Needless to say, my wife will arrange and pay for the care of the children while my wife is working.

4   I want a wife who will take care of *my* physical needs. I want a wife who will keep my house clean. A wife who will pick up after me. I want a wife who will keep my clothes clean, ironed, mended, replaced when need be, and who will see to it that my personal things are kept in their proper place so that I can find what I need the minute I need it. I want a wife who cooks the meals, a wife who is a *good* cook. I want a wife who will plan the menus, do the necessary grocery shopping, prepare the meals, serve them pleasantly, and then do the cleaning up while I do my studying. I want a wife who will care for me when I am sick and sympathize with my pain and loss of time from school. I want a wife to go along when our family takes a vacation so that someone can continue to care for me and my children when I need a rest and change of scene.

5   I want a wife who will not bother me with rambling complaints about a wife's duties. But I want a wife who will listen to me when I feel the need to explain a rather difficult point I have come across in my course of studies. And I want a wife who will type my papers for me when I have written them.

6   I want a wife who will take care of the details of my social life. When my wife and I are invited out by my friends, I want a wife who will take care of

the babysitting arrangements. When I meet people at school that I like and want to entertain, I want a wife who will have the house clean, will prepare a special meal, serve it to me and my friends, and not interrupt when I talk about the things that interest me and my friends. I want a wife who will have arranged that the children are fed and ready for bed before my guests arrive so that the children do not bother us. I want a wife who takes care of the needs of my guests so that they feel comfortable, who makes sure that they have an ashtray, that they are passed the hors d'oeuvres, that they are offered a second helping of the food, that their wine glasses are replenished when necessary, that their coffee is served to them as they like it.

And I want a wife who knows that sometimes I need a night out by   7
myself.

I want a wife who is sensitive to my sexual needs, a wife who makes   8
love passionately and eagerly when I feel like it, a wife who makes sure that I am satisfied. And, of course, I want a wife who will not demand sexual attention when I am not in the mood for it. I want a wife who assumes the complete responsibility for birth control, because I do not want more children. I want a wife who will remain sexually faithful to me so that I do not have to clutter up my intellectual life with jealousies. And I want a wife who understands that *my* sexual needs may entail more than strict adherence to monogamy. I must, after all, be able to relate to people as fully as possible.

If, by chance. I find another person more suitable as a wife than the   9
wife I already have, I want the liberty to replace my present wife with another one. Naturally, I will expect a fresh, new life; my wife will take the children and be solely-responsible for them so that I am left free.

When I am through with school and have a job, I want my wife to   10
quit working and remain at home so that my wife can more fully and completely take care of a wife's duties.

My God, who *wouldn't* want a wife?   11

▶ Building Vocabulary

1. After checking a dictionary for Brady's specific use of each of the following words, write out their definitions:
   a. attendant (par. 3)
   b. adequate (par. 3)
   c. peers (par. 3)
   d. tolerate (par. 3)
   e. rambling (par. 5)
   f. replenished (par. 6)
   g. monogamy (par. 8)

2. Write an original sentence for each word.

▶ Thinking Critically about the Argument

Understanding the Writer's Argument

1. What made Brady think about wanting a wife for herself?
2. How would a wife help the writer continue her education?
3. In what way would a wife help the writer around the house?
4. Why does the writer want someone to help her take care of the children?
5. How would a wife change the writer's sex life?
6. What kind of freedom does the writer want, finally?

Understanding the Writer's Techniques

1. What is Brady's major claim in this essay? Consider the ironic meaning of her essay, and decide if she ever truly expresses her claim. Explain your answer.
2. What are the implied warrants in this essay? How do you know?
3. What minor propositions does Brady give to show that she wants a wife?
4. What pattern of coherence among the minor propositions do you detect? Why does the writer include them in the order she does? Would you change the order at all?
5. What is the effect of Brady's use of the word "I"? Do you find it effective? Why or why not?
6. What is the tone here? Explain your answer.
7. Why does the writer separate the idea that "sometimes I need a night out by myself" in paragraph 7? What rhetorical purpose does this serve?
8. What is the effect of the rhetorical question at the end of the essay and of the use of the phrase "My God" and the word "wouldn't" in italics?

Exploring the Writer's Argument

1. Brady wrote this essay two years before she and her husband separated. How does this knowledge change your opinion of the essay, if at all?
2. This essay was published in 1971. Do you think that this essay could be published in a major magazine today? Why or why not? Do husbands still expect their wives to perform all of these duties without help? Explain what has changed.
3. Brady lists many domestic duties traditionally assigned to the homemaker. What "wifely responsibilities" exist today that she doesn't mention?
4. In what ways are Brady's arguments old fashioned? In what ways are they relevant to today's men and women?

▶Ideas for Writing Arguments

Prewriting

What kind of help do you need in life? What kind of person would you need? If you are living at home, would it be helpful to have a student of your own?

Writing a Guided Argument

Write an essay titled "I Want a Student."

1. Begin your essay by identifying yourself as a student. You will argue that you want a student to help you with your life as a student.
2. Offer a brief personal story (as Brady does in par. 2) to explain why you decided you wanted your own student.
3. Using Brady as a guide, support your main idea with supporting points, explaining the various activities your very own student could help you with in your life as a student.
4. Organize your points in an effective order, using transition words and phrases to improve the flow from paragraph to paragraph.
5. Use repetition in your language for rhetorical effect.
6. End your essay with a question, making that question as effective and dramatic as possible.

Thinking, Arguing, and Writing Collaboratively

Help to divide the class into two groups: one consisting of all the men in the class and the other consisting of all the women. Working in these groups, have the men come up with reasons why husbands (and boyfriends) need extra help, and have the women list reasons why wives (and girlfriends) need help. Each group should assign a representative to put the reasons on the board. The class should discuss the effectiveness of each reason.

Writing about the Text

Write an essay about the use of irony in this essay. What is the effect of writing such an emotional essay in such a straightforward style? Discuss Brady's use of humor.

More Writing Ideas

1. In your journal, explain which of Brady's complaints you find most effective and which you find most whiny or weak.

2. In a paragraph, argue for or against this statement: "Men should stay home while women go out and earn a living."

3. Write an essay arguing that it is more difficult to be a man in today's society than it is to be a woman.

NICOLAS KRISTOF
Love and Race

Born in 1959, Nicolas Kristof was raised in Oregon, educated at Harvard, and won a Rhodes scholarship to Oxford University in England. He and his wife, also a journalist, won a Pulitzer Prize for their work in China during the Tiananmen Square uprising. Kristof writes a regular column for the New York Times. *In this selection, he sings the praises of the current rise in marriage between the races.*

▶ Prereading: Thinking about the Essay in Advance

Do you know any interracial couples? If so, what problems do they face, if any, and why? If you do not know any, what problems do you think they might face in society today?

▶ Words to Watch

genome (par. 6) entire code for DNA in a cell
superficial (par. 7) unimportant, only on the surface
miscegenation (par. 10) mixing of races
guru (par. 13) leader and guide
surge (par. 14) sharp rise

1   In a world brimming with bad news, here's one of the happiest trends: Instead of preying on people of different races, young Americans are falling in love with them.

2   Whites and blacks can be found strolling together as couples even at the University of Mississippi, once the symbol of racial confrontation.

3   "I will say that they are always given a second glance," acknowledges C. J. Rhodes, a black student at Ole Miss. He adds that there are still misgivings about interracial dating, particularly among black women and a formidable number of "white Southerners who view this race-mixing as abnormal, frozen by fear to see Sara Beth bring home a brotha."

4   Mixed-race marriages in the U.S. now number 1.5 million and are roughly doubling each decade. About 40 percent of Asian-Americans and 6 percent of blacks have married whites in recent years.

Still more striking, one survey found that 40 percent of Americans   5
had dated someone of another race.

In a country where racial divisions remain deep, all this love is an enor-   6
mously hopeful sign of progress in bridging barriers. Scientists who study
the human genome say that race is mostly a bogus distinction reflecting very
little genetic difference, perhaps one-hundredth of 1 percent of our DNA.

Skin color differences are recent, arising over only the last 100,000   7
years or so, a twinkling of an evolutionary eye. That's too short a period
for substantial genetic differences to emerge, and so there is perhaps 10
times more genetic difference within a race than there is between races.
Thus we should welcome any trend that makes a superficial issue like
color less central to how we categorize each other.

The rise in interracial marriage reflects a revolution in attitudes. As   8
recently as 1958 a white mother in Monroe, N.C., called the police after
her little girl kissed a black playmate on the cheek; the boy, Hanover
Thompson, 9, was then sentenced to 14 years in prison for attempted
rape. (His appeals failed, but he was released later after an outcry.)

In 1963, 59 percent of Americans believed that marriage between   9
blacks and whites should be illegal. At one time or another 42 states
banned intermarriage, although the Supreme Court finally invalidated
these laws in 1967.

Typically, the miscegenation laws voided any interracial marriages,   10
making the children illegitimate, and some states included penalties such
as enslavement, life imprisonment, and whippings. My wife is Chinese-
American, and our relationship would once have been felonious.

11   At every juncture from the 19th century on, the segregationists warned that granting rights to blacks would mean the start of a slippery slope, ending up with black men marrying white women. The racists were prophetic.

12   "They were absolutely right," notes Randall Kennedy, the Harvard Law School professor and author of a dazzling new book, "Interracial Intimacies," to be published next month. "I do think [interracial marriage] is a good thing. It's a welcome sign of thoroughgoing desegregation. We talk about desegregation in the public sphere; here's desegregation in the most intimate sphere."

13   These days, interracial romance can be seen on the big screen, on TV shows, and in the lives of some prominent Americans. Former Defense Secretary William Cohen has a black wife, as does Peter Norton, the software guru. The Supreme Court justice Clarence Thomas has a white wife.

14   I find the surge in intermarriage to be one of the most positive fronts in American race relations today, building bridges and empathy. But it's still in its infancy.

15   I was excited to track down interracial couples at Ole Miss, thinking they would be perfect to make my point about this hopeful trend. But none were willing to talk about the issue on the record.

16   "Even if people wanted to marry [interracially], I think they'd keep it kind of quiet," explained a minister on campus.

17   For centuries, racists warned that racial equality would lead to the "mongrelization" of America. Perhaps they were right in a sense, for we're increasingly going to see a blurring of racial distinctions. But these distinctions acquired enormous social resonance without ever having much basis in biology.

▶ Building Vocabulary

Explain the meaning of the following examples of figurative language. Rewrite the sentences by putting the figure of speech in your own words.

1. "all this love is an enormously hopeful sign of progress in *bridging barriers*." (par. 6)
2. "Skin color differences are recent, arising over only the last 100,000 years or so, a *twinkling of an evolutionary eye*." (par. 7)
3. "the segregationists warned that granting rights to blacks would mean the start of a *slippery slope*." (par. 11)
4. "these distinctions acquired enormous social *resonance*." (par. 17)

▶ Thinking Critically about the Argument

Understanding the Writer's Argument

1. Why is it significant that interracial couples exist at the University of Mississippi?

2. What lessons does the writer suggest we learn from the statistic that skin color differences are a relatively recent development evolutionarily?
3. What were segregationists afraid of in the 19th century?
4. Explain Randall Kennedy's quote, "We talk about desegregation in the public sphere; here's desegregation in the most intimate sphere." Paraphrase his quote.
5. What evidence does the writer give that interracial marriages are becoming more mainstream?
6. Why wouldn't students at Ole Miss discuss intermarriage with Kristof?

Understanding the Writer's Techniques

1. What is the writer's major proposition? Where is it best stated?
2. What minor propositions does the writer use to support his major proposition?
3. What evidence does the writer use to support his minor propositions? Make a rough outline of the essay's argument.
4. How effective is Kristof's use of statistics in paragraphs 4 through 7?
5. Does the writer only rely on rational arguments? What other kinds of appeals can you find? Explain your answer.
6. What is the persuasive effect of the writer explaining in paragraph 10 that he is in an interracial marriage?
7. How effective is the last paragraph?

Exploring the Writer's Argument

1. Do you find paragraphs 2 and 3 in Kristof's essay contradictory? Why or why not?
2. If racial differences are not that important and have little basis in biology, why does Kristof repeat his argument about racial distinctions in paragraph 17? Does he have a rhetorical reason? Could you strengthen his point here?
3. Do you think the structure of Kristof's essay is effective? Why or why not? Could you suggest a better structure? How would you structure the essay if you were assigned to write a column on the same issue?
4. Why does Kristof use the example of Hanover Thompson in paragraph 8? Why that example? He could have found a much more tragic example from the early part of the 20th century. There were many lynchings of African Americans who merely looked at a white woman in a way she didn't like. Why, then, does he offer an example from 1958?

▶Ideas for Writing Arguments

Prewriting

How common is interracial marriage where you live? Why do you think that is? Write about whether you think it is getting more common, and explain why it is or why it is not.

Writing a Guided Argument

Write an essay about a lifestyle that still is not accepted fully in society (for example, openly gay couples or unmarried couples living together). Argue that you see an improvement in the level of tolerance toward that lifestyle.

1. Begin your essay with a declaration that things are getting better.
2. Continue by offering examples or statistics to bolster your claim. Do some research, if you must, to gather evidence and, preferably, quotes. Save at least two pieces of evidence for later in your essay, under step 6.
3. While keeping an impartial distance to your writing, establish an optimistic tone.
4. In the next section, discuss the history of your chosen subject.
5. Develop and discuss the idea of opposing views to your subject.
6. Provide evidence to show how tolerance is increasing by offering evidence.
7. Link your ideas with well-developed transitions.
8. In your conclusion, link the fears opponents have about your subject with the reality or the coming reality in society.

Thinking, Arguing, and Writing Collaboratively

In small groups, share your papers that grew out of the Writing a Guided Argument assignment. Discuss suggestions for improvements in tone and word choice. Also, help your classmates to develop evidence for their essays by paying close attention to any pieces of evidence that are irrelevant and by helping with any awkward phrasing.

Writing about the Text

Write an essay in which you evaluate Kristof's use of statistics in this essay. Which do you find most impressive or effective for helping his claim? Which are less effective? What other statistics would you have liked to see?

More Writing Ideas

1. Are there any negative effects of interracial relationships on the children of those unions? Write in your journal about this topic.
2. Write a paragraph about why you think someone would be opposed to interracial marriage? What are people afraid of? Is there anything you could say to alleviate their fears?
3. In an essay, write about Kristof's statement in his conclusion that "we're increasingly going to see a blurring of racial distinctions." How would life in the United States change if he is correct? How is it already heading in that direction?

ANN PATCHETT
Kissing Cousins

Ann Patchett was born in Los Angeles in 1963 and moved to Nashville, Tennessee, with her family at the age of six. She was educated at Sarah Lawrence College and at the prestigious Writer's Workshop at the University of Iowa. She is the author of four novels: The Patron Saint of Liars *(1992),* Taft *(1994),* The Magician's Assistant *(1997), and* Bel Canto *(2001), which won the PEN/Faulkner award for fiction. Her book about an enduring friendship,* Truth & Beauty, *appeared in 2004. She also has written for many publications, including the* Chicago Tribune, The Village Voice, GQ, Elle, Gourmet, *and* Vogue. *This selection appeared in 2002.*

▶ Prereading: Thinking about the Essay in Advance

What do you think of first cousins becoming romantically involved? Can you imagine falling in love with your first cousin? Why do you think there is a stigma on first cousins marrying?

▶ Words to Watch

star-crossed (par. 1) ill-fated
nominal (par. 3) almost nothing
lethal (par. 3) deadly
stigma (par. 5) part of someone's identity that causes shame
taboos (par. 5) things banned because of morality or social custom
pyromaniac (par. 8) one who enjoys lighting fires

1   Thanks to 12 years of Catholic single-sex education, a lack of brothers, and an overdeveloped interest in reading as a child, I grew up in a world almost completely devoid of boys. Except, of course, for those boys I was related to. I had 25 first cousins, and I remember many summer family reunions eating sand-infused slices of sheet cake on the beaches of Southern California, so lost in the cousin crush of the moment that I could hardly swallow. These feelings were for the most part unexpressed and interchangeable (I liked cousin Lenny as much his brother Greg). One crush, however, started when I was 8 and proved hearty enough to follow me into adulthood. Whenever this cousin and I were on the same side of the country there were dinners, hand-holding, and a certain amount of sighing. Alas, we would be perfect for each other if only we weren't cousins. But we were, and so, feeling genetically star-crossed we always said good night and went our separate ways.

2   It turns out we didn't have to.

3   Popular mythology often takes the place of science. Lemmings do not, in fact, hurl themselves into the sea by the thousands to drown, and the country folk in the film "Deliverance" were not the product of parents who failed to take the initiative to go any farther than their aunts' and uncles' houses to look for a spouse. An article published recently in *The Journal of Genetic Counseling* says that the increased risk of birth defects to children born of first cousins is nominal. This isn't exactly breaking news, either; research has been in for some time. Could it be that we are so unnerved by the idea of the union of cousins that we didn't even want to hear about it? The fact that marriage between first cousins is illegal in 24 states will probably go the way of laws that banned interracial marriage. The norm is capable of change. After all, my grandmother was forbidden to serve apple pie with cheddar cheese when she was a young waitress in Kansas. (The combination was once believed to be as lethal as cousin love.)

4   Certainly in just about every other place in the world, marrying your first cousin is an unremarkable event. For centuries royalty has had to look in the bank of immediate relatives to find suitable mates. Who would be good enough for a Hapsburg but another Hapsburg? The notion that there was something genetically weakening, if not downright creepy, about intermarriage is one that is distinctly American. Perhaps it is born from a distaste of what our ancestors left behind when they boarded their ships to the New World. What is thought of as essential in the highest social classes of other countries is seen as a mark of the most backward and impoverished factions of our own. Now we find out that all of those jokes about Appalachian families are utterly baseless.

5   Still, to think that the laws against close family marriages are entirely based on a concern over the medical well-being for the child that might come of that union seems to miss a large part of the point: marrying a cousin at 60 carries almost the same burden of stigma as marrying a cousin at 16. It's one of those things we're not supposed to do, and

these days sexually active Americans have precious few limitations. For better or worse, we cling to the few taboos we have left. If the *Journal of Genetic Counseling* told us that there would be no major medical repercussions from reproduction with your brother or aunt, I don't think we would heave a national sigh of relief and say, well, as long as there are no medical issues. . . . Remember Oedipus and Jocasta? The story didn't turn out too well for them.

If you had to mark out the boundaries of incest, some of us are going to put first cousins on one side of the line and some are going to put them on the other. A friend of mine from Los Angeles recently met a first cousin once removed from Israel who she never knew existed. They fell madly in love at a family reunion in Spain. While they are working through cultural differences, a language barrier, and a long commute, the only thing that gives her a moment's pause is the blood tie, even though they have no plans to have children. Yet it seems impossible that a little thing like a common relative should ruin her chances for happiness. 6

Other cousins, the ones who were more like the pseudo-siblings of your entire youth, may take more consideration. But true love is a rare and wonderful thing, and if you happen to find it with a first cousin in one of the 24 states of the union that will still put you in jail for your marriage, the wisest choice may simply be moving. There are enough of those couples in America now to merit an extensive and thoughtful Web site, cousincouples.com. They supply not only support and inspirational stories but also a very helpful map to show you just what your state thinks of your love life. 7

I, for one, am glad to have grown up in an era that made me feel that following through on any of my earlier crushes would have been akin to my being a pyromaniac. For me, cousin love was like a set of romantic training wheels: safe, steady little things that screwed onto the real wheels of the bike I wasn't actually big enough to ride. Watching the boys swim out into the ocean at those sunburned family reunions, I got to have all the fun without the chance of actually getting hurt. As for the cousin I thought I was in love with, after a few years we turned out not to get along at all. That had nothing to do with our being related but I thank my lucky gene pool that it kept me from marrying him. 8

▶ Building Vocabulary

This selection requires knowledge of some history and art. Identify the following terms and explain their significance for this article:

1. the film "Deliverance" (par. 3)
2. Hapsburg (par. 4)
3. Appalachian (par. 4)
4. Oedipus and Jocasta (par. 5)

▶ Thinking Critically about the Argument

Understanding the Writer's Argument

1. What does Patchett mean when she writes that she was "so lost in the cousin crush of the moment that I could hardly swallow"? (par. 1)
2. What are some myths about cousin marriage?
3. How does the writer describe these myths?
4. What does Patchett mean when she says that "The notion that there was something genetically weakening, if not downright creepy, about intermarriage is one that is distinctly American"? (par. 4)
5. Why is the first cousin relationship on the borderline between acceptability and disgust, according to the writer?
6. How many states in the United States allow first cousins to marry?
7. What was the most positive thing for the writer about having crushes on her cousins?

Understanding the Writer's Techniques

1. What is the writer's major proposition? Where is it best expressed? If you can't find it, why do you think that is? If you can't find it, put her claim into your own words.
2. Why does the writer begin her essay with a recollection of her experiences with her many cousins? What argumentative purpose does this serve?
3. Outline the essay to highlight the minor propositions.
4. What evidence or support does the writer present for her minor propositions?
5. Which evidence in the essay do you think is the most effective? Why?
6. How effective is the writer's insistence in paragraph 7 that "true love" is the most important thing here?
7. In her closing, the writer moves away from saying that "cousin love" is a positive thing and says that it was only a good thing as "romantic training wheels." Why does she shy away from completely endorsing cousin love?

Exploring the Writer's Argument

1. Does Patchett's last sentence contradict the rest of her essay and its message of tolerance? Why or why not? Explain.
2. Many anthropologists believe that the taboo against incest is ingrained in humans as a survival instinct; the species would get stronger, evolutionarily, if people ventured out to other families rather than taking mates from their own families. They say the taboo exists for good reason. Do you agree or not, and why? What would Patchett say to that?

3. Do you think that Patchett's conclusion helps or hurts her argument? Explain your answer. Refer to question 7 in the "Understanding the Writer's Techniques" assignment.

▶Ideas for Writing Arguments

Prewriting

What were some beliefs you had when you were a child that you now know were false, were myths? Where did those myths come from? How did they come to be dispelled? Did you learn the truth from books? From friends? From parents? From siblings? How did you feel when you learned the truth?

Writing a Guided Argument

Write an essay in which you examine a popular myth you grew up with (for example, that your father was the strongest man in the world or that there was a tooth fairy or Santa Claus). Argue that those mythologies were wrong, and dispel them for your reader.

1. Begin your essay with a recollection of growing up with a myth, and explain the myth's origins.
2. Write about your good or bad memories of the myth.
3. Note how the myth from your childhood affects your life today.
4. Write your major proposition, dispelling the myth.
5. In the next few paragraphs, write minor propositions in which you support the idea in your major proposition.
6. Offer specific examples or anecdotes to support each of your minor propositions.
7. Attempt to use a poetic or nostalgic tone.
8. Close by discussing whether or not you are glad that you believed the myth when you were younger.

Thinking, Arguing, and Writing Collaboratively

Assist in dividing the class into three parts. Each group should prepare for a debate on "cousin love," doing research on the Web (you may visit the Web site Patchett suggests, cousincouples.com) and in the library. Each group should develop some familiarity with the history and practice of cousin marriage around the world. The aim of the debate is to win based on persuasive illustration. Stage the debate, with one group arguing in favor of cousin marriage and the other arguing against it. The third group will act as a jury. The jury should deliberate, vote on the winner, and make a presentation explaining in a written statement the results of the vote.

Writing about the Text

Patchett is a novelist and is known for her prose style. Write an essay in which you examine how Patchett adapts techniques from writing fiction to the essay form. Look especially at how she sets a scene. Does she have any characters? How is her word choice and tone affected?

More Writing Ideas

1. Visit the Web site cousincouples.com, which Patchett mentions in paragraph 7. Record your impressions of the Web site's content in your journal.
2. Research one of the terms in the "Building Vocabulary" exercise, and write a paragraph explaining how it relates to the idea of incest.
3. In paragraph 5, Patchett writes, "For better or worse, we cling to the few taboos we have left." Besides incest, what other taboos do we have? Write an essay in which you answer this question, offering an explanation of each one as well as a judgment about whether we should still hold on to that taboo.

Andrew Sullivan
Let Gays Marry

Andrew Sullivan was born in 1963 in a small town in England. He went to Oxford University and Harvard University, where he earned his Ph.D. in 1989. He was editor at The New Republic *magazine at the age of 27. Sullivan, who is openly homosexual, wrote* Virtually Normal: An Argument About Homosexuality *(1995), a book about gay rights. He resigned from* The New Republic *in 1996 and continues to write widely for many publications.* The Conservative Soul: How We Lost It, How to Get It Back, *appeared in 2006. In this selection, Sullivan makes the case for allowing homosexual couples to marry in civil ceremonies.*

▶ Prereading: Thinking about the Essay in Advance

Do you agree with the title of this essay? Should homosexuals be able to marry? Why or why not? If you agree that gays should marry, what do you think would be some common arguments against it?

▶ Words to Watch

subvert (par. 2) overturn
sanction (par. 6) officially approve of
fidelity (par. 7) faithfulness

"**A** state cannot deem a class of persons a stranger to its laws," de- 1
clared the Supreme Court last week. It was a monumental statement. Gay men and lesbians, the conservative court said, are no longer
strangers in America. They are citizens, entitled, like everyone else, to
equal protection—no special rights, but simple equality.

For the first time in Supreme Court history, gay men and women 2
were seen not as some powerful lobby trying to subvert America, but as
the people we truly are—the sons and daughters of countless mothers
and fathers, with all the weaknesses and strengths and hopes of everybody else. And what we seek is not some special place in America but
merely to be a full and equal part of America, to give back to our society
without being forced to lie or hide or live as second-class citizens.

That is why marriage is so central to our hopes. People ask us why 3
we want the right to marry, but the answer is obvious. It's the same reason anyone wants the right to marry. At some point in our lives, some of
us are lucky enough to meet the person we truly love. And we want to
commit to that person in front of our family and country for the rest of
our lives. It's the most simple, the most natural, the most human instinct
in the world. How could anyone seek to oppose that?

Yes, at first blush, it seems like a radical proposal, but, when you think 4
about it some more, it's actually the opposite. Throughout American history, to be sure, marriage has been between a man and a woman, and in
many ways our society is built upon that institution. But none of that need
change in the slightest. After all, no one is seeking to take away anybody's
right to marry, and no one is seeking to force any church to change any
doctrine in any way. Particular religious arguments against same-sex marriage are rightly debated within the churches and faiths themselves. That
is not the issue here: there is a separation between church and state in this
country. We are only asking that when the government gives out *civil* marriage licenses, those of us who are gay should be treated like anybody else.

Of course, some argue that marriage is *by definition* between a man 5
and a woman. But for centuries, marriage was *by definition* a contract in
which the wife was her husband's legal property. And we changed that.
For centuries, marriage was *by definition* between two people of the same
race. And we changed that. We changed these things because we recognized that human dignity is the same whether you are a man or a woman,
black or white. And no one has any more of a choice to be gay than to be
black or white or male or female.

Some say that marriage is only about raising children, but we let 6
childless heterosexual couples be married (Bob and Elizabeth Dole, Pat
and Shelley Buchanan, for instance). Why should gay couples be
treated differently? Others fear that there is no logical difference between allowing same-sex marriage and sanctioning polygamy and
other horrors. But the issue of whether to sanction multiple spouses
(gay or straight) is completely separate from whether, in the existing

institution between two unrelated adults, the government should discriminate between its citizens.

7   This is, in fact, if only Bill Bennett could see it, a deeply conservative cause. It seeks to change no one else's rights or marriages in any way. It seeks merely to promote monogamy, fidelity, and the disciplines of family life among people who have long been cast to the margins of society. And what could be a more conservative project than that? Why indeed would any conservative seek to oppose those very family values for gay people that he or she supports for everybody else? Except, of course, to make gay men and lesbians strangers in their own country, to forbid them ever to come home.

▶ Building Vocabulary

This essay is making a strong point, and thus it is trying to undermine the opposition's position. List five words or phrases in this essay that aim to strengthen the writer's position and weaken the opposition's. Explain how each word does this.

▶ Thinking Critically about the Argument

Understanding the Writer's Argument

1. Explain in your own words what the Supreme Court means by "A state cannot deem a class of persons a stranger to its laws."
2. Why is marriage so important to gays and lesbians, according to Sullivan?
3. According to Sullivan, what is the difference in the debate between the civil and religious worlds?
4. What is Sullivan's answer to those who say that marriage is by definition between a man and a woman?
5. How does he respond to those who say marriage is only for procreation?
6. Why is gay marriage actually a "conservative project"? Explain what this means.

Understanding the Writer's Techniques

1. Is the writer's major proposition the same as the title? If so, show where it appears in the essay. If not, what is the major proposition?
2. Analyze paragraph 2 and explain why it is effective.
3. What are the writers' minor propositions? Outline the body of the essay.
4. For what argumentative purpose does the writer make the distinction between marriage within a religion and civil marriage?

5. How would you characterize the writer's tone? Why do you think he wrote the essay in this tone? Do you think the fact that this appeared in *Newsweek*, a magazine read by a wide audience, made a difference? Why or why not?
6. Paraphrase the writer's argument in paragraph 5. Is it effective? Why or why not?
7. What minor proposition do you think is the writer's most effective?
8. Analyze the writer's use of the word "home" in paragraph 7.

Exploring the Writer's Argument

1. Sullivan is both openly gay and openly conservative. What is conservatism? How might Sullivan's two identities clash? Do you see evidence of the clash in his essay? Does he reconcile them persuasively?
2. Answer Sullivan's question in paragraph 3.
3. Sullivan says in paragraph 4 that "there is a separation of church and state in this country." Do you think that is absolutely true? How does the religious faith of our leaders affect policy, more specifically, policy toward homosexuality and gay marriage? Examine recent statements made by the president of the United States and members of Congress about the issue and compare them to Sullivan's assertions. Do you think he might persuade them? Explain your answer.

▶ Ideas for Writing Arguments

Prewriting

Will gay marriage inevitably be legalized? Write down some of your thoughts about how that might come about or why it would not come about.

Writing a Guided Argument

Many people think that the legalization of gay marriage is only a matter of time. What does that mean? Argue in an essay that gay marriage will or will not be legal nationally within the next 10 years.

1. Begin your essay with a quote from Sullivan's essay that asserts the moral right of gays to marry.
2. Continue with an analysis of how other social progress has been made.
3. Compare that progress with the advent of gay marriage, and make your claim in the form of a prediction.
4. Give at least two minor propositions for why you think gay marriage will or will not soon be legal nationally.

5. Support your ideas with further evidence from other areas of civil rights.
6. Imagine a point the opposition might make; rebut the opposition's point.
7. Conclude your essay with an appeal to the reader's emotions and sense of morality.

Thinking, Arguing, and Writing Collaboratively

Exchange papers from your Writing a Guided Argument assignment with a classmate. Read the student's paper for the success of the argument. Outline the student's essay, listing his or her major proposition and minor propositions, with an indication of the support the student gives. Write a couple of paragraphs to the student, one praising the positive aspects of the paper and the other explaining what is weak and could be improved. Return the paper and your outline and notes.

Writing about the Text

In an essay, compare Sullivan's argument about gay marriage with Ann Patchett's argument about marriage between first cousins in "Kissing Cousins." How are their arguments similar, and how are they different?

More Writing Ideas

1. Gay marriage issues have filled the news recently with officials in some cities and states issuing marriage licenses and performing ceremonies for gay couples. Check newspaper and magazine articles and write a journal entry about your reactions to these official acts.
2. In 2003 the Supreme Court handed down a landmark decision in *Lawrence v. Texas* that has a bearing on gay marriage. The court struck down sodomy laws in Texas and other states that made homosexual sex a crime. Write a paragraph summarizing either the court's majority opinion (striking down the sodomy laws), or the dissent (which was written by the justices who wanted to uphold them). What were their claims?
3. In an essay, defend either the majority decision or the dissenting opinion referred to in item 2 above. Use evidence from the texts to make your case.

BARBARA KANTROWITZ
Unmarried, with Children

Barbara Kantrowitz was educated at Cornell University and Columbia University. She is married with two children and lives in New York City. She has written for many magazines and newspapers, including the New York Times, *the* Philadelphia Inquirer, Newsday, Martha Stewart Living, *and* Newsweek, *where this article appeared in 2001 and where she is now senior editor. In this essay, Kantrowitz discusses the ever-shifting face of the American family, especially the mainstream acceptance of single-parent families.*

▶ Prereading: Thinking about the Essay in Advance

How has the American family changed in the past 20 years? 10 years? 5 years? What was a "traditional" family years ago, and what is a "traditional" family today?

▶ Words to Watch

negotiating (par. 1) dealing with
postmodern (par. 2) contemporary
demographers (par. 3) scientists who study patterns of human populations
stigma (par. 4) part of one's identity that seems shameful
watershed (par. 4) significant
serendipitous (par. 9) chance
futile (par. 14) without effect

Just imagine what would happen if June and Ward Cleaver were negotiat- 1
ing family life these days. The scenario might go something like this: they meet at the office (she's in marketing; he's in sales) and move in together after dating for a couple of months. A year later June gets pregnant. What to do? Neither feels quite ready to make it legal and there's no pressure from their parents, all of whom are divorced and remarried themselves. So little Wally is welcomed into the world with June's last name on the birth certificate. A few years later June gets pregnant again with the Beav. Ward's ambivalent about second-time fatherhood and moves out, but June decides to go ahead on her own. In her neighborhood, after all, single motherhood is no big deal; the lesbians down the street adopted kids from South America, and the soccer mom next door is divorced with a live-in boyfriend.

Figures released last week from the 2000 Census show that this post- 2
modern June would be almost as mainstream as the 1950s version. The number of families headed by single mothers has increased 25 percent since 1990, to more than 7.5 million households. Contributing to the numbers are a high rate of divorce and out-of-wedlock births. For most of the

past decade, about a third of all babies were born to unmarried women, compared with 3.8 percent in 1940. Demographers now predict that more than half of the youngsters born in the 1990s will spend at least part of their childhood in a single-parent home. The number of single fathers raising kids on their own is also up; they now head just over 2 million families. In contrast, married couples raising children—the "Leave It to Beaver" models—account for less than a quarter of all households.

3   Demographers and politicians will likely spend years arguing about all this and whether the shifts are real or just numerical flukes. But one thing everyone does agree on is that single mothers are now a permanent and significant page in America's diverse family album. "We can encourage, pressure, preach, and give incentives to get people to marry," says Stephanie Coontz, author of "The Way We Never Were" and a family historian at the Evergreen State College in Olympia, Wash. "But we still have to deal with the reality that kids are going to be raised in a variety of ways, and we have to support all kinds of families with kids."

4   This new breed of single mother doesn't fit the old stereotype of an unwed teen on welfare. She's still likely to be financially insecure, but she could be any age and any race. The median age for unmarried mothers is the late 20s, and the fastest-growing category is white women. She may be divorced or never-married. Forty percent are living with men who may be the fathers of one or more of their children; as the Census numbers also showed, there's been nearly a 72 percent increase in the number of cohabiting couples, many of whom bring along children from previous relationships. She may also be a single mother by choice. Unwed motherhood has lost much of its stigma and has even been glamorized by celebrity role models like Rosie O'Donnell and Calista Flockhart. "Twenty years ago middle-class women believed it took a man to have a child, but that's no longer true," says Rosanna Hertz, chair of the women's studies department at Wellesley College. "We've reached a watershed moment."

5   More women are better educated and better able to support themselves—so a husband is no longer a financial prerequisite to motherhood. That's a huge social change from the past few decades. Carolyn Feuer, 30, a registered nurse from New York, decided not to marry her boyfriend when she became pregnant with Ryan, now 6. "It wouldn't have been a good marriage," she says. "It's better for both of us this way, especially my son." Her steady salary meant she had choices. "I had an apartment," she says. "I had a car. I felt there was no reason why I shouldn't have the baby. I felt I could give it whatever it needed as far as love and support and I haven't regretted it for even a minute since."

6   For many women, the barrier to marriage may be that they care too much about it, not too little, and they want to get it right. If they can't find the perfect soulmate of their dreams, they'd rather stay single. So they're postponing that walk down the aisle until after college, grad school, or starting a career and putting a little money in the bank. "Para-

doxically, more people today value marriage," says Frank Furstenberg, professor of sociology at the University of Pennsylvania. "They take it seriously. That's why they're more likely to cohabit. They want to be sure before they take the ultimate step." The average age of first marriage is now 25 for women and 27 for men—up from 20 and 23 in 1960. That's the highest ever, which leaves plenty of time for a live-in relationship to test a potential partner's compatibility. "Today it's unusual if you don't live with someone before you marry them," says Andrew Cherlin, a sociologist at Johns Hopkins University. "Before 1970, it wasn't respectable among anyone but the poor."

Some of these women are adult children of divorce who don't want to make their own offspring suffer the pain of watching a parent leave. They see living together as a kind of trial marriage without the legal entanglements that make breaking up so hard to do—although research indicates that cohabiting couples don't have a much better track record. "They're trying to give their marriages a better chance," says Diane Sollee, founder of the Coalition for Marriage, Family, and Couples Education. "They're not trying to be immoral and get away with something."   7

And if the first (or the second) relationship doesn't work out, many women think there's no reason to forgo motherhood. Wellesley researcher Hertz has been studying middle-class single mothers older than 35. Most of the 60 women she has interviewed in-depth became pregnant "accidentally." While their babies may have been unplanned, they were not unwanted. Hertz says that for many of these women, the decision to become a mother was all about the modern version of "settling." In the old days a woman did that by marrying Mr. Almost Right. Now settling means having the baby even if you can't get the husband. "When I started this project in the mid-'90s," Hertz says, "these women were tough to find. Now they're all over—next door, at the playground, in your kid's classroom. They've become a normal part of the terrain."   8

Not all single mothers by choice wait for a serendipitous pregnancy. There are so many options: sperm banks, adoption. New Yorker Gail Janowitz, a market researcher in her mid-40s, decided to adopt two years ago. She always wanted to be a mother, but never married. "As I got older," she says, "I didn't know if the timing of meeting a man was going to work out. I thought, well, I'll do the child part first." A year ago she adopted Rose, now 18 months old, in Kazakhstan. Although there have been difficult moments, Janowitz says she has no regrets. "I've never stopped knowing it was the right thing to do," she says. "I think I will still have the opportunity or the option, hopefully, to get married. But right now, I have a family."   9

Even under the very best of conditions, single motherhood is a long, hard journey for both mother and children. No one really knows the long-term consequences for youngsters who grow up in these new varieties of single-parent and cohabiting homes. Much of the research in the past on   10 alternative living arrangements has concentrated on children of divorce, who face very different issues than youngsters whose mothers have chosen to be single from the start or are cohabiting with their children's fathers or other partners. "We need to start paying attention to how these kids" living in cohabiting homes are doing, says Susan Brown, a sociologist at Bowling Green State University in Ohio. "All the evidence we have suggests that they are not doing too well."

11   Single mothers in general have less time for each individual child than two parents, and cohabiting relationships are less stable than marriages. That means that children living in these families are more likely to grow up with a revolving set of adults in their lives. And the offspring of single parents are more likely to skip the altar themselves, thus perpetuating the pattern of their childhood. "Children living outside marriage are seven times more likely to experience poverty and are 17 times more likely to end up on welfare and to have a propensity for emotional problems, discipline problems, early pregnancy, and abuse," says Robert Rector, a senior research fellow at the Heritage Foundation, a conservative think tank. "It can be a recipe for disaster."

12   The average kid in a single-parent family looks much the same emotionally as children who grow up in the most conflicted two-parent homes, says Larry Bumpass, a sociologist at the University of Wisconsin. But, he adds, "the average is not the script written for every child. The outcomes are not all negative; it's just a matter of relative probability . . . the majority will do just fine." Lyn Freundlich, who is raising two boys in Boston with their father, Billy Brittingham, says her home is as stable as any on the block. Freundlich and Brittingham have no plans to marry even though they've been living together for 13 years. "It's not important to me," says Freundlich, 36, who works for the Boston AIDS Action Committee. "Marriage feels like a really unfair institution where the government validates some relationships and not others. I can't think of any reason compelling enough to become part of an institution I'm uncomfortable with." When she was pregnant with their first son, Jordan, now 6, Brittingham's parents "waged a campaign for us to get married," she says. His father was relieved when they decided to draft a will and sign a medical proxy. These days, the possibility of marriage hardly crosses her mind. "I'm so busy juggling all the details of having a two-career family, taking care of my kids, seeing my friends, and having a role in the community that it's just not something I think about," she says.

13   If Freundlich isn't thinking about marriage, a lot of politicians are—from the White House on down. In a commencement address at Notre Dame on Sunday, President George W. Bush planned to stress the need to strengthen families and assert that "poverty has more to do with troubled lives than a troubled economy," according to an aide. Bush believes funding religious initiatives is one way Washington can foster family stability. Policies to encourage marriage are either in place or under discussion around the country. Some states, such as Arizona and Louisiana, have es-

tablished "covenant" marriages in which engaged couples are required to get premarital counseling. It's harder to get divorced in these marriages. Utah allows counties to require counseling before issuing marriage licenses to minors and people who have been divorced. Florida now requires high-school students to take marriage-education classes that stress that married people are statistically healthier and wealthier.

Some researchers who study the history of marriage say that such efforts may be futile or even destructive. "Giving incentives or creating pressures for unstable couples to wed can be a huge mistake," says family historian Coontz. "It may create families with high conflict and instability—the worst-case scenario for kids." Other scientists say that lifelong marriage may be an unrealistic goal when humans have life expectancies of 80 or older. In their new book, "The Myth of Monogamy," David Barash and Judith Lipton say that in the natural world, monogamy is rare. And even among humans, it was probably the exception throughout much of human history. In "Georgiana: Duchess of Devonshire," biographer Amanda Foreman details bed-hopping among the 18th-century British aristocracy that would make even a randy Hollywood icon blush.   14

If a long and happy marriage is an elusive goal for couples in any century, most women—even those scarred by divorce—say it's still worth pursuing. When Roberta Lanning, 37, of Woodland Hills, Calif., became pregnant with her fifth child after a bitter divorce, she decided not to marry her boyfriend and raise Christian, now 9, on her own. As a child of divorce herself, she never wanted to raise a family on her own. "Single motherhood is not a good thing," she says. "It's definitely one hurdle after another." And despite everything, she hasn't given up. "It's been my heart's desire to have a father and mother in a structured home situation" for Christian, she says. "It just hasn't happened for me. Believe me, I've certainly been looking." If she finds the right man, chances are he'll probably have a couple of kids of his own by now, too.   15

▶ Building Vocabulary

Explain in your own words the meanings of the following phrases and words. Use clues from the surrounding text to help you understand or use reference texts:

1. soccer mom (par. 1)
2. out-of-wedlock births (par. 2)
3. median age (par. 4)
4. cohabiting couples (par. 4)
5. legal entanglements (par. 7)
6. Mr. Almost Right (par. 8)
7. think tank (par. 11)

   8. religious initiatives (par. 13)
   9. bed-hopping (par. 14)
10. aristocracy (par. 14)

▶ Thinking Critically about the Argument

Understanding the Writer's Argument

1. June and Ward Cleaver were the parents in the TV series *Leave It to Beaver*, which showed an extremely traditional family in the 1950s. Why would the writer's hypothetical June Cleaver in paragraph 1 be mainstream today?
2. Why are so many families today headed by single moms?
3. Why does Stephanie Coontz say that people need to accept all kinds of families?
4. Who is today's single mother, and how has the profile changed?
5. Why are more and more women choosing to adopt or get artificially inseminated?
6. What are the different opinions the writer presents about the effect of single parenthood on children?
7. Why would conservatives' religious initiatives to foster traditional marriages "be futile or even destructive"? (par. 14)

Understanding the Writer's Techniques

1. What is the writer's claim? Does she place it effectively? If so, explain. If not, where would you put it?
2. What is the argumentative effect of the scenario outlined in paragraph 1?
3. In paragraph 5, the argument shifts. How would you characterize this shift?
4. Outline the minor propositions the writer gives for her claim. Which proposition is most interesting? Is that also the most effective? What is the weakest? What kind of evidence does the writer use to support her minor propositions?
5. What is the effect of the sentences at the beginning of paragraphs 13, 14, and 15 that act as transitions?
6. How effective is the writer's discussion in paragraphs 10 through 12 about how single-parent families affect the lives of children?
7. How does the writer rebut Robert Rector's quote in paragraph 11? Is her technique effective? Explain the effect the final example of Roberta Lanning has on the writer's argument.

Exploring the Writer's Argument

1. The writer of this essay has obviously done a great deal of reporting. She uses several single mothers as examples. Do you find this excessive? Are some of the examples more persuasive than others, and, more important, are they *meant* to be persuasive? If not, what is their purpose? If so, how are they persuasive?

2. Do you find this essay completely coherent? The concept of single motherhood is a wide topic, and the writer does a lot of work to tie everything together, exploring all the different reasons why women would be single parents or would choose that lifestyle. Where in the essay do you think the discussion becomes too broad?

3. The writer uses many quotes and opinions of other writers and thinkers, but rarely comes out and expresses her own opinions. Examine where in the essay the writer's own ideas stand out. Does she hide behind her research? Explain your answer.

▶ Ideas for Writing Arguments

Prewriting

Are there any examples in your life, or in the lives of your family members or friends, that show that children suffer from divorce? Write a few notes about some of the negative effects of divorce on children.

Writing a Guided Argument

Kantrowitz seems to think that "a long and happy marriage is an elusive goal," but she also says that divorce is usually difficult for everyone involved. Write an essay about how people give up on marriages too readily and why they should seek counseling if they are considering divorce.

1. Open with an example of how divorce can be harmful to everyone involved in a marriage.
2. Indicate that perhaps married couples need to be less hasty in getting divorces.
3. Give at least two grounds for your claim.
4. Use a tone of concerned detachment in your essay.
5. Support your ideas with statistics from Kantrowitz's essay.
6. Give an example of a success story by describing a couple at risk of divorce who sought counseling.
7. Conclude your essay by referring to the divorce rate and explaining why the rate is alarming.

Thinking, Arguing, and Writing Collaboratively

In small groups of three or four, choose two different quotes from single mothers in Kantrowitz's essay. Compare the women's approaches to the situation and discuss which you think is the more positive attitude. Present your opinions to the class.

Writing about the Text

Andrew Sullivan's "Let Gays Marry" states that most gay people want the opportunity to marry. Many observers think that gay marriage will soon be a reality: it already is in Canada and Massachusetts, and some American cities have provided marriage licenses to gay couples. Write an essay explaining what lessons homosexuals could learn about marriage from Kantrowitz's essay. Argue that gays should still want to get married or that they should avoid the institution.

More Writing Ideas

1. In your journal, freewrite about the topic of adoption. Do not edit your writing. Write nonstop for at least 15 minutes. When you finish, exchange your journal with another student. Do you see any potential major propositions in your classmate's freewriting?
2. Do you think men—or women—are to blame for the high rate of divorce in this country? Write a paragraph defending your position.
3. Write an essay in the form of a letter to one of the experts quoted in Kantrowitz's essay, arguing against their position. Do research on the Web or in the library if necessary to build evidence for your claim.

3 Literary Arguments: Getting to the Point about Literature and the Arts

Art as a reflection of life engages our minds and passions, and writers—from Sir Philip Sidney (*A Defense of Poesy*) of the Renaissance era to today's Joyce Carol Oates (*Uncensored: Views & (Re)views,* 2005), Peter Travers (film critic for *Rolling Stone*), and innumerable others—produce logical arguments about works of literature and the arts. Works that now fill our libraries, computers, iPods, museums, concert halls, movie houses, and television screens make artistic endeavors and critiques of them more accessible than ever. On the Internet, for example, you can read reviews and essays about almost any artistic subject. Chat rooms devoted to commentary on the arts abound. And more formal arguments, as well, are available through cyberspace; on the Movie Query Engine (http://www.mrqe.com/), for example, you can find links to thousands of past and current film reviews—almost a hundred essays about the movie *Spider-Man 3* alone. (You'll read one of them later on in this chapter.) People *argue* about literature and the arts; that is, following the general language we have used in this book, writers present a debatable point of view and back it up with appropriate details so that, with their reasoned deliberations, they can get us to believe what they believe.

No doubt you have read some literary arguments already—a review of a book, a movie, or a television show. Perhaps even in high school one of your instructors asked you to check some critic's view of a novel you had to read in class—*Adventures of Huckleberry Finn, A Tale of Two Cities, The Catcher in the Rye,* or *The Color Purple,* for example. Certainly, as you take more and more courses in literature, art, and communications, you will confront impassioned arguments about the merits (or failings) of this short story or that art show or some recent series on television. As an intelligent reader you have to bring to bear the same level of attention and focus that you bring to any argument, just what you practiced in Chapters 1 and 2 and what you will refine as you read through the essays throughout the rest of this book. We will present guidelines to consider as you read a literary essay so that you can determine for yourself how well the writer draws on the conventions of reasoned arguments.

Just as important as reading literary arguments is the almost certain assignment you're bound to receive to *write* a literary argument. Your instructors may ask you to provide your own commentary on a poem, short story, novel, film, sculpture, painting, or musical composition. We include all such assignments in our view of the activity of literary argument—making an assertion about a work of art and presenting logical support for the assertion.

READING ARGUMENTS ABOUT LITERATURE AND THE ARTS

Critics and students of the arts take a variety of approaches to their subject matter, yet they usually apply some key principles in developing and presenting their arguments.

Discovery

The writer of a literary argument must know deeply the details of the piece under review. That is, the writer must be able to identify and describe the key elements of the work of art. An essay about *Hamlet*, for example, must convince readers that the writer understands who the major characters are, what seminal actions take place, where the scene is set, and what dialogue reveals Shakespeare's main points in the play. But having this knowledge and showing it off in a comprehensive summary of the work are different notions. A good essay about literature almost never relies on a detailed plot summary to make its point. True, to defend an element of the argument a writer will have to provide evidence that often depends on summaries of actions or character behavior or influential external events. An essay about a painting would surely describe elements of it to help readers visualize the vital features of the artwork and might also include historical references and related details about the painter's life. An essay about a poem, short story, or novel would assuredly draw on quotes from the piece and, if secondary sources impart significant information, from statements by reliable critics and reviewers. However, a summary implies that the reader doesn't know the selection well enough to connect the essay with the work in question or that the reader won't take the time to look up the work. A summary also makes it easy for the essay writer to avoid coming to the point.

Certainly, book, film, and television reviews rely more heavily on plot summaries than general literary essays because the reviewer's job is to provide details of a work assumed to be unknown to readers of the critical essay. A review of a new film would require some details of the setting and the characters' exploits and interactions. Yet even here, an experienced reviewer (like Manohla Dargis in the review of *Spider-Man 3* on pages 127–129), intimate with plot details, will not provide a full description of the selection, allowing readers the opportunity to see the film or read the book on their own and reap the delights or pains of it unencumbered by a full knowledge of the events in the work. Reviewers almost always assume that readers will want to see for themselves, thereby confirming the reviewer's opinions of the work at hand.

We have to make an essential point about using quoted or paraphrased material in a literary essay, which, in fact, is like all other essays in this regard. The writer must clearly acknowledge the source of every citation. In the case of reviews of single works, citation is often a routine affair; the reader knows pretty much from the outset of the essay just what piece the reviewer will deal with. But in essays that draw substantially on a variety of sources—from the work itself and from others who have commented on it—the writer must cite sources. And writers choose from a variety of formats in naming their source material, from parenthetical citations and informal bibliographies, to abbreviated footnoting systems, to formal methods developed by professional organizations such as the Modern Language Association (MLA) and the American Psychological Association (APA), to long-used systems advanced in highly regarded texts, such as *The Chicago Manual of Style* and Kate Turabian's *A Manual for Writers of Research Papers, Theses, and Dissertations*. The essays that you will read later in this chapter show a number of the options available to writers who cite source material. In Part 6 of this book, you can examine a student-prepared argumentative research paper that relies on the citation system promulgated by the MLA (see pages 489–497).

Interpretation

A literary argument provides the writer's interpretation of a piece by explaining and analyzing it in the context of the debatable position taken in the essay. The writer lays out the meaning or meanings of the work as she sees it.

Modern thinkers and scholars generally discredit the notion of one exact meaning in an artistic endeavor. The selection may have one meaning intended by the artist in the historical moment of production, but over the years, different levels of interpretation come into play, adding new views and broadening the context of the work. In the poem "Ozymandias" by the 19th-century Romantic poet Percy Bysshe Shelley, for example, (read the poem on page 98), the poet shows the absurdity of a tyrant's assertion of his own awesome power; the ancient king Ozymandias has built a statue of himself to celebrate his "cold command" as "king of kings," yet the statue now is a "colossal wreck" amid "lone and level sands" that "stretch far away." Some of the bloodiest tyrants in history—Adolph Hitler, Josef Stalin, Mao Zedong, Saddam Hussein—came to power long after the poem was written and continued to produce great monuments to their might and authority. These more immediate events for modern readers bring strong new meanings to the poem. One could argue that even with the evidence of Ozymandias's folly, the mighty and powerful fail to see that material things easily disintegrate and those who put their faith in them are doomed to ineffectuality and ultimate failure. Acute interpretation takes into account the many possible meanings of a work as a critic teases out meanings.

Merely providing an interpretation is not enough, however. The writer must offer supporting details as evidence for the meanings set forth in an essay. In the example of modern tyrants who do not see the lesson of Ozymandias, one might cite the innumerable statues, photographs, and paintings of Stalin and Hussein, now largely desecrated by angry citizens in Russia and Iraq, or the failure of Mao's political and economic reforms in China, pretty much overridden by subsequent leaders after his death. And the supporting evidence must hew to the debatable position the writer has stated. These pointers, you should recall, are variations on the Aristotelian equation we explored in Chapter 1: **Argument = Statement + Proof**.

Ozymandias

I met a traveler from an antique land
Who said: Two vast and trunkless legs of stone
Stand in the desert . . . Near them, on the sand,
Half sunk, a shattered visage lies, whose frown,
And wrinkled lip, and sneer of cold command
Tell that its sculptor well those passions read
Which yet survive, stamped on these lifeless things,
The hand that mocked them, and the heart that fed.

And on the pedestal these words appear:
"My name is Ozymandias, king of kings:
Look on my works, ye Mighty, and despair!"

Nothing beside remains. Round the decay
Of that colossal wreck, boundless and bare
The lone and level sands stretch far away.
                                    —*Percy Bysshe Shelley*

Evaluation

In this element of literary interpretation, the writer-critic provides an assessment of the work. What is the artistic merit of the piece? The claim of the argument usually embeds an assertion, which, of course, is another way of saying that the critic is providing an assessment. Consider the following evaluations of Shelley's poem:

- The imagery in "Ozymandias" is of such high visual quality that the sensory details of the fallen statue show exactly what the flesh-and-blood king himself must have looked like during his reign.
- Despite the rich imagery of a material statue, Shelley fails to account for a tyrant's deeds and actions, which have devastating effects on individuals, their progeny, their surroundings, and the future of their governmental structures.

You can see that these are essentially opposite opinions of the poem. Each one makes an assertion about the imagery, and each one arrives at a different conclusion about its artistic merit. The first writer would provide specific examples from the poem to link the visage of a cracked stone statue and the features of a human being, perhaps even referring to facial features of today's tyrants. The second writer, apparently believing that Shelley misses a major point about the rule of tyrants, would have to show that the imagery does not account for events that go beyond the material—the devastating human toll of Stalin's and Hussein's now well-known massacres of their people, for example. The opinions embedded in each of these evaluations clearly emanate from the writers' interpretations of the poem and the writers' ability to identify—provide essential supporting evidence for—the key elements of the work.

In the following paragraph by David Michaelis, from his essay "Sgt. Pepper's Words," about the Beatles' 1967 album, for *The American Scholar*, note the interaction among discovery, interpretation, and evaluation as the writer advances his argument:

From *Introducing the Beatles* in 1963 to *Revolver* in 1966, the Beatles had supplemented the traditional release of new hit singles with annual appearances of two-sided LPs, the covers of which, though increasingly brash, and inventive, gave no warning of what Sgt. Pepper would unleash. Inside and out, everything about the new record was narrative. It was bursting to tell a story. The Beatles made their regular instruments, from bass guitar to drums, sound like voices that had something fresh to say, while making the harpsichord and the fiddle, as well as classical instruments from India, seem integral to the most far-out aspirations of rock 'n' roll. It was the first rock album to insert orchestral scoring for narrative effects—one of many ways in which Sgt. Pepper was created more in the manner of filmmaking than by the conventions of the music industry. And if the recording processes devised in the Abbey Road studios gave Sgt. Pepper the aura of a mod film, the sumptuous packaging that the Beatles insisted upon clothed the album in its most characteristic quality: readability. Here was the first record ever to publish its lyrics on the back of its cover. The songs told a story that was connected by a theme and that could be read cover to cover.

Reading Literary Arguments: A Checklist

- Has the writer stated an arguable position? Does the statement pass the test of justification? (See page 6.)
- Has the writer avoided detailed plot summary, yet included important elements of the work in question so readers see that the writer understands the key elements of the piece?
- Has the writer provided evidence? Does the writer support effectively the claims and the minor propositions of the argument?
- Overall, has the writer convinced you that the major premise is viable and believable?
- Are all sources fully acknowledged and cited in an acceptable format?

WRITING ARGUMENTS ABOUT LITERATURE AND THE ARTS

As stated before—and no doubt you've found this to be true on your own—many courses in college will require you to write a short literary argument. Certainly your English literature courses will expect you to read and argue about a poem, short story, or novel or to synthesize your thoughts around some controlling idea regarding a group of literary works. In addition, your history instructor might ask for a review of a new book on the Kennedy years, or your art instructor may require a comparison between two paintings, Sargent's *Madame X* and Picasso's *Woman in White,* for example. Or in a basic comparative and contrast assignment, you might choose a topic around the arts, like comparing two sonnets by Shakespeare; the three Spider-Man films; the *Ocean's Eleven, Ocean's Twelve,* and *Ocean's Thirteen* productions; or the two film versions of *King Kong.* Your basic challenge in any one of these assignments will be to make an appropriate argument built on a debatable point of view. You have seen in Chapter 2 how to approach the task of narrowing a topic and developing from it a thesis that makes a claim. And you've also examined some strategies for supporting your claim, organizing the grounds of your argument, checking your assumptions, and dealing with opposing points of view. All these strategies pertain in the literary argument as well.

Use the following checklist as you consider developing your own literary argument. Then examine the annotated student paper on a poem by e. e. cummings. Finally, read the literary arguments of professional writers who ask you to consider key works through the lenses of their own analyses.

Writing Literary Arguments: A Checklist

Examine the work very carefully. Read the literary selection very slowly; study the painting thoroughly; watch the film attentively. If you're reporting on a story or poem, for example, a first reading rarely provides you with a clear sense of what the writer is up to. You have to read the material more than once in order to appreciate the emotional and intellectual impact that the writer has aimed for. The separate elements of the story will come into clearer focus on rereading, and you will see the logical pattern of the work, making your own argument easier to assert.

Ignore nothing. Attentive reading means that everything in the piece is worth noting. Good literature, as in all good art, includes nothing extraneous: each word and sentence, each brushstroke and color, each musical note and timbre should contribute to the overall effect intended by the artist. You must assume that everything serves a purpose. Pay attention to details as you read closely, and use the details to support and strengthen your argument.

Keep your personal prejudices at bay. An effective literary argument analyzes what is happening in a work of art, not what your own philosophy or moral commitments are. The artist is presenting a point of view that you must understand without preconceived notions of right and wrong, good or bad, weak or strong. Once you understand the writer's position you will no doubt draw on your own life's view to evaluate it, but you must make clear what your prejudices are and realize that they are separate from the work of art itself. Your view of the sanctity of marriage and the necessary devotion between a husband and wife should not prejudice your understanding of Kate Chopin's "The Story of an Hour" (pages 108–110).

State your thesis clearly so that the reader knows your position on the topic. As we pointed out in Chapter 2, a thesis is the key to a strong essay. You don't always have to include the thesis in your essay (although it's usually a good idea to do so), but you must always be able to state it clearly, whether or not you use it in your paper.

Use only the language of literary analysis that you truly understand. Words such as *theme, symbol, moral, tone, diction, connotation, denotation, figure, irony, metaphor,* and *point of view* (there are many others), may be key to literary argument, but when you write about literature you shouldn't bandy them about unless you understand precisely what they mean. Students often confuse irony—the use of language to suggest the opposite of what the writer states directly—with sarcasm, which is a heavy-handed form of irony in an effort to hurt by means of ridicule or sharp criticism. And symbol, or symbolism, is a much maligned term as well: a symbol is not some exotic literary device but simply a person, place, or thing that stands for or strongly suggests something in addition to itself, generally an abstract idea more important than the object itself. A diamond engagement ring, for example, is not only a gift signifying betrothal but also a symbol of fidelity, commitment, morality, and so on. Your English instructors no doubt will review many of these terms with you, and several extensive glossaries of literary terms are available in book form or online. Many literature anthologies contain back-of-book glossaries of essential terms. Consult these resources for clarification if you have any problems.

Avoid plot summaries. Student writers often mistake plot summary for interpretation and evaluation, and you don't want to fall into that trap. Don't tell the story again. A literary argument is not a book report. Always assume that your reader has some familiarity with the work in question or can check it easily for more information. Few people will read an analysis of a work with which they are completely unfamiliar (except a current review of an unknown work, perhaps).

Use direct quotations carefully and sparingly. Rely mostly on references in your own words to the work you are discussing. Certainly a well-chosen direct quotation can drive home a point successfully, but merely stringing together one quote after another will never serve you well. Of course, if you are writing about a writer's style or explaining what a few complex lines mean, you will have to quote directly. But on the whole, use a quote when you have a specific reason for doing so—otherwise, use your own language.

Consider one of the many possible approaches to writing a literary argument.

- *Write about the theme of the work*. Make an assertion about what you think the artist's main point is in the poem, short story, novel, or other work. A theme is not a moral, message, or bit of advice; it is the underlying issue of the piece. Especially in literature, don't think of the theme as the artist's attempt to provide guidance on how to live our lives. Your basic question about theme should be: What is the writer attempting to say here?

- *Write about the characters in the work*. Here you would focus on the way the writer develops the people in the work and how they relate to the events of the book. Can you determine why a character reacts in a certain way? Do you understand the relations that the writer has set up among the characters? What do the characters learn? How do you feel about the characters and why?

- *Write about the structure of the work*. Literary genres—poems, short stories, novels, memoirs, dramas, screenplays, works of nonfiction—have their own structural requirements. How does the particular work relate to the conventions of the genre? An inventive poet of the early 20th century, e. e. cummings, (you will examine one of his works further on in this chapter), chose to avoid conventional punctuation, even going so far as to write his own name in all lowercase letters. In his novels, William Faulkner broke down the expected chronological sequence in narrative, disrupting temporal events as the writer moves back and forth in time. Why did the writer choose the structure that shapes the work? How do the chapters or stanzas or acts relate to each other?

- *Write about the plot and setting.* The actions and place and time of the piece are important elements in works of fiction and poetry. If you write about the plot, examine the links between and among events and the effect they have on the characters. If you write about the setting, identify the critical features of the place in which the action occurs and explain why you think the author chose the particular setting for the work. Consider the order of the events and why the author has arranged them in the sequence you identify. Examine the period of time that the work embraces. Again, a by now familiar caution: don't provide an exhaustive summary of the work, even if you are writing about the plot.

- *Write about the tone of the work.* The tone is the author's attitude toward the subject. How does the author feel about the characters and events in the selection? Is the tone sentimental, impartial, ironic, sarcastic, humorous, coy, angry? And why has the author chosen this tone?

- *Write about language and style.* What pattern of imagery do you find? How do figurative expressions contribute to the piece? What structural elements do you notice about the sentences? Are they short, long, simple, complex? What special qualities of style do you note?

A Student's Literary Argument

Responding to an assignment to write a literary argument about poetry studied in class, one student, Harry Singh, chose the poem "in Just-" by e. e. cummings.

After considering a variety of options and following the suggestions in this chapter section, he wrote the following paper. Answer the questions after you finish reading the poem and the student's written work.

in Just-

in Just-
spring   when the world is mud-
luscious the little
lame balloonman

whistles   far   and wee

and eddieandbill come
running from marbles and
piracies and it's
spring

when the world is puddle-wonderful

the queer
old balloonman whistles
far   and   wee
and bettyandisbel come dancing

   from hop-scotch and jump-rope and

it's
spring
and
        the
                goat-footed

balloonMan   whistles
far
and
wee

                                        — e. e. cummings

Delights and Dangers of Childhood

E. E. Cummings's poems show an inventive, playful use of words and sentence structure to force readers to consider common ideas and feelings in a new context. The poem "in Just-" presents an entirely familiar world of children at play in the spring. Yet the poet's unusual use of language shows us the subtle dangers lurking about the delights and pleasures we all associate with childhood.

Cummings uses words and images that reflect a child's perception of the world. He calls the world "mud-luscious" and "puddle-wonderful." With those phrases we can feel a child's delight at springtime. The games abandoned at the balloonman's call—"marbles and / piracies" and "hop-scotch and jump-rope"—accurately show us children at play. Cummings runs the names of the children together on the page so that we hear them just as children would say them, "eddieandbill" and "bettyandisbel." In addition, the balloonman "whistles far and wee," a child's excited expression certainly. The words "it's spring" are repeated twice, again to show the innocent excitement of youngsters outdoors after the spring rain.

But beneath this simple world is a much more complex one. The balloonman has a peculiar, ominous power over the children. They stop everything, running and dancing to see him. On one level, of course, it is not surprising for children to greet a neighborhood visitor who sells balloons. Yet Cummings calls him "lame," "queer," and "goat-footed." In Greek mythology, the satyrs, creatures who enjoyed wild merrymaking, were humanlike gods with goats' features. By alluding to the satyrs, the poet implies something sinister.

Margin annotations:

Evaluation: writer states his opinion "playful use," "unusual use"

Writer introduces argumentative thesis succinctly in the first paragraph

Details drawn directly from the poem support language issue

Writer avoids summarizing the poem yet provides his interpretation of key lines

Singh explains the allusion. *Fact*: satyrs are Greek mythological characters who enjoy wild merrymaking; *interpretation*: something sinister implied

The phrase for the sound of the balloonman's whistle, "far and wee," which is used three times in this poem of twenty-four very short lines, also suggests something unusual, even dangerous. Why "far"? Will the sound transport the children far away? Can children far away hear it? Although Cummings's piper is more contemporary—he uses a whistle instead of a flute—the poet certainly is alluding here to the Pied Piper of Hamelin, who enchanted all the children with his magic flute and lured them away from their town.

> Writer interprets elements of poem's structure, repetition of phrase, and indicates another allusion—Pied Piper.

In a sense, then, the poem may be viewed as a story of the loss of innocence awaiting children as they grow up. In a secure world of play there are no troubles. But evil and danger are imminent, maybe even necessary for passage into adulthood. These ideas help call attention to the phrase "in Just–"/ spring." (Cummings probably used an uppercase letter for the j in Just for emphasis. The only other capital letter in the poem is for the word Man in balloonMan, when the word appears for the third time. Even the children's names are set in lowercase letters.)

> Writer explains his view of the poem's theme, a key element in Singh's argument

> Evidence to support interpretation of theme: analysis of key phrase, "in Just–"

Does the word Just mean "only," suggesting that spring alone, the season of growth and renewal, is the time of joy in a child's life? Or is the message darker, perhaps even ironic? If spring is "just," meaning fair or honorable, where is the justice in children (or their childhoods) being stolen away? Perhaps Cummings is saying that spring is not just at all, that its delights are merely seductions. What makes the poem so compelling and provocative is that the poet raises the questions but provides no definite answers.

1. What arguable assertion does the writer make about the poem? How effective is it? What argument could someone offer to oppose Singh's thesis?
2. How effective is the writer's use of quotations (he includes many of the poet's exact words)? Why has he chosen to draw so many words and phrases directly from the poem?
3. Has the writer convinced you of the validity of his argument? Why or why not?

LITERARY ARGUMENTS FOR READING AND ANALYSIS

DANIEL P. DENEAU
Chopin's "The Story of an Hour"

Novelist and short story writer Kate Chopin (1850–1904) first published "The Story of an Hour" in 1894, and many see it as a classic, a short story about a young wife momentarily freed from a stifling marriage. In his essay about the story, Daniel P. Deneau examines a single passage, the point at which the main character, Louise Mallard, feels something that "was approaching to possess her" and to which "she abandoned herself." Deneau is professor emeritus in the English Department at Minnesota State University–Moorehead. He has written many articles about literature, including this selection on Kate Chopin's much discussed story. The essay originally appeared in the journal Explicator *in 2003. Read Chopin's brief story below, followed by Deneau's argument about it.*

KATE CHOPIN
The Story of an Hour

1   Knowing that Mrs. Mallard was afflicted with a heart trouble, great care was taken to break to her as gently as possible the news of her husband's death.

2   It was her sister Josephine who told her, in broken sentences; veiled hints that revealed in half concealing. Her husband's friend Richards was there, too, near her. It was he who had been in the newspaper office when intelligence of the railroad disaster was received, with Brently Mallard's name leading the list of "killed." He had only taken the time to assure himself of its truth by a second telegram, and had hastened to forestall any less careful, less tender friend in bearing the sad message.

3   She did not hear the story as many women have heard the same, with a paralyzed inability to accept its significance. She wept at once, with

sudden, wild abandonment, in her sister's arms. When the storm of grief had spent itself she went away to her room alone. She would have no one follow her.

There stood, facing the open window, a comfortable, roomy armchair. 4 Into this she sank, pressed down by a physical exhaustion that haunted her body and seemed to reach into her soul.

She could see in the open square before her house the tops of trees 5 that were all aquiver with the new spring life. The delicious breath of rain was in the air. In the street below a peddler was crying his wares. The notes of a distant song, which some one was singing reached her faintly, and countless sparrows were twittering in the eaves.

There were patches of blue sky showing here and there through the 6 clouds that had met and piled one above the other in the west facing her window.

She sat with her head thrown back upon the cushion of the chair, 7 quite motionless, except when a sob came up into her throat and shook her, as a child who has cried itself to sleep continues to sob in its dreams.

She was young, with a fair, calm face, whose lines bespoke repression and even a certain strength. But now there was a dull stare in her eyes, whose gaze was fixed away off yonder on one of those patches of blue sky. It was not a glance of reflection, but rather indicated a suspension of intelligent thought.

There was something coming to her and she was waiting for it, fear- 8 fully. What was it? She did not know; it was too subtle and elusive to name. But she felt it, creeping out of the sky, reaching toward her through the sounds, the scents, the color that filled the air.

Now her bosom rose and fell tumultuously. She was beginning to rec- 9 ognize this thing that was approaching to possess her, and she was striv-ing to beat it back with her will—as powerless as her two white slender hands would have been.

When she abandoned herself a little whispered word escaped her 10 slightly parted lips. She said it over and over under her breath: "free, free, free!" The vacant stare and the look of terror that had followed it went from her eyes. They stayed keen and bright. Her pulses beat fast, and the coursing blood warmed and relaxed every inch of her body.

She did not stop to ask if it were or were not a monstrous joy that 11 held her. A clear and exalted perception enabled her to dismiss the sug-gestion as trivial.

She knew that she would weep again when she saw the kind, tender 12 hands folded in death; the face that had never looked save with love upon her, fixed and gray and dead. But she saw beyond that bitter mo-ment a long procession of years to come that would belong to her ab-solutely. And she opened and spread her arms out to them in welcome.

There would be no one to live for her during those coming years; she 13 would live for herself. There would be no powerful will, bending hers in that blind persistence with which men and women believe they have a right to impose a private will upon a fellow-creature. A kind intention or a cruel intention made the act seem no less a crime as she looked upon it in that brief moment of illumination.

14   And yet she had loved him—sometimes. Often she had not. What did it matter! What could love, the unsolved mystery, count for in face of this possession of self-assertion which she suddenly recognized as the strongest impulse of her being!

15   "Free! Body and soul free!" she kept whispering.

16   Josephine was kneeling before the closed door with her lips to the keyhole, imploring for admission. "Louise, open the door! I beg; open the door—you will make yourself ill. What are you doing, Louise? For heaven's sake open the door."

17   "Go away. I am not making myself ill." No; she was drinking in a very elixir of life through that open window.

18   Her fancy was running riot along those days ahead of her. Spring days, and summer days, and all sorts of days that would be her own. She breathed a quick prayer that life might be long. It was only yesterday she had thought with a shudder that life might be long.

19   She arose at length and opened the door to her sister's importunities. There was a feverish triumph in her eyes, and she carried herself unwittingly like a goddess of Victory. She clasped her sister's waist, and together they descended the stairs. Richards stood waiting for them at the bottom.

20   Some one was opening the front door with a latchkey. It was Brently Mallard who entered, a little travel-stained, composedly carrying his grip-sack and umbrella. He had been far from the scene of accident, and did not even know there had been one. He stood amazed at Josephine's piercing cry; at Richards' quick motion to screen him from the view of his wife.

21   But Richards was too late.

22   When the doctors came they said she had died of heart disease—of joy that kills.

DANIEL P. DENEAU
Chopin's "The Story of an Hour"

1   The much-anthologized "The Story of an Hour" (1894) is surely Kate Chopin's best-known piece of short fiction. Innumerable students, ranging from the very naive to the very sophisticated, must have grappled with the story in discussions and essays. As all readers should agree,

Louise Mallard receives a great shock, goes through a rapid sequence of reactions, is in a sense awakened and then seems to drink in "a very elixir of life" (354), and finally receives another shock, a reversal, which proves lethal. Probably equally clear to all or to most readers are Chopin's economy, the significance of the open window and the spring setting, the power which she assigns to "self-assertion," and the bold dramatic irony with which the story concludes. About one issue, at least among readers of anthologies, there may be continuing debate: is Louise a normal, understandable, sympathetic woman, or is she an egocentric, selfish monster or anomaly? And, as more sophisticated readers may ask, is the degree of "self-assertion" or freedom that she thinks she has attained a real possibility in a world of normal human relationships? Obviously readers' preconceptions about love and marriage and independence will dictate different answers to these questions. At one crucial point, however, this relatively clear and realistic story becomes problematic, perhaps even enigmatic—that is, the passage in which Chopin attempts to account for the direct cause of Louise's awakening:

> There was something coming to her and she was waiting for it, fear-   2
> fully. What was it? She did not know; it was too subtle and elusive to
> name. But she felt it, creeping[1] out of the sky, reaching toward her
> through the sounds, the scents, the color that filled the air.
>
> Now her bosom rose and fell tumultuously. She was beginning to   3
> recognize this thing that was approaching to possess her, and she was
> striving to beat it back with her will—as powerless as her two white
> hands would have been.
>
> When she abandoned herself a little whispered word escaped her   4
> slightly parted lips. She said it over and over under her breath: "Free,
> free, free!" The vacant stare and the look of terror that had followed it
> went from her eyes. They stayed keen and bright. Her pulses beat fast,
> and the coursing blood warmed and relaxed every inch of her body.
> (353)

This "something," this "it,"[2] which oddly arrives from the sky, exerts   5
a powerful physical influence on Louise and leaves her with a totally new perspective on her self and her place in the scheme of things. In a limited space, and without the assistance of a psychological vocabulary, Chopin may have been forced to rely on the indefinite, the unidentified, which, as best we can judge, is some powerful force, something supernatural, something beyond the realm of mundane experience or the rule of logic.[3] If immediately after learning of the death of her husband Louise had gone through a rapid logical process leading to a celebration of her total freedom, she might have seemed to be a hard, calculating, and therefore unsympathetic woman. Or to put the point in another way: since she has neither the physical nor moral strength to "beat . . . back" her attacker, which she begins to recognize but sadly never names, her responsibility is

abrogated. In addition, one of the problems presented by the passage is the fact that Louise meets the "something" with both fear and anticipation. Clearly what occurs is some type of sexual experience, one that at first seems, except for the anticipation, like a terrifying rape, but one that evolves into something sensually stimulating and relaxing, and, of course, spiritually illuminating. In short, a rape seems to have an ironic outcome.

6   There can be no doubt that the crucial passage becomes a fairly explicit description of a sexual union. One of the meanings of the verb "possess" is "to have sexual intercourse with (a woman)" (OED),[4] and this meaning was certainly known to Chopin, as illustrated by the climactic—that word, unfortunately, is inevitable—passage of "The Storm," the sexual union of Alcee and Calixta: "And when he possessed her, they seemed to swoon together at the very borderland of life's mystery" (595).[5] Moreover, the third paragraph quoted above does suggest coitus and postcoital reactions: the "abandonment," the "slightly parted lips," the "keen and bright eyes," and especially the final sentence—"Her pulses beat fast, and the coursing blood warmed and relaxed every inch of her body."

7   With no male aggressor-partner named in the text, only a "something," readers naturally will speculate. For me, two possibilities exist—both supernatural—of which, time after time, I am reminded as I contemplate the passage: one is classical, pagan; the other, Christian. The former is Leda and the swan-Zeus, a potent, sinister force which creeps from the "sky," attacks, and engenders a world-shaking course of events.[6] But the passage is about more than fear, force, and sex; it is also about anticipation, pleasure, and ultimately enlightenment. Thus, I am also reminded of the descent of the Christian Holy Spirit,[7] who is associated with conception, renewal, empowerment, inspiration, enlightenment, and freedom.[8] Louise does indeed receive an infusion of knowledge from a source that seems beyond human understanding or even naming. Add to these subjective responses Chopin's "belief" that genuine sexual passion itself may help the blind see: after Edna Pontellier's first sexual union with Arobin, she has various reactions; however, "above all, there was understanding. She felt as if a mist had been lifted from her eyes, enabling her to look upon and comprehend the significance of life, that monster made up of beauty and brutality" (967).

8   "The Story of an Hour" lacks the kind of diagrammatic clarity that some readers may expect, mainly or even exclusively, as I have tried to suggest, because of one curious passage. Chopin's desire to transform her protagonist from a woman with a "dull stare in her eyes" (353) to one with "a feverish triumph in her eyes," a woman who carries "herself unwittingly like a goddess of Victory" (354), required a force of exceptional intensity, a force as intense as a combination of a rape, a visitation by the Holy Spirit, and a sexual union—or, in short, a deus ex machina. It is no wonder that in a mere seven sentences this force remains perplexing,

probably enigmatic. One final point, however, is perfectly clear: having experimented with one very condensed account of an awakening—the account of a mere hour—Chopin later proceeded to create one of the masterpieces of American Literature—the slowly paced, psychologically credible, many-staged awakening of Edna Pontellier.[9]

Notes

1. In one other notable place in her short fiction Chopin used the verb "creeping." See the sexually charged "The Night Comes Slowly" (366).
2. Madonne M. Miner recognizes the importance of the "something" passage (31), but she does not scrutinize it sufficiently. "The unnameable is, of course, her self-consciousness that is embraced once she names her experience as emancipation and not destitution" (63). Angelyn Mitchell observes that "freedom ravishes" Louise and, quite correctly, that the passage is "loaded with sexual imagery" (62).
3. Cf. "Athenaise": "If she ever came to such knowledge [of her own mind], it would be by no intellectual research, by no subtle analyses or tracing of actions to their source. It would come to her as the song to the bird, the perfume and color to the flower" (433).
4. The editor of the OED adds a surprising note: "this sense [was] suggested in private correspondence in 1969 by Professor W. Empson." The meaning should have been commonly known much earlier.
5. Bert Bender finds the diction "wooden" and "ironically conventional" (266). I doubt that a similar charge could be made about the crucial passage in "The Story of an Hour. "
6. Recall Yeats, "Leda and the Swan," esp. 11. 5 and 6: "How can those terrified vague fingers push / The feathered glory from her loosing thighs?"
7. Chopin would have been well aware of the Christian view of the Holy Spirit (Ghost). See in /particular "At Cheniere Caminada" (317) and *The Awakening* (893).
8. Various Epistles associate the Holy Spirit with freedom. See, for example, 2 Cor. 3.17, as well as Isa. 61.1.
9. After completing this paper, I was pleased to find Jacqueline Padgett's paragraph in which she refers to an "annunciation" (101) in "The Story of an Hour."

Works Cited

Bender, Bert. "Kate Chopin's Lyrical Short Stories." *Studies in Short Fiction* 11 (1974): 257–66.

Chopin, Kate. *The Complete Works of Kate Chopin*. Ed. Per Seyersted. Baton Rouge: Louisiana State UP, 1969.

Miner, Madonne M. "Veiled Hints: An Affective Stylist's Reading of Kate Chopin's 'The Story of an Hour.'" *The Markham Review* 11 (Winter 1982): 29–32.

Mitchell, Angelyn. "Feminine Double Consciousness in Kate Chopin's 'The Story of an Hour.'" *CEA Magazine* 5.1 (1992): 59–64.

Padgett, Jacqueline Olson. "Kate Chopin and the Literature of the Annunciation, with a Reading of 'Lilacs.'" *Louisiana Literature* 11.1 (1994): 97–107.

Papke, Mary E. *Verging on the Abyss: The Social Fiction of Kate Chopin and Edith Wharton.* New York: Greenwood, 1990.

"Possess." Def. 3b. *The Oxford English Dictionary.* 2nd ed. 1989.

▶ Responding to the Essay

1. In his opening, Deneau writes about how "naïve" and "sophisticated" readers might read Chopin's story differently. He also writes in generalities about "most readers" and uses words like "obviously." Do you find his opening and choice of language effective? Why or why not?

2. After his first paragraph Deneau includes a three-paragraph quotation from Chopin's story. Is this an effective strategy for a literary argument? Why or why not?

3. What is Deneau's claim in this essay? Where does he state it most clearly?

4. In his essay, Deneau likens the events of the quoted passage to a rape. How effective is his description of the event as a kind of rape? Do you think he is going too far? Why or why not?

5. Which myths and religious stories does the writer refer to? How does his discussion of them contribute to his argument?

6. At the close of his essay, the writer refers to Edna Pontellier, a character in Chopin's novel *The Awakening*, which Deneau sees as an outgrowth of "The Story of an Hour." Whether or not you have read the novel, do you think this strategy of referring to an outside work is effective, or does it weaken the argument? Explain.

7. Examine the notes appended to the essay. What do they add to the argument? Why hasn't Deneau integrated the information in these notes into the essay itself?

▶ Responding in Writing

1. Deneau writes that readers have had debates about "The Story of an Hour," and he lists two debates: one that "readers of anthologies" might have, and one that more sophisticated readers might have. In a few paragraphs, state your position on both of these points.

2. What Louise Mallard experiences, it seems to Deneau, is a moment of freedom. Write a narrative about a time when you yourself have experienced such a moment. What was it like? Would you describe it in the terms Chopin uses? Why or why not?
3. Write an argumentative essay in which you analyze the last section of Chopin's story.
4. Write a paragraph-by-paragraph summary of Deneau's argument.

ROBERT E. FLEMING
Wallace Stevens' "The Snow Man" and Hemingway's "A Clean, Well-Lighted Place"

Robert E. Fleming is a literary critic and professor emeritus of English at the University of New Mexico. He is the coeditor, with Richard W. Lewis, of a scholarly edition of a previously unpublished Ernest Hemingway book, Under Kilimanjaro *(2005), and the author of many articles about Hemingway. In this selection, which was published in* American Notes and Queries *(ANQ) in April 1989, Fleming shows how it is likely that, although Hemingway once punched poet Wallace Stevens in the face, the fiction writer took a central conceit from "The Snow Man" for his own story. Note Fleming's use of a now outdated system to acknowledge sources, in which his references appear in footnotes, as opposed to internal parenthetical citations.*

The relationship between Wallace Stevens and Ernest Hemingway is best remembered for the one-sided fist fight between the two in February of 1936. According to a letter Hemingway wrote on 27 February 1936, Hemingway knocked Stevens down several times because he had insulted Hemingway's sister Ursula at a party. According to Hemingway, Stevens spent several days in the hospital, but an impartial witness said that the poet was seen in public the day after the fight, wearing sunglasses to conceal bruises.[1]   1

It is possible, however, that there is a more meaningful connection between the two. In "The Snow Man," first published in *Poetry* in 1921, Stevens uses the same existential image that Hemingway was to use in "A Clean, Well-Lighted Place," first published in *Scribner's Magazine* in 1933.[2] The image is that of nothing, not *nothing* as one normally uses the word, but what Carlos Baker describes as "Something—a Something called Nothing which is so huge, terrible, overbearing, inevitable, and omnipresent that, once experienced, it can never be forgotten."[3]   2

No external evidence that Hemingway had read "The Snow Man" exists. Both Michael Reynolds in *Hemingway's Reading, 1910–1940* and Brasch and Sigman in *Hemingway's Library: A Composite Record* indicate that the only Stevens work owned by Hemingway was *The Man with the*   3

Blue Guitar (1937), and that the only copy of *Poetry* in his personal library was the January 1923 issue which contained six of his own poems.[4] Nevertheless, Hemingway borrowed books regularly during his Paris years and could easily have seen "The Snow Man" either in *Poetry* or in *Harmonium* (1923).

4   After detailing a barren, snowy landscape observed by a "mind of winter," suggestive of modern life as perceived by modern existential man, Stevens concludes his fifteen-line poem by stating that his protagonist, "nothing himself," sees "Nothing that is not there *and the nothing that is*" (my emphasis).[5] The distinction is exactly the same as that paraphrased by Baker, writing of Hemingway's depiction of *nada* or nothing, the second *nothing* in Stevens' last line is not the mere absence of something, but an entity in itself, a force so powerful that only the strongest mind can perceive it and survive.

5   In his five-page story, Hemingway explores the theme more fully and goes a step beyond Stevens. After closing the cafe where an elderly customer has been lingering, trying to forget his loneliness and his suicidal thoughts, one of Hemingway's two waiters discloses that he shares the old man's sense of horror at the nothingness that pervades the universe. "It was a nothing that he knew too well. It was all a nothing and a man was nothing too. It was only that and light was all it needed and a certain cleanness and order. Some lived in it and never felt it but he knew it all was nada y pues nada y nada y pues y nada. Our nada who art in nada, nada be thy name thy kingdom nada thy will be nada in nada as it is in nada."[6]

6   To modern man, nothingness is such a powerful force that only the strongest can bear to perceive it, furthermore, since it is the only force in the universe, the wise man will worship it, however ironically.

7   Whatever their personal differences, Stevens and Hemingway shared a bleak view of the universe. It seems quite possible that Hemingway, reading the last line of "The Snow Man," felt moved to write his own artistic response to the plight of modern humanity.

Notes

1. *Ernest Hemingway: Selected Letters, 1917–1961*, ed. Carlos Baker (New York: Scribner's, 1981), pp. 438–39. See also Baker, *Ernest Hemingway: A Life Story* (New York: Scribner's, 1969), p. 285, and Jeffrey Meyers, *Hemingway: A Biography* (New York: Harper & Row, 1985), pp. 273–75.
2. *Poetry*, 19 (Oct. 1921), 4–5; *Scribner's Magazine*, 93 (March 1933), 149–50.
3. Carlos Baker, *Hemingway: The Writer as Artist* (Princeton: Princeton Univ. Press, 1963), p. 124.

4. Michael S. Reynolds, *Hemingway's Reading, 1910–1940* (Princeton: Princeton Univ. Press, 1981), pp. 85, 188; James Brasch and Joseph Sigman. *Hemingway's Library: A Composite Record* (New York: Garland, 1981), p. 356.
5. Wallace Stevens, *Poems* (New York: Vintage Books, 1959), p. 23.
6. Ernest Hemingway, "A Clean, Well-Lighted Place," *The Short Stories of Ernest Hemingway* (New York: Scribner's, 1961), p. 383.

▶ Responding to the Essay

1. In what ways is the opening of Fleming's essay effective? How does the writer use humor? Where does the introduction end? Explain your answers.
2. What does "existential" mean? How is that concept important to Fleming's argument?
3. What is Fleming's major proposition? How do you know?
4. Why does the writer make a point in paragraphs 4 and 5 to mention the lengths of Stevens's poem and Hemingway's story?
5. In what ways does Fleming convincingly connect the two works?
6. Have you read either of the two works? Does it matter in regard to your appreciation of the argument? Why or why not? Does it incline you to read the two selections? Why or why not?
7. How does Fleming use definition in his essay? Comparison and contrast?
8. What is your impression of the writer's use of quotations from the two pieces in question? Are there too many? Too few? Just enough? Support your answer with references to the text.

▶ Responding in Writing

1. Write your own reaction to discussions of "nothingness." Do you see attention to the concept in any movies or books you are aware of? If so, which ones? If not, why not?
2. Paragraph 6 of Fleming's essay is an opinion. Is it grammatically correct? Write an essay in which you agree or disagree with Fleming's statement—and in which you explain it.
3. Write an essay of your own comparing two works of art. You may look at a poem and a story, as Fleming does, or you may discuss a movie and a story, a movie and a song—it doesn't matter what media the works are in. The goal is to identify a common theme and write an essay explaining how the theme is shared between the two works.

CARRIE O'MALEY
Dickinson's "I Started Early—Took My Dog—"

Emily Dickinson was a poet from Amherst, Massachusetts, during the 19th century. Her gnomic verse still draws a wide following among readers of all ages who respond to the passion and succinct expression in her poetry. Carrie O'Maley published this interesting view of one of Dickinson's poems in the journal Explicator *in 2003. In her essay, O'Maley reprints the whole of "I Started Early—Took My Dog—"; her argument disputes the conventional wisdom about the poem, which says that Dickinson is describing a sexual encounter. Rather, says O'Maley, she is talking about both sex and death. Read the poem carefully before you start the essay.*

I started Early—Took my Dog—
And visited the Sea—
The Mermaids in the Basement
Came out to look at me—

And Frigates—in the Upper Floor
Extended Hempen Hands—
Presuming Me to be a Mouse—
Aground—upon the Sands

But no Man moved Me—till the Tide
Went past my simple Shoe
And past my Apron—and my Belt
And past my Bodice—too—

And made as He would eat me up—
As wholly as a Dew
Upon a Dandelion's Sleeve—
And then—I started—too

And He—He followed—close behind—
I felt His Silver Heel
Upon my Ankle—Then my Shoes
Would overflow with Pearl—

Until We met the Solid Town—
No One He seemed to know—
And bowing—with a Mighty look—
At me—The Sea withdrew—

1   Critics have concluded that the main theme in Emily Dickinson's "I Started Early—Took My Dog—" (1862) is a male/female sexual encounter. They dispute whether the encounter is malicious or consensual.

Lynn Shakinovsky argues that the Sea is a symbol of power and masculinity working against the weak woman: "Poem 520 concerns itself, on the one hand, with the play of power between the female narrator and the Sea who is figured as male." The narrator is undisputedly a woman in all criticisms, and the fact that Dickinson assigns masculine pronouns to describe the secondary character makes this assumption irrefutable. The womanly narrator is depicted as a "Mouse," whereas the male figure is posed as a "Frigate" in the Sea, descriptions that fit typical stereotypes of the aggressive male and the passive female.

Although the poem includes strong metaphors alluding to a corporal   2
meeting between a man and a woman, many other phrases suggest a near-death experience. The Sea, although representing the male in a sexual encounter, is also a metaphor for Death, and Dickinson's use of the capitalized pronoun "He" shows the importance of this proverbially feared phenomenon. Indeed, the "basement" in the first stanza is the scary part of death, its power to make most humans run in fear. Additionally, Dickinson says that "Frigates—in the Upper Floor/Extended Hempen Hands." The "Hands" are likely the hands of Death reaching down to take the narrator captive.

Most critics, however, view "Hempen Hands" as symbolic of male   3
sexual dominance. According to Shakinovsky, "The welcoming, 'extending' hands of the Frigate are not entirely friendly and contain a slight sense of threat, as 'Hempen' implies the possibility of trapping, tying, and strangling." However, she fails to recognize the severe tonal switch in the third stanza:

But no Man moved Me—till the Tide   4
Went past my simple Shoe—
And past my Apron—and my Belt
And past my Bodice—too—.

The switch seems to imply that the narrator, at first fearful of her first   5
sexual experience, is unsure of what is coming, but the ease in which the man approaches her wipes these fears away. Indeed, Jonnie Guerra argues that there is a lack of power in either the man or woman and that the pair share an intense mutual attraction: "The man's advances entice the female speaker as those of other men have not: according to the speaker's own report, he alone has 'moved' her." But I contend that the encounter is with death, wherein death first frightens her and then beckons her with a calming rush.

In the same way a virgin may at first fear sex, most humans fear   6
death. The touch of Death seems to ease the narrator, much as the gentle touch of a lover may ease a virgin during her first sexual encounter. The transaction is nearly complete in the fourth stanza, as death "made as He would eat me up—/As wholly as a Dew."

7   Guerra points out that the control possessed by both the male and Death in the second stanza has been completely handed to the narrator by the fifth stanza: "He—He followed—close behind—/ I felt His Silver Heel/Upon my Ankle—Then my Shoes / Would overflow with Pearl." Thus, not only does the male follow the female's lead, he possesses a "Silver Heel." This grandiose description of the male's body part stresses the luxurious quality of the sexual encounter. Likewise, Guerra notes, "even when the speaker feels 'His Silver Heel' on her 'Ankle,' his touch is made to seem not irritating, but desirable, for her shoes overflow with 'Pearl,' an image that Dickinson privileges for things she deems precious." This passing of control makes it evident that the pair share not only the aggressive power, but an intense mutual attraction as well. Likewise, the narrator overtakes death, and the fear that goes along with such a wondrous event has turned into acceptance. The narrator is at once at the same level as both death and her sexual partner, and she finds that neither being should be feared.

8   Shakinovsky claims that the final stanza reiterates male power and control, writing, "His power is conveyed again by the idea of control and choice that is implicit in the fact that his withdrawal at the end of the poem is presented not only as voluntary but also as temporary." However, when the pair meet "the Solid Town" in the last stanza, the end appears as an intrusion that neither welcomes. It was not the male who met the town, nor was it the female. Rather, Dickinson distinctly uses the pronoun "We" to signify that the lovers experience this sad ending together.

9   The poem is convincingly about both a first enjoyable sexual encounter and a brush with death. The allusions to each experience are impassioned, and the emotions associated with each phenomenon are universal. It is a strange paradox that Dickinson simultaneously describes one of the greatest pleasures of human life—sexual relations between men and women—and one of human beings' most feared experiences, death. The fact that the two experiences fall on opposite sides of life's spectrum of anticipated to feared events demonstrates that Dickinson understood that life is filled with both pleasure and pain. However, the ending of the poem shows that the narrator has embraced both sex and death. In refreshing contrast to all of Dickinson's poems and musings on death, "I Started Early—Took My Dog—" shows that the poet recognized that life brings joy and ecstasy along with darker pains, and that those seeming opposites are intimately related.

Works Cited

Dickinson, Emily. "I Started Early—Took My Dog—." *The Complete Poems of Emily Dickinson*. Ed. Thomas H. Johnson. Boston: Little Brown. 1960.

Guerra, Jonnie G. "Dickinson's 'I Started Early—Took My Dog—.'" *Explicator* 50.2 (1992): 78.

Shakinovsky, Lynn. "No Frame of Reference: The Absence of Context in Emily Dickinson's Poetry." *The Emily Dickinson Journal* 3.2 (1994). 15 November 2001 <http://cwru.edu/EDIS/journal/articles/III.2.Shakinovsky.html>.

▶ Responding to the Essay

1. The opening presents what other critics have thought about Dickinson's poem. Is this rhetorical strategy effective? Why or why not? How does this strategy continue throughout O'Maley's essay?
2. Who is the writer's intended audience for this essay? How do you know? How does audience affect the writer's tone? Give specific examples.
3. What is O'Maley's claim? Where does she state it in a single sentence?
4. O'Maley never mentions the possibility that Dickinson herself ever had a near-death experience. Does that weaken her argument? Why or why not?
5. In the course of her essay, O'Maley engages in close readings of each of Dickinson's stanzas. Which of O'Maley's readings is most effective? Why?
6. What is O'Maley's argument in her closing? Is this an effective way to close her essay? Explain your answer.

▶ Responding in Writing

1. O'Maley writes that the poem is about both sex and death, but she never mentions what Dickinson herself had intended her poem to be about. Write an analysis of why some critics might avoid discussing the intentions of the authors whose work they are reading.
2. Write about your own feelings on the relation between sex and other pleasures and death. How do we reconcile them? How does poetry ease or complicate the discussion, do you think?
3. Write a literary argument of your own about "I Started Early—Took My Dog—."

CAROLINE WEBER
Tabloid Princess:
Review of *The Diana Chronicles* by Tina Brown

Caroline Weber is an associate professor of French at Columbia University's Barnard College. She earned her undergraduate degree from Harvard University in 1991 and her Ph.D. in French literature from Yale University in 1998. She has taught at the University of Pennsylvania. She has published numerous articles on French history and thinkers, and she is the author of Terror and its Discontents: Suspect Words and the French Revolution *(2003) and* Queen of Fashion: What Marie-Antoinette Wore to the French Revolution *(2006), which helps make her an informed critic of royalty. Here she writes a review of a book by Tina Brown about the "People's Princess," Diana, Princess of Wales, who was killed in 1997 while fleeing the paparazzi trying to take pictures of her.*

1   Admittedly, I'm biased. On July 29, 1981, when Lady Diana Spencer married Prince Charles, I was in London with my family. I was 11, and like millions of people, I couldn't get enough of the "Shy Di" fairy tale; ugly (O.K., gangly) duckling meets handsome (O.K., gangly) prince and becomes luminous royal swan. In the new couple's honor, I spent a month's allowance on wedding memorabilia. My prize purchase was a Diana coffee mug with a wide-brimmed ceramic hat. "Only the girls are going in for this lot," the sales clerk grumbled. He might have been talking about the fairly princess myth itself. Sometimes against their better judgment, women the world over were entranced by the prospect of untold leisure, unequaled glamour and redemptive metamorphosis that this particular myth promised. Ladies, let's be honest: who really among US hasn't dreamed of becoming a princess?

2   With "The Diana Chronicles," Tina Brown breathes new life into the saga of this royal "icon of blondness" by astutely revealing just how powerful, and how marketable, her story became in the age of modern celebrity journalism. Indeed, while Diana named Camilla Parker Bowles as the third party in her unhappy union, she might also have mentioned a fourth: the media. "She was way ahead of her contemporaries in foreseeing a world where celebrity was, so to speak, the coin of the realm," Brown writes. "An aristocrat herself, Diana knew that the aristocracy of birth was now irrelevant. All that counted now was the aristocracy of exposure." And Brown offers an insightful, absorbing account of the pas de deux into which, to her eventual peril, Diana joined with the paparazzi.

3   As the former editor of *Vanity Fair* and the *New Yorker*, Brown certainly has the authority to examine the Princess of Wales as a creation and a casualty of the media glare. Perhaps not incidentally, Brown's own

London, England: Diana smiles and shakes hands of adoring fans.

years in the spotlight were bookended by Diana's rise and fall. In July 1981, Brown appeared as a "royalty expert" on the "Today" show's coverage of the Wales wedding. Then the editor of the British gossip magazine *Tatler*, Brown recalls that "the wedding did for the sales of *Tatler* . . . what the O.J. Simpson chase did for the ratings of CNN. It put us on the map."

After Diana's death in August 1997, Brown again placed the maga-   4
zine over which she presided—this time, the *New Yorker*—"in the middle" of what was still "the biggest tabloid story in the world," by publishing a special issue devoted to the princess' memory. Brown stressed the dramatic difference between the Windsors' self-styled identity ("local, modest, unsurprising" guarantors of British tradition) and Diana's (global superstar, unapologetically "shrewd . . . at press relations"). The conflicted relationship between the two had been, the historian Simon Schama noted in the same issue, a "wedding of the past and the future: the Radetzky March meets the Tatler cover girl. . . . But, as it turned out, the past and the future couldn't get along." What's more—as Brown's book demonstrates, and as the recent film "The Queen" has also made clear— the future was bound to win, even if it claimed its own leading avatar in the process.

In fact, Diana's conquest of the camera was bittersweet from the start.   5
In February 1967, when she was 5, her mother, Frances, began an extramarital liaison that led to her parents' acrimonious divorce. Diana's father, Johnnie Spencer, retaliated against Frances by gaining custody of the children. But his stiff-upper-lip reaction to the trauma ("speaking in

words of one syllable . . . and sitting morosely for hours staring out of the window") made him ill-suited to handle its effects on his offspring, for whom he was able to show affection only by taking "amateur movies and still photographs" of them. As a result, Brown notes, "Diana grew up associating the camera with love," and striving to give it what it appeared to want in return. Her brother, Charles, told Sally Bedell Smith, a previous biographer, that when Johnnie was filming Diana, "she would automatically sort of make gestures and strike poses." Honing her star power became, Brown observes, the bereft little girl's "own way of surviving."

6   In theory, this was useful preparation for her relationship with Prince Charles, which first made it into the newspapers in September 1980. By this time, the British press was in a full-scale backlash against "the culture of deference" that had long dominated its society pages. Since Rupert Murdoch's acquisition of "the prurient News of the World" in 1969 and his reinvigoration, a year later, of the *Sun* "as a rollicking, up-yours tabloid featuring bare-breasted pinups every day," England had entered a "racier media age" in which the staid House of Windsor "was acquiring the stale, curdled taste of a British Rail cheese sandwich." Because "pictures of a middle-aged Princess Margaret churning grandly around the dance floor in her caftan in Mustique hardly moved product"—and Brown should know, having trumpeted that princess' "Mustique mystique" for *Tatler*—"the guessing game of the Prince of Wales's love life was the sole excitement for the media." And what excitement it was. The prince was Europe's most eligible bachelor, and his romantic exploits became fodder for an increasingly rapacious media machine.

7   Before Diana, Charles had tried to evade the tabloids' scrutiny by bedding married women, "because the need for secrecy made them 'safe.'" But when he began appearing publicly with Diana—the 19-year-old debutante with a "soft, peachy complexion" and legs that seemed "to extend up to her ears like Bambi"—secrecy ceased to be an option. The paparazzi went wild for the girl who was not only (as an aristocrat, Protestant and self-proclaimed virgin) an ideal royal bride, but also a magnificently photogenic subject. Notwithstanding her "Shy Di" nickname, born of her habit of glancing up coyly at the camera from beneath batting eyelashes, Diana proved "a natural at giving the press what they wanted": gorgeous pictures. According to Brown, "the hack pack fell in love with her."

8   Winning the affection of the press was not, however, the same thing as winning the affection of Prince Charles, as Diana would soon be devastated to learn. One of the more striking revelations in "The Diana Chronicles" is that it was the media just as much as the royal family—ready for Charles to stop dithering and settle down—that propelled him into marriage with a woman he didn't love. A former royal-watcher for the *Sun* told Brown: "We really got behind Diana and pushed her towards him. I am absolutely convinced that we the media forced Charles to marry her."

The prince's heart belonged to his married girlfriend, Camilla Parker   9
Bowles (now his second wife), but as heir to the throne, he was neither
encouraged nor expected to follow his heart. The problem was that the
tabloids—and Diana, who consumed them avidly—insisted on a different
story line: He's in Love. Other biographers have attributed the subsequent unraveling of the Waleses' marriage to Charles's cruelty (Andrew
Morton) or Diana's mental illness (Sally Bedell Smith), but Brown chalks
the disaster up to the bride's naive belief in a tabloid fiction. She and the
media became partners in ignoring the warning signs from the groom
himself, like his now notorious reply when, receiving news of the couple's engagement in February 1981, a BBC reporter asked Charles if he
and his fiancée were in love: "Whatever 'in love' means." Amazingly,
Brown points out, "the print press literally erased" the phrase "from their
accounts. No one, it seems, wanted to break the spell." Least of all Diana,
who answered the reporter's "love" question with a giggle: "Of course."

The bride was in for a rude awakening. And though most of the   10
Waleses' sordid domestic drama has already been covered at length elsewhere, Brown perceptively highlights the media's starring role. Once
married to Charles, Diana chafed at playing second fiddle not only to
Camilla but also to Queen Elizabeth. While still a newlywed, she was
deeply offended when Charles offered his mother a drink before her. "I
always thought it was the wife first—stupid thought," she complained afterward. Brown observes that first offering drinks to an older woman—
queen or not—"was only basic good manners" and concludes: "Stupid
thought, yes, or maybe something worse: the onset of superstar entitle-
ment. . . . Six months of adulation from the press had begun to reshape
Diana's worldview." Offended by the Windsors' failure to appreciate the
qualities everyone else seemed to admire, she turned increasingly to the
tabloids to nourish and sustain her.

To that end, Diana became a master of press manipulation, regularly   11
leaking tips and planting stories about both herself and her enemies. She
also understood the incomparable power of the image, which led her, at
the height of her problems with Charles, to pose for a photograph alone
in front of the Taj Mahal, "the monument to marital love." In one of the
book's many new interviews, John Travolta tells Brown about his leg-
endary dance with Diana at the White House in 1985: "I thought, she not
only knows who she is, she knows what this is—and how big this is. She
was so savvy about the media impact of it all."

Yet Diana's savvy had its limits. For although her public-relations   12
wizardry enabled her repeatedly to upstage and—with the tell-all interviews she did in 1992 and 1995—humiliate the Windsors, it did more than
just give the monarchy an appealing, "human" face. By inviting the press
to share in her most intimate experiences, the princess abolished every
last vestige of celebrity privacy. And by providing the press with picture
after dazzling, salable picture, she stoked "the media's inexhaustible

appetite for celebrity images." In an extended meteorological conceit, Brown observes: "The sunshine of publicity in which Diana would at first be happy to bask, posing and smiling for the cameras, grew steadily hotter and harsher. As the superheated imperatives of an invasive press bumped up increasingly against the milder human necessity of privacy, scattered rains gave way to drenching gales and then to spectacular and finally lethal hurricanes. . . . Diana herself had accelerated the climate change that ended up making her life literally impossible." Mistakenly, she thought she could "control the genie she had released."

13   But the genie pursued her to the end, right into the Pont de l'Alma tunnel in Paris, where a high-speed paparazzi chase culminated in the princess' death. Lying unconscious and badly wounded in the wreckage of a black Mercedes, Diana continued to inspire the frenzied photographers. As the picture editor of the *Sun* confessed to Brown, that very evening he initially agreed to pay £300,000 to one of the shutterbugs who had followed the Mercedes into the tunnel for snapshots of its mangled blond occupant. "Even as Diana struggled for life," Brown writes, "she was being sold as an exclusive."

▶ Responding to the Essay

1. Weber begins her essay with her own personal story. Is this an effective opening? Why or why not?
2. What is the writer's claim in this essay? Is Weber arguing something about Brown's book, or about Diana's life? Explain your answer.
3. This essay was published in the *New York Times Book Review*, which has an audience that is highly educated. How does that fact affect the essay? Offer at least two examples to support your answer.
4. Weber spends some time discussing the life and career of Tina Brown. Why does she use this strategy?
5. How does the writer use process analysis in this essay?
6. Weber goes through Diana's life history in this essay. In what ways does this strengthen or weaken her argument?
7. Where does Weber's conclusion begin? Is it an effective conclusion? Why or why not?

▶ Responding in Writing

1. Write a comparison of this review and the works by Deneau, O'Maley, and Fleming. How are the writers' strategies similar? How are they different? How do the intended audiences affect the varying approaches? How well does each qualify as a strong (or weak) literary argument?
2. Write an argumentative essay about the current culture of celebrity. How is celebrity, in Tina Brown's term, "the coin of the realm"?

3. Write an essay about "the incomparable power of the image" (par. 11) in which you argue about two works of art—literary and (or) visual (film, photographs, paintings, for example). State your major proposition carefully.

MANOHLA DARGIS
Superhero Sandbagged

Manohla Dargis is one of the chief film critics for the New York Times. *She was formerly a film writer at the* Village Voice, *the film critic for the* Los Angeles Times, *and the editor of the film section at* LA Weekly. *She has written for a variety of publications, including* Film Comment *and* Sight and Sound. *She is the author of* LA Confidential *(2003).*

If ever a movie had a case of the blues and the blahs, it's *Spider-Man 3*, the third and what feels like the end of Sam Raimi's big-screen comic-book adaptations. (Ready or not, the studio is talking about a fourth.) Aesthetically and conceptually wrung out, fizzled rather than fizzy, this latest installment in the spider-bites-boy adventure story shoots high, swings low and every so often hits the sweet spot, but mostly just plods and plods along, as if its heart were pumping tired radioactive blood.

Maybe it's middle age. In fictional terms Spider-Man aka Peter Parker aka Tobey Maguire looks like he's pushing 23, but there's something about the guy that shrieks midlife crisis. Peter is still hitting the books and still snapping photographs for *The Daily Bugle*, run by the flattop blowhard J. Jonah Jameson (J. K. Simmons, in clover, as usual). It's a living, kind of, enough for an enviably situated dump in Manhattan with artfully peeling walls and a fabulous picture window through which Peter regularly bounds into the air in full superhero drag. (The neighbors in this part of town evidently always keep the blinds drawn.) It's a calling, sort of, though it's also started to feel a bit like punching the clock.

The programmatic screenplay credited to Mr. Raimi, his brother Ivan Raimi (a third Raimi brother, Ted, plays a tiny role in the picture) and Alvin Sargent certainly feels more like work than play. The big selling point in *Spider-Man 3* is that Spider-Man or Peter or some combination of the two discovers his so-called dark side when an inky extraterrestrial glob (a symbiote in Marvel-speak) spreads its gooey tentacles over his body, turning his suit and soul black. Though there's something dubious about the idea that black still conveys evil in our culture, pop or otherwise (tell it to Batman and Barack Obama, for starters), the idea of messing with Spider-Man's squeaky-clean profile, smearing it with dirt, a touch of naughtiness, seems too good to resist.

4   It's also too good to be true. There's no knowing if the problem is bottom-line reserve, or lack of imagination or creative nerve, but Spider-Man's voyage into darkness turns out to be little more than an overnighter. The goo transforms Spider-Man, but the alteration barely registers. There's some wacky, misguided nonsense involving Peter's super-inflated ego and Mr. Raimi's apparent desire to direct a musical. As well as fleeting nastiness with a resurrected foe, Flint Marko (Thomas Haden Church), recently escaped from prison. Marko has the makings of a super-antagonist, and Mr. Church brings a touching delicacy to the few short scenes in which you can see his face, the skin pulled back so tightly that you fear his jagged cheekbones might pierce right through.

5   With his hard-body physique and a striped shirt that evokes a 1930s chain gang, Marko also feels and looks like a fugitive from an earlier era, one of the film's many such nostalgic flourishes. Marko's earthbound trudge makes it seem as if he's dragging a literal ball and chain, not just the baggage of a sick daughter and a cranky missus (Theresa Russell, in and out like the Flash). And when he rises from a bed of sand after a "particle atomizer" scrambles his molecules, his newly granulated form shifts and spills apart, then lurches into human form with a heaviness that recalls Boris Karloff staggering into the world as Frankenstein's monster. There's poetry in this metamorphosis, not just technological bravura, a glimpse into the glory and agony of transformation.

6   It's this combination of exaltation and dread that can come with radical life change that made the first film work as well as it did. The first *Spider-Man* never soared, but there was something very appealing about the image of a skinny, geeky adolescent struggling to rise to the occasion of his newfound powers, like a 97-pound weakling tiptoeing on the beach after getting with the Charles Atlas program. Part of the allure of superheroes, of course, is how they serve as wish fulfillments for the faithful, allowing their mild-mannered fans to settle scores and snare the babe by proxy. But nothing seems to put a damper on interesting self-doubt faster than fame, or so this film and its lead character both seem intent on proving.

7   Success may not have spoiled Mr. Raimi as it has Peter Parker, but it seems as if it has zapped his gracious good humor, which was so critical to the first two films. The story this time unfolds as a series of increasingly dreary and teary melodramatic encounters regularly interrupted by special-effects-laden fights. As it happens, the over-all shape does recall a Busby Berkeley musical—snappy story, lavish number, snappy story, lavish number—but without the snap or fun. Peter ignores his girlfriend, Mary Jane (Kirsten Dunst), so she reaches out to her friend and his frenemy, Harry Osborn (James Franco), aka Son of the Green Goblin (Willem Dafoe, revived in flashback), while Peter turns to his Aunt May (Rosemary Harris), who shovels the manure with grace.

8   And so it goes as the Sandman cometh and goeth and a twerp named Eddie Brock (Topher Grace, running fast with a small role) throws a

couple of monstrous hissy fits. Bryce Dallas Howard shows up to smile at the camera, as does a marvelous Bruce Campbell, who almost swallows it whole. Ms. Dunst looks a bit lost, at times even bereft, but you want to catch hold of her story line and follow her home. When she tramps across the screen, this wispy, sad-eyed beauty turns into Melancholy Girl, able to melt hearts in a single glance. For his part Mr. Maguire needs to stop relying on those great big peepers of his: simply widening your eyes to attract attention does not cut it when you're over 30.

It's hard not to think that Mr. Raimi would rather follow Ms. Dunst to   9 wherever her story might take them, too. And while Marko is mainly around to show off the franchise's snazzy special effects, it feels as if the director has put quite a bit of himself into the Sandman, whose struggle to find a form that suits his talents has the sting of a metaphor. The bittersweet paradox of this franchise is that while the stories have grown progressively less interesting the special effects have improved tremendously, becoming at once more plausible—when Spider-Man swings through the urban canyons he finally looks almost real—and more spectacular. In Sandman you see the vestiges of Mr. Raimi's personal touch slipping through a nearly empty hourglass.

▶ Responding to the Essay

1. How does Dargis encapsulate her feelings about the movie *Spider-Man 3* in the first sentence of the essay? Is this opening effective? Why or why not? What is your reaction to the phrase, "the blues and the blahs"?
2. What is Dargis's claim in this essay? Where does she state it clearly?
3. Who is the audience for this essay? How do you know?
4. Where do you find examples here of humor? How does humor contribute to the essay?
5. Dargis uses part of her essay to give a plot summary of *Spider-Man 3*. How does the summary either strengthen or weaken the argument?
6. Paragraph 5 states, "Part of the allure of superheroes, of course, is how they serve as wish fulfillments for the faithful, allowing their mild-mannered fans to settle scores and snare the babe by proxy." Explain this statement and evaluate it—is Dargis right? Why or why not?
7. How effective is Dargis's conclusion? Explain your answer.

▶ Responding in Writing

1. Write an argumentative review of a movie you love and respect or dislike.
2. Read another of Dargis's movie reviews from the *New York Times* and compare it to her review of *Spider-Man 3*.
3. Write an argumentative essay in which you explore the genre of superhero or action movies.

Part Two

Contemporary Debates

Arguments Pro and Con

4 ▸Rap Culture: Is It Too Negative?

R ap music—now often referred to (purists would say inaccurately) as hip-hop—started in the cities, in poor, largely African-American neighborhoods. At parties, disc jockeys, or DJs, played records—the then-current music technology—and some began to experiment with moving the record back and forth under the needle, manipulating the beats on the record. Rap's basic paradigm solidified when masters of ceremony, called MCs, picked up a microphone at those parties and began reciting rhyming poems. This spoken-word performance gave the new music the name of *rap*. Rap was a revolutionary music, and early performers such as Grandmaster Flash were interested in its power to reach black youth and expose the conditions in the inner cities. In the early 1990s, a form of rap called "gangsta rap" emerged out of Los Angeles and expressed the frustration evident in the inner cities. The stance of gangsta rappers included threatening the police (whom they saw as their enemies), dealing drugs, carrying guns, taking advantage of women, and expressing a callous attitude toward everything except money.

A controversy emerged: One side claimed that the violence and crime depicted in rap music is a realistic reflection of poor urban neighborhoods and that rappers, like all artists, aim to transform what they see into art. Those on the other side of the debate—especially but not exclusively media observers and politicians—see rap music as overly and unnecessarily negative and maintain that rap artists do more harm than good. These critics charge that rap glorifies violence and crime and alienates and provokes neighborhood police. The debate has raged for years and still rages. In London in 2006, the popular tabloid *Daily Mail* ran a piece called "Rap Music Blamed for Teen Pregnancy." In New York City in 2007, a hip-hop musical, *In the Heights*, opened on Broadway.

In the first selection that follows, a college student argues that rap is moving the black community in the wrong direction. In the second selection, a magazine columnist insists that we should not call upon artists to censor themselves.

GREG JONES
Rap Fans Desire a More Positive Product

This selection appeared in the Daily Cougar, *the student newspaper for the University of Houston, in the summer of 2002. The writer, Greg Jones, was a communications major at the school. In this selection, Jones makes a distinction between "old school," conscience-raising hip-hop and what he perceives as the more negative message appearing currently in rap music.*

▶ **Prereading: Thinking about the Essay in Advance**

Do you listen to rap music? Why or why not? What associations does rap music have for you? Do you agree with the title of this essay?

▶ **Words to Watch**

materialism (par. 2) concern with money and possessions
disenfranchisement (par. 2) exclusion from power
ideology (par. 4) belief system
entrepreneurship (par. 6) position as owner of a business
reparations (par. 6) money as payment for suffering, as in slavery

1   In the early stage of rap music before the bling bling era, rap music was the CNN for poor and working-class blacks in America. Songs such as "The Message" and "Fight the Power" raised the conscience levels of people and the need for social change in America.

2   Then, in the early 1990s, greedy, out-of-touch record executives took control of the art form and made materialism the main priority, over the continued disenfranchisement of blacks, latinos, and poor whites.

3   I believe the billion-dollar rap industry, which has a great influence on American culture, needs to take a turn for the better by going back to its roots. Record executives use rap artists for major profits at the expense of the African-American poor and working-class people that actually experience what these rappers are rapping about.

4   Many people wonder why anyone should make a big deal out of negative rap music, because they believe it is only entertainment. Most fans know many of the artists such as Dr. Dre and Jay Z actually don't perform many of the activities they claim. This ideology is wrong and lacks serious thought. The reason we listen to music is because it makes us feel emotions such as joy, sadness, motivation, or even relaxation.

5   In other words, it affects the soul of an individual. The imbalance in rap music is consistently reflected on the radio and shown on the video programs such as "Rap City." The images presented are not an actual account of how blacks are living as a whole.

As a kid growing up on the West side of Chicago I saw many images I thought were good because I saw them over and over again. For example, I thought gang banging was good because it was around me. The same concept applies to music. Blacks in America have many concerns such as police brutality, entrepreneurship, reparations, election reform, employment, quality health care, and quality education. This is what the art form needs to reflect instead of promoting materialism and violence. 6

Black music has historically always voiced the concerns of issues in America that effect their way of living. Instead, rappers and even some R&B and rock artists admit to committing crimes consistently on records, thus promoting some of the worst elements our society has to offer. Songs such as "Hood Rich" or "My Neck/My Back" have become the norm. 7

Record executives such as Jimmy Iovine, L.A. Reid, Tommy Mottola, Andrew Herrera, Bryan Turner, Russell Simmons, Tony Brown, and Ted Fields don't want positive images seen or heard, because it will interfere with the millions they make off young, uneducated, and misled black rappers from the inner cities of America. 8

Female rapper Foxy Brown and former rapper Mase both have gone on record saying they portrayed negative images on albums and videos because the record executives forced them to do so in order to sell more records. This is the norm also for the entire music industry. Just look at Britney Spears. 9

What can cure the problems of negative images of Black America presented in rap and other forms of music? 10

Music fans of all backgrounds must e-mail and write letters to the major record company executives and voice their concerns. Also don't buy the music when you hear songs such as "Big Pimpin'." 11

Music fans can turn off the television and the radio when these images are displayed. Music listeners must e-mail and write the executives of the products that pay for advertising space on rap shows and in magazines such as *Vibe* and *The Source.* If companies such as the Coca-Cola Corporation do not take the concerns seriously, then music fans must stop buying their products. 12

Positive artists such as Common, Black Star, Dead Pres., KRS1, Mos Def, Gang Star, Goodie Mob, Pharoahe Monch, and The Roots must get more requests on the radio and rap video programs. 13

The most important aspect is to shift the focus from the rap artist and put the heat on the record executives who run the major distributors such as Universal and AOL/Time Warner. 14

The executives are responsible for what is seen and heard, not the artist. So the next time you have issues with a song such as "Money, Cash, Hoes," send Russell Simmons an e-mail, or just don't buy the album. 15

▶ Building Vocabulary

The writer of this essay assumes knowledge of a few topical phrases relating to the world of music and rap music in particular. Identify the following terms, and explain their relevance to rap music:

1. bling bling (par. 1)
2. gang banging (par. 6)
3. R&B (par. 7)

▶ Thinking Critically about the Argument

Understanding the Writer's Argument

1. What does Jones mean in paragraph 1 when he writes that "rap music was the CNN for poor and working-class blacks in America"?
2. What change came over rap music in the early 1990s, according to the writer?
3. Why does Jones put so much emphasis on the financial situations of the record executives and the fans of rap music?
4. What are some of the issues facing blacks in America, according to Jones? Do you think rap music addresses some of these? How?
5. Why don't record executives want positive images in rap music? Why are the record executives responsible for the negative images in rap, as opposed to the artists, as Jones says in paragraph 15?
6. Which rap musicians does Jones cite for presenting a positive message? Whom does he cite as being negative?

Understanding the Writer's Techniques

1. Why does Jones start his essay with a short history of rap music?
2. What is the major proposition here? Is it simply the statement in paragraph 3, or is there another aspect to the argument? What minor proposition does Jones present to show that rap needs to "take a turn for the better"? What evidence does Jones give to support the minor proposition?
3. What is the tone in this essay? Who is the audience, and how does that affect the tone? Explain your answer. This is an emotional issue for Jones, but do you sense emotion? Where? If not, why?
4. How effective is Jones's mini-recollection in paragraph 6? What purpose does it serve in his argument?
5. Jones's essay shifts strategy with his question in paragraph 10. What is the shift, and is his rhetorical question effective? Does his essay maintain coherence despite the shift?

6. In his conclusion, the writer returns to his major proposition, but there has been a change. What is that change, and is the conclusion effective?

7. What is your view of the title? If you could change it, would you? What would you call the essay?

Exploring the Writer's Argument

1. Jones implies in his first paragraph that "poor and working-class blacks in America" only get their identity and news from rap music and that music in general is the biggest influence on Americans. Do you think this is true? Why or why not?

2. This essay was written by a college student. Do you expect him to have these views? How does this fact alter your reception of his argument?

3. Are you convinced by Jones's argument in paragraph 7 regarding his opinion that rappers who admit to committing crimes promote "the worst elements our society has to offer"? Why or why not?

4. In paragraph 7, Jones cites the song "My Neck/My Back" as being one of the "worst elements" in society that rap glorifies. This song, however, is about two consenting adults having sex. Knowing this, do you accept or reject Jones's argument? Why?

5. Do you agree that record executives are responsible for the content of rap records but that the artists are not? Why or why not?

6. What in this essay's argument do you think is effective? Too simple or generalized? Which of Jones's points do you think are well reasoned? Open to question or serious disagreement?

▶ Ideas for Writing Arguments

Prewriting

Jot down notes on what images you see on TV or in the movies and how they affect you negatively.

Writing a Guided Argument

A *genre* is an artistic form. Write an essay in which you argue that some genre other than rap music is responsible for negative effects on children. Be specific. Don't just write about movies—write about action movies or horror films. Don't just write about TV shows—write about *The Simpsons* or reality programming, for example.

1. Begin your essay by explaining a little about the history of the particular medium.

2. Write your major proposition clearly and place it prominently in your essay.

3. Give at least two minor propositions for why you think your medium has negative effects on children.
4. Offer ample evidence for your minor propositions in the form of anecdotes or examples.
5. Decide who is mostly responsible for the continuing popularity of that genre.
6. Make sure to use proper transitions in your essay to ensure coherence.
7. In the conclusion of your essay, offer solutions that will minimize the damage done by your chosen offending genre.

Thinking, Arguing, and Writing Collaboratively

Play a song from the gangsta rap era in class, and in small groups analyze the music and lyrics for what you consider positive or helpful to society. Present your findings to the class and solicit their objections. Rebut their objections as a group.

Writing about the Text

Jones states in paragraph 5 that music "affects the soul of an individual." How well has he developed that idea? Do you think music has that much influence on people? Has the essay convinced you of that? Does Jones's argument depend on that statement being true? If so, and if it is not true, does the essay still work? Address these questions in an essay that analyzes "Rap Fans Desire a More Positive Product."

More Writing Ideas

1. In your journal, outline an essay about how you are personally affected by music.
2. Find the lyrics to one of the songs cited by Jones, and analyze it in a paragraph based on his ideas.
3. When novels were first becoming popular in the late 1700s, people accused the form of having a terrible effect on young people. When jazz became popular in the 1920s, critics leveled the same accusation at that music. In the 1950s, when rock 'n' roll was becoming popular, the same thing happened. Research the history of the popular reception of one of these art forms. In an essay, compare the reaction against rap music with the reaction of those who thought novels, jazz, or rock 'n' roll were going to have a negative effect on youth. How are the two situations similar? How are they different?

BARBARA EHRENREICH
Ice-T: The Issue Is Creative Freedom

Biologist Barbara Ehrenreich (she got her Ph.D. from Rockefeller University in 1968) became involved in political activism during the Vietnam War and began writing on topics such as feminism, class in America, and health care. Her books include The American Health Empire: Power, Profits, and Politics *(1970) and* The Hearts of Men: American Dreams, the Flight from Commitment *(1983), and* Blood Rites: Origins and History of the Passions of War *(1998). She has written for the* Progressive, In These Times, *the* Nation, Time, *and many other magazines. Her book* Nickel and Dimed: On (Not) Getting by in America *(2001), recounting her experience working in low-class jobs, was a best-seller. Her most recent work is* Dancing in the Streets: A History of Collective Joy *(2007). In 1992, rap artist Ice-T released a rock song called "Cop Killer." The reaction among the public and politicians was swift and angry. As Ehrenreich mentions in this selection, even the president at the time, George H. Bush, offered his opinion that Ice-T was "sick." Ehrenreich's essay, which appeared in* Time *magazine that year, argues that everyone was overreacting.*

▶ Prereading: Thinking about the Essay in Advance

What is the first emotion that comes to mind when you think of a song titled "Cop Killer"? What do you think Ehrenreich means by "the issue is creative freedom"?

▶ Words to Watch

taboo (par. 1) against social customs
paroxysm (par. 2) attack of violent emotion
boycott (par. 2) protest that takes the form of refusing to take part in
sedition (par. 2) act of trying to overthrow those in power
hyperbole (par. 4) exaggeration
decorum (par. 5) the social norm
demagogues (par. 5) dangerously charismatic speakers
miscreants (par. 6) delinquents

I ce-T's song "Cop Killer" is as bad as they come. This is black anger—   1
raw, rude, and cruel—and one reason the song's so shocking is that in postliberal America, black anger is virtually taboo. You won't find it on TV, not on the *McLaughlin Group* or *Crossfire,* and certainly not in the placid features of Arsenio Hall or Bernard Shaw. It's been beaten back into the outlaw subcultures of rap and rock, where, precisely because it is taboo, it sells. And the nastier it is, the faster it moves off the shelves.

As Ice-T asks in another song on the same album, "Goddamn what a brotha gotta do / To get a message through / To the red, white, and blue?"

2   But there's a gross overreaction going on, building to a veritable paroxysm of white denial. A national boycott has been called, not just of the song or Ice-T, but of all Time Warner products. The president himself has denounced Time Warner as "wrong" and Ice-T as "sick." Ollie North's Freedom Alliance has started a petition drive aimed at bringing Time Warner executives to trial for "sedition and anarchy."

3   Much of this is posturing and requires no more courage than it takes to stand up in a VFW hall and condemn communism or crack. Yes, "Cop Killer" is irresponsible and vile. But Ice-T is as right about some things as he is righteous about the rest. And ultimately, he's not even dangerous—least of all to the white power structure his songs condemn.

4   The "danger" implicit in all the uproar is of empty-headed, suggestible black kids, crouching by their boom boxes, waiting for the word. But what Ice-T's fans know and his detractors obviously don't is that "Cop Killer" is just one more entry in pop music's long history of macho hyperbole and violent boast. Flip to the classic-rock station, and you might catch the Rolling Stones announcing "the time is right for violent revoloo-shun!" from their 1968 hit "Street Fighting Man." And where were the defenders of our law-enforcement officers when a white British group, the Clash, taunted its fans with the lyrics: "When they kick open your front door / How you gonna come / With your hands on your head / Or on the trigger of your gun?"

5   "Die, Die, Die Pig" is strong speech, but the Constitution protects strong speech, and it's doing so this year more aggressively than ever. The Supreme Court has just downgraded cross burnings to the level of bonfires and ruled that it's no crime to throw around verbal grenades like "nigger" and "kike." Where are the defenders of decorum and social stability when prime-time demagogues like Howard Stern deride African Americans as "spear chuckers"?

6   More to the point, young African Americans are not so naive and suggestible that they have to depend on a compact disc for their sociology lessons. To paraphrase another song from another era, you don't need a rap song to tell which way the wind is blowing. Black youths know that the police are likely to see them through a filter of stereotypes as miscreants and potential "cop killers." They are aware that a black youth is seven times as likely to be charged with a felony as a white youth who has committed the same offense, and is much more likely to be imprisoned.

7   They know, too, that in a shameful number of cases, it is the police themselves who indulge in "anarchy" and violence. The U.S. Justice Department has received 47,000 complaints of police brutality in the past six

Musician Ice-T explains to reporters his reasons for pulling "Cop Killer" from his "Body Count" album in Los Angeles, Calif., on July 28, 1992. Ice-T pulled "Cop Killer" from the album because of threats against Time Warner and Warner Bros. (Bob Galbraith/AP images)

years, and Amnesty International has just issued a report on police brutality in Los Angeles, documenting forty cases of "torture or cruel, inhuman, or degrading treatment."

Menacing as it sounds, the fantasy in "Cop Killer" is the fantasy of   8
the powerless and beaten down—the black man who's been hassled once too often ("A pig stopped me for nothin'!"), spread-eagled against a police car, pushed around. It's not a "responsible" fantasy (fantasies seldom are). It's not even a very creative one. In fact, the sad thing about "Cop Killer" is that it falls for the cheapest, most conventional image of rebellion that our culture offers: the lone gunman spraying fire from his AK-47. This is not "sedition"; it's the familiar, all-American, Hollywood-style pornography of violence.

Which is why Ice-T is right to say he's no more dangerous than   9
George Bush's pal Arnold Schwarzenegger, who wasted an army of cops

in *Terminator 2*. Images of extraordinary cruelty and violence are marketed every day, many of far less artistic merit than "Cop Killer." This is our free market of ideas and images, and it shouldn't be any less free for a black man than for other purveyors of "irresponsible" sentiments, from David Duke to Andrew Dice Clay.

10   Just, please, don't dignify Ice-T's contribution with the word *sedition*. The past masters of sedition—men like George Washington, Toussaint L'Ouverture, Fidel Castro, or Mao Zedong, all of whom led and won armed insurrections—would be unimpressed by "Cop Killer" and probably saddened. They would shake their heads and mutter words like "infantile" and "adventurism." They might point out that the cops are hardly a noble target, being, for the most part, honest working stiffs who've got stuck with the job of patrolling ghettos ravaged by economic decline and official neglect.

11   There is a difference, the true seditionist would argue, between a revolution and a gesture of macho defiance. Gestures are cheap. They feel good, they blow off some rage. But revolutions, violent or otherwise, are made by people who have learned how to count very slowly to ten.

▶ Building Vocabulary

1. For the following words, write definitions (attempt to understand their meanings from the context of the essay, or look them up in a dictionary), and write a sentence of your own using each word:
   a. placid (par. 1)
   b. subcultures (par. 1)
   c. veritable (par. 2)
   d. denounced (par. 2)
   e. posturing (par. 3)
   f. detractors (par. 4)
   g. indulge (par. 7)
   h. ghettos (par. 10)
   i. adventurism (par. 10)
   j. defiance (par. 11)
2. Ehrenreich mentions a number of people and institutions from recent and distant history. Identify these people, and explain how they are relevant to Ehrenreich's argument:
   a. Arsenio Hall (par. 1)
   b. Bernard Shaw (par. 1)
   c. Time Warner (par. 2)
   d. Ollie (Oliver) North (par. 2)
   e. VFW (par. 3)
   f. Rolling Stones (par. 4)
   g. Howard Stern (par. 5)
   h. Amnesty International (par. 7)

i. Arnold Schwarzenegger (par. 9)
j. David Duke (par. 9)
k. Andrew Dice Clay (par. 9)
l. George Washington (par. 10)
m. Toussaint L'Ouverture (par. 10)
n. Fidel Castro (par. 10)
o. Mao Zedong (par. 10)

▶Thinking Critically about the Argument

Understanding the Writer's Argument

1. Paraphrase the writer's first two sentences.
2. According to the writer, why does "angry" rap sell?
3. What is the writer's opinion of Ice-T's song "Cop Killer"? What is her opinion of the song's most outspoken critics?
4. How does the writer place Ice-T's song in the perspective of music history?
5. How does "Cop Killer" relate to the harsh realities of the criminal justice system and police brutality, according to the writer?
6. What is the writer's main criticism of "Cop Killer"?
7. What, according to the writer, is the difference between "revolution and a gesture of macho defiance"? Why is one more impressive than the other?

Understanding the Writer's Techniques

1. What is the intended argumentative effect of Ehrenreich's confrontational opening?
2. Where does Ehrenreich's introduction end? Where is her claim? Is it placed in her introduction? Explain.
3. What are the writer's minor propositions? Which makes her point most effectively? Which is weakest?
4. Compare and contrast the kinds of support Jones and Ehrenreich use to make their arguments. Do they both rely equally on reasonable propositions? Does one rely more on an emotional appeal? Explain your answers.
5. Analyze Ehrenreich's use of transitions. Which is most impressive?
6. What kinds of support does the writer use to bolster her minor propositions?
7. Why is the writer's conclusion effective? Explain your answer. How does it help the essay to cohere?

Exploring the Writer's Argument

1. How do you think Jones would react to Ehrenreich's points that Ice-T and his songs are "not even dangerous" (par. 3) and that "young African Americans are not so naive and suggestible that they have to depend on a compact disc for their sociology lessons" (par. 6)? What is your reaction to those statements?
2. Do you think Ehrenreich's placing Ice-T in the stream of music history in paragraph 4 is effective? Why or why not?
3. Do you find Ehrenreich's arguments in paragraph 9—that (1) rap is no more dangerous than action movies, and (2) there is free speech, so rap artists can say anything they want—compatible? Why or why not?
4. How effective is Ehrenreich's comparison of Ice-T to the "past masters of sedition"? Do you think this is a fair comparison? Is it an effective argumentative technique? Explain your answers.

▶ Ideas for Writing Arguments

Prewriting

What other elements of popular culture might be considered dangerous, and why? What is your position?

Writing a Guided Argument

Choose an activity that many critics agree is dangerous, such as riding motorcycles or skydiving, and write an essay defending the right of people to do it.

1. Begin your essay by explaining your topic and summarizing the main objections on the grounds of its danger.
2. Write your major proposition clearly.
3. Use a tone that is similar to Ehrenreich's.
4. Offer at least three minor propositions to explain why critics of your chosen action are overreacting.
5. Support your ideas with vivid examples and, if possible, statistics.
6. For at least one of your minor propositions, explain that other activities that are not criticized are at least, if not more, dangerous.
7. Pick out one word that the critics would use to describe your chosen action (for example, some might call skydiving "suicidal"), and close your essay as Ehrenreich does, with a long analysis of how that word is not apt in describing the action.

Thinking, Arguing, and Writing Collaboratively

With the class divided into two arbitrary groups, have one group take Jones's position that rap music is dangerous and have the other group argue, as Ehrenreich does, that it is harmless. As a group, think of arguments and facts to add to those already explored by the writer whose position you are taking, and fix weaknesses in his or her argument. You may do research and bring in examples from home or the library. Take notes on your intragroup discussion, and use your notes to prepare for a debate on the issue of rap music. Present your position to the class as a group, with each member of the group presenting a certain aspect of your argument. As a class, discuss which group's argument was stronger, and explain why.

Writing about the Text

Compare Ehrenreich's argument in this essay with her argument in "From Stone Age to Phone Age" in Chapter 1. Ehrenreich wrote "Ice-T: The Issue Is Creative Freedom" in 1992, and "From Stone Age to Phone Age" in 1999. What development do you see in the writer's style? What is the difference in argumentative technique? How does the tone in her essays differ?

More Writing Ideas

1. In a journal entry, write notes about the word *sedition*. All the "past masters of sedition" Ehrenreich lists were seditious long ago. What examples of true sedition or anarchy, if any, can you identify today?
2. In paragraph 3, Ehrenreich makes a point about American rhetoric, saying that arguing against rap music is "posturing and requires no more courage than it takes to stand up in a VFW hall and condemn communism or crack." In a paragraph, explain this quote, and give at least two examples of this kind of posturing and rhetoric that you have seen.
3. Write an essay in which you analyze an artistic medium other than music, such as movies, television, books, or radio. Explain how, as Ehrenreich notes, "precisely because it is taboo, it sells" (par. 1). How does the medium exploit the public's desire for "outlaw subcultures" or the shocking?

5 ▶ SUVs: Safe or Dangerous?

There you are, driving down the highway, when in your rearview mirror you see a grille, bearing down on you. You start to change lanes, putting on your signal, but the driver of the sport utility vehicle (SUV) behind you blasts the horn, passes you with annoyance on the right, and whips in front of you. The thing is huge, and if there was a pileup on the highway, that driver would probably survive sooner than you. You start considering—maybe this isn't such a bad thing, a big-engine, large-size car that like a neighborhood bully can keep smaller cars in their place. But your conscience might ask: What about fuel mileage? Aren't we trying to deal with global warming? Are these big vehicles safe for those not driving them?

The sport utility vehicle is mostly a middle class phenomenon in the United States and Canada, where the history of ecologically aware gasoline consumption and auto emission reduction is undistinguished, particularly in America. In many parts of the world, gasoline prices are so high through deliberate government taxation that the big-car phenomenon is largely nonexistent. In a consumer-driven society, where gasoline prices are relatively low despite recent spikes, auto manufacturers are giving buyers what they want—big, bigger, biggest automobiles with little attention to safety, energy conservation, and dangerous greenhouse gases. Many consumers who pay attention to environmental matters do purchase small, fuel-efficient automobiles, and both American and foreign automakers have brought a number of environment-friendly vehicles to the marketplace. But the big car as a symbol of power and success has never faded from the American identity. The bigger the car the more status it affords.

On the positive side, the SUV gives a large family more room to sit comfortably and store the big items of everyday life: carriages, strollers, boxes and bags from wholesale food suppliers, hockey sticks, and bicycles, to name a few. And many new frills like back-seat television screens, computer-based maps and voice directions, and heated and air-conditioned seats add to the attractiveness of the large-size vehicle.

SUVs wouldn't raise so many questions, perhaps, if there weren't so many of them and if their effects on the natural world were not so open to question.

The two essays in this chapter suggest that the answer to the question in the chapter title is "Yes, SUVs are both safe *and* dangerous." To whom are they safe, and to whom are they dangerous—those are the issues. In "Terror on the Roads," Kim Pittaway argues that people who drive SUVs care only about themselves. In "Did My Car Join Al Qaeda?" Woody Hochswender, an SUV driver, defends himself against perceived charges that he's a bad person, and in the process tries to defend all SUV owners.

KIM PITTAWAY
Terror on the Roads

Kim Pittaway is the former editor in chief of Chatelaine, *Canada's largest-circulation woman's magazine, in which this essay originally appeared. She is now a freelance editor, writer, and consultant. In her selection, Pittaway criticizes the very notion of sport utility vehicles (SUVs). She writes that not only are SUVs dangerous to the environment, but they also are dangerous to other drivers not driving SUVs, a situation not unlike an arms race. And furthermore, she says, SUV owners are simply jerks.*

▶ Prereading: Thinking about the Essay in Advance

What is your opinion of SUVs? Do you drive one? If so, why? If not, would you drive one? Why or why not?

▶ Words to Watch

decapitate (par. 2) cut off the head of someone
refrain (par. 4) something repeated
dismal (par. 4) depressing and lacking in hope
derided (par. 5) dismissed with contempt
mitigate (par. 5) lessen
deterrence (par. 6) act of discouraging a dangerous situation
legitimate (par. 6) correct or well reasoned
illusory (par. 7) consisting of deceptive ideas

1   If you drive a gas-guzzling SUV, then you're supporting terrorist groups. That's the controversial claim of the Detroit Project, which earlier this year launched a television ad campaign featuring "George," an SUV owner and pawn o'terror. Each time George gases up, says the ad, he's lining the pockets of terrorist organizations because the gas he's buy-

"We breed them for aggressiveness."

ing comes from countries that support terrorism. Guess the gas purchased by those of us driving smaller cars must come from somewhere else. . . .

Normally, I'd be lining up to applaud anyone who slags SUVs, but I think the Detroit Project has missed its mark. It's true that SUVs are gas-hogging smog-mobiles (they're permitted to emit more than five times as much smog-causing nitrogen oxide as cars). But when it comes to SUVs—especially the big ones—the terror I'm most concerned about is the terror they create on the roads right here at home. Ever seen an SUV bearing down behind you on the highway, shiny grille sitting at about your head-height, all the better to decapitate you? Sure strikes terror in my heart.

Now, I'm not completely opposed to utility vehicles. If you're a farmer hauling bales of hay and farm equipment, go for it. If you're routinely driving into the woods—the real woods, with rutted dirt tracks and the occasional fallen tree in your path, not the level-gravel-road-to-the-cottage woods—then maybe I'll buy the argument that you need one. But from what I've seen, the only time most SUV drivers go off-road is when they drive into a mall parking lot, and the biggest obstacle most drive over is the curb.

"But I need my SUV—it's all about safety!" is the SUV driver's refrain. Well, turns out we've been sold a bill of goods about the safety of these terror-mobiles. SUVs have a dismal safety record. According to Keith Bradsher, *New York Times* reporter and author of *High and Mighty:*

SUVs: The World's Most Dangerous Vehicles and *How They Got That Way* (PublicAffairs), the occupant death rate in SUVs is six per cent higher than it is for cars, largely because top-heavy SUVs have a deadly tendency to roll over. Add to that the fact that SUV drivers tend to overestimate the safety and braking capacity of their vehicles, making them more likely to drive too fast on bad roads or in crummy weather, and, well, it's an accident waiting to happen.

5   And when it does happen, if you're a non-SUV driver, you'd better hope you're nowhere around. When SUVs meet cars and minivans, you can guess who wins. The problem is twofold: when an SUV hits a lighter vehicle, all of the force of that collision gets transferred to whatever it has hit. Plus these beasts are so high off the ground that their grilles don't hit the reinforced side panels or bumpers of other cars. Instead, they come crashing through your windows and, well, take your friggin' head off. Want proof? According to researchers at the U.S. National Highway Traffic Safety Administration quoted by Bradsher, if you're in a car hit by an SUV, you're nearly three times as likely to be killed than if you'd been hit by another car. Automakers initially derided these results—but then quietly began to make design changes to try to mitigate them. (Even scarier: as more of these vehicles start to move into the second-hand market, the drivers will be younger—and likely less experienced.)

6   Makes you want to be in an SUV rather than hit by one, doesn't it? And that's the reason I've heard some SUV drivers cite when explaining their vehicle of choice. Call it vehicular deterrence: like nuclear deterrence, you've gotta have one because the other guy has one, and that way, we'll all be safe, each in our own personal weapon-on-wheels. I guess it's a legitimate argument, if you go for that "every driver for herself" school of morality.

7   I can hear SUV drivers everywhere screaming at me. It's a nice change, because usually when I'm behind the wheel, I'm screaming at them. And it turns out that some of what I've been screaming at them is accurate: according to the market research conducted by the automakers themselves, and reported in *High and Mighty*, SUV drivers are more likely than the rest of us to be—how shall I put this?—jerks. They tend to be insecure and vain, lack confidence in their driving skills, be self-centered and rarely take part in volunteer work. Oh yeah, and apparently they don't care if their illusory safety fouls the air and threatens the lives of other drivers. Jerks? You betcha.

8   When SUVs meet cars and minivans, you can guess who wins.

▶ Building Vocabulary

In her essay, Pittaway uses a number of colloquial terms and phrases. Identify and define each of the following, and explain why she uses them instead of more formal terms or phrases.

1. pawn o'terror (par. 1)
2. lining the pockets (par. 1)
3. slags (par. 2)
4. all the better to (par. 2)
5. go for it (par. 3)
6. sold a bill of goods (par. 4)
7. crummy (par. 4)
8. take your friggin' head off (par. 5)
9. you've gotta have one (par. 6)
10. You betcha. (par. 7)

▶ Thinking Critically about the Argument

Understanding the Writer's Argument

1. What does the Detroit Project think of SUVs?
2. What problem does Pittaway have with the Detroit Project's campaign?
3. How, according to Pittaway, are SUVs dangerous to people driving cars?
4. Under what conditions would Pittaway not begrudge a person owning an SUV?
5. Are SUVs safe for those who drive them, according to Pittaway? Why or why not?
6. What does the age of a driver have to do with Pittaway's argument?
7. How is driving an SUV analogous to the nuclear arms race, according to Pittaway?
8. Why are SUV drivers more likely to be "jerks," according to Pittaway?

Understanding the Writer's Techniques

1. Why does Pittaway open her essay with a statement she doesn't think is the most effective argument against SUVs?
2. What is the tone of the essay? Who do you think is the intended audience, and how does that affect the tone?
3. Does the title suit the rest of the essay? Why or why not?

4. What is the central claim? Where does the writer state it most clearly?
5. What are Pittaway's minor propositions? Which do you think is the most effective? Why?
6. What evidence does Pittaway offer to prove that SUVs are actually a danger to their drivers? Is her evidence effective?
7. What is behind Pittaway's claim that SUVs are dangerous to drivers of cars? Don't people have a right to drive cars that will be safer in case of a collision? What does Pittaway say to that argument? Do you find her retort effective?
8. Do you think that the conclusion is effective? Why or why not? Does it feel like an ad hominem attack?

Exploring the Writer's Argument

1. What is your view of the use of colloquialisms in the selection? The combative tone? Why does the writer call SUV drivers "jerks"? Does this help or hurt her argument? Explain your answer.
2. Pittaway decides in her essay not to argue against SUVs by looking at their environmental impact. Do you think this was a mistake? How could you fit environmental issues into her argument?
3. Why does the writer focus her argument so much on safety? Is this the most effective argument?

▶ Ideas for Writing Arguments

Prewriting

Write a few sentences about motorcycles, another vehicle often targeted by critics for their safety record. In what ways are they dangerous, do you think? Useful? What reasons other than safety can you think of for not allowing motorcycles on the roads? Why do people drive motorcycles? Should every state have a helmet law for motorcycle drivers?

Writing a Guided Argument

Write an essay in which you argue that motorcycles should (or should not) not be allowed on American roads.

1. Begin with a paragraph that sums up views that you do not think make the strongest argument by supporters of your position.
2. Next, explain, instead, what you think is the real issue with motorcycles.
3. Use a relaxed tone, and do not hold back from making fun of motorcycle riders or their critics, based on your position.

4. Next, explain your major proposition by arguing your first minor proposition.
5. Include some statistics as evidence for your argument.
6. Argue two more minor propositions, offering ample evidence.
7. End your essay with an ad hominem attack on motorcycle riders or their critics, on the basis that your arguments make it impossible to think of motorcycle riders or their critics as anything but "jerks" (or your own word).

Thinking, Arguing, and Writing Collaboratively

In small groups of three or four, exchange your Writing a Guided Argument papers. Offer suggestions in the form of a paragraph or two to help your classmate develop his or her essay. Offer, from your own research, anything that might add to your peer's argument.

Writing about the Text

Pittaway's essay appeared in a Canadian women's magazine. Write an essay in which you argue that Pittaway should have attempted to publish her essay in a different publication, preferably in the United States. Which publication would have been better? Why?

More Writing Ideas

1. In your journal, write about the SUV drivers you know or you have seen recently. Do they "need" their SUV? Why do they drive their SUV?
2. Do some research on the impact of SUVs on the environment and write a paragraph or two about the issue.
3. Write an essay in which you defend SUV drivers. You might need to do research to gather evidence for this position.

WOODY HOCHSWENDER
Did My Car Join Al Qaeda?

A former reporter and fashion columnist for the New York Times, *Woody Hochswender has also edited for* Esquire *magazine. He is the author of* The Buddha in Your Rearview Mirror *(2007), a book that attempts to apply the lessons of Buddhism to everyday life. In this selection, Hochswender, who lives in Connecticut, defends his use of the small truck known as the SUV, or sport utility vehicle.*

▶ Prereading: Thinking about the Essay in Advance

The SUV famously gets very low gas mileage, and thus conservationists accuse drivers of SUVs of being wasteful. What do you think about drivers of SUVs? If a friend or someone in your family has an SUV, do you agree with the purchase? Why or why not?

▶ Words to Watch

petrodollars (par. 2) money from oil and gasoline
transmigrate (par. 2) move
implicate (par. 3) accuse of guilt
insidious (par. 4) sinister, dangerous
propensity (par. 6) tendency
harrowing (par. 6) terrifying
voracious (par. 8) hungry

1   I drive a large, four-wheel-drive vehicle. Does that mean I'm a bad person?

2   You might think so, from all the sturm und drang we've heard lately from the Virtuous Ones who insist that America's fuel consumption—indeed, our very style of life—is somehow responsible for the enmity toward us in the Middle East, not to mention the rest of the world. A series of TV commercials put together by the columnist Arianna Huffington and Lawrence Bender, the Hollywood producer behind "Pulp Fiction," have even linked SUVs with Mideast terrorism. The idea is that the petrodollars transmigrate from the Gas 'n' Go to the oil sheiks to the hands of maniacs wielding AK-47s.

3   Leaving aside for the moment that this is trendy, illogical thinking—and leaving aside also the odd sensation of being lectured on socially responsible behavior by the producer of "Pulp Fiction"—isn't this really a backdoor way of blaming America for Sept. 11 and other crimes like it? Those who implicate Americans—particularly our adventurous habits, offbeat choices and breathtaking freedoms, including the freedom to drive to a poetry reading followed by dinner at a French restaurant in the midst of a raging snowstorm—validate the terrorists as essentially right.

4   Where I live, about 100 miles north of New York City, at least half of all the vehicles you see on the road are SUVs or other light trucks. They make a great deal of sense. This is not just because we have plenty of long steep driveways and miles and miles of dirt roads. We also have had more than 70 inches of snow this winter. When the sun goes down and the melted snow re-freezes, the roads are covered with insidious stretches of black ice.

Four-wheel-drive vehicles allow workers to get to and from their   5
jobs, and parents to transport their children safely to school, sporting
events, ballet classes and the rest. Yes, there is something vaguely obscene
about driving solo to the supermarket in Beverly Hills to pick up a carton
of milk in your two-ton Navigator. But not so much in Portland or Green
Bay or Chicago.

The well-publicized notion that SUVs are actually unsafe, based   6
on their propensity to roll over, does not take into account personal
responsibility. Rollover accidents tend to be something the driver has a
substantial degree of control over. I choose not to whip around corners or
to follow others so closely and at such high speeds that I have to make
harrowing emergency stops. I drive so as not to roll over.

However, if some drunken driver veers across the center divider—a   7
situation I have no control over—I would prefer that my 9-year-old and I
not be inside a Corolla. From the standpoint of a reasoned individualism,
SUVs are safer in many situations than cars. I think a lot of intelligent
people realize that.

Of course, SUVs use a lot of gas. This goes for my wife's all-wheel-   8
drive Volvo as well as for my voracious mistress, my 1989 GMC. But a
car's miles-per-gallon rating is only one measure of fuel efficiency. Miles
driven is another. People who drive light trucks quickly learn not to drive
around aimlessly. We tend to combine trips and to keep engines finely
tuned and tires properly inflated. It all comes down to home economics.

What are we supposed to do now, turn our SUVs in? En masse? Only   9
the independently wealthy can treat their cars purely as fashion items.

The SUV-bashers' argument also falls apart on macro-economic   10
grounds. Were we to somehow cut our national fuel consumption by
20 percent, would that deprive the terrorism sponsors of cash? Unfortunately, the world oil market is, well, a market. Even if America were energy independent, there is no guarantee that Exxon, Texaco, and Getty—
or, for that matter, France, the Netherlands, and Japan—would cease
buying oil from Middle Eastern states.

My guess is that this campaign has less to do with politics and eco-   11
nomics than with an American tendency to mind everybody else's business. So busybodies, let me ask you a question. How big is your house?
Ms. Huffington's is reported to be 9,000 square feet. We all know what it
costs to heat and air-condition a joint like that. A couple of years ago I replaced the aging oil furnace in my 3,000-square-foot house with a new
fuel-injected system. It saves me about 800 gallons of oil a year. Hey,
that's almost precisely the yearly fuel consumption of my GMC. I think
of that as progress for me, as a world citizen. Maybe I'm not such a bad
person after all.

▶ Building Vocabulary

Hochswender uses some common phrases and idioms to enrich his essay. Below are some that he uses. Explain what each phrase or idiom means, and use each in a sentence:

1. sturm und drang (par. 2)
2. whip around corners (par. 6)
3. home economics (par. 8)
4. en masse (par. 9)
5. macro-economic (par. 10)
6. energy independent (par. 10)
7. busybodies (par. 11)
8. a joint (par. 11)

▶ Thinking Critically about the Argument

Understanding the Writer's Argument

1. What is the major objection against driving SUVs, according to the writer? What is he being accused of?
2. What does the writer mean when he says, "Those who implicate Americans . . . validate the terrorists as essentially right"? (par. 3)
3. How does the SUV make life easier for the writer?
4. Why is the SUV safer than a smaller car?
5. The writer admits in paragraph 8 that the SUV uses a great deal of gasoline. How does he defend himself against the accusation of being wasteful?
6. The writer says that "the SUV-bashers' argument also falls apart on macro-economic grounds." (par. 10) What does he mean by this? How does the argument fall apart, according to him?

Understanding the Writer's Techniques

1. What do you think about the opening? Is it effective?
2. Who is the audience? How does that affect the tone of this essay?
3. Where does the writer express his major proposition most clearly and fully?
4. Hochswender has several minor propositions, and they are essentially of two kinds: propositions that are positive reasons to own SUVs and propositions that are rebuttals to perceived oppositions. Make an outline of the propositions offered in the body of his essay.
5. In paragraph 7, the writer mentions his 9-year-old child. Why does he do that? What is the effect of bringing a child into the argument?

6. In paragraph 7, the writer states, "I think a lot of intelligent people realize that." To what is he referring, and what argumentative purpose does this serve?
7. Which minor proposition do you find most effective? Why?
8. What do you think of the conclusion?
9. Why does the writer echo his statement from the beginning of the essay?

Exploring the Writer's Argument

1. One of the writer's arguments is that he drives "so as not to roll over." (par. 6) Why is this proposition weak? Could you strengthen his argument in this section?
2. One objection that some people have to SUVs that the writer doesn't mention is that although they might be safer for those driving them, they can be dangerous to those in smaller cars in the event of an accident. What might the author say to defend against this charge?
3. Paragraph 9 is short, but it includes an interesting idea. Paraphrase the idea, and think of a rebuttal to the point.

▶ Ideas for Writing Arguments

Prewriting

Make a list of lifestyle choices that you have made, actions that you perform often, or decisions that still have an impact on your life now (smoking, piercing), that people might have objections to, and try to come up with answers to objections.

Writing a Guided Argument

Woody Hochswender saw an aspect of his lifestyle that the media and people around him were attacking, and he wrote an essay defending himself. Write an essay in which you identify an aspect of *your* lifestyle that someone conceivably could object to on moral grounds, and defend yourself against the charges. For example, you might smoke cigarettes or cigars; you might consume alcohol; you might like loud music.

1. Begin by explaining your lifestyle choice to your reader, appealing to the reader's compassion.
2. Continue by describing the person or people who accuse you of acting poorly because of your lifestyle choice.
3. Next, offer a minor proposition that explains a positive side of your choice.

4. Then explain one of the objections to your choice, and give your rebuttal.
5. Repeat the process in order, alternating a positive idea with a rebuttal.
6. Emphasize an emotional appeal to the reader.
7. Conclude the essay with a reiteration of the beginning appeal.

Thinking, Arguing, and Writing Collaboratively

In small groups, compare the lists you made for the Prewriting exercise. Allow your fellow students to help you choose a lifestyle choice that would be best for the Writing a Guided Argument assignment, and then ask them for objections to your choice. Collect their answers and use them in your rebuttals.

Writing about the Text

In an essay, answer Hochswender's question to his audience in the negative—that no, he is not a bad person, but argue that he has a bad argument. Analyze his argument for him, focusing on how successful his individual points are. Address each minor proposition in his essay, and offer some suggestions for revisions.

More Writing Ideas

1. In your journal, freewrite about this topic: freedoms you enjoy that might hurt other people. Write for 15 minutes without editing your writing. Then exchange your writing with a partner and discuss your ideas as a possible basis for an essay.
2. Write a paragraph in which you critique the argumentative basis for this statement: "Everyone does it, so I should be allowed to also." Is there anything valid about that reasoning? Explain your answer fully.
3. Terrorism, of course, is the reason Hochswender wrote this essay in the first place. He was upset that people accused him and other SUV drivers of supporting terrorism. Write an essay about other day-to-day activities that you think unintentionally might support terrorism—television programs, ubiquitous cell phones, video games, for example.

6 ▶ Wal-Mart: Good or Evil?

Wal-Mart is a retail corporation based in Bentonville, Arkansas. But that statement is like simply saying that Michael Jordan was a basketball player who played in Chicago—the statement doesn't capture how important and dominant Wal-Mart is. It's clear that Wal-Mart is the Michael Jordan of companies—it's the best at what it does, which is to sell products at its more than 5,700 stores in more than 15 countries. It has revenues of more than $350 billion a year. Wal-Mart is the largest private employer in the United States, providing wage-earning opportunities to people here as well as around the globe. Founded in 1962, the company has in less than a half a century become the most widely argued-over corporation in the world. What is there to argue about? To be fair, some opposition to Wal-Mart might be fear of the powerful, but there's more to it than that. Wal-Mart has been accused of allowing poor working conditions, of paying low wages, of not providing health care, and of fighting union activity. And several lawsuits have been filed against the company on the grounds of gender discrimination.

This chapter includes two opposing views on Wal-Mart. The title of "What's Right about Wal-Mart," by Jack and Suzy Welch, is not a question, which tells you which side of the argument the Welches are on. Jack Welch, the former CEO of General Electric, and his wife, Suzy, argue that Wal-Mart has a huge impact on the economy in this country and that the effects are mainly positive. Wal-Mart keeps prices down, which helps customers, and it keeps competition going among its suppliers, always a good thing for the financial system. Paul Krugman, an economist who writes a column for the *New York Times*, disagrees. He thinks that Wal-Mart has destroyed jobs rather than added to the workforce. Prices may go down, yes, but so do wages, which is a disaster for the working person.

Jack and Suzy Welch
What's Right about Wal-Mart

Jack Welch is the former CEO of General Electric. During his time at the company, from 1981 to 2000, he grew GE from about a $14 billion company to about a $400 billion company. Business leaders consider him one of the great executives of the 20th century, and he certainly had one of the most successful careers. Many people complain about his retirement plan, which pays him more than $8 million a year, but others feel he deserves the rewards, considering the job he did. Suzy Welch is Jack Welch's third wife. She was the editor of the Harvard Business Review, *but was forced to resign when investigators revealed that she and Welch were having an affair while she was reporting on him. The two have written a book together,* Winning *(2005), and they cowrite a column for* Business Week *magazine, which is the source for this selection.*

▶ Prereading: Thinking about the Essay in Advance

Do you shop at Wal-Mart on a regular basis? Have you ever shopped there or even been inside a Wal-Mart? If you have been inside a Wal-Mart, what was your impression? How did it differ from the popular culture image of Wal-Mart? Did you think about the popular culture image when you were shopping? Why or why not? If you've never been inside a Wal-Mart, why do you think that is?

▶ Words to Watch

fervently (par. 1) in a passionate way
concede (par. 4) admit something with reluctance
credentials (par. 6) experience that qualifies someone for something
galore (par. 6) in abundance
conspiracy (par. 10) agreement between people to act in a certain way
lambaste (par. 12) criticize viciously
leverage (par. 13) advantage over others
upside (par. 13) positive aspects of a situation

> *Is Wal-Mart a force for good or evil in the world?*
> —Anonymous, Exeter, N.H.

1   We have heard this question again and again in recent months, but it was posed perhaps most fervently by the high school student above. He added: "You claim business is good for society—but Wal-Mart destroys it."

Destroys it? No way.   2

Maybe it's politically incorrect these days to say this, but Wal-Mart   3
helps individuals, communities, and whole economies prosper.

Without question, Wal-Mart is huge and getting more so. Its business   4
model is threatening to rivals and its purchasing power frightening to suppliers. But that doesn't make Wal-Mart bad—just a fat target for critics who,
for reasons of their own, won't concede how Wal-Mart improves lives.

Take individuals. Most obviously, Wal-Mart's prices have a positive   5
impact on the quality of life of millions of consumers. No other retailer offers so many good products for so little, from groceries to school supplies
to medicine. The net effect: Wal-Mart does more to hold down household
expenses than any social or government program.

In addition, Wal-Mart provides its employees with tremendous ac-   6
cess to upward mobility, even those with modest educational credentials. There are stories galore of employees who started on the floor or
as cashiers and worked their way up to management positions. And
with Wal-Mart's international growth, you are now seeing career
paths that can start in merchandising in Texas, move to logistics in
Arkansas, and end up in divisional leadership positions in Europe and
Asia. Only the military rivals Wal-Mart when it comes to providing
training and opportunity for individuals who have no other way to
breakout of a paycheck-to-paycheck lifestyle and into a whole new
world of possibility.

Wal-Mart's low prices and large workforce, of course, have a cumula-   7
tive effect on the local and national economies where the company oper-
ates. Low prices keep inflation down, while the employees' purchasing
power keeps demand high.

This is evil?   8

There are critics who claim that Wal-Mart destroys communities by   9
wiping out mom-and-pop stores—the little pharmacies, hardware, and
grocery stores—that took much better care of customers and employees.
These critics are nostalgic for a time that never was.

Yes, Wal-Mart has meant the end of many local stores. And yes, at some   10
of them, customers might have been greeted by name when they walked in
the door. But those customers chose to shop at Wal-Mart when it came to
town because low prices, apparently, meant more to their quality of life
than a wave and a smile. No conspiracy, just the free market at work.

As for taking better care of employees—nonsense. In most small   11
towns the storeowner drove the best car, lived in the fanciest house, and
belonged to the country club. Meanwhile, employees weren't exactly
sharing the wealth. They rarely had life insurance or health benefits and
certainly did not receive much in the way of training or big salaries. And
few of these storeowners had plans for growth or expansion: Their lives
were nicely set. That was good for them but a killer for employees seeking life-changing careers.

12 Critics also lambaste Wal-Mart for being brutal to its suppliers. Be it swing sets or beef jerky, you sell to Wal-Mart on its terms, or you don't sell at all.

13 We'd say this is pretty true. Wal-Mart's huge market share gives it enormous leverage. One of us (Jack) negotiated for decades with Wal-Mart buyers at General Electric, and they were never unethical or unfair. Just tough. GE won plenty of rounds and lost a few. But losing had its upside. It forced GE to look inside to see how it could do its job better by lowering manufacturing costs, for instance, or being more flexible in how a product was packaged.

14 Ultimately, prices stayed low, and the customer won. And that is what drives Wal-Mart—keeping its customers satisfied—and why it keeps increasing sales and profits.

15 Yes, there will be "casualties" of Wal-Mart's success: competitors that fold, jobs lost. But in that way, Wal-Mart is no different than Toyota. When Toyota arrived in the 1970s, it was accused of upsetting the status quo. Decades later most people accept that Toyota simply had a better way of doing business. Its value proposition to consumers was a wake-up call to the auto industry, raising standards and requiring companies that had lost their edge to reinvent themselves and start making better cars for a lot less. And that's the Wal-Mart story. It's a great company that helps consumers win and employees grow. And as long as it does, it will, too.

▶ Building Vocabulary

The Welches use various phrases from popular culture and business. For each of the following, explain what the phrase means and use it in your own sentence.

1. politically incorrect (par. 3)
2. upward mobility (par. 6)
3. logistics (par. 6)
4. management positions (par. 6)
5. purchasing power (par. 7)
6. mom-and-pop (par. 9)
7. free market (par. 10)
8. status quo (par. 15)
9. value proposition (par. 15)
10. wake-up call (par. 15)

▶ Thinking Critically about the Argument

Understanding the Writers' Argument

1. How, according to the Welches, does Wal-Mart help individuals?

2. What are the advantages of working for Wal-Mart, according to the writers?
3. What are the economic effects of Wal-Mart's operating in a community?
4. Why do critics of Wal-Mart long for the days of mom-and-pop stores? What do the writers say to that criticism?
5. What do critics of Wal-Mart say is the effect that the retailer has on suppliers? What do the writers say about that criticism?
6. What is the parallel the writers draw between Wal-Mart and Toyota?

Understanding the Writers' Techniques

1. Do you find the writers' technique of using a quote to start their essay effective or not? Explain.
2. What is the central claim? Where do the writers express it best?
3. What are the writers' minor propositions? List them in the form of an outline.
4. How does Jack Welch's reputation as one of the great CEOs of his time help his essay? Explain.
5. How do the short paragraphs punctuate the argument?
6. In paragraph 10, the Welches write, "No conspiracy, just the free market at work," but they don't explain the statement. They don't quote anyone as accusing Wal-Mart of a conspiracy. Do you think this helps or hurts their argument? Why?
7. How does the writers' use of Jack Welch's business relationship in paragraph 13 help or hurt their argument?
8. Is the concluding paragraph effective? Why or why not?

Exploring the Writers' Argument

1. What arguments against Wal-Mart do Jack and Suzy Welch omit in their defense of the company?
2. In paragraph 5, the writers state that the "net effect" of Wal-Mart's power is that the company "does more to hold down household expenses than any social or government program." Some would argue that the government should be doing this job. What do you think? What would the Welches say to that argument?
3. How successful is the argument in paragraph 10 that even though Wal-Mart has meant the demise of a great many local stores, what is most important is that low prices have prevailed? Do you agree that this is the most important outcome? Is there anything more important than keeping prices low so that people can afford to buy more things? What, for example?

▶Ideas for Writing Arguments

Prewriting

Where do you shop in your community? Where do you get groceries? Where do you buy electronics or books or coffee? Are there any independently owned stores where you shop?

Writing a Guided Argument

Write an essay in which you argue that Starbucks, McDonald's, Burger King, Dairy Queen or some chain other than Wal-Mart is or is not good for your community.

1. Begin with a quote that you find on the Internet that poses the question you will answer in your essay.
2. Next, state your major proposition clearly.
3. Using an assured tone, explain up front what your three minor propositions will be.
4. Support your minor propositions with examples and facts.
5. Do not hesitate to use your own experiences as evidence to support your propositions.
6. Refer to the Welches' argument (or Paul Krugman's) at least once in your essay.
7. Start your conclusion with a concession to the other side.
8. Close your essay with a restatement of your strongest minor proposition.

Thinking, Arguing, and Writing Collaboratively

In small groups, exchange the essays you wrote for your Writing a Guided Argument assignment with a fellow student. Offer suggestions in the form of a paragraph or two to help your classmate develop his or her argument.

Writing about the Text

Scrutinize the Welches' points in paragraph 6 about the opportunities Wal-Mart offers to employees. Argue that their analogy with the military is either accurate or spurious and whether it is one of the strongest points or one of the weakest. You might have to do some research on the Internet to back up your points.

More Writing Ideas

1. Write in your journal about your experience shopping in big-box stores such as Wal-Mart and Target.

2. Write a paragraph or two that argues for or against this statement: "It doesn't matter that Wal-Mart ensures low prices: It makes America boring and homogenous."

3. Write an essay that explores the idea of being able to resist Wal-Mart's predominance. What can the private citizen do if he or she is not happy with Wal-Mart's hold on the world economy?

Paul Krugman
Low Pay, Few Benefits

Economist Paul Krugman was born in 1952 on Long Island, New York. He got his undergraduate degree at Yale University and his Ph.D. in economics at MIT. He has taught at his alma maters and at the London School of Economics, and he is currently a professor at Princeton University. He worked for the Reagan White House on the Council of Economic Advisers. He has written for many publications, including the Economist, *the* Harvard Business Review, Fortune, *and* Slate, *but he is best known as the author of a twice-weekly column on the op-ed page of the* New York Times. *He has spoken strongly against the Bush administration, not only about economic topics, but also about political matters. In this selection, Krugman speaks out against Wal-Mart's treatment of its workers. The religious-values critique he refers to in his second paragraph was a television advertisement by a group called Wake-Up Wal-Mart; the ad suggested that Wal-Mart was treating its employees in an anti-Christian way.*

▶ Prereading: Thinking about the Essay in Advance

Do you think it is fair that Wal-Mart has so much impact on the economy of the United States? How is it possible that one corporation can be such an influence on a whole country?

▶ Words to Watch

stagnant (par. 1) not growing
war room (par. 2) place to devise and implement strategies
critique (par. 2) argument against something
organizational (par. 3) relating to the way something is organized
innovation (par. 3) act of inventing something new
defy (par. 4) challenge or go against someone
core (par. 5) most important part
speculation (par. 9) reasoning based on a lack of evidence

1   Wal-Mart isn't just America's largest private employer. It's also a symbol of the state of our economy, which is growing even as living standards for average working Americans fall or remain stagnant. And Wal-Mart is a huge, and hugely profitable, company that pays badly and offers minimal benefits.

2   Attacks on Wal-Mart have hurt its image, and perhaps even its business. The company has set up a campaign-style war room to devise responses. So how did Wal-Mart respond to this recent religious-values critique?

3   Wal-Mart can claim, with considerable justice, that its business practices make America as a whole richer. The fact is that Wal-Mart sells many products more cheaply than traditional stores, and that its low prices aren't solely or even mainly the result of the low wages it pays: Wal-Mart has been able to reduce prices largely because it has brought genuine technological and organizational innovation to the retail business.

4   It's harder for Wal-Mart to defend its pay and benefits policies. The company could try to argue that despite its awesome size and market dominance, it cannot defy the laws of supply and demand, and therefore is forced to pay low wages (though I would disagree).

5   But instead, Wal-Mart decided to insult our intelligence by claiming to be, of all things, an engine of job creation. Judging from its response to the religious-values campaign, the assertion that Wal-Mart "creates 100,000 jobs a year" is now the core of the company's public-relations strategy.

Creating Jobs?

6   It's true that the company is getting bigger every year. But adding 100,000 people to Wal-Mart's workforce does not mean adding 100,000 jobs to the economy. On the contrary, there's every reason to believe that as Wal-Mart expands, it destroys at least as many jobs as it creates, and drives down workers' wages in the process.

7   Think about what happens when Wal-Mart opens a store in a previously untouched city or county. The new store takes sales away from stores that are already in the area; these stores lay off workers or even go out of business.

When Wal-Mart Comes to Town

8   Because Wal-Mart's stores employ fewer workers per dollar of sales than the smaller stores they replace, overall retail employment surely goes down, not up, when Wal-Mart comes to town. And if the jobs lost come from employers who pay more than Wal-Mart does, overall wages will fall.

9   This isn't just speculation on my part. A recent study used sophisticated statistical analysis to estimate the effects on jobs and wages as Wal-Mart spread out from its original center in Arkansas. The authors found that retail employment did, indeed, fall when Wal-Mart arrived in a new

Hamden, Connecticut: SHOP TILL YOU DROP: On the busiest retail shopping day of the year, early bird shoppers looking for day after Thanksgiving sales enter the Wal-Mart department store in the Hamden Mart after the 6:00 AM opening. A line to enter Wal-Mart started forming at 4:00 AM and the queue ran almost the length of Hamden Mart before the 6:00 AM opening. November 28, 2003

county. It's not clear whether overall employment rose or fell when a Wal-Mart store opened. But it's clear that average wages fell.

So Wal-Mart has chosen to defend itself with a really poor argument.   10
If that's the best the company can come up with, it's going to keep losing the public-relations war with its critics. Maybe it should consider an alternative strategy, such as paying higher wages.

▶ Building Vocabulary

In his column, Krugman—as an economist—uses various terms and phrases from the academic discipline of economics. For each of the following economic terms and phrases, write a definition and offer at least one example from the world of business.

1. living standards (par. 1)
2. business practices (par. 3)
3. low wages (par. 3)
4. retail (par. 3)
5. benefits policies (par. 4)
6. laws of supply and demand (par. 4)

7. public-relations strategy (par. 5)
8. lay off (par. 7)
9. statistical analysis (par. 9)

▶ Thinking Critically about the Argument

Understanding the Writer's Argument

1. How is Wal-Mart a symbol of our economy, according to Krugman?
2. What does Krugman say that Wal-Mart can claim it has done for the United States?
3. How has Wal-Mart been able to lower prices?
4. Why, according to the writer, does Wal-Mart's business practices ensure that it must pay low wages?
5. Why does Krugman think that Wal-Mart is insulting our intelligence when it claims to be "of all things, an engine of job creation"?
6. Why doesn't "adding 100,000 people to Wal-Mart's workforce . . . mean adding 100,000 jobs to the economy," according to Krugman?
7. What, according to Krugman, happens to wages when Wal-Mart comes to town?

Understanding the Writer's Techniques

1. Why does Krugman begin his essay by explaining what Wal-Mart is not?
2. What is the claim in this essay? Where does the writer state it most clearly?
3. Krugman is an economist. What is the argumentative effect of the economic analysis Krugman uses in this essay?
4. What is the tone here? How does the fact that Krugman writes regularly in perhaps the most prominent place in the most prestigious newspaper in the world affect his tone?
5. What evidence does the writer cite to support his minor proposition that when Wal-Mart opens a store in a community, overall wages fall?
6. Analyze the transitions Krugman uses in his essay to link his various points.
7. How effective is Krugman's conclusion?

Exploring the Writer's Argument

1. Krugman spends a good deal of his essay criticizing Wal-Mart for not fighting their public relations well, or rather for defending themselves with weak arguments. How is Krugman constructing his argument in an indirect way by using this technique?

2. Does Krugman seem to be upset with Wal-Mart for simply being large? How can you tell? Is he expecting Wal-Mart to be something it is not? Explain your answer.
3. Krugman cites a study but doesn't give more information other than a very thin summary of it. Are you convinced by this piece of evidence? Why or why not? If not, what would satisfy you?

▶ Ideas for Writing Arguments

Prewriting

Think about the institutions with which you come into contact often: a local bank or supermarket, your university administration, a government bureaucracy, the department of motor vehicles, or some similar institution. What is it about this institution that bothers you?

Writing a Guided Argument

Write an essay in which you criticize an institution with which you come into contact regularly and which you think is disturbing or unfair in some way.

1. Open your essay by stating in clear, forceful language what your chosen institution signifies to you.
2. Write your major proposition.
3. Offer at least three minor propositions that explain why the institution should be changed.
4. Connect each of your minor propositions with the importance that you attributed to the institution as a result of step 1.
5. Explain what the institution's defenders would say, in general, to your arguments.
6. Bring your essay to a close with an answer to the institution's imagined defenders.

Thinking, Arguing, and Writing Collaboratively

In groups of four or five class members, discuss Krugman's economic argument based on your own interests. Krugman most likely does not have to shop at Wal-Mart, but many people do. What does Wal-Mart mean to you personally or to people you know? Examine how your answers to this question affect your reading of this essay and the Welches' essay. Come together as a class to talk about how we bring our own experiences to the reading of any essay.

Writing about the Text

Do some research on Paul Krugman. Where can you place him in the spectrum of economists from socialist to laissez-faire capitalists, and where can you place him in the political spectrum from left to right? Write an essay in which you evaluate Krugman's essay based on what you know about his economic and political affiliations.

More Writing Ideas

1. In your journal, write notes toward an essay attacking stores like Wal-Mart based on an aesthetic argument about what they do to America's neighborhoods.
2. Do some research online about Wal-Mart's health insurance policy for its employees. Write a paragraph summarizing the policy and another paragraph analyzing its effects.
3. Krugman says that Wal-Mart should pay higher wages to help poor people in America. Wal-Mart would argue that its low prices already help poor people in America. Write an essay that attempts to break this pattern of argument, based on your own Internet research.

7 Animal Rights: Should They Compromise Human Needs?

I n recent years the idea of *animal* rights has gained many supporters. Animal rights advocates believe that other species should exist without human interference. Modern researchers have argued that animals feel pain and emotions and, in some cases, are capable of reasoning. Organizations such as the People for the Ethical Treatment of Animals (PETA) go so far as to claim that drinking milk is immoral because it causes the cows suffering. Some animal rights advocates are more moderate and abstain from eating meat from big commercial farms or become vegetarians altogether. Some will not wear leather.

Most people, if pressed, will agree that we do not need to eat hamburgers to live, but what happens when it is a question of life and death? For example, what if the suffering of animals can help save the lives of humans who are sick with disease? Many drugs and procedures that humans rely on for health emerged through medical research on animals.

In the selections that follow, written by two writers of vastly different backgrounds and viewpoints, notice how emotional the arguments for or against animal experimentation can be.

JANE MCCABE
Is a Lab Rat's Fate More Poignant than a Child's?

Jane McCabe was a wife and mother living in northern California when she published this essay in Newsweek. *She is not a professional writer, nor is she a public person. Her only qualification for writing is that she believes strongly in animal experimentation and has a deeply personal stake in the issue. Her daughter has an incurable disease, and hope for a cure lies mostly in the ability of scientists to continue doing experiments on animals. In this selection, McCabe argues passionately that animal experimentation must continue.*

▶ Prereading: Thinking about the Essay in Advance

Think about the question posed in the title. Consider giving an answer to that question. What about the fate of a chimpanzee? A pet dog's fate? A cat's? Where would you personally draw the line and why?

▶ Words to Watch

stark (par. 1) plain, harsh
cystic fibrosis (par. 1) a disease that appears in early childhood affecting the digestive system and the lungs
supplemental (par. 4) making up for something lacking
enzymes (par. 5) molecules that help biological function
antibiotics (par. 5) drugs designed to fight bacterial infection
diabetes (par. 5) a disease caused by a low level of insulin, the hormone in the body that controls the level of sugar in the blood
semblance (par. 6) an outward appearance or likeness
poignant (par. 7) deeply affecting the emotions
eloquent (par. 9) forcefully expressive and persuasive

1   I see the debate about using animals in medical research in stark terms. If you had to choose between saving a very cute dog or my equally cute, blond, brown-eyed daughter, whose life would you choose? It's not a difficult choice, is it? My daughter has cystic fibrosis. Her only hope for a normal life is that researchers, some of them using animals, will find a cure. Don't misunderstand. It's not that I don't love animals, it's just that I love Claire more.

2   Nine years ago I had no idea that I would be joining the fraternity of those who have a vital interest in seeing that medical research continues. I was a very pregnant woman in labor; with my husband beside me I gave birth to a 7-pound 1-ounce daughter. It all seemed so easy. But for the next four months she could not gain weight. She was a textbook case of failure to thrive. Finally a hospital test of the salt content in her sweat led to the diagnosis of cystic fibrosis.

3   The doctor gave us a little reason for hope. "Your daughter will not have a long life, but for most of the time, it will be a good life. Her life expectancy is about 13 years, though it could be longer or shorter. As research continues, we're keeping them alive longer."

4   "As research continues." It's not a lot to rely on but what's our alternative? We haven't waited passively. We learned how to take care of our little girl; her medical problems affect her digestion and lungs. We protected her from colds, learned about supplemental vitamins and antibiotics. We moved to California where the winters aren't so harsh and the

(People for the Ethical Treatment of Animals/AP)

cold and flu season isn't so severe. Our new doctor told us that the children at his center were surviving, on the average, to age 21. So far, our daughter is doing well. She is a fast runner and plays a mean first base. She loves her friends and is, in general, a happy little girl. All things considered, I feel very lucky.

How has research using animals helped those with CF? Three times a   5
day my daughter uses enzymes from the pancreas of pigs to digest her food. She takes antibiotics tested on rats before they are tried on humans. As an adult, she will probably develop diabetes and need insulin—a drug developed by research on dogs and rabbits. If she ever needs a heart-lung transplant, one might be possible because of the cows that surgeons practiced on. There is no animal model to help CF research, but once the CF gene is located, new gene-splicing techniques may create a family of mice afflicted with the disease. Researchers would first learn to cure the mice with drugs, then cautiously try with humans.

There are only about 10,000 people with CF in the United States. But   6
the number of people dependent on research is much larger. Walk with me through the Children's Hospital at Stanford University: here are the youngsters fighting cancer, rare genetic illnesses, immunological diseases.

Amid their laughter and desperate attempts to retain a semblance of childhood, there is suffering.

7   I think the motivation of animal-rights activists is to cut down on the suffering in this world, but I have yet to hear them acknowledge that people—young and old—suffer, too. Why is a laboratory rat's fate more poignant than that of an incurably ill child?

8   There are advocates for animals who only seek to cut down on "unnecessary research." They don't specify how to decide what is unnecessary, but they do create an atmosphere in which doing medical research is seen as distasteful work. I think that's wrong. Researchers should be thanked, not hassled.

9   Every time I see a bumper sticker that says "Lab animals never have a nice day," a fantasy plays in my brain. I get out of my car, tap on the driver's window and ask to talk. In my fantasy, the other driver gets out, we find a coffee shop and I show her photos of my kids. I ask her if she has ever visited Children's Hospital. I am so eloquent that her eyes fill with tears and she promises to think of the children who are wasting away as she considers the whole complicated issue of suffering.

10   I have other fantasies, too, that a cure is found for what ails my daughter, that she marries and gives us some grandchildren, and does great work in her chosen profession, which at this moment appears to be cartooning or computer programming. We can still hope—as long as the research continues.

▶ Building Vocabulary

1. In this essay, the writer uses several medical terms. Find at least five and write definitions for each.
2. Sometimes, writers use idiomatic phrases that they assume their reader will either know or understand from context. Rewrite the following phrases in your own language:
   a. the fraternity of those (par. 2)
   b. a textbook case (par. 2)
   c. plays a mean first base (par. 4)
   d. cut down on (par. 7)
   e. who are wasting away (par. 9)

▶ Thinking Critically about the Argument

Understanding the Writer's Argument

1. Why does McCabe begin her essay by admitting that she sees the issue of animal experimentation "in stark terms"? What does she mean? Why does she see the choice between child and animal as "stark"?

2. Why does McCabe place herself in the "fraternity of those who have a vital interest in seeing that medical research continues"? Why does she use the word "fraternity"? (par. 2)
3. In paragraph 4, McCabe mentions all the things that her husband and she have done for their daughter. What is she implying? In what ways has animal experimentation helped McCabe's daughter?
4. What other diseases can animal experimentation give hope for? Why does McCabe mention only children with diseases in paragraph 6?
5. In paragraph 7, McCabe repeats the title question, but in different words. What is the difference?
6. According to McCabe, what is the result of animal rights advocates making vague claims that research is "unnecessary"?
7. What is McCabe's reason for including her fantasy about confronting the driver? (par. 9)

Understanding the Writer's Techniques

1. What is McCabe's major proposition and where does she place it? Is it effective where it is? Explain.
2. What is the effect of McCabe's "stark" admission in paragraph 1? If this admission is part of the warrant behind her claim, why does she state it? Why can this warrant not remain implied?
3. What other implied or stated warrants affect McCabe's argument?
4. Who is McCabe's audience? How does her audience affect the tone of the essay?
5. Paraphrase McCabe's argument. Write one sentence for each paragraph explaining the function of that paragraph.
6. What examples does McCabe use to back up her major proposition?
7. McCabe's argument is emotional. What emotional appeals does she make?
8. Discuss the conclusion. Is it effective? Why or why not?
9. **(Mixing modes)** How does McCabe use narrative and illustration together? Does she do it successfully? Why or why not?

Exploring the Writer's Argument

1. What is your emotional reaction to the essay? Does the writer pull your "heart-strings" too much? Look at your list of emotional appeals from question 7, above. Which of McCabe's emotional appeals are unfair appeals? Which do you think are fair?
2. What logical appeals could you think of to complement McCabe's argument?
3. McCabe writes that any criticism of animal experimentation is harmful. What reason does she give for this position? What do you think of her argument?

4. McCabe offers examples of her daughter's suffering, but never mentions the sufferings of the animals that are experimented upon. Is this a weakness in her argument? Why or why not?

▶ Ideas for Writing Arguments

Prewriting

Invent another bumper sticker (see paragraph 9) that either supports or challenges animal experimentation.

Writing a Guided Argument

Write an argument that supports animal experimentation, but assume that you, like McCabe, are a parent, friend, or relative of a seriously ill child who has been helped and perhaps can be cured by furthering animal experimentation.

1. Begin your essay by expressing the rules. What is your warrant, and what is your claim?
2. Address the expectations of the opposition.
3. State your first minor proposition to support your claim.
4. Support your first proposition with evidence.
5. State your second minor proposition.
6. Support your second proposition with evidence from McCabe's essay. Use her own words to prove your point.
7. End your essay by expressing, once again, how surprising your position is. Explain why your point of view lends your position more credibility.

Thinking, Arguing, and Writing Collaboratively

Work in small groups of three or four. List ways in which humans assert their superiority over animals. Which of these ways are acceptable ethically? Report the differences of opinion in your group, including reasons for your various claims.

Writing about the Text

Because McCabe is a parent, it is natural for her to argue for the value of her child's life over that of anonymous animals. In what ways does her identity weaken her position? Does she anticipate the issue of her identity in her essay? If not, how could she anticipate it? If so, could she do better and would doing so strengthen her argument?

More Writing Ideas

1. Jeremy Bentham, a 19th-century English philosopher, in considering the rights of animals, said, "The question is not, 'Can they reason?' nor, 'Can they talk?' But rather, 'Can they suffer?'" Do you agree with this view, or are the other questions that he mentions worth considering? Write an essay agreeing or disagreeing with Bentham.
2. Some animals kill each other. Humans are, essentially, just animals with the ability to reason. If animals can kill each other for food, why can't we kill animals to prolong our own lives? Does our ability to reason take away our right to use animals for experimentation, food, or sport?
3. Many people wear leather or eat meat but still believe that animal experimentation is wrong. Write an essay about people wanting to have the issue of animal rights their own way. What is your position on the issue? Do you have a double standard? Justify your position.
4. Working with your list of claims and evidence from your collaborative work, write an essay in which you defend one human use of animals—for example, for food or in fashion. Choose a specific use, as in harvesting caviar or wearing leather belts.

JANE GOODALL
A Question of Ethics

Jane Goodall, born in 1934 in London, England, is best known for her work studying chimpanzees in the wild. In 1960, at the age of 26, with no college degree or formal training, she began to study chimps at the Gombe Stream Reserve in Tanzania in eastern Africa, working as a secretary to fund her work. By watching the chimps closely, she was able to gain their trust. Soon she saw differences between the individual chimps. She was the first scientist to note that chimps are not strictly vegetarian and that the species uses tools, something previously thought to be purely a human trait. Goodall wrote many books about her work, including My Friends the Wild Chimpanzees *(1967),* In the Shadow of Man *(1971),* The Chimpanzees of Gombe: Patterns of Behavior *(1986),* Through a Window: My Thirty Years with the Chimpanzees of Gombe *(1990), and* The Chimpanzee: The Living Link Between Man and Beast *(1992). She has received several awards for her research and for conservation, including the prestigious Albert Schweitzer Award. In this essay, Goodall displays her signature thoughtfulness and humanism.*

▶ **Prereading: Thinking about the Essay in Advance**

Ethics is the branch of philosophy that deals with moral obligations and duties. What is more ethical: protecting the rights and lives of animals or looking for cures for human diseases? Make two columns, one for each side of the issue, and jot down as many reasons as you can under each heading.

▶ **Words to Watch**

fuzzy (par. 1) unclear
distinction (par. 1) difference
vaccines (par. 2) medicines that prevent a disease
surly (par. 2) bad tempered
sentient (par. 3) capable of feeling
dilemma (par. 3) problem with two unsatisfactory alternatives
vigorously (par. 4) with great energy
apathy (par. 5) lack of interest

1   David Greybeard first showed me how fuzzy the distinction between animals and humans can be. Forty years ago I befriended David, a chimpanzee, during my first field trip to Gombe in Tanzania. One day I offered him a nut in my open palm. He looked directly into my eyes, took the nut out of my hand and dropped it. At the same moment he very gently squeezed my hand as if to say, I don't want it, but I understand your motives.

2   Since chimpanzees are thought to be physiologically close to humans, researchers use them as test subjects for new drugs and vaccines. In the labs, these very sociable creatures often live isolated from one another in 5-by-5-foot cages, where they grow surly and sometimes violent. Dogs, cats and rats are also kept in poor conditions and subjected to painful procedures. Many people would find it hard to sympathize with rats, but dogs and cats are part of our lives. Ten or 15 years ago, when the use of animals in medical testing was first brought to my attention, I decided to visit the labs myself. Many people working there had forced themselves to believe that animal testing is the only way forward for medical research.

3   Once we accept that animals are sentient beings, is it ethical to use them in research? From the point of view of the animals, it is quite simply wrong. From our standpoint, it seems ridiculous to equate a rat with a human being. If we clearly and honestly believe that using animals in research will, in the end, reduce massive human suffering, it would be difficult to argue that doing so is unethical. How do we find a way out of this dilemma?

One thing we can do is change our mind-set. We can begin by questioning the assumption that animals are essential to medical research. Scientists have concluded that chimpanzees are not useful for AIDS research because, even though their genetic makeup differs from ours by about 1 percent, their immune systems deal much differently with the AIDS virus. Many scientists test drugs and vaccines on animals simply because they are required to by law rather than out of scientific merit. This is a shame, because our medical technology is beginning to provide alternatives. We can perform many tests on cell and tissue cultures without recourse to systemic testing on animals. Computer simulations can also cut down on the number of animal tests we need to run. We aren't exploring these alternatives vigorously enough.   4

Ten or 15 years ago animal-rights activists resorted to violence against humans in their efforts to break through the public's terrible apathy and lack of imagination on this issue. This extremism is counterproductive. I believe that more and more people are becoming aware that to use animals thoughtlessly, without any anguish or making an effort to find another way, diminishes us as human beings.   5

▶ Building Vocabulary

For each of the following words, write both a definition and a sentence of your own:

1. fuzzy (par. 1)
2. surly (par. 2)
3. sentient (par. 3)
4. dilemma (par. 3)
5. vigorously (par. 4)
6. apathy (par. 5)
7. counterproductive (par. 5)

▶ Thinking Critically about the Argument

Understanding the Writer's Argument

1. Why does Goodall start her essay with the story of giving the nut to the chimp David Greybeard?
2. According to Goodall, how are lab animals treated, and what does this do to their behavior? What are other physical and emotional effects of experimentation on animals?
3. Why did Goodall visit the labs where animal experimentation was taking place? (par. 2)

4. In paragraph 3, the writer questions whether it is "ethical" to use animals in medical research. What does she mean here by ethical? In your own words, what is the "dilemma" Goodall refers to in paragraph 3?
5. Goodall thinks that people should change their "mind-set" about animal experimentation. What is the current mind-set of people about the issue?
6. How can people change the way that they think about animal experimentation, according to the writer?
7. Goodall says that extreme forms of protest are "counterproductive," alluding to violence by activists against people who use animals for medical research. What are *productive* ways of changing people's minds about the issue?

Understanding the Writer's Techniques

1. Which sentence in the essay states the writer's claim?
2. Goodall is known as a scientist with a heart, a person who cares about all creatures of Earth. How does knowing this information influence how you perceive her argument?
3. What are Goodall's warrants for this essay? Who is her audience, and how does that affect the tone of the essay?
4. Make an outline of the essay, paraphrasing the argument.
5. What form of reasoning does Goodall use in this essay, deductive or inductive? What kind of evidence does she use?
6. Although this is mostly a reasoned argument, it is about an emotional issue. Can you locate the places where she appeals to her readers' emotions?

Exploring the Writer's Argument

1. Goodall makes many assumptions in her essay. For example, she interprets David Greybeard's behavior as a kindly, understanding response. Is this the only way we can interpret his behavior? What other assumptions does Goodall ask her readers to make?
2. The workers who worked at the labs, according to Goodall, "forced themselves" to believe that what they were doing was okay. Is this good logic? Do you see any logical fallacies here or elsewhere in her essay?
3. Goodall seems to offer solutions to the problem of animal experimentation when, in paragraph 3, she says that "if we clearly and honestly believe that using animals in research will, in the end, reduce massive human suffering, it would be difficult to argue that doing so is unethical." What burden does this place on her argument? Do you think she gives enough evidence for her own side?

4. In paragraph 4, the writer states that people have to change their mind-set, and then, in the last sentence, she writes that she thinks that people's minds are changing. Are these statements contradictory? Why or why not?

▶ Ideas for Writing Arguments

Prewriting

List the moral, or ethical, arguments for and against the use of medical research on animals.

Writing a Guided Argument

In paragraph 3, Goodall poses a dilemma: We want to be ethical, but if animals suffer, how can it be ethical to harm them for any reason? Write a letter to Jane Goodall in which you satisfy Goodall's grounds for her own argument: She says that if we believe that animal experimentation will "reduce massive human suffering, it would be difficult to argue that doing so is unethical." Argue that animal experimentation is ethical because of this reason.

1. Start your essay by quoting Goodall from paragraph 3.
2. Next, state your major proposition, using Goodall's own words against her. Focus on establishing the correct tone in your first paragraph.
3. In the next paragraph, write your first minor proposition using a logical appeal.
4. Offer evidence to support your proposition.
5. Next, write a paragraph in which you offer another minor proposition, but this time use an emotional appeal.
6. Offer evidence to support your proposition.
7. In your concluding paragraph, make it clear to Goodall that you are correct on moral or ethical grounds, again repeating, for rhetorical reasons, her ideas.

Thinking, Arguing, and Writing Collaboratively

In small groups of four or five, discuss the dilemma explored in your Writing a Guided Argument paper. Where is the issue of animal experimentation headed in the future? Will people change their minds? Will protests lead to more violence, as Goodall warns against? Can animal experimentation ever end, realistically?

Writing about the Text

Goodall presents her essay as a reasoned argument, but much of what she writes is an emotional appeal presented as logic. Write an essay in which you explore the question of whether one can write about animal experimentation without an excess of emotion.

More Writing Ideas

1. Many people argue that animals can't understand their own death so their suffering is not as severe as human suffering. Do you agree or disagree? Outline your reasons in a persuasive essay.
2. David Greybeard showed Goodall "how fuzzy the distinction between animals and humans can be." What are other "fuzzy" distinctions between animals and humans? Are there clear distinctions?
3. On the basis of some research, write an essay about the similarities between the struggle for animal rights and other modern struggles for rights, such as the civil rights movement, the fight for gay rights, or the struggle for female suffrage.

8 ▶ Stem Cell Research and Use: Yes or No?

What are stem cells? We hear so much about them frequently in the news. Politicians talk about them in one way, scientists in another, but what are stem cells in fact? According to the National Institutes of Health Web site on the topic, "Stem cells have two important characteristics that distinguish them from other types of cells. First, they are unspecialized cells that renew themselves for long periods through cell division. The second is that under certain physiologic or experimental conditions, they can be induced to become cells with special functions such as the beating cells of the heart muscle or the insulin-producing cells of the pancreas."

The promise of stem cells is that they might be able to help cure a variety of debilitating diseases, from spinal cord injuries to Parkinson's disease to diabetes and heart disease. There are two types of stem cells: embryonic stem cells and adult stem cells. The controversy in the United States has centered mostly on embryonic stem cells because harvesting the cells requires destroying the embryo or cloning human cells.

You can see the volatility of the issue: it plays into the long-standing debate about how to define human life and its beginnings and who should determine the viability of a fetus—scientists, doctors, policy makers and elected officials, or the woman who carries the developing embryo. Anti-abortion supporters claim that life begins at the moment of conception; pro-abortion supporters say life begins only at birth. Scientists and physicians line up on both sides of the debate. Religious leaders have weighed in vociferously on the moral implications of the inquiry. Politicians and celebrities such as former First Lady Nancy Reagan and film and television star Michael J. Fox, a victim of Parkinson's disease, support embryonic stem cell research; others, such as Rush Limbaugh, a conservative talk show host, and actor-director Mel Gibson, oppose it.

In this chapter, Michael Kinsley, in "False Dilemma on Stem Cells," writes about the hypocrisy endemic to the debate over stem cells: If everyone is worried about stem cells being destroyed, then we should look at fertility clinics, which "murder" many, many millions every year. He attempts to puncture the traditional arguments against the therapeutic use

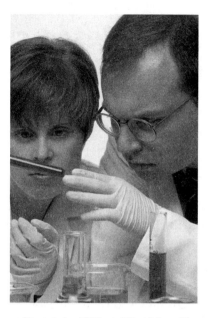

of stem cells. Gary Rosen in "What Would a Clone Say?" deplores the practice, arguing that therapeutic use of stem cells is the beginning of a slippery slope into moral gray areas that human beings do not want to enter. If we value life so little, he says, then why not clone people and harvest them for organs. What's the difference, really, he asks.

MICHAEL KINSLEY

False Dilemma on Stem Cells

Michael Kinsley is a journalist and currently a columnist for Time *magazine. Born in 1952 in Michigan, Kinsley was educated at Harvard University and worked on the school newspaper, the* Harvard Crimson. *He was awarded a Rhodes scholarship and studied at Oxford University. He then went back to Harvard for law school and eventually earned his J.D. from George Washington University. He was editor at the* New Republic *and a host on CNN's popular television show* Crossfire *for six years, representing the liberal view. In 1995 he moved to Seattle to become the founding editor of* Slate, *the online magazine. He left that position in 2002, in part because he was diagnosed with Parkinson's disease. He later went to the* Los Angeles Times *as the editorial page editor. Later he wrote a weekly column for the* Washington Post. *In July of 2006, Kinsley underwent brain surgery for his illness and survived. In this selection, published just five days before his operation, Kinsley argues that all the traditional arguments against the use of stem cells are disingenuous or miss the point.*

▶ **Prereading: Thinking about the Essay in Advance**

What do you think about using stem cells from human embryos to advance the cause of medicine? Do you think it's moral or immoral? Why? When does life begin, in your opinion: at conception, some time during pregnancy, or at birth?

▶ **Words to Watch**

objective (par. 1) without bias
analyst (par. 1) someone who picks apart an issue
ailment (par. 1) illness
conception (par. 2) fertilization of an egg by a sperm
womb (par. 3) uterus
backlash (par. 3) reaction against an event or trend
fathom (par. 9) understand at all
righteousness (par. 9) goodness
subset (par. 10) group that's part of another group

The issue of stem cell research—which is back before the Senate—is often described as a moral dilemma, but it simply is not. Or at least it is not the moral dilemma often used in media shorthand: the rights of the unborn vs. the needs of people suffering from diseases that embryonic stem cells might cure. As one of those people myself (I have Parkinson's), I am not an objective analyst of what the U. S. government's continuing near-ban on stem cell research is costing our society and the world. Naturally, I think it's costing too much. No other potential therapy—including adult stem cells—is nearly as promising for my ailment and others. Evaluate that as you wish.

Against this, you have the fact that embryonic stem cells are extracted from human embryos, killing the latter in the process. If you believe that embryos a few days after conception have the same human rights as you or me, killing innocent embryos is obviously intolerable. But do opponents of stem cell research really believe that? Stem cell research tests that belief, and sharpens the basic right-to-life question, in a way abortion never has.

Here's why. Stem cells used in medical research generally come from fertility clinics, which produce more embryos than they can use. This isn't an accident—it is essential to their mission of helping people have babies. Often these are "test tube babies": the product of an egg fertilized in the lab and then implanted in a womb to develop until birth. Controversy about test-tube babies has all but disappeared. Vague science-fiction alarms have been crushed by the practical evidence, and potential political backlash, of grateful, happy parents.

4   In any particular case, fertility clinics try to produce more embryos than they intend to implant. Then—like the Yale admissions office (only more accurately)—they pick and choose among the candidates, looking for qualities that make for a better human being. If you don't get into Yale, you have the choice of attending a different college. If the fertility clinic rejects you, you get flushed away—or maybe frozen until the day you can be discarded without controversy.

5   And fate isn't much kinder to the embryos that make this first cut. Usually several of them are implanted in the hope that one will survive. Or, to put it another way, in the hope that all but one will not survive. And fertility doctors do their ruthless best to make these hopes come true.

6   In short, if embryos are human beings with full human rights, fertility clinics are death camps—with a side order of cold-blooded eugenics. No one who truly believes in the humanity of embryos could possibly think otherwise.

7   And, by the way, when it comes to respecting the human dignity of microscopic embryos, nature—or God—is as cavalier as the most godless fertility clinic. The casual creation and destruction of embryos in normal human reproduction is one reason some people, including me, find it hard to make the necessary leap of faith to believe that an embryo and, say, Nelson Mandela are equal in the eyes of God.

8   Proponents of stem cell research like to emphasize that it doesn't cost the life of a single embryo. The embryos killed to extract their stem cells were doomed already. But this argument gives too much ground, and misses the point. If embryos are human beings, it's not okay to kill them for their stem cells just because you were going to kill them, or knowingly let them die, anyway. The better point—the killer point, if you'll pardon the expression—is that if embryos are human beings, the routine practices of fertility clinics are far worse—both in numbers and in criminal intent—than stem cell research. And yet, no one objects, or objects very loudly. President Bush actually praised the work of fertility clinics in his first speech announcing restrictions on stem cells.

9   Even strong believers in abortion rights (I'm one) ought to acknowledge and respect the moral sincerity of many right-to-lifers. I cannot share, or even fathom, their conviction that a microscopic dot—as oblivious as a rock, more primitive than a worm—has the same human rights as anyone reading this article. I don't have their problem with the question of when human life begins. (When did "human" life begin during evolution? Obviously, there is no magic point. But that doesn't prevent us from claiming humanity for ourselves and denying it to the embryo-like entities we evolved from.) Nevertheless, abortion opponents deserve respect for more than just their right to hold and express an opinion we disagree with. Excluding, of course, the small minority who believe that their righteousness puts them above the law, sincere right-to-lifers de-

serve respect as that rarity in modern American politics: a strong interest group defending the interest of someone other than themselves.

Or so I always thought—until the arrival of stem cells. Moral sincerity is not impressive if it depends on willful ignorance and indifference to logic. Not every opponent of stem cell research deserves to have his or her debater's license taken away. There are a few, no doubt, who are as horrified by fertility clinics as they are by stem cell research, and a subset of this subset may even be doing something about it. But these people, if they exist, are not a political force strong enough to stop a juggernaut of medical progress that so many other people are desperate to encourage. The vast majority of people who oppose stem cell research either haven't thought it through, or have thought it through and don't care.   10

I wish they would think again.   11

▶ Building Vocabulary

1. Kinsley's essay includes several words that come from other languages. Define each of the following words, and identify the source language.
   a. dilemma (par. 1)
   b. embryonic (par. 1)
   c. eugenics (par. 6)
   d. cavalier (par. 7)
   e. juggernaut (par. 10)
2. Identify and explain the following references, looking them up in reference works if necessary.
   a. stem cell (par. 1)
   b. Parkinson's (par. 1)
   c. death camps (par. 6)
   d. Nelson Mandela (par. 7)

▶ Thinking Critically about the Argument

Understanding the Writer's Argument

1. What is the "shorthand" the media use to frame the stem cell debate, according to Kinsley?
2. Why does Kinsley say he isn't an "objective analyst" in the debate over stem cells?
3. Why does Kinsley say that stem cell research "sharpens the basic right-to-life question, in a way abortion never has"?
4. Why has the debate over test-tube babies disappeared, according to Kinsley?
5. How, according to Kinsley, is a fertility clinic like the Yale admissions office?

6. Why does Kinsley say that nature is "cavalier" with embryos?
7. Why does Kinsley find it difficult to compare Nelson Mandela with an embryo?
8. Kinsley writes that the proponents of stem cell research miss the point when they argue that embryos killed to gather stem cells were doomed already. What does he mean?
9. Why, according to Kinsley, has his respect for right-to-lifers been shaken because of the stem cell debate?

Understanding the Writer's Technique

1. What is Kinsley's major proposition? Which sentence do you think sums up that proposition most clearly? What would you include to make that sentence more inclusive of Kinsley's entire argument?
2. How does the writer maintain a detached tone despite the fact that stem cell research could help his personal condition?
3. How does Kinsley use comparison and contrast strategies in the essay? How effective are they? How can this technique backfire? Does it here?
4. What is the effect of using only Nelson Mandela's name, and nobody else's, in the course of this essay?
5. Judge the effectiveness of paragraph 8. What do you think is the most powerful sentence in the paragraph?
6. What is the effect of Kinsley's connecting his conclusion with his introduction?
7. What is your reaction to the one-sentence last paragraph? Is it effective or not? Explain your answer.

Exploring the Writer's Argument

1. Kinsley writes in paragraph 1 that the issue of stem cells is "often described as a moral dilemma, but it simply is not. Or at least it is not the moral dilemma often used in media shorthand . . ." Do you think Kinsley thinks it is some kind of moral dilemma? How would you characterize the moral dilemma based on the essay?
2. How does God fit into Kinsley's essay? Is this an argument about religion or the uses of religion?
3. Do you think Kinsley's analogy is fair in paragraph 9 when he writes that arguing over the beginnings of the human species "doesn't prevent us from claiming humanity for ourselves and denying it to the embryo-like entities we evolved from"?

▶ Ideas for Writing Arguments

Prewriting

One of the logical conclusions one could draw from Kinsley's argument is that fertility clinics should be shut down. What do you think of this conclusion? Is it absurd? Why or why not?

Writing a Guided Argument

Write a satirical essay arguing that fertility clinics should all be shut down, using Kinsley's argument as your starting point.
1. Begin your essay with a quote from Kinsley's essay.
2. State your major proposition clearly in your first paragraph.
3. Admit that this seems like an extreme position, but that it is the sensible one.
4. Offer at least three minor propositions, drawing from Kinsley's argument.
5. Illustrate your essay with a hypothetical trip to a fertility clinic.
6. Use a combative tone, as if no other argument could reasonably be made.
7. Address at least one view of the opposition.
8. Rebut the opposition's argument.
9. Close your essay with a conclusion, followed by a one-sentence final paragraph.

Thinking, Arguing, and Writing Collaboratively

In small groups of four or five, exchange your Writing a Guided Argument papers with each member of your group. Each student should read the essays of the other students in the group, marking them up. Then each student should write a paragraph commenting on how successful the argument is. Then collect your essay from the other members and use the comments to revise your paper.

Writing about the Text

Kinsley's essay appeared in the *Washington Post*. Write an essay in which you explore why the *Post* is either a good place or a bad place to publish his essay if he's trying to convince as many people as possible to come over to his position. Include a short discussion of where you might want to publish this.

More Writing Ideas

1. Write a journal entry about your thoughts on stem cell research. Are you absolutely decided on the issue, or do you have some ambivalence? How has Kinsley influenced your position, if at all?
2. Write two or three paragraphs explaining as best you can the concept of a moral dilemma.
3. Write an essay in which you argue that stem cell research should be an issue that the states, and not the federal government, should decide. How is the banning of stem cell research unconstitutional? Or do you think the ban is protected by the Constitution?

GARY ROSEN
What Would a Clone Say?

Gary Rosen is the managing editor of Commentary *magazine, a publication that in recent years has been the home for neoconservative thought. He was senior editor of the Manhattan Institute's* City Journal. *He is the author of* American Compact: James Madison and the Problem of Founding *(1999), many articles in the* Wall Street Journal, *and he is the editor of an anthology,* The Right War? The Conservative Debate on Iraq *(2005). A graduate of Stanford University, he received his Ph.D. in political science from Harvard University in 1996. In this selection, Rosen argues that human cloning for therapeutic reasons—for example, to grow embryonic stem cells—is morally wrong.*

▶ **Prereading: Thinking about the Essay in Advance**

Do you think human cloning should be allowed? Why or why not? Is it unethical to clone humans only to the embryo stage? What if cloning humans might supply organs for people in need?

▶ **Words to Watch**

tony (par. 1) stylish and high-class
cliques (par. 1) small, insular groups that exclude others
furtive (par. 1) in a way that appears to be hiding something
nascent (par. 6) not fully formed, in the process of becoming
Bible-thumper (par. 7) someone evangelizing loudly and intrusively
injunction (par. 7) order to stop doing something
meliorative (par. 7) in a way as to make something better
skirmish (par. 8) fight
petri dish (par. 9) a dish used in a laboratory used to grow bacterial cultures

You know from the start that there's something creepy about Kathy H.,   1
the narrator of *Never Let Me Go*, Kazuo Ishiguro's recent and widely
acclaimed coming-of-age novel. Though Kathy's fond memories of ado-
lescence are set at a tony English boarding school, with its cliques and
pranks and furtive hookups, it's clear that she is not child of privilege. As
we learn to our dismay, she and her peers are clones—members of a caste
created and trained for no other purpose than to provide healthy organs
for the sick and feeble.

Genetic duplicates are hardly new to literature and pop culture—   2
think of Huxley's worker-drone Epsilons in *Brave New World*—but Ishiguro's protagonist is different. Despite the novel's fantastic premise and
Kathy's gruesome lot, she is unmistakably a person—not a monster or a
menace or a comic device but a young woman struggling to figure out
who she is and what she wants. *Never Let Me Go* is something of a cultural
landmark: a subtle, sympathetic portrait of the inner life of a clone.

The imaginative leap that Ishiguro takes is instructive. Today most   3
people condemn the very thought of cloning for reproduction—that is, to
make a child. But with the exception of the religious right, Americans increasingly embrace cloning for research, with its promise of miracle cures
for our most debilitating ills. Ishiguro's tale flips this emerging consensus
on its head. What's upsetting about Kathy isn't her existence as a clone
but rather the fate that has been assigned to her: to die young, used up for
the medical benefit of others. She is at once a literary protest against research cloning and, by virtue of her strength as a character, a quiet sug-
gestion that reproductive cloning may not be so troubling after all.

A bill now before Congress would allow federally financed stem-cell   4
research on embryos that would otherwise be thrown out by fertility clinics. Abortion foes hope to head off the legislation with their own propos-
als encouraging alternate sources of stem cells. But all of this is just a
warm-up. The issue hovering in the background is cloning, what scientists call somatic cell nuclear transfer (S.C.N.T.). For researchers in the
field, as well as for the various interests that lobby on their behalf—universities, patient groups, the biotech industry—the real prize is public
support for work not just on "spare" embryos but also on cloned ones.

Embryonic stem cells can develop into almost any of the body's spe-   5
cialized cells, a capacity that gives them enormous therapeutic potential
(as yet unrealized) for the treatment of diseases like Alzheimer's and diabetes. They might also make it possible to cultivate new tissue for failing
organs. Researchers fear, however, that the immune systems of would-be
patients will reject stem cells whose DNA is foreign to them. How to solve
the problem? By drawing stem cells from embryonic clones of the patients themselves.

This is a far cry, of course, from the system of organ farming that   6
furnishes the horrifying backdrop of *Never Let Me Go*. The nascent being

destroyed in research cloning is no larger than the dot atop this printed "i"—not a fetus and certainly not a baby. Indeed, advocates like the Coalition for the Advancement of Medical Research have energetically denounced any cloning that might result in reproduction. The one "clear, bright line" that shouldn't be crossed, said the group's president, is the "implantation" of a clone in a woman's uterus.

7   Still, you don't have to be a raving Bible-thumper to entertain moral doubts about so-called therapeutic cloning ("therapeutic," that is, for potential patients; not such a great deal for the embryos). All you need is a bit of Kant from Ethics 101, especially the part about treating other people, presumably even proto-people, not as a means to your own ends but as ends in themselves. It is an injunction hard to square with the literature on S.C.N.T., with its talk of "harvesting" and "programming" stem cells. The language of the scientists and their supporters is clinical, meliorative and humane, but it gives off an unmistakable whiff of cannibalism.

8   Some see the cloning debate as just another skirmish in the abortion war. After all, if it is permissible to abort an embryo, what could be wrong with putting it to some lifesaving use instead? But abortion is an ordeal unsought by the woman who faces it, a tragedy of circumstance. There is, by contrast, nothing accidental or contingent about creating nascent human life with the declared aim of destroying it. It is the deliberate use of one (developing) person as the instrument of another, a practice that should give pause even to those who ardently favor abortion rights.

9   As for Ishiguro's doomed Kathy H., is she a proto-type of future clones? Certainly not in the harsh fate she suffers as a "donor." No one is going to deny the rights of a clone that escapes the petri dish, which helps to explain why the proponents of research cloning so noisily forswear any intention of producing babies. The first actual child born of S.C.N.T. will make it that much more difficult to treat other clones as raw material for experimentation.

10   What may most surprise us about that first child is its ordinariness. Critics worry that clones will be grotesque puppets, the manufactured playthings of their creators, lacking all individuality. But Ishiguro allows us to glimpse a different possibility. Though Kathy is a genetic duplicate, she is nobody's double or distorted reflection. She is her own person, indeed a young woman of growing self-awareness and independence. If she really existed, she might even be in Washington just now, raising her voice against the evils of therapeutic cloning.

▶ Building Vocabulary

1. In this essay, Rosen uses several literary terms and references. Identify the following and write an explanation of each.

    a. Kazuo Ishiguro (par 1)
    b. coming-of-age novel (par. 1)
    c. "Brave New World" (par. 2)
    d. protagonist (par. 2)
    e. comic device (par. 2)
    f. Kant (par. 7)
2. Write definitions and your own sentences for the following words:
    a. caste (par. 1)
    b. premise (par. 2)
    c. capacity (par. 5)
    d. furnishes (par. 6)
    e. denounced (par. 6)
    f. humane (par. 7)
    g. contingent (par. 8)
    h. forswear (par. 9)
    i. grotesque (par. 10)

▶Thinking Critically about the Argument

Understanding the Writer's Argument

1. Why does Rosen think that the "imaginative leap that Ishiguro takes is instructive"? Instructive of what?
2. Rosen says that the argument between abortion supporters and abortion foes over the use of embryonic stem cells is a "warm-up" for the big fight. What is this big fight he sees coming?
3. What, according to Rosen, are scientists concerned about when it comes to using embryonic stem cells in therapies?
4. What does Rosen think is the most reasonable argument from the world of philosophy against the use of therapeutic cloning?
5. What does Rosen see is wrong about the language scientists use when talking about cloning?
6. What does Rosen think is the moral distinction between using an embryo from an abortion and using one that has been cloned?

Understanding the Writer's Technique

1. Why does Rosen start his argument with a discussion of a novel that you and other readers might not have read? Is this an effective strategy? Why or why not?
2. What is Rosen's major proposition in this essay? Where does he state it most clearly? Why does it appear where it does?
3. Who is the ideal audience for this selection, do you think? What is the tone of the essay? How does the tone fit the audience?

4. Why does Rosen use the scientific term "S.C.N.T." rather than just us- ing the word "cloning"? What is the rhetorical effect on the reader?
5. What is the effect on the reader of Rosen's use of Kant? Who was Kant?
6. Why does Rosen close his essay by imagining a cloned person fight- ing for her rights? What is the effect on the reader?

Exploring the Writer's Argument

1. Rosen uses Kazuo Ishiguro's novel *Never Let Me Go* (2005) as the jumping-off point for his argument, but it's unclear if Ishiguro would agree with Rosen's reading of his book. Are there any points you think Ishiguro might disagree with that Rosen takes for granted? Ex- plain your answer.
2. Where in the essay does Rosen's language or tone seem objectionable or at least uncivil? Why has he chosen such an approach?
3. Rosen writes, "Some see the cloning debate as just another skirmish in the abortion war." Do you agree with this statement? Why or why not?

►Ideas for Writing Arguments

Prewriting

Do a focused 10- to 15-minute freewrite about the ethical problems facing reproductive cloning, that is, cloning people with the object of producing children.

Writing a Guided Argument

Write an essay in which you argue that reproductive cloning should or should not be legalized.

1. Begin with a definition of reproductive cloning and how it works. Check reliable external resources in books or journals and (or) the Web.
2. Finish your introduction with your major proposition in which you state clearly which side of the argument you are on.
3. Indicate the arguments of critics on the opposite side of your argu- ment. Be fair in your presentation.
4. Explain why the opposition is wrong, and why your position on cloning is correct.
5. Affect a tone of compassionate urgency in your essay.
6. End your essay by citing expert testimony that supports your view.

Thinking, Arguing, and Writing Collaboratively

Split your class into two groups, and organize a debate. One side will argue for therapeutic cloning, and the other will argue against it. Vote within your group for a team leader who will begin an initial discussion on the topic and assign small groups to do research. and determine who will make which arguments. Then, after the debate, write a short paper about the presentation by the group you found more convincing. How did the group convince you? What strategies were most effective?

Writing about the Text

Rosen's argument seems a little muddled in that he treats together the ideas of cloning for reproduction and cloning for therapeutic reasons. Write an essay in which you argue that Rosen is purposefully, for rhetorical reasons, conflating the two ideas.

More Writing Ideas

1. In your journal, write an entry about whether you think Rosen's use of the term "cannibalism" in paragraph 7 is fair.
2. Write two or three paragraphs about other technologies that seemed unethical when they were first introduced, but soon came to seem obviously ethical.
3. Read Kazuo Ishiguro's novel *Never Let Me Go* and write an essay in which you argue whether the novelist would agree with Rosen's position in "What Would a Clone Say?"

9 ▸ The Death Penalty: Should We Take a Human Life?

D oes a government have the right to put one of its citizens to death for any reason? Does the death penalty violate the "cruel and unusual" punishment clause in the Eighth Amendment of the U.S. Constitution?

After World War II, many European and industrialized nations signed the *Universal Declaration of Human Rights* and banned the death penalty within their borders. The United States, however, kept the death penalty. The debate has intensified in this country over the fairness and humaneness of the punishment. One argument focuses on whether it is fair to execute a convict who is mentally ill or retarded. Another highlights the fact that a disproportionate number of people on death row are African-Americans. A question here remains: Are blacks punished with execution more frequently than whites, and if so, why, and what does that say about our use of the death penalty? One other objection to capital punishment is that humans administer it and humans make mistakes. Innocent people have gone to their death.

Defenders of the death penalty, however, say that besides being a deterrent to people who might commit capital crimes in the future, execution fulfills a need by society for retribution—the public demands and deserves to see wrongdoers punished severely.

In the selections that follow, Terry Golway deals with the issue of people unjustly convicted of murder. David Gelernter, who was almost killed by a mail bomb sent by the Unabomber (a secretive terrorist who sent bombs by mail at the end of the 20th century), argues that we should administer the death penalty as the triumph of rationality over emotion. What do you think about the topic? As you read these two selections, consider why you feel the way you do about the death penalty. Is there a rational way to approach the subject, or are arguments only accessible through the emotions? How does that question affect these essays? In Part V, you can read another selection about capital punishment. In the renowned essay "A Hanging," George Orwell, writing in the early 1930s, expresses his disgust for executions by showing one to his readers. His vivid and carefully chosen descriptions evoke a feeling of moral decay.

TERRY GOLWAY
Wrongly Convicted?

Terry Golway teaches U.S. history at Kean University in Union, New Jersey. He is the author of For the Cause of Liberty: A Thousand Years of Ireland's Heroes *(2000),* So Others Might Live: A History of New York's Bravest—The FDNY from 1700 to the Present *(2002),* Washington's General: Nathanael Greene and the Triumph of the American Revolution *(2004), and other books. In this selection, published in* America, *the "National Catholic Weekly," where he has been a columnist since 1995, Golway argues that not only is it possible for people to be wrongly convicted of crimes; it also happens all the time. For this simple reason, the death penalty, he says, doesn't make sense.*

▶ Prereading: Thinking about the Essay in Advance

Do you think the argument that some people are wrongly convicted is a good enough reason to abolish the death penalty? Has DNA testing changed your opinion? If so, how?

▶ Words to Watch

ordeal (par. 4) difficult experience
unseemly (par. 6) improper or inappropriate
successive (par. 8) following in order
cleared (par. 9) freed of guilt
gratitude (par. 10) feeling of being thankful
proposition (par. 11) statement of opinion
import (par. 13) significance

1   Scott Fappiano spent more than 20 years in prison in New York. He was convicted of a brutal crime in 1985—the rape of a woman married to a police officer in Brooklyn.

2   His trial was not exactly open and shut. Although the victim identified Fappiano as her attacker by looking at photographs, he was, in fact, about five inches shorter than the man she had described, and he had shorter hair. Extensive blood tests failed to establish any connection between Fappiano and the crime. Nevertheless, in 1985 he was convicted of the crime and sentenced to 50 years.

3   He is free today because a group called the Innocence Project took up his case, demanded DNA testing and proved what Fappiano had said all along: he was innocent. The State of New York, which had custody of him for nearly half of his 44 years on earth, released him earlier this year.

What do you say when you have spent more than 20 years in prison   4
for a crime you didn't commit? Scott Fappiano simply said he was glad
his ordeal was over and that the injustice had come to an end. His 69-
year-old mother said she felt that her son had been kidnapped, but finally
had returned.

In a sense, he was kidnapped—an innocent person taken away   5
against his will by an imperfect justice system, imperfect because it is administered by flawed human beings who probably get it right most of the
time but clearly not all of the time.

Scott Fappiano received a long sentence for a crime he did not com-   6
mit. How many prisoners in the United States today have received a far
worse sentence—death—for crimes they did not commit? At a time when
Americans have embraced the death penalty with unseemly enthusiasm,
this question ought to haunt prosecutors, judges and juries.

Death penalty advocates argue that the system has built-in checks   7
and procedures that nearly eliminate the chance that an innocent person
could be convicted of a capital crime and sentenced to death. But is that
really the case?

In 1991 a man named Jeffrey Mark Deskovic was convicted of raping   8
and murdering a young woman in Peekskill, NY. New York did not have
a death-penalty statute at the time because two successive New York governors, Hugh Carey and Mario Cuomo, vetoed death-penalty legislation
annually. Had they not done so, Jeffrey Mark Deskovic surely would have
received a death sentence.

But he did not commit that crime. He maintained his innocence for   9
years and asked the local prosecutor, Jeanine Pirro, to examine DNA evidence that he believed would prove his case. The prosecutor's office declined to do so. But earlier this year, the Innocence Project took up
Deskovic's case, a new prosecutor looked at the DNA evidence, and
Deskovic was cleared of the crime after spending 15 years in prison.

Without the support of the Innocence Project, Deskovic, Fappiano   10
and other wrongly convicted people in New York and elsewhere might
still be in prison. The staff and lawyers of this not-for-profit legal clinic
deserve the gratitude of all who pray for justice, for the clinic's mission is
nothing less than the overturning of injustice. In the last year alone, the
Innocence Project has helped free five prisoners wrongly convicted of
murder in New York.

The Innocence Project relies on DNA evidence to return the unjustly   11
convicted to freedom. Since 1989 nearly 200 people have been released,
because of DNA evidence, from prison for crimes they did not commit.
The Innocence Project is pushing for the routine collection of genetic material from convicted felons. That seemingly sensible proposition, however, has drawn some opposition from civil libertarians, who fear the
growth of government-maintained DNA databases.

12   With two million people serving time in American prisons, the Innocence Project's mission could hardly be more urgent. How many of those
two million have been wrongly convicted? The number certainly is small,
but the presence of even one innocent person in prison mocks the very
notion of justice. Once imprisoned, as Deskovic discovered, inmates and
their continued pleas of innocence generally go unheard. Judges, prosecutors and the public at large generally do not regard convicted felons as
sympathetic or credible figures.

13   All of this, of course, takes on even greater import when the death
penalty becomes part of the equation. We know, thanks to the Innocence
Project, that people have been wrongly convicted of crimes. Shouldn't
that give death penalty supporters pause? Do they believe that the system
is flawless, or do they believe that the occasional innocent executed in the
name of justice is the tragic price we must pay for law and order?

14   After Deskovic was released earlier this year, Barry Scheck, a lawyer
who has been one of the driving forces behind the Innocence Project, directed his remarks to death penalty supporters. "This is the fifth man to
be exonerated in a murder case in New York State in the past 10 months,"
he noted. "And for all those who are thinking that it might be a good idea
to reinstate capital punishment in this state, please, please, please look at
the evidence in front of you."

15   The evidence in front of New Yorkers—in front of all of us—was a
live human being wrongly sent to prison for a murder he didn't commit
He lost 15 years of his life thanks to a miscarriage of justice.

16   But at least he did not lose his life. Do we really wish to take that risk?

▶ Building Vocabulary

This selection assumes a general familiarity with terms related to the legal
system. Identify and write definitions for the following:
1. open and shut (par. 2)
2. convicted (par. 2)
3. custody (par. 3)
4. administered (par. 5)
5. prosecutors (par. 6)
6. advocates (par. 7)
7. capital crime (par. 7)
8. statute (par. 8)
9. legislation (par. 8)
10. legal clinic (par. 10)
11. felons (par. 11)
12. civil libertarians (par. 11)
13. exonerated (par. 14)
14. reinstate (par. 14)
15. miscarriage of justice (par. 15)

▶ Thinking Critically about the Argument

Understanding the Writer's Argument

1. Why was Scott Fappiano convicted of his crime? Why was he eventually released from prison?
2. Why does Golway (and Fappiano's mother) say that Fappiano was "kidnapped"?
3. According to Golway, how do death penalty advocates defend the system?
4. What happened to Jeffrey Mark Deskovic?
5. What is the Innocence Project, and what does it do?
6. Who objects to what the Innocence Project is doing, and what is their objection?
7. What is the point Barry Scheck makes in paragraph 14?

Understanding the Writer's Techniques

1. Why does Golway open his essay with the story of Scott Fappiano?
2. What is the writer's major proposition? Where does he state it most clearly?
3. In paragraph 6, Golway writes that the question of how many other innocent people had been sentenced to death "ought to haunt prosecutors, judges, and juries." What is he implying here?
4. Write an outline of Golway's argument. Why does he use this kind of order to make his argument?
5. Golway uses several rhetorical questions in his essay. What is the effect of these questions?
6. Why does Golway tell the stories of both Scott Fappiano and Jeffrey Mark Deskovic?
7. Why does Golway end his essay with a brief, two-sentence paragraph? What is the rhetorical effect of this?

Exploring the Writer's Argument

1. Does Golway do a good enough job evoking emotion in his readers? Did you have an emotional reaction to this essay? Why or why not, in your opinion? How could you make his essay more emotional?
2. How does Golway make the case that the justice system in the United States is both perfect and flawed? Explain.
3. In his essay, David Gelernter writes about our administration of the death penalty, "That we are botching things does not entitle us to give up." He means that even though the way we use the penalty is not perfect, we still should use it. What would Golway say to that statement?

▶ Ideas for Writing Arguments

Prewriting

Some states have issued moratoriums on the death penalty—orders that say that no executions can be carried out—because of the possibility that innocent people can be executed. What do you think? Should states put a hold on their executions until some later date?

Writing a Guided Argument

In 2000, Illinois Governor George Ryan, a Republican and former supporter of the death penalty, instituted a moratorium on all executions. Thirteen inmates on death row had had their convictions overturned. From 1977 to 2000, Illinois put 12 people to death and released 13 because they were found to be innocent. Write an essay in which you argue that all states should or should not do the same. You might need to do some research to learn about the various arguments for either side and to gather narrative evidence.

1. Open your essay with the story of a convicted murderer.
2. Use a proper and effective transition to move into a well-articulated major proposition.
3. Have at least two reasons of your own to back up your position and express them as minor propositions.
4. Support your ideas with facts taken from your research.
5. Support one of your reasons with another narrative culled from your research.
6. Explain to your reader where you got your narrative evidence.
7. Rebut the opposing view with a recapitulation of your points.
8. Close your essay with an appeal to the reader's emotions.

Thinking, Arguing, and Writing Collaboratively

Divide into three equal groups. Each group should prepare for a debate on the use of the death penalty. You may conduct research in the library or online. The aim of your research and preparation should be to develop arguments for your position. Stage the debate so that the groups only find out on the day of the debate which side they are arguing for. One group should argue for the death penalty, the second against it, and the third should act as the jury. After an opening statement from each group, each member of the debating groups should have a chance to make one argument for his or her side, followed by a rebuttal from the other side. After everyone takes a turn, the jury will vote on the winner and explain its decision to the class.

Writing about the Text

Write an essay about Golway's style in this essay. How does his use of questions help (or hinder) his rhetorical approach? How effective are the many short paragraphs?

More Writing Ideas

1. In your journal, write about what somone falsely accused of a murder could do.
2. In the next essay, David Gelernter writes that "we execute murderers in order to make a communal proclamation: that murder is intolerable. A deliberate murderer embodies evil so terrible that it defiles the community." Write a few paragraphs in which you explore the notion that the state is included in the category "deliberate murderer."
3. Write an essay in which you argue for or against the death penalty based solely on ethical grounds. If you need to, you should do some research into the subject of ethics.

DAVID GELERNTER
What Do Murderers Deserve?

David Gelernter is a professor of computer science at Yale. In 1991 he published a book, Mirror Worlds, *that some say predicted the Internet. In 1993, he was the victim of a letter bomb, and survived, but he had a long rehabilitation period. He is a leading figure in the field of artificial intelligence. He is the author of* The Muse in the Machine *(1994),* 1939: The Lost World of the Fair *(1995),* Drawing a Life: Surviving the Unabomber *(1997), and* Americanism: The Fourth Great Western Religion *(2007). His near-death experience informs this selection, in which he discusses what punishment murderers, including his would-be murderer (who did succeed in taking the lives of three people), deserve.*

▶ Prereading: Thinking about the Essay in Advance

Why does a country have the right to execute one of its citizens? What is the political rationale for keeping the death penalty?

▶ Words to Watch

penitent (par. 1) those who ask for forgiveness
defiles (par. 4) morally stains
equivocation (par. 6) lack of commitment
reverting (par. 9) returning

inclination (par. 10) tendency
sanctity (par. 14) holiness
capricious (par. 15) impulsive
faculties (par. 18) abilities
bestiality (par. 22) animal-like behavior
smitten (par. 24) attacked

1   No civilized nation ever takes the death penalty for granted; two recent cases force us to consider it yet again. A Texas woman, Karla Faye Tucker, murdered two people with a pickaxe, was said to have repented in prison, and was put to death. A Montana man, Theodore Kaczynski, murdered three people with mail bombs, did not repent, and struck a bargain with the Justice Department; he pleaded guilty and will not be executed. (He also attempted to murder others and succeeded in wounding some, myself included.) Why did we execute the penitent and spare the impenitent? However we answer this question, we surely have a duty to ask it.

2   And we ask it—I do, anyway—with a sinking feeling, because in modern America, moral upside-downness is a specialty of the house. To eliminate race prejudice we discriminate by race. We promote the cultural assimilation of immigrant children by denying them schooling in English. We throw honest citizens in jail for child abuse, relying on testimony so phony any child could see through it. Orgasm studies are okay in public high schools but the Ten Commandments are not. We make a point of admiring manly women and womanly men. None of which has anything to do with capital punishment directly, but it all obliges us to approach any question about morality in modern America in the larger context of this country's desperate confusion about elementary distinctions.

3   Why execute murderers? To deter? To avenge? Supporters of the death penalty often give the first answer, opponents the second. But neither can be the whole truth. If our main goal were deterring crime, we would insist on public executions—which are not on the political agenda, and not an item that many Americans are interested in promoting. If our main goal were vengeance, we would allow the grieving parties to decide the murderer's fate; if the victim had no family or friends to feel vengeful on his behalf, we would call the whole thing off.

4   In fact, we execute murderers in order to make a communal proclamation: that murder is intolerable. A deliberate murderer embodies evil so terrible that it defiles the community. Thus the late social philosopher Robert Nisbet: "Until a catharsis has been effected through trial, through the finding of guilt and then punishment, the community is anxious, fearful, apprehensive, and above all, contaminated."

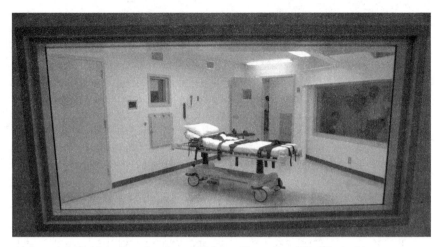

Alabama's lethal injection chamber at Holman Correctional Facility in Atmore, Alabama. (Dave Martin/AP images)

Individual citizens have a right and sometimes a duty to speak. A   5
community has the right, too, and sometimes the duty. The community
certifies births and deaths, creates marriages, educates children, fights
invaders. In laws, deeds, and ceremonies it lays down the boundary
lines of civilized life, lines that are constantly getting scuffed and needing renewal.

When a murder takes place, the community is obliged, whether it   6
feels like it or not, to clear its throat and step up to the microphone.
Every murder demands a communal response. Among possible responses, the death penalty is uniquely powerful because it is permanent
and can never be retracted or overturned. An execution forces the community to assume forever the burden of moral certainty; it is a form of
absolute speech that allows no waffling or equivocation. Deliberate murder, the community announces, is absolutely evil and absolutely intolerable, period.

Of course, we could make the same point less emphatically if we   7
wanted to—for example, by locking up murderers for life (as we sometimes do). The question then becomes: is the death penalty overdoing it?
Should we make a less forceful proclamation instead?

The answer might be yes if we were a community in which murder   8
was a shocking anomaly and thus in effect a solved problem. But we are
not. Our big cities are full of murderers at large. "One can guesstimate,"
writes the criminologist and political scientist John J. DiIulio, Jr., "that we
are nearing or may already have passed the day when 500,000 murderers,
convicted and undetected, are living in American society."

DiIulio's statistics show an approach to murder so casual as to be de-   9
praved. We are reverting to a pre-civilized state of nature. Our natural

bent in the face of murder is not to avenge the crime but to shrug it off, except in those rare cases when our own near and dear are involved. (And even then, it depends.)

10   This is an old story. Cain murders Abel and is brought in for questioning: where is Abel, your brother? The suspect's response: how should I know? "What am I, my brother's keeper?" It is one of the very first statements attributed to mankind in the Bible; voiced here by an interested party, it nonetheless expresses a powerful and universal inclination. Why mess in other people's problems? And murder is always, in the most immediate sense, someone else's problem, because the injured party is dead.

11   Murder in primitive societies called for a private settling of scores. The community as a whole stayed out of it. For murder to count, as it does in the Bible, as a crime not merely against one man but against the whole community and against God—that was a moral triumph that is still basic to our integrity, and that is never to be taken for granted. By executing murderers, the community reaffirms this moral understanding by restating the truth that absolute evil exists and must be punished.

12   Granted (some people say), the death penalty is a communal proclamation; it is nevertheless an incoherent one. If our goal is to affirm that human life is more precious than anything else, how can we make such a declaration by destroying life?

13   But declaring that human life is more precious than anything else is not our goal in imposing the death penalty. Nor is the proposition true. The founding fathers pledged their lives (and fortunes and sacred honor) to the cause of freedom; Americans have traditionally believed that some things are more precious than life. ("Living in a sanitary age, we are getting so we place too high a value on human life—which rightfully must always come second to human ideas." Thus E.B. White in 1938, pondering the Munich pact ensuring "peace in our time" between the Western powers and Hitler.) The point of capital punishment is not to pronounce on life in general but on the crime of murder.

14   Which is not to say that the sanctity of human life does not enter the picture. Taking a life, says the Talmud (in the course of discussing Cain and Abel), is equivalent to destroying a whole world. The rabbis used this statement to make a double point: to tell us why murder is the gravest of crimes, and to warn against false testimony in a murder trial. But to believe in the sanctity of human life does not mean, and the Talmud does not say it means, that capital punishment is ruled out.

15   A newer objection grows out of the seemingly random way in which we apply capital punishment. The death penalty might be a reasonable communal proclamation in principle, some critics say, but it has become so garbled in practice that it has lost all significance and ought to be dropped. DiIulio writes that "the ratio of persons murdered to persons executed for murder from 1977 to 1996 was in the ballpark of 1,000 to 1";

the death penalty has become in his view "arbitrary and capricious," a "state lottery" that is "unjust both as a matter of Judeo-Christian ethics and as a matter of American citizenship."

We can grant that, on the whole, we are doing a disgracefully bad job 16 of administering the death penalty. After all, we are divided and confused on the issue. The community at large is strongly in favor of capital punishment; the cultural elite is strongly against it. Our attempts to speak with assurance as a community come out sounding in consequence like a man who is fighting off a choke-hold as he talks. But a community as cavalier about murder as we are has no right to back down. That we are botching things does not entitle us to give up.

Opponents of capital punishment tend to describe it as a surrender to 17 our emotions—to grief, rage, fear, blood lust. For most supporters of the death penalty, this is exactly false. Even when we resolve in principle to go ahead, we have to steel ourselves. Many of us would find it hard to kill a dog, much less a man. Endorsing capital punishment means not that we yield to our emotions but that we overcome them. (Immanuel Kant, the great advocate of the death penalty precisely on moral grounds, makes this point in his reply to the anticapital-punishment reformer Cesare Beccaria—accusing Beccaria of being "moved by sympathetic sentimentality and an affectation of humanitarianism.") If we favor executing murderers it is not because we want to but because, however much we do not want to, we consider ourselves obliged to.

Many Americans, of course, no longer feel that obligation. The death 18 penalty is hard for us as a community above all because of our moral evasiveness. For at least a generation, we have urged one another to switch off our moral faculties. "Don't be judgmental!" We have said it so many times, we are starting to believe it.

The death penalty is a proclamation about absolute evil, but many of us 19 are no longer sure that evil even exists. We define evil out of existence by calling it "illness"—a tendency Aldous Huxley anticipated in his novel *Brave New World* (1932) and Robert Nisbet wrote about in 1982: "America has lost the villain, the evil one, who has now become one of the sick, the disturbed. . . . America has lost the moral value of guilt, lost it to the sickroom."

Our refusal to look evil in the face is no casual notion; it is a powerful 20 drive. Thus we have (for example) the terrorist Theodore Kaczynski, who planned and carried out a hugely complex campaign of violence with a clear goal in mind. It was the goal most terrorists have: to get famous and not die. He wanted public attention for his ideas about technology; he figured he could get it by attacking people with bombs.

He was right. His plan succeeded. It is hard to imagine a more compelling proof of mental competence than this planning and carrying out 21 over decades of a complex, rational strategy. (Evil, yes; irrational, no; they are different things.) The man himself has said repeatedly that he is perfectly sane, knew what he was doing, and is proud of it.

22   To call such a man insane seems to me like deliberate perversity. But many people do. Some of them insist that his thoughts about technology constitute "delusions," though every terrorist holds strong beliefs that are wrong, and many nonterrorists do, too. Some insist that sending bombs through the mail is ipso facto proof of insanity—as if the 20th century had not taught us that there is no limit to the bestiality of which sane men are capable.

23   Where does this perversity come from? I said earlier that the community at large favors the death penalty, but intellectuals and the cultural elite tend to oppose it. This is not (I think) because they abhor killing more than other people do, but because the death penalty represents absolute speech from a position of moral certainty, and doubt is the black-lung disease of the intelligentsia—an occupational hazard now inflicted on the culture as a whole.

24   American intellectuals have long differed from the broader community—particularly on religion, crime and punishment, education, family, the sexes, race relations, American history, taxes and public spending, the size and scope of government, art, the environment, and the military. (Otherwise, I suppose, they and the public have been in perfect accord.) But not until the late '60s and '70s were intellectuals finally in a position to act on their convictions. Whereupon they attacked the community's moral certainties with the enthusiasm of guard dogs leaping at throats.* The result is an American community smitten with the disease of intellectual doubt—or, in this case, self-doubt.

25   The failure of our schools is a consequence of our self-doubt, of our inability to tell children that learning is not fun and they are required to master certain topics whether they want to or not. The tortured history of modern American race relations grows out of our self-doubt; we passed a civil-rights act in 1964, then lost confidence immediately in our ability to make a race-blind society work; racial preferences codify our refusal to believe in our own good faith. During the late stages of the cold war, many Americans laughed at the idea that the American way was morally superior or the Soviet Union was an "evil empire"; some are still laughing. Within their own community and the American community at large, doubting intellectuals have taken refuge (as doubters often do) in bullying, to the point where many of us are now so uncomfortable at the prospect of confronting evil that we turn away and change the subject.

26   Returning then to the penitent woman and the impenitent man: the Karla Faye Tucker case is the harder of the two. We are told that she repented of the vicious murders she committed. If that is true, we would still have had no business forgiving her, or forgiving any murderer. As Dennis Prager has written apropos this case, only the victim is entitled to

---

*I have written about this before in "How the Intellectuals Took Over (And What to Do About It)," *Commentary*, March 1997.

forgive, and the victim is silent. But showing mercy to penitents is part of our religious tradition, and I cannot imagine renouncing it categorically.

Why was Cain not put to death, but condemned instead to wander 27
the earth forever? Among the answers given by the rabbis in the Midrash is that he repented. The moral category of repentance is so important, they said, that it was created before the world itself. I would therefore consider myself morally obligated to think long and hard before execut-ing a penitent. But a true penitent would have to have renounced (as Karla Faye Tucker did) all legal attempts to overturn the original convic-tion. If every legal avenue has been tried and has failed, the penitence window is closed. Of course, this still leaves the difficult problem of telling counterfeit penitence from the real thing, but everything associ-ated with capital punishment is difficult.

As for Kaczynski, the prosecutors who accepted the murderer's plea- 28
bargain say they got the best outcome they could, under the circumstances, and I believe them. But I also regard this failure to execute a cold-blooded impenitent terrorist murderer as a tragic abdication of moral responsibility. The tragedy lies in what, under our confused system, the prosecutors felt compelled to do. The community was called on to speak unambiguously. It flubbed its lines, shrugged its shoulders, and walked away.

Which brings me back to our moral condition as a community. I can 29
describe our plight better in artistic than in philosophical terms. The most vivid illustrations I know of self-doubt and its consequences are the paintings and sculptures of Alberto Giacometti (who died in 1966). Gia-cometti was an artist of great integrity; he was consumed by intellectual and moral self-doubt, which he set down faithfully. His sculpted figures show elongated, shriveled human beings who seem corroded by acid, eaten-up to the bone, hurt and weakened past fragility nearly to death. They are painful to look at. And they are natural emblems of modern America. We ought to stick one on top of the Capitol and think it over.

In executing murderers, we declare that deliberate murder is ab- 30
solutely evil and absolutely intolerable. This is a painfully difficult procla-mation for a self-doubting community to make. But we dare not stop try-ing. Communities may exist in which capital punishment is no longer the necessary response to deliberate murder. America today is not one of them.

▶ Building Vocabulary

1. In this essay, Gelernter uses several words and phrases that derive from other languages. Look up the following and write a definition for each:
   a. catharsis (par. 4)
   b. anomaly (par. 8)
   c. cavalier (par. 16)
   d. ipso facto (par. 22)

e. apropos (par. 26)
f. abdication (par. 28)
2. Identify and define the following:
  a. assimilation (par. 2)
  b. retracted (par. 6)
  c. depraved (par. 9)
  d. integrity (par. 11)
  e. incoherent (par. 12)
  f. evasiveness (par. 18)
  g. abhor (par. 23)
  h. plea-bargain (par. 28)

▶Thinking Critically about the Argument

Understanding the Writer's Argument

1. Why does the writer choose the Tucker and Kaczynski cases to start his essay? Why does he think that in modern America, "moral up-side-downness is a specialty of the house"? Explain this quote.
2. What is the rationale for executing murderers, according to Gelernter?
3. Why does John DiIulio's statistic in paragraph 8 "show an approach to murder so casual as to be depraved"?
4. How does the writer characterize the progress in crime and punishment from primitive society to today? (par. 11) What does he say to the objection that capital punishment is not administered effectively?
5. What is "bloodlust"? In your own words, summarize Gelernter's answer to the objection that being a supporter of the death penalty is "bloodlust."
6. What is perverse about calling a murderer insane? (par. 22)
7. Why is "self-doubt" such a problem in the United States, according to the writer?
8. What do Giacometti's sculptures have to do with the death penalty?

Understanding the Writer's Techniques

1. What sentence best states Gelernter's major proposition? What is his major argumentative purpose in this essay? Is he trying to convince the reader? Explain.
2. Paraphrase the argument in paragraph 3.
3. What is the writer's overall tone? How and why does he develop this tone? Who is his audience?
4. What is the persuasive effect of the writer's argument in paragraph 9? Does it work? Explain your answer.

5. Analyze the writer's use of quotes from other writers. How well does he succeed in using them to advance his own claim?
6. Do you find effective the writer's argument in paragraph 13, that life isn't always the most precious thing? Explain.
7. Does paragraph 14 find the writer backing off from the earlier argument? Why or why not?
8. How effective is the conclusion?

Exploring the Writer's Argument

1. Analyze Gelernter's argument in paragraph 16. Do you think that his point is valid? Why or why not? What do you think of this statement: "That we are botching things does not entitle us to give up"? Do you think he's right? Explain.
2. Gelernter says that America is morally upside-down. He cites, for one, the fact that we try to right racial discrimination by affirmative action. Isn't calling for the death for murderers just as morally upside-down? Does he address this issue sufficiently? Explain your answers.
3. Gelernter was the victim of attempted murder by the hands of Theodore Kaczynski. To what degree do you think Gelernter's argument is affected by his experience? Explain your answer, addressing specifically the section in paragraphs 20 through 22.

▶ Ideas for Writing Arguments

Prewriting

Freewrite for 15 minutes about the difference between your emotions about the death penalty and your intellectual consideration of the subject. Which do you trust more? Why?

Writing a Guided Argument

The Unabomber, Kaczynski, almost killed Gelernter and succeeded in killing three people. Investigate the Unabomber case and his trial. Why, despite the fact that Kaczynski never repented, did he not get the death penalty for his premeditated crimes? Write an essay in which you argue that it was right that he was spared and got the punishment he deserved, or that he should have been executed. Address Gelernter's statement in paragraph 28 that the community "flubbed its lines, shrugged its shoulders, and walked away."

1. Begin your essay with a summary of the case.
2. State your major proposition clearly.
3. Establish a tone of objectivity throughout your essay, while still being persuasive.
4. Offer at least three well-placed minor propositions to support your major proposition.
5. Support your minor propositions with examples and facts.
6. Refer to Gelernter's essay and argument at least twice.
7. Build up to what you think is your strongest minor proposition.
8. Close your essay with a classical argument for or against the death penalty in general, depending on your position.

Thinking, Arguing, and Writing Collaboratively

In small groups, exchange drafts of the paper you wrote for the Writing a Guided Argument assignment with a fellow student. Write a paragraph of comments to help your peer develop his or her argument. Exchange your paper with another student and compare the feedback. Are they consistent? Why or why not?

Writing about the Text

Write an essay expanding on your consideration of Gelernter's tone and analyzing how his tone affects his argumentative claim. Do you think it helps or hurts his argument? Pay attention, especially, to whether he ever gets cynical. What is his tone in paragraph 24?

More Writing Ideas

1. In your journal, write notes for an essay that examines whether or not you consider life imprisonment a "cruel and unusual" punishment.
2. Write a paragraph in which you argue for this idea: "Penitence doesn't matter—if someone does a crime, they must be punished."
3. Based on Gelernter's arguments on self-doubt and his comments in paragraphs 2 and 25, write an essay in which you argue that Gelernter would be against affirmative action, explaining why you think that is true.

Part Three

Perspectives on Critical Issues

10 The Internet: How Do We Relate to Each Other in Cyberspace?

I n the past decade, we have witnessed a major change in the way we live our lives. When the Internet started in the 1970s and 1980s, only governments and scientists used it in order to exchange information. In the early 1990s, consumer technology advanced and Marc Andreeson developed the extraordinary graphical browser, Mosaic, which became Netscape Navigator. Soon, the World Wide Web was big news. We forget, but before the Internet, people had to shop in person at stores or through the use of catalogs. People wrote letters to each other. People got their news from the radio or newspapers. Now, because of the new technologies everything has changed, from basic communication between family members and friends to dating to politics. Almost all business done around the world involves the Internet at some point.

With the rise of such a revolutionary technology has come an army of writers trying to understand the change and trying to explain it to their readers. The following four selections suggest the wide range of arguments you will find about the Internet. In "Anyone Need a Friend?" Libby Copeland shows how Craigslist fills the need of lonely people seeking companionship by means of the Internet. In "I Surf, Therefore I Am," Judith Levine explores the dangers of students relying on the Internet in doing research. Beth Brophy writes about the variety of online dating problems in "Saturday Night and You're All Alone? Maybe You Need a Cyberdate" and is able to push her own point of view on the topic without being confrontational. Finally Joshua Green, writing for a student newspaper, argues for a balanced assessment of YouTube as a social networking engine.

LIBBY COPELAND
Anyone Need A Friend?

Libby Copeland, born in 1976 and educated at the University of Pennsylvania, is a staff writer for the Washington Post. *She covers politics for the* Post. *In this selection, which appeared in the style section of that newspaper in 2004, she discusses with good humor and some pathos the phenomenon of lonely people looking for friends on the online listing service Craigslist. "I'm not a loser," she quotes one lonely man as saying, but Copeland isn't so sure.*

Prereading: Thinking about the Essay in Advance

What can the Internet offer you in moments of loneliness? If you or someone you know had ever turned to the Internet at such moments, what was the outcome? If not, what stopped you from trying to connect with other people in cyberspace?

Words to Watch

modernity (par. 1) state of living in the modern world
plaintively (par. 1) in a sad way
anonymity (par. 2) state of not being identified by name
desolation (par. 2) overwhelming despair and loneliness
frankness (par. 5) utter honesty, almost to a fault
quintessentially (par. 10) essentially, in a pure way
inordinate (par. 13) beyond reasonable limits
laborious (par. 15) requiring a lot of effort

1   When you think of personals you think of romance—SWM, 6'1", green eyes, ISO trim classy lady—but there are plenty of people out there solely in need of friendship, an end to their loneliness, the disease of modernity. Which is why on Craigslist, the free online classifieds, there are sections called Strictly Platonic and Activity Partners, where people post messages like "Lunch anyone?" and "terminally bored at work, let's IM" and, most plaintively, "Looking for Best Friend."

2   To read these queries is to realize how needy people are, even if they express it only under a cloak of Internet anonymity. There are people on Craigslist who want to see movies with you, go dancing with you, take trips to Atlantic City with you, if only you will e-mail them. There is a sense that it doesn't really matter who you are, that anyone is better than no one, that no fate is worse than being alone. Imagine the desolation of the guy in Ashburn, who writes, near midnight on a Saturday, "Looking for some conversation to help pass the rest of the night," or the desperation of the woman in the Chelsea neighborhood of Manhattan who posts "help i need valium" at 5:25 a.m.

A 22-year-old guy in Arlington writes a message at 8:18 on a Friday   3
night: "New in town—anybody out there without plans tonight?"

Anybody at all?   4

Tennessee Williams wrote that we're all sentenced to solitary confine-   5
ment inside our own skins, but really, there's no need to be so dramatic.
Sometimes you're just sick of talking to the bartender. People have
formed friendships on the Internet for as long as it's been around, and it
doesn't seem that surprising someone might use free classifieds to, say,
seek a tennis partner. But there's a painful frankness to many of the requests at Craigslist.org. Many of the messages seem to have been posted
hurriedly, in fits of anger or desperation.

"I'm not a loser," writes a guy looking for female friends.   6

"Whatever happened to loyal friends??" asks a 21-year-old girl on the   7
San Francisco section of the Web site. "Not these catty scenester/hipster
bitches who have [had sex with] half of your exes."

"I am in a relationship with someone I love and we have a beautiful   8
little boy," writes a young woman in Silver Spring who is looking for a
male friend. "I do not plan on leaving him, I want it to work. But I am not
happy. I feel that my man is putting me last. . . . I just want someone who
I can have intelligent conversations with from time to time. I cannot talk
to my man without him falling asleep."

Scientists have studied loneliness and found it may be bad for you,   9
something about stress and blood pressure. If that's true, then modernity
is bad for you, because there's something quintessentially modern about
the way we experience loneliness: living alone, orbiting each other in
bars, nursing cold coffee in cafes, checking our voice mail and finding it
empty. You phone your mother in Fort Lauderdale and she talks about
her second husband and her book club, and you realize when she says,
"How are you?," that she doesn't really want to know.

And there's something quintessentially urban about this loneliness,   10
maybe even quintessentially Washington, with all the people here who
come and go.

"Everybody just moves," says Darlene Macy of Woodbridge, a com-   11
puter programming teacher who posted a message on Craigslist looking
for men and women to hang out with. It said. "I'm 24, in okay shape, love
animals, funny, and down to earth—just don't like going home to an
empty house."

All those empty houses! All those apartments kept clean for guests   12
who never arrive. All those wineglasses growing dusty. And that bottle
of cabernet sauvignon, bought years ago, sitting in an otherwise empty
wine rack, until one day you decide to get drunk watching "Will &
Grace."

An inordinate number of Washingtonians who frequent the site   13
(named after founder Craig Newmark) are looking for Strictly Platonic relationships, compared with Craigslist fans in well-trafficked cities such as
New York, Boston, Los Angeles and San Francisco. What does it mean

that so many people here yearn for basic human interaction—small talk, the pleasure of a stranger's company at lunch?

14   In D.C. there is "sort of a stern-faced desperation that people have on their faces as they drive to work," says Nicole Franklin-Kern, who is originally from central Ohio, where she says people are friendlier. "I think everybody has this force field that they put up around them." Franklin-Kern is 31, married, bored with her temp job and bored with her social life. She's been in the area for seven months, and she lives in a big apartment complex in Silver Spring, where her neighbors are mostly strangers. "I probably hear more coming through the wall than I would ever hear in a conversation," she says.

15   Franklin-Kern, who's into Wicca, posts a query on Craigslist—"Neo-pagan needs a break"—looking for friends and job connections. She gets almost 50 responses. Then she engages in the laborious process of getting to know these people by e-mail, figuring out who's normal and who might be into kiddie porn.

16   "I call it de-freaking," she says.

17   Just as it's possible to be married and lonely, it's possible to be alone and content. But you can't will yourself into it. The lonelier you are, the lonelier you are. Loneliness clings to you with a slightly sour smell, keeping people at a distance. It feels like confirmation of your worst fears. Remember that girl in seventh grade with thick glasses and lime green sweat pants, the one who always laughed at the wrong moments, and the only time people talked to her was when she brought in cupcakes for her own birthday?

18   That's you. Drinking ice water in the Italian restaurant, alone, aware that all the couples are looking at you. You smile at another diner and he looks away as if he knows. He knows. The waitress comes up and tells you the specials, and you want to stop her when she gets to the scallops but you let her finish, as if someone else at your table might want them. You get the feeling that she feels bad for you, but not bad enough to ever want to sit with you.

19   Ryan Hajen, 23, another Craigslister, worked as a waiter at a Bennigan's through college and learned to distinguish the people who were content to eat alone from the ones who were embarrassed. Those comfortable with solitude, he noticed, didn't look around worriedly or rush through their meals.

20   Now that Hajen has taken to eating alone, he's been trying to achieve this Zen-like state. He is new to the area, working in Washington as a government economist and living with his girlfriend in an area of Alexandria where there's little to do. Instead of going straight home after work, he sometimes eats alone in the city, grabbing street literature beforehand so he has something to keep himself occupied. He practices seeming "natural." Recently, while eating alone in a Chinese restaurant near Dupont

Circle, he overheard a table of young women discussing World War II, and he briefly joined their conversation. This felt like a triumph.

"The primary goal of it was to not come across as some kind of a stalker," Hajen says.   21

The lonely guy talking to strangers. We have all seen him, and we fear becoming him. He shows up sometimes on chat lines and park benches. Andre Dickerson sees him sometimes at Stetson's Famous Bar and Grill on U Street. Dickerson, 23, has started frequenting Stetson's every Thursday night at 7:30 by himself, after deciding he needs to get out of the house even if there's no one to get out with. And when he sits there, eating a half-price turkey burger, he often sees this older fellow by himself, talking to everyone. The old guy talks to the bartender even when she's not listening. He talked to Dickerson one time. "He just started rambling on about something," Dickerson says.   22

We all need friendship, or something like it. Through his Craigslist posting, Dickerson has a regular lunch partner. Hajen was able to meet with a young woman to have dinner, and though it felt strange at first, he was relieved to find that she, too, was just looking for a friend. Franklin-Kern invited a nice couple on a group hike, and has scheduled an interview for a job at a nonprofit she learned about through a Craigslist contact. And a young woman in Alexandria named Michelle Sprecher, who posted a message saying she'd always wanted a gay best friend, received a reply from a bisexual drag queen known as Lola the Fabulous.   23

He seems nice enough, Sprecher says. She thinks she may wind up meeting with him "in a very public place."   24

▶ Building Vocabulary

In her article, Copeland makes several references to pop culture phenomena. For each of the following words or terms, define and explain its connotations in popular culture.

 1. SWM (par. 1)
 2. Platonic (par. 1)
 3. Chelsea neighborhood (par. 2)
 4. Fort Lauderdale (par. 9)
 5. "Will & Grace" (par. 12)
 6. temp job (par. 14)
 7. Wicca (par. 15)
 8. Neopagan (par. 15)
 9. Bennigan's (par. 19)
10. Zen-like state (par. 20)
11. stalker (par. 21)
12. drag queen (par. 23)

▶ **Thinking Critically about the Argument**

Understanding the Writer's Argument

1. What is Craigslist? What are its Strictly Platonic and Activity Partners sections for?
2. What do the messages on Craigslist Strictly Platonic and Activity Partners boards make Copeland realize?
3. What does Copeland mean that there's no need to be as dramatic as the Tennessee Williams quote she paraphrases?
4. Why does Copeland say in paragraph 9 that modernity is bad for you?
5. Why, according to Copeland, is there "something quintessentially urban about this loneliness" she sees on the Web?
6. Why, according to Copeland and the people she quotes in her essay, is Washington, D.C., a place where so many people are looking for "Strictly Platonic" relationships?
7. What is "de-freaking," and why is it necessary?
8. What does Copeland mean when she writes, "The lonelier you are, the lonelier you are"?
9. Why is Ryan Hajen worried about coming across as a "stalker"?

Understanding the Writer's Techniques

1. How effective is Copeland's opening? Explain.
2. What is Copeland's major proposition? Make an outline of her minor propositions. Which is the most effective, and why?
3. What is the tone of Copeland's argument? Could one object to her tone? Why?
4. Paraphrase Copeland's argument in paragraph 9. Do you find it effective? Why or why not?
5. Copeland wrote this essay for the *Washington Post*, which is a D.C. paper but is also read by people outside the region. What is the argumentative effect of the discussion of Washington, D.C.?
6. Do you think that Copeland's conclusion is effective? Explain your answer.

Exploring the Writer's Argument

1. Copeland loads her essay with quotes from the Strictly Platonic and Activity Partners boards. What is the cumulative effect on you, the reader, of reading all these quotes? Do you feel Copeland is helping her own argument, or is she burdening it? Explain.
2. Copeland doesn't spend any time discussing dating online. Why? Do you think this might help her argument, or not? Explain your answer.

3. In the penultimate paragraph of her essay, Copeland offers a "where are they now" type happy ending, and then mutes that happiness by showing how wary Sprecher is of her new friend. Do you think this is the correct ending? Should Copeland be more positive with her ending, or is this the correct note to end on? Explain.

▶ Ideas for Writing Arguments

Prewriting

In what ways can life in the modern world ever make people feel lonely? How can technology and the way people work and are entertained make them feel disconnected from others? Can it instead offer the antidote to true loneliness? Freewrite about the topic of loneliness in the modern world.

Writing a Guided Argument

In her essay, Copeland writes that scientists have studied loneliness and have discovered that it's bad for a person's health. She writes that if that is true, then modernity is bad for us, because "there's something quintessentially modern about how we experience loneliness: living alone, orbiting each other in bars, nursing cold coffee in cafes, checking our voice mail and finding it empty." Write an essay called "Get a (Modern) Life!" in which you challenge the notion that modernity is bad for us. Try to persuade people to take part in the above activities (and others of your devising).

1. Open your essay by explaining why life among other people is so burdensome.
2. Offer as an alternative the idea that modern life, with its distractions and opportunities for isolation, is the best way to experience existence.
3. Write your major proposition clearly and forcefully.
4. Offer your reader at least three ways in which modern life can make people's lives better by giving them solitude and time to themselves.
5. Gear your essay and your ideas toward college students.
6. Write a conclusion that affirms modern practices as a valid way of life in the 21st century.

Thinking, Arguing, and Writing Collaboratively

In small groups of three or four, exchange your Writing a Guided Argument papers. Offer suggestions in the form of a paragraph or two to help your classmate develop his or her essay.

Writing about the Text

Read Joshua Green's essay (pages 234–236). Write an essay in which you compare and contrast the styles of Green's and Copeland's arguments. Which do you think is the stronger argument? How are their styles similar and different? Make your case using many direct comparisons of quotes from the two essays.

More Writing Ideas

1. In your journal, write an entry in which you comment on when you were last very lonely. What did you do about it?
2. Write two or three paragraphs in the form of ad copy for Craigslist's Strictly Platonic or Activity Partners sections.
3. Write an essay in which you argue that Internet dating either is or is not a useful and valid way to meet people.

JUDITH LEVINE
I Surf, Therefore I Am

Author and journalist Judith Levine was born in 1952 in New York City. She is an activist for free speech and sex education, the founder of the feminist group No More Nice Girls, and is active in the National Writers Union. She has published many articles in Ms., Mother Jones, *and the* Village Voice, *among other publications. She is the author of* My Enemy, My Love: Women, Men, and the Dilemmas of Gender *(1992, 2003) and* Harmful to Minors: The Perils of Protecting Children from Sex *(1999), a book that rethinks how we approach the topic of sexuality in children and teenagers. The following selection, which examines the content of what we read when we surf the Internet, appeared in the online magazine* Salon *in its Mothers Who Think column in 1997.*

▶ Prereading: Thinking about the Essay in Advance

Is reading on the Web the same as reading in the book or magazine or newspaper? Does the information stick with you as long? What kind of reading leaves your head the quickest?

▶ Words to Watch

bestowed (par. 1) donated
scant (par. 4) not sufficient
encumbrance (par. 5) a burden
corral (par. 5) organize

etiology (par. 5) cause, as of a disease
promiscuous (par. 5) casual
gleaned (par. 7) picked up, gathered
think tanks (par. 8) institutions often founded for political research
stratospheric (par. 12) extremely high
relinquishing (par. 12) giving up

"O bviously, I'm somebody who believes that personal computers are   1
empowering tools," Bill Gates said after he bestowed a $200 mil-
lion gift to America's public libraries so they could hook up to the Internet.

"People are entitled to disagree," Gates said. "But I would invite   2
them to visit some of these libraries and see the impact on kids using
this technology."

Well, I have seen the impact, and I disagree. Many of my students—   3
undergraduate media and communications majors at a New York
university—have access to the endless information bubbling through cyberspace, and *it is not* empowering.

Most of the data my students Net is like trash fish—and it is hard for   4
them to tell a dead one-legged crab from a healthy sea bass. Scant on
world knowledge and critical thinking skills, they are ill-equipped to interpret or judge the so-called facts, which they insert into their papers
confidently but in no discernible order.

Their writing often "clicks" from info-bit to info-bit, their arguments   5
free of that gluey, old-fashioned encumbrance—the transitional sentence.
When I try to help them corral their impressions into coherent stories, I
keep hearing the same complaint: "I can't concentrate." I've diagnosed
this phenomenon as epidemic attention deficit disorder. And I can't help
but trace its etiology, at least in part, to the promiscuous pointing and
clicking that has come to stand in for intellectual inquiry.

These students surf; therefore, they do not read. They do not read   6
scholarly articles—which can be trusted because they are juried or challenged because they are footnoted. They do not read books—which tell
stories and sustain arguments by placing idea and metaphor one on top of
the other, so as to hold weight, like a stone wall. Even the journalism students read few magazines and even fewer newspapers, which are edited
by people with recognizable and sometimes even admitted cultural and
political biases and checked by fact-checkers using other edited sources.

On the Net, nobody knows if any particular "fact" is a dog. One stu-   7
dent handed in a paper about tobacco companies' liability for smokers'
health, which she had gleaned almost entirely from the Web pages of the
Tobacco Institute. Did she know what the Tobacco Institute is? Apparently not, because she had done her research on the Net, and was de-
prived of the modifying clause, "a research organization supported by
the tobacco industry," obligatory in any edited news article.

8   Another young woman, writing about teen pregnancy, used data generated by the Family Research Council, which, along with other right-wing Christian think tanks, dominates the links on many subjects related to family and sexuality and offers a decidedly one-sided view.

9   A teacher at another school told me one of her students had written a paper quoting a person who had a name but no identifying characteristics. "Who's this?" the professor asked. "Someone with a Web page," the young man said.

10   If there is no context on the Net, neither is there history. My friend who teaches biology told me her students propose research that was completed, and often discredited, 50 years ago. "They go online," she said, "where nothing has been indexed before 1980."

11   A San Francisco librarian interviewed on National Public Radio worried that, space and resources strained as they are, more computers will inevitably mean fewer books. Another commentator on the Gates gift suggested that the computers would not be very valuable without commensurate human resources—that is, trained workers to help people use them.

12   At New York's gleaming new Science, Industry, & Business Library (SIBL), you can sit in an ergonomically correct chair at one of several hundred lovely color computer terminals and call up, among hundreds of other databases, the powerful journalistic and legal service Nexis/Lexis. But since Nexis/Lexis is in great demand, you have about 45 minutes at the screen, half of which the inexperienced user will blow figuring out the system, because there is only one harassed staff person to assist all the computer-users. Then you'll learn that the library cannot afford the stratospheric fees for downloading the articles. So most users, I imagine, will manage to copy out quotes from a couple of articles before relinquishing the seat to the next person waiting for the cyber-kiosk.

13   Unlike a paper or microfilm version of the same pieces, which could be photocopied or copied at leisure onto a pad or laptop, the zillion articles available on the library's Nexis/Lexis are more or less unavailable—that is, to no avail. Useless.

14   Technology may empower, but how and to what end will that power be used? What else is necessary to use it well and wisely? I'd suggest, for a start, reading books—literature and history, poetry and politics—and listening to people who know what they're talking about. Otherwise, the brains of those kids in Gates's libraries will be glutted with "information" but bereft of ideas, rich in tools but clueless about what to build or how to build it. Like the search engines that retrieve more than 100,000 links or none at all, they will be awkward at discerning meaning, or discerning at all.

▶ Building Vocabulary

Write definitions of the following and use them in sentences of your own:

1. discernible (par. 4)
2. epidemic (par. 5)
3. obligatory (par. 7)
4. ergonomically correct (par. 12)
5. glutted (par. 14)
6. bereft (par. 14)

▶ Thinking Critically about the Argument

Understanding the Writer's Argument

1. What does Levine mean when she says in paragraph 4 that "most of the data my students Net is like trash fish"?
2. What is "the transitional sentence" (par. 5), and why is it important?
3. What is attention deficit disorder?
4. Why, according to Levine, is it important to read books, magazines, and newspapers?
5. Levine's student handed in a paper about tobacco for which she got research only from the Tobacco Institute. Why was Levine less than happy about this?
6. What is the risk, according to Levine, with adding so many computers to libraries?
7. What are the downsides to Lexis/Nexis at the public library?

Understanding the Writer's Techniques

1. What is the argumentative effect in the beginning of Levine's essay, when she openly disagrees with Bill Gates, chairman and founder of Microsoft and an expert of computers?
2. Where does Levine articulate her major proposition most clearly? What minor propositions does Levine offer to support her ideas?
3. Analyze why Levine places her minor propositions in the order she does. Is there a strategy at work? Explain your answer.
4. How would you characterize the tone that Levine uses in this essay? Is it effective in helping her argument?
5. What popular saying about computers does Levine satirize in the first sentence of paragraph 7?
6. What evidence does Levine use to support her idea that students today are not aware of the source of what they are reading online?
7. How effective is Levine's conclusion? Why does she return her discussion to Bill Gates's libraries?

Exploring the Writer's Argument

1. Levine wrote this article for *Salon* magazine, a publication that is available only on the Web. How can she publish an article criticizing online writing in an online magazine? How does that affect the writing? Explain your answer.
2. Prove Levine wrong. Pretend that you are doing a research paper on a topic such as abortion or flag burning. Go to the Internet and print out four articles: two should be "trash fish," as Levine says in paragraph 4, and two should be from a respectable news source.
3. In paragraphs 12 and 13, it seems as if Levine relies too much on one example. What point is she trying to make? What could she do to improve this section? Explain fully.

▶ Ideas for Writing Arguments

Prewriting

In your Web-surfing time between classes, pay close attention to your reading habits online. Write notes later analyzing whether what you read is worth reading.

Writing a Guided Argument

Librarians and communities around the country still debate whether libraries should provide access to the Internet. Free Internet access in libraries is, in some communities, the only way for people to get online. However, through ease of availability, everyone has access to pornography and information that could harm others. Software filters can stop viewers from visiting some sites, but the filters are imperfect and many people believe filters violate First Amendment rights to free speech. Write an essay in which you argue that Internet access in libraries should or should not be censored. Do some research in the library (not online) to gather evidence for your position.

1. Open your essay by briefly outlining the issue.
2. Write your major proposition clearly and in strong language.
3. Affect a tone similar to Levine's.
4. Explain your minor propositions, offering ample support in the form of fact and examples.
5. Entertain one opposing view with a clear rebuttal.
6. Close your essay by referring in some useful way to the First Amendment.

Thinking, Arguing, and Writing Collaboratively

In small groups, exchange your Writing a Guided Argument papers with another student. Spend at least 15 minutes going through your classmate's paper, commenting on the following categories: (1) strength of basic argument, (2) argumentative effect of support, (3) grammar and quality of the prose, and (4) transitions. Write a short paragraph for your classmate about each of these categories, and give back the paper. Review your peer's comments, and discuss any questions you have.

Writing about the Text

Expand on question 4 in the Understanding the Writer's Techniques section. Levine seems to have a cynical edge to her tone. Write an essay that analyzes the use of cynicism and irony in her article.

More Writing Ideas

1. How has the way you get your news and information changed over the past few years? What do you rely on the Internet for? Answer these questions in a journal entry. Compare your answers with those of a classmate. Are your answers similar? Different? How?
2. Just how real is the threat to books by computers, the Internet, Web sites, e-mail, and so on? Write an extended paragraph to argue your position.
3. Write an essay in the form of a letter from Bill Gates to Judith Levine defending his decision to give $200 million to libraries to hook up to the Internet.

BETH BROPHY

Saturday Night and You're All Alone?
Maybe You Need a Cyberdate

A Washington, D.C. journalist who has written for Forbes *magazine and* USA Today, *Beth Brophy is the author of* My Ex-Best Friend (2003), *a mystery novel about a suburban mother who solves a friend's murder. In this selection, which appeared in* U.S. News & World Report *in 1997, Brophy demystifies the subject of online dating by giving her take on everything from safety to the question of whether flirting online is actually cheating.*

▶ **Prereading: Thinking about the Essay in Advance**

Have you tried online dating? Do you know anyone who has? What was your experience or your friend's experience? Was it a positive one? Negative? Why?

▶ **Words to Watch**

infatuation (par. 3) romantic obsession
dalliance (par. 5) casual romance
clandestine (par. 6) secret
tryst (par. 6) illicit love affair
relented (par. 6) gave up
paradox (par. 7) something seemingly self-contradictory
personas (par. 7) personalities a person puts forth in front of other people

1   *Forget roses, candlelit dinners, pillow talk—or even two people in the same room. And read on for answers to those burning questions.*

2   **How is cyberdating different from meeting at a club?** It's a lot different. Everybody in cyberspace is tall, thin, blond, and rich—at least in theory. Without physical cues to provide a reality check—how someone looks or speaks, or whether he leaves his dirty socks on the floor—the person on the other end can be imagined as the ideal lover. The blank computer screen becomes a projection for hopes and dreams.

3   **I meet lots of people on the Net, but most of my romances last only a day or two. How come?** It's easy to deceive in cyberspace, but it's also easy to fall into premature intimacy. Revealing secrets to a stranger can be intoxicating and, like most stimulants, dangerous. The Internet "seems to be laced with truth serum," says therapist Marshall Jung, co-author of *Romancing the Net.* "All this truth-telling puts enormous pressure on fledgling relationships." So it's no wonder that the cycle of "love, infatuation, and disappointment may take three weeks," says MIT sociology professor Sherry Turkle, author of *Life on the Screen.*

4   Unlike real time, which involves annoying waits in traffic, time in cyberspace is compressed. Sometimes that leads to impulsive actions. Old-fashioned mail, on the other hand, allows time for reflection, for letting a passionate letter sit overnight, or even for tearing it up.

5   **My husband says I spend too much time online. He's worried I'll find somebody else. Is he a control freak, or what?** The relationship gurus of popular culture disagree as to whether extramarital cyber-romance is cheating or not. John Gray, omnipresent author of the bestseller *Men Are From Mars, Women Are From Venus,* gets huffy about online dalliance. "Indulging in sexual arousal is adultery as far as your partner is concerned,"

(Web site www.cyberdating.net)

he says. "It's not innocent and harmless; it's a betrayal." Advice columnist Ann Landers is more pragmatic: "It's not adultery; it's just foolishness," she says, "and a little bit on the sick side."

6   Cyber-romance can strain a marriage, sometimes to the breaking point. One woman, an attractive professional in her mid-30s, compares chat rooms to the temptation of drugs. Her husband's clandestine four-month Internet romance with a married woman living in another state nearly wrecked their 10-year marriage. "He wouldn't have gone to a singles bar. A friend or client might have seen him," she says. When she asked him why their monthly bill for using the Net exceeded $200, she says, her husband told her, "I'm in love with the perfect woman and I'm leaving you." His "true love" was planning to leave her husband, but plans changed following an out-of-state tryst. "Each of them thought the other was the greatest—until they actually met," the woman says. Her husband begged to come back. She relented, and they're now in marriage counseling. So ask yourself why you're spending more time online than with your husband.

7   **I met this woman on the Net two months ago. She thinks I'm "Cowboy," a daring Hollywood stuntman. But really I'm just a quiet, skinny accountant. Now she wants a face to face. Help!** Meet her, come clean, and hope she's been lying, too. As Cowboy's dilemma illustrates, cyberspace can lead to a curious paradox: The anonymity of a computer screen makes people bolder and often leads them to try on more daring personas. At the same time, cyberspace allows users to exert tight control over information flow, which can lead to deception and disappointment. "Online is simply a starting point. You don't already have a relationship. You have a cyberflirtation," says Rosalind Resnick, host of the Web site *LoveSearch.com,* a combination dating site, personal data base, and advice column.

8   **I've been e-mailing somebody for three months who lives 60 miles away. I drop hints about a face to face, but he's slow on the uptake. Should I ask him directly?** Sure, but be prepared for rejection. The sad fact is some people are better suited to being behind the screen—they don't want to reveal themselves in person. "True intimacy is not one aspect of the self, it's all aspects," Turkle says. "They may not be up for the lack of fantasy and the challenge of commitment." If that happens, say goodbye and try again.

9   **I've heard there are weirdos on the Net, like the case of that woman who traded fantasies with a guy in an S&M chat room, met him in person and later was found strangled. Is online romance safe?** Yes, there are some strange people online. But there are weirdos everywhere—in cyberspace, in singles bars, at parties, maybe even in

the apartment next door. For some people, the Net offers an opportunity they despair of finding elsewhere. Melinda Stevenson, who works for a Washington, D.C., international organization, says between her age and a long commute that left her exhausted at the end of the day, she'd stopped investing energy in dating. "I'm in my 40s," Stevenson says. "I'd given up."

But then she received an e-mail from "Bob," an avid sailor who   10
lived in the Annapolis area. For six weeks, she and Bob e-mailed daily. Finally, Stevenson says, she "tossed out conventional wisdom" and invited him for dinner. He showed up 30 minutes later bearing "flowers, a bottle of wine, no ax—I checked." Their worst fears about each other (that she would be grossly overweight; that he would sport a comb-over hairdo) didn't materialize. Their first date lasted 10 hours—no touching, but "there was an electric sense between us," she says. After a few hours, he politely inquired if they could "share a bracket" (Web talk for hug). Three weeks later he said, "I love you." And five months after that, he proposed. The couple recently returned from their Hawaiian honeymoon.

I hear the Internet is a good place for shy people to meet others. Is it   11
true? Cyberdating, says Frances Maier, general manager of Match.Com, an online personals ad service, "is not about lonely hearts. The Internet is a screener. Generally, the people on it have higher incomes and better jobs." Some shy people find that the Net allows them to meet someone outside their immediate geographic area. For example, attorney Heather Williams and 911 dispatcher Gerald Harrington, both divorced, lived 200 miles away from each other. After meeting in a chat room in December 1995, they e-mailed for two weeks, then talked on the phone. A month later Harrington drove to meet Williams. "I am a shy person who does not interact with people I do not know," he says, but the opportunity to build a relationship online first smoothed the way. "I felt totally at ease after several minutes and knew this was someone I could feel comfortable with." Within a few months, Harrington packed up his belongings and moved to Hollidaysburg, PA, to be with Williams. He proposed nine months later. They plan to marry in June.

Sound like a Valentine's Day fairy tale? In cyberspace, just as in face-   12
to-face dating, things often don't work out so perfectly. Luckily, the Internet also has a Web site for divorce.

▶ Building Vocabulary

1. Brophy uses phrases in her essay from the world of computers. Often, when a new technology is adopted, terminology from the technology it replaced seeps into its vocabulary. For example, we still say we "dial" the phone when the phone dial, the rotary phone, is long gone. Find

at least three computer phrases in Brophy's essay with origins outside the world of computers, and explain why you think they were
adopted.

2. In her essay, Brophy uses figurative language. In the following sentences, replace the italicized phrases with your own words:
   a. without physical cues to *provide a reality check* (par. 2)
   b. Is he *a control freak,* or what? (par. 5)
   c. I *drop hints* about a *face to face,* but he's *slow on the uptake.* (par. 8)
   d. she'd *stopped investing energy* in dating (par. 9)
   e. that he would *sport* a comb-over hairdo (par. 10)
   f. the opportunity to *build a relationship* online first *smoothed the
   way* (par. 11)

▶ Thinking Critically about the Argument

Understanding the Writer's Argument

1. What is cyberdating?
2. Why can every person on a cyberdate be "the ideal lover"? (par. 2)
3. Why can cyberdating often be so intense and accelerated?
4. Does Brophy think that some online flirting is adultery? Explain.
5. Why is it that dating online makes people "bolder and often leads
   them to try on more daring personas"? (par. 7)
6. Does Brophy give any examples of success stories online? What
   are they?
7. In what way is the Internet a "screener"?

Understanding the Writer's Techniques

1. What is Brophy's major proposition? Does she have one? Explain.
2. What are the minor propositions in this essay? Make a list of the
   points Brophy makes.
3. Why do you think Brophy wrote this essay in the form of an advice
   column? How does the advice column format act as a series of rhetorical questions? Is it an effective way to cover her topic? Why or
   why not?
4. Who is Brophy's audience? How does that affect her tone?
5. How important is Brophy's use of quotes from experts in this essay?
   Do they help to convince you?
6. Evaluate Brophy's conclusion. Why does she end on the note she does?
   Explain.

Exploring the Writer's Argument

1. How good is Brophy's advice? What would you agree with? Disagree
   with? What would you add to her discussion? What would you like
   to see her address that she hasn't touched on?

2. Things move quickly on the Internet. Trends change almost weekly, it seems. Brophy's essay was written in 1997, ages ago in Internet years. Are any of her points outdated (so to speak)? Explain your answer.
3. In paragraph 3, Brophy suggests that the Internet encourages people to tell the truth (too much), and in paragraph 7, she suggests that the Internet encourages people to lie about themselves. Is this a contradiction? Does it affect her argument? How? Explain your answers.

▶ Ideas for Writing Arguments

Prewriting

How has e-mail changed the way people communicate?

Writing a Guided Argument

Write an essay that argues that people should write more letters (snail mail) and less e-mail.

1. Open your essay with an anecdote showing that e-mail can be a problem (for example, a misunderstanding or a message sent in anger).
2. Refer to paragraph 4 in Brophy's essay.
3. Move your argument into an articulation of your major proposition.
4. Offer a minor proposition that supports writing letters.
5. Expand on your idea with examples and other support.
6. Write a minor proposition in which you contrast e-mail with snail mail.
7. Repeat steps 4 through 6.
8. Adopt a tone of authority on the subject.
9. Close your essay with a positive anecdote about snail mail to counterbalance the anecdote you told at the beginning. You may refer to your intro if you like.

Thinking, Arguing, and Writing Collaboratively

In two or three paragraphs, write your own online personal ad. How can you persuade someone to answer your ad, purely through your description of yourself. Write your ad without lying about anything. When you are finished, exchange ads with a classmate. Is your classmate's ad persuasive? How are your ads similar? How are they different?

Writing about the Text

Write an essay that expands on this sentence by Brophy: "The blank computer screen becomes a projection for hopes and dreams."

More Writing Ideas

1. Find and print or cut out 10 personal ads, either from a local paper or online. In your journal, analyze the ads. Do you see any similarities? Differences?
2. Find an advice column in your local paper or online. Pick one of the questions and write your own advice to the writer in an extended paragraph.
3. Write an essay in which you argue that cyberdating is pathetic and that people should seek love in other, more social places.

JOSHUA GREEN
YouTube: Maker of Dreams, Destroyer of Lives

Undergraduate student Joshua Green wrote "YouTube: Maker of Dreams, Destroyer of Lives" in 2007 for the Pitt News, *the student newspaper at the University of Pittsburgh, which bills itself on its Web site as "One of America's Great Student Newspapers." In his essay, Green implies he enjoys and has respect for YouTube, but he has some fun here with the way people have knee-jerk reactions to striking images. On-demand video has its limitations.*

▶ Prereading: Thinking about the Essay in Advance

If you haven't already done so, have a look at YouTube online. What kinds of videos have you already watched or can imagine yourself watching there? Is there anything worthwhile?

▶ Words to Watch

cease (par. 2) stop
peyote buttons (par. 8) cacti that have hallucinatory properties
hygiene (par. 10) practice of cleanliness
PETA (par. 11) People for the Ethical Treatment of Animals, an animal rights organization
behaviorists (par. 13) scientists who study the behavior of animals and humans
snuff film (par. 15) pornographic film that ends in a murder

1   Recently I was shown a video on YouTube that I just can't get over. Now, I am no stranger to YouTube—it was where I first learned about the Michael Richards[1] debacle. It was also where I kept up with the

---

[1.] Michael Richards played Kramer on *The Jerry Seinfeld Show*, and in a standup comedy routine exploded in a racist tirade on November 17, 2006. [Editor's note]

epic Donald Trump/Rosie O'Donnell rivalry.[2] It was the place that I learned of a video called "Spirit of Truth"[3]—if you haven't seen it, watch it immediately.

So in a way, YouTube is one of our generation's finest outlets for media, entertainment and news. It shows raw, unedited moments that never cease to inform and amaze us. The site has reached a level of journalistic integrity equal to or greater than that of the Fox News Channel—on which, by the way, YouTube has many great videos; might I suggest the documentary "Outfoxed." 2

However, the most recent video I viewed was one called "Kitty Washing Machine." In it, an orange cat is placed in what appears to be some kind of oversized microwave. A few buttons and knobs are pressed, and the cat immediately senses danger. 3

Water begins shooting from below where the cat is standing, and the feline immediately becomes psychotic. It jumps around as water and soap are sprayed all around the inside of the machine, pawing at the window, begging for someone to free it from the hell it hath encountered. 4

The video finishes with a clip of the cat wrapped in a towel, being dried. 5

Now, to be totally honest, I am not the biggest fan of cats. They're the kind of creatures that want you to pet them, but just as you succumb to their wishes, their claws come out. They sleep more than 20 hours a day and they poop in perfectly good sandboxes. So when I saw this video, my reaction was slightly more than a chuckle. I enjoyed the video, so I decided to show it to my girlfriend. I figured, "Hey, she has a cat! She'll love this!" 6

She didn't. 7

She didn't even crack a smile. But once I saw the negative reaction the video received from her, I started thinking. What would I think if a huge cat picked me up and sent me through a car wash? First, I'd wonder if I had accidentally consumed peyote buttons, but after I realized the whole thing was real, what would I think? Well, I guess I'd be terrified that a cat of that size somehow came into existence, but what would I think after I accepted it? I immediately felt bad for my initial reaction to the video. I figured it was just another dumb YouTube video that would lose its pizazz after a couple days. 8

However, there was a report on CNN.com that indicated that this video may have more of an effect than I ever imagined. 9

---

2. At the end of 2006 and continuing well into the next year, Donald Trump, the millionaire mogul, and Rosie O'Donnell, the outspoken talk-show host and comedian, engaged in what the media called a catfight, verbally attacking each other. [Editor's note]

3. A video by preacher Don Vincent, who claims to be God and to come from "the Kingdom of Heaven." The evangelist's unpredictable behavior, including repeated swearing and rap presentations with dance made his video a popular site for visitors to YouTube, on which "The Kingdom of Heaven" first appeared in 2006. [Editor's note]

10   Apparently Andres Diaz, the owner and inventor of the machine—called the Pet Spa—fears that he may suffer financial loss because of this negative portrayal of the feline hygiene experience. Diaz assures that the Pet Spa is more humane than any traditional pet cleansing technique. One thousand five hundred units have been sold worldwide—mostly to vets and pet shops.

11   Then, naturally, a PETA representative had to chime in with her own brilliant observations about this controversy. According to her, Diaz is a cat-hating, money-hungry, jerk face with a poopie head—I'm paraphrasing. She even went as far as saying that "using this machine is as ridiculous as tossing toddlers in the dishwasher."

12   Well, I completely agree. The life of a toddler is equivalent to the life of a cat, and "tossing" a 3-year-old child is about as bad as bathing a house pet. Now I'm glad that this video surfaced. Finally, we can put this money fiend out of a job. Selling 40 of these machines each year is just 41 too many.

13   Never mind that the machine was created by a group of veterinarians, animal behaviorists and engineers. This one cat on YouTube hated it. Hence, it is wrong.

14   And shame on everyone who laughed as hard as I first did upon first seeing this video. Isn't a calendar with pictures of cats in Halloween costume, given to you by your strange aunt, enough to tickle your funny bones? Isn't Garfield a surplus of cat humor? Wasn't the movie "Catwoman" funnier than anything else feline-related?

15   This is an example of the kind of power Internet video has. Through these Web sites, smiles can be brought to people's faces, or lives can be completely destroyed. Because of what appears to be a kitty snuff film, the creator of an invention used by evil, animal-hating veterinarians all over the globe will be stopped.

▶ Building Vocabulary

For each of the following words, write a definition (minding its context) and a sentence of your own making.

1. debacle (par. 1)
2. epic (par. 1)
3. succumb (par. 6)
4. pizazz (par. 8)
5. paraphrasing (par. 11)
6. surfaced (par. 12)

▶ Thinking Critically about the Argument

Understanding the Writer's Argument

1. What pop culture phenomena has the writer kept up with through YouTube?
2. Why does the writer call YouTube "one of our generation's finest outlets for media, entertainment and news"?
3. What is the video "Kitty Washing Machine" about?
4. Why does the cat video amuse the writer so much?
5. What is the writer's girlfriend's reaction to the video? Why?
6. Why does the inventor of the Pet Spa fear financial loss because of the video on YouTube?
7. What does the writer think about the PETA representative's argument that using the Pet Spa "is as ridiculous as tossing toddlers in the dishwasher"?
8. Why does the writer point out that the Pet Spa was designed by "veterinarians, animal behaviorists and engineers"?

Understanding the Writer's Techniques

1. Why does Green open his essay by praising YouTube?
2. Where does the writer state his major proposition most clearly?
3. How does he play with traditional emotional appeals to make his point?
4. How does Green employ causal analysis in his essay?
5. What is the effect of the writer's use of the word "I" in this essay? Do you find it effective? Why or why not?
6. Green uses irony to help make his point in this essay. Where does he use irony most effectively? What is the difference between irony and sarcasm, and where in Green's essay do you detect sarcasm? Do you think the writer's tone suits his subject? Why or why not?
7. How does this essay's argument turn on the sentence, "Well, I completely agree"?
8. Do you think that Green's conclusion is effective? Why or why not?

Exploring the Writer's Argument

1. Green published this essay in a college newspaper. Do you think he could have published the essay in a mainstream publication? Somewhere on the Web? Explain your answer.

2. In his essay, Green uses many colloquialisms and eye-catching phrases. Choose at least three that you find particularly effective and explain your choices.
3. Cat lovers make up a very significant part of the general population. Do you think that Green is aware of this reality? How do you know? How has awareness of cat lovers influenced his argument in the essay?
4. Why does the writer defend YouTube? Is he serious about the claim that YouTube is "one of our generation's finest outlets"? How do you know?
5. What do you make of the statement "The life of a toddler is equivalent to the life of a cat"? How does the statement help Green's argument? Hurt it?

▶ Ideas for Writing Arguments

Prewriting

In what ways does a service like YouTube enhance modern life? How does it diminish it? Which do you think is the more compelling argument?

Writing a Guided Argument

Write an essay for your own school newspaper in which you challenge YouTube as a modern cultural phenomenon.

1. Call your essay either "YouTube: Maker of Dreams" *or* "YouTube: Destroyer of Lives."
2. Begin with a paragraph that explains the YouTube phenomenon and what it has to offer.
3. Write a clearly stated proposition to indicate your argument.
4. Depending on your position, provide an anecdote that characterizes what you see as the success (or problem) with YouTube.
5. Carefully identify some of the major points that critics could make on the other side of the argument and show the weaknesses of their positions.
6. Use irony if it serves your purpose in the essay.
7. Through your language and sentence structure, show an awareness of your audience. Use colloquialisms and slang terms to make your argument lively.

Thinking, Arguing, and Writing Collaboratively

Form small groups of three or four. Find a video on YouTube, or watch one your professor assigns to your group. Write a paragraph or two arguing for or against the video for its content, and then have everybody else in your group read your paragraph. What was the difference in your reactions to the video? What kinds of appeals did you and your group make? Discuss the distance between your reactions, and report to the class on your group's experiences.

Writing about the Text

Green's essay is notable mostly for its use of irony and sarcasm. Write an essay in which you analyze his use of these rhetorical devices. How do you feel about their use in Green's essay? How does the use of irony and sarcasm depend greatly on an understanding of audience?

More Writing Ideas

1. Write a journal entry in which you pretend to be Green trying to persuade his girlfriend that the Pet Spa video is actually funny.
2. On the Web, visit www.petspausa.com, the Internet home of the Pet Spa, the subject of the video in question in Green's essay, and try to find a video of the Pet Spa in use either on that site or on YouTube. Write a paragraph or two about your own reaction to the Pet Spa.
3. Write an essay exploring Green's notion that lives can be destroyed because of the Web. What does he mean, and can you think of other examples?

11 Campus Violence: What Is the Answer?

The image is haunting: April 16, 2007. Dozens of dead bodies under sheets, police milling about, citizens of a shocked nation once again glued to their television screens. The word of the Virginia Tech massacre has just hit the airwaves, and family and friends of students are calling. Is my child safe? Is my brother okay? Is my boyfriend alive? Cell phones sound off from under the sheets.

Before the slaughter at Virginia Tech, the country had suffered through several shootings in high schools, such as the 1999 Columbine massacre in Jefferson County, Colorado. And in what seems like the distant past we recall the horror of the shooting by Charles Whitman at the University of Texas in 1966. But Seung-Hui Cho at Virginia Tech killed more people than in any other school shooting, and the enormity of the act is indelible on our consciousness.

The debate rages: Why? Why in settings of supposed hope and promise—our schools and colleges—has seemingly purposeless butchery taken the lives of innocents? Was it apathy on campus to students in psychological trouble? Was it weak or absent gun control laws that made weapons just about as uncomplicated to purchase as a quart of milk? Was it a lack of campus security, an easy target for shrinkage in the face of perennial tax reductions and budget cuts? The debate stormed in the media for a short time after each horror, but in the 24-hour news cycle, it faded away rather quickly. Yet for students and their parents the possibility of uncontrolled violence on campuses looms even now as a potential reality of terror. Especially on college campuses, where many students live away from home without the close contact of family and friends does the issue of violence remain a constant fear, and for good reason. Students, faculty, staff, and parents have joined in establishing watchdog groups, committees, associations, therapy groups, and counseling programs, for example, in bold efforts to forestall other tragedies. Metal detectors, the searching of knapsacks, and restrictive curfew policies are familiar entities in some places. Yet many people worry that even painful vigilance may not prevent another outburst in some bucolic setting at some unsuspecting institution. Others worry that restrictions and watchdog groups can have a stultifying effect on campus freedoms and wonder if it is even possible to maintain a place where students are completely safe and free from fear.

This chapter collects four essays published within the three weeks following the Virginia Tech massacre. In "Feeling Safe Isn't Safe," Michael Barone takes the opportunity to raise the issue of concealed weapon laws, pointing out that in his view, if Virginia Tech had allowed weapons on its campus instead of being a "gun-free zone," the massacre never would have happened. He marshals the examples of Florida and Michigan as two states that are safe and allow concealed weapons. Warren Goldstein, in "Why It's OK to Rat on Other Students," writes in support of students informing on each other. Calling himself a "dyed-in-the-wool civil libertarian," Goldstein nevertheless wants students to "rat out" each other to avoid tragedy. In "How Safe Are America's Campuses?" Jodi S. Cohen and Rex W. Huppke report on concerns of parents, but conclude that a focus on students' mental health is perhaps the best bet in the war against campus violence. Finally, Adam Gopnik writes in the *New Yorker* that the Virginia Tech massacre is a sign that America needs gun control laws like those in Europe: ban semiautomatic weapons, which are not for hunting game, only humans.

MICHAEL BARONE
Feeling Safe Isn't Safe

Michael Barone is a senior writer for U.S. News & World Report, *in which "Feeling Safe Isn't Safe" appeared in 2007. Born in 1944 in Michigan, Barone received his B.A. from Harvard University in 1966 and his law degree from Yale in 1969. He is the author of several books, including* Our Country: The Shaping of America from Roosevelt to Reagan *(1990),* The New Americans: How the Melting Pot Can Work Again *(2001),* Hard America, Soft America: Competition vs. Coddling and the Battle for the Nation's Future *(2004), and* Our First Revolution: The Remarkable British Uprising That Inspired America's Founding Fathers *(2007). He is also the principal author of* The Almanac of American Politics, *a reference work published biannually by the National Journal Group. In this selection, Barone argues that although he was against Florida's 1987 law allowing people to carry concealed weapons, today he feels that he was wrong, and the Virginia Tech massacre might not have happened if people other than criminals had been able to bring guns onto campus.*

▶ **Prereading: Thinking about the Essay in Advance**

What is your opinion of gun control laws today? Do you think ordinary citizens should be able to carry concealed weapons? Why or why not? Do you think it's possible that the gun laws are fine as they stand, but that they are just not being enforced well enough?

▶ Words to Watch

revoked (par. 3) canceled officially
trustworthy (par. 3) dependable and honest
repeal (par. 4) revoke something, such as a law
unfounded (par. 4) groundless, unsupported by fact
decree (par. 5) official pronouncement
advocate (par. 7) supporter

The murders two weeks ago at Virginia Tech naturally set off a cry in   1
the usual quarters—the *New York Times*, the London-based *Economist*—for stricter gun control laws. Democratic officeholders didn't chime in, primarily because they believe they were hurt by the issue in 2000 and 2004, but most privately agree.

What most discussions of this issue tend to ignore is that we have two   2
tracks of political debate and two sets of laws on gun control. At the federal level there has been a push for more gun control laws since John Kennedy was assassinated in 1963, and some modest restrictions have been passed. At the state level something entirely different has taken place. In 1987 Florida passed a law allowing citizens who could demonstrate that they were law abiding and had sufficient training to obtain permits on demand to own and carry concealed weapons. In the succeeding 20 years many other states have passed such laws, so that today you can, if you meet the qualifications, carry concealed weapons in 40 states with 67 percent of the nation's population (including Vermont, with no gun restrictions at all).

When Florida passed its concealed-weapons law, I thought it was a   3
terrible idea. People would start shooting each other over traffic altercations; parking lots would turn into shooting galleries. Not so, it turned out. Only a very, very few concealed-weapons permits have been revoked. There are only rare incidents in which people with concealed-weapons permits have used them unlawfully. Ordinary law-abiding people, it turns out, are pretty trustworthy.

Unfounded fears

I'm not the only one to draw such a conclusion. When she was Michi-   4
gan's attorney general, Democrat Jennifer Granholm opposed the state's concealed-weapons law, which took effect in 2001. But now, as governor, she's not seeking its repeal. She says that her fears—like those I had about Florida's law 20 years ago—proved to be unfounded. So far as I know, there are no politically serious moves to repeal any state's concealed weapons laws. In most of the United States, as you go to work, shop at

the mall, go to restaurants, and walk around your neighborhood, you do so knowing that some of the people you pass by may be carrying a gun. You may not even think about it. But that's all right. Experience has shown that these people aren't threats.

5   Virginia has a concealed-weapons law. But Virginia Tech was, by the decree of its administrators, a "gun-free zone." Those with concealed-weapons permits were not allowed to take their guns on campus and were disciplined when they did. A bill was introduced in the House of Delegates to allow permit holders to carry guns on campus. When it was sidetracked, a Virginia Tech administrator hailed the action and said that students, professors, and visitors would now "feel safe" on campus. Tragically, they weren't safe. Virginia Tech's "gun-free zone" was not gun free. In contrast, killers on other campuses were stopped by faculty or bystanders who had concealed-weapons permits and brandished their guns to stop the killing.

6   We may hear more about gun control at the national level. The D.C. Circuit Court of Appeals recently ruled that the District of Columbia's ban on handguns violates the Second Amendment's right "to keep and bear arms." Judge Laurence Silberman's strong opinion argues that this is consistent with the Supreme Court's ruling in a 1939 case upholding a federal law banning sawed-off shotguns; limited regulation is allowed, Silberman wrote, but not a total ban. Somewhere on the road between a law banning possession of nuclear weapons and banning all guns the Second Amendment stands in the way. This is the view as well of the liberal constitutional law scholar Laurence Tribe. The Supreme Court may take the case,which is in conflict with other circuits' rulings.

7   If it upholds the D.C. decision, there is still room for reasonable gun regulation. The mental health ruling on the Virginia Tech killer surely should have been entered into the instant check data-base to prevent him from buying guns. The National Rifle Association is working with gun control advocate Rep. Carolyn McCarthy to improve that database. But even as we fine-tune laws to make sure guns don't get into the wrong hands, maybe the opinion elites will realize that in places, where gun ownership is wide-spread, we're safer than in a "gun-free zone."

▶Building Vocabulary

Identify or define each of the following words and terms based on their context:
1. quarters (par. 1)
2. chime in (par. 1)
3. law-abiding (par. 2)
4. altercations (par. 3)
5. attorney general (par. 4)
6. brandished (par. 5)

7. sawed-off shotguns (par. 6)
8. fine-tune (par. 7)

▶ Thinking Critically about the Argument

Understanding the Writer's Argument

1. What was the reaction in the media and among Democrats after the Virginia Tech massacre?
2. What, according to Barone, are the "two tracks of political debate" over gun control laws in this country?
3. What was Barone's original reaction to Florida's concealed weapons law? What is his feeling now?
4. What does Barone say proves his point that people with concealed weapons aren't threats?
5. What pre-massacre debate on the Virginia Tech campus does Barone discuss? What is its significance, in his view?
6. What has the D.C. Circuit Court of Appeals ruled about the District of Columbia's laws on gun control? What is the possible future for the case?
7. What are some suggestions that Barone offers for "reasonable gun regulation"?
8. Who is the "opinion elite"?

Understanding the Writer's Techniques

1. Why does Barone open his essay with a review of the debate over gun control laws and illustrations of steps taken nationally and locally to deal with the issue? Is this opening effective? Explain.
2. What authority does Barone cite to support his claim about the Florida concealed weapon law?
3. What is Barone's claim in this essay?
4. Barone's essay appeared in *U.S. News & World Report*, a magazine for a very wide audience. How does that fact affect his tone?
5. What are Barone's minor propositions?
6. How does the writer employ an ethical appeal in this essay?
7. How does the writer use the rhetorical strategy of definition in this essay? Explain.
8. Is Barone's conclusion effective? Why or why not?

Exploring the Writer's Argument

1. Barone's opening paragraph strikes a tone that one could describe as derisive. Why does he use such a tone? Does this opening weaken or strengthen his argument? Why or why not?

2. The writer argues in paragraph 5 that Virginia Tech's "gun-free zone" policy was a foolish one. As evidence, he states that bystanders or faculty at other schools have stopped gunmen by brandishing weapons. Barone does not, however, offer any examples. Does this strategy weaken his argument? Why or why not?
3. In paragraph 6, Barone writes about a case from the D.C. Circuit Court of Appeals striking down a ban on handguns, based on the Second Amendment. He writes that one of the judges in that case wrote that the decision is consistent with the Supreme Court ruling banning sawed-off shotguns. Is this contradictory? Does Barone do a good job explaining this seeming paradox and marshaling it for his own uses? Explain your answer.

▶ Ideas for Writing Arguments

Prewriting

Do you think people should carry guns everywhere in their lives? Make two columns: CARRY and DON'T CARRY, and under each column, write down as many reasons for each side as possible within ten minutes.

Writing a Guided Argument

Write an essay in the form of a letter to the governor of your state in which you argue that he or she should or should not sign a concealed weapon law. First, find out what the law is in your state. If your state does not have such a law, argue for or against instituting that law. If your state does have such a law, argue for or against extending the law.

1. Open with a reference to the Virginia Tech massacre.
2. Next, refer to the Barone essay.
3. Use a self-assured tone that intimates that the other side's arguments mean nothing.
4. Write your claim in a clear thesis statement.
5. Argue at least three minor propositions.
6. Appeal to the governor's emotions using examples.
7. Close with clear policy suggestions.

Thinking, Arguing, and Writing Collaboratively

In small groups of four or five, read the original language of the Second Amendment from the U.S. Constitution: "A well regulated militia being necessary to the security of a free State, the right of the People to keep and bear arms shall not be infringed." Try to decide as a group what the

framers meant by the wording and how it relates to weapons that exist today. Reach a consensus among the group members and then come together
as a class and share your group's conclusions. Discuss as a class the dis-
crepancies, if any, among the conclusions.

Writing about the Text

Write an essay that analyzes Barone's assertion that he has been con-
verted to his present position, as has the governor of Michigan. Is his use
of this technique effective? How can Barone improve this technique?

More Writing Ideas

1. In your journal, write about the point Barone makes that "as you go
   to work, shop at the mall, go to restaurants, and walk around your
   neighborhood, you do so knowing that some of the people you pass
   by may be carrying a gun." He suggests that you might not even
   think about the point. Think about it now.
2. Write a couple of paragraphs considering the question of whether
   you would ever carry a concealed weapon to class. Why would you
   carry one, or why wouldn't you? Try to get rid of all your previous
   notions about right and wrong and just try to consider whether it's a
   good idea or not.
3. Watch Michael Moore's film *Bowling for Columbine*. Write an essay in
   the form of a review of the ideas in that movie, relating them to
   Barone's argument.

WARREN GOLDSTEIN
Why It's OK to Rat on Other Students

*Warren Goldstein is an associate professor of history and chair of the History
Department at the University of Hartford, in Connecticut. He earned his B.A.
and Ph.D. at Yale University, and has taught at SUNY/Old Westbury, in Long
Island, New York. He is the author of* Playing for Keeps: A History of Early
Baseball *(1989) and* William Sloane Coffin, Jr: A Holy Impatience *(2004),
and the coauthor of* A Brief History of American Sports *(1993). He has also
written numerous articles and essays for such publications as the* New York
Times, *the* Washington Post, *the* Nation, *and the* Chronicle of Higher Education, *in which this selection appeared in May 2007. Goldstein argues that although he is a "dyed-in-the-wood civil libertarian," he still feels that there needs
to be a culture on campus that allows students and professors to speak up when
they suspect something might be amiss with a fellow student.*

▶ Prereading: Thinking about the Essay in Advance

Have you ever been tempted to tell the authorities about something a fellow student has done, that you suspect he or she has done, or that you fear he or she might do? What would you do if you were ever in that position?

▶ Words to Watch

academy (par. 1) the community of teachers and students at colleges and universities
ethic (par. 2) system of standards
bucolic (par. 4) relating to the countryside
rants (par. 6) overblown speeches
equanimity (par. 6) evenness of temper
persistent (par. 16) continuing despite obstacles
promiscuity (par. 16) wide-ranging casual sexual behavior
loathe (par. 18) hate intensely
proactive (par. 20) taking initiative

1   Like many people in the academy, I have found myself uneasily stewing over the murders at Virginia Tech. My students and I have spent far too much time glancing over at our classroom door, wondering whether we would have been able to hold it shut if a gunman had wanted in; would I have had the courage of Liviu Librescu, who students said died protecting them?

2   I was lucky; I didn't have to deal with Seung-Hui Cho, unlike my poor colleagues in the Virginia Tech English department, who had formed a departmental task force to discuss him. At least they tried. They resisted the status quo on most campuses, the "live and let live," anti-authoritarian ethic of individualism that dominates so much of American life, especially that organized around the young.

3   Look, I'm a dyed-in-the-wool civil libertarian who's publicly condemned the USA Patriot Act, the FBI, and the trumped-up "war on terror," and I've given a half-dozen speeches (one the night of September 11, 2001) defending civil liberties in time of war. But I'm suggesting that we adopt campus versions of New York City's Metropolitan Transportation Authority slogan: If You See Something, Say Something.

4   Some years ago, in the bucolic little college town in Massachusetts where my wife and I raised our three children, some middle-schoolers boarded a school bus carrying a couple of pipe bombs in a shoebox. The wonder, of course, is that those sensitive devices survived the bumpy New England ride. But they did, and when the young engineers showed their handiwork to fellow students, someone reported the bombs to the

assistant principal, who retrieved them (what was he thinking?), dismissed school, and called the bomb squad.

Within hours my kids knew the identities of the four students who'd   5
made the bombs, and I soon learned the names from them—not from the
school, which showed itself exceptionally attentive to the rights of the
boys who had threatened the lives of dozens, if not hundreds, of their fellow students. We never got a report, never had an investigative piece in
the local newspaper, only learned in the most distant sort of way that
first, the students had been disciplined, and then, that they were back at
school. No apology from anyone. After all, they were just juveniles. (This
was before the massacre at Columbine High School.)

I ruined dinner parties with rants about my neighbors' equanimity in   6
the face of near disaster. It turns out that a group of kids had known for
weeks, even months, that the bomb makers were practicing in their back-
yards. Didn't their parents have some responsibility for knowing what
their children were up to? But the highly educated people in our college
town did not want to talk about it. Now, I hope, we can begin a long-over-
due public discussion about how we encourage and defend our students'
civil liberties—while doing a lot more to enhance their safety.

To start, we need to confront the problem that nearly all our students,   7
like our children, believe that "ratting out" a friend or fellow student is a
far worse offense than shutting up and allowing a couple of pipe bombs
to ride to school on a bumpy school bus. I tried to talk to my kids' friends
about that, as I did to my own students at the time. I was whistling into a
nor'easter. There are more descriptive metaphors.

Last week I raised these issues with my classes, and I heard about a   8
roommate who had turned a pizza box into a dartboard for an X-Acto
knife. Laughing as the blade went into a face on the box, the knife thrower
told his roommate, "This could be you." My student and his other roommate "got rid of him" by talking to someone in student affairs. I got the
impression they just emphasized the guy's weirdness, and that they didn't
get along with him. Great. So now our knife thrower lives someplace else
on the campus. "Do you think I should report him?" my student asked.
"Yes," I answered, "I do—to someone in genuine authority."

"It's easier," another student said, not to look too closely—and cer-   9
tainly not to "report" anything. Of course it is. The campus cop might not
take you seriously; a professor might laugh. "You might be wrong, and
they might think you're a sissy for being afraid," said still another guy.

In college-student culture, you don't rat. Not about your fake ID, not   10
about the drug dealer in the next dorm, not about the gun you heard
about across campus, not about the fraternity's term-paper bank, not
about an athlete's no-show "job." After all, another student explained, the
one time she told on her brothers as a kid, her father did little, and her
brothers beat her up, yelling "snitches get stitches." But college students

are on their way to becoming adults. (That's why we don't immediately call their parents when they stop attending class.) And adults need to move beyond adolescent peer bonding.

11   Maybe we should talk to them about what that means.

12   And maybe we should ask ourselves the same question. As academics, we believe in expanding the sources of knowledge as much as possible. To do intellectual work, we need access to books, journals, newspapers, and archives. Why, then, on a university campus, do we not do everything in our power to gain access to all the available information about our students? We faculty members could take a page from the example of those Virginia Tech English professors, and share impressions of our students on a more regular basis.

13   Oddly, we may need to acknowledge that our students, particularly the 18- to 20-year-olds, are less grown up than previous generations. Our student-affairs officials have been educating us about the "millennium generation," with their hovering "helicopter parents" who use cellphones to keep psychological umbilical cords connected. Nor are we, when we adopt our role as parents, guilt free. A colleague once told me that "we are having trouble with our daughter's [a college sophomore] political-science class." "We?" I asked, dissolving in laughter. But perhaps today's students do need—expect—something more from us.

14   In my university, even senior faculty members teach a full load, mostly undergraduates in relatively small classes. But that's hardly the case in big universities with large lecture classes and lots of teaching assis-

tants. That makes it hard to get to know your students (and admit it, you're more interested in your own research, right?). Plus we have legitimate concerns about students' privacy. No one wants a confidential "watch" list in an academic department. We're supposed to be teachers, not snoops. Still . . . on most campuses, we could do a lot more than we do.

It's the students who really know their fellow students, much better   15
than we ever will. They live, eat, and party with them; they hang out with or pass one another in the bathrooms and common rooms, weight rooms, dining halls and the bookstore, the library and local bars. They have an enormous amount of information about one another. As a community, we need to develop ways of inviting them to share that information, especially when it seems to veer in particularly weird directions.

We could even provide some guidelines (as one of my students re-   16
quested): Tell someone about persistent violent talk. About someone who never speaks. Really oddball loner behavior. Yes, even someone obsessed with violent video games. Fierce racism and homophobia. Calling women "hos" or ranting about promiscuity. Unmistakable "creepiness." Students have a good feel for that—we need to help them trust their instincts. We need to help female students not be afraid to report harassment—electronic as well as physical. According to my own unscientific survey over the years, too often they would rather let offensive behavior pass than become known as the "bitch" who "reported" someone. Or they're afraid to be singled out for retaliation by the harasser.

The kind of behavior I'm proposing here may make many of us un-   17
comfortable. But comfort is hardly the highest value of a university. Particularly in the humanities, teaching that doesn't make our students uncomfortable at some point isn't really good teaching, since it doesn't challenge them. Nor ought comfort to be the measure of a community's achievement. It surely would have been easier, more comfortable, for most African-Americans to continue living under segregation in the 1960s; it took a movement and an exceptional leader to help them defy the status quo and risk their lives for a more just world.

I loathe the endlessly repeated slogan, but I love the idea that we take   18
responsibility for ourselves; that we get nosier—yes, I said that, nosier—than usual. I'm not proposing that we become a nation of campus informers, but if we're going to have a chance of stopping future massacres, those of us on campuses are going to have to spend as much time talking about community members' responsibility to the whole as we talk about the right to "do one's own thing."

Look, I know we can't draw a clear line here. But at least let's debate   19
how we might draw some kind of line.

Breaking out of the prohibition on "ratting out," and playing a more   20
proactive role as faculty members, will surely result in some, maybe even much, harmless behavior being reported to authorities, some of whom

will react in heavy-handed ways. Some colleges may get sued. Or some parents and students may flock to a campus that is rethinking what the safety of the community demands. And we'll all know each other a little better, perhaps a little more than makes us comfortable.

21   Welcome to a university that just might be able to stop the next massacre. And maybe not—but we'd be trying harder, and insisting that there are values higher than individualism and "do your own thing."

22   A student of mine, I'm just remembering, flipped out before I got to class late one day a couple of weeks ago and stomped out. The other students told me the story, but he hasn't been back, and I haven't followed up. Not good.

▶ Building Vocabulary

The writer uses several idiomatic words or phrases in this selection that you might not be familiar with. Rewrite the following in your own words:

1. resisted the status quo (par. 2)
2. live and let live (par. 2)
3. anti-authoritarian (par. 2)
4. dyed-in-the-wool civil libertarian (par. 3)
5. trumped-up (par. 3)
6. whistling into a nor'easter (par. 7)
7. no-show "job" (par. 10)
8. adolescent peer bonding (par. 10)
9. take a page from (par. 12)
10. heavy-handed (par. 20)
11. flock to (par. 20)

▶ Thinking Critically about the Argument

Understanding the Writer's Argument

1. What does Goldstein admire about the faculty of the English Department at Virginia Tech in their dealings with Seung-Hui Cho?
2. With what disclaimer does Goldstein preface his support for "campus versions of . . . If You See Something, Say Something"?
3. What story does Goldstein tell about what happened in the town where he lived with his family?
4. What does Goldstein think the authorities did wrong in that situation?
5. Why do so many kids think that "ratting out" someone is such a bad act?

6. What happened in the situation of the student with the X-Acto knife and the pizza box?
7. What do students fear from authorities if they do "rat out" another student?
8. Why does the writer think students today are less grown up than other generations?
9. What does the writer suggest students look out for in their fellow students?
10. What will be the result for campuses that decide to revisit the usual policies, according to Goldstein?

Understanding the Writer's Techniques

1. What is the writer's claim in this essay?
2. Does Goldstein place his minor propositions in any strategic order? Explain.
3. Who is Goldstein's audience for this essay? How do you know? Do you think that view of audience affects his tone? Explain.
4. What kinds of appeals does the writer use in this essay?
5. Analyze Goldstein's use of narrative here. Is it effective? Why or why not?
6. Goldstein repeats the phrase "rat out" often in this essay. Is his repeated use of the phrase effective or not? Explain.
7. How well constructed is Goldstein's conclusion? What is strong about it? Weak? Explain.

Exploring the Writer's Argument

1. Analyze Goldstein's discussion of civil libertarianism in paragraph 2. Does Goldstein demonstrate that there is a conflict between what he is claiming in his essay and his political stance of civil libertarianism? Explain your answer.
2. In paragraph 12 Goldstein writes, "As academics, we believe in expanding the sources of knowledge as much as possible. To do intellectual work, we need access to books, journals, newspapers, and archives. Why, then, on a university campus, do we not do everything in our power to gain access to all the available information about our students?" Is this a valid argument? What are its strengths and weaknesses?
3. Analyze Goldstein's argument in paragraph 17. Do you agree with his analogy between people not willing to "rat out" fellow students and African-Americans who didn't challenge segregation? Explain what he means and why he has a valid or invalid argument.

▶ Ideas for Writing Arguments

Prewriting

How do you describe yourself politically? Are you conservative? Liberal? Middle-of-the-road? What does that mean when it comes to different issues, such as civil liberties, privacy, and gun control? Write for 10 minutes nonstop to consider some of these questions.

Writing a Guided Argument

Write an essay in which you outline your political stance and your feelings about Goldstein's suggestions for a culture of "tattle-tales" on campus as a hedge against violence.

1. Open your essay with a reference to the Virginia Tech massacre and your own emotional reaction to it.
2. Follow with a clear statement of your political philosophy.
3. Then, write your major proposition, linking it with your political philosophy.
4. Employ a tone of equanimity, showing how you are constantly open to new suggestions.
5. Use a short narrative as evidence for your claim.
6. Write at least two minor propositions as lessons you learned from the narrative.
7. Use both ethical and emotional appeals in your essay.
8. Close with another short narrative that underlines your major proposition.

Thinking, Arguing, and Writing Collaboratively

In small groups of three or four, discuss the possible audience for Goldstein's essay. Come up with at least two passages that you think are directed at each of the following audiences: (1) students, (2) faculty members, (3) administration members, (4) parents. Explain why your group thinks each passage could be persuasive to that audience, and then convene as a class and discuss your groups' answers.

Writing about the Text

Write an essay about Goldstein's use of narrative as evidence in his essay. Write about at least three passages in Goldstein's essay and judge them for their effectiveness. Write about what you would do if you were Goldstein revising this essay. Would you increase the amount of narrative? Decrease it? Explain your response.

More Writing Ideas

1. Write a journal entry in which you try to think of arguments against "If You See Something, Say Something," an idea Goldstein defends in his essay.
2. Write a paragraph or two about the gender issues here. If you have a female roommate who starts acting as Goldstein describes in paragraph 16, should you report her?
3. Goldstein implies that students have an especially good feel for "unmistakable creepiness" (paragraph 16). Write an essay in which you agree or disagree with this observation. Without mentioning names, draw on your own (or your friends') experiences in which you noticed (or did not notice) strange behavior in a fellow student.

JODI S. COHEN AND REX W. HUPPKE
How Safe Are America's Campuses?

Rex W. Huppke is a staff reporter for the Chicago Tribune *and Jodi S. Cohen is a higher education reporter for that paper. In their article, they look at studies and talk to academics to determine the actual level of violence on college campuses. According to an administrator at Northeastern University in Boston, "there are so few homicides on college campuses that you're much safer there than you are in almost any other venue." Suicide's a much bigger problem. But mistakes can happen, and then a Virginia Tech can happen, so schools are scrambling to balance the safety and the civil liberties of their students.*

▶ **Prereading: Thinking about the Essay in Advance**

How safe do you feel when you're at school? Do you ever get nervous about school violence, or do you just go about your business without thinking about it?

▶ **Words to Watch**

sentries (par. 1) military personnel assigned to guard duty
grapple (par. 5) struggle
maelstrom (par. 6) situation that is very confusing or turbulent
venue (par. 8) place where an event takes place
psyches (par. 17) mental states
despondent (par. 20) depressed, in despair
rampage (par. 28) outburst of violence

1   At the end of a week that shook the nation's already tenuous sense of safety, Lileana Folmar and her 16-year-old daughter stopped and examined one of more than 1,000 emergency call boxes posted like sentries along the walkways of the University of Illinois' Chicago campus.

2   "If someone presses this button, how long does it take for someone to get here?" Folmar asked a student tour guide.

3   Mother and daughter stood 650 miles from Blacksburg, VA, and the horror that shattered Virginia Tech, but the images were fresh in their minds.

4   "I want my girl to be safe," said Folmar, whose daughter is a junior at Hoffman Estates High School. "How safe is this school? This area? What kind of training does the security have?"

5   As Americans grapple with the scope and senselessness of the carnage at Virginia Tech, parents preparing to set loose their children on campuses across the country feel more compelled than ever to ask colleges and universities: How will you protect my child?

6   As with so many questions that have spun out from the maelstrom in Blacksburg, this one is not easily answered. What can a university do to ensure another troubled student won't decide to kill?

7   Hard and fast assurances are hard to come by. But for parents, there are realities that at least give perspective to the horror, and the uniqueness, of last week's tragedy.

No "Epidemic" of Violence

8   "There's no epidemic of campus violence," said Jack Levin, director of the Brudnick Center on Conflict and Violence at Northeastern University in Boston. "In fact, there are so few homicides on college campuses that you're much safer there than you are in almost any other venue."

9   Other experts agree that of all the places young adults spend their time, a college campus likely provides the largest safety net. There are resident advisers in dorms, counseling centers, campus police, peers.

10   Still, students in need of help, like the Virginia Tech gunman, can fall through the cracks. But how can a school pinpoint those who fit the profile of a killer?

11   "If what we are looking for is some scientific perfect solution, that if we just unravel these incidents carefully enough we will find the key and put the key in the lock and prevent this from happening again, that is extraordinarily naïve in my view," said Gary Pavela, director of student judicial programs at the University of Maryland at College Park. "A lot of things were done right at Virginia Tech, and it still didn't work."

12   Levin said the typical mass murderer, including Virginia Tech shooter Seung Hui Cho, has suffered from years of chronic depression and frustration, blames everyone but himself for his problems and is socially isolated.

But many who fit that profile will never go on to harm others. They   13
may, however, try to kill themselves.

About 9 percent of college students say they have seriously consid-   14
ered attempting suicide, according to a 2006 study by the American
College Health Association. Nearly 18 percent said they suffered from
depression.

"When you think about those numbers, you realize there are a lot of   15
struggling students out there," said Joseph Hermes, director of the counseling center at the University of Illinois at Chicago.

In 2004, after six suicides at New York University, the school required   16
new students to go through an orientation that included dramatic presentations of the challenges of college life, including depression.

The Virginia Tech slayings will spur higher-education leaders to re-   17
examine how they tend to students' psyches. Some work in that vein has
already begun.

Penn State University recently created a research center to gather data   18
from counseling centers across the country. But Ben Lock, national coordina-
tor for the new Center for the Study of College Student Mental Health, said
it's also imperative that school officials on the same campus collaborate.

"[They] need to have, as much as possible, the ability for information   19
to flow between the people who need to be in the know," Locke said. "If
there is a student really in distress and distressing others, colleges and
universities need to do the best that they can to find ways to work as a
collaborative team around those students."

Providing despondent students with help can be legally and logisti-   20
cally difficult.

Unless a student is an immediate threat to himself or others, school   21
officials are restricted by privacy and anti-discrimination laws. In most
cases they can't inform parents of problems their children might be having, whether they involve mental illness, poor grades or underage drinking. Even classmates and professors who may be at risk can't be told.

Last fall, George Washington University settled a lawsuit brought by   22
a former student who was involuntarily suspended after he sought help
for depression. The amount of the settlement was not disclosed.

"I always felt we were in a double bind," said George Washington   23
President Stephen Trachtenberg, "If you have concerns about a student, if
you act too passively or don't act at all, you have neglected the interests
of others and perhaps even that student. But if you act too aggressively,
you run the risk of having violated that student's rights."

Enlisting the Students

Dr. Gary Slutkin, head of the Chicago Project for Violence Prevention and   24
founder of the anti-violence group CeaseFire, said university officials

may want to consider enlisting students to be their eyes and ears on campus, looking and listening for people who show signs of needing help.

25   "To prevent this, you need to have a network that is more than counselors in their offices," Slutkin said.

26   He posited that a large campus could hire perhaps 30 students, train them to recognize the signs of isolation and depression and then pay them to spend time each day walking the dorms, talking to people, seeking out those who might feel isolated.

27   During the tour Folmar and her daughter took Friday at UIC, the majority of questions involved tuition, academic majors, class size and housing.

28   Bloomington, IL., resident Randy Pearson said he's more concerned about his daughter living in a city than he is about a shooting rampage.

29   "The big thing happens so rarely," he said. "You have to have some faith in humanity overall to let your kid leave the house."

30   When questions of safety did come up, Daniel DiCesare, the university's assistant director of admissions, told parents about the university's emergency call boxes and its police force of 70 officers.

31   "I know for parents and students going to college anywhere, safety is a concern," DiCesare said. "We were reminded of that this week at Virginia Tech. From the university's perspective, UIC really takes safety seriously."

32   But questions about safety will continue, even if the answers remain out of reach.

33   "Sometimes there are questions that don't have fast, easy answers," said Trachtenberg, the George Washington president. "And this is one."

A Father's View

34 C. Bryan Cloyd, a Virginia Tech accounting and information systems professor, is the father of Austin Cloyd (right), one of the 32 victims killed in Blacksburg, VA. The former University of Illinois professor had this to say about campus security in the wake of the tragedy:

35   "Universities are vulnerable places and then need to be. We can't put scanners on all of our doors. We don't want to be airport security at a university. There are probably some things we can learn from this.

36   "I want to challenge our public officials to think about what we could learn from this and think objectively, not emotionally, about what we can learn and what we can do better. But in a free society, we have to balance the cost and the benefits of all of that, and certainly a university setting is the epitome of that free society."

▶ **Building Vocabulary**

Write definitions of the following and use them in sentence of your own:

1. tenuous (par. 1)

2. compelled (par. 5)
3. assurances (par. 7)
4. naive (par. 11)
5. imperative (par. 18)
6. logistically (par. 20)

▶ **Thinking Critically about the Argument**

Understanding the Writers' Argument

1. What do the writers say is the question on parents' minds as the parents bring their children to college?
2. What is one of the statements that the writers say "at least give perspective to the horror, and the uniqueness, of" the Virginia Tech massacre?
3. What, according to Gary Pavela, of the University of Maryland, is the reality of security on college campuses?
4. What is the reality about suicide on college campuses, according to the writers?
5. What have some colleges done to improve mental health on campuses?
6. How is helping students and protecting their rights sometimes in conflict?
7. What does the head of the Chicago Project for Violence Protection propose?

Understanding the Writers' Techniques

1. What is the writers' claim? Do they express it clearly? If so, where? If not, how is it expressed?
2. What grounds do Cohen and Huppke offer to support their claim?
3. How do the writers use narrative to support their claim?
4. Analyze the transitions the writers use in their essay. Which are most effective?
5. In paragraphs 20 through 23 the writers discuss the problems of dealing with depressed students. How do Cohen and Huppke make their own claims on the issue known?
6. Analyze the writers' use of quotations to support their claim.
7. How effective is the writers' conclusion? Explain.

Exploring the Writers' Argument

1. This essay is a newspaper article written by reporters; it is not an editorial. Does that make the claim more difficult to spot? Why or why not?

2. This essay is about school violence, and was written with the Virginia Tech massacre in mind. Why do the writers spend so much time discussing suicide? How do they show its relevance to the argument?
3. How effective do you find the section headings? Why do the writers break the essay into sections?
4. The writers use quotations by officials at many universities, but don't spend a great deal of space on any one university. Is this a strength or a weakness of the essay? Explain your point of view.

▶ Ideas for Writing Arguments

Prewriting

If you were writing a newspaper article about how your school is managing security, and you had to do some interviews for your research, who would you interview, and why?

Writing a Guided Argument

You are to write an essay about the state of violence on your campus: how violent is your campus, and what is the administration doing to prevent violence? Include suicide as a form of violence. Find two people in the school administration or faculty and interview them for this essay. You may tape your interview or simply take notes.

1. Open your essay with a short narrative setting the scene.
2. Take a purely neutral tone, as if your essay is going to run as a news article.
3. Write your major proposition clearly near the beginning of your essay.
4. Break your essay into three sections in which you cover your minor propositions.
5. Use quotes from your interviews to support your minor propositions.
6. Make sure you cover what your college's procedures are for dealing with violent offenders.
7. Close with a quote from one of your interviewees.

Thinking, Arguing, and Writing Collaboratively

In small groups of three or four, exchange your Writing a Guided Argument papers. Offer suggestions in the form of a paragraph or two to help your classmates develop their essays. Return the papers to your peers and continue exchanging papers until everyone in your group has read and commented on your paper. Then revise your paper based on the comments you have received.

Writing about the Text

In their essay, the writers refer several times to parents dropping their children off at school, or parents being concerned about their children at school. Men and women attending college are adults, almost always 18 years or older. Can't people who are of age take care of themselves in college? Write an essay in which you argue that the writers' essay is weakened by this fact or is not weakened by this fact.

More Writing Ideas

1. In your journal, write about whether you ever fear for your safety when you're at college. Compare how you feel about your safety when you're off campus.
2. Write a paragraph or two in which you consider how colleges can best identify and help depressed and "despondent" students.
3. Pretend that you have a roommate who has demonstrated disturbing behavior and made threatening comments. Write an essay about how you would react and what steps you would or would not take.

ADAM GOPNIK
Shootings

Adam Gopnik was born in 1956 in Philadelphia but reared in Montreal, Canada, where his parents were professors at McGill University. Gopnik took his undergraduate degree at that school. He writes regularly for the New Yorker *magazine, in which this article appeared in April 2007. From 1995 to 2000, Gopnik and his family lived in Paris, where he wrote a column for the* New Yorker *called "Paris Journals." In 2000 he published a collection of those columns called* Paris to the Moon. *In "Shootings," Gopnik uses the Virginia Tech massacre as a jumping-off point for his argument about the gun control laws in the United States: semiautomatic weapons are legal here. In places where they are illegal, these kinds of massacres don't happen anymore. He says that "the point of lawmaking is not to act as precisely as possible, in order to punish the latest crime; it is to act as comprehensively as possible, in order to prevent the next one."*

▶ Prereading: Thinking about the Essay in Advance

What do you know about the gun control laws in this country? What about the ones in your state? If you're aware of the laws, do you agree or disagree with them? Why?

▶ Words to Watch

eccentric (par. 1) strange, not normal
heartrending (par. 1) horribly sad
intervening (par. 2) something that happens in between two things
narcissism (par. 2) excessive self-love as a reaction to a low self-esteem
subsequent (par. 4) happening after something
notorious (par. 5) well-known for something bad

1   The cell phones in the pockets of the dead students were still ringing when we were told that it was wrong to ask why. As the police cleared the bodies from the Virginia Tech engineering building, the cell phones rang, in the eccentric varieties of ring tones, as parents kept trying to see if their children were O.K. To imagine the feelings of the police as they carried the bodies and heard the ringing is heartrending; to imagine the feelings of the parents who were calling—dread, desperate hope for a sudden answer and the bliss of reassurance, dawning grief—is unbearable. But the parents, and the rest of us, were told that it was not the right moment to ask how the shooting had happened—specifically, why an obviously disturbed student, with a history of mental illness, was able to buy guns whose essential purpose is to kill people—and why it happens over and over again in America. At a press conference, Virginia's governor, Tim Kaine, said, "People who want to . . . make it their political hobby horse to ride, I've got nothing but loathing for them. . . . At this point, what it's about is comforting family members . . . and helping this community heal. And so to those who want to try to make this into some little crusade, I say take that elsewhere."

2   If the facts weren't so horrible, there might be something touching in the Governor's deeply American belief that "healing" can take place magically, without the intervening practice called "treating." The logic is unusual but striking: the aftermath of a terrorist attack is the wrong time to talk about security, the aftermath of a death from lung cancer is the wrong time to talk about smoking and the tobacco industry, and the aftermath of a car crash is the wrong time to talk about seat belts. People talked about the shooting, of course, but much of the conversation was devoted to musings on the treatment of mental illness in universities, the problem of "narcissism," violence in the media and in popular culture, copycat killings, the alienation of immigrant students, and the question of Evil.

Some people, however—especially people outside America—were ea- 3
ger to talk about it in another way, and even to embark on a little crusade.
The whole world saw that the United States has more gun violence than
other countries because we have more guns and are willing to sell them to
madmen who want to kill people. Every nation has violent loners, and they
tend to have remarkably similar profiles from one country and culture to
the next. And every country has known the horror of having a lunatic get
his hands on a gun and kill innocent people. But on a recent list of the fourteen worst mass shootings in Western democracies since the nineteen-
sixties the United States claimed seven, and, just as important, no other
country on the list has had a repeat performance as severe as the first.

In Dunblane, Scotland, in 1996, a gunman killed sixteen children and 4
a teacher at their school. Afterward, the British gun laws, already restrictive, were tightened—it's now against the law for any private citizen in
the United Kingdom to own the kinds of guns that Cho Seung-Hui used
at Virginia Tech—and nothing like Dunblane has occurred there since. In
Quebec, after a school shooting took the lives of fourteen women in 1989,
the survivors helped begin a gun-control movement that resulted in legislation bringing stronger, though far from sufficient, gun laws to Canada.
(There have been a couple of subsequent shooting sprees, but on a
smaller scale, and with far fewer dead.) In the Paris suburb of Nanterre,
in 2002, a man killed eight people at a municipal meeting. Gun control became a key issue in the presidential election that year, and there has been
no repeat incident.

So there is no American particularity about loners, disenfranchised 5
immigrants, narcissism, alienated youth, complex moral agency, or Evil.
There is an American particularity about guns. The arc is apparent. Forty
years ago, a man killed fourteen people on a college campus in Austin,
Texas; this year, a man killed thirty-two in Blacksburg, Virginia. Not
enough was done between those two massacres to make weapons of mass
killing harder to obtain. In fact, while campus killings continued—
Columbine being the most notorious, the shooting in the one-room Amish
schoolhouse among the most recent—weapons have gotten more lethal,
and, in states like Virginia, where the N.R.A. is powerful, no harder to buy.

Reducing the number of guns available to crazy people will neither 6
relieve them of their insanity nor stop them from killing. Making it
more difficult to buy guns that kill people is, however, a rational way to
reduce the number of people killed by guns. Nations with tight gun
laws have, on the whole, less gun violence; countries with somewhat restrictive gun laws have some gun violence; countries with essentially no
gun laws have a lot of gun violence. (If you work hard, you can find a
statistical exception hiding in a corner, but exceptions are just that.
Some people who smoke their whole lives don't get lung cancer, while
some people who never smoke do; still, the best way not to get lung
cancer is not to smoke.)

7   It's true that in renewing the expired ban on assault weapons we can't guarantee that someone won't shoot people with a semi-automatic pistol, and that by controlling semi-automatic pistols we can't reduce the chances of someone killing people with a rifle. But the point of lawmaking is not to act as precisely as possible, in order to punish the latest crime; it is to act as comprehensively as possible, in order to prevent the next one. Semiautomatic Glocks and Walthers, Cho's weapons, are for killing people. They are not made for hunting, and it's not easy to protect yourself with them. (If having a loaded semi-automatic on hand kept you safe, cops would not be shot as often as they are.)

8   Rural America is hunting country, and hunters need rifles and shot-guns—with proper licensing, we'll live with the risk. There is no reason that any private citizen in a democracy should own a handgun. At some point, that simple truth will register. Until it does, phones will ring for dead children, and parents will be told not to ask why.

▶ Building Vocabulary

For each of the following phrases, explain from the context or your own research what Gopnik means:

1. press conference (par. 1)
2. hobby horse (par. 1)
3. copycat killings (par. 2)
4. repeat performance (par. 3)
5. municipal meeting (par. 4)
6. disenfranchised immigrants (par. 5)
7. alienated youth (par. 5)
8. moral agency (par. 5)

▶ Thinking Critically about the Argument

Understanding the Writer's Argument

1. What does Gopnik think about Governor Tom Kaine's statement at his press conference? Why?
2. Why does the writer think the time after a crisis is the perfect time to talk about politics?
3. What does Gopnik say about how the rest of the world views gun violence in the United States?
4. What were the reactions of the British and Canadian governments to gun violence in their countries?
5. What is the difference, according to Gopnik, between the violence in Austin in 1996 and the violence in Virginia in 2007?
6. What does Gopnik think is "a rational way to reduce the number of people killed by guns"?
7. What, according to Gopnik, is the point of lawmaking?

Understanding the Writer's Techniques

1. What is Gopnik's claim in this essay? Where is it most clearly expressed? What are the grounds he provides for his claim?
2. Who is the audience for this essay? Offer examples to explain your answer.
3. What is the writer's tone in this essay? Offer examples to explain your answer.
4. How does Gopnik use emotional appeals in his essay? Explain.
5. How does Gopnik use causal analysis in his essay? Is it effective? Why or why not?
6. How effective is the discussion of the American character in paragraph 5? Why?
7. Why, in paragraph 7, does Gopnik explain to his reader what the point of lawmaking is not, before he explains what it is? Do you think this is an effective rhetorical technique? Why or why not?
8. How effective is the closing paragraph? Why?

Exploring the Writer's Argument

1. Do you think that Gopnik's opening is too emotional, or is it effective? Why? Is it possible for a piece of writing to be both effective and *too* emotional or *too* coldly logical? Explain.
2. In paragraph 4 of his essay, Gopnik includes a list of incidents of gun violence from countries other than the United States. What effect does this list have on the reader? What is Gopnik's intention here, do you think?
3. This essay appeared in the *New Yorker*, which is read by a highly educated audience. How do you think that fact affects the tone of this essay? Offer examples to support your point.

▶ Ideas for Writing Arguments

Prewriting

Have you or someone you know ever owned a gun? Why or why not? Have you ever fired a handgun? Why or why not? Do you think handguns are useful objects for the private citizen?

Writing a Guided Argument

Gopnik writes that "there is no reason that any private citizen in a democracy should own a handgun." Write an essay in which you argue for or against Gopnik's statement.

1. Begin with a paragraph that refers to Gopnik's essay and restates his claim.

2. Next, explain your own claim in response to Gopnik's.
3. Outline your minor propositions in support of your claim.
4. Use an ethical appeal in your essay.
5. Support each of your minor propositions with facts, hypothetical situations, and (or) emotional appeals.
6. Use strong transitions.
7. Address at least one view from the opposition's perspective.
8. Rebut the opposition's argument.
9. End your essay with another reference to Gopnik's argument, recapitulating why you think he is correct or incorrect.

Thinking, Arguing, and Writing Collaboratively

Exchange your Writing a Guided Argument essay with another member of the class. Has your partner written an effective paper? Write a note to your partner about how he or she could improve (1) the statement of the claim, (2) the statement of the grounds for the claim, and (3) the amount and effectiveness of the evidence the author uses.

Writing about the Text

Write an essay discussing Gopnik's use of ethical appeals in this essay. Are his appeals effective? What could he do to strengthen those appeals?

More Writing Ideas

1. Write a journal entry considering Gopnik's proposition that a tragedy is actually the perfect time to discuss more than just supporting the victims. What does he mean? Do you agree?
2. Write a paragraph or two about violence as portrayed in the media. Do you think violence in movies, music, and video games are in any way responsible for massacres? Consider the use by the Virginia Tech killer of the South Korean film *Old Boy* in his communiqués to the news media.
3. Write an essay in which you argue in support of or in opposition to the following proposition: "When guns are outlawed, only outlaws will have guns."

12 ▶ Work, Money, and Class: Who Benefits?

As economists tell us, the middle class in the United States is shrinking and the gulf that has always existed between the rich and the poor is getting wider. The rich are getting richer, the poor are getting poorer, and everybody is trying to figure out why. Although politicians pass tax cuts or raise and lower interest rates to help the economy, people suffer from poverty in our own country. Meanwhile, while poverty rises, Americans are still working harder. While many Europeans have 35-hour workweeks and four weeks of vacation a year, Americans are veritable workaholics. Although officially, we have a 40-hour workweek in this country, it is not unusual for people to work 50-, 60-, even 70-hour weeks on a regular basis.

How do our attitudes toward work and working affect our policies and our lives? Linda Hishman expresses alarm in her essay, "Off to Work She Should Go." The current trend of married mothers leaving the workforce, she believes, is especially bad because it is the educated women who leave their jobs in the greatest numbers. In "The Case Against Chores," novelist Jane Smiley takes a leisurely look at how one's feelings toward work develop at home. She raises the interesting point that many people don't love what they do because they are taught not to as children. Conservative writer David Brooks takes on a mystery, explaining patiently in "The Triumph of Hope Over Self-Interest" why the middle class and poor don't vote for politicians who might make their lives easier. He argues that we just don't want to believe that we're not rich. If you criticize the wealthy, you criticize us all, this argument goes, because we all want to see ourselves as rich people. Some writers use their pen to try to expose what they see as injustice and inequality. Herbert J. Gans, in "Fitting the Poor into the Economy," doesn't like the attitude of Americans toward the poor. He says we have a notion of the poor as "too lazy or morally deficient to deserve assistance," an attitude, in Gans's opinion, that causes needless suffering. These four writers, all writing on a related topic, show the range of approaches to the timeless issues of work, money, and class.

LINDA HIRSHMAN
Off to Work She Should Go

Linda Hirshman was born in 1944 in Cleveland. She has a law degree from the University of Chicago and a Ph.D. in philosophy from the University of Illinois, Chicago. She is a former professor of philosophy and women's studies at Brandeis University. She is the author of The Women's Guide to Law School *(1999) and* Get to Work: A Manifesto for Women of the World *(2006), and the coauthor of* Hard Bargains: The Politics of Sex *(1998). In* Get to Work, *Hirshman argues that men should share the burden of child care and that when educated women leave the workforce, they are harming their cause. Her blog,* Get to Work, *is at gettoworkmanifesto.com/blog. In this essay, published in the* New York Times *in 2007, Hirshman takes as her starting point recently released government statistics that show married mothers leaving the workforce. She argues that this is a serious and negative trend, one that can be partially addressed by changing the tax code.*

▶ Prereading: Thinking about the Essay in Advance

Do you have or plan to have children? If so, do you plan to work while raising your children? Why should mothers go to college if they are just going to stay home and take care of children?

▶ Words to Watch

number crunchers (par. 1) slang for people who work with numbers, such as accountants and statisticians
magnitude (par. 2) size
revive (par. 3) come back with some energy
exodus (par. 4) mass flight from something
speculate (par. 6) guess
allocates (par. 12) distributes
pool (par. 12) group of possible participants

1   The United States Bureau of Labor Statistics recently published its long-awaited study, "Trends in Labor Force Participation of Married Mothers of Infants." "In recent years," the number crunchers reported, "the labor force participation of married mothers, especially those with young children, has stopped its advance."

2   Sixty percent of married mothers of preschool children are now in the work force, four percentage points fewer than in 1997. The rate for mar-

ried mothers of infants fell by about six percentage points, to 53.5 percent. The bureau further reports that the declines "have occurred across all educational levels and, for most groups, by about the same magnitude."

In sum, sometime well before the 2000 recession, wives with infants and toddlers began leaving the work force. And they stayed out even after the economy began to revive.   3

For several years, experts have been arguing about the "opt-out" revolution—the perception that there has been an exodus of young mothers from the work force. Heather Boushey of the Center for Economic and Policy Research called the opt-out revolution a myth, and asserted that married mothers don't drop out any more than other women in a bad economy. The new report is strong evidence that something really is going on.   4

Why are married mothers leaving their jobs? The labor bureau's report includes some commonsense suggestions, but none that fully explains the situation. New mothers with husbands in the top 20 percent of earnings work least, the report notes. As Ernest Hemingway said, the rich do have more money. So they also have more freedom to leave their jobs. But why do they take the option? It's easier in the short term, sure, but it's easier to forgo lots of things, like going to college or having children at all. People don't—nor should they—always do the easier thing.   5

The authors also speculate that the pressure of working and running a household is great. They do not say, however, that working hours have increased as participation has declined. Educated women, they report, work 42.2 hours a week on average and those with professional degrees, 45—hardly the "80-hour week" of legend.   6

Poorer mothers can less afford child care, and because they earn less, their opportunity costs of not working are lower, the authors suggest. But for these women, lost income cuts deeper. And this factor, like the average number of hours worked, has not changed since 1997.   7

What has changed in the last decade is that the job of motherhood has ramped up. Mothers today spend more time on child care than women did in 1965, a time when mothers were much less likely to have paying jobs, family scholars report.   8

The pressure to increase mothering is enormous. For years, women have been on the receiving end of negative messages about parenting and working. One conservative commentator said the lives of working women added up to "just a pile of pay stubs." When the National Institute of Child Health reported recently that long hours in day care added but a single percentage point to the still-normal range of rambunctious behavior in children, newspaper headlines read, "Day Care, Behavior Problems Linked in Study."   9

Should we care if women leave the work force? Yes, because participation in public life allows women to use their talents and to powerfully affect society. And once they leave, they usually cannot regain the income   10 or status they had. The Center for Work-Life Policy, a research organization founded by Sylvia Ann Hewlett of Columbia, found that women lose an average of 18 percent of their earning power when they temporarily leave the work force. Women in business sectors lose 28 percent.

11   And despite the happy talk of "on ramps" back in, only 40 percent of even high-powered professionals get back to full-time work at all.

12   That the most educated have opted out the most should raise questions about how our society allocates scarce educational resources. The next generation of girls will have a greatly reduced pool of role models.

13   But what is to be done? Organizations like Moms Rising and the Mothers Movement Online have stepped up the pressure for reforms like flexible work hours and paid parental leave. Such changes probably would help lower-income women in the most unforgiving workplaces. But they are unlikely to affect the behavior of the highly educated women with the highest opt-out rates.

14   We could make an effort to change men's attitudes. Sociologists have found that mothers (rich and poor) still do twice the housework and child care that fathers do, and even the next generation of males say they won't sacrifice work for home. But in the short term, it might be easier to change the tax code.

15   In most American marriages, wives earn less than their husbands. Since the tax code encourages joint filing (by making taxes lower for those who do), many couples figure that the "extra" dollars the wife brings in will be piled on top of the husband's income and taxed at the highest rates, close to 50 percent, according to estimates made by Ed McCaffery, a tax professor at the University of Southern California. Considering the cost of child care, couples often conclude that her working adds nothing to the family treasury.

16   If married couples were taxed as the separate income earners they often are, women would be liberated from some of the pressure to reduce their "labor force participation," as the labor bureau would say.

17   Labor statistics are always couched in such dry language, but it reveals a powerful reality: working mothers, rich and poor, struggle with their competing commitments. Now that we have seen the reality, it is time to address it.

▶ Building Vocabulary

For each of the following institutions, look up and explain any political affiliations, if it is a private or governmental body, and in your own words, what it does:

1. United States Bureau of Labor Statistics (par. 1)
2. Center for Economic and Policy Research (par. 4)
3. National Institute of Child Health (par. 9)

4. Center for Work-Life Policy (par. 10)
5. Moms Rising (par. 13)
6. Mothers Movement Online (par. 13)

▶ Thinking Critically about the Argument

Understanding the Writer's Argument

1. What is the conclusion of the study by the U.S. Bureau of Labor Statistics?
2. What is the "opt-out" revolution?
3. How does the new study provide evidence of the opt-out revolution?
4. What speculations does the study make for the reasons for the opt-out revolution?
5. What, according to Hirshman, is the real reason for the opt-out revolution?
6. Who is pressuring women to "increase mothering," according to Hirshman?
7. Why does the writer think that we should care about the opt-out revolution?
8. What does Hirshman think can be done to reverse the opt-out revolution?

Understanding the Writer's Techniques

1. What is the rhetorical effect of Hirshman's starting her essay with a quote from the U.S. Bureau of Labor Statistics study?
2. Which sentence best states Hirshman's major proposition? Is the sentence effectively placed? Explain.
3. Write an outline of the minor propositions in the essay. Which is the most effective argument?
4. What is the writer's tone? Who is her audience, and how does the audience relate to the tone she uses?
5. Where does Hirshman use causal analysis in her essay? Is her use of this rhetorical strategy effective? Explain your answers.
6. Where do you find emotional appeals in the essay? Do you find them effective? Why or why not?
7. Paraphrase the argument in paragraphs 14 through 16.
8. Do you think Hirshman's final paragraph is effective, or is it too short and cursory? Explain your answer.

Exploring the Writer's Argument

1. Analyze Hirshman's argument in paragraph 10. Do you think her point is the most valid one she could come up with? How could one argue that Hirshman is being presumptuous in this paragraph?

2. Hirshman writes in paragraph 14 that to change the amount women work, we "could make an effort to change men's attitudes . . . . But in the short term, it might be easier to change the tax code." Do you think this point evades the issue? Do you think Hirshman's essay requires more focus on the problem of men? Explain your answers.
3. Do you think Hirshman's discussion of taxes near the end of her essay is effective? Boring? Inconsequential? Explain your answers?

▶Ideas for Writing Arguments

Prewriting

Some men choose the role of "househusband," staying home and taking care of their children while the mother of the children goes to work. What are your feelings about this arrangement?

Writing a Guided Argument

Write an essay arguing that more men should stay home and take care of their children while their wives go out into the workforce. Check library or online sources for quotes and (or) statistics in support of this proposition before you begin your essay.

1. Open your essay with a quote from one of your sources, citing that source as an authority.
2. Write your major proposition clearly and forcefully.
3. Offer at least three minor propositions that explain why men should stay home with their children.
4. At least one of your minor propositions should be an emotional appeal to your reader.
5. Support at least one of your minor propositions with another quote or statistic from one of your sources.
6. Anticipate critics' objections to your major proposition.
7. Close your essay with a conclusion that offers a particular policy change that the federal or state government could implement to make more men stay home with their children.

Thinking, Arguing, and Writing Collaboratively

After dividing into four equal groups, read your essays from the Writing a Guided Argument essay out loud to each other within your group. Agree by consensus which essay has the strongest argument in your group. Discuss the strengths of the strongest essay and develop a list of some of the weaknesses of the weaker essays. Form a list of "lessons" to be learned from this exercise and share them with the class.

Writing about the Text

Write an essay exploring the paragraph structure of Hirshman's essay. Note that many are just a few sentences in length. What do the sentences tell you about the writer's intended audience? Do short paragraphs enhance an argumentative presentation? Or do they "dumb down" the discussion? Address these issues in an essay.

More Writing Ideas

1. Write a journal entry about the demands working mothers face every day. Look at the problem as a journey through a typical day and try to imagine as many details as you can.
2. Hirshman suggests that one of the problems with mothers not working enough is the attitudes of men. Write two or three paragraphs in which you try to come up with ways to change men's attitudes.
3. Write an essay in which you argue for or against the proposition that women who are working at home, taking care of their children, are doing more for society than those women who go out into the workforce.

JANE SMILEY
The Case Against Chores

Novelist Jane Smiley was born in Los Angeles in 1950 and was reared near St. Louis, Missouri. She was educated at Vassar College and the Writer's Workshop at the University of Iowa. Her novels include The Age of Grief *(1987),* A Thousand Acres *(1991), for which she won the Pulitzer Prize for fiction, and* Horse Heaven *(2000). She has written for many publications, including the* New Yorker, *the* New York Times Magazine, *the* Nation, *and, reflecting her interest in horses,* Practical Horseman. *This selection appeared in* Harper's *in 1995 and has an argument that most children would celebrate.*

▶ Prereading: Thinking about the Essay in Advance

How can parents rear their children to appreciate the value of work? Who do you know who loves work? Hates work? How do you feel about work?

▶ Words to Watch

unrelenting (par. 1) not weakening in force
gleaned (par. 2) found out
pastimes (par. 2) activities

alienated (par. 2) separated from one's true interests
tack (par. 5) put on a horse's saddle and bridle
bales (par. 5) piles
humaneness (par. 5) basic kindness

1   I've lived in the upper Midwest for twenty-one years now, and I'm
here to tell you that the pressure to put your children to work is unrelenting. So far I've squirmed out from under it, and my daughters have
led a life of almost tropical idleness, much to their benefit. My son, however, may not be so lucky. His father was himself raised in Iowa and put
to work at an early age, and you never know when, in spite of all my husband's best intentions, that early training might kick in.

2   Although "chores" are so sacred in my neck of the woods that almost
no one ever discusses their purpose, I have over the years gleaned some
of the reasons parents give for assigning them. I'm not impressed. Mostly
the reasons have to do with developing good work habits or, in the absence of good work habits, at least habits of working. No such thing as a
free lunch, any job worth doing is worth doing right, work before play, all
of that. According to this reasoning, the world is full of jobs that no one
wants to do. If we divide them up and get them over with, then we can go
on to pastimes we like. If we do them "right," then we won't have to do
them again. Lots of times, though, in a family, that *we* doesn't operate.
The operative word is *you*. The practical result of almost every child-labor
scheme that I've witnessed is the child doing the dirty work and the parent getting the fun: Mom cooks and Sis does the dishes; the parents plan
and plant the garden, the kids weed it. To me, what this teaches the child
is the lesson of alienated labor: not to love the work but to get it over
with; not to feel pride in one's contribution but to feel resentment at the
waste of one's time.

3   Another goal of chores: The child contributes to the work of maintaining the family. According to this rationale, the child comes to understand what it takes to have a family, and to feel that he or she is an important, even indispensable member of it. But come on. Would you really
want to feel loved primarily because you're the one who gets the floors
mopped? Wouldn't you rather feel that your family's love simply exists
all around you, no matter what your contribution? And don't the parents
love their children anyway, whether the children vacuum or not? Why lie
about it just to get the housework done? Let's be frank about the other
half of the equation too. In this day and age, it doesn't take much work at
all to manage a household, at least in the middle class—maybe four hours
a week to clean the house and another four to throw the laundry into the
washing machine, move it to the dryer, and fold it. Is it really a good idea
to set the sort of example my former neighbors used to set, of mopping

the floor every two days, cleaning the toilets every week, vacuuming every day, dusting, dusting, dusting? Didn't they have anything better to do than serve their house?

Let me confess that I wasn't expected to lift a finger when I was grow-   4
ing up. Even when my mother had a full-time job, she cleaned up after me, as did my grandmother. Later there was a housekeeper. I would leave my room in a mess when I headed off for school and find it miraculously neat when I returned. Once in a while I vacuumed, just because I liked the pattern the Hoover made on the carpet. I did learn to run water in my cereal bowl before setting it in the sink.

Where I discovered work was at the stable, and, in fact, there is no   5
housework like horsework. You've got to clean the horses' stalls, feed them, groom them, tack them up, wrap their legs, exercise them, turn them out, and catch them. You've got to clip them and shave them. You have to sweep the aisle, clean your tack and your boots, carry bales of hay and buckets of water. Minimal horsekeeping, rising just to the level of humaneness, requires many more hours than making a few beds, and horsework turned out to be a good preparation for the real work of adulthood, which is rearing children. It was a good preparation not only because it was similar in many ways but also because my desire to do it, and to do a good job of it, grew out of my love of and interest in my horse. I can't say that cleaning out her bucket when she manured in it was an actual joy, but I knew she wasn't going to do it herself. I saw the purpose of my labor, and I wasn't alienated from it.

Probably to the surprise of some of those who knew me as a child, I   6
have turned out to be gainfully employed. I remember when I was in seventh grade, one of my teachers said to me, strongly disapproving, "The trouble with you is you do only what you want to do!" That continues to be the trouble with me, except that over the years I have wanted to do more and more.

My husband worked hard as a child, out-Iowa-ing the Iowans, if such a   7
thing is possible. His dad had him mixing cement with a stick when he was five, pushing wheelbarrows not long after. It's a long sad tale on the order of two miles to school and both ways uphill. The result is, he's a great worker, much better than I am, but all the while he's doing it he wishes he weren't. He thinks of it as work; he's torn between doing a good job and longing not to be doing it at all. Later, when he's out on the golf course, where he really wants to be, he feels a little guilty, knowing there's work that should have been done before he gave in and took advantage of the beautiful day.

Good work is not the work we assign children but the work they   8
want to do, whether it's reading in bed (where would I be today if my parents had rousted me out and put me to scrubbing floors?) or cleaning their rooms or practicing the flute or making roasted potatoes with rosemary and Parmesan for the family dinner. It's good for a teenager to

suddenly decide that the bathtub is so disgusting she'd better clean it herself. I admit that for the parent, this can involve years of waiting. But if she doesn't want to wait, she can always spend her time dusting.

▶ Building Vocabulary

Explain these colloquialisms in Smiley's essay:

1. that early training might kick in (par. 1)
2. in my neck of the woods (par. 2)
3. I wasn't expected to lift a finger (par. 4)
4. I have turned out to be gainfully employed (par. 6)
5. he's torn between doing a good job (par. 7)

▶ Thinking Critically about the Argument

Understanding the Writer's Argument

1. Why have Smiley's daughters avoided any work, and why might her son not be so lucky?
2. What are the reasons people give chores to their children?
3. What does Smiley think is the result of giving kids the dirty work in a job?
4. What is "alienated labor"?
5. What is Smiley's answer to the rationale that putting kids to work "contributes to the work of maintaining the family"? (par. 3)
6. What activity kept Smiley from being alienated from work? How did this happen?
7. What was Smiley's husband's childhood like? What has been the result, as it relates to his work habits?

Understanding the Writer's Techniques

1. What is the major proposition of this essay?
2. This essay appeared in *Harper's*, a magazine that attracts a highly educated, relatively wealthy readership. How does that fact affect the writer's tone?
3. How does Smiley attempt to appeal to her readers' emotions in this essay?
4. How does Smiley rebut the arguments in favor of giving chores to children? How effective are her rebuttals?
5. What minor propositions does Smiley offer to support her argument against chores?
6. Which is Smiley's strongest paragraph? Explain your response.
7. Smiley writes about a subject she loves, horses, in paragraph 5. Analyze her use of language in that paragraph. How does she make the paragraph effective?

8. How effective is Smiley's conclusion? Explain.

Exploring the Writer's Argument

1. Smiley admits in paragraph 4 that the very thing she's arguing for is how she was reared. Does that make her argument suspect? Why or why not? If so, how? If not, how does she overcome that limitation in her argument?

2. Smiley writes at the beginning of her essay that her daughters "have led a life of almost tropical idleness." Later, at the end of her essay, she writes that kids should do work that is good for them (i.e., that doesn't alienate them from the work). Are these two statements contradictory? Why or why not?

3. Smiley writes that she lives in the Midwest, and she seems to imply that this is important to her argument. Do you think it is? Explain where she refers to her geographical location and how she makes her essay universal despite this focus.

▶ Ideas for Writing Arguments

Prewriting

Jot down some notes on the following questions: What did your parents, grandparents, or other family members do during your upbringing that you don't agree with? What did they do right?

Writing a Guided Argument

In her essay, Smiley is giving parental advice. Write an essay with the title "The Case Against . . ." in which you argue that parents should avoid doing something that you don't agree with. For example, argue against spankings, letting kids go out on bicycle rides by themselves, or allowing them to attend rap concerts.

1. Begin your essay by explaining your own personal relationship with your chosen subject.
2. In the next section, lay out at least two arguments the opposition might have.
3. Write your major proposition.
4. Rebut the arguments with effective support.
5. Adopt an informal tone, much like Smiley's.
6. About halfway through your argument, write a personal reminiscence that illustrates the correct way to go about things.
7. Offer at least two minor propositions to support your argument.
8. Close your essay with a discussion of how you will approach the rearing of your children in relation to this topic.

Thinking, Arguing, and Writing Collaboratively

In groups of four or five, discuss alternate opposition arguments from those you present in your Writing a Guided Argument essay, and come up with possible rebuttals. Jot down notes and incorporate them into your essay's final draft.

Writing about the Text

Write an essay in which you analyze Smiley's informal style. What is informal here? How does she keep the reader relaxed? How does the fact that Smiley is a novelist come through in the essay?

More Writing Ideas

1. In your journal, freewrite about this topic: fun work. Do not edit your writing. Write for at least 15 minutes. When you are done, read over your unedited writing to see if there are any propositions that could be used as the basis for an essay.
2. What are your feelings about those people who have domestic help, such as maids, butlers, and chauffeurs? Is it really necessary to have that kind of help? Write an extended paragraph on the topic.
3. Write an essay in which you argue that children should stop receiving an allowance at age 14 and work for their own money.

DAVID BROOKS
The Triumph of Hope Over Self-Interest

David Brooks is a senior editor at the conservative magazine the Weekly Standard *and is the author of* Bobos in Paradise: The New Upper Class and How They Got There *(2001) and* Paradise Drive: How We Live Now (and Always Have) in the Future Tense *(2005). He is also a contributing editor at* Newsweek *and the* Atlantic Monthly, *writes for the* New York Times Magazine, *and recently began a twice weekly column in the* New York Times. *He is also a regular commentator on National Public Radio. He was educated at the University of Chicago and started his career as a newspaper reporter. In this selection, Brooks explains why people don't vote for politicians who support policies that will help them.*

▶ Prereading: Thinking about the Essay in Advance

What are your feelings about those who are more wealthy than you are? Do you envy them? Do you want to be like them? Do you resent them? Why do you react as you do?

▶ Words to Watch

populist (par. 2) appealing to the common people
overdetermined (par. 3) having many reasons
savaged (par. 5) destroyed
appointed (par. 7) furnished
resentment (par. 8) feeling of anger and being injured
sommeliers (par. 10) waiter in a restaurant who helps customers choose
    wine
eau (par. 10) French for "water"
subsumes (par. 18) overwhelms

Why don't people vote their own self-interest? Every few years   1
the Republicans propose a tax cut, and every few years the Democrats pull out their income distribution charts to show that much of the
benefits of the Republican plan go to the richest 1 percent of Americans or
thereabouts. And yet every few years a Republican plan wends its
way through the legislative process and, with some trims and amendments, passes.

The Democrats couldn't even persuade people to oppose the repeal of   2
the estate tax, which is explicitly for the mega-upper class. Al Gore, who
ran a populist campaign, couldn't even win the votes of white males who
didn't go to college, whose incomes have stagnated over the past decades
and who were the explicit targets of his campaign. Why don't more Americans want to distribute more wealth down to people like themselves?

Well, as the academics would say, it's overdetermined. There are sev-   3
eral reasons.

People vote their aspirations.   4

The most telling polling result from the 2000 election was from a   5
Time magazine survey that asked people if they are in the top 1 percent
of earners. Nineteen percent of Americans say they are in the richest 1
percent and a further 20 percent expect to be someday. So right away
you have 39 percent of Americans who thought that when Mr. Gore
savaged a plan that favored the top 1 percent, he was taking a direct
shot at them.

It's not hard to see why they think this way. Americans live in a cul-   6
ture of abundance. They have always had a sense that great opportunities
lie just over the horizon, in the next valley, with the next job or the next
big thing. None of us is really poor; we're just pre-rich.

Americans read magazines for people more affluent than they are   7
(*W*, *Cigar Aficionado*, *The New Yorker*, *Robb Report*, *Town and Country*) because they think that someday they could be that guy with the tastefully
appointed horse farm. Democratic politicians proposing to take from the
rich are just bashing the dreams of our imminent selves.

8   **Income resentment is not a strong emotion in much of America.**

9   If you earn $125,000 a year and live in Manhattan, certainly, you are surrounded by things you cannot afford. You have to walk by those buildings on Central Park West with the 2,500-square-foot apartments that are empty three-quarters of the year because their evil owners are mostly living at their other houses in L.A.

10   But if you are a middle-class person in most of America, you are not brought into incessant contact with things you can't afford. There aren't Lexus dealerships on every corner. There are no snooty restaurants with water sommeliers to help you sort though the bottled eau selections. You can afford most of the things at Wal-Mart or Kohl's and the occasional meal at the Macaroni Grill. Moreover, it would be socially unacceptable for you to pull up to church in a Jaguar or to hire a caterer for your dinner party anyway. So you are not plagued by a nagging feeling of doing without.

11   **Many Americans admire the rich.**

12   They don't see society as a conflict zone between the rich and poor. It's taboo to say in a democratic culture, but do you think a nation that watches Katie Couric in the morning, Tom Hanks in the evening and Michael Jordan on weekends harbors deep animosity toward the affluent?

13   On the contrary. I'm writing this from Nashville, where one of the richest families, the Frists, is hugely admired for its entrepreneurial skill and community service. People don't want to tax the Frists—they want to elect them to the Senate. And they did.

14   Nor are Americans suffering from false consciousness. You go to a town where the factories have closed and people who once earned $14 an hour now work for $8 an hour. They've taken their hits. But odds are you will find their faith in hard work and self-reliance undiminished, and their suspicion of Washington unchanged.

15   **Americans resent social inequality more than income inequality.**

16   As the sociologist Jennifer Lopez has observed: "Don't be fooled by the rocks that I got, I'm just, I'm just Jenny from the block." As long as rich people "stay real," in Ms. Lopez's formulation, they are admired. Meanwhile, middle-class journalists and academics who seem to look down on megachurches, suburbia and hunters are resented. If Americans see the tax debate as being waged between the economic elite, led by President Bush, and the cultural elite, led by Barbra Streisand, they are going to side with Mr. Bush, who could come to any suburban barbershop and fit right in.

17   **Most Americans do not have Marxian categories in their heads.**

18   This is the most important reason Americans resist wealth redistribution, the reason that subsumes all others. Americans do not see society as a layer cake, with the rich on top, the middle class beneath them and the working class and underclass at the bottom. They see society as a high school cafeteria, with their community at one table and other communi-

ties at other tables. They are pretty sure that their community is the nicest, and filled with the best people, and they have a vague pity for all those poor souls who live in New York City or California and have a lot of money but no true neighbors and no free time.

All of this adds up to a terrain incredibly inhospitable to class-based   19
politics. Every few years a group of millionaire Democratic presidential aspirants pretends to be the people's warriors against the overclass. They look inauthentic, combative rather than unifying. Worst of all, their basic message is not optimistic.

They haven't learned what Franklin and Teddy Roosevelt and even   20
Bill Clinton knew: that you can run against rich people, but only those who have betrayed the ideal of fair competition. You have to be more hopeful and growth-oriented than your opponent, and you cannot imply that we are a nation tragically and permanently divided by income. In the gospel of America, there are no permanent conflicts.

▶ Building Vocabulary

Write out definitions for the following words from Brooks's essay, and use them each in a sentence:

1. stagnated (par. 2)
2. abundance (par. 6)
3. affluent (par. 7)
4. imminent (par. 7)
5. incessant (par. 10)
6. taboo (par. 12)
7. animosity (par. 12)
8. aspirants (par. 19)

▶ Thinking Critically about the Argument

Understanding the Writer's Argument

1. Why do Republicans want to cut the taxes of the richest 1 percent of Americans?
2. What is the estate tax? Who benefits from it?
3. Why do so many Americans think they're in the richest 1 percent? What does Brooks mean when he says that "none of us is really poor; we're just pre-rich"? (par. 6)
4. Why, according to Brooks, do Americans admire the rich?
5. What does Brooks mean by "Marxian categories"? (par. 17)
6. What, according to Brooks, did Franklin Roosevelt, Teddy Roosevelt, and Bill Clinton know that made them popular politicians?
7. What is the "gospel of America"? (par. 20)

Understanding the Writer's Techniques

1. What is Brooks's major proposition in this essay?
2. Why does Brooks start with a question?
3. Brooks uses only one statistic in his essay, the *Time* poll. Is this single information enough to help his case? Explain.
4. Does Brooks put his minor propositions in any strategic order? Explain.
5. How does Brooks use causal analysis to advance his argument? Is it an effective rhetorical strategy? Why or why not?
6. What is the argumentative effect of Brooks's section headings? Do they help or hurt his argument?
7. Analyze Brooks's analogies in paragraph 18. Are they effective? Why or why not?
8. How effective is Brooks's conclusion? What is its strongest element?

Exploring the Writer's Argument

1. Brooks is a conservative, yet he seems to work in this essay to give away one of the secrets of the Republican party's success: that often people who should vote Democratic do not. Why would he want to expose this secret?
2. In his essay, Brooks uses many vivid examples. Choose at least three that you find particularly effective and explain your choices.
3. Do you agree with Brooks's argument in paragraph 10 that people in middle-class America outside of New York City do not resent rich people? Why or why not?

▶ Ideas for Writing Arguments

Prewriting

Are there any activities you take part in regularly that you know are counterproductive to your safety or health or to the safety or health of other people? Jot down some ideas for an essay on the topic.

Writing a Guided Argument

Write an essay that attempts to explain why someone might take part in an activity that not everyone would understand. For example, explain why people still smoke although they know it is bad for them or why people live in cities that are often hit with natural disasters.

1. Begin your essay with a rhetorical question.
2. Describe the activity you are going to explain.
3. State your major proposition.

4. Offer at least three reasons why people take part in the activity you've chosen to write about.
5. After each reason, support the idea with evidence in the form of examples.
6. In the next section, offer a solution to the problem: How can one stop doing the activity?
7. Close with a switch to a neutral, detached discussion of the issue.

Thinking, Arguing, and Writing Collaboratively

In groups of four or five, study one of the magazines Brooks mentions in paragraph 7, or find another magazine geared for a luxury readership. Each group should examine a different magazine. What images support Brooks's position that middle-class readers essentially are "wannabes" who see themselves in the places of the rich? Discuss the images, and present your findings to the class.

Writing about the Text

Write an essay that analyzes Brooks's use of irony. Choose at least three passages from Brooks's essay that you find particularly ironic. Explain how what Brooks says and what he means are two different things. How does irony fit into Brooks's overall tone, and how effective is it?

More Writing Ideas

1. In your journal, illustrate at least three times in the past few days when you observed class to be an issue between two or more people.
2. Write a paragraph or two that explores celebrity worship in our culture as the worship of the rich.
3. In an essay, argue that Americans should be more class conscious, and explain how this might come about.

HERBERT J. GANS
Fitting the Poor into the Economy

Herbert J. Gans, a professor of sociology at Columbia University, was born in Germany in 1927. The rise of the Nazis caused his family to flee to England in 1938. Gans came to America in 1940 and subsequently became a U.S. citizen. He went to the University of Chicago and then earned a Ph.D. at the University of Pennsylvania. He has been a professor at Pennsylvania Teachers College and M.I.T. Gans has written many of books about class and culture in America, including The War Against the Poor *(1995),* Making Sense of America *(1999), and* Democracy and the News *(2003). In this*

selection, Gans examines the attitudes Americans have about the poor, espe-
cially the way in which people blame the poor for their own poverty.

▶ Prereading: Thinking about the Essay in Advance

What are the reasons for poverty in a rich country like America? Do
people blame the poor for their poverty? Are there any realistic solutions to the problem?

▶ Words to Watch

allocations (par. 1) money given for a specific purpose
affluent (par. 1) wealthy
onus (par. 2) responsibility
scapegoats (par. 2) those falsely blamed for a problem
antidote (par. 4) solution to a problem
inroads (par. 6) progress
paltry (par. 7) small, insignificant
dereliction (par. 8) serious shortcoming
spawned (par. 11) been the source for
utopian (par. 11) unrealistically idealistic

1   The notion of the poor as too lazy or morally deficient to deserve assistance seems to be indestructible. Public policies limit poor people to
substandard services and incomes below the subsistence level, and Congress and state legislatures are tightening up even on these miserly
allocations—holding those in the "underclass" responsible for their own
sorry state. Indeed, labeling the poor as undeserving has lately become
politically useful as a justification for the effort to eliminate much of the
antipoverty safety net and permit tax cuts for the affluent people who do
most of the voting.

2   Such misplaced blame offers mainstream society a convenient eva-
sion of its own responsibility. Blaming poor men and women for not
working, for example, takes the onus off both private enterprise and government for failing to supply employment. It is easier to charge poor unmarried mothers with lacking family values than to make sure that there
are jobs for them and for the young men who are not marriageable because they are unable to support families. Indeed, the poor make excellent scapegoats for a range of social problems, such as street crime and
drug and alcohol addiction. Never mind the reversal of cause and effect
that underlies this point of view—for centuries crime, alcoholism, and
single motherhood have risen whenever there has not been enough work
and income to go around.

China: Workers sewing blue jeans in garment factory in the city of Shenzhen.

The undeserving underclass is also a useful notion for employers as   3
the economy appears to be entering a period of long-term stagnation. Jobs
are disappearing—some displaced by labor-saving technologies, others
exported to newly industrializing, low-wage countries, others lost as
companies "downsize" to face tougher global competition. Indeed, the
true rate of unemployment—which includes involuntary part-time workers and long-term "discouraged" workers who have dropped out of the
job market altogether—has remained in double digits for more than a
generation and no longer seems to drop during times of economic
strength. Labeling poor people as lacking the needed work ethic is a politically simple way of shedding them from a labor market that will most
likely never need them again.

The most efficient antidote to poverty is not welfare but full employ-   4
ment. In the short run, therefore, today's war against the poor should be
replaced with efforts to create jobs for now-surplus workers. New Deal–
style programs of large-scale governmental employment, for example,
can jump-start a slow economy. Besides being the fastest way to put people to work, a public-works program can improve the country's infrastructure, including highways, buildings, parks, and computer databases.

In addition, private enterprise and government should aim to stimu-   5
late the most promising labor-intensive economic activities and stop encouraging new technology that will further destroy jobs—reviving, for
example, the practice of making cars and appliances partly by hand. A

parallel policy would tax companies for their use of labor-saving technology; the revenues from this tax would pay for alternative jobs for people in occupations that technology renders obsolete. This idea makes good business as well as social sense: human workers are needed as customers for the goods that machines now produce.

6   To distribute the jobs that do exist among more people, employers could shorten the work day, week, or year. Several large manufacturing companies in Western Europe already use worksharing to create a 35-hour week. Making significant inroads on U.S. joblessness may require reducing the work week to 30 hours.

7   A more generous welfare system would go a long way toward solving the problems of the remainder: those who cannot work or cannot find jobs. By persisting in the belief that poor people deserve their fate, society can easily justify a paltry and demeaning welfare system that pays recipients only about one-quarter of the median income. A system that paid closer to half the median income, by contrast, would enable those without work to remain full members of society and thus minimize the despair, anger, and various illnesses, as well as premature mortality, distinctive to the poor.

8   For such antipoverty policies to gain acceptance, mainstream America will have to unlearn the stereotype of poor people as immoral. Most of the poor are just as law-abiding as everyone else. (While a minority of poor people cheat on their welfare applications, an even larger minority of affluent people cheat on their tax returns—yet the notion of undeservingness is never applied to the middle or upper classes.) In admitting that the phenomena now explained as moral dereliction are actually traceable to poverty, Americans will force themselves to find solutions, not scapegoats, to the country's problems.

9   Most of the people assigned to today's undeserving underclass are the first victims of what is already being called the future "jobless economy." In the long run, if the cancer of joblessness spreads more widely among the population, large numbers of the present middle class will have to adapt to the reality that eventually most workers may no longer be employed full time. In that case, more drastic job-creation policies will be needed, including a ban on additional job-destroying technology and the establishment of permanent public employment modeled on the kind now associated with military spending. Worksharing would most likely be based on a 24-hour week.

10   At that point, everyone would in fact be working part time by today's standards, and new ways to maintain standards of living would have to be found. One approach, already being discussed in Europe, is a universal, subsistence-level income grant. This "demogrant," a twenty-first-century version of the $1,000-per-person allotment that presidential candidate George McGovern proposed in 1972, would be taxed away from people still working full time. In any case, private and government agen-

cies should begin now to study what policies might be needed to preserve the American way of life when the full-time job will no longer be around to pay for the American Dream.

It is possible, of course, that new sources of economic growth will   11
suddenly develop to revive the full employment and prosperity of the post–World War II decades. And some labor-saving technologies may, in the long run, create more jobs than they destroy; that may well be the case for computers, which have spawned a large sector of the economy. Such happy outcomes cannot be counted on to materialize, however, and there remains the danger that the war on the poor will continue as the politically most convenient path. We will undoubtedly find that when the economy begins to threaten the descendants of today's middle and even affluent classes with becoming poor, and then "undeserving," policies that today seem utopian will be demanded, and quickly.

▶ Building Vocabulary

This selection assumes a general familiarity with basic economic and political terms and concepts. Identify and write definitions for the following:

1. subsistence level (par. 1)
2. safety net (par. 1)
3. private enterprise (par. 2)
4. underclass (par. 3)
5. stagnation (par. 3)
6. downsize (par. 3)
7. work ethic (par. 3)
8. welfare (par. 4)
9. New Deal (par. 4)

▶ Thinking Critically about the Argument

Understanding the Writer's Argument

1. What responsibility does Gans say mainstream society has toward the poor? (par. 2)
2. Why, historically, are crime, alcoholism, and single motherhood common?
3. Why is the idea of an "undeserving underclass" something employers can use to shed responsibility, according to Gans?
4. What does Gans suggest in place of welfare, or does he think welfare is all right?
5. What are people on welfare paid in proportion to the average income? What does Gans think welfare recipients should be paid? Why?

6. How can shortening the 40-hour workweek reduce poverty, according to Gans?
7. What is a "demogrant"? How is it designed to help?

Understanding the Writer's Techniques

1. What is Gans's claim? Where does he express it best?
2. What grounds does Gans offer to support his claim?
3. Outline Gans's argument. How does he structure his points?
4. What is the nature of the switch in Gans's argument from paragraph 3 to paragraph 4?
5. How does Gans's position as a professor of sociology at Columbia University, an Ivy League school, help his essay? Explain.
6. What is the author's tone? Explain your answer fully, showing examples from the essay that led to your answer.
7. Is Gans's closing effective? Why or why not?

Exploring the Writer's Argument

1. Gans objects to society blaming the "underclass" for various social problems. He wants to take the responsibility off the poor. Is that, however, considering poor people as children who can't be held accountable for their actions? Is that what he's saying? Explain your answer fully? Do you agree?
2. In his essay (page 278), David Brooks writes about how people don't always act in their own political best interest. Do you see any arguments, implied or overt, in Brooks's essay that could help the poor with the problems Gans identifies? Explain.
3. Gans makes some radical suggestions to improve life in America. Do you think any of his suggestions are feasible? Why or why not?
4. In paragraph 8, Gans writes that if people change their minds about the poor, that will allow new policies to take shape. Do you agree with his assessment? Explain your answer.

▶Ideas for Writing Arguments

Prewriting

What do you think are the effects, psychologically, of being unemployed? What are the psychological effects of making too little money in a job? Write notes on your thoughts.

Writing a Guided Argument

Write an essay arguing that a New Deal–style project, such as building a hypothetical high-speed highway from Los Angeles to New York (or some other comparably huge project of your own devising) would improve the economy.

1. Open your essay with a discussion of the problems of unemployment and poverty in our society, as described by Gans.
2. Write your major proposition, proposing your project.
3. Offer at least three minor propositions that explain why this project would benefit the economy.
4. Explain the long-term positive economic effects of full employment.
5. Use effective transitions to move from point to point.
6. Predict a possible objection to the project, and rebut that point.
7. Bring your essay to a close by illustrating how your project would provide a great convenience to everyone.

Thinking, Arguing, and Writing Collaboratively

After dividing into four equal groups, have members of each group read their essays from the Writing a Guided Argument assignment out loud. Select your group's strongest essay, and as a group help the writer to improve any weak points. List the strengths of the essay. Read the four strongest essays to the whole class, and discuss the strengths and weaknesses of each.

Writing about the Text

Write an essay that explores the concept of what it means to be "undeserving," as Gans defines it. Is this a useful concept? Does Gans make good use of it in his essay? What does it mean to "deserve" your economic fate? Do we have any control at all? Is there upward mobility in the United States?

More Writing Ideas

1. In your journal, speculate on what it would be like to live in poverty in a wealthy country like the United States.
2. In a paragraph or two, explore the responsibility you have personally as a citizen of this country to the poor of the country.
3. Write an essay in which you argue that the poor are actually *more* moral than the rich in the United States.

13 The Media: Do We Control It, or Does It Control Us?

In our media-saturated culture, there are hundreds of newspapers and magazines, hundreds of channels on cable television offering news, editorials, entertainment, sports, movies, and music videos. How can the media *not* influence us? Wherever we turn the media bombard us. Magazine cover stories pull us into the lives of celebrities and the devastation of wars. Almost every film we want to watch is available at our local video store. Video cameras are getting smaller and cheaper, so that few events can escape taping. Since the early 1900s, when movies started, through the 1950s, when television became a popular medium (and advertisers discovered its power), the images created by Hollywood, the TV industries, and the advertising companies on Madison Avenue have become as familiar to us as our own family members. We read and watch for entertainment and versions of the news, but we are also aware that the media manipulate us at the same time. In a seemingly endless supply, new media possibilities thrust themselves on our lives. Cell phones ring and BlackBerrys glow in every human space and accomplish more and more tasks. With our portable phones we can send and receive text messages, take photographs and videos, store messages, and access e-mail. Today's cell phone, computer, and iPod make last year's models obsolete. Indeed Tony Sachs and Sal Nunziato in "Spinning into Oblivion" in this chapter mark the demise of record stores and record albums, which can no longer prosper in the era of downloads.

Some would argue that even adults cannot resist the onslaught of the media, but what about children? Children learn about the world, in part, by imitating what they see. Parents influence their children by offering themselves as behavioral models. But children today witness what they normally wouldn't see in real life—on television, in periodicals, and in the movies. What, for example, is the effect of video gunfights on children? This topic is the subject of one of the most bitterly fought debates today. In an age when children have gone to school with guns and shot their teachers and classmates, the question arises: How responsible are the media for these tragedies? And if they are responsible, can we really ask them to stop showing what people want to see? Violence and sex sell, and so that is what shows up in the media. But are images of violence and sex enough to make youngsters imitate what they see, or are children media savvy enough today to have sufficient distance from what they view? How can parents protect their children?

Karen Springen, a parent of two girls, explores one response. She explains in "Why We Tuned Out" that she is simply not letting her children watch any TV or movies. To some, this might seem extreme. Although she might disagree with Springen, Wendy Kaminer, like Springen, chooses to focus on solutions, with vastly different results. In "Toxic Media," Kaminer examines the danger of government censorship and finds that prospect to be scarier than the scariest slasher film. As you read, consider the role that the media play in your life and whether we could or should set limits on this ever-present phenomenon in the modern world.

KAREN SPRINGEN
Why We Tuned Out

Karen Springen has written for Newsweek *since the 1980s, and focuses on health, social issues, and parenting. She has also written freelance articles for many magazines, including* Vegetarian Times, Working Woman, *and* Elle. *Springen was educated at Stanford University and got her master's degree in journalism from Columbia University. She has taught there and at Northwestern University. Springen and her husband live in Chicago and are the parents of two daughters who are the subjects of this selection about the decision to keep the children from watching television.*

▶ Prereading: Thinking about the Essay in Advance

Were you allowed to watch television when you were a child? What effect did it have on you, do you think?

▶ Words to Watch

inquisitive (par. 2) asking a lot of questions
cartwheels (par. 2) a gymnastic move in which, arms and legs extended, one turns over sideways like a wheel
puritanical (par. 4) overly moral
outcasts (par. 4) those excluded from a group
cringed (par. 7) reacted out of pain or disgust
crusading (par. 7) acting as if on a mission
ridicule (par. 7) being made fun of, mockery

"What's your favorite TV show?" our girls' beloved ballet instruc-   1
tor asked each pint-size dancer in her class. Our oldest daughter, Jazzy, didn't know how to answer. She shrugged. Her moment of
awkwardness results from a decision my husband, Mark, and I made five
years ago. We don't allow our kids to watch TV. Period. Not at home, not
at friends' houses; and they don't watch videos or movies, either. We
want our daughters, Jazzy, now nearly 6, and Gigi, 3, to be as active as
possible, physically and mentally. So when a babysitter asked whether
Jazzy, then 1 year old, could watch TV, we thought about it—and said no.

When we look at our inquisitive, energetic daughters, we have no re-   2
grets. And our reading of the research makes us feel even better. Nielsen
Media Research reports that American children 2 through 11 watch three
hours and 16 minutes of television every day. Kids who watch more than
10 hours of TV each week are more likely to be overweight, aggressive
and slow to learn in school, according to the American Medical Association. For these reasons, the American Academy of Pediatrics recommends no TV for children younger than 2 and a maximum of two hours a
day of "screen time" (TV, computers or videogames) for older kids. We
are convinced that without TV, our daughters spend more time than
other kids doing cartwheels, listening to stories and asking such interesting questions as "How old is God?" and "What makes my rubber ducks
float?" They also aren't haunted by TV images of September 11—because
they never saw them.

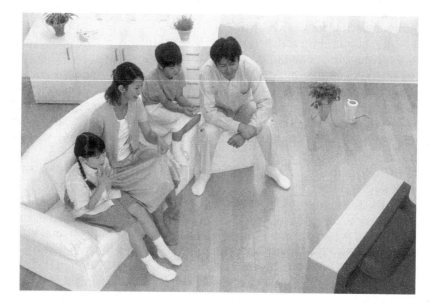

3   Going without TV in America has its difficult moments. When I called my sister, Lucy, to make arrangements for Thanksgiving, she warned that her husband was planning to spend the day watching football. We're going anyway. We'll just steer the girls toward the playroom. And some well-meaning friends tell us our girls may be missing out on good educational programming. Maybe. But that's not what most kids are watching. Nielsen Media Research reports that among children 2 through 11, the top-five TV shows in the new fall season were "The Wonderful World of Disney," "Survivor: Thailand," "Yu-Gi-Oh!", "Pokémon" and "Jackie Chan Adventures."

4   Will our happy, busy girls suffer because they're not participating in such a big part of the popular culture? Will they feel left out in school when they don't know who won on "Survivor"? "Kids are going to make fun of them," warns my mother-in-law. And a favorite child psychiatrist, Elizabeth Berger, author of "Raising Children With Character," cautions that maintaining a puritanical approach may make our kids into social outcasts. "Part of preparing your children for life is preparing them to be one of the girls," she says. "It's awful to be different from the other kids in fourth grade."

5   Our relatives all watch TV. So did we. I was born in 1961, the year Newton Minow, then the chairman of the U.S. Federal Communications Commission, called television a "vast wasteland." But I loved it. My sister, Katy, and I shared a first crush on the TV cartoon hero Speed Racer. Watching "Bewitched" and "The Brady Bunch" and, later, soap operas gave us an easy way to bond with our friends. Am I being selfish in not wanting the same for our children?

6   So far, our daughters don't seem to feel like misfits. We have no problem with the girls enjoying products based on TV characters. The girls wear Elmo pajamas and battle over who can sit on a big Clifford stuffed animal. From books, they also know about Big Bird, the Little Mermaid and Aladdin. And they haven't mentioned missing out on "Yu-Gi-Oh!" cartoon duels. Dr. Miriam Baron, who chairs the American Academy of Pediatrics committee on public education, says I'm helping our kids be creative, independent learners and calls our decision "awesome." And Mayo Clinic pediatrician Daniel Broughton, another group member, says that "there's no valid reason" the girls need to view television.

7   As the girls grow older, we can't completely shield them from TV anyway. We'll probably watch Olympic rhythmic gymnastics; the girls love it. And if Jazzy's favorite baseball team, the Cubs, ever make the World Series, we'll tune in. Last Monday Jazzy's music teacher showed "The Magic School Bus: Inside the Haunted House." Though "Magic School Bus" is a well-regarded Scholastic product, I still cringed, wondering why the kids weren't learning about vibrations and sounds by singing and banging on drums. But I kept silent; I'd never require my kids to

abstain in school. Like Jean Lotus, the Oak Park, Ill., mom who founded the anti-TV group the White Dot and who also reluctantly allows her kids to view TV in school, I'm wary of being seen "as the crusading weirdo." But some public ridicule will be worth it if I help get even a few people to think twice before automatically turning on the tube. Now it's time for me to curl up with the girls and a well-worn copy of "Curious George."

▶ Building Vocabulary

Identify and explain the following references, looking them up in reference works if necessary:

1. Nielsen Media Research (par. 2)
2. American Medical Association (par. 2)
3. *Survivor* (par. 4)
4. Federal Communications Commission (par. 5)
5. Mayo Clinic (par. 6)
6. Scholastic (par. 7)
7. *Curious George* (par. 7)

▶ Thinking Critically about the Argument

Understanding the Writer's Argument

1. What is negative about the statistic that, on average, children watch more than three hours of television a day?
2. Why is it difficult to go without TV in America, according to Springen?
3. Why does Springen list the top five TV shows for children in the fall of 2002?
4. What did Newton Minow mean in 1961 when he called TV a "vast wasteland"?
5. Did Springen watch TV as a kid? What did she watch? How did it affect her?
6. Do Springen's girls know anything about what's on TV?
7. Will Springen always bar her children from watching TV? Explain.

Understanding the Writer's Techniques

1. What is Springen's major proposition? Where does she articulate it best in her essay?
2. What are Springen's minor propositions? List them in the form of an outline.

3. How does Springen use transitions effectively to build coherence in her essay? Analyze her use of transitions. Could you improve them? How?
4. What point is Springen making when she lists the top five TV shows for children ages 2 to 11 in paragraph 3?
5. What is the effect of Springen's quoting Elizabeth Berger in paragraph 4? Why does she do this? Does it help or hurt her argument? Explain.
6. What is your reaction to paragraph 6? Do you find it persuasive? Why or why not?
7. Do you find the last paragraph persuasive? Why or why not?
8. What is the effect of the title? What meanings can you suggest for the phrase "tuned out"?

Exploring the Writer's Argument

1. Springen's daughters did not see images of the September 11 attacks. The children were young, and the images are disturbing. But if Springen's no-TV rule remains in place, her children will most likely miss out on the images that help shape American culture. Do you think that the children are missing out or will miss out on becoming involved Americans? Or are they better off without those images? Do we rely on those images today? Explain your answers.
2. Is Springen's essay presumptuous? Is she telling people how to rear their children or is she merely sharing her own experiences? Is she too self-congratulatory or appropriately proud? Explain your view of how Springen's argument is affected by how she presents her subject.
3. What does Springen's point about her children doing cartwheels and asking interesting questions contribute to the argument? Is a lack of TV the only reason they do these things? Explain your response. Do you know any children who are active and imaginative yet also watch TV? Explain your answers.

▶Ideas for Writing Arguments

Prewriting

What is it about television that you think has a *positive* effect on children? Are there any programs that kids like that are also educational and make them think? Jot down some notes on the topic.

Writing a Guided Argument

Write an essay in which you argue that television is good for children. You might have to do some research by watching television during those hours when children watch—Saturday mornings and weekday afternoons.

1. Begin with a paragraph that introduces your reader to the subject through an anecdote or interesting example.
2. Write your claim clearly.
3. Establish a tone early on of self-importance—make sure your reader understands that you are absolutely sure of your argument.
4. Allow two rhetorical questions that put voice to the opposition's viewpoint—for example, "Doesn't television make kids lazy?"
5. Answer the rhetorical questions with persuasive grounds to back up your claim.
6. Use effective transitions to maintain coherence.
7. Close your essay by asserting that you are going to let your children watch television.

Thinking, Arguing, and Writing Collaboratively

In small groups of three or four, exchange your Writing a Guided Argument papers. Offer suggestions in the form of a paragraph or two to help your classmate develop his or her essay. After revising the essay at home, meet with the same partner to discuss the success of the revisions.

Writing about the Text

Consider the weaknesses in Springen's essay. What are the major problems in her argument? Write an essay in the form of a letter to Springen in which you point out at least three criticisms you have of her essay.

More Writing Ideas

1. Write notes for an essay on the effect advertising has on children.
2. Write a paragraph or two that argues that even if TV isn't great for children, it's great for *parents.*
3. Write an essay that explores the idea of popular culture and its importance. What is popular culture, and what is its effect on our lives?

TONY SACHS AND SAL NUNZIATO
Spinning into Oblivion

Sal Nunziato and Tony Sachs are co-owners of NYCD, which at one point was a bricks-and-mortar record store in Manhattan. They started selling CDs online, but had to close the physical store in 2005. Both have written for the Huffington Post. *On their blog, located at www.nycdonline.blogspot.com/, Nunziato and Sachs, or as they call themselves, Sal and Tony, give their pointed opinions on new music releases. In this selection, published in 2007, the writers argue that the record companies, which complain about illegal downloads, actually dug their own graves by eliminating single recordings and raising album prices.*

▶ Prereading: Thinking about the Essay in Advance

When you buy music, do you purchase single songs or do you always buy the entire album? Why? How do you get your music? Do you buy CDs or do you download songs? Why?

▶ Words to Watch

counterpart (par. 2) person corresponding to another
scrupulous (par. 2) having moral integrity
haven (par. 4) safe place
maligned (par. 4) spoken badly of
dearth (par. 6) shortage
foisting (par. 9) pushing on
gloat (par. 15) smugly rejoice
obsolete (par. 16) no longer useful or relevant

1   Despite the major record labels' best efforts to kill it, the single, according to recent reports, is back. Sort of.

2   You'll still have a hard time finding vinyl 45s or their modern counterpart, CD singles, in record stores. For that matter, you'll have a tough time finding record stores. Today's single is an individual track downloaded online from legal sites like iTunes or eMusic, or the multiple illegal sites that cater to less scrupulous music lovers. The album, or collection of songs—the de facto way to buy pop music for the last 40 years—is suddenly looking old-fashioned. And the record store itself is going the way of the shoehorn.

3   This is a far cry from the musical landscape that existed when we opened an independent CD shop on the Upper West Side of Manhattan in 1993. At the time, we figured that as far as business ventures went, ours was relatively safe. People would always go to stores to buy music. Right? Of course, back then there were also only two ringtones to choose from—"riiiiinnng" and "ringring."

4   Our intention was to offer a haven for all kinds of music lovers and obsessives, a shop that catered not only to the casual record buyer ("Do you have the new Sarah McLachlan and uh is there a Beatles greatest hits CD?") but to the fan and oft-maligned serious collector ("Can you get the Japanese pressing of 'Kinda Kinks'? I believe they used the rare mono mixes"). Fourteen years later, it's clear just how wrong our assumptions were. Our little shop closed its doors at the end of 2005.

5   The sad thing is that CDs and downloads could have coexisted peacefully and profitably. The current state of affairs is largely the result of shortsightedness and boneheadedness by the major record labels and the Recording Industry Association of America, who managed to achieve the opposite of everything they wanted in trying to keep the

music business prospering. The association is like a gardener who tried to rid his lawn of weeds and wound up killing the trees instead.

In the late '90s, our business, and the music retail business in general, was booming. Enter Napster, the granddaddy of illegal download sites. How did the major record labels react? By continuing their campaign to eliminate the comparatively unprofitable CD single, raising list prices on album-length CDs to $18 or $19 and promoting artists like the Backstreet Boys and Britney Spears—whose strength was single songs, not albums. The result was a lot of unhappy customers, who blamed retailers like us for the dearth of singles and the high prices.   6

The recording industry association saw the threat that illegal downloads would pose to CD sales. But rather than working with Napster, it tried to sue the company out of existence—which was like thinking you've killed all the roaches in your apartment because you squashed the one you saw in the kitchen. More illegal download sites cropped up faster than the association's lawyers could say "cease and desist."   7

By 2002, it was clear that downloading was affecting music retail stores like ours. Our regulars weren't coming in as often, and when they did, they weren't buying as much. Our impulse-buy weekend customers were staying away altogether. And it wasn't just the independent stores; even big chains like Tower and Musicland were struggling.   8

Something had to be done to save the record store, a place where hard-core music fans worked, shopped and kibitzed—and, not incidentally, kept the music business's engine chugging in good times and in lean. Who but these loyalists was going to buy the umpteenth Elton John hits compilation that the major labels were foisting upon them?   9

But instead, those labels delivered the death blow to the record store as we know it by getting in bed with soulless chain stores like Best Buy and Wal-Mart. These "big boxes" were given exclusive tracks to put on new CDs and, to add insult to injury, they could sell them for less than our wholesale cost. They didn't care if they didn't make any money on CD sales. Because, ideally, the person who came in to get the new Eagles release with exclusive bonus material would also decide to pick up a high-speed blender that frappeed.   10

The jig was up. It didn't matter that even a store as small as ours carried hundreds of titles you'd never see at Best Buy and was staffed by people who actually knew who Van Morrison was, or that Tower Records had the entire history of recorded music under one roof while Costco didn't carry much more than the current hits. A year after our shop closed, Tower went out of business—something that would have been unthinkable just a few years earlier. The customers who had grudgingly come to trust our opinions made the move to online shopping or lost interest in buying music altogether. Some of the most loyal fans had been soured into denying themselves the music they loved.   11

12   Meanwhile, the recording industry association continues to give the impression that it's doing something by occasionally threatening to sue college students who share their record collections online. But apart from scaring the dickens out of a few dozen kids, that's just an amusing sideshow. They're not fighting a war any more than the folks who put on Civil War regalia and reenact the Battle of Gettysburg are.

13   The major labels wanted to kill the single. Instead they killed the album. The association wanted to kill Napster. Instead it killed the compact disc. And today it's not just record stores that are in trouble, but the labels themselves, now belatedly embracing the Internet revolution without having quite figured out how to make it pay.

14   At this point, it may be too late to win back disgruntled music lovers no matter what they do. As one music industry lawyer, Ken Hertz, said recently, "The consumer's conscience, which is all we had left, that's gone, too."

15   It's tempting for us to gloat. By worrying more about quarterly profits than the bigger picture, by protecting their short-term interests without thinking about how to survive and prosper in the long run, record-industry bigwigs have got what was coming to them. It's a disaster they brought upon themselves.

16   We would be gloating, but for the fact that the occupation we planned on spending our working lives at is rapidly becoming obsolete. And that loss hits us hard—not just as music retailers, but as music fans.

▶ Building Vocabulary

Sachs and Nunziato use several colloquialisms in their essay. For each of the following, "translate" the colloquialism, based on its context, into plain English:

 1. de facto (par. 2)
 2. going the way of the shoehorn (par. 2)
 3. boneheadedness (par. 5)
 4. granddaddy (par. 6)
 5. cropped up (par. 7)
 6. kibitzed (par. 9)
 7. chugging (par. 9)
 8. umpteenth (par. 9)
 9. The jig was up. (par. 11)
10. fans had been soured (par. 11)
11. scaring the dickens (par. 12)
12. record-industry bigwigs (par. 15)

▶ Thinking Critically about the Argument

Understanding the Writers' Argument

1. What, according to Sachs and Nunziato, is the way people listen to music singles these days?
2. What were the writers' intentions in opening a record store in 1993? How long was the record store open?
3. What do the writers mean when they say the record industry "is like a gardener who tried to rid his lawn of weeds and wound up killing the tree instead"?
4. What did the record industry do after Napster started up in the late 1990s, according to the writers?
5. Why did unhappy customers blame retailers for the high prices and lack of singles, according to the writers?
6. What, according to the writers, is the problem with record stores closing?
7. What's wrong with the "big box" stores' approach to selling music?
8. Why do the writers insist that the record industry "brought upon themselves" the current situation?

Understanding the Writers' Techniques

1. Why do the writers open their essay with a rundown of lost technologies?
2. What is the major proposition in this piece? How do the writers lead up to it? Is this lead-up effective or not? Why?
3. What are the minor propositions that support the idea that the record industry brought their ruin on themselves?
4. What evidence do the writers supply to prove that the record industry is responsible for their own problems?
5. Who is the audience for this essay? How do you know?
6. What is your opinion of the writers' conclusion? Is it effective or not? Explain your answer.

Exploring the Writers' Argument

1. In paragraph 4, the writers indicate that their assumptions were wrong. What were these assumptions? Do they carry those assumptions over to this essay? Explain your answers.
2. How successful is the writers' argument that the recording industry "wanted to kill the single. Instead they killed the album"? Is that a fair argument? Why or why not?

3. Sachs and Nunziato write that "the occupation we planned on spending our working lives at is rapidly becoming obsolete." One could argue that this is just a result of technology advancing. Is their entire argument a result of sour grapes? Why or why not?

▶ Ideas for Writing Arguments

Prewriting

Although music is easy to download online, for many people, movies are still too big to download quickly at the quality people want. But eventually technological barriers will fall and people will start downloading movies in great numbers. How do you feel about this coming technological advancement? Will you download movies? Why or why not?

Writing a Guided Argument

Write an essay in which you argue that the movie industry needs to take drastic measures if it doesn't want people to start pirating movies in large numbers by downloading them. Propose those measures.

1. Open your essay with a pithy statement summing up the problem for the movie industry.
2. Follow with your major proposition directly after your opening.
3. State your minor propositions.
4. Write at least two substantial suggestions to the movie industry as your minor propositions.
5. Anticipate at least one argument for why pirating of movies is a good thing, and refute that argument.
6. Use strong transitions to bind your argument.
7. Close your essay with a warning to the movie industry that if it doesn't change, pirating will be its fault.

Thinking, Arguing, and Writing Collaboratively

In small groups of three or four, discuss the problem explored in your Writing a Guided Argument papers. Collect the best ideas and have one person in your group take notes. At the end of a period of discussion, share the ideas with your classmates in the other groups.

Writing about the Text

Write an essay about the writers' use of emotional appeals in this essay, which are somewhat disguised as logical arguments. How do the writers anticipate their readers' objections to their arguments through emotional appeals? What are possible reader objections?

More Writing Ideas

1. In your journal, write an entry about the state of music today in the age of legal and illegal downloads. Are people still listening to music? Are people still playing music? Is the situation bad, just okay, or really good?
2. In two or three paragraphs, write about your own experience with downloading music without paying for it. Have you ever been tempted? Have you succumbed to that temptation? Write about how it *felt*.
3. Pretend that you have a time machine and are able to travel back to 1998. Write an essay in the form of a letter to the Recording Industry Association of America, offering the industry advice on how *it* can help avert the catastrophe the writers write about.

WENDY KAMINER
Toxic Media

Lawyer and writer Wendy Kaminer is a contributing editor for the Atlantic Monthly *and is on the board of the libertarian legal organization the American Civil Liberties Union. She is the author of* Sleeping with Extra-Terrestrials: I'm Dysfunctional, You're Dysfunctional *(1992),* It's All the Rage: Crime and Culture *(1995),* The Rise of Irrationalism and Perils of Piety *(1999), and* Free for All: Defending Liberty in America Today *(2002). She also writes freelance for the* New York Times, *the* Wall Street Journal, *the* Nation, *and* Newsweek. *This essay, which appeared in the* American Prospect, *for which Kaminer is a senior correspondent, warns against the danger of censorship gone out of control.*

▶ Prereading: Thinking about the Essay in Advance

Is there anything on television you'd like to see censored? What, and why?

▶ Words to Watch

ceasefire (par. 1) a break in fighting
concomitant (par. 2) accompanying
centrist (par. 3) politically between the extremes of liberal and conservative
complemented (par. 3) made complete or matched up with
bipartisan (par. 4) having members from both parties
stringent (par. 8) strict and unbending
abhors (par. 9) hates
hyperbolic (par. 10) wildly exaggerated
dearth (par. 10) a lack of, insufficient amount
de facto (par. 12) in reality, even if not official

1   Like Claude Rains in Casablanca, Al Gore is shocked!, shocked! that the entertainment industry is marketing violent material to minors. Countering Hollywood's macho entertainments with some macho rhetoric of his own, he gave the industry six months to "clean up its act" and declare a "ceasefire" in what he apparently sees as the media's war against America's children.

2   No one should be surprised by the vice president's threat to impose government regulations on the marketing of popular entertainments, which immediately followed the issuance of a new Federal Trade Commission (FTC) report on the subject. As his choice of running mate [Joseph Lieberman] made clear, Gore is positioning himself as the moral voice of the Democratic Party—replete with Godliness and a desire to cleanse the culture. With a concomitant promise to protect ordinary Americans from rapacious corporations, Gore is an early twenty-first-century version of a nineteenth-century female Progressive—a Godloving social purist with a soft spot for working families and, not so incidentally, women's rights.

3   Many Victorian women's rights activists, like Frances Willard of the Women's Christian Temperance Union and Julia Ward Howe, enthusiastically supported the suppression of "impure" or "vicious" literature, which was blamed for corrupting the nation's youth. "Books are feeders for brothels" according to the notorious nineteenth-century antivice crusader Anthony Comstock, for whom the nation's first obscenity law was named. Gun violence is fed by violent media, Al Gore, Joseph Lieberman, and others assert. The new FTC report was commissioned by President Clinton immediately after the 1999 shootings at Columbine High. That was when centrist politicians (and commentators) were touting the new "commonsense" view of youth violence: It was caused by both the availability of firearms and the availability of violent media. Gun control would be complemented by culture control.

4   So in June 1999, two Democratic senators, Lieberman and the usually thoughtful Kent Conrad of North Dakota, joined with [Senators] Trent Lott and John McCain in proposing federal legislation requiring the labeling of violent audio and visual media. These requirements, which were to be enforced by the FTC, were amendments to the cigarette labeling act. (When politicians revisit their bad ideas, critics like me repeat themselves. I discussed this proposed bill and the bipartisan drive to censor in a November 23, 1999, *American Prospect* column, "The Politics of Sanctimony.")

5   Advocates of censorship often charge that media can be "toxic" (as well as "addictive") like tobacco and other drugs. By describing whatever film or CD they disdain as a defective product, they undermine the view of it as speech. (We should regulate pornography the way we regulate exploding Ford Pintos, one feminist antiporn activist used to say; she

seemed to consider *Playboy* an incendiary device.) In endorsing Internet filtering programs, Gore has remarked that minors should be protected from "dangerous places" on the Internet—in other words, "dangerous" speech. Some Web sites should effectively be locked up, just as medicine cabinets are locked up to protect children from poisons, the vice president remarked at a 1997 Internet summit.

Once you define violent or sexually explicit media as toxic products, it is not terribly difficult to justify regulating their advertising, at least, if not their distribution and production. Commercial speech generally enjoys constitutional protection, but as advocates of marketing restrictions assert, the First Amendment does not protect false or misleading advertising or ads promoting illegal activities. That's true but not necessarily relevant here. Campaigns marketing violent entertainment to children may be sleazy, but they don't promote an illegal activity (the sale of violent material to minors is not generally criminal); and they're not deceptive or unfair (many popular entertainments are just as bad as they purport to be). Ratings are not determined or mandated by the government (not yet, anyway), so why should it be a federal offense for industry executives to violate the spirit of their own voluntary codes?   6

Effective regulation of media marketing campaigns would require new federal legislation that would entangle the government in the production of popular entertainments. What might this legislation entail? Ratings and labeling would be mandatory, supervised by the FTC (or some other federal agency), and any effort to subvert the ratings system would be a federal offense. Testifying before the Senate Commerce Committee on September 12, 2000, Lieberman promised that regulation of the entertainment industry would focus on "how they market, not what they produce," but that promise ignores the effect of marketing considerations on content.   7

Some may consider the decline of violent entertainments no great loss, imagining perhaps that slasher movies and violent video games will be the primary victims of a new federal labeling regime. But it's not hard to imagine a docudrama about domestic abuse or abortion, or a coming-of-age story about a gay teen, receiving the same restricted rating as a sleazy movie about a serial murderer. In any case, a stringent, federally mandated and monitored rating and labeling system will not enhance parental control; it's a vehicle for bureaucratic control. Federal officials, not parents, will determine what entertainment will be available to children when they devise and enforce the ratings.   8

Some claim that federal action is justified, nonetheless, by an overriding need to save lives. At the September 12 hearing inspired by the FTC report, several senators and other witnesses vigorously condemned   9 the entertainment industry for "literally making a killing off of marketing to kids," in the words of Kansas Republican Sam Brownback. He called upon the industry to stop producing the entertainments he abhors. Lieberman charged that media violence was "part of a toxic mix that has turned some of our children into killers." Lynne Cheney, former head of the National Endowment for the Humanities, declared that "there is a problem with the product they market, no matter how they market it." Democratic Senator Fritz Hollings proposed giving the Federal Communications Commission the power to impose a partial ban on whatever programming it considers violent and harmful to minors.

10   What all this hyperbolic rhetoric obscured (or ignored) was the dearth of hard evidence that violent media actually turns "children into killers." In fact, the FTC study on which would-be censors rely found no clear causal connection between violent media and violent behavior. "Exposure to violent materials probably is not even the most important factor" in determining whether a child will turn violent, FTC Chairman Robert Pitofsky observed. The most he would say was that exposure to violent media "does seem to correlate with aggressive attitudes, insensitivity toward violence, and an exaggerated view of how much violence occurs in the world."

11   This is not exactly a defense of media violence, but it may present a fairly balanced view of its effects, which do not justify limitations on speech. Living in a free society entails a commitment not to prohibit speech unless it clearly, directly, and intentionally causes violence. If violent entertainment can be regulated by the federal government because it allegedly causes violence, so can inflammatory political rhetoric, like assertions that abortion providers kill babies. Anti-abortion rhetoric probably has even a clearer connection to violence than any violent movie, but both must be protected. If Disney can be brought under the thumb of federal regulators, so can Cardinal Law when he denounces abortion as murder.

12   It's unfortunate and ironic that apparently amoral corporations, like Disney or Time-Warner, stand as champions and beneficiaries of First Amendment rights. As gatekeepers of the culture, they're not exactly committed to maintaining an open, diverse marketplace of ideas. Indeed, the de facto censorship engineered by media conglomerates may threaten public discourse nearly as much as federal regulation. And neither our discourse nor our culture is exactly enriched by gratuitously violent media.

13   But speech doesn't have to provide cultural enrichment to enjoy constitutional protection. We don't need a First Amendment to protect popular, inoffensive speech or speech that a majority of people believe has social value. We need it to protect speech that Lynne Cheney or Joseph Lieberman consider demeaning and degrading. Censorship campaigns often begin with a drive to protect children (or women), but they rarely end there.

▶ Building Vocabulary

1. Write out the meanings of the following idioms:
   a. the moral voice (par. 2)
   b. cleanse the culture (par. 2)
   c. a soft spot for working families (par. 2)
   d. entangle the government (par. 7)
   e. making a killing off (par. 9)
   f. under the thumb (par. 11)
   g. marketplace of ideas (par. 12)

2. Identify and define the following references, and explain their significance to American culture:
   a. Federal Trade Commission (par. 2)
   b. Victorian (par. 3)
   c. Ford Pintos (par. 5)
   d. slasher movies (par. 8)
   e. National Endowment for the Humanities (par. 9)
   f. Cardinal Law (par. 11)

▶ Thinking Critically about the Argument

Understanding the Writer's Argument

1. What does it mean that Al Gore is "shocked!, shocked!" about the entertainment industry's marketing of violence? What is the writer referring to here? Why is Kaminer not surprised by Gore's threat to the entertainment industry?
2. What is the history of labeling media? According to Kaminer, what are the risks of labeling entertainment?
3. What does the First Amendment not protect when it comes to advertising?
4. What is Kaminer's view of the politicians and their opinions as quoted in paragraph 9? What does Kaminer think is more of a risk to America than media violence?
5. What, according to Kaminer, is the problem with the argument that media violence is a direct cause of the rise in violence?
6. Why does Kaminer think it's odd that large media corporations "stand as champions and beneficiaries of First Amendment rights"? (par. 12)

Understanding the Writer's Techniques

1. What is Kaminer's major proposition? Where does it appear?

2. Why does the writer start her essay with the voices of politicians? How does she portray them? What argumentative effect does her opening have?
3. Why does Kaminer give the history of politicians' attempts to regulate media? What point is she making? Is it effectively done? Why or why not?
4. What tone is the writer taking in this essay? Give examples to explain your answer.
5. How do paragraphs 9 and 10 support Kaminer's position?
6. List two or three of her most effective transitions, and explain why they are effective.
7. Is the conclusion effective? What makes it so, or how could it be improved?

Exploring the Writer's Argument

1. In paragraph 6, Kaminer complains that "once you define violent or sexually explicit media as toxic products, it is not terribly difficult to justify regulating their advertising, at least, if not their distribution and production." Do you agree with her statement? Do you still think it is difficult, no matter what a politician or other public figure might say? Why or why not?
2. Do you think Kaminer's occasionally combative tone strengthens or weakens her argument? Explain your answer.
3. Although this essay was written recently, in 2000—after the shootings at Columbine High School in 1999 and after other school shootings— do you think Kaminer would have any reason today to change her mind about her claim? Why or why not? Can you think of any reason Kaminer would change her mind? Explain your response.

▶ **Ideas for Writing Arguments**

Prewriting

Warning labels now appear on video games and television shows to indicate violence, sexually explicit material, and so on. What is your opinion of those labels? Are they helpful? Why or why not? Write some notes on your feelings and the reasons for your feelings.

Writing a Guided Argument

Write an essay arguing for or against the warning labels on television shows. Do some research online or in the library to determine the origin of the labels. Who made the networks include them, or did the networks put them in on their own?

1. Open your essay with an account of watching television and noticing a label on a show.
2. Link your experience with your major proposition by using a transition.
3. Give the history of the labels and a partial list, for your reader's information, of the labels.
4. Explain in brief why you are for or against the labels.
5. In the next section, offer your minor propositions.
6. Support your minor propositions with examples and facts you gleaned from your research.
7. Address the issue of television as "toxic media."
8. Establish a tone that has some irony and cynicism.
9. Rebut at least one possible objection to your argument.
10. Close your essay with a discussion of how the television industry is doing things the right way, or offer a proposal to address the problem.

Thinking, Arguing, and Writing Collaboratively

Help to divide the class into two equal groups. One group should take Kaminer's position that violence in the media does not warrant censorship, and the other should take Easterbrook's position that violence at least warrants self-censorship. As a group, think of arguments and facts to add to those already given by the writer whose position you are taking and try to remedy weaknesses you might see. Take notes on your group discussion and prepare an outline for a debate. Debate the issue, and afterwards reconvene as a class to discuss the success of the structure of the debate and how effective the arguments your group added were. Discuss what you left out or improved.

Writing about the Text

Write an essay that expands on the following sentence by Kaminer: "Campaigns marketing violent entertainment to children may be sleazy, but they don't promote an illegal activity (the sale of violent material to minors is not generally criminal); and they're not deceptive or unfair (many popular entertainments are just as bad as they purport to be)." (par. 6)

More Writing Ideas

1. In your journal, write an entry about your feelings on the First Amendment.
2. If violent media is one possible risk that we face in an open society, what other risks are there? Write one or two paragraphs outlining the various dangers that arise from living as we do in a free country.
3. Find an item in the media (a song, a clip from a movie, a television show, a radio show, or a newspaper or magazine advertisement, for example) that you find particularly offensive and bad for society, then defend it in an essay. Defend the piece's right to be created, distributed, and marketed, addressing each of these rights in order.

14 ▶ The Environment: How Can We Preserve It?

Will we leave any natural resources for our children and our children's children? That's the urgent question from the environmentalist movement. Humankind is the only species able to alter the climate artificially and pollute the land, water, and air, and we certainly have done that. The Industrial Revolution marked a move away from an agricultural economy to one dominated by machines and factories. Trains, running on coal fuel, belched out black smoke and fouled the atmosphere. Factories dumped chemicals into rivers and harbors. Not until relatively recently did scientists understand the extent to which 200 years of industrialization was damaging the world we live in.

Nature writers helped bring to light the diversity of plants and animals and moved readers to try to protect this diversity. Many writers mobilized to persuade people (especially legislators and politicians) to sit up and take notice and to understand that how they act affects the rest of the world. "Think globally, act locally" became one of the slogans of environmentalism. Much of the recent conversation has focused on global warming and trying to reduce greenhouse gases, which result from the burning of coal or gasoline. The gases warm the atmosphere and have upset Earth's climate. Scientists warn that if humanity doesn't stop global warming, many species will become extinct.

New York Times columnist Bob Herbert, in "No Margin for Error," attempts to frighten his readers into caring about the future of the coral reefs. Verlyn Klinkenborg, in "Out of the Wild," uses a different and more genteel strategy to underline the wonder of the natural world, telling the story of surprising a sick fox in the writer's barn. Barry Lopez in "Apologia" takes this sense of wonder to an extreme in his account of a road trip. Feeling guilty for all the animals he sees dead on the road, he takes his time to pay tribute to them. Fiction writer Wendell Berry, in "In Distrust of Movements," agrees with these writers, but he has no patience for the environmentalist movement or any other movement. In his essay, he circles his subject until arriving at a prescription—have respect for the Earth, and everything will be okay.

BOB HERBERT
No Margin for Error

Bob Herbert was born in Brooklyn in 1945 and started his career as a reporter for the Star-Ledger, *a Newark, New Jersey, newspaper. He worked in television news for NBC before returning to newspaper writing in 1993 as a columnist for the* New York Times *op-ed page. Called the conscience of the op-ed page, he has won numerous awards, including the American Society of Newspaper Editors award for distinguished newspaper writing. His book,* Promises Betrayed: Waking Up from the American Dream, *appeared in 2005. Herbert has taught journalism at Brooklyn College and the Columbia University Graduate School of Journalism. Herbert is known for having a strong moral compass in his columns, and in this selection, he takes a look at global warming and its effects on the world's coral reefs.*

▶ Prereading: Thinking about the Essay in Advance

What do you think is the greatest threat to Earth as a result of global warming? What effects have we felt already as a result?

▶ Words to Watch

disintegrate (par. 1) fall apart
emissions (par. 5) things released or given off
phenomena (par. 7) things that occur
indisputable (par. 9) impossible to doubt
catastrophic (par. 12) causing terrible damage
epochs (par. 14) long period of time

1   Global warming is already attacking the world's coral reefs and, if nothing is done soon, could begin a long-term assault on the vast West Antarctic Ice Sheet. If the ice sheet begins to disintegrate, the worldwide consequences over the next several centuries could well be disastrous.

2   Coral reefs are sometimes called the rain forests of the oceans because of the tremendous variety of animal and plant life that they support.

3   "They're the richest ocean ecosystem, and if they are destroyed or severely damaged, a lot of the biological diversity simply goes away," said Dr. Michael Oppenheimer, a professor of geosciences and international affairs at Princeton who is an expert on climate change.

4   Dr. Oppenheimer and Brian C. O'Neill, a professor at Brown, have an article in the current issue of *Science* magazine that addresses some of the long-term dangers that could result if nothing is done about global warming.

One of the things that is not widely understood about the greenhouse   5
gases that are contributing to the warming of the planet is that once they
are spewed into the atmosphere, they stay there for centuries, and in
some cases, millenniums. So a delay of even a decade or so in reducing
those emissions can make it much more difficult—and costly—to slow the
momentum of the warming and avert the more extreme consequences.

In their article, Dr. Oppenheimer and Dr. O'Neill suggest that public   6
officials and others trying to determine what levels of global warming
would actually be dangerous could use the destruction of the world's
coral reefs as one of their guides.

Coral reefs, which are breathtakingly beautiful natural phenom-   7
ena, tend to thrive in water temperatures that are only slightly below
the maximum temperature at which they can survive. There is not
much margin for error. Even allowing for some genetic adaptation, a
sustained increase in water temperatures of as little as a couple of degrees Fahrenheit can result in widespread coral reef destruction in just
a few years.

A number of factors are already contributing to the destruction of   8
coral reefs, and global warming is one of them. As the earth's temperature continues to rise, global warming will most likely become the chief
enemy of what Dr. Oppenheimer calls "these wonderful sources of biological diversity."

The threat to coral reefs is clear and indisputable. Much less clear is   9
the danger that global warming presents to the West Antarctic Ice Sheet.

10   "We really don't know with any level of certainty what amount of warming would destroy the ice sheet or how quickly that would happen," said Dr. Oppenheimer. He and Dr. O'Neill wrote, "In general, the probability is thought to be low during this century, increasing gradually thereafter."

11   There is not even agreement among scientists on the amount of warming necessary to begin the destruction. But what is clear is that if the ice sheet were to disintegrate, the consequences would be profound. So you don't want to play around with this. You want to make sure it doesn't happen.

12   "We know," said Dr. Oppenheimer, "that if the ice sheet were destroyed, sea levels would rise about five meters, which would be catastrophic for coastal regions. That would submerge much of Manhattan below Greenwich Village, for instance. It would drown the southern third of Florida, an area inhabited by about four million people."

13   Five meters is approximately 16 feet. Tremendous amounts of housing, wetlands and farming areas around the world would vanish. Large portions of a country like Bangladesh, on the Bay of Bengal, would disappear.

14   So what could actually set this potential catastrophe in motion? Dr. Oppenheimer has looked back at past geological epochs. "There is some evidence," he said, "that when the global temperature was warmer by about four degrees Fahrenheit than it is today the ice sheet disintegrated."

15   It is now estimated that if we do nothing to stem the rise of global warming, the increase in the earth's temperature over the course of this century will be between 3 and 10.5 degrees Fahrenheit. That is a level of warming that could initiate the disintegration of the ice sheet. And stopping that disintegration, once the planet gets warm, may be impossible.

▶ Building Vocabulary

In this essay, Herbert uses several terms from the world of ecology and earth science. Identify and write definitions for the following:

1. global warming (par. 1)
2. rain forests (par. 2)
3. ecosystem (par. 3)
4. geosciences (par. 3)
5. climate change (par. 3)
6. greenhouse gases (par. 5)
7. wetlands (par. 13)

▶ Thinking Critically about the Argument

Understanding the Writer's Argument

1. What are coral reefs? Why are they so special?

2. Why is time of the essence when dealing with issues of global warming?
3. How are coral reefs a good gauge of the destruction wrought by global warming?
4. What is the West Antarctic Ice Sheet, and why should we care what happens to it?
5. What is the main cause of global warming?

Understanding the Writer's Techniques

1. What is Herbert's major proposition? Where does he express it most clearly?
2. Why does Herbert begin his essay with such a confrontational paragraph? Explain how it affects his argument.
3. This essay lists the effects of global warming. Identify these effects in the order that Herbert presents them. Which is most surprising or powerful? Why?
4. Why does Herbert present his argument in the order that he does?
5. Why does Herbert pause in his argument to explain how many feet five meters is, after he has already mentioned much of the destruction that might occur if the ice sheet melts?
6. How does the concluding paragraph help to wrap up Herbert's argument?

Exploring the Writer's Argument

1. There are a few places in this short essay when Herbert repeats information. Why does he repeat himself? Is the strategy effective or is it a weakness in the essay?
2. Herbert doesn't spend much time explaining what his readers could do to help the coral reefs or the ice sheet. Is this a weakness in his essay? Explain your answer.
3. Herbert praises the coral reefs and explains why it would be terrible if they were lost, but at the end of his essay he doesn't mention them again. Why? Does this omission weaken his essay? Why or why not?

▶ Ideas for Writing Arguments

Prewriting

Herbert says that people are the problem. What can you do yourself to help stop global warming, if it is such a problem?

Writing a Guided Argument

One of the sayings in the environmental movement is "think globally, act locally." Activists say that if many people do little things to conserve resources, then we will see the benefits worldwide. Write an essay in the form of an open letter to the other students in your college arguing that they can act locally to help the environment. (You might have to do a little bit of research to gather evidence.)

1. Open your essay with an explanation of the problem and why it is urgent that we protect the environment.
2. Write your major proposition, and explain how students can play a role in this effort.
3. Next, show how students can be wasteful and act in ways that harm the environment.
4. Offer your minor propositions in the next section, showing exactly what students can do to help protect the environment.
5. Support your minor propositions with facts and process analysis, giving your reader a "how-to" for each.
6. Affect a tone that reflects the seriousness and urgency of the topic.
7. Explain to your reader that students are important because they are the future leaders of the world.
8. Bring your essay to a close on an ominous note, explaining what might happen if students don't take a role.

Thinking, Arguing, and Writing Collaboratively

In groups of four or five, discuss the ideas presented in your Writing a Guided Argument assignment. Jot down notes, and incorporate your peers' opinions—making sure they suit your essay—in your final draft.

Writing about the Text

In this essay, Herbert depends for his evidence almost entirely on the single article in *Science* magazine by Drs. Michael Oppenheimer and Brian C. O'Neill. Where in Herbert's essay do you, as the reader, desire more varied evidence? Or do you not need more? Write an essay in which you analyze how Herbert's essay is either strengthened or weakened by having only one source?

More Writing Ideas

1. In your journal, write an entry assessing your own activities when it comes to saving or wasting natural resources.
2. Some people, despite all scientific evidence for global warming, have denied that it's happening at all. Do some research and in several paragraphs, summarize the arguments of those who don't believe in global warming.

3. Many countries have tried to reduce the effects of global warming. One of those efforts, the Kyoto Conference, was an international meeting brokered under the power of the United Nations. The conference drafted the Kyoto Protocol, which called for countries to reduce emissions and other greenhouse gases. Most industrial nations agreed to adhere to Kyoto, but the United States, which causes most of the emissions in the world, refused to agree. Do some research on the topic, and write an essay that argues either for or against the United States agreeing to the Kyoto Protocol.

VERLYN KLINKENBORG
Out of the Wild

Verlyn Klinkenborg lives on a small farm in upstate New York, from which he writes his popular "The Rural Life" column on the editorial page of the New York Times. *He published a collection of the columns in 2003. Klinkenborg comes from a family of Iowa farmers. His unique vision as someone from the country who lived in the city and then returned to the country makes his essays poignant and touching. He is also the author of* Making Hay *(1986),* The Rural Life *(2004), and* Timothy, or Notes of an Abject Reptile *(2007). A member of the editorial board of the* New York Times, *he has written for the* New Yorker, Harper's, Esquire, National Geographic, *and* Mother Jones, *among others. In this essay Klinkenborg narrates his face-to-face meeting with a wild animal and is forced to rethink his preconceptions.*

▶ Prereading: Thinking about the Essay in Advance

Have you or someone you know ever encountered a wild animal? What was the reaction—fear, awe, surprise, respect, or some other emotion?

▶ Words to Watch

bale (par. 1) pile bound together
transgression (par. 1) act of crossing a forbidden boundary
frigid (par. 3) bitterly cold
platonic (par. 4) perfect and idealistic in form
vertebrae (par. 5) backbones

The other morning I lifted a bale of hay from a loose pile of bales on   1
the barn floor, and a fox jumped out from under it. The fox ran to the back of the barn and turned to watch me. It paced a few steps, uncertain,

and then scurried under the door and out into the cold rain. It was a moment of pure transgression. All the old story lines broke apart—the ones about farmers and foxes and chickens—and just when the old story had been going so well. The fox had stolen a couple of our chickens. I had chased it off several times. It would lope up the hill in the middle pasture and sit on the ridge looking back at me, waiting for my next move. We hated to lose the chickens, and we hated the fox for taking them, but it was a conventional hatred, a part we knew we were supposed to play.

2   But there are no stories in which the fox sleeps overnight in the barn on a bed of hay only a few feet from three horses in a run-in shed and a big, campaigning dog in his kennel. In all the traditional tales the fox keeps its distance, a playful distance perhaps, always respecting the invisible boundary between wildness and not-wildness. But the other morning that fox ignored the boundary completely.

3   The reason was obvious. It was dying from a terrible case of sarcoptic mange, an all-too-common disease caused by mites that infest the skin and cause severe inflammation and hair loss. Foxes with mange die of malnutrition or they freeze to death. The night had been frigid, with a blowing, soaking rainfall. Even the driest den would have been insufferable, and so the fox took refuge in a burrow among hay bales in a dry barn.

4   My wife and I have been seeing foxes ever since we moved to this place. They skirted the far edge of the pasture at a businesslike trot, keeping watch as if they knew that someday we'd give in and get chickens. But because they always kept their distance, they were platonic foxes, storybook foxes with sharp muzzles and thick red fur and bushy tails and the gloss of wild health. They looked the way they were supposed to look, the way you imagine a fox looks. The binoculars only confirmed what we knew we'd find, the very idea of Vulpes vulpes. Every now and then a fox would get hit by a car on the nearby highway, and one of us would wonder aloud if it was our fox and we would miss it in advance. And yet there was always another fox crossing the pasture.

5   But seeing this nearly hairless fox shivering at the barn door, its tail a pitiful file of vertebrae under bare flesh, I couldn't help thinking what a thin concept of wildness I had been living with. The wild I imagined was where the archetypes lived, negotiating their survival. Each animal in the wild embodied its species, which means that it lived up to its portrait in "The Sibley Guide to Birds" or "Walker's Mammals of the World." And though I had a rough idea of how creatures died in the wild, I had never come across an animal driven out of the wild— across that taboo boundary and into my barn—by its suffering. The fox and I looked at each other, only a few feet apart. If it had been a dog I could have helped it. But even the pity in my eyes reminded it that it had come too close.

▶ Building Vocabulary

Define and write a sentence of your own using each of the following words:

1. scurried (par. 1)
2. lope (par. 1)
3. businesslike (par. 4)
4. archetypes (par. 5)
5. embodied (par. 5)
6. taboo (par. 5)

▶ Thinking Critically about the Argument

Understanding the Writer's Argument

1. What does the writer have against the fox at the beginning of his essay?
2. Why does Klinkenborg think it unusual that the fox was taking refuge in his barn?
3. Why *was* the fox in the barn?
4. What is the normal behavior of foxes around the writer's farm?
5. What is the writer's usual view of "wildness"? How has it changed after his run-in with the fox?

Understanding the Writer's Techniques

1. What is Klinkenborg's major proposition? Is it a clear statement? If so, what is it? If not, what do you think it is?
2. The essay is essentially a narrative and attempts to move its readers emotionally. How does the writer build an emotional appeal to his readers?
3. Analyze the use of transitions. How do they move the essay along?
4. This essay aims for an urban readership, and the writer must educate his readers about the rural life. How does Klinkenborg get this information into his essay?
5. What are the warrants in this essay? Are they implied or explicit?
6. Most of the writer's explicit argument is in the final paragraph. How effective is his conclusion?

Exploring the Writer's Argument

1. Klinkenborg writes that if the fox had been a dog, he "could have helped it." Do you think that makes him seem heartless? Or is he merely being realistic? Could he have helped the fox, do you think? Should he have?

2. The writer speaks as a gentleman-farmer, an observer of nature who is educated. Do you believe he is a real farmer? Is his voice authentic? Defend your answers.
3. What relation does the essay imply between humans and animals? Why might you agree or disagree with the relation as Klinkenborg suggests it?

▶ Ideas for Writing Arguments

Prewriting

What did people have to do to domesticate animals like dogs, cats, pigs, and cows? Why did they do it? What do humans gain from domesticating animals?

Writing a Guided Argument

Many of us have pets for companionship and safety, and they are reliable and veritable members of the family. Every once in a while, however, we get a glimpse of just how much they are still animals. Write an essay in which you argue that a pet such as a dog or cat remains, in part, wild, no matter how domesticated it is.

1. Open your essay with a short narrative about a time when you saw the wild animal inside of a pet come through.
2. Next, write a major proposition that argues that pets are, in part, wild.
3. State at least two or three minor propositions to support your position.
4. Show examples to illustrate your minor propositions.
5. Establish a tone that shows how you are amused by the idea of pets being wild.
6. Somewhere near the end, break the normal tone of your essay to express that although it is amusing that pets can be wild, there is something a bit frightening about the fact.
7. Close your essay by reestablishing the normal tone.

Thinking, Arguing, and Writing Collaboratively

In groups of four or five students, share your papers that grew out of the Writing a Guided Argument assignment. Discuss the success of the opening narrative and the examples offered to support the minor propositions. Can the passages be improved by omission or rewriting? Can the argument be improved by altering the facts?

Writing about the Text

Write an essay in which you analyze Klinkenborg's style in "Out of the Wild." How does the writer succeed in creating an argument out of a situation he encounters on his farm? He is writing for a newspaper for the biggest city in the United States. How does his rural, laid-back style work?

More Writing Ideas

1. In your journal, freewrite on the topic of boundaries between humans and animals. Write for at least 15 minutes, but do not edit your work as you go. After the time is up, look at what you wrote, and take notes on anything that might be the basis for an essay.
2. Write a paragraph or two in which you explore how nature asserts itself in a city.
3. Write an essay in which you defend or challenge people's efforts to assist animals in the wild—a beached whale or an injured bird, for example. Should humankind help beasts in the wild, or should we leave them to the fate to which nature has led them?

Barry Lopez
Apologia

Barry Lopez was born in 1945 in rural California and now lives in Oregon. He is a short story and nonfiction writer best known for his nature writing, especially Arctic Dreams *(1986), which won the National Book Award for nonfiction. He is also the author of* Crow and Weasel *(1990) and* Field Notes *(1994), among other books, and the editor of* Home Ground: Language for an American Landscape *(2006). In this selection, Lopez tells the story of a road trip turned deadly—for animals in the wild.*

▶ Prereading: Thinking about the Essay in Advance

Have you ever run over an animal or seen one run over? What did you feel, if anything? Do you ever feel grief at seeing a dead animal on the road?

▶Words to Watch

maniacally (par. 1) in a crazy way
cornea (par. 2) the membrane that covers the eye
seers (par. 5) people who can see the future
carcass (par. 9) dead body of an animal
tawny (par. 11) of an orange-brown color
gunnysack (par. 11) a bag made from a rough material
cloister (par. 12) place in a monastery where monks live; considered
    secluded
macadam (par. 14) road surface made of asphalt mixed with rocks
fractious (par. 15) irritable and complaining
beryl (par. 16) a hard mineral consisting of many colors
mandibular (par. 18) relating to the jaw
limpid (par. 21) clear and calm
exculpation (par. 23) to free someone from blame
lavabo (par. 25) a ceremony in a Catholic mass in which a congregant rit-
    ually washes his hands

1   A few miles east of home in the Cascades I slow down and pull over for two raccoons, sprawled still as stones in the road. I carry them to the side and lay them in sun-shot windblown grass in the barrow pit. In eastern Oregon along U.S. 20, black-tailed jackrabbits lie like welts of sod—three, four, then a fifth. By the bridge over Jordan Creek, just shy of the Idaho border in the drainage of the Owyhee River, a crumpled adolescent porcupine leers up almost maniacally over its blood-flecked teeth. I carry each one away from the pavement into a cover of grass or brush out of decency, I think. And worry. Who are these animals, their lights gone out? What journeys have fallen apart here?

2   I do not stop to remove each dark blister from the road. I wince before the recently dead, feel my lips tighten, see something else, a fence post, in the spontaneous aversion of my eyes, and pull over. I imagine white silk threads of life still vibrating inside them, even if the body's husk is stretched out for yards, stuck like oiled muslin to the road. The energy that once held them erect leaves like a bullet, but the memory of that energy fades slowly from the wrinkled cornea, the bloodless fur.

3   The raccoons and, later, a red fox carry like sacks of wet gravel and sand. Each animal is like a solitary child's shoe in the road.

4   Once a man asked, Why do you bother?

5   You never know, I said. The ones you give some semblance of burial, to whom you offer an apology, may have been like seers in a parallel culture. It is an act of respect, a technique of awareness.

6   In Idaho I hit a young sage sparrow—thwack against the right fender in the very split second I see it. Its companion rises from the same spot

but a foot higher, slow as smoke, and sails off clean into the desert. I rest the walloped bird in my left hand, my right thumb pressed to its chest. I feel for the wail of the heart. Its eyes glisten like rain on crystal. Nothing but warmth. I shut the tiny eyelids and lay it beside a clump of bunch-grass. Beyond a barbed-wire fence the overgrazed range is littered with cow flops. The road curves away to the south. I nod before I go, a ridiculous gesture, out of simple grief.

I pass four spotted skunks. The swirling air is acrid with the rup- 7
ture of each life.

Darkness rises in the valleys of Idaho. East of Grand View, south of 8
the Snake River, nighthawks swoop the roads for gnats, silent on the wing as owls. On a descending curve I see two of them lying soft as clouds in the road. I turn around and come back. The sudden slowing down and my K-turn at the bottom of the hill draw the attention of a man who steps away from a tractor, a dozen yards from where the birds lie. I can tell by his step, the suspicious tilt of his head, that he is wary, vaguely proprietary. Offended, or irritated, he may throw the birds back into the road when I leave. So I wait, subdued like a penitent, a body in each hand.

He speaks first, a low voice, a deep murmur weighted with awe. He 9
has been watching these flocks feeding just above the road for several evenings. He calls them whippoorwills. He gestures for a carcass. How odd, yes, the way they concentrate their hunting right on the road, I say. He runs a finger down the smooth arc of the belly and remarks on the small whiskered bill. He pulls one long wing out straight, but not roughly. He marvels. He glances at my car, baffled by this out-of-state courtesy. Two dozen nighthawks career past, back and forth at arm's length, feeding at our height and lower. He asks if I would mind—as though I owned it—if he took the bird up to the house to show his wife. "She's never seen anything like this" He's fascinated. "Not close."

I trust, later, he will put it in the fields, not throw the body in the 10
trash, a whirligig.

North of Pinedale in western Wyoming on U.S. 189, below the Gros 11
Ventre Range, I see a big doe from a great distance, the low rays of first light gleaming in her tawny reddish hair. She rests askew, like a crushed tree. I drag her to the shoulder, then down a long slope by the petals of her ears. A gunnysack of plaster mud, ears cold as rain gutters. All of her doesn't come. I climb back up for the missing leg. The stain of her is darker than the black asphalt. The stains go north and off to the south as far as I can see.

On an afternoon trafficless, quiet as a cloister, headed across South 12
Pass in the Wind River Range, I swerve violently but hit a bird, and then try to wrestle the gravel-spewing skid in a straight line along the lip of an embankment. I know even as I struggle for control the irony of this: I could easily pitch off here to my own death. The bird is dead somewhere

in the road behind me. Only a few seconds and I am safely back on the road, nauseated, light-headed.

13   It is hard to distinguish among younger gulls. I turn this one around slowly in my hands. It could be a western gull, a mew gull, a California gull. I do not remember well enough the bill markings, the color of the legs. I have no doubt about the vertebrae shattered beneath the seamless white of its ropy neck.

14   East of Lusk, Wyoming, in Nebraska, I stop for a badger. I squat on the macadam to admire the long claws, the perfect set of its teeth in the broken jaw, the ramulose shading of its fur—how it differs slightly, as does every badger's, from the drawings and pictures in the field guides. A car drifts toward us over the prairie, coming on in the other lane, a white 1962 Chevrolet station wagon. The driver slows to pass. In the bright sunlight I can't see his face, only an arm and the gesture of his thick left hand. It opens in a kind of shrug, hangs briefly in limp sadness, then extends itself in supplication. Gone past, it curls into itself against the car door and is still.

15   Farther on in western Nebraska I pick up the small bodies of mice and birds. While I wait to retrieve these creatures I do not meet the eyes of passing drivers. Whoever they are, I feel anger toward them, in spite of the sparrow and the gull I myself have killed. We treat the attrition of lives on the road like the attrition of lives in war: horrifying, unavoidable, justified. Accepting the slaughter leaves people momentarily fractious, embarrassed. South of Broken Bow, at dawn, I cannot avoid an immature barn swallow. It hangs by its head, motionless in the slats of the grille.

16   I stop for a rabbit on Nebraska 806 and find, only a few feet away, a garter snake. What else have I missed, too small, too narrow? What has gone under or past me while I stared at mountains, hay meadows, fencerows, the beryl surface of rivers? In Wyoming I could not help but see pronghorn antelope swollen big as barrels by the side of the road, their legs splayed rigidly aloft. For animals so large, people will stop. But how many have this habit of clearing the road of smaller creatures, people who would remove the ones I miss? I do not imagine I am alone. As much sorrow as the man's hand conveyed in Nebraska, it meant gratitude too for burying the dead.

17   Still, I do not wish to meet anyone's eyes.

18   In Southwestern Iowa, outside Clarinda, I haul a deer into high grass out of sight of the road and begin to examine it. It is still whole, but the destruction is breathtaking. The skull, I soon discover, is fractured in four places; the jaw, hanging by shreds of mandibular muscle, is broken at the symphysis, beneath the incisors. The pelvis is crushed, the left hind leg unsocketed. All but two ribs are dislocated along the vertebral column, which is complexly fractured. The intestines have been driven forward into the chest. The heart and lungs have ruptured the chest wall at the base of the neck. The signature of a tractor-trailer truck: 80,000 pounds at 65 mph.

In front of a motel room in Ottumwa I finger-scrape the dry, stiff car-   19
casses of bumblebees, wasps, and butterflies from the grille and head-
light mountings, and I scrub with a wet cloth to soften and wipe away
the nap of crumbles, the insects, the aerial plankton of spiders and mites.
I am uneasy cleaning so many of the dead. The carnage is so obvious.

In Illinois, west of Kankakee, two raccoons as young as the ones in Ore-   20
gon. In Indiana another raccoon, a gray squirrel. When I make the left turn
into the driveway at the house of a friend outside South Bend, it is evening,
hot and muggy. I can hear cicadas in a lone elm. I'm glad to be here.

From the driveway entrance I look back down Indiana 23, toward In-   21
diana 8, remembering the farm roads of Illinois and Iowa. I remember
how beautiful it was in the limpid air to drive Nebraska 2 through the
sand hills, to see how far at dusk the land was etched east and west of
Wyoming 28. I remember the imposition of the Wind River Range in a
hard, blue sky beneath white ranks of buttonhook clouds, windy hay
fields on the Snake River plain, the welcome of Russian olive trees and
willows in western creek bottoms. The transformation of the heart such
beauty engenders is not enough tonight to let me shed the heavier memory, a catalog too morbid to write out, too vivid to ignore.

I stand in the driveway now, listening to the cicadas whirring in the   22
dark tree. My hands grip the sill of the open window at the driver's side,
and I lean down as if to speak to someone still sitting there. The weight I
wish to fall I cannot fathom, a sorrow over the world's dark hunger.

A light comes on over the porch. I hear a deadbolt thrown, the shiver   23
of a door pulled free. The words of atonement I pronounce are too inept
to offer me release. Or forgiveness. My friend is floating across the tree-
shadowed lawn. What is to be done with the desire for exculpation?

"Later than we thought you'd be," he says.   24

I do not want the lavabo. I wish to make amends.   25

"I made more stops than I thought I would," I answer. "Well, bring in   26
your things. And whatever I can take," he offers.

I anticipate, in the powerful antidote of our conversation, the reassur-   27
ance of a human enterprise, the forgiving embrace of the rational. It waits
within, beyond the slow tail-wagging of two dogs standing at the screen
door.

▶ Building Vocabulary

1. Go through this essay again and list at least 10 of the animals mentioned. Write a short description of each, using reference works, if
   necessary.
2. For each of the following words, write a definition:
   a. leers (par. 1)
   b. wince (par. 2)
   c. semblance (par. 5)

d. walloped (par. 6)
e. acrid (par. 7)
f. penitent (par. 8)
g. supplication (par. 14)
h. atonement (par. 23)

▶ Thinking Critically about the Argument

Understanding the Writer's Argument

1. What are the Cascades? Why is Lopez driving east through them? Where is he going?
2. Why does Lopez carry the bodies of dead animals to the side of the road? What does Lopez mean by "What journeys have fallen apart here?" (par. 1) How do you know?
3. List the different encounters Lopez has with people along his trip, and explain the nature of each encounter.
4. What does Lopez mean in paragraph 5 that offering a "semblance of burial" to a dead animal on the road is "a technique of awareness"? Where does this phrase come from?
5. Why does Lopez write that his nod to the bird in paragraph 6 is a "ridiculous gesture"?
6. Why doesn't Lopez tell his friend what he had been thinking at the end of his essay?
7. Paraphrase the following sentence: "I anticipate, in the powerful antidote of our conversation, the reassurance of a human enterprise, the forgiving embrace of the rational." (par. 27)

Understanding the Writer's Techniques

1. This essay's argument is complicated. It is not as simple as it seems at first glance. What is Lopez's claim, and where does he state it? If he doesn't state it, why not?
2. Comment on Lopez's use of transitions. How do they contribute to the coherence of the essay and his portrayal of the passage of time?
3. Why does Lopez write about the man who asks him "Why do you bother?" in paragraph 4?
4. What tense does the writer use for the verbs is this essay? Why do you think Lopez uses this tense? Is it effective? Why or why not?
5. What is the effect of the transition between paragraphs 12 and 13? At first, the reader thinks Lopez has driven away from his near-accident, and then the reader realizes that Lopez has turned around. How does he explain this?

6. What three descriptions in Lopez's essay do you think help his position the most?
7. Why does Lopez describe the driver of the Chevrolet driving past him in paragraph 14?
8. Why does Lopez make paragraph 17 one sentence? Is it effective? If so, how, and if not, why not?
9. What is the rhetorical effect of the last section of the essay, after Lopez has pulled into his friend's driveway?
10. What is your opinion of the last paragraph? Is it effective? How does it contribute to the essay's message?

Exploring the Writer's Argument

1. Lopez describes carefully the dead animals he finds. What is your reaction to his descriptions? Do you find the descriptions beautiful? Repulsive? Attractive? Why would he make them so? Explain your answers.
2. The language that Lopez uses in this essay is lyrical, but some readers also might consider it unnecessarily flowery and overwritten. Which do you think it is? Do you think the language in this essay is appropriate? Why or why not?
3. Do you agree with Lopez's statement in paragraph 15 that "we treat the attrition of lives on the road like the attrition of lives in war: horrifying, unavoidable, justified." Is this an apt simile? Why or why not?

▶ Ideas for Writing Arguments

Prewriting

What kind of purely legal and natural behavior do people engage in as a matter of course that we would have to apologize for or defend?

Writing a Guided Argument

Write a narrative argumentative essay also called "Apologia," in which you apologize for or defend some frequent action you take, or action you believe requires apology or defense. For example, you might apologize for last-minute, all-night vigils before a major test; for deciding to break off a relationship with someone you liked; or for refusing to give money to a homeless person begging for help.

1. Begin your narrative at the moment when you first start doing something that needs explaining. Do not start before this.

2. After you establish your story, fill in the back story, explaining anything your reader needs to know.
3. Attempt a lyrical style and tone in your essay, adding descriptions where appropriate.
4. Continue your story, breaking it up into episodes.
5. Offer your reader part of your argument after each episode.
6. Use effective transitions to move your essay along chronologically.
7. Close your essay with a section that ends the narrative and widens the discussion of the lesson you have learned (and which your reader can presumably learn) from your narrative.

Thinking, Arguing, and Writing Collaboratively

In groups of four or five, share experiences that you have had in nature when you felt either superior as humans (perhaps crushing a line of ants) or small as humans (perhaps watching a major storm). Make a list of the kinds of experiences that can make us feel one way or the other.

Writing about the Text

In this essay, Lopez uses many similes, such as in paragraph 11 when describing the dead deer: "She rests askew, like a crushed tree." Write an essay analyzing Lopez's use of figurative language, such as similes and metaphors, and how it helps his argument.

More Writing Ideas

1. In your journal, write a beautiful description of something not ordinarily seen as beautiful—such as withered trees, a sick old dog or cat, or a beaten-up automobile, for example.
2. Write a couple of paragraphs about a trip you took that led you to think about something you hadn't thought about before.
3. *Merriam-Webster's Collegiate Dictionary* defines *apologia* as "a defense especially of one's opinions, position, or actions" but also lists it as a synonym of "apology." Does the definition surprise you? Do you think this essay is a defense at all, or an apology? Write an essay in which you analyze the extent to which this essay is an apologia as *Webster's* defines it, and to what extent it is an apology. What would Lopez be apologizing for? What would he be defending?

WENDELL BERRY
In Distrust of Movements

Prolific Kentucky writer Wendell Berry was born in 1934. He was edu-
cated at the University of Kentucky. He is the author of 32 books of essays,
poetry, and fiction. His collections of poetry include There Is Singing
Around Me *(1976),* Traveling at Home *(1989),* Entries: Poems *(1994),*
and Window Poems *(2007). His novels include* Remembering *(1988),* A
World Lost *(1996), and* Andy Catlett: Early Travels *(2006). He is also*
the author of essay collections Standing on Earth: Selected Essays
(1991), Sex, Economy, Freedom, & Community *(1993), and* Another
Turn of the Crank *(1995). He has taught English at New York University*
and his alma mater, the University of Kentucky. Berry lives on a farm in
Port Royal, Kentucky. In this selection, originally published in 1999, Berry
expresses his impatience with organized environmental efforts and offers an
alternative way to make a difference.

▶ **Prereading: Thinking about the Essay in Advance**

Have you ever given money to a cause? Why or why not? What do you
think are the most respectable nonprofit organizations? Why?

▶ **Words to Watch**

watersheds (par. 4) area of land that drains into a body of water
advocates (par. 5) people who support something
preemption (par. 8) action that comes before something else can happen
irradiation (par. 8) treating food with radiation to kill germs
reconciled (par. 10) have accepted that something is going to happen
erosion (par. 14) a wearing-away from water or air
husbandry (par. 16) science and art of farming
profound (par. 18) very great
reductionist (par. 23) oversimplified
hubris (par. 24) excessive arrogance and pride
appropriate (par. 25) claim or use something as one's own

1   I must burden my readers as I have burdened myself with the knowledge that I speak from a local, some might say a provincial, point of view. When I try to identify myself to myself I realize that, in my most immediate reasons and affections, I am less than an American, less than a Kentuckian, less even than a Henry Countian, but am a man most involved with and concerned about my family, my neighbors, and the land that is daily under my feet. It is this involvement that defines my citizenship in the larger entities. And so I will remember, and I ask you to remember, that I am not trying to say what is thinkable everywhere, but rather what it is possible to think on the westward bank of the lower Kentucky River in the summer of 1998.

2   Over the last twenty-five or thirty years I have been making and remaking different versions of the same argument. It is not "my" argument, really, but rather one that I inherited from a long line of familial, neighborly, literary, and scientific ancestors. We could call it "the agrarian argument." This argument can be summed up in as many ways as it can be made. One way to sum it up is to say that we humans can escape neither our dependence on nature nor our responsibility to nature—and that, precisely because of this condition of dependence *and* responsibility, we are also dependent upon and responsible for human culture.

3   Food, as I have argued at length, is both a natural (which is to say a divine) gift and a cultural product. Because we must *use* land and water and plants and animals to produce food, we are at once dependent on and responsible to what we use. We must know both how to use and how to care for what we use. This knowledge is the basis of human culture. If we do not know how to adapt our desires, our methods, and our technology to the nature of the places in which we are working, so as to make them productive *and to keep them so,* that is a cultural failure of the grossest and most dangerous kind. Poverty and starvation also can be cultural products—if the culture is wrong.

4   Though this argument, in my keeping, has lengthened and acquired branches, in its main assumptions it has stayed the same. What has changed—and I say this with a good deal of wonder and with much thankfulness—is the audience. Perhaps the audience will always include people who are not listening, or people who think the agrarian argument is merely an anachronism, a form of entertainment, or a nuisance to be waved away. But increasingly the audience also includes people who take this argument seriously, because they are involved in one or more of the tasks of agrarianism. They are trying to maintain a practical foothold on the earth for themselves or their families or their communities. They are trying to preserve and develop local land-based economies. They are trying to preserve or restore the health of local communities and ecosystems

and watersheds. They are opposing the attempt of the great corporations to own and control all of Creation.

In short, the agrarian argument now has a significant number of friends. As the political and ecological abuses of the so-called global economy become more noticeable and more threatening, the agrarian argument is going to have more friends than it has now. This being so, maybe the advocate's task needs to change. Maybe now, instead of merely propounding (and repeating) the agrarian argument, the advocate must also try to see that this argument does not win friends too easily. I think, myself, that this is the case. The tasks of agrarianism that we have undertaken are not going to be finished for a long time. To preserve the remnants of agrarian life, to oppose the abuses of industrial land use and finally correct them, and to develop the locally adapted economies and cultures that are necessary to our survival will require many lifetimes of dedicated work. This work does not need friends with illusions. And so I would like to speak—in a friendly way, of course—out of my distrust of "movements."

I have had with my friend Wes Jackson a number of useful conversations about the necessity of getting out of movements—even movements that have seemed necessary and dear to us—when they have lapsed into self-righteousness and self-betrayal, as movements seem almost invariably to do. People in movements too readily learn to deny to others the rights and privileges they demand for themselves. They too easily become unable to mean their own language, as when a "peace movement" becomes violent. They often become too specialized, as if they cannot help taking refuge in the pinhole vision of the industrial intellectuals. They almost always fail to be radical enough, dealing finally in effects rather than causes. Or they deal with single issues or single solutions, as if to assure themselves that they will not be radical enough.

And so I must declare my dissatisfaction with movements to promote soil conservation or clean water or clean air or wilderness preservation or sustainable agriculture or community health or the welfare of children. Worthy as these and other goals may be, they cannot be achieved alone. They cannot be responsibly advocated alone. I am dissatisfied with such efforts because they are too specialized, they are not comprehensive enough, they are not radical enough, they virtually predict their own failure by implying that we can remedy or control effects while leaving the causes in place, Ultimately, I think, they are insincere; they propose that the trouble is caused by *other* people; they would like to change policy but not behavior.

The worst danger may be that a movement will lose its language either to its own confusion about meaning and practice, or to preemption by its enemies. I remember, for example, my naive confusion at learning that it was possible for advocates of organic agriculture to look upon the "organic method" as an end in itself. To me, organic farming was attractive both as a way of conserving nature and as a strategy of survival for small farmers. Imagine my surprise in discovering that there could be huge "organic" monocultures. And so I was somewhat prepared for the recent attempt of the United States Department of Agriculture to appropriate the "organic" label for food irradiation, genetic engineering, and other desecrations by the corporate food economy. Once we allow our language to mean anything that anybody wants it to mean, it becomes impossible to mean what we say. When "homemade" ceases to mean neither more nor less than "made at home," then it means anything, which is to say that it means nothing. The same decay is at work on words such as "conservation," "sustainable," "safe," "natural," "healthful," "sanitary," and "organic." The use of such words now requires the most exacting control of context and the use immediately of illustrative examples.

9   Real organic gardeners and farmers who market their produce locally are finding that, to a lot of people, "organic" means something like "trustworthy." And so, for a while, it will be useful for us to talk about the meaning and the economic usefulness of trust and trustworthiness. But we must be careful. Sooner or later, Trust Us Global Foods, Inc., will be upon us, advertising safe, sanitary, natural food irradiation. And then we must be prepared to raise another standard and move on.

10   As you see, I have good reasons for declining to name the movement I think I am a part of. I call it The Nameless Movement for Better Ways of Doing—which I hope is too long and uncute to be used as a bumper sticker. I know that movements tend to die with their names and slogans, and I believe that this Nameless Movement needs to live on and on. I am reconciled to the likelihood that from time to time it will name itself and have slogans, but I am not going to use its slogans or call it by any of its names. After this, I intend to stop calling it The Nameless Movement for Better Ways of Doing, for fear it will become the NMBWD and acquire a headquarters and a budget and an inventory of T-shirts covered with language that in a few years will be mere spelling.

11   Let us suppose, then, that we have a Nameless Movement for Better Land Use and that we know we must try to keep it active, responsive, and intelligent for a long time. What must we do?

12   What we must do above all, I think, is try to see the problem in its full size and difficulty. If we are concerned about land abuse, then we must see that this is an economic problem. Every economy is, by definition, a land-using economy. If we are using our land wrong, then something is wrong with our economy. This is difficult. It becomes more difficult when we recognize that, in modern times, every one of us is a member of the economy of everybody else. Every one of us has given many proxies to the economy to use the land (and the air, the water, and other natural gifts) on our be-

half. Adequately supervising those proxies is at present impossible; withdrawing them is for virtually all of us, as things now stand, unthinkable.

But if we are concerned about land abuse, we have begun an extensive   13
work of economic criticism. Study of the history of land use (and any local history will do) informs us that we have had for a long time an economy that thrives by undermining its own foundations. Industrialism, which is the name of our economy, and which is now virtually the only economy of the world, has been from its beginnings in a state of riot. It is based squarely upon the principle of violence toward everything on which it depends, and it has not mattered whether the form of industrialism was communist or capitalist, the violence toward nature, human communities, traditional agricultures, and local economies has been constant. The bad news is coming in from all over the world. Can such an economy somehow be fixed without being radically changed? I don't think it can.

The Captains of Industry have always counseled the rest of us to "be   14
realistic." Let us, therefore, be realistic. Is it realistic to assume that the present economy would be just fine if only it would stop poisoning the earth, air, and water, or if only it would stop soil erosion, or if only it would stop degrading watersheds and forest ecosystems, or if only it would stop seducing children, or if only it would quit buying politicians, or if only it would give women and favored minorities an equitable share of the loot? Realism, I think, is a very limited program, but it informs us at least that we should not look for bird eggs in a cuckoo clock.

Or we can show the hopelessness of single-issue causes and single-   15
issue movements by following a line of thought such as this: We need a continuous supply of uncontaminated water. Therefore, we need (among other things) soil-and-water-conserving ways of agriculture and forestry that are not dependent on monoculture, toxic chemicals, or the indifference and violence that always accompany big-scale industrial enterprises on the land. Therefore, we need diversified, small-scale land economies that are dependent on people. Therefore, we need people with the knowledge, skills, motives, and attitudes required by diversified, small-scale land economies. And all this is clear and comfortable enough, until we recognize the question we have come to: *Where are the people?*

Well, all of us who live in the suffering rural landscapes of the   16
United States know that most people are available to those landscapes only recreationally. We see them bicycling or boating or hiking or camping or hunting or fishing or driving along and looking around. They do not, in Mary Austin's phrase, "summer and winter with the land." They are unacquainted with the land's human and natural economies. Though people have not progressed beyond the need to eat food and drink water and wear clothes and live in houses, most people have progressed beyond the domestic arts—the husbandry and wifery of the world—by which those needful things are produced and conserved. In

fact, the comparative few who still practice that necessary husbandry and wifery often are inclined to apologize for doing so, having been carefully taught in our education system that those arts are degrading and unworthy of people's talents. Educated minds, in the modern era, are unlikely to know anything about food and drink or clothing and shelter. In merely taking these things for granted, the modern educated mind reveals itself also to be as superstitious a mind as ever has existed in the world. What could be more superstitious than the idea that money brings forth food?

17   I am not suggesting, of course, that everybody ought to be a farmer or a forester. Heaven forbid! I *am* suggesting that most people now are living on the far side of a broken connection, and that this is potentially catastrophic. Most people are now fed, clothed, and sheltered from sources, in nature and in the work of other people, toward which they feel no gratitude and exercise no responsibility.

18   We are involved now in a profound failure of imagination. Most of us cannot imagine the wheat beyond the bread, or the farmer beyond the wheat, or the farm beyond the farmer, or the history (human or natural) beyond the farm. Most people cannot imagine the forest and the forest economy that produced their houses and furniture and paper; or the landscapes, the streams, and the weather that fill their pitchers and bathtubs and swimming pools with water. Most people appear to assume that when they have paid their money for these things they have entirely met their obligations. And that is, in fact, the conventional economic assumption. The problem is that it is possible to starve under the rule of the conventional economic assumption; some people are starving now under the rule of that assumption.

19   Money does not being forth food. Neither does the technology of the food system. Food comes from nature and from the work of people. If the supply of food is to be continuous for a long time, then people must work in harmony with nature. That means that people must find the right answers to a lot of questions. The same rules apply to forestry and the possibility of a continuous supply of forest products.

20   People grow the food that people eat. People produce the lumber that people use. People care properly or improperly for the forests and the farms that are the sources of those goods. People are necessarily at both ends of the process. The economy, always obsessed with its need to sell products, thinks obsessively and exclusively of the consumer. It mostly takes for granted or ignores those who do the damaging or the restorative and preserving work of agriculture and forestry. The economy pays poorly for this work, with the unsurprising result that the work is mostly done poorly. But here we must ask a very realistic economic question: Can we afford to have this work done poorly? Those of us who know something about land stewardship know that we cannot afford to pay poorly for it, because that means simply that we will

not get it. And we know that we cannot afford land use without land stewardship.

One way we could describe the task ahead of us is by saying that we   21
need to enlarge the consciousness and the conscience of the economy. Our economy needs to know—and care—what it is doing. This is revolutionary, of course, if you have a taste for revolution, but it is also merely a matter of common sense. How could anybody seriously object to the possibility that the economy might eventually come to know what it is doing?

Undoubtedly some people will want to start a movement to bring   22
this about. They probably will call it the Movement to Teach the Economy What It Is Doing—the MTEWIID. Despite my very considerable uneasiness, I will agree to participate, but on three conditions.

My first condition is that this movement should begin by giving up   23
all hope and belief in piecemeal, one-shot solutions. The present scientific quest for odorless hog manure should give us sufficient proof that the specialist is no longer with us. Even now, after centuries of reductionist propaganda, the world is still intricate and vast, as dark as it is light, a place of mystery, where we cannot do one thing without doing many things, or put two things together without putting many things together. Water quality, for example, cannot be improved without improving farming and forestry, but farming and forestry cannot be improved without improving the education of consumers—and so on.

The proper business of a human economy is to make one whole thing   24
of ourselves and this world. To make ourselves into a practical wholeness with the land under our feet is maybe not altogether possible—how would *we* know?—but, as a goal, it at least carries us beyond *hubris*, beyond the utterly groundless assumption that we can subdivide our present great failure into a thousand separate problems that can be fixed by a thousand task forces of academic and bureaucratic specialists. That program has been given more than a fair chance to prove itself, and we ought to know by now that it won't work.

My second condition is that the people in this movement (the   25
MTEWIID) should take full responsibility for themselves as members of the economy. If we are going to teach the economy what it is doing, then we need to learn what *we* are doing. This is going to have to be a private movement as well as a public one. If it is unrealistic to expect wasteful industries to be conservers, then obviously we must lead in part the public life of complainers, petitioners, protesters, advocates and supporters of stricter regulations and saner policies. But that is not enough. If it is unrealistic to expect a bad economy to try to become a good one, then we must go to work to build a good economy. It is appropriate that this duty should fall to us, for good economic behavior is more possible for us than it is for the great corporations with their miseducated managers and their greedy and oblivious stockholders. Because it is possible for us, we must try in every way we can

to make good economic sense in our own lives, in our households, and in our communities. We must do more for ourselves and our neighbors. We must learn to spend our money with our friends and not with our enemies. But to do this, it is necessary to renew local economics, and revive the domestic arts. In seeking to change our economic use of the world, we are seeking inescapably to change our lives. The outward harmony that we desire between our economy and the world depends finally upon an inward harmony between our own hearts and the creative spirit that is the life of all creatures, a spirit as near us as our flesh and yet forever beyond the measures of this obsessively measuring age. We can grow good wheat and make good bread only if we understand that we do not live by bread alone.

26   My third condition is that this movement should content itself to be poor. We need to find cheap solutions, solutions within the reach of everybody, and the availability of a lot of money prevents the discovery of cheap solutions. The solutions of modern medicine and modern agriculture are all staggeringly expensive, and this is caused in part, and maybe altogether, by the availability of huge sums of money for medical and agricultural research.

27   Too much money, moreover, attracts administrators and experts as sugar attracts ants—look at what is happening in our universities. We should not envy rich movements that are organized and led by an alternative bureaucracy living on the problems it is supposed to solve. We want a movement that is a movement because it is advanced by all its members in their daily lives.

28   Now, having completed this very formidable list of the problems and difficulties, fears and fearful hopes that lie ahead of us, I am relieved to see that I have been preparing myself all along to end by saying something cheerful. What I have been talking about is the possibility of renewing human respect for this earth and all the good, useful, and beautiful things that come from it. I have made it clear, I hope, that I don't think this respect can be adequately enacted or conveyed by tipping our hats to nature or by representing natural loveliness in art or by prayers of thanksgiving or by preserving tracts of wilderness—though I recommend all those things. The respect I mean can be given only by using well the world's goods that are given to us. This good use, which renews respect—which is the only currency, so to speak, of respect—also renews our pleasure. The callings and disciplines that I have spoken of as the domestic arts are stationed all along the way from the farm to the prepared dinner, from the forest to the dinner table, from stewardship of the land to hospitality to friends and strangers. These arts are as demanding and gratifying, as instructive and as pleasing as the so-called fine arts. To learn them, to practice them, to honor, and reward them is, I believe, our profoundest calling. Our reward is that they will enrich our lives and make us glad.

▶ Building Vocabulary

Write out a definition for each of the following words, then write a sentence using it:

1. invariably (par. 6)
2. naive (par. 8)
3. undermining (par. 13)
4. degrading (par. 14)
5. oblivious (par. 25)
6. formidable (par. 28)

▶ Thinking Critically about the Argument

Understanding the Writer's Argument

1. Wes Jackson is the founder of the Land Institute, which does research on agriculture. Why does Berry mention Jackson at the beginning of his essay? How does this help you to understand the Nameless Movement for Better Land Use in paragraph 11?
2. What kinds of movements is Berry talking about in the title? What does he see as the main problems with movements? What does he say is the worst problem, and how does it have larger implications for society?
3. Who are the "Captains of Industry"? (par. 14) Why are they important to Berry's argument?
4. What does Berry mean when he writes that "we should not look for bird eggs in a cuckoo clock"?
5. Paraphrase Berry's crucial argument in paragraph 15.
6. Berry lives in the country. What cues does Berry give you to express that information?
7. What point is Berry making when he writes that "we are involved now in a profound failure of imagination"? (par. 18)
8. What is the Movement to Teach the Economy What It Is Doing? What does he demand from the movement?
9. What are the "domestic arts"? What do they have to do with Berry's argument?
10. Berry says in paragraph 28 that he has been preparing to say "something cheerful." What is that cheerful thing?

Understanding the Writer's Techniques

1. What is Berry's claim? In what sentence does he express it most clearly?

2. Berry organizes this essay in three sections. Make an outline in which you paraphrase the essential argument in each section, and then analyze how the argument moves from one to the other. How does he develop his claim?

3. Make a shorter outline in which you analyze the second section in Berry's essay. How does Berry move from identifying a problem in paragraph 15 to his demand for conditions starting in paragraph 22?

4. What is Berry's tone? Point out the uses of irony in the essay. How does irony contribute to Berry's intent?

5. Why doesn't Berry use the real names of movements? What is the effect of making up names for hypothetical movements?

6. What is the argumentative purpose of Berry's accusations regarding the "Captains of Industry"? Is it effective? How is it effective or how is it not?

7. Who is Berry's audience for this essay? What assumption about the audience does he imply in his conclusion?

8. Evaluate the success of Berry's concluding paragraph. Does he tie his essay together? If so, how? If not, why not?

Exploring the Writer's Argument

1. Berry's introduction lists "dealing . . . in effects rather than causes" (par. 6) as one of his grievances against movements. In what way does Berry take his own advice here and concentrate on causes rather than effects? In what way does he *not* take his own advice?

2. Why doesn't Berry argue against nonprofit organizations, which are the organizations working for these "single causes"? Instead, he targets "movements." What are the implications of the choice for his argument and for how you understand the essay?

3. How effective are Berry's arguments in support of his statement in paragraph 16, that in taking modern conveniences for granted "the modern educated mind reveals itself also to be as superstitious a mind as ever has existed in the world"?

4. Write a response to Berry's accusation that because people don't think of wheat when they eat bread, "we are involved now in a profound failure of imagination." (par. 18)

▶ Ideas for Writing Arguments

Prewriting

How do you pay your respects to nature—or do you at all? What do you do that Berry states in his conclusion everyone should do?

Writing a Guided Argument

Write an essay that attempts to prove that you, a modern educated mind, are not alienated from the everyday items and activities that you consume or are engaged in and that you do what Berry asks in his conclusion, that you use "well the world's goods that are given to us."

1. Begin by explaining to your reader why you are writing this essay—to defend yourself against Wendell Berry's accusations.
2. Continue with a brief personal story in which you illustrate your lack of alienation from nature.
3. Link your illustration with a major proposition.
4. Support your main point with a number of minor propositions.
5. Expand each minor proposition with details and examples that explain your grounds for believing yourself to understand and live in accordance with Berry's demands.
6. End your essay with a paragraph that extends your use of goods to a larger philosophy of living.

Thinking, Arguing, and Writing Collaboratively

In small groups, share your papers that grew out of the Writing a Guided Argument assignment. Discuss possible weak examples of your respectful use of nature and possible objections that a reader might have. Brainstorm in your groups about how you might address these objections or weaknesses in your essay. Take notes, and incorporate your notes into your final draft.

Writing about the Text

All of the essays in this book are arguments of some sort. Some argue for simple policy changes, whereas Berry's essay is qualitatively different. He is calling for his readers to change their belief systems, to look at the world in a whole new way. Find another essay in this book that calls for the same kind of radical shift in thinking, and compare and contrast Berry's essay with that selection. How are the arguments similar? Different? Which is more successful, and why?

More Writing Ideas

1. In your journal, list the causes identified in paragraph 2 of this essay, and do some research to find which nonprofit organizations are the leaders of those movements. Which are you drawn to? Why?
2. In an extended paragraph, explore Berry's idea from paragraph 12 that "every one of us is a member of the economy of everybody else."

3. Write an essay in which you argue that even in private life, Berry's statement in paragraph 26 is true: "the availability of a lot of money prevents the discovery of cheap solutions."

15 ► Globalization: How Are We Interconnected?

That shirt or blouse you're wearing: if you check the label don't be surprised to find that a factory in China or Taiwan or Sri Lanka produced the garment. Odds are that the gasoline in your car comes from somewhere in the Middle East and that the car itself might emerge from an assembly line managed by a corporate unit in Japan. Your favorite beer—if it's Heinekin it's from Holland; Dos Equis from Mexico; Stella Artois from Belgium; Medalla from Puerto Rico. And the tiny microchips in your computer and printer—well, they could originate in any industrialized center of the world.

Throughout Europe, despite complaints and some attacks, McDonald's is an omnipresent entity. Men and women in Rome, London, Beijing, Cairo, and Warsaw wear American-styled jeans—and T-shirts with mostly nonsensical combinations of English words and phrases blazoned across the front. American-style supermarkets with American goods (M&Ms, Doritos, Band-Aids) crop up in South America, Europe, Mexico, and many other countries. Our corn, wheat, and barley reach the corners of the globe.

Welcome to globalization in the 21st century. The word *globalization* is a convenient term that identifies the economic and social interconnections—some would say interdependence—of people and countries across the world. Globalization can distinguish the spread and melding of cultures. It can indicate the use of outsourcing work from one country to another where labor costs are low or tax advantages more significant. Globalization often encompasses the principle of free trade: low taxes on imported products help bring low-cost merchandise to local markets from far-off continents. Companies expanding offices and services and becoming multinational corporations contribute to the idea of globalization. The advantages of the hands-across-the-globe dynamic are numerous and provide a spectrum of opportunities unavailable in a cloistered nationalistic environment: enrichment, engagement, advancement, better lives.

But critics point to the dark shadows that globalization spreads. Cheap labor in one country means that another country with perhaps higher living standards and better pay for workers may lose jobs in large

341

numbers. Some labor groups in Western nations oppose free trade for that very reason: lower taxes mean that foreign manufacturers can ply their wares at rock-bottom prices because of cheap labor, thereby challenging the local manufacturing sector. And countries with tight national identities often bemoan the infiltration of another country's language and customs into their own. Many citizens of France abhor the use of English words now so much a part of the French lexicon—*le sandwich* and *le drug store*, for example.

It's useful to remember that globalization doesn't describe what individual people do. A man in India who gets a job at a call center for a multinational computer company isn't engaging in globalization; he's trying to support his family. A woman in China who leaves her family in their rural town and moves to the city to make sneakers for an American company and drinks Coke on her lunch break isn't globalizing; she's just living her life. Yet the political, social, and economic implications of globalization have a profound effect on citizens falling under its umbrella.

So, controversy rages. Opinions vary. Arguments fly. How are we interconnected? How should we be interconnected? Is globalization a blessing or a curse?

The four essays in this chapter try to capture the large social movements of globalization and the individual experiences of people in its path. Thomas L. Friedman connects social and economic issues in "Globalization, Alive and Well": "Countries that don't trade in goods and services," he says, "also tend not to trade in ideas, pluralism or tolerance." Veteran travel writer William Ecenbarger, in his essay "We Are the World," ponders America's cultural imperialism. Everywhere in the world, now, he says, America's cultural artifacts are the world's artifacts. Lewis M. Branscomb, a former Harvard scholar of public policy and an astrophysicist who has worked for government, warns in "Innovate or Perish" that we're resting on our laurels while the rest of the world is catching up; he places the blame squarely in the lap of the administration and Congress, writing that unless they "free up more money for education and science, the U.S. will continue to drift down the path to economic mediocrity." Finally, Bob Davis, John Lyons, and Andrew Batson of the *Wall Street Journal* write in "Wealth of Nations" about the effect globalization has had on income inequality around the world. They focus on both broad economic changes and the individual decisions people have to make in places like China and Mexico as their economic reality changes.

THOMAS L. FRIEDMAN
Globalization, Alive and Well

Thomas L. Friedman has written for the New York Times *since 1981. He has reported for the paper from Beirut in Lebanon, Jerusalem in Israel, New York,*

and Washington, D.C. Since 1995 he has served as the paper's foreign-affairs columnist. In all he has won three Pulitzer Prizes. He is the author of From Beirut to Jerusalem *(1989), which won the National Book Award for nonfiction, and* The Lexus and the Olive Tree: Understanding Globalization *(2000). Friedman was born in Minneapolis in 1953 and went to Brandeis University and Oxford University.* The World is Flat *(2005) received the Financial* Times *Business Book of the Year Award. In January 1989, Friedman took up a new assignment in Washington as the* Times' *chief diplomatic correspondent. His sobering and intelligent columns on all topics touching American foreign policy and events around the world are read widely and are influential. In this column, published a year after the September 11 attacks, Friedman scoffs at those who said that 9/11 would end the process of globalization.*

▶ Prereading: Thinking about the Essay in Advance

What is globalization? Do you see its effects in your life? What does globalization have to do with terrorism?

▶ Words to Watch

integration (par. 1) act of combining
pampered (par. 3) comfortable financially
abject (par. 3) hopeless, complete
subsidies (par. 3) money given from a government to a company to help
    it function
ideology (par. 4) system of beliefs

1   If one were having a contest for the most wrongheaded prediction about the world after 9/11, the winner would be the declaration by the noted London School of Economics professor John Gray that 9/11 heralded the end of the era of globalization. Not only will Sept. 11 not be remembered for ending the process of global financial, trade and technological integration, but it may well be remembered for bringing some sobriety to the antiglobalization movement.

2   If one thing stands out from 9/11, it's the fact that the terrorists originated from the least globalized, least open, least integrated corners of the world: namely, Saudi Arabia, Yemen, Afghanistan and northwest Pakistan. Countries that don't trade in goods and services also tend not to trade in ideas, pluralism or tolerance.

3   But maybe the most important reason why globalization is alive and well post-9/11 is that while pampered college students and academics in the West continue to debate about whether countries should globalize, the two biggest countries in the world, India and China—who represent one-third of humanity—have long moved beyond that question. They have decided that opening their economies to trade in goods and services is the best way to lift their people out of abject poverty and are now focused simply on how to globalize in the most stable manner. Some prefer to go faster, and some prefer to phase out currency controls and subsidies gradually, but the debate about the direction they need to go is over.

4   "Globalization fatigue is still very much in evidence in Europe and America, while in places like China and India, you find a great desire for participation in the economic expansion processes," said Jairam Ramesh, the Indian Congress Party's top economic adviser. ". . . Even those who are suspicious now want to find a way to participate, but in a way that manages the risks and the pace. So we're finding ways to 'glocalize,' to do it our own way. It may mean a little slower growth to manage the social stability, but so be it. . . . I just spent a week in Germany and had to listen to all these people there telling me how globalization is destroying India and adding to poverty, and I just said to them, 'Look, if you want to argue about ideology, we can do that, but on the level of facts, you're just wrong.'"

5   That truth is most striking in Bangalore, India's Silicon Valley, where hundreds of thousands of young Indians, most from lower-middle-class families, suddenly have social mobility, motor scooters and apartments after going to technical colleges and joining the Indian software and engineering firms providing back-room support and research for the world's biggest firms—thanks to globalization. Bangalore officials say each tech job produces 6.5 support jobs, in construction and services.

"Information technology has made millionaires out of ordinary peo-   6
ple [in India] because of their brainpower alone—not caste, not land, not
heredity," said Sanjay Baru, editor of India's Financial Express. "India is
just beginning to realize that this process of globalization is one where we
have an inherent advantage."

Taking advantage of globalization to develop the Indian I.T. industry   7
has been "a huge win in terms of foreign exchange [and in] self-
confidence," added Nandan Nilekani, chief executive of Infosys, the Indian
software giant. "So many Indians come and say to me that 'when I walk
through immigration at J.F.K. or Heathrow, the immigration guys look at
me with respect now.' The image of India changed from a third-world
country of snake charmers and rope tricks to the software brainy guys."

Do a majority of Indians still live in poor villages? Of course. Do we   8
still need to make globalization more fair by compelling the rich Western
countries to open their markets more to those things that the poor countries are best able to sell: food and textiles? You bet.

But the point is this: The debate about globalization before 9/11 got   9
really stupid. Two simple truths got lost: One, globalization has its upsides and downsides, but countries that come at it with the right institutions and governance can get the best out of it and cushion the worst.
Two, countries that are globalizing sensibly but steadily are also the ones
that are becoming politically more open, with more opportunities for
their people, and with a young generation more interested in joining the
world system than blowing it up.

▶ Building Vocabulary

Friedman uses some common expressions in his essay to make his prose
feel familiar. Use each of the following terms in a sentence of your own
based on how they are used in the essay:

1. alive and well (par. 3)
2. pampered (par. 3)
3. abject poverty (par. 3)
4. phase out (par. 3)
5. in evidence (par. 4)
6. social mobility (par. 5)
7. back-room support (par. 5)
8. third-world country (par. 7)
9. simple truths (par. 9)

▶Thinking Critically about the Argument

Understanding the Writer's Argument

1. What is globalization in your own words?
2. Who is John Gray? What was his prediction after 9/11, and why is he wrong, according to Friedman?
3. Where were the 9/11 terrorists from? Why is that significant to Friedman?
4. What does Friedman mean when he says that China and India have moved past the question of whether globalization is alive and well?
5. What does Jairam Ramesh mean by the word "glocalize" (par. 4), and why is this desirable?
6. In Friedman's view, what effect is globalization having on India?
7. What effect does globalization have on how Indians are viewed around the world, according to Friedman? Explain.
8. What two truths about globalization were forgotten before 9/11, according to Friedman?

Understanding the Writer's Techniques

1. What is Friedman's major proposition?
2. How does the writer structure his essay? Make an outline that reflects the flow of his argument.
3. What kinds of evidence does Friedman offer to back up his position?
4. Paraphrase Friedman's argument in paragraph 3. Is it effective?
5. What is the effect of the quotes Friedman offers? Are they persuasive? Why or why not?
6. Which quote is the most effective? Which is the least effective? Why?
7. What is Friedman's tone in this essay? How do you know?
8. How do paragraphs 8 and 9 work together to make up a complete conclusion? Explain.

Exploring the Writer's Argument

1. Friedman depends in this essay on India as a test country for his claim. Is this convincing enough? Why doesn't he include examples from other countries? Explain your answers.
2. What aspects (if any) of Friedman's argument cause you to have confidence in his conclusions? What aspects of his argument cause you to distrust him (if any)?
3. Friedman does not include in his argument the idea that there are many people in developing countries who do not want globalization because they resent the influence of more developed countries, like the United States. Why, do you think, does Friedman not discuss this point?

▶ Ideas for Writing Arguments

Prewriting

What social implications do you see as a result of globalization? Think about foods you eat, music you listen to, clothes you wear, and so on.

Writing a Guided Argument

Write an essay in which you argue that there is (or is not) a link between globalization and terrorism. Refer to Friedman's argument at least once in your essay.

1. Open your essay with a discussion of the relation between terrorism and one's economic situation.
2. Offer your claim in a clear statement.
3. Back up your claim with strong grounds for why globalization might prevent or cause terrorism.
4. Use examples to demonstrate the grounds for your claim.
5. Link your paragraphs with strong transitions to improve the coherence of the essay.
6. End by restating your claim in other words.

Thinking, Arguing, and Writing Collaboratively

In groups of four or five, discuss how globalization has already deeply affected our lives and has for many years. List the ways in which this has happened, and choose the three most important ones to present to the class. As a class, discuss the future of globalization and how it will affect the United States.

Writing about the Text

Write an essay in which you explore the positive aspects of globalization as Friedman sees it. What are the "upsides," as he puts it? What are the main factors that will promote these upsides? How can the common person promote upsides? How does religion play a role?

More Writing Ideas

1. In your journal, freewrite about social mobility. Do not edit your writing. Write nonstop for at least 15 minutes. When you are done, exchange journal entries with another student in your class. How do your responses compare? Contrast?

2. Write a two- or three-paragraph letter in which you, as a "pampered college student," take issue with Friedman's statement that we shouldn't "debate about whether countries should globalize."
3. Antiglobalization groups have protested around the world, most famously in Seattle in 1999, when protesters smashed the facades of Starbucks stores. Read about the antiglobalization forces, and write an essay in which you argue that they are either justified in their protests or wrong and being unrealistic.

WILLIAM ECENBARGER
We Are the World

William Ecenbarger won the 1979 Pulitzer Prize for his part in the Philadelphia Inquirer's *team coverage of the Three Mile Island nuclear accident. He is a former contributing editor for* Reader's Digest *and winner of the Travel Journalist of the Year award from the Society of American Travel Writers. He lives in Lancaster, Pennsylvania. Ecenbarger is the author of* Walkin' the Line: A Journey from Past to Present Along the Mason-Dixon *(2000). In this essay, which appeared in the* Times-Picayune *(New Orleans) in 2003, Ecenbarger tells vignettes from his world travels in which he encountered American food (Burger King), music (Britney Spears), and sports (baseball) everywhere from Buenos Aires to Kuala Lumpur to Fiji.*

▶ Prereading: Thinking about the Essay in Advance

What does the phrase "American cultural imperialism" mean? Have you ever experienced it, either in person or on television or in the movies? Do you think that's a fair phrase to describe the phenomenon, or do you think there should be a different phrase?

▶ Words to Watch

oracular (par. 1) signifying something mystical and full of import
gist (par. 1) essential meaning
unrepentant (par. 2) without remorse
moored (par. 4) tied up
indignant (par. 8) angry with a strong reason
bartering (par. 12) trading
substantive (par. 16) full of practical importance
photogenic (par. 16) looking good in photos
cacophony (par. 25) loud, various noise
daft (par. 30) lacking common sense (used in the U.K.)

A t 5 a.m. I am awakened by the voice of the pilot, who delivers his 1
words as though they were oracular. The gist is that the No. 3 engine
is leaking oil, we're going out to sea to dump most of our fuel, and then
we're going to make an emergency landing in Asuncion, Paraguay. I have
an appointment at 10 a.m. in Buenos Aires, but that doesn't seem important now.

The cabin is prickly with tension, but we land without incident. 2
Shaken passengers on the DC-10 begin filing off the plane. The heat slams
into me as I step down to the runway and think that Paraguay brings to
my mind a Banana Republic dictatorship peopled by unrepentant Nazis. I
will learn later that the nation recently became democratized, but right
now I'm looking at a line of khaki-clad soldiers with slung carbines,
standing as though glued to the tarmac by their shadows, glowering like
sullen watchdogs.

The leader of these carabineros, a balding man with a face like a pall- 3
bearer, is checking passports and furrowing his brow with self-importance. He returns mine with a look Patton might direct toward a deserter.
I am wondering whether anyone ever tries to sneak IN to Paraguay.

There are vintage DC-3s parked all over the airport, their tails low to 4
the ground and their fuselages tilted at 30 degrees, just like in Terry and the
Pirates or Steve Canyon. The airport access road is lined with billboards for
Coca Cola and Kent cigarettes. The latter shows two tanned Americans,
Ken and Barbie, smoking as they lean on a white convertible parked at a
palm-fringed lagoon in which is moored a yacht flying Old Glory.

· · ·

There are a few places on Earth where an American can get away 5
from America, but I haven't been to any of them recently.

Most of the world has literally become a Mickey Mouse operation. 6
The USA reigns supreme as the exporter of music, film, television, sports,
food and hundreds of consumer products ranging from Levis to Pampers
to Barbie dolls.

American travelers are discovering that the sun never sets on the U.S. 7
popular culture empire. Madonna writhes and jiggles and kisses Britney
Spears on MTV from Rangoon to Rio de Janeiro. I visited a Burger King in
Kuala Lumpur, a Pizza Hut on Fiji and a McDonald's in Buenos Aires. I
turned on my hotel television in Taipei to find Geraldo interviewing Elvis
impersonators.

In Hanoi, I saw former Viet Cong soldiers standing in line wearing 8
New York Yankee baseball caps waiting to see movies such as "Platoon"
and "Apocalypse Now." From my hotel room in Manila, I watched protesters against American policies burning the Stars and Stripes while

wearing Nikes and Levis, righteously indignant right down to their Calvin Klein underwear . . .

.   .   .

9   In many Asian and Latin American cities, hanging out at the local American fast-food restaurant is part of the trendy youth lifestyle. Conspicuous consumption takes on a new meaning in Bangkok, where the McDonald's restaurants have floor-to-ceiling windows. The better, I was advised by a local doctor, to be seen.

10   Unlike their U.S. counterparts, Dunkin' Donut stores in Asia do the bulk of their business at night. They are a gathering place for young professional men to impress their dates. Meanwhile, Coke and Pepsi are slugging it out on the Serengeti Plain and in the tin-roofed kampungs of Malaysia.

11   I was in a cab whiz-banging from the airport into downtown Bangkok, and it was a real white-knuckler. I peeked at the speedometer and tried to convert 127 kilometers into miles per hour. The driver didn't speak English, but nevertheless he lip-synched along with Ray Charles, whose voice was coming from a speaker inches behind my right ear . . . "just an old sweet song keeps Georgia on my mind."

12   We stopped for a red light and I saw two young Thai boys, wearing Mohawk haircuts and Guns N' Roses T-shirts, standing in front of a Pizza Hut, bartering with tourists in English over pirated music cassettes. Paula Abdul was going for $1. The driver pointed across the street to a long line waiting to get into the latest Sylvester Stallone epic. He shrugged philosophically, lit a Marlboro and hooked up with Simon and Garfunkel, "What's that you say, Mrs. Robinson . . . ?"

.   .   .

13   MTV, with all its nymphets in underwear, screaming guitars, and guys with earrings and gold chains, is wrapped around the globe like an extension cord, and it is nothing less than the defining influence of a new international youth culture. These days a 17-year-old Malaysian has more in common with a 17-year-old Chilean than with a 40-year-old Malaysian.

14   The emphasis on American music can turn wretched at times. In Suva, capital of Fiji, I watched four perfectly talented local doctors make fools of themselves trying to play light jazz for the Americans in the audience; I've heard various versions of "Feelings" played in Manila, Bangkok and Nairobi—and heard it sung over and over at a karaoke bar in Santiago.

15   From Togo to Tegucigalpa, people are doing the same thing: sitting in front of their televisions watching American programs and American commercials. Couch potatoes are sprouting up along the Amazon, the Nile and the Ganges.

Even local TV takes its cues from the Americans. The local news in   16
Taipei is delivered by blow-dried mannequins who confuse the substantive with the merely photogenic. Just like the Americans on action news,
they exchange quips, give the temperature at the airport (the last place
anyone needs to know the temperature) and at the sign-off, pound their
stack of 8-by-11-inch papers endlessly into the table.

In Taipei, I had some time on my hands and felt like a bit of the National Pastime. So I plunked down and watched the Weichuan Dragons   17
battle the Brother Hotel Elephants in an important Taiwan Professional
Baseball League contest.

"Play ball" is now a global cry, and they're tying on the spikes from   18
Australia to Zaire. About 100 million people are playing organized baseball—and only about one in every five is an American. Baseball is now
the International Pastime.

Baseball isn't the only American game gone global. Some 300 million   19
Chinese watched the 1992 Super Bowl, and National Basketball Association games are telecast to 90 nations, including Reykjavik, Iceland, where
they love the Boston Celtics.

·   ·   ·

Some American advertisers don't even bother to dub their spots in   20
the local language, figuring that English is understood in many places,
and even if it's not, it carries a certain snob appeal. In fact, the sun never
sets on the English language.

English has long been spoken in cockpits and control towers the   21
world over, and now it is becoming a language for universal communication, because of the dominance of American popular culture.

With 700 million people using it, English ranks second only to Chinese in number of speakers, but it is spoken commonly in more countries   22
than any other language. Indeed, the number of non-native users of the
English language now outnumber those who were born into it.

Perhaps *New York Times* columnist Thomas Friedman summed it up   23
best in his book, "The Lexus and the Olive Tree: Understanding Globalization." He wrote, "On top of it all, globalization has a distinctly American face. It wears Mickey Mouse ears, it eats Big Macs, it drinks Coke or
Pepsi and it does its computing on an IBM or Apple laptop, using Windows 98. . . . In most societies, most people cannot distinguish anymore
between American power, American exports, American cultural assaults,
American cultural exports and plain vanilla globalization. They are now
all wrapped into one."

·   ·   ·

I have just flown over the Rift Valley, where Darwinists believe   24
mankind began at least 2.7 million years ago, and now I sit in an outdoor

restaurant in a small market town near Nairobi, sampling grilled wildebeest and smoked impala with my Kenyan host.

25   Around us the market throbs like a helicopter. It is a thicket of humanity, and everyone is talking earnestly, rapidly, as though if they stop for an instant they will crumble to dust in the red clay ground. The cacophony is like an over-populated marsh. We are interrupted by a young boy, who seems to have stepped off a page of National Geographic. He extends toward me a wood-carving of a tribal mask.

26   "He wants to trade you," says my companion.

27   "What does he want?"

28   He talks to the boy in Swahili and then answers. "He wants anything from America. A T-shirt, a cassette, a baseball cap. As long as it's from America." In my bag I find a gray sweatshirt that says "New York Giants."

29   The boy's eyes widen in appreciation, and we make a deal. Later the boy comes back and takes my picture with a Polaroid camera. And then he offers to come to the United States and work as my "assistant."

30   "Our young people are absolutely daft about America," says my host, a Kenyan of English ancestry. "It is said that Kenyan children hope for two things—to go to heaven, and to go to America . . ."

▶ Building Vocabulary

1. Ecenbarger is a world traveler, and he makes reference here to people, places, and things you might never have heard of. Identify each of the following terms and references:
   a. Banana Republic dictatorship (par. 2)
   b. carabineros (par. 3)
   c. Terry and the Pirates, Steve Canyon (par. 4)
   d. Old Glory (par. 4)
   e. Rangoon (par. 7)
   f. Viet Cong (par. 8)
   g. Conspicuous consumption (par. 9)
   h. Simon and Garfunkel (par. 12)
   i. nymphets (par. 13)
   j. "Feelings" (par. 14)
   k. wildebeest, impala (par. 24)
   l. National Geographic (par. 25)
2. Explain the meaning of the following examples of figurative language.
   a. "The cabin is *prickly with tension.*" (par. 2)
   b. "standing as *though glued to the tarmac by their shadows,* glowering like *sullen watchdogs.*" (par. 2)
   c. "with a face like *a pallbearer.*" (par. 3)
   d. "*the sun never sets on the U.S. popular culture empire*" (par. 7)
   e. "Coke and Pepsi *are slugging it out*" (par. 10)

f. "is *wrapped around the globe like an extension cord*" (par. 13)

g. "delivered by *blow-dried mannequins*" (par. 16)

h. "the market *throbs like a helicopter*. It is a *thicket of humanity*" (par. 25)

▶ Thinking Critically about the Argument

Understanding the Writer's Argument

1. What does Ecenbarger mean when he writes, "Most of the world has literally become a Mickey Mouse operation"? What expression is he playing with here?
2. What is the significance of "former Viet Cong soldiers standing in line wearing New York Yankee baseball caps waiting to see movies such as 'Platoon' and 'Apocalypse Now'"?
3. How do people in Bangkok see McDonald's and young men in Asia see Dunkin' Donuts?
4. Why is it that "These days, a 17-year-old Malaysian has more in common with a 17-year-old Chilean than with a 40-year-old Malaysian"?
5. What bothers Ecenbarger about the ubiquity of American music?
6. How is the style of American local news spreading around the world?
7. How are sports part of global culture, according to Ecenbarger?
8. In what way is English a dominant language around the world, according to Ecenbarger?

Understanding the Writer's Techniques

1. Ecenbarger opens his essay with a story of landing at an airport in Paraguay. How does he craft his opening to support his claim effectively?
2. What is Ecenbarger's claim in this essay, and where does he state it most clearly?
3. What is the tone of the writer's essay? Give at least three examples to support your answer.
4. Who is the audience for this essay? Explain your answer.
5. What is Ecenbarger's central claim? Where is it stated most clearly? Why does he place it where he does? Is it effectively placed? Explain.
6. What grounds for his claim does Ecenbarger include in this essay?
7. How does the writer use narrative to make his essay effective?
8. How effective is Ecenbarger's final scene? Explain your answer.

Exploring the Writer's Argument

1. Ecenbarger has traveled around the world in his career. How important are his credentials to you as a reader? If he had just started traveling, would it make much of a difference? Does he make a point of explaining his experience? Explain your answers.

2. By writing the statement, "There are a few places on Earth where an American can get away from America, but I haven't been to any of them recently," Ecenbarger seems to be suggesting that one would want to get away from America. Do you think that's what he means? Why would that be a desirable goal? Explain your answers.
3. How does Ecenbarger use humor in this essay? Is it an important aspect of his argument? Explain.

▶Ideas for Writing Arguments

Prewriting

Record as many instances as you can of advertising that you encounter throughout one 24-hour period. Carry around a little notebook and jot down a few words listing where and what the advertising was. You should record logos you happen to see, jingles you inadvertently hear as you walk past an open window—be as liberal in your definition of advertising as you'd like.

Writing a Guided Argument

We live in America, so of course American culture is everywhere. Advertising, especially, is everywhere. Write an essay in which you analyze the amount of advertising and corporate presence you experience in your life, based on the Prewriting activity.

1. Open your essay with a story of encountering a large number of corporate messages.
2. Lead up to a clear statement of your claim.
3. Next, offer several more examples of American corporate advertising culture.
4. Use a humorous tone, if possible, but make it clear that this is serious business.
5. Offer grounds for your claim.
6. Use an ethical appeal to make a value judgment about advertising in America.
7. Close by including another story of encountering a particularly poignant aspect of American advertising.

Thinking, Arguing, and Writing Collaboratively

In small groups of three or four, discuss the issues you raised in your Writing a Guided Argument analyses. How were your experiences different, and how were they the same? How did you approach the issue of advertising culture differently and similarly? Have one person in your group write down these differences and similarities. Then, come together as a class and discuss how individual responses are important in culture.

Writing about the Text

In his essay, Ecenbarger uses a great many popular culture references. Write an essay in which you analyze his use of references. How does Ecenbarger succeed in making his argument more effective using these references? How does this affect his style? How is his use of references related to his perceived audience? Was it necessary for Ecenbarger to use so many references?

More Writing Ideas

1. In your journal, write a 10-minute focused freewrite about your travel experiences outside the United States. If you haven't been outside the United States, write a focused freewrite from the point of view of a traveler to your hometown who has never been there before. What would they notice?
2. Write a paragraph or two in which you explore the notion that obsession with cultural products from America might be in conflict with the foreign policy of the country.
3. Write an essay in which you argue for or against the idea that English should become the official language of the Internet.

LEWIS M. BRANSCOMB
Innovate or Perish

Lewis M. Branscomb is a professor emeritus of public policy and corporate management at Harvard University and a research associate at the Scripps Institution of Oceanography. He received his B.A. in physics from Duke University in 1945 and Ph.D. in physics from Harvard in 1949. An astrophysicist, he directed the U.S. National Bureau of Standards from 1969 to 1972. Three U.S. presidents have appointed him to various government advisory boards. Among other books, he is the coauthor of Taking Technical Risks: How Innovators, Executives, and Investors Manage High-Tech Risk *(2000). In this essay, which appeared in the* Los Angeles Times *in 2006, Branscomb argues that the United States has been losing its competitive edge globally for some time, and that things are only getting worse.*

▶ Prereading: Thinking about the Essay in Advance

When you picked your major, or when you think about picking your major, do you think about what would be most useful to your country? Why or why not? How is innovation important to the United States, and what part do young people play in developing innovation?

▶ Words to Watch

discourse (par. 3) way of speaking
erosion (par. 4) withering away
consistently (par. 9) in a way that is regular and constant
blunted (par. 11) made dull
restrictive (par. 11) tight, not lenient
stagnant (par. 12) stale, not moving
mediocrity (par. 14) quality that is average

1   The United States is losing its competitive advantage and may soon lose its innovative edge. It does not invest fully in resources most critical for sustained high-tech leadership, and the most talented and productive regions of the Third World challenge our dominance with skills and efforts only we once possessed.

2   The origins of the decline can be traced to the 1960s, when the U.S. trade surplus in high-tech manufactured goods began slipping. By 1972, the surplus had disappeared.

3   In the 1980s, U.S. manufacturers rapidly lost market share in high-tech goods to companies based in Asia. "Japan Inc." was the presumed threat, and the Reagan administration's buzzword was "competitiveness." I served on one of President Reagan's special commissions on competitiveness, but like most such commissions, it was chiefly intended to stave off congressional pressure to remake the U.S. economy in Japan's image. Competitiveness was so overused in political discourse that the news media called it the "C-word." Meanwhile, Japanese electronics manufacturers drove their U.S. counterparts out of business.

4   In the 1990s, the Japanese real estate bubble burst, and U.S. business leaders stopped reading books about Japanese "quality circles" and Theory Z and started implementing Japan's "lean" production technologies. The erosion of U.S. market share in high-tech goods slowed and in some cases reversed. The Japanese industrial image shrank to its normal size, and U.S. productivity grew once again.

5   The 21st century has brought globalization and the emergence of such new high-tech competitors as China and India. Outsourcing technically skilled jobs has become the chief indicator of a newly perceived U.S. com-

parative weakness. For instance, the salary of one engineer or chemist in the U.S. is equivalent to five in China and 11 in India. This time the buzzword is "innovation."

A country's capacity for innovation is hard to measure. Academics   6
define the term as the successful commercial introduction of a novel product, service or business model. Innovations spawned by new science may generate whole new industries.

The U.S. talent for innovation is still the envy of the world. With but   7
one-quarter of the world's scientists and engineers, we perform one-third of the world's research. Our primary high-tech competitors struggle to imitate, let alone duplicate, our private venture-capital industry. Top engineering graduates of Stanford University would rather start a company than work for a well-established high-tech corporation. I know of no university outside the U.S. whose engineering students are such eager entrepreneurs.

But the economic facts paint a grim picture. The U.S. annually im-   8
ports $24 billion more in high-tech products than we export. Our share of global production has fallen from 30% to 17% in the last two decades. The U.S. is closing chemical plants (70 in 2004, 40 last year) and constructing only one new billion-dollar plant. By contrast, there are 50 chemical plants under construction in China. U.S.-owned firms' share of all new patents awarded is now less than one-third.

This may only worsen because the number of U.S. students pursuing   9
technical careers is declining. About 59% of undergraduates in China study engineering. In Japan, the number is 66%. In the U.S., only 32%. Nor is the pre-college engineer pipeline promising. In head-to-head matchups with other countries, U.S. high school seniors consistently score lower in general mathematical and scientific knowledge.

To offset our generally poor K–12 education, universities and colleges   10
have recruited the best and brightest foreign students to fill their graduate-school programs. But this source is drying up because the quality of foreign schools is improving, work opportunities abroad are multiplying, the United States's image as the best place to "lead a good life" is declining, and the U.S. government has not kept pace with foreign governments' emphasis on nurturing innovation.

Some U.S. responses to 9/11 have further blunted our innovative   11
edge. More restrictive visa policies and other regulations have discouraged many foreign students from studying here. Proposed regulations would force U.S. universities to police their laboratories to prevent certain foreign students from using some equipment. A new, vaguely defined category of scientific information called "sensitive but unclassified" allows government agencies to halt publication of new research in the name of national security.

But 9/11 is not solely to blame for the failure of federal government   12
policies to address the economic requirements for a vigorous technical base for commercial innovation. A few examples:

- Since 1990, federal support of research in mathematics, engineering and the physical sciences has been stagnant. Federal funding (in constant dollars) of research in non-defense-related areas, except medicine, is lower today than it was 25 years ago. U.S. research and development spending by both private industry and government has been falling as a percentage of gross domestic product since 2000.
- The U.S. venture-capital industry is shying away from more exciting but risky innovations. Only about 1% of venture firms' money now seeds such promising high-tech innovations as high-capacity data storage using holography and nanotech devices for use in new surgical methods.
- Chiefly for ideological reasons, the Bush administration has not promoted an expansion of stem-cell research, has declined to pursue the implications of global climate change and has failed to mount a balanced research effort to reduce U.S. energy dependency.

13   But state and local governments and the private sector are also needed in the national response to our innovation challenge. The seedbeds for science-based innovation are concentrated in a few urban areas marked by networks of resources and relationships, angel investors, local and state government programs to stimulate creation of new companies, and a large supply of technically savvy entrepreneurs. Although federal policy did little to create these nuclei of a competitive industrial economy, it provided incentives to help them grow. Regrettably, it increasingly erects more barriers than it offers incentives.

14   Adoption of the recommendations contained in a new National Academy of Sciences report titled "Rising Above the Gathering Storm" may help reverse the erosion of the intellectual soil from which U.S. innovation grows. But unless the Bush administration and Congress rein in the rising budget deficit to free up more money for education and science, the U.S. will continue to drift down the path to economic mediocrity.

▶ Building Vocabulary

In his essay, Branscomb uses uses various terms and phrases from the business and economics world. Identify and define each of the following:

1. Third World (par. 1)
2. trade surplus (par. 2)
3. real estate bubble (par. 4)
4. "quality circles" (par. 4)
5. Theory Z (par. 4)
6. market share (par. 4)
7. productivity (par. 4)
8. entrepreneurs (par. 7)

9. gross domestic product (par. 12)
10. venture capital (par. 12)
11. private sector (par. 13)
12. angel investors (par. 13)

▶Thinking Critically about the Argument

Understanding the Writer's Argument

1. What does Branscomb think might happen to the United States's economic competitive advantage and why?
2. When did the decline in American economic dominance happen? What happened in the 1980s?
3. How did America's fortune change from the 1990s to the early 21st century?
4. Why is "the U.S. talent for innovation . . . still the envy of the world," according to Branscomb?
5. What, according to the writer, has happened in the schools that bodes poorly for the United States?
6. How have U.S. responses to the 9/11 attacks "blunted our innovative edge"?
7. Why is the venture capital industry in the United States not investing in high-tech innovations?
8. Why did the Bush administration decline to invest federal money in certain high-tech industries, according to Branscomb?
9. What does Branscomb see as a crucial development if local and state governments are going to get the resources they need to foster innovation?

Understanding the Writer's Techniques

1. How effective is Branscomb's opening? Why does he open with such a bold statement?
2. What is the audience for the essay? How does the tone relate to the audience here?
3. What is the central claim of this essay? Where does the writer state it most clearly?
4. What are Branscomb's minor propositions? Which is the most effectively stated? Explain your answer.
5. Are there any ethical or emotional appeals here? Explain your answer.
6. Analyze Branscomb's use of transitions. How do they help push his argument further?
7. What are the warrants in this essay? Are they implied or explicit?
8. Do you think that the essay's conclusion is effective? Why or why not?

Exploring the Writer's Argument

1. How do you account for the fact that "U.S. high school seniors consistently score lower in general mathematics and scientific knowledge" than many other countries? Are American students less smart? Are American teachers less competent? Are American science industries less attractive as career endpoints? Consider some of these questions as you consider your response to the general weakness in science education highlighted by Branscomb. Does Branscomb still get his point across clearly?
2. Near the end of his essay, Branscomb includes a list of bullet points, examples of how 9/11 isn't responsible for all the ways in which the federal government isn't contributing to innovation. Only two of the three supply reasons. Which of the examples doesn't contain a reason? Do you find the lack of supporting detail a weakness in the argument? Explain.
3. Branscomb never explains what readers can do to improve the situation. Is that a problem with the argument? Explain your answer.

▶Ideas for Writing Arguments

Prewriting

Branscomb, for the most part, writes about innovation in general, but he does mention such areas of innovation as stem cell research, climate change research, nanotech, holography, and so forth. What do you think is the most promising line of high-tech research the United States should be investing more money into? You will likely need to do some research of your own, online or in the library. Do a 10-minute freewrite to focus your reasons.

Writing a Guided Argument

Write an essay in the form of a letter to the president in which you argue that the United States should heavily fund one particular kind of high-tech research, based on your Prewriting exercise.

1. Begin your essay with a clear and bold statement of your claim.
2. Use an authoritative but respectful tone.
3. Explain the reasons you think your chosen line of research is important.
4. Write a paragraph in which you use narrative along with an emotional appeal to support your claim.
5. Argue your minor propositions using ethical appeals.
6. Explain the positive effects on the country that fully funding this research would have.

7. Close your essay with a pessimistic warning about what would happen if the government didn't fund your chosen research.

Thinking, Arguing, and Writing Collaboratively

In small groups of three or four, exchange your Writing a Guided Argument papers. On a separate piece of paper, write a paragraph or two that analyzes the effectiveness of the following three areas: (1) opening, (2) clarity of the statement of the claim, and (3) the use of emotional or ethical appeals. Then continue exchanging essays until everyone in the group has read everyone else's essay. Then collect your essay and revise it based on the comments you received.

Writing about the Text

Write an essay in which you analyze how pessimistic or optimistic Branscomb is about the issue of innovation in the United States. Which do you think he is? Do you think his optimism or pessimism is warranted? What do *you* think?

More Writing Ideas

1. In your journal, write an entry in response to Exploring the Writer's Argument question 3. What can we do to improve the situation?
2. Write one or two paragraphs about how outsourcing can affect the American economic competitive advantage in both positive and negative ways.
3. In the very first sentence of his essay, Branscomb writes that the United States "is losing its competitive advantage and may soon lose its innovative edge." This assumes that America has both a competitive advantage and an innovative edge. Assume that this is true. Write an essay analyzing in what aspect the United States is *not* a leader. You may choose as narrow or as broad an aspect as you'd like.

BOB DAVIS AND JOHN LYONS
Wealth of Nations

Bob Davis and John Lyons are staff writers for the Wall Street Journal. *In this selection, filed from Puebla, Mexico, in 2007, they write about the effects of globalization on that city. They say that education is the key for pulling people out of poverty. Skilled workers are able to buy homes, but unskilled laborers are vulnerable as companies search for a lower-wage labor market. The story Davis and Lyons tell is of an uncertain world in which Mexican workers who can are fleeing their homes and heading north to the United States, where they know they can find jobs.*

▶ Prereading: Thinking about the Essay in Advance

How has globalization affected your own financial situation, do you think? Can you think of any examples of how people you know have been affected? What do you think the effect has been on Chinese farmers? Mexican garment workers? Midwestern steel workers?

▶ Words to Watch

intensified (par. 2) got stronger
boon (par. 3) great benefit
vibrant (par. 6) full of energy
profound (par. 8) very great and deep
sentiment (par. 14) feelings
alienation (par. 15) estrangement from
tariffs (par. 18) taxes levied on imported goods
neonatal (par. 27) related to a newborn child
populace (par. 34) general public
decamped (par. 37) suddenly left

1   Like millions of other low-wage workers here, Hermenegildo Flores was supposed to benefit from Mexico's decision to open its economy to foreign trade and investment in the 1990s. For a time, he did. As U.S. companies boosted purchases from Mexican factories, Mr. Flores's salary nearly doubled to $68 a week in 2001.

2   Then foreign competition from places like India, Pakistan and El Salvador intensified: Mr. Flores, who sewed pockets onto blue jeans, says his foreman "would go around shouting, 'If you don't work harder, we are going to shut this plant down and move it to Central America.'" Today, Mr. Flores is unemployed, having accepted a $900 buyout in April after the company switched to new machines.

3   A decade ago, the globalization of commerce promised to be a boon to low-wage workers in developing nations. As wealthy nations shed millions of jobs making apparel, electronics, and other goods, economists predicted that low-skilled workers in Latin America and Asia would benefit because there would be greater demand for their labor—and better wages.

4   In some ways, globalization delivered as promised. But there was an unexpected consequence. As trade, foreign investment and technology have spread, the gap between economic haves and have-nots has fre-

quently widened, not only in wealthy countries like the U.S. but in poorer ones like Mexico as well. Many economists now say that the biggest winners by far are those with the education and skills to take advantage of new opportunities, leaving many lagging far behind. Incomes of low-skilled workers may rise, but incomes of skilled workers rise a lot faster.

"While globalization was expected to help the less skilled . . . in developing countries, there is overwhelming evidence that these are generally not better off, at least not relative to workers with higher skill or education levels," write economists Pinelopi Koujianou Goldberg of Yale University and Nina Pavcnik of Dartmouth in the spring issue of the Journal of Economic Literature.   5

Globalization deserves credit for helping lift many millions out of poverty and for improving standards of living of low-wage families. In developing countries around the world, globalization—defined as trading and participating in the global economy—has created a vibrant middle class that has elevated the standards of living for hundreds of millions of people. That's particularly true in China, where the incomes of low-skilled workers have consistently risen. The poor in countries like Vietnam and elsewhere in Southeast Asia have also benefited greatly since those countries have opened their economies. In many developing countries around the world, life expectancies and health care have improved, as have educational opportunities.   6

But because globalization is also creating more inequality, it is raising questions about how much inequality countries can bear and whether these gaps could ultimately produce a backlash that will undermine trade and investment liberalization around the world.   7

Many developing nations seem to be following in the footsteps of the U.S., where the income gap has grown sharply since the early 1970s. A 2006 study of Latin America, a region long marked by profound gaps between rich and poor, by World Bank economists Guillermo Perry and Marcelo Olarreaga found that the income divide deepened after economic liberalization in nine of the 12 countries examined.   8

While that could partly be explained by Latin America's slow rate of economic growth, income gaps are widening in fast-growing Asian nations as well, including Thailand and India. It's even grown in the past decade in South Korea, a country long known for an egalitarian commitment to education.   9

Then there's China. One of the fastest-growing economies in the world has generated significant wage gains for its rank and file. Yet income inequality is also growing because of the huge gains being posted by the upper crust. Between 1984 and 2004, China's income inequality as measured by the Gini index—zero is perfect equality and 100 is perfect inequality—increased to 47 from 29, according to World Bank researchers Martin Ravallion and Shaohua Chen. From 2000 to 2005, per-capita income of the   10 bottom 10% of urban households in China rose 26% while those at the top saw gains of 133%.

11   While Mexico hasn't experienced the spectacular growth of China, wages of low-skilled workers have improved in the past four years. Since 2000, the percentage of Mexicans living in poverty has fallen below 20% for the first time ever in the nation's history.

12   Even so, skilled, workers in Mexico still earn far more relative to unskilled workers than they did before liberalization. In 2004, those in the top 10th percentile earned 4.7 times more than those in the bottom 10th, compared with four times as much in 1987, according to Columbia University economists Eric Verhoogen and Kensuke Teshima.

13   By other measures, income inequality is far greater. The World Bank, for instance, estimates that the top 10% of Mexicans accounted for 39% of the country's total spending in 2004, while the bottom 10% accounted for less than 2%.

14   The benefits of globalization have elevated the standards of living for hundreds of millions of people. Yet the consequences of widening income inequality are also profound. Those without much education or skills often find themselves stuck in jobs in the underground economy that don't pay health-care or pension benefits. That's boosted immigration to better-off regions domestically or to the U.S. and Europe, where anti-immigrant sentiment is surging.

15   Growing inequality also feeds the populist argument that globalization is a sucker's game that benefits only the elites. In Latin America, that sense of alienation has powered populist presidential candidates who won in Ecuador, Bolivia, Nicaragua and Venezuela and came close to carrying Mexico last year. In China, the ruling Communist Party worries that support for liberalization could crumble. The government needs to "safeguard social fairness and justice and ensure that all of the people share in the fruits of reform and development," said Chinese Premier Wen Jiabao in March.

16   How does globalization boost inequality? The question is too fresh to have definitive answers, but it's clear that international competition forces local firms to add skilled workers who can handle newer technology and shed workers who can't. Foreign firms bring new technology to developing nations and boost demand there for skilled workers by paying 10% to 20% more than domestic firms, says Dirk Willem te Velde, a research fellow at the Overseas Development Institute, a United Kingdom think tank.

17   Access to education also plays an important role. Developing nations rarely crank out enough college-trained workers to match growing demand, boosting the wages for fresh graduates. Unskilled workers who get laid off can't find retraining and add to the pool of workers looking for low-wage work.

The effects of globalization are vividly on display in Puebla, a lively   18
city of 1.5 million known for its baroque churches and colonial architec-
ture. Located between the port of Veracruz and Mexico City, 70 miles to
the northwest, Puebla has long been a center of trade and textile. As with
the rest of Mexico, its industries were protected after World War II by
high walls of tariffs and quotas, and by restrictions on foreign investment.

During the 1970s, those barriers helped produce rapid economic   19
growth, but the system collapsed in a debt crisis and deep recession that
swept through Latin America in the 1980s. To restart the economy, Mexico
began dismantling its import barriers in the mid-1980s and tied itself
tightly to the world economy through the North American Free Trade
Agreement, or Nafta, with the U.S. in 1994, and a passel of other trade ac-
cords since then. At the time, Mexico's politicians and economists predicted that globalization would produce many new jobs in Mexico, especially for those at the bottom, as companies that produce low-skilled
goods set up shop south of the border.

"Mexican wages will not remain low if we are capable of growing,"   20
said Mexico's then-President, Carlos Salinas, in 1991 when he was promoting Nafta.

For a time, that turned out to be true. Towel-maker Industrias Cobitel   21
SA picked up two big new U.S. customers after Nafta and doubled the
number of production workers to 250 by 2000. Exports accounted for 40%
of the company's sales in 2000, about triple the percentage before Nafta.
Business was so brisk that many employers didn't care whether new hires
had much schooling.

But foreign investment and competition also prompted a big demand   22
for skilled labor. Local companies that had gotten by with outmoded machinery either upgraded or closed.

Volkswagen AG, the city's largest private employer, has had an espe-   23
cially large impact on the local economy. The company for years produced "Vochos," as VW Beetles are called in Mexico, on an old-fashioned
production line where dents were banged out with mallets. But as Mexico
opened its economy, VW ratcheted up the demands on its work force.

The company started building the new Beetle in Puebla in 1998 and   24
followed with other models aimed at hard-to-please U.S. buyers. New
machinery was imported. Now welds are done by lasers. Robots paint
the exteriors of cars for an even finish. In the past decade, the company
has doubled the number of engineers to 700 and is planning to add 100
more this year. They make between $400 and $600 a week and are college
graduates.

At the same time, VW slashed its Puebla work force by about 15%   25
since 2000 to 14,000, mostly eliminating assembly jobs, and outsourced
production of seats, steering wheels and wire harnesses to factories in a
sprawling industrial park outside the gates of the manicured VW campus.

Assembly workers at those factories are paid about one-third the $225 a week VW line workers make. Many auto-parts companies won't hire laid-off VW workers, figuring they can't make the financial adjustment.

26   Ricardo Mosqueda Martinez lost his job at VW and worked for a time at a parts supplier. "When I first saw the paycheck, I thought to myself, is this a joke?" he says. He didn't last long there. Like many other VW employees, Mr. Martinez ended up in Puebla's informal economy, working as a gypsy taxi driver and doing other jobs.

27   For Poblanos, as Puebla natives are called, with the right education, globalization has also opened opportunities that were absent in Mexico just a decade ago. Victor Pasilla, the 30-year-old son of a hospital security guard, makes $600 a week designing oxygen sensors for a Puebla start-up, Biomedical integral SA, which hopes to build neonatal surgical beds for export. "It's been a big leap," says Mr. Pasilla, who has outfitted his parents' home, where he still lives, with its first telephone and computer. "My parents are quite proud that their children are moving upwards."

28   The surge of well-to-do residents has changed Puebla's look. In the once-poor south of the city, housing developments of small, brightly colored homes, each topped with water tanks, have opened for young families who have become eligible for mortgage financing. There are also two new shopping malls with international clothing stores, including Zara and Massimo Dutti.

29   Low-paid textile or auto-parts workers don't shop at Zara, although many now frequent the local Wal-Mart, which offers food, clothing and appliances at good prices. Low-wage workers live as they have for many years, in cramped urban tenements ringed with razor wire to keep out thieves.

30   Part of Mexico's problem is that U.S. manufacturers looking for bargain prices have rerouted orders to China, where wages are even lower. Cobitel, Puebla's towel maker, had to cut payroll after a big South Carolina textile customer shifted orders to China in 2004. Overall, Mexican textile jobs that pay health benefits, which peaked at 195,000 in 2000, fell by one-third to 127,000 this year, according to Labor Ministry statistics.

31   But China's success doesn't fully explain the puzzle of growing global income inequality. If it did, China's low-wage workers would have seen especially fast growth in income, reducing income inequality. While low wage workers have benefited, it's elite workers that have benefited most. In part, that's because the companies in China doing work for overseas markets usually look for a set of skills few Chinese have, such as foreign-language fluency and technical knowledge.

32   Investment by Japanese and Korean companies has transformed the coastal city of Dalian, as crumbling slums and boarded-up factories have given way to new shopping malls and fancy apartment complexes. But the accompanying surge in real-estate prices has made Dalian nearly un-

affordable for lower-paid locals, who often complain they are being literally pushed out of the city.

"The fact that ordinary people in Dalian can't afford to buy a house in the city center is indisputable. The city government should reflect on this," one Dalian resident using the name Mu Fan wrote in a comment on a government-sponsored Web site.   33

Such social tensions have become an increasing political problem for the Communist Party, whose legitimacy rests on its ability to deliver a broad improvement in the populace's standard of living. Wary of being identified as favoring an urban elite, leaders have this year expanded social programs for the poorest and campaigned against wealthy people who flout tax and family-planning laws.   34

Expanded education can ease inequality, as more workers qualify for skilled jobs. In Mexico, the income gap has diminished somewhat since 2000, partly reflecting improved education levels. Since 2000, for instance, Puebla State Popular Autonomous University, a large private university, has added undergraduate degrees in such specialties as bionics, electronics and software and is planning to add degrees in biotechnology, power-grid administration and plastics.   35

Another major factor: So many Poblanos have given up on their home turf and migrated to the U.S. that competition has eased somewhat for lower-skilled jobs. The greater number of Poblanos working abroad has also increased the amount of cash being sent back home, boosting the incomes of many residents. In the past decade, New York has become a magnet for many Poblanos, so much so that mole poblano, a Puebla specialty, is now widely available for sale in the borough of Queens.   36

Mr. Flores, the unemployed tailor, has two brothers who have decamped for the U.S. but says he doesn't want to follow suit because he doesn't want to leave his wife and daughter. Instead, Mr. Flores is looking for work as a day laborer, building homes for Puebla's surging new middle class. "I have a fight in front of me trying to find work," he says.   37

▶ Building Vocabulary

Define each of the following and use each in a sentence of your own:

1. lagging (par. 4)
2. backlash (par. 7)
3. egalitarian (par. 9)
4. per-capita (par. 10)
5. populist (par. 15)
6. quotas (par. 18)
7. outmoded (par. 22)
8. indisputable (par. 33)
9. flout (par. 34)

▶ Thinking Critically about the Argument

Understanding the Writers' Argument

1. Why is Hermenegildo Flores unemployed?
2. How has globalization both helped low-wage workers and opened up a new problem in the countries where they live?
3. How, according to the writers, are many developing nations "following in the footsteps of the U.S." economically?
4. How dramatically has China's income inequality in the past few years?
5. How does Mexico's growth and income inequality compare to China's?
6. What are the consequences of income inequality, according to the writers?
7. How does globalization cause an increase in income inequality, according to the writers? What is the role of education in income inequality?
8. What was NAFTA? What changes since NAFTA have made the biggest impact on Puebla?
9. How has free trade caused jobs to leave Puebla and move to China? What has been the effect on both Mexico and China?
10. Why is Mr. Flores staying in Mexico and not moving to the United States?

Understanding the Writers' Techniques

1. Why do the writers open their essay with the story of Hermenegildo Flores? Is his story an effective opening? Why or why not?
2. What is the writers' claim in this essay?
3. What are the writers' warrants for their claim? Are their warrants implied or explicit?
4. Who is the writers' audience? How would you describe the tone?
5. Do the writers' use ethical or emotional appeals? Why or why not, do you think?
6. Analyze the writers' use of statistics. Is it effective? Why or why not?
7. How do the writers use causal analysis? Is it effective? Why or why not?
8. How effective is the writers' conclusion, in which they return to the story of Hermenegildo Flores?

Exploring the Writers' Argument

1. The writers wait quite a while to explain why income inequality is undesirable. Is that a weakness of this argument? A strength? Explain your answer.

2. The writers write about Puebla, Mexico, in paragraphs 1 through 3, but don't get back to Puebla until paragraph 18, and then don't return until the very end of the essay. Is this a strength or a weakness in the selection? Explain.
3. The writers use China and Mexico as examples of developing nations that are being changed by globalization. Do the writers strike a good balance between their discussions of the two countries? Support your impression by direct reference to passages in the selection.

▶ Ideas for Writing Arguments

Prewriting

The writers argue that income inequality is a problem. Do you agree? Why or why not?

Writing a Guided Argument

Write an essay in which you support or oppose the idea that inequality among incomes is a terrible thing for society.

1. Open your essay with a discussion of the experiences of two very different hypothetical families: a poor family and a rich family in your community.
2. Next, explain why you think this is or is not a bad thing.
3. Use an even, dispassionate tone, while making it very clear what your position is.
4. Write your claim in a clear sentence.
5. Write the grounds for your claim clearly before you offer evidence.
6. Make the warrants for your claim explicit.
7. Argue at least two minor propositions in separate paragraphs.
8. Close your essay by returning to your hypothetical families and whether they are happy.

Thinking, Arguing, and Writing Collaboratively

In small groups of three or four, exchange your Writing a Guided Argument papers. Offer suggestions in the form of a paragraph or two to help your classmate develop his or her essay.

Writing about the Text

Analyze the writers' use of data, statistics, and expert testimony. How do the details strengthen the argument? Which data do you find most effective? Ineffective? What do the quoted statements from economists add to the piece?

More Writing Ideas

1. In your journal, consider how economics affects immigration—legal and illegal.
2. Write a paragraph or two in which you connect this essay to the arguments of the Welches and Krugman in Chapter 6, on Wal-Mart.
3. All around you are products the origin of which you probably aren't aware. Spend some time going through your clothes, your electronics, your car, and your other belongings, discovering where they were manufactured. For products for which you don't find an identifying label, try to find out their country of origin. Write an essay analyzing what you discovered.

16 ▶ Terrorism: How Should We Meet the Challenge?

The planes crash into the World Trade Center and the Pentagon on September 11, 2001, shocking what many saw as a complacent nation. All of a sudden, Americans are vulnerable to sneak attack. The country went into mourning. For whom? For what? For the dead, yes, the more than 2,700 murdered. It seemed that most of us had some direct or indirect connection to someone who died that day. But Americans have also mourned their innocence, their lost way of life. The world since 9/11 has grown darkly complex. Two wars later, we are trying to deal with many issues raised by the attacks: What is the nature of patriotism? How can we balance our open society and our civil liberties with national security? Is it possible to defend ourselves against terrorism at all? And if not, then how can we prepare for the next attacks? How do we heal? The questions go on and on, and there seem to be few answers.

There are viewpoints, though. Reshma Memon Yaqub, a Muslim-American writer expresses her fear of being blamed for terrorism in "You People Did This." She counsels education to counter the ignorance that leads to violence. In "Words Fail, Memory Blurs, Life Wins," novelist Joyce Carol Oates offers a humanist-reading of our response to terrorism. We'll all be okay, she says, if we trust life. Finally, Jeffrey Rosen in "Bad Luck," cautions us against exaggerating the terrorist threat. Sometimes argumentative essays can make hopeful claims!

RESHMA MEMON YAQUB
You People Did This

Reshma Memon Yaqub is a writer living in Maryland who, after the attacks on America on September 11, found herself faced with a familiar prejudice. As a Muslim-American, she knew immediately that she would have to deal with people's misconceptions. Yaqub, a graduate of the University of Pennsylvania, is a writer for Worth *magazine and has written for the* St. Louis

Post-Dispatch, *the* Washington Post, Parents, Men's Health, *and* Reader's Digest, *among other publications. She currently writes a monthly consumer-help column for* Good Housekeeping. *This selection, which contains her thoughts soon after the attacks, was published in* Rolling Stone.

▶ Prereading: Thinking about the Essay in Advance

How much do you know about Islam? What were the different reactions to Muslims in the United States after the events of 9/11?

▶ Words to Watch

miscarry (par. 4) lose a fetus, which is expelled dead
travesty (par. 5) a grotesque, twisted version of something
epithets (par. 6) abusive, insulting words
assailant (par. 6) attacker
decry (par. 8) express strong disapproval

1   As I ran through my neighborhood on the morning of September 11th, in search of my son, who had gone to the park with his baby sitter, I wasn't just afraid of another hijacked plane crashing into us. I was also afraid that someone else would get to my son first, someone wanting revenge against anyone who looks like they're from "that part of the world." Even if he is just one and a half years old.

2   I know I wasn't just afraid that the building where my husband works, a D.C. landmark, might fall on him. I was also afraid that another American might stop him on the street and harass him, or hurt him, demanding to know why "you people" did this. As soon as we heard the news, 7 million American Muslims wondered in terror, "Will America blame me?"

3   When our country is terrorized, American Muslims are victimized twice. First, as Americans, by the madmen who strike at our nation, at our physical, mental and emotional core. Then we're victimized again, as Muslims, by those Americans who believe that all Muslims are somehow accountable for the acts of some madmen, that our faith—that our God, the same peace-loving God worshiped by Jews and Christians—sanctions it.

4   It didn't matter when the federal building in Oklahoma City blew up that a Muslim didn't do it. That a Christian man was responsible for the devastation in Oklahoma City certainly didn't matter to the thugs who terrorized a Muslim woman there, nearly seven months pregnant, by attacking her home, breaking her windows, screaming religious slurs. It didn't matter to them that Sahar Al-Muwsawi, 26, would, as a result, miscarry her baby. That she would bury him in the cold ground, alongside other victims of the Oklahoma City bombing, after naming him Salaam, the Arabic word for "peace."

But that travesty and hundreds like it certainly were on my mind   5
that Tuesday morning. And they were reinforced every time a friend
called to check on my family and to sadly remind me, "It's over for us.
Muslims are done for."

Even as we buckled under the same grief that every American was   6
feeling that day, American Muslims had to endure the additional burden
of worrying for our own safety, in our own hometowns, far from hijackers
and skyscrapers. Shots would be fired into the Islamic Center of Irving,
Texas; an Islamic bookstore in Virginia would have bricks thrown
through its windows; a bag of pig's blood would be left on the doorstep
of an Islamic community center in San Francisco; a mosque near Chicago
would be marched on by 300 people shouting racist epithets. A Muslim of
Pakistani origin would be gunned down in Dallas; a Sikh man would be
shot and killed in Mesa, Arizona (possibly by the same assailant who
would go on to spray bullets into the home of a local Afghani family).

And those were just the cases that were reported. I know I didn't re-   7
port it when a ten-year-old neighborhood boy walked by and muttered,
"Terrorist," as I got into my car. My neurosurgeon friend didn't report
that a nurse at the prominent Washington hospital where they both work
had announced in front of him that all Muslims and Arabs should be
rounded up and put into camps, as Japanese were in World War II. My
family didn't report that we're sick with worry about my mother-in-law,
another sister-in-law and my niece, who are visiting Pakistan, with their
return uncertain.

In the days to come, in the midst of the darkness, there is some light.   8
A neighbor stops by to tell me that he doesn't think Muslims are responsible for the acts of madmen. Strangers in Starbucks are unusually
friendly to me and my son, reaching out as if to say, "We know it's not
your fault." The head of a church told me his congregation wants to
come and put its arms around us, and to help in any way possible—by
cleaning graffiti off a mosque, by hosting our Friday prayers, whatever
we needed. President Bush warns Americans not to scapegoat Muslims
and Arabs. He even visits a mosque, in a show of solidarity. Congress
swiftly passes a resolution to uphold the civil rights of Muslims and
Arabs, urging Americans to remain united. Jewish and Christian leaders
publicly decry the violence against Muslims. At a mosque in Seattle,
Muslim worshippers are greeted by members of other faiths bringing
them flowers.

There's something America needs to understand about Islam. Like   9
Judaism, like Christianity, Islam doesn't condone terrorism. It doesn't allow it. It doesn't accept it. Yet, somehow, the labels *jihad, holy war* and
suicide martyrs are still thrown around. In fact, jihad doesn't even mean
holy war. It's an Arabic word that means "struggle"—struggle to please
God. And suicide itself is a forbidden act in Islam. How could anyone believe that Muslims consider it martyrdom when practiced in combination

with killing thousands of innocents? Anyone who claims to commit a politically motivated violent act in the name of Islam has committed a hate crime against the world's 1.2 billion Muslims.

10   It is not jihad to hijack a plane and fly it into a building. But in fact there was jihad done that Tuesday. It was jihad when firemen ran into imploding buildings to rescue people they didn't know. It was jihad when Americans lined up and waited to donate the blood of their own bodies. It was jihad when strangers held and comforted one another in the streets. It was jihad when rescue workers struggled to put America back together, piece by piece.

11   Yes, there were martyrs made that Tuesday. But there were no terrorists among them. There were only Americans, of every race and religion, who, that Tuesday, took death for us.

▶ Building Vocabulary

Define and use each of the following words in a sentence of your own, making sure that you use the word as Yaqub uses it in her essay.

1. core (par. 3)
2. sanctions (par. 3)
3. slurs (par. 4)
4. buckled (par. 6)
5. scapegoat (par. 8)
6. condone (par. 9)

▶ Thinking Critically about the Argument

Understanding the Writer's Argument

1. In the beginning of her essay, why does Yaqub run to find her son on the morning of September 11, 2001? Why is she afraid for her husband?
2. Why and how do people harass Muslims in America when terrorism strikes America? What examples does Yaqub give of Muslims being harassed? Why aren't all incidents of harassment reported?
3. How does Yaqub show that not all people she comes into contact with harass her?
4. What do most people think *jihad* is? What is it, in fact?
5. What does Yaqub mean when she says that anybody who commits an act of terrorism "in the name of Islam has committed a hate crime" against all Muslims?

Understanding the Writer's Techniques

1. What is Yaqub's major proposition? Where in the essay does she state it?
2. Why does Yaqub mention that there are 7 million Muslims in the United States? She also states that there are 1.2 billion in the world. Is she setting up a deliberate comparison? Explain your answer.
3. Which examples that Yaqub gives of Muslims being harassed are the most effective? How does her title project the sense of harassment?
4. What is the emotional impact of Yaqub quoting her friend as saying, "It's over for us. Muslims are done for"?
5. How does Yaqub use transitions to maintain coherence in her essay? Are there any places you think need stronger transitions? Where?
6. In paragraph 10, Yaqub uses the word *jihad* over and over. What is the argumentative effect of this technique?
7. How effective is Yaqub's conclusion? Why?

Exploring the Writer's Argument

1. In what way does Yaqub's description convince you of her fears? Do you think they are warranted based on her essay? In what ways does she build your trust? Or do you distrust her? If so, why?
2. In paragraph 8, Yaqub mentions actions by the president and Congress to make sure that Americans show tolerance of Islam and Muslims. In what ways are their actions useful? Do you think that after 9/11, President George W. Bush's visits helped matters? Why or why not?
3. How do Yaqub's examples of *jihad* in paragraph 10 support her definition of the word?

▶ Ideas for Writing Arguments

Prewriting

During and after the 9/11 attacks, men and women across the country took the opportunity to perform both great and completely rotten acts. Draw a line down the middle of the page and make two lists headed NOBLE and IGNOBLE. Fill in each column as best you can.

Writing a Guided Argument

Write an essay in which you argue that although times of adversity and crisis lead to displays of both the best humankind has to offer and the worst, one of these always dominates. Feel free to be as optimistic or pessimistic as you'd like.

1. Open your essay with a summary of the events of 9/11.
2. After this, give one example of a noble act and one example of an ignoble act.
3. Write your claim that one tendency is the dominant one.
4. Build your case by giving grounds for your claim.
5. Analyze what it is about human nature that led you to make your claim.
6. Offer examples to back up your case.
7. Link paragraphs with appropriate transitions.
8. In your conclusion, offer a suggestion for how to tilt people's behavior in the direction of nobility.

Thinking, Arguing, and Writing Collaboratively

Exchange draft versions of your Writing a Guided Argument assignment with a classmate. Review your partner's essay for its success in following the guidelines and how well it succeeds on its own. What are the paper's greatest strengths? Weaknesses? Write one or two paragraphs that will help your partner take the paper to the next draft.

Writing about the Text

Yaqub uses a variety of rhetorical strategies in this essay—narration, comparison, definition, and illustration, for example. Write an essay examining some of these strategies and their effect on the essay. How does mixing the modes advance the argument?

More Writing Ideas

1. Write in your journal about why you think the Department of Homeland Security's color coding terror alert system does more harm than good or more good than harm. Pick your side.
2. In a paragraph or two, explore the notion of how America's reaction to terrorism is bound to change if it becomes more common.
3. Read some accounts of how Germans and Japanese people in the United States were treated during World War II, how the Japanese were put into internment camps in California, and how, during the Vietnam and Korean wars, Asian Americans were treated. Compare any of those episodes in American history with the most recent episode of the treatment of Muslim Americans after 9/11.

JOYCE CAROL OATES
Words Fail, Memory Blurs, Life Wins

Novelist, short story writer, essayist, poet, and teacher Joyce Carol Oates was born in 1938 in Lockport in upstate New York. She has been writing novels since the age of 14, and she hasn't stopped since. She went to Syracuse University where she won the coveted Mademoiselle *fiction contest. She graduated at the top of her class at Syracuse and went to graduate school at the University of Wisconsin. During her career, she has published more than 75 books. To comments that she is a "workaholic," she has responded, "I am not conscious of working especially hard, or of 'working' at all. Writing and teaching have always been, for me, so richly rewarding that I don't think of them as work in the usual sense of the word." Her novels, which are noted for their unflinching eye on the noble as well as the profane aspects of human life, include* Them *(1969),* Bellefleur *(1980),* Solstice *(1984),* Black Water *(1992),* Blonde *(2000), and* The Gravedigger's Daughter *(2007), among many others. In this essay, from the* New York Times *on New Year's Eve 2001, Oates argues that terrorism cannot destroy basic human hope.*

▶ Prereading: Thinking about the Essay in Advance

After September 11, 2001, people in the United States were nervous and on edge. How long did people's nerves remain raw? Are they still? How long does the grieving process take in the wake of such an event?

▶ Words to Watch

demonized (par. 1) caused someone or something to seem evil
palliative (par. 2) soothing and alleviating pain
invests (par. 4) to give someone or something a characteristic
visceral (par. 6) directly from the emotions rather than from rational thought
aphorisms (par. 6) short statements representing a larger truth
crevices (par. 9) small openings in something
amnesia (par. 9) state of forgetfulness

Since Sept. 11, what might be called the secondary wave of the terrorist attacks has been nearly as traumatic to some of us as the attacks themselves: our discovery that we have been demonized and that because we are Americans, we are hated; because we are Americans, we are seen to be deserving of death. "Words fail us" was the predominant cliché   1 in the days immediately after the attacks, but for some, even intellectuals in other secular democracies, words have been too easily and cheaply produced; they matter-of-factly declared, "The United States had it coming."

2   The closest I've knowingly come to a "senseless" violent death was during an airline flight from New Orleans to Newark when turbulence so rocked, shook, and rattled the plane that it seemed the plane could not endure and would break into pieces. White-faced attendants were strapped into their seats, and the rest of us, wordless, very still except for the careenings and lurchings of the plane, sat with eyes fixed forward and hands clenched into fists. In the earlier, less alarming stages of the turbulence, the passenger beside me had remarked that turbulence "per se" rarely caused plane crashes, that crashes were caused by "mechanical failure" or bad takeoffs or landings. But now he was silent, for we'd passed beyond even the palliative value of words.

3   If I survive this, I vowed, I will never fly again. No doubt every passenger on the flight was making a similar vow. If—survive!—never again.

4   The utterly physical—visceral—adrenaline-charged—sensation that you may be about to die is so powerful that it invests the present tense with an extraordinary lucidity and significance. To imagine the next stage as it has been experienced by countless fellow human beings—when the plane actually disintegrates, or begins to fall, or, in the case of hijacked planes, nears the targets chosen by "martyrs" in the holy war—is to re-experience symptoms of anxiety that culminate in the mind simply blanking out: as words fail us in extremis, so do coherent sensations fail us.

5   We flew through the turbulence. If there was a narrative developing here it was not to be a narrative of tragedy or even melodrama but one that lends itself to a familiar American subgenre, the anecdote.

6   As soon as such an experience—whether anecdotal or tragic—is over, we begin the inevitable process of "healing": that is, forgetting. We extract from the helpless visceral sensation some measure of intellectual summary or control. We lie to ourselves: we revise experience to make it light-hearted and amusing to others. For in what other way is terror to be tamed, except recycled as anecdotes or aphorisms, a sugary coating to hide the bitter pellet of truth within?

7   How many airplane flights I've taken since that day I vowed I would never fly again, I can't begin to estimate. Dozens, certainly. Perhaps more than 100. The promise I'd made to myself in extremis was quickly broken, though it was a reasonable promise and perhaps my terror-stricken mind was functioning more practically than my ordinary mind, uncharged by adrenaline.

8   Yet the fact is: Words fail us. There is the overwhelming wish to "sum up"—"summarize"—"put into perspective." As if typed-out words pos-

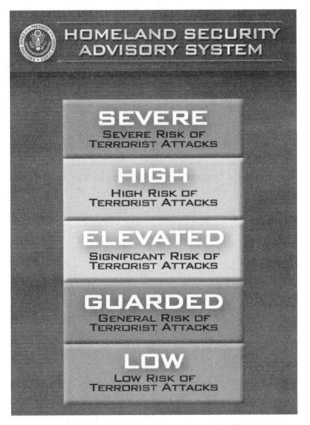

The color-coded terrorism warning system is shown
Tuesday, March 12, 2002, in Washington. The five-level
system is a response to public complaints that broad terror
alerts issued by the government since the Sept. 11, 2001,
attacks raised alarm without providing useful guidance.
(AP Photo/Joe Marquette)

sessed such magic and could not, instead, lead to such glib summations
as "The United States had it coming."

Admittedly, having survived that rocky airplane flight, I could not   9
long retain its significance in my mind, still less in my emotions. Amnesia
seeps into the crevices of our brains, and amnesia heals. The present tense
is a needle's eye through which we thread ourselves—or are threaded—
and what's past is irremediably past, to be recollected only in fragments.
So, too, the collective American experience of the trauma of Sept. 11 has
begun already to fade and will continue to fade, like previous collective
traumas: the shock of Pearl Harbor, the shock of President John F.
Kennedy's assassination.

10   The great narrative of our planet isn't human history but the history of evolving life. Environments alter, and only those species and individuals that alter with them can survive.

11   "Hope springs eternal in the human breast" may be a cliché, but it is also a profound insight. Perhaps unfairly, the future doesn't belong to those who only mourn, but to those who celebrate.

12   The future is ever-young, ever forgetting the gravest truths of the past.

13   Ideally we should retain the intellectual knowledge that such traumas as the terrorist attacks have given us, while assimilating and moving beyond the rawness of the emotional experience. In this season of unease, as ruins continue to smolder, we celebrate the fact of our existence, which pity, terror and visceral horror have made more precious, at least in our American eyes.

▶ Building Vocabulary

1. Write a paragraph describing a car or train trip in which you use at least five words that help bring the events to life.
2. For each of the following words, write a definition and a sentence of your own:
   a. turbulence (par. 2)
   b. lucidity (par. 4)
   c. melodrama (par. 5)
   d. cliché (par. 11)
   e. gravest (par. 12)

▶ Thinking Critically about the Argument

Understanding the Writer's Argument

1. What does Oates mean by the "secondary wave of the terrorist attacks"? (par. 1)
2. Who, after the 9/11 attacks, said that America "had it coming"? Why doesn't Oates mention any of them?
3. How does Oates describe the feeling of impending death? What happens, in her opinion?
4. What does "in extremis" mean? How does Oates use it here?
5. According to Oates, what is the natural way people deal with harrowing situations?
6. What does Oates mean when she writes in paragraph 9 that "The present tense is a needle's eye through which we thread ourselves"? What does this have to do with 9/11?
7. How does hope come out of forgetfulness, according to Oates?

Understanding the Writer's Techniques

1. What is Oates's major proposition? Where does she state it most clearly?
2. Is her major proposition in an effective place? Why or why not?
3. What is Oates's rhetorical intent in this essay? Is she trying to convince her reader of something? If so, of what? If not, what is she trying to do?
4. How well does Oates's title reflect the argument in her essay?
5. How does Oates connect paragraph 1 with paragraph 2? There doesn't seem to be any transition. How does this affect her argument?
6. How does Oates's repetition of the phrase "words fail us" help to hold the essay together?
7. Analyze Oates's concluding paragraph. Is it effective? Why or why not?

Exploring the Writer's Argument

1. Do you agree with Oates that one can call the idea that Americans are to blame for terrorism "the secondary wave of the terrorist attacks"? Explain.
2. Oates says that the "future is ever-young," and that we forget quickly, thus gaining hope. Do you think that is always true with tragedies? Is that true for everyone? Explain your answers.
3. Do our minds always blur when we are in situations "in extremis"? How can we change that?
4. Do you think Oates's conclusion is too analytical for such an emotional topic, or do you think she gets the emotion across properly? Explain your answer.

▶ Ideas for Writing Arguments

Prewriting

What did the United States do, if anything, to deserve the attacks on the World Trade Center and the Pentagon on 9/11? Write some notes on the subject.

Writing a Guided Argument

Write a letter in the form of an argumentative essay in which you take issue with those people who say about 9/11, "The United States had it coming."

1. Open your essay by summarizing the argument that the United States had it coming. Give at least three arguments that can be made for this position.

2. Write that you can understand why the opposition feels as it does, but that you disagree.
3. Write your major proposition.
4. For each of the opposition arguments, write a paragraph in rebuttal.
5. Explain how the opposition's idea can be dangerous.
6. In the next section, explain how the United States can change the minds of people around the world.
7. In your conclusion, restate your major proposition and assess how successful the United States is being in convincing the world that it is not responsible for being attacked.

Thinking, Arguing, and Writing Collaboratively

In groups of four or five, exchange drafts of the essays that grew out of your Writing a Guided Argument assignment. After making general comments about the success of your partner's paper, write a paragraph or two about the effectiveness of the conclusion. How well has your partner succeeded in tying the paper together? Is the conclusion appropriate?

Writing about the Text

How does Oates, as a novelist, use her gifts of description and narration (and her powers of imagination) to help her argument? Write an essay in which you analyze both (1) how Oates is led to her conclusion because she is a fiction writer, and (2) how her fiction writing leads her to write this essay as it is written.

More Writing Ideas

1. In your journal, write about a "senseless violent death" that you may have witnessed or heard about.
2. Write a paragraph or two in which you explore the implications of Oates's assertion that "the future doesn't belong to those who only mourn, but to those who celebrate."
3. People who suffer tragedies and crises deal with lingering effects for years, or perhaps for their entire lives. In an essay, argue that, contrary to what Oates says, people never completely get over tragedies.

JEFFREY ROSEN
Bad Luck: Why Americans Exaggerate the Terrorist Threat

A teacher at George Washington Law School in Washington, D.C., Jeffrey Rosen holds degrees from Harvard, Balliol, and Oxford Universities. He is a staff writer for the New Republic, *in which this essay first appeared. He is the author of* The Unwanted Gaze: The Destruction of Privacy in America *(2000), in which he draws on a broad historical perspective to examine the right of privacy in a variety of cultures. Most recently he has written* The Supreme Court: The Personalities and Rivalries That Defined America *(2007). In this essay, Rosen examines the response to terrorism in America. As you can see from the title, he finds our fears overblown.*

▶ Prereading: Thinking about the Essay in Advance

What does the phrase "bad luck" suggest to you? What connections can you make between the notion of misfortune and terrorism?

▶ Words to Watch

vulnerability (par. 3) weakness, helplessness
assaulted (par. 6) attacked
scenarios (par. 7) outlines of a plan of likely events
melodramatically (par. 7) in an exaggerated or over-emotional manner
arbitrary (par. 8) determined by chance or whim, not logic or reason
calamities (par.8) disasters; catastrophes
egregious (par. 9) extremely bad; shocking
inegalitarian (par. 11) not supporting equal political, economic, and legal
  rights for all human beings

The terrorist threat is all too real, but newspapers and TV stations   1
around the globe are still managing to exaggerate it. As new cases of anthrax infection continue to emerge, the World Health Organization is begging people not to panic. But tabloid headlines like this one from *The Mirror* in London send a different message: "panic." A Time/CNN poll found that nearly half of all Americans say they are "very" or "somewhat" concerned that they or their families will be exposed to anthrax, even though only a handful of politicians and journalists have been targeted so far.

This isn't surprising. Terrorism is unfamiliar, it strikes largely at ran-   2
dom, and it can't be easily avoided by individual precautions. Criminologists tell us that crimes with these features are the most likely to create hysteria. If America's ability to win the psychological war against terrorism depends upon our ability to remain calm in the face of random violence, our reaction to similar threats in the past is not entirely reassuring.

In the academic literature about crime, scholars have identified a par-   3
adox: "Most surveys discover that people apparently fear most being a victim of precisely those crimes they are least likely to be victims of," writes Jason Ditton of the University of Sheffield. "Little old ladies apparently worry excessively about being mugged, but they are the least likely to be mugging victims." Women worry most about violent crime, though they have the lowest risk of being victims, while young men worry the

least, though they have the highest risk. And because of their physical vulnerability, women tend to worry more about violence in general, even when the risk of experiencing a particular attack is evenly distributed. In a Gallup poll at the end of September, 62 percent of women said they were "very worried" that their families might be victimized by terrorist attacks. Only 35 percent of the men were similarly concerned.

4   Why are people most afraid of the crimes they are least likely to experience? According to Wesley Skogan of Northwestern University, "it may be the things we feel we can't control or influence, those uncontrollable risks, are the ones that make people most fearful." It's why people fear flying more than they fear being hit by a car. We think we can protect ourselves against cars by looking before crossing the street—and therefore underestimate the risk, even though it is actually higher than being killed in a plane crash.

5   People also overestimate the risk of crimes they have never experienced. The elderly are no more fearful than anyone else when asked how safe they feel when they go out at night. That's because many senior citizens don't go out at night, or they take precautions when they do. But when surveys ask how safe they would feel if they did go out at night more often, old people say they would be very afraid, since they have less experience to give them context. Instead they tend to assess risk based on media hype and rumors. "To be able to estimate the probability of an event occurring, you first have to know the underlying distribution of those events, and second the trend of those events—but when it comes to crime, people usually get both hugely wrong," writes Ditton.

6   The media is partly to blame. A survey by George Gerbner, former dean of the Annenberg School at the University of Pennsylvania, found that people who watch a lot of television are more likely than occasional viewers to overestimate their chances of being a victim of violence, to believe their neighborhood is unsafe, to say fear of crime is a very serious problem, to assume that crime is rising, and to buy locks, watchdogs, and guns. And this distortion isn't limited to television. Jason Ditton notes that 45 percent of crimes reported in the newspaper involve sex or violence, even though they only represent 3 percent of crimes overall. When interviewed about how many crimes involve sex or violence, people tend to overestimate it by a factor of three or four. People believe they are more likely to be assaulted or raped than robbed, even though the robbery rate is much higher.

7   Will sensationalistic reports of worst-case terrorist scenarios exaggerate people's fear of being caught in an attack? There's every reason to believe that they will because of the media's tendency to exaggerate the scope and probability of remote risks. In a book called *Random Violence*, Joel Best, then of Southern Illinois University, examined the "moral panics" about a series of new crimes that seized public attention in the 1980s

and '90s: freeway violence in 1987, wilding in 1989, stalking around 1990, kids and guns in 1991, and so forth. In each case, Best writes, television seized on two or three incidents of a dramatic crime, such as freeway shooting, and then claimed it was part of a broader trend. By taking the worst and most infrequent examples of criminal violence and melodramatically claiming they were typical, television created the false impression that everyone was equally at risk, thereby increasing its audience.

The risk of terrorism is more randomly distributed than the crimes the   8
media has hyped in the past. This makes it even more frightening because it is hard to avoid through precautions. (The anthrax envelopes were more narrowly targeted than the World Trade Center attack, of course, but they still infected postal workers.) Contemporary Americans, in particular, are not well equipped to deal with arbitrary threats because, in so many realms of life, we refuse to accept the role of chance. In his nineteenth-century novel *The Gilded Age*, Mark Twain described a steamship accident that killed 22 people. The investigator's verdict: "nobody to blame." This attitude was reflected in nineteenth-century legal doctrines such as assumption of risk, which refused to compensate victims who behaved carelessly. In the twentieth century, by contrast, the United States developed what the legal historian Lawrence Friedman has called an expectation of "total justice"—namely, "the general expectation that somebody will pay for any and all calamities that happen to a person, provided only that it is not the victim's 'fault,' or at least not solely his fault."

This effort to guarantee total justice is reflected throughout American   9
society—from the regulation of product safety to the elimination of legal doctrines like assumption of risk. Since September 11 the most egregious display of this total justice mentality has been the threat by various personal injury lawyers to sue the airlines, security officials, and the architects of the World Trade Center on behalf of the victims' families. One of their claims: Flaws in the design of the twin towers may have impeded escape.

Given America's difficulty in calculating and accepting unfamiliar   10
risk, what can be done, after September 11, to minimize panic? Rather than self-censoring only when it comes to the ravings of Osama bin Laden, the broadcast media might try to curb its usual focus on worst-case scenarios. Wesley Skogan found that when people were accurately informed about the real risk, they adjusted their fears accordingly. Politicians also need to be careful about passing on unspecified but terrifying threats of future attacks. In the middle of October the Justice Department warned that a terrorist attack might be imminent, but didn't say what the attack might be, or where it might strike. The vagueness of the warning only increased public fear and caused people to cancel travel plans. But it didn't make anyone more secure.

While Americans learn to take sensible precautions, we need   11
to also learn that there is no insurance against every calamity or

compensation for every misfortune. There is something inegalitarian about risk: It singles out some people from the crowd for no good reason and treats them worse than everybody else. But even in the United States, there is no such thing as perfect equality or total justice. If the first foreign attack on U.S. soil helps teach Americans how to live with risk, then perhaps we can emerge from this ordeal a stronger society as well as a stronger nation.

▶ Building Vocabulary

Determine the meanings of the familiar words that follow by using your knowledge of prefixes, roots, and suffixes and your understanding of compound words—that is, two words put together to form a new word. Define each word in the list; then explain how the parts of the word contribute to the definition. Check your definitions in a dictionary.

1. criminologists (par. 2)
2. uncontrollable (par. 4)
3. underestimate (par. 4)
4. precautions (par. 5)
5. watchdogs (par. 6)
6. freeway (par. 7)
7. steamship (par, 8)
8. self-censoring (par. 10)
9. worst-case (par. 10)
10. misfortune (par 11)

▶ Thinking Critically about the Argument

Understanding the Writer's Argument

1. Who, according to Rosen, is to blame for America's anxiety about different kinds of threats?
2. What paradox does Rosen identify in paragraph 3?
3. According to the writer, why are people afraid of the crimes they are least likely to experience? Why do they overestimate the risk of crimes that they never have experienced?
4. Why does the writer feel that "sensationalist reports of worst-case terrorist scenarios" will exaggerate people's fear of being caught in an attack?
5. Why are contemporary Americans not equipped to deal with arbitrary threats, according to Rosen?
6. What, according to the writer, can we do to minimize panic, given our difficulty to calculate and accept unfamiliar risk?

Understanding the Writer's Techniques

1. What is Rosen's major proposition? Which sentence or two do you think best sums it up? How would you state the proposition in your own words?

2. Why does the writer use the words "Bad Luck" as the opening of his title? How does the statement after the colon in the title help establish the writer's purpose in the essay?

3. How has Rosen used cause-and-effect strategies in this essay? In what way does the title establish the audience's expectations of a cause-and-effect analysis?

4. Rosen uses many external sources for expert testimony to support his argument. What is the effect of the statistical reports he cites? What is the effect of the quotes from scholars, writers, and university professors? What is the effect of the quotation drawn from Mark Twain in paragraph 8? In what ways do you find the evidence he presents convincing?

5. Rosen has considerable legal training. How does his knowledge of the law and legal issues contribute to the way he builds his case in this essay?

6. In what ways does the last paragraph serve as an effective conclusion to the essay? How does the last paragraph relate to the introductory paragraph?

7. How does Rosen maintain a tone of calm and logic despite the frightening topic of terrorism?

Exploring the Writer's Argument

1. Why might you agree or disagree with the idea that the media are exaggerating the terrorist threat? In what ways do the newspapers you read or the television news programs you watch contribute to your fears of terrorism? Or do you think that the media respond appropriately to terrorist threats?

2. How do you think that people can learn to remain calm in the face of random violence?

3. How effective is Rosen's point about why people fear flying more than they fear automobiles?

4. Why do you think Americans refuse to accept the role of chance? In what ways do you think our expectation of total justice is a good thing? A bad thing? How much should we support the 19th-century idea of "nobody to blame" when it comes to accidents?

5. Rosen complains about personal injury lawyers who try to sue airlines, security officials, and World Trade center architects on behalf of the 9/11 victims. Why might you agree or disagree with his position? How has

the "total justice" belief affected recent controversies at fast-food restaurants like McDonald's? Accidental injuries or deaths in doctors' offices or hospitals? Automobile accidents?

▶Ideas for Writing Arguments

Prewriting

In what ways do you think that we have to take terrorist threats seriously, even when they are ambiguous?

Writing a Guided Argument

Terrorist threats have reached new highs across the world, and whereas nobody supports panic in response to them, many people—government authorities included—believe that we have to take these threats seriously, both as a society and as individuals. Write an essay in which you argue that we should take terrorist threats seriously—that is, write an essay opposing Rosen's proposition.

1. Open your essay with an introduction to the notion of terrorist threats, and cite one or two of the most recent examples.
2. Introduce and deal with the *opposing* argument—that most of the threats *are* exaggerated and that we should not panic when we hear about imminent threats.
3. State your major proposition about how the threats are not exaggerated and that we must take them seriously.
4. Offer at least two minor propositions to back up your major proposition. Draw on recent threats you know of that require more than "sensible precautions"—Rosen's point in the last paragraph. Offer suggestions about how we should respond in the light of threats and subsequent government warnings.
5. Present statistics, quotations, or cases to reinforce your argument.
6. Establish a calm tone that uses logic as opposed to emotional appeal.
7. Use appropriate transitions to link your points.

Thinking, Arguing, and Writing Collaboratively

In small groups, discuss the possibilities inherent in Rosen's tenth paragraph: that the broadcast media can and should "curb its usual focus on worst-case scenarios." In what ways might this idea, if acted upon, keep people calm? In what ways does the suggestion fringe on censorship on potentially misinforming the public?

Writing about the Text

Write a brief essay in which you analyze Rosen's use of expert testimony. How do the quotes, paraphrases, and survey data strengthen the piece? What shortfalls do you see in drawing on expert testimony in the way that Rosen has?

More Writing Ideas

1. Write a journal entry about your own response to a recent terrorist threat.
2. In an extended paragraph, define "random violence" as you understand the use of the term today.
3. Write an essay called "The Responsibilities of the Media" in which you argue that newspapers, radio, and television have important responsibilities in providing information to American citizens. Include your views on how well the media are meeting those responsibilities.

Part Four

Six Classic Arguments

PLATO
The Allegory of the Cave

Plato (c. 427–347 B.C.) was born into a wealthy family in Athens, Greece. He turned early to philosophy, studying under the famous philosopher Socrates, who had the reputation of a "gadfly," a person who challenged the traditional ideas of society. His pestering of the powerful men in Athens led to Socrates' conviction on trumped-up charges of corrupting the youth of Athens. He was executed in 399 B.C. Soon after, Plato founded the Academy, a school of philosophy, and began writing his famous works, inquiries into philosophical topics in the form of conversations starring Socrates. Plato portrays his mentor as interrogating members of Athenian society, breaking down their assumptions and leading to an abstract discussion about a philosophical subject such as virtue or love. Some of these dialogues are the Phaedo, Symposium, Crito, *and* Meno.*

Plato's most famous dialogue is the Republic, *perhaps the most influential work in all of world philosophy. The* Republic *inquires into what it means to live the good life, especially as it pertains to government's role in that endeavor. "The Allegory of the Cave" is perhaps the most influential passage in that influential work. Plato introduces his idea of Forms or Ideas, the idea that there is a "real" world outside of the one the everyday person experiences, and the ones who can discover that world are philosophers. As you read, consider how Socrates attempts to persuade Glaucon of his position.*

1   And now, I said, let me show in a figure how far our nature is enlightened or unenlightened: Behold! human beings living in an underground den, which has a mouth open towards the light and reaching all along the den; here they have been from their childhood, and have their legs and necks chained so that they cannot move, and can only see before them, being prevented by the chains from turning round their heads. Above and behind them a fire is blazing at a distance, and between the fire and the prisoners there is a raised way; and you will see, if you look, a low wall built along the way, like the screen which marionette players have in front of them, over which they show the puppets.

2   I see.

3   And do you see, I said, men passing along the wall carrying all sorts of vessels, and statues and figures of animals made of wood and stone and various materials, which appear over the wall? Some of them are talking, others silent.

4   You have shown me a strange image, and they are strange prisoners.

5   Like ourselves, I replied; and they see only their own shadows, or the shadows of one another, which the fire throws on the opposite wall of the cave.

6   True, he said; how could they see anything but the shadows if they were never allowed to move their heads?

And of the objects which are being carried in like manner they would   7
only see the shadows?

Yes, he said.   8

And if they were able to converse with one another, would they not   9
suppose that they were naming what was actually before them?

Very true.   10

And suppose further that the prison had an echo which came from   11
the other side, would they not be sure to fancy when one of the passersby
spoke that the voice which they heard came from the passing shadow?

No question, he replied.   12

To them, I said, the truth would be literally nothing but the shad-   13
ows of the images.

That is certain.   14

And now look again, and see what will naturally follow if the prison-   15
ers are released and disabused of their error. At first, when any of them is
liberated and compelled suddenly to stand up and turn his neck round
and walk and look towards the light, he will suffer sharp pains; the glare
will distress him and he will be unable to see the realities of which in his
former state he had seen the shadows; and then conceive some one saying
to him, that what he saw before was an illusion, but that now, when he is
approaching nearer to being and his eye is turned towards more real existence, he has a clearer vision—what will be his reply? And you may further imagine that his instructor is pointing to the objects as they pass and
requiring him to name them—will he not be perplexed? Will he not fancy
that the shadows which he formerly saw are truer than the objects which
are now shown to him?

Far truer.   16

And if he is compelled to look straight at the light, will he not have a   17
pain in his eyes which will make him turn away to take refuge in the objects of vision which he can see, and which he will conceive to be in reality clearer than the things which are now being shown to him?

True, he said.   18

And suppose once more, that he is reluctantly dragged up a steep   19
and rugged ascent, and held fast until he is forced into the presence of the
sun himself, is he not likely to be pained and irritated? When he approaches the light his eyes will be dazzled and he will not be able to see
anything at all of what are now called realities.

Not all in a moment, he said.   20

He will require to grow accustomed to the sight of the upper world.   21
And first he will see the shadows best, next the reflections of men and
other objects in the water, and then the objects themselves; then he will
gaze upon the light of the moon and the stars and the spangled heaven;
and he will see the sky and the stars by night better than the sun or the
light of the sun by day?

Certainly.   22

23   Last of all he will be able to see the sun, and not mere reflections of him in the water, but he will see him in his own proper place, and not in another; and he will contemplate him as he is.

24   Certainly.

25   He will then proceed to argue that this is he who gives the season and the years, and is the guardian of all that is in the visible world, and in a certain way the cause of all things which he and his fellows have been accustomed to behold?

26   Clearly, he said, he would first see the sun and then reason about him.

27   And when he remembered his old habitation, and the wisdom of the den and his fellow-prisoners, do you not suppose that he would felicitate himself on the change, and pity them?

28   Certainly, he would.

29   And if they were in the habit of conferring honors among themselves on those who were quickest to observe the passing shadows and to remark which of them went before, and which followed after, and which were together; and who were therefore best able to draw conclusions as to the future, do you think that he would care for such honors and glories, or envy the possessors of them? Would he not say with Homer, Better to be the poor servant of a poor master, and to endure anything, rather than think as they do and live after their manner?

30   Yes, he said, I think that he would rather suffer anything than entertain these false notions and live in this miserable manner.

31   Imagine once more, I said, such an one coming suddenly out of the sun to be replaced in his old situation; would he not be certain to have his eyes full of darkness?

32   To be sure, he said.

33   And if there were a contest, and he had to compete in measuring the shadows with the prisoners who had never moved out of the den, while his sight was still weak, and before his eyes had become steady (and the time which would be needed to acquire this new habit of sight might be very considerable) would he not be ridiculous? Men would say of him that up he went and down he came without his eyes; and that it was better not even to think of ascending; and if any one tried to loose another and lead him up to the light, let them only catch the offender, and they would put him to death.

34   No question, he said.

35   This entire allegory, I said, you may now append, dear Glaucon, to the previous argument; the prison-house is the world of sight, the light of fire is the sun, and you will not misapprehend me if you interpret the journey upwards to be the ascent of the soul into the intellectual world according to my poor belief, which, at your desire, I have expressed—whether rightly or wrongly God knows. But, whether true or false, my opinion is that in the world of knowledge the idea of good appears last of all, and is seen only with an effort; and, when seen, is also inferred to be the univer-

sal author of all things beautiful and right, parent of light and of the lord of light in this visible world, and the immediate source of reason and truth in the intellectual; and that this is the power upon which he who would act rationally either in public or private life must have his eye fixed.

I agree, he said, as far as I am able to understand you.   36

Moreover, I said, you must not wonder that those who attain to this   37
beautiful vision are unwilling to descend to human affairs; for their souls are ever hastening into the upper world where they desire to dwell; which desire of theirs is very natural, if our allegory may be trusted.

Yes, very natural.   38

And is there anything surprising in one who passes from divine con-   39
templations to the evil state of man, misbehaving himself in a ridiculous manner; if, while his eyes are blinking and before he has become accustomed to the surrounding darkness, he is compelled to fight in courts of law, or in other places, about the images or the shadows of images of justice, and is endeavouring to meet the conceptions of those who have never yet seen absolute justice?

Anything but surprising, he replied.   40

Any one who has common sense will remember that the bewilder-   41
ments of the eyes are of two kinds, and arise from two causes, either from coming out of the light or from going into the light, which is true of the mind's eye, quite as much as of the bodily eye; and he who remembers this when he sees any one whose vision is perplexed and weak, will not be too ready to laugh; he will first ask whether that soul of man has come out of the brighter light, and is unable to see because unaccustomed to the dark, or having turned from darkness to the day is dazzled by excess of light. And he will count the one happy in his condition and state of being, and he will pity the other; or, if he have a mind to laugh at the soul which comes from below into the light, there will be more reason in this than in the laugh which greets him who returns from above out of the light into the den.

That, he said, is a very just distinction.   42

Responding to the Essay

1. What is Plato's argument? What is an allegory, and why does he use the form to make his claim rather than just stating it right away? Explain.
2. Is the dialogue format effective here? Is Glaucon a real part of the conversation with Socrates? Defend your answers.
3. In many Platonic dialogues, Socrates appears as a combative and a tough debater. Do you see any evidence of that in this selection? Explain.
4. Analyze Plato's use of syllogistic argument in this selection. Trace his reasoning, especially throughout the first section.

5. How does Plato contrast the people who live in the world of shadows with the ones who have seen the light? What is he saying about himself, do you think?

Responding in Writing

1. How are Plato's ideas in this essay relevant to modern life? Write an essay in which you argue that the influence of this selection is apparent in your experience.
2. Do some research on Plato on the Internet, and write a short history of his ideas, focusing on how the *Republic*'s political philosophy influenced Western political science.
3. Write your own allegory that brings to life a belief you have about college.

JONATHAN SWIFT
A Modest Proposal

Satirist and poet Jonathan Swift (1667–1745), one of the greatest prose writers in the history of English literature, was born in Dublin, Ireland, where he is still a national hero. After studying in Ireland, he was forced for political reasons to emigrate to England, where he read widely and went into the Anglican Church as a clergyman. He worked for the church his entire life, but soon realized his gift for writing. Swift composed poems and prose satires, including A Tale of a Tub *(1704), which makes a target of the corruption he saw among the religious and educational leaders of his time. Again, because of a change in the political winds, he returned to Dublin as dean of St. Patrick's Cathedral and lived in the city for the rest of his life. In 1726 Swift published* Gulliver's Travels, *which was a wide-ranging satire that took aim at all 18th-century society as he saw it. Swift always fought for the rights of Ireland against what he saw as English oppression, publishing many articles for the cause, including the series of letters written as "M.B. Drapier" that helped foil English plans that might have hurt the Irish economy.*

In this selection, which he wrote in 1729, Swift uses all his powers of satire to propose, tongue in cheek, that Ireland could solve its problems of poverty if the Irish ate their own children. Pay close attention as you read to see how his argument works through the device of irony.

1   It is a melancholy object to those who walk through this great town or travel in the country, when they see the streets, the roads, and cabin doors, crowded with beggars of the female-sex, followed by three, four, or six children, all in rags and importuning every passenger for an alms. These mothers, instead of being able to work for their honest livelihood,

are forced to employ all their time in strolling to beg sustenance for their helpless infants, who, as they grow up, either turn thieves for want of work, or leave their dear native country to fight for the Pretender in Spain, or sell themselves to the Barbadoes.

I think it is agreed by all parties that this prodigious number of children in the arms, or on the backs, or at the heels of their mothers, and frequently of their fathers, is in the present deplorable state of the kingdom a very great additional grievance; and therefore whoever could find out a fair, cheap, and easy method of making these children sound, useful members of the commonwealth would deserve so well of the public as to have his statue set up for a preserver of the nation. 2

But my intention is very far from being confined to provide only for the children of professed beggars; it is of a much greater extent, and shall take in the whole number of infants at a certain age who are born of parents in effect as little able to support them as those who demand our charity in the streets. 3

As to my own part, having turned my thoughts for many years upon this important subject, and maturely weighted the several schemes of other projectors, I have always found them grossly mistaken in their computation. It is true, a child just dropped from its dam may be supported by her milk for a solar year, with little other nourishment; at most not above the value of two shillings, which the mother may certainly get, or the value in scraps, by her lawful occupation of begging; and it is exactly at one year old that I propose to provide for them in such a manner as instead of being a charge upon their parents or the parish, or wanting food and raiment for the rest of their lives, they shall on the contrary contribute to the feeding, and partly to the clothing, of many thousands. 4

There is likewise another great advantage in my scheme, that it will prevent those voluntary abortions, and that horrid practice of women murdering their bastard children, alas, too frequent among us, sacrificing the poor innocent babes, I doubt, more to avoid the expense than the shame, which would move tears and pity in the most savage and inhuman breast. 5

The number of souls in this kingdom being usually reckoned one million and a half, of these I calculate there may be about two hundred thousand couples whose wives are breeders; from which number I subtract thirty thousand couples who are able to maintain their own children, although I apprehend there cannot be so many under the present distresses of the kingdom; but this being granted, there will remain an hundred and seventy thousand breeders. I again subtract fifty thousand for those women who miscarry, or whose children die by accident or disease within the year. There only remain an hundred and twenty thousand children of poor parents annually born. The question therefore is, how this number shall be reared and provided for, which, as I have already said, under the present situation of affairs, is utterly impossible by all the methods hitherto proposed. For we can neither employ them in handicraft or agriculture; we neither build houses (I mean in the country) nor 6 cultivate land. They can very seldom pick up a livelihood by stealing till they arrive at six years old, except where they are of towardly parts; although I confess they learn the rudiments much earlier, during which time they can however be looked upon only as probationers, as I have been informed by a principal gentleman in the county of Cavan, who protested to me that he never knew above one or two instances under the age of six, even in a part of the kingdom so renowned for the quickest proficiency in that art.

7   I am assured by our merchants that a boy or girl before twelve years old is no salable commodity; and even when they come to this age they will not yield above three pounds, or three pounds and half a crown at most on the Exchange; which cannot turn to account either to the parents or the kingdom, the charge of nutriment and rags having been at least four times that value.

8   I shall now therefore humbly propose my own thoughts, which I hope will not be liable to the least objection.

9   I have been assured by a very knowing American of my acquaintance in London, that a young healthy child well nursed is at a year old a most delicious, nourishing, and wholesome food, whether stewed, roasted, baked or boiled; and I make no doubt that it will equally serve in a fricassee or a ragout.

10   I do therefore humbly offer it to public consideration that of the hundred and twenty thousand children, already computed, twenty thousand may be reserved for breed, whereof only one fourth part to be males, which is more than we allow to sheep, black cattle, or swine; and my reason is that these children are seldom the fruits of marriage, a circumstance not much regarded by our savages, therefore one male will be sufficient to serve four females. That the remaining hundred thousand may at a year old be offered in sale to the persons of quality and fortune through the kingdom, always advising the mother to let them suck plentifully in the last month, so as to render them plump and fat for a good table. A child will make two dishes at an entertainment for friends; and when the family dines alone, the fore or hind quarter will make a reasonable dish, and seasoned with a little pepper or salt will be very good boiled on the fourth day, especially in winter.

11   I have reckoned upon a medium that a child just born will weigh twelve pounds, and in a solar year if tolerably nursed increaseth to twenty-eight pounds.

12   I grant this food will be somewhat dear, and therefore very proper for landlords, who, as they have already devoured most of the parents, seem to have the best title to the children.

13   Infant's flesh will be in season throughout the year, but more plentiful in March, and a little before and after. For we are told by a grave author, an eminent French physician, that fish being a prolific diet, there are more children born in Roman Catholic countries about nine months after Lent than at any other season: therefore, reckoning a year after Lent, the mar-

kets will be more glutted than usual, because the number of popish infants is at least three to one in this kingdom; and therefore it will have one other collateral advantage, by lessening the number of Papists among us.

I have already computed the charge of nursing a beggar's child (in   14
which list I reckon all cottagers, laborers, and four fifths of the farmers) to be about two shillings per annum, rags included: and I believe no gentleman would repine to give ten shillings for the carcass of a good fat child, which, as I have said, will make four dishes of excellent nutritive meat, when he hath only some particular friend or his own family to dine with him. Thus the squire will learn to be a good landlord, and grow popular among the tenants; the mother will have eight shillings net profit, and be fit for work till she produces another child.

Those who are more thrifty (as I must confess the times require) may   15
flay the carcass; the skin of which artificially dressed will make admirable gloves for ladies, and summer boots for fine gentlemen.

As to our city of Dublin, shambles may be appointed for this purpose   16
in the most convenient parts of it, and butchers we may be assured will not be wanting; although I rather recommend buying the children alive, and dressing them hot from the knife as we do roasting pigs.

A very worthy person, a true lover of his country, and whose virtues I   17
highly esteem, was lately pleased in discoursing on this matter to offer a refinement upon my scheme. He said that many gentlemen of this kingdom, having of late destroyed their deer, he conceived that the want of venison might be well supplied by the bodies of young lads and maidens, not exceeding fourteen years of age nor under twelve, so great a number of both sexes in every county being now ready to starve for want of work and service; and these to be disposed of by their parents, if alive, or otherwise by their nearest relations. But with due deference to so excellent a friend and so deserving a patriot, I cannot be altogether in his sentiments; for as to the males, my American acquaintance assured me from frequent experience that their flesh was generally tough and lean, like that of our schoolboys, by continual exercise, and their taste disagreeable; and to fatten them would not answer the charge. Then as to the females, it would, I think with humble submission, be a loss to the public, because they soon would become breeders themselves: and besides, it is not improbable that some scrupulous people might be apt to censure such a practice (although indeed very unjustly) as a little bordering upon cruelty; which, I confess, hath always been with me the strongest objection against any project, how well so ever intended.

But in order to justify my friend, he confessed that this expedient was   18
put into his head by the famous Psalmanazar, a native of the island Formosa, who came from thence to London above twenty years ago, and in conversation told my friend that in his country when any young person happened to be put to death, the executioner sold the carcass to persons of quality as a prime dainty; and that in his time the body of a plump girl of fifteen, who was crucified for an attempt to poison the emperor, was

sold to his Imperial Majesty's prime minister of state, and other great mandarins of the court, in joints from the gibbet, at four hundred crowns. Neither indeed can I deny that if the same use were made of several plump young girls in this town, who without one single groat to their fortunes cannot stir abroad without a chair, and appear at the playhouse and assemblies in foreign fineries which they never will pay for, the kingdom would not be the worse.

19   Some persons of a desponding spirit are in great concern about that vast number of poor people who are aged, diseased, or maimed, and I have been desired to employ my thoughts what course may be taken to ease the nation of so grievous an encumbrance. But I am not in the least pain upon that matter, because it is very well known that they are every day dying and rotting by cold and famine, and filth and vermin, as fast as can be reasonably expected. And as to the younger laborers, they are now in almost as hopeful a condition. They cannot get work, and consequently pine away for want of nourishment to a degree that if at any time they are accidentally hired to common labor, they have not strength to perform it; and thus the country and themselves are happily delivered from the evils to come.

20   I have too long digressed, and therefore shall return to my subject. I think the advantages by the proposal which I have made are obvious and many, as well as of the highest importance.

21   For first, as I have already observed, it would greatly lessen the number of Papists, with whom we are yearly overrun, being the principal breeders of the nation as well as our most dangerous enemies; and who stay at home on purpose to deliver the kingdom to the Pretender, hoping to take their advantage by the absence of so many good Protestants, who have chosen rather to leave their country than to stay at home and pay tithes against their conscience to an Episcopal curate.

22   Secondly, the poorer tenants will have something valuable of their own, which by law may be made liable to distress, and help to pay their landlord's rent, their corn and cattle being already seized and money a thing unknown.

23   Thirdly, whereas the maintenance of an hundred thousand children, from two years old and upwards, cannot be computed at less than ten shillings a piece per annum, the nation's stock will be thereby increased fifty thousand pounds per annum, besides the profit of a new dish introduced to the tables of all gentlemen of fortune in the kingdom who have any refinement in taste. And the money will circulate among ourselves, the goods being entirely of our own growth and manufacture.

24   Fourthly, the constant breeders, besides the gain of eight shillings sterling per annum by the sale of their children, will be rid of the charge of maintaining them after the first year.

Fifthly, this food would likewise bring great custom to taverns, where the vintners will certainly be so prudent as to procure the best receipts for dressing it to perfection, and consequently have their houses frequented by all the fine gentlemen, who justly value themselves upon their knowledge in good eating; and a skillful cook, who understands how to oblige his guests, will contrive to make it as expensive as they please.   25

Sixthly, this would be a great inducement to marriage, which all wise nations have either encouraged by rewards or enforced by laws and penalties. It would increase the care and tenderness of mothers toward their children, when they were sure of a settlement for life to the poor babes, provided in some sort by the public, to their annual profit instead of expense. We should see an honest emulation among the married women, which of them could bring the fattest child to the market. Men would become as fond of their wives during the time of their pregnancy as they are now of their mares in foal, their cows in calf, or sows when they are ready to farrow; nor offer to beat or kick them (as is too frequent a practice) for fear of a miscarriage.   26

Many other advantages might be enumerated. For instance, the addition of some thousand carcasses in our exportation of barreled beef, the propagation of swine's flesh, and improvement in the art of making good bacon, so much wanted among us by the great destruction of pigs, too frequent at our tables, which are no way comparable in taste or magnificence to a well-grown, fat yearling child, which roasted whole will make a considerable figure at a lord mayor's feast or any other public entertainment. But this and many others I omit, being studious of brevity.   27

Supposing that one thousand families in this city would be constant customers for infants' flesh, besides others who might have it at merry meetings, particularly weddings and christenings, I compute that Dublin would take off annually about twenty thousand carcasses, and the rest of the kingdom (where probably they will be sold somewhat cheaper) the remaining eighty thousand.   28

I can think of no one objection that will possibly be raised against this proposal, unless it should be urged that the number of people will be thereby much lessened in the kingdom. This I freely own, and it was indeed one principal design in offering it to the world. I desire the reader will observe, that I calculate my remedy for this one individual kingdom of Ireland and for no other that ever was, is, or I think ever can be upon earth. Therefore let no man talk to me of other expedients: of taxing our absentees at five shillings a pound: of using neither clothes nor household furniture except what is of our own growth and manufacture: of utterly rejecting the materials and instruments that promote foreign luxury: of curing the expensiveness of pride, vanity, idleness, and gaming in   29 our women: of introducing a vein of parsimony, prudence, and temperance: of learning to love our country, in the want of which we differ even from Laplanders and the inhabitants of Topinamboo: of quitting our animosities and factions, nor acting any longer like the Jews, who were murdering one another at the very moment their city was taken: of being a little cautious not to sell our country and conscience for nothing: of teaching landlords to have at least one degree of mercy toward their tenants: lastly, of putting a spirit of honesty, industry, and skill into our shopkeepers; who, if a resolution could be now taken to buy only our native goods, would immediately unite to cheat and exact upon us in the price, the measure and the goodness, nor could ever yet be brought to make one fair proposal of just dealing, though often and earnestly invited to it.

30   Therefore I repeat, let no man talk to me of these and the like expedients, till he hath at least some glimpse of hope that there will ever be some hearty and sincere attempt to put them in practice.

31   But as to myself, having been wearied out for many years with offering vain, idle, visionary thoughts, and at length utterly despairing of success, I fortunately fell upon this proposal, which, as it is wholly new, so it hath something solid and real, of no expense and little trouble, full in our own power, and whereby we can incur no danger in disobliging England. For this kind of commodity will not bear exportation, the flesh being of too tender a consistence to admit a long continuance in salt, although perhaps I could name a country which would be glad to eat up our whole nation without it.

32   After all, I am not so violently bent upon my own opinion as to reject any offer proposed by wise men, which shall be found equally innocent, cheap, easy, and effectual. But before something of that kind shall be advanced in contradiction to my scheme, and offering a better, I desire the author or authors will be pleased maturely to consider two points. First, as things now stand, how they will be able to find food and raiment for an hundred thousand useless mouths and backs. And secondly, there being a round million of creatures in human figure throughout this kingdom, whose sole subsistence put into a common stock would leave them in debt two millions of pounds sterling, adding those who are beggars by profession to the bulk of farmers, cottagers, and laborers, with their wives and children who are beggars in effect; I desire those politicians who dislike my overture, and may perhaps be so bold to attempt an answer, that they will first ask the parents of these mortals whether they would not at this day think it a great happiness to have been sold for food at a year old in the manner I prescribe, and thereby have avoided such a perpetual scene of misfortunes as they have since gone through by the oppression of landlords, the impossibility of paying rent without money or trade, the want of common sustenance, with neither house nor clothes to cover them from the inclemencies of the weather, and the most inevitable prospect of entailing the like or greater miseries upon their breed forever.

I profess, in the sincerity of my heart, that I have not the least per-   33
sonal interest in endeavoring to promote this necessary work, having
no other motive than the public good of my country, by advancing our
trade, providing for infants, relieving the poor, and giving some pleasure to the rich. I have no children by which I can propose to get a
single penny; the youngest being nine years old, and my wife past
childbearing.

Responding to the Essay

1. What is Swift's major proposition? What is the true nature of his argument? Explain.
2. Where in the essay does Swift come closest to criticizing openly the
   English and especially the rich? Is he ever openly critical to the poor
   Irish Catholics? Offer evidence for your answers.
3. Analyze the structure of Swift's essay. How does he build this argument slowly? Make an outline in which you trace his reasoning.
4. Discuss the title of the essay. Why use the word *modest*? What is modest about his argument? Is there irony in the title too? How does it
   play out in his essay? Defend your answers.

Responding in Writing

1. Write a modest proposal of your own on a social problem of your
   choosing. For example, perhaps propose an ironic solution for the
   War on Terrorism.
2. Research the life of Jonathan Swift, focusing on his political beliefs.
   How did he fight for them during his life, and how does he reveal
   them in "A Modest Proposal"?
3. In small groups, make a list of two columns: In one column, list
   Swift's minor propositions in this essay. In the other column, list the
   corresponding serious arguments hiding behind the propositions.
   Present your list to the class.

Virginia Woolf
Professions for Women

Virginia Woolf (1882–1941) was born Virginia Stephen in London into a
wealthy and influential family. As an adult she moved with her brother to
the Bloomsbury area of the city, where they became friends with many lead-
ing lights of their generation, including writers, painters, scholars, and crit-
ics. She met her husband, Leonard Woolf, in this group, and later they

founded Hogarth Press, which published many important works including her own books. Mrs. Dalloway *(1925),* To the Lighthouse *(1927), and* The Waves *(1931) are among the most famous of Woolf's novels, which she wrote in the modernist technique called "stream of consciousness." Her fiction depicted the flow of her characters' thoughts. Woolf also published many essays and works of criticism, some of which were collected in* The Common Reader *(1925). After a lifelong struggle with depression, Woolf committed suicide by filling her pockets with rocks and walking into the Thames River.*

Woolf was always concerned with the situation of women in society, especially women who had a desire for independence, as she did. Her writing on the topic is well known, especially the long essays A Room of One's Own *(1929) and* Three Guineas *(1938). In 1931, Woolf gave a lecture on feminism, which she shortened and published later the same year as "Professions for Women." In this selection, Woolf picked up on the idea of the Angel in the House, which she took from a famous Victorian poem, and described how women must fight against preconceptions about their abilities and feelings and against how men try to suppress them.*

1   When your secretary invited me to come here, she told me that your Society is concerned with the employment of women and she suggested that I might tell you something about my own professional experiences. It is true I am a woman; it is true I am employed; but what professional experiences have I had? It is difficult to say. My profession is literature; and in that profession there are fewer experiences for women than in any other, with the exception of the stage—fewer, I mean, that are peculiar to women. For the road was cut many years ago—by Fanny Burney, by Aphra Behn, by Harriet Martineau, by Jane Austen, by George Eliot—many famous women, and many more unknown and forgotten, have been before me, making the path smooth, and regulating my steps. Thus, when I came to write, there were very few material obstacles in my way. Writing was a reputable and harmless occupation. The family peace was not broken by the scratching of a pen. No demand was made upon the family purse. For ten and sixpence one can buy paper enough to write all the plays of Shakespeare—if one has a mind that way. Pianos and models, Paris, Vienna and Berlin, masters and mistresses, are not needed by a writer. The cheapness of writing paper is, of course, the reason why women have succeeded as writers before they have succeeded in the other professions.

2   But to tell you my story—it is a simple one. You have only got to figure to yourselves a girl in a bedroom with a pen in her hand. She had only to move that pen from left to right—from ten o'clock to one. Then it occurred to her to do what is simple and cheap enough after all—to slip a few of those pages into an envelope, fix a penny stamp in the corner, and drop the envelope into the red box at the corner. It was thus that I became a journal-

ist; and my effort was rewarded on the first day of the following month—a very glorious day it was for me—by a letter from an editor containing a cheque for one pound ten shillings and sixpence. But to show you how little I deserve to be called a professional woman, how little I know of the struggles and difficulties of such lives, I have to admit that instead of spending that sum upon bread and butter, rent, shoes and stockings, or butcher's bills, I went out and bought a cat—a beautiful cat, a Persian cat, which very soon involved me in bitter disputes with my neighbors.

What could be easier than to write articles and to buy Persian cats 3 with the profits? But wait a moment. Articles have to be about something. Mine, I seem to remember, was about a novel by a famous man. And while I was writing this review, I discovered that if I were going to review books I should need to do battle with a certain phantom. And the phantom was a woman, and when I came to know her better I called her after the heroine of a famous poem, The Angel in the House. It was she who used to come between me and my paper when I was writing reviews. It was she who bothered me and wasted my time and so tormented me that at last I killed her. You who come of a younger and happier generation may not have heard of her—you may not know what I mean by the Angel in the House. I will describe her as shortly as I can. She was intensely sympathetic. She was immensely charming. She was utterly unselfish. She excelled in the difficult arts of family life. She sacrificed herself daily. If there was a chicken, she took the leg; if there was a draught she sat in it—in short she was so constituted that she never had a mind or a wish of her own, but preferred to sympathize always with the minds and wishes of others. Above all—I need not say it—she was pure. Her purity was supposed to be her chief beauty—her blushes, her great grace. In those days—the last of Queen Victoria—every house had its Angel. And when I came to write I encountered her with the very first words. The shadow of her wings fell on my page; I heard the rustling of her skirts in the room. Directly, that is to say, I took my pen in hand to review that novel by a famous man, she slipped behind me and whispered: "My dear, you are a young woman. You are writing about a book that has been written by a man. Be sympathetic; be tender; flatter; deceive; use all the arts and wiles of our sex. Never let anybody guess that you have a mind of your own. Above all, be pure." And she made as if to guide my pen. I now record the one act for which I take some credit to myself, though the credit rightly belongs to some excellent ancestors of mine who left me a certain sum of money—shall we say five hundred pounds a year—so that it was not necessary for me to depend solely on charm for my living. I turned upon her and caught her by the throat. I did my best to kill her. My excuse, if I were to be had up in a court of law, would be that I acted in self-defense. Had I not killed her she would have killed me. She would have plucked the heart out of my writing. For, as I found, directly I put pen to paper, you cannot review even a novel without having a mind of your own, without expressing what you think to be the truth about human relations, morality, sex. And all these questions, according to the Angel in the House, cannot be dealt with freely and openly by women; they must charm, they must conciliate, they must—to put it bluntly—tell lies if they are to succeed. Thus, whenever I felt the shadow of her wing or the radiance of her halo upon my page, I took up the inkpot and flung it at her. She died hard. Her fictitious nature was of great assistance to her. It is far harder to kill a phantom than a reality. She was always creeping back when I thought I had dispatched her. Though I flatter myself that I killed her in the end, the struggle was severe; it took much time that had better have been spent upon learning Greek grammar; or in roaming the world in search of adventures. But it was a real experience; it was an experience that was bound to befall all women writers at that time. Killing the Angel in the House was part of the occupation of a woman writer.

4   But to continue my story. The Angel was dead; what then remained? You may say that what remained was a simple and common object—a young woman in a bedroom with an inkpot. In other words, now that she had rid herself of falsehood, that young woman had only to be herself. Ah, but what is "herself"? I mean, what is a woman? I assure you, I do not know. I do not believe that you know. I do not believe that anybody can know until she has expressed herself in all the arts and professions open to human skill. That indeed is one of the reasons why I have come here—out of respect for you, who are in process of showing us by your experiments what a woman is, who are in process of providing us, by your failures and successes, with that extremely important piece of information.

5   But to continue the story of my professional experiences. I made one pound ten and six by my first review; and I bought a Persian cat with the proceeds. Then I grew ambitious. A Persian cat is all very well, I said; but a Persian cat is not enough. I must have a motor car. And it was thus that I became a novelist—for it is a very strange thing that people will give you a motor car if you will tell them a story. It is a still stranger thing that there is nothing so delightful in the world as telling stories. It is far pleasanter than writing reviews of famous novels. And yet, if I am to obey your secretary and tell you my professional experiences as a novelist, I must tell you about a very strange experience that befell me as a novelist. And to understand it you must try first to imagine a novelist's state of mind. I hope I am not giving away professional secrets if I say that a novelist's chief desire is to be as unconscious as possible. He has to induce in himself a state of perpetual lethargy. He wants life to proceed with the utmost quiet and regularity. He wants to see the same faces, to read the same books, to do the same things day after day, month after month, while he is writing, so that nothing may break the illusion in which he is living—so that nothing may disturb or disquiet the mysterious nosings about, feelings round, darts, dashes and sudden discoveries of that very shy and illusive spirit, the imagination. I suspect that this state is the

same both for men and women. Be that as it may, I want you to imagine me writing a novel in a state of trance. I want you to figure to yourselves a girl sitting with a pen in her hand, which for minutes, and indeed for hours, she never dips into the inkpot. The image that comes to my mind when I think of this girl is the image of a fisherman lying sunk in dreams on the verge of a deep lake with a rod held out over the water. She was letting her imagination sweep unchecked round every rock and cranny of the world that lies submerged in the depths of our unconscious being. Now came the experience, the experience that I believe to be far commoner with women writers than with men. The line raced through the girl's fingers. Her imagination had rushed away. It had sought the pools, the depths, the dark places where the largest fish slumber. And then there was a smash. There was an explosion. There was foam and confusion. The imagination had dashed itself against something hard. The girl was roused from her dream. She was indeed in a state of the most acute and difficult distress. To speak without figure she had thought of something, something about the body, about the passions which it was unfitting for her as a woman to say. Men, her reason told her, would be shocked. The consciousness of what men will say of a woman who speaks the truth about her passions had roused her from her artist's state of unconsciousness. She could write no more. The trance was over. Her imagination could work no longer. This I believe to be a very common experience with women writers—they are impeded by the extreme conventionality of the other sex. For though men sensibly allow themselves great freedom in these respects, I doubt that they realize or can control the extreme severity with which they condemn such freedom in women.

These then were two very genuine experiences of my own. These were   6
two of the adventures of my professional life. The first—killing the Angel in the House—I think I solved. She died. But the second, telling the truth about my own experiences as a body, I do not think I solved. I doubt that any woman has solved it yet. The obstacles against her are still immensely powerful—and yet they are very difficult to define. Outwardly, what is simpler than to write books? Outwardly, what obstacles are there for a woman rather than for a man? Inwardly, I think, the case is very different; she has still many ghosts to fight, many prejudices to overcome. Indeed it will be a long time still, I think, before a woman can sit down to write a book without finding a phantom to be slain, a rock to be dashed against. And if this is so in literature, the freest of all professions for women, how is it in the new professions which you are now for the first time entering?

Those are the questions that I should like, had I time, to ask you. And   7
indeed, if I have laid stress upon these professional experiences of mine, it is because I believe that they are, though in different forms, yours also. Even when the path is nominally open—when there is nothing to prevent a woman from being a doctor, a lawyer, a civil servant—there are many phantoms and obstacles, as I believe, looming in her way. To discuss and

define them is I think of great value and importance; for thus only can the labour be shared, the difficulties be solved. But besides this, it is necessary also to discuss the ends and the aims for which we are fighting, for which we are doing battle with these formidable obstacles. Those aims cannot be taken for granted; they must be perpetually questioned and examined. The whole position, as I see it—here in this hall surrounded by women practising for the first time in history I know not how many different professions—is one of extraordinary interest and importance. You have won rooms of your own in the house hitherto exclusively owned by men. You are able, though not without great labour and effort, to pay the rent. You are earning your five hundred pounds a year. But this freedom is only a beginning; the room is your own, but it is still bare. It has to be furnished; it has to be decorated; it has to be shared. How are you going to furnish it, how are you going to decorate it? With whom are you going to share it, and upon what terms? These, I think, are questions of the utmost importance and interest. For the first time in history you are able to ask for them; for the first time you are able to decide for yourselves what the answers should be. Willingly would I stay and discuss those questions and answers—but not tonight. My time is up; and I must cease.

Responding to the Essay

1. Woolf originally gave as a speech what is now this essay. Why did Woolf keep the trappings of the speech when she published the essay? Why not recast it as a straight essay? How does making it a speech help the argument?
2. What is the Angel in the House? Why is she an "Angel"? How does Woolf use description of the Angel to advance her argument?
3. How does Woolf use a humble tone in this essay? Is her humbleness honest, or is she being ironic? Explain your answer.
4. How does Woolf use contrast analysis in this essay to highlight the different stages of women's freedom?

Responding in Writing

1. Identify the women writers Woolf mentions in paragraph 1 and explain how each of them struggled (if they did) against their own Angels in the House.
2. In groups, discuss the idea that men today face certain obstacles in their work life and in their own head that are unique to their gender. What do you think Woolf would say to your speculations? Make a list of these obstacles and how they manifest themselves. Compare your group's work with the rest of the class.
3. Write an essay in which you bring Woolf's problems up to date. Does a woman, even after all the advances of more than 70 years, still have "phantoms and obstacles . . . looming in her way"? (par. 7)

GEORGE ORWELL
A Hanging

George Orwell (whose real name was Eric Blair) was born in India in 1903 and died in London at the age of 47. During his short life, he became famous for his political writing, especially his political novels. Orwell's parents were members of the Indian Civil Service, and, after his education at Eton College in England, at the age of 19, Orwell joined the Indian Imperial Police in Burma, which he wrote about in his novel Burmese Days *(1934) and in various essays. One of those essays, "Killing an Elephant," expresses his disillusion with British colonialism. His politics shifted to the left and he became a socialist. He left Burma, traveled around Europe in self-enforced poverty, and wrote his first book about the experience,* Down and Out in Paris and London *(1933). Soon, in the mid-1930s, he joined many writers and intellectuals from all over the Western world in fighting with the Republicans against the Fascists in the Spanish Civil War.* Homage to Catalonia *(1938) tells of his experiences in the war. Orwell was wounded, and, when the Communists attempted to eliminate their allies on the far left, he fought against them and was forced to flee for his life.*

His most famous books, however, are Animal Farm *(1945), a modern fable that attacked the Soviet system of communism by setting the events among animals on a farm; and* 1984 *(1949), a novel about a frightening future.* 1984 *introduced the phrase "Big Brother" into the English language. In the years after his death, Orwell has become renowned for above all things his clarity of writing and his clarity of moral thought. In "A Hanging," written in 1931, Orwell tells of an experience watching an execution in Burma. This classic essay betrays his feelings about capital punishment, but he remains somewhat ambiguous. Elsewhere, Orwell wrote, "Society, apparently, cannot get along without capital punishment—for there are some people whom it is simply not safe to leave alive—and yet there is no one, when the pinch comes, who feels it right to kill another human being in cold blood."*

I t was in Burma, a sodden morning of the rains. A sickly light, like yellow tinfoil, was slanting over the high walls into the jail yard. We were waiting outside the condemned cells, a row of sheds fronted with double bars, like small animal cages. Each cell measured about ten feet by ten and was quite bare within except for a plank bed and a pot of drinking water. In some of them brown silent men were squatting at the inner bars, with their blankets draped round them. These were the condemned men, due to be hanged within the next week or two.   1

One prisoner had been brought out of his cell. He was a Hindu, a puny wisp of a man, with a shaven head and vague liquid eyes. He had a thick, sprouting moustache, absurdly too big for his body, rather like the moustache of a comic man on the films. Six tall Indian warders were guarding him and getting him ready for the gallows. Two of them stood by with rifles with fixed bayonets, while the others handcuffed him,   2 passed a chain through his handcuffs and fixed it to their belts, and lashed his arms tight to his sides. They crowded very close about him, with their hands always on him in a careful, caressing grip, as though all the while feeling him to make sure he was there. It was like men handling a fish which is still alive and may jump back into the water. But he stood quite unresisting, yielding his arms limply to the ropes, as though he hardly noticed what was happening.

3   Eight o'clock struck and a bugle call, desolately thin in the wet air, floated from the distant barracks. The superintendent of the jail, who was standing apart from the rest of us, moodily prodding the gravel with his stick, raised his head at the sound. He was an army doctor, with a grey toothbrush moustache and a gruff voice. "For God's sake hurry up, Francis," he said irritably. "The man ought to have been dead by this time. Aren't you ready yet?"

4   Francis, the head jailer, a fat Dravidian in a white drill suit and gold spectacles, waved his black hand. "Yes sir, yes sir," he bubbled. "All iss satisfactorily prepared. The hangman iss waiting. We shall proceed."

5   "Well, quick march, then. The prisoners can't get their breakfast till this job's over."

6   We set out for the gallows. Two warders marched on either side of the prisoner, with their files at the slope; two others marched close against him, gripping him by arm and shoulder, as though at once pushing and supporting him. The rest of us, magistrates and the like, followed behind. Suddenly, when we had gone ten yards, the procession stopped short without any order or warning. A dreadful thing had happened—a dog, come goodness knows whence, had appeared in the yard. It came bounding among us with a loud volley of barks, and leapt round us wagging its whole body, wild with glee at finding so many human beings together. It was a large woolly dog, half Airedale, half pariah. For a moment it pranced round us, and then, before anyone could stop it, it had made a dash for the prisoner, and jumping up tried to lick his face. Everyone stood aghast, too taken aback even to grab at the dog.

7   "Who let that bloody brute in here?" said the superintendent angrily. "Catch it, someone!"

8   A warder, detached from the escort, charged clumsily after the dog, but it danced and gambolled just out of his reach, taking everything as part of the game. A young Eurasian jailer picked up a handful of gravel and tried to stone the dog away, but it dodged the stones and came after us again. Its yaps echoed from the jail walls. The prisoner, in the grasp of the two warders, looked on incuriously, as though this was another formality of the hanging. It was several minutes before someone managed to catch the dog. Then we put my handkerchief through its collar and moved off once more, with the dog still straining and whimpering.

9   It was about forty yards to the gallows. I watched the bare brown back of the prisoner marching in front of me. He walked clumsily with his

bound arms, but quite steadily, with that bobbing gait of the Indian who never straightens his knees. At each step his muscles slid neatly into place, the lock of hair on his scalp danced up and down, his feet printed themselves on the wet gravel. And once, in spite of the men who gripped him by each shoulder, he stepped slightly aside to avoid a puddle on the path.

It is curious, but till that moment I had never realised what it means to destroy a healthy, conscious man. When I saw the prisoner step aside to avoid the puddle, I saw the mystery, the unspeakable wrongness, of cutting a life short when it is in full tide. This man was not dying, he was alive just as we were alive. All the organs of his body were working—bowels digesting food, skin renewing itself, nails growing, tissues forming—all toiling away in solemn foolery. His nails would still be growing when he stood on the drop, when he was falling through the air with a tenth of a second to live. His eyes saw the yellow gravel and the grey walls, and his brain still remembered, foresaw, reasoned—reasoned even about puddles. He and we were a party of men walking together, seeing, hearing, feeling, understanding the same world; and in two minutes, with a sudden snap, one of us would be gone—one mind less, one world less.   10

The gallows stood in a small yard, separate from the main grounds of the prison, and overgrown with tall prickly weeds. It was a brick erection like three sides of a shed, with planking on top, and above that two beams and a crossbar with the rope dangling. The hangman, a greyhaired convict in the white uniform of the prison, was waiting beside his machine. He greeted us with a servile crouch as we entered. At a word from Francis the two warders, gripping the prisoner more closely than ever, half led, half pushed him to the gallows and helped him clumsily up the ladder. Then the hangman climbed up and fixed the rope round the prisoner's neck.   11

We stood waiting, five yards away. The warders had formed in a rough circle round the gallows. And then, when the noose was fixed, the prisoner began crying out on his god. It was a high, reiterated cry of "Ram! Ram! Ram! Ram!", not urgent and fearful like a prayer or a cry for help, but steady, rhythmical, almost like the tolling of a bell. The dog answered the sound with a whine. The hangman, still standing on the gallows, produced a small cotton bag like a flour bag and drew it down over the prisoner's face. But the sound, muffled by the cloth, still persisted, over and over again: "Ram! Ram! Ram! Ram! Ram!"   12

The hangman climbed down and stood ready, holding the lever. Minutes seemed to pass. The steady, muffled crying from the prisoner went on and on, "Ram! Ram! Ram!" never faltering for an instant. The superintendent, his head on his chest, was slowly poking the ground with his stick; perhaps he was counting the cries, allowing the prisoner a fixed number—fifty, perhaps, or a hundred. Everyone had changed colour. The Indians had gone grey like bad coffee, and one or two of the bayonets were wavering. We looked at the lashed, hooded man on the drop, and   13 listened to his cries—each cry another second of life; the same thought was in all our minds; oh, kill him quickly, get it over, stop that abominable noise!

14   Suddenly the superintendent made up his mind. Throwing up his head he made a swift motion with his stick. "Chalo!" he shouted almost fiercely.

15   There was a clanking noise, and then dead silence. The prisoner had vanished, and the rope was twisting on itself. I let go of the dog, and it galloped immediately to the back of the gallows; but when it got there it stopped short, barked, and then retreated into a corner of the yard, where it stood among the weeds, looking timorously out at us. We went round the gallows to inspect the prisoner's body. He was dangling with his toes pointed straight downwards, very slowly revolving, as dead as a stone.

16   The superintendent reached out with his stick and poked the bare body; it oscillated, slightly. "*He's* all right," said the superintendent. He backed out from under the gallows, and blew out a deep breath. The moody look had gone out of his face quite suddenly. He glanced at his wristwatch. "Eight minutes past eight. Well, that's all for this morning, thank God."

17   The warders unfixed bayonets and marched away. The dog, sobered and conscious of having misbehaved itself, slipped after them. We walked out of the gallows yard, past the condemned cells with their waiting prisoners, into the big central yard of the prison. The convicts, under the command of warders armed with lathis, were already receiving their breakfast. They squatted in long rows, each man holding a tin pannikin, while two warders with buckets marched round ladling out rice; it seemed quite a homely, jolly scene, after the hanging. An enormous relief had come upon us now that the job was done. One felt an impulse to sing, to break into a run, to snigger. All at once everyone began chattering gaily.

18   The Eurasian boy walking beside me nodded towards the way we had come, with a knowing smile: "Do you know, sir, our friend (he meant the dead man), when he heard his appeal had been dismissed, he pissed on the floor of his cell. From fright—Kindly take one of my cigarettes, sir. Do you not admire my new silver case, sir? From the boxwallah, two rupees eight annas. Classy European style."

19   Several people laughed—at what, nobody seemed certain.

20   Francis was walking by the superintendent, talking garrulously: "Well, sir, all hass passed off with the utmost satisfactoriness. It wass all finished—flick! like that. It iss not always so—oah, no! I have known cases where the doctor wass obliged to go beneath the gallows and pull the prisoner's legs to ensure decease. Most disagreeable!"

21   "Wriggling about, eh? That's bad," said the superintendent.

22   "Ach, sir, it iss worse when they become refractory! One man, I recall, clung to the bars of hiss cage when we went to take him out. You will

scarcely credit, sir, that it took six warders to dislodge him, three pulling at each leg. We reasoned with him. 'My dear fellow,' we said, 'think of all the pain and trouble you are causing to us!' But no, he would not listen! Ach, he wass very troublesome!"

I found that I was laughing quite loudly. Everyone was laughing.   23
Even the superintendent grinned in a tolerant way. "You'd better all come out and have a drink," he said quite genially. "I've got a bottle of whisky in the car. We could do with it."

We went through the big double gates of the prison, into the road.   24
"Pulling at his legs!" exclaimed a Burmese magistrate suddenly, and burst into a loud chuckling. We all began laughing again. At that moment Francis's anecdote seemed extraordinarily funny. We all had a drink together, native and European alike, quite amicably. The dead man was a hundred yards away.

Responding to the Essay

1. What is Orwell's claim in this essay? Is there an explicit statement in which he states his claim? If not, how does the essay succeed without one?
2. Explain how Orwell's description of the jail and the weather help him to make his point. Give specific examples. What is the significance of the dog for Orwell's argument?
3. Between paragraphs 9 and 10, Orwell begins thinking about the morality of executing the prisoner. What triggers his thoughts? Is this an effective technique, or is it too abrupt and transparent a transition?
4. How does Orwell's description of the immediate aftermath of the execution affect his argument? Is it acceptable that he describes it so matter-of-factly? Why or why not?

Responding in Writing

1. How might you or might you not change your views on capital punishment if someone in your circle of family and friends was murdered?
2. David Gelernter writes, in Chapter 9, that "Even when we resolve in principle to go ahead [with the death penalty], we have to steel ourselves." What does Gelernter mean, and how does Orwell's essay reflect this idea? Write an essay to explore the meaning of Gelernter's statement.
3. How does the fact that Orwell writes this essay as a narrative help or harm his argument? What does his choice of form *not* allow him to do? What are the inherent strengths and limitations of this rhetorical mode?

RACHEL CARSON
The Obligation to Endure

Writer and scientist Rachel Carson (1907–1964) helped make modern environmentalism a popular cause. After getting her master's degree in zoology from Johns Hopkins University in 1932, she went to work for the U.S. government as a scientist and writer, eventually working her way up to the position of editor in chief of all publications for the U.S. Fish and Wildlife Service. During her career in government, Carson wrote freelance works, becoming well known for her ability to move her readers on topics such as nature and conservation. From 1952, when she resigned from her job, she wrote full time, producing such books as The Sea Around Us *(1952) and* The Edge of the Sea *(1955).*

The wide use of pesticides (especially the insecticide DDT) to improve agricultural production without a thought to the cost in wildlife alarmed Carson, and she wrote Silent Spring *(1962) to warn against the practice. The book and her articles helped convince President John F. Kennedy to order an investigation, for which Carson testified before Congress. Her appearance gave rise to legislation that limited the industrial and agricultural use of harmful chemicals and led eventually to the founding of the Environmental Protection Agency.*

In this selection, an excerpt from Silent Spring, *Carson lays out her case against DDT and other chemicals, arguing that humans need to be more responsible with the lives of their fellow animals.*

1   The history of life on earth has been a history of interaction between living things and their surroundings. To a large extent, the physical form and the habits of the earth's vegetation and its animal life have been molded by the environment. Considering the whole span of earthly time, the opposite effect, in which life actually modifies its surroundings, has been relatively slight. Only within the moment of time represented by the present century has one species—man—acquired significant power to alter the nature of his world.

2   During the past quarter century this power has not only increased to one of disturbing magnitude but it has changed in character. The most alarming of all man's assaults upon the environment is the contamination of air, earth, rivers, and sea with dangerous and even lethal materials. This pollution is for the most part irrecoverable; the chain of evil it initiates not only in the world that must support life but in living tissues is for the most part irreversible. In this now universal contamination of the environment, chemicals are the sinister and little recognized partners of radiation in changing the very nature of the world—the very nature of this life. Strontium 90, released through nuclear explosions into the air, comes

to earth in rain or drifts down as fallout, lodges in soil, enters into the grass or corn or wheat grown there, and in time takes up its abode in the bones of a human being, there to remain until his death. Similarly, chemicals sprayed on croplands or forests or gardens lie long in soil, entering into living organisms, passing from one to another in a chain of poisoning and death. Or they pass mysteriously by underground streams until they emerge and, through the alchemy of air and sunlight, combine into new forms that kill vegetation, sicken cattle, and work unknown harm on those who drink from once-pure wells. As Albert Schweitzer has said, "Man can hardly even recognize the devils of his own creation."

It took hundreds of millions of years to produce the life that now in-   3
habits the earth—eons of time in which developing and evolving the di-versifying life reached a state of adjustment and balance with its sur-roundings. The environment, rigorously shaping and directing the life it supported, contained elements that were hostile as well as supporting. Certain rocks gave out dangerous radiation: even within the light of the sun, from which all life draws its energy, there were short-wave radiations with power to injure. Given time—time not in years but in millennia—life adjusts, and a balance has been reached. For time is the essential ingredi-ent; but in the modern world there is no time.

The rapidity of change and the speed with which new situations are   4
created follow the impetuous and heedless pace of man rather than the deliberate pace of nature. Radiation is no longer merely the background radiation of rocks, the bombardment of cosmic rays, the ultraviolet of the sun that have existed before there was any life on earth; radiation is now the unnatural creation of man's tampering with the atom. The chemicals to which life is asked to make its adjustment are no longer merely the cal-cium and silica and copper and all the rest of the minerals washed out of the rocks and carried in rivers to the sea; they are the synthetic creations of man's inventive mind, brewed in his laboratories, and having no coun-terparts in nature.

To adjust to these chemicals would require time on the scale that is   5
nature's; it would require not merely the years of a man's life but the life of generations. And even this, were it by some miracle possible, would be futile, for the new chemicals come from our laboratories in an endless stream; almost five hundred annually find their way into actual use in the United States alone. The figure is staggering and its implications are not easily grasped—500 new chemicals to which the bodies of men and ani-mals are required somehow to adapt each year, chemicals totally outside the limits of biologic experience.

Among them are many that are used in man's war against nature.   6
Since the mid-1940s over 200 basic chemicals have been created for use in killing insects, weeds, rodents, and other organisms described in the modern vernacular as "pests"; and they are sold under several thousand different brand names.

7　　　These sprays, dusts, and aerosols are now applied almost universally to farms, gardens, forests, and homes—nonselective chemicals that have the power to kill every insect, the "good" and the "bad," to still the song of birds and the leaping of fish in the streams, to coat the leaves with a deadly film, and to linger on in soil—all this though the intended target may be only a few weeds or insects. Can anyone believe it is possible to lay down such a barrage of poisons on the surface of the earth without making it unfit for all life? They should not be called "insecticides," but "biocides."

8　　　The whole process of spraying seems caught up in an endless spiral. Since DDT was released for civilian use, a process of escalation has been going on in which ever more toxic materials must be found. This has happened because insects, in a triumphant vindication of Darwin's principle of the survival of the fittest, have evolved super races immune to the particular insecticide used, hence a deadlier one has always to be developed—and then a deadlier one than that. It has happened also because, for reasons to be described later, destructive insects often undergo a "flareback," or resurgence, after spraying, in numbers greater than before. Thus the chemical war is never won, and all life is caught in its violent crossfire.

9　　　Along with the possibility of the extinction of mankind by nuclear war, the central problem of our age has therefore become the contamination of man's total environment with such substances of incredible potential for harm—substances that accumulate in the tissues of plants and animals and even penetrate the germ cells to shatter or alter the very material of heredity upon which the shape of the future depends.

10　　　Some would-be architects of our future look toward a time when it will be possible to alter the human germ plasm by design. But we may easily be doing so now by inadvertence, for many chemicals, like radiation, bring about gene mutations. It is ironic to think that man might determine his own future by something so seemingly trivial as the choice of an insect spray.

11　　　All this has been risked—for what? Future historians may well be amazed by our distorted sense of proportion. How could intelligent beings seek to control a few unwanted species by a method that contaminated the entire environment and brought the threat of disease and death even to their own kind? Yet this is precisely what we have done. We have done it, moreover, for reasons that collapse the moment we examine them. We are told that the enormous and expanding use of pesticides is necessary to maintain farm production. Yet is our real problem not one of *overproduction*? Our farms, despite measures to remove acreages from production and to pay farmers *not* to produce, have yielded such a staggering excess of crops that the American taxpayer in 1962 is paying out more than one billion dollars a year as the total carrying cost of the surplus-food storage program. And is the situation helped when one branch of the Agriculture Department tries to reduce production while another states, as it did in 1958, "It is believed generally that reduction of crop acreages under provisions of the Soil Bank will stimulate interest in use of chemicals to obtain maximum production on the land retained in crops."

All this is not to say there is no insect problem and no need of control.   12
I was saying, rather, that control must be geared to realities, not to mythical situations, and that the methods employed must be such that they do not destroy us along with the insects.

Responding to the Essay

1. What is Carson's major proposition? What minor propositions does she offer to support her main one?
2. In what order does Carson present her minor propositions? Why does she put them in that order?
3. How does Carson use emotional language to help her claim?
4. How does Carson deftly connect man's invention and use of chemicals with the threat of the atomic bomb? How was this notion radical in 1962?
5. Do you find Carson's conclusion convincing? Why or why not?

Responding in Writing

1. Look at Bob Herbert's essay "No Margin for Error." How are Herbert's and Carson's arguments different? Similar? Explain your answer.
2. In groups of four or five students, investigate the levels of chemicals that are present in your drinking water. This information is readily available on the Internet. Then split up and do research into the danger of each chemical on humans and on the environment. Present your findings to the class.
3. Write an essay in which you argue that not all of the changes made by modern society have caused disastrous effects on the environment but that some might, in fact, have helped the environment.

MARTIN LUTHER KING JR.

I Have a Dream

The Reverend Martin Luther King Jr., civil rights leader and Nobel Peace Prize winner, was born in 1929 in Atlanta, Georgia. He went to traditionally black Morehouse College, where both his father and grandfather had studied. He then attended Crozer Theological Seminary and Boston University, from which he earned his doctorate. King then became a pastor in Montgomery, Alabama, and a member of the National Association for the Advancement of Colored People. He began organizing for the civil rights movement. King believed in nonviolent protest, the technique for civil disobedience he took from Gandhi. He organized major protests all over the South as president of the Southern Christian Leadership Conference, a civil rights group.

King was arrested and assaulted and his house was bombed, but he continued to speak, write, and lead. In the summer of 1963, he directed the March on Washington, in which 250,000 people participated. The emotional and rhetorical culmination of the march was King's "I Have a Dream" speech, printed here, which was immediately recognized as one of the major speeches in American history. King's work ended in 1968, when he was assassinated in Memphis, Tennessee, but the legacy of this speech—which blends brilliantly the emotional rhythms of religious oratory and allusions to American guarantees of freedom—stands as one of his greatest achievements. As you read, pay close attention to how King is able to manipulate his audience emotionally with a strong rational argument.

1   I am happy to join with you today in what will go down in history as the greatest demonstration for freedom in the history of our nation.

2   Fivescore years ago, a great American, in whose symbolic shadow we stand today, signed the Emancipation Proclamation. This momentous decree came as a great beacon light of hope to millions of Negro slaves who had been seared in the flames of withering injustice. It came as a joyous daybreak to end the long night of their captivity.

3   But one hundred years later, the Negro still is not free; one hundred years later, the life of the Negro is still sadly crippled by the manacles of segregation and the chains of discrimination; one hundred years later, the Negro lives on a lonely island of poverty in the midst of a vast ocean of material prosperity; one hundred years later, the Negro is still languishing in the corners of American society and finds himself in exile in his own land.

4   So we've come here today to dramatize a shameful condition. In a sense we've come to our nation's capital to cash a check. When the architects of our republic wrote the magnificent words of the Constitution and the Declaration of Independence, they were signing a promissory note to which every American was to fall heir. This note was the promise that all men, yes, black men as well as white men, would be guaranteed the unalienable rights of life, liberty, and the pursuit of happiness.

5   It is obvious today that America has defaulted on this promissory note in so far as her citizens of color are concerned. Instead of honoring this sacred obligation, America has given the Negro people a bad check; a check which has come back marked "insufficient funds." We refuse to believe that there are insufficient funds in the great vaults of opportunity of this nation. And so we've come to cash this check, a check that will give us upon demand the riches of freedom and the security of justice.

We have also come to this hallowed spot to remind America of the   6
fierce urgency of now. This is no time to engage in the luxury of cooling off
or to take the tranquilizing drug of gradualism. Now is the time to make
real the promises of democracy; now is the time to rise from the dark and
desolate valley of segregation to the sunlit path of racial justice; now is the
time to lift our nation from the quicksands of racial injustice to the solid
rock of brotherhood; now is the time to make justice a reality for all God's
children. It would be fatal for the nation to overlook the urgency of the
moment. This sweltering summer of the Negro's legitimate discontent will
not pass until there is an invigorating autumn of freedom and equality.

Nineteen sixty-three is not an end, but a beginning. And those who   7
hope that the Negro needed to blow off steam and will now be content,
will have a rude awakening if the nation returns to business as usual.

There will be neither rest nor tranquility in America until the Negro is   8
granted his citizenship rights. The whirlwinds of revolt will continue to
shake the foundations of our nation until the bright day of justice emerges.

But there is something that I must say to my people who stand on the   9
warm threshold which leads into the palace of justice. In the process of
gaining our rightful place we must not be guilty of wrongful deeds.

Let us not seek to satisfy our thirst for freedom by drinking from the   10
cup of bitterness and hatred. We must forever conduct our struggle on the
high plane of dignity and discipline. We must not allow our creative
protest to degenerate into physical violence. Again and again we must
rise to the majestic heights of meeting physical force with soul force.

The marvelous new militancy which has engulfed the Negro commu-   11
nity must not lead us to a distrust of all white people, for many of our
white brothers, as evidenced by their presence here today, have come to
realize that their destiny is tied up with our destiny and they have come
to realize that their freedom is inextricably bound to our freedom. This offense we share mounted to storm the battlements of injustice must be carried forth by a biracial army. We cannot walk alone.

And as we walk, we must make the pledge that we shall always   12
march ahead. We cannot turn back. There are those who are asking the
devotees of civil rights, "When will you be satisfied?" We can never be
satisfied as long as the Negro is the victim of the unspeakable horrors of
police brutality.

We can never be satisfied as long as our bodies, heavy with fatigue of   13
travel, cannot gain lodging in the motels of the highways and the hotels
of the cities. We cannot be satisfied as long as the Negro's basic mobility is
from a smaller ghetto to a larger one.

We can never be satisfied as long as our children are stripped of their   14
self-hood and robbed of their dignity by signs stating "for whites only."
We cannot be satisfied as long as a Negro in Mississippi cannot vote and a
Negro in New York believes he has nothing for which to vote. No, we are

not satisfied, and we will not be satisfied until justice rolls down like waters and righteousness like a mighty stream.

15   I am not unmindful that some of you have come here out of excessive trials and tribulation. Some of you have come fresh from narrow jail cells. Some of you have come from areas where your quest for freedom left you battered by the storms of persecution and staggered by the winds of police brutality. You have been the veterans of creative suffering. Continue to work with the faith that unearned suffering is redemptive.

16   Go back to Mississippi; go back to Alabama; go back to South Carolina; go back to Georgia; go back to Louisiana; go back to the slums and ghettos of the northern cities, knowing that somehow this situation can, and will be changed. Let us not wallow in the valley of despair.

17   So I say to you, my friends, that even though we must face the difficulties of today and tomorrow, I still have a dream. It is a dream deeply rooted in the American dream that one day this nation will rise up and live out the true meaning of its creed—we hold these truths to be self-evident, that all men are created equal.

18   I have a dream that one day on the red hills of Georgia, sons of former slaves and sons of former slave-owners will be able to sit down together at the table of brotherhood.

19   I have a dream that one day, even the state of Mississippi, a state sweltering with the heat of injustice, sweltering with the heat of oppression, will be transformed into an oasis of freedom and justice.

20   I have a dream my four little children will one day live in a nation where they will not be judged by the color of their skin but by the content of their character. I have a dream today!

21   I have a dream that one day, down in Alabama, with its vicious racists, with its governor having his lips dripping with the words of interposition and nullification, that one day, right there in Alabama, little black boys and black girls will be able to join hands with little white boys and white girls as sisters and brothers. I have a dream today!

22   I have a dream that one day every valley shall be exalted, every hill and mountain shall be made low, the rough places shall be made plain, and the crooked places shall be made straight and the glory of the Lord will be revealed and all flesh shall see it together.

23   This is our hope. This is the faith that I go back to the South with.

24   With this faith we will be able to hear out of the mountain of despair a stone of hope. With this faith we will be able to transform the jangling discords of our nation into a beautiful symphony of brotherhood.

25   With this faith we will be able to work together, to pray together, to struggle together, to go to jail together, to stand up for freedom together, knowing that we will be free one day. This will be the day when all of God's children will be able to sing with new meaning—"my country 'tis of thee; sweet land of liberty; of thee I sing; land where my fathers died,

land of the pilgrims' pride; from every mountain side, let freedom ring"—and if America is to be a great nation, this must become true.

So let freedom ring from the prodigious hilltops of New Hampshire.   26

Let freedom ring from the mighty mountains of New York.   27

Let freedom ring from the heightening Alleghenies of Pennsylvania.   28

Let freedom ring from the snow-capped Rockies of Colorado.   29

Let freedom ring from the curvaceous slopes of California.   30

But not only that.   31

Let freedom ring from Stone Mountain of Georgia.   32

Let freedom ring from Lookout Mountain of Tennessee.   33

Let freedom ring from every hill and molehill of Mississippi, from   34
every mountainside, let freedom ring.

And when we allow freedom to ring, when we let it ring from every   35
village and hamlet, from every state and city, we will be able to speed up that day when all of God's children—black men and white men, Jews and Gentiles, Catholics and Protestants—will be able to join hands and to sing in the words of the old Negro spiritual, "Free at last, free at last; thank God Almighty, we are free at last."

Responding to the Essay

1. In his introduction, King echoes another great speech, Lincoln's Gettysburg Address. Compare and contrast the arguments in those two speeches.
2. King uses many different metaphors and similes. Which are the strongest? The weakest? Do you think he has too many different ones, or does his strategy work? Defend your answers.
3. King's essay makes use of religious and biblical speech. How does his speech actually use references and phrases from the Bible, and where does his speech just carry the cadences and rhythms of biblical rhetoric? How does repetition figure in his technique?
4. How effective is King's ending? Why does he end on a quote from an old Negro spiritual?
5. King subscribed to the protest technique of nonviolence, and he spent considerable time convincing people to remain nonviolent in the face of great abuse. How can we reconcile his ideas of nonviolence with his language in paragraph 5? Explain.

Responding in Writing

1. Do some research to discover what led King, in his life, to the point at which he came to make a speech before 200,000 people on the Mall in Washington, D.C.
2. More than 40 years have passed since King delivered his speech at the March on Washington. In groups, discuss whether King's hopes

and his dream have been fulfilled. Write your answers down, and compare them with the answers of the other groups.

3. The King family holds the copyright to the "I Have a Dream" speech. Investigate the various battles they have waged with people and companies they thought were infringing on the copyright. Write an essay in which you either defend the King family's action or in which you argue that the speech is the property of the entire country, as it was delivered during a massive public event.

4. Seek out an audio file or video of King delivering the "I Have a Dream" speech. Write an essay that contrasts experiencing the speech visually or aurally and reading it.

Part Five

A Casebook of Arguments
on Americans' Eating Habits:
Are We What We Eat?

People today work more hours than ever before. They rush from school to work to home to school again. Families used to eat together at home, but today there frequently is nobody to stay at home to cook wholesome, nutritious, and healthy meals. Instead, we grab whatever we can on the run and eat on our way to school or work, on the street, or in our cars.

What is more convenient than fast food? As we get busier, McDonald's, Burger King, and other fast-food chains get busier and busier too. But these restaurants aren't serving carrot and celery sticks. They serve red meat and fried food—high-calorie, high-carbohydrate, high-fat meals that taste good.

Americans face a public health crisis. Heart disease is the number one cause of death in the country, and a disturbing percentage of Americans are morbidly obese. Obviously there is some connection between fast-food restaurants and Americans' unhealthy eating habits—but who is at fault? Obese customers have filed lawsuits against the fast-food companies, which, they feel, are responsible for their health problems. Are companies so adept at marketing and making their food so attractive that Americans cannot resist? Is it the lack of time available and the lack of quick, healthful food? Or are the overweight to blame for their own actions? And, of course, in the media, everyone is slim, and glamorous. How does that situation affect how we eat?

The selections in this casebook provide multiple perspectives on these issues. Paul Rozin and Andrew B. Geier, in "Want Fewer Fries with That?" argue that all the subtle little signals we get from our eating environment are causing the obesity epidemic in this country, and that if we get better cues, we'll be healthier. Shannon Brownlee, in "We're Fatter but Not Smarter," sees the problem in growing portion sizes (as opposed to the portion sizes eaten by the relatively thin French, who eat fatty foods in small amounts). David Zinczenko, in "Don't Blame the Eater," also blames the companies, arguing that children are particularly susceptible to their misrepresentations. Adam Cohen, in "The McNugget of Truth in the Lawsuits Against Fast-Food Restaurants," argues that restaurants ignore these lawsuits at their own peril. Sometimes writers use satire to get their point across. Jonathan Rauch, in "The Fat Tax," proposes that the government penalize overweight people for every pound they gain. Michele Ingrassia wonders why it seems that black girls are more comfortable with their bodies than white girls in "The Body of the Beholder." Jay Walljasper, in "The Joy of Eating," takes a more leisurely journey through the problems of how Americans are alienated from their food and sees some hope in the organic arm of the environmentalist movement. Ellen Goodman, in "The Culture of Thin Bites Fiji," and Dawn Mackeen, in "Waifs on the Web," take more journalistic looks at two phenomena: an island nation formally obsessed with gaining weight and a subculture of young girls in America who are obsessed with losing weight at any cost.

As you read these essays, pay attention to how the writers use their reported facts to make their points.

PAUL ROZIN AND ANDREW B. GEIER
Want Fewer Fries with That?

Paul Rozin and Andrew B. Geier are in the psychology department at the University of Pennsylvania. Rozin, a professor of psychology, received his undergraduate degree from the University of Chicago in 1956 and his Ph.D. in biology and psychology from Harvard University in 1961. He has taught at the University of Pennsylvania since 1963 and has done a great deal of research on the cultural significance of food. Geier received his B.A. from Yale University in 2003 and is finishing his Ph.D. in experimental clinical psychology. He does research in issues related to eating disorders and patterns. In this essay, published in the April 6, 2007, issue of the Chronicle of Higher Education, *Rozin and Geier argue that the "so-called obesity epidemic could be halted by minor changes in the eating environment," by which they mean a culture of health in general and smaller portion sizes at restaurants in particular.*

O n a flight from Philadelphia to Chicago that one of us took some time   1
ago, a full lunch was served at 4 p.m. Six of the nine passengers in sight ate all of it. Simply put, it was there. And in a study conducted with people who have amnesia, and who therefore cannot remember that they have just eaten, the subjects consumed second and even third lunches when the food was offered.

In short, whether or not we are physiologically hungry, when we are   2
served food, we eat it—usually in its entirety. It may be hard to understand how a species that behaves in such a way could have survived over hundreds of thousands of years. The answer is that until recently humans did not live in an environment in which palatable food appeared out of nowhere. People had to expend effort to get food. That meant they did not become overweight.

But in the modern developed world, our food environment has been   3
turned upside down. In our ancestors' world, food was scarce and required effort to obtain. Now it is plentiful, tasty, cheap, and accessible with minimal effort. Furthermore, we now have an enormous variety of choices, and variety encourages intake. And the menu includes "super foods," developed through millennia of cultural advances and modern food technology. Chocolate is a prime example: Nothing in nature provides the sweetness, fatty texture, appealing aroma, and calorie density that a piece of chocolate delivers.

4   It is an irony of eating that one has to expend energy, in foraging for food, in order to gain energy. Animals are designed to spend the least amount of energy possible to get the maximum energy from eating. They are optimal foragers, or energy misers. That holds for precultural humans as well.

5   There is no doubt that a food-regulation system exists in humans. It has been demonstrated in the laboratory, and it is revealed by the fact that, even with food readily available, many people keep their weight relatively constant for years without monitoring how much they weigh.

6   But in the developed world, food has become so palatable and so accessible, and requires so little energy to find and eat, that our natural regulation system is overwhelmed. Scientists have shown the same effect in rats when they are exposed in cages to abundant amounts of very appealing food.

7   Enter obesity. To our own peril, we can now succeed at what we evolved to do: Take in energy while expending virtually none.

8   In the last decade or so, a number of psychologists, nutritionists, and physiologists—including Kelly D. Brownell of Yale, James O. Hill of the University of Colorado, David A. Levitsky and Brian C. Wansink of Cornell, Marion Nestle of New York University, Barbara J. Rolls of Pennsylvania State University, and our group—have come to the conclusion that, in the developed world, increasing obesity can be attributed primarily to the environment in which we live and eat.

9   It is remarkable how even small environmental changes can lead to large increases in weight, as most changes occur over and over: every meal, every day, every year. An increase in food intake of simply one apple a day, for a year, with everything else constant, will lead to an increase in weight of about eight pounds a year. On the other hand, walking an extra block a day for a year, with everything else constant, will produce a weight loss of about five pounds a year.

10   American adults gained about 1.4 pounds a year over the 10-year period from 1991 to 2000. That amounts to eating less than an extra quarter of an apple a day, holding other consumption and the level of energy expenditure constant. Thus the undeniable increase in obesity in the developed world could actually be eliminated by very small changes in habits or the environment. The so-called obesity epidemic need not be thought of as a deep sickness in modern society, but rather an undesirable trend that could be altered with modest changes, like replacing one sugared soft drink a day with a diet soda, or parking a block farther from the office.

11   American suburban life—with the car next to the door; remote-controlled appliances; the almost continuous availability of high-calorie, palatable snacks; the shift from daily food acquisition to a weekly trip to the supermarket; and ever-increasing portion sizes—encourages energy imbalance.

Does it have to be that way? The answer is clearly no. Perhaps the   12
best illustration of that is another wealthy, developed country: France.
The French are much less fat than Americans—according to recent figures
from the World Health Organization and the U.S. Centers for Disease
Control and Prevention, 8 percent of French adults qualify as obese, compared with about 31 percent of Americans.

Obviously that is not because French food is unappealing. Nor can it   13
be because French food is lower in calories. In fact, the French diet has a
higher percentage of total fat and saturated fat than the American diet. So
how do the French do it? Our group, in collaboration with Claude Fis-
chler, of France's National Center for Scientific Research, has found several interesting points.

One is that although the French spend more time eating each day   14
than Americans do, they have fewer eating occasions. Almost all of their
eating occurs at two meals—extended lunches and dinners.

In addition, the French pay more attention to the experience of eat-   15
ing—the taste and feel of the food in their mouths—than to the consequences of eating for their arteries and waistlines, and as a result feel less
ambivalence about food than Americans do. The French eat more fat than
we do, and they enjoy their food more.

But although eating fewer snacks helps to limit calorie intake, neither   16
longer meals nor greater unadulterated pleasure in eating can explain
why the French are thinner.

To understand the smaller French waistline, we have to appreciate a   17
fundamental French-American difference. The French prize moderation
in consumption, and quality in their diet. There are very few, if any, all-
you-can-eat restaurants in France.

Americans put more emphasis on abundance and quantity; love and   18
caring are expressed by offering a lot of food, as much as by providing
high-quality food. Just consider our most famous holiday meal, Thanksgiving dinner—the success of which is gauged by how stuffed the guests
are afterward.

It is also likely that the French expend more energy in an average day   19
than do Americans. French people have fewer energy-saving gadgets,
and most of them live in an environment where it is easier to shop for
food and other goods on foot than by car, with many local bakers, butchers, and greengrocers easily accessible.

One reason for the lower French body weight that we have been in-   20
vestigating is portion size: The French serve less food at meals than
Americans do, and hence they eat less. Even McDonald's in Paris serves
less, with the same menu items containing fewer calories—for instance,
there are fewer fries in a serving and fewer ounces in a large soda. The
same is true at pizzerias, Chinese restaurants, and other fast-food empori-
ums in France.

21   In addition, food in supermarkets that comes in individual portions, such as single-serving yogurt cups, has fewer calories. When we compared supermarkets, we found that the most common yogurt sizes in Paris and Philadelphia are 127 and 225 grams, respectively. Even French fruits are smaller, so when a French person and an American eat an apricot, the French person consumes fewer calories.

22   Many investigators have shown, in the laboratory or at eating establishments, that people eat less when they are offered smaller portions—even when they can have second helpings.

23   That is a remarkable fact. If the French ate two yogurt containers, or two apricots, they would lose the advantage they gain from small portion sizes. What stops them from doing that?

24   Basically, consumption norms, ideas about what is a proper portion, are responsible. People commonly assume that a proper portion of something of at least modest size is one. It is OK to eat a very large sandwich—say, a 12-inch submarine—but odd to eat two 6-inch ones.

25   In a 2006 article with Gheorghe Doros in *Psychological Science*, we named that phenomenon "unit bias." We demonstrated it in a number of ways. For instance, we left pretzels in the lobby of an apartment house as free snacks for the residents. When we offered full pretzels (containing 300 calories each), people consumed 71 percent more calories than when we offered pretzels cut in half. Of course, people could take a second half-pretzel, but most didn't.

26   It is not only the food portion that is subject to unit bias, but also the serving instrument or receptacle: the size of the glass, plate, or serving spoon. At other times in the same lobby, we left out a big bowl of peanut M&M's with either a tablespoon or a quarter-cup scoop tethered to the bowl. A sign urged individuals to serve themselves as much as they wanted. With the scoop, four times as large as the tablespoon, people took 75 percent more candy. Of course, they could have dipped the tablespoon in repeatedly, but they tended not to do so.

27   One serving seems right. Unit bias therefore suggests that small reductions in portion size would reduce food intake.

28   There are two possible problems with using unit bias to help control weight gain. One is that people might compensate for smaller portions of one food by eating more of something else. However, the evidence from laboratory studies—particularly by Barbara Rolls and her colleagues—and from the lighter weight of the French suggests that people do not completely compensate for reduced portion size.

29   The second is that the metabolism of people who reduce their intake may become more efficient and slow down, so that their weight would not decrease as much as expected. Although increased efficiency at using energy has been shown with long-term and substantial reductions in food intake (as with many diets), there is no evidence that it occurs with very small changes in portion size.

We believe that the so-called obesity epidemic could be halted by mi- 30
nor changes in the eating environment. Reducing the portion sizes of
food sold in supermarkets or served in restaurants by an imperceptible
amount (say, a few percent) would be a good first step.

If food companies and restaurants chose to cut their portion sizes by a 31
small amount and charged the same, they would make a little more
money, people would lose weight, and we would have a slightly healthier
population. That seems to us like an irresistible idea.

Responding to the Essay

1. How effective is the opening? The writers include two pieces of evidence for the proposition "whether we are physiologically hungry,
   when we are served food, we eat it"—one is an anecdote, the other
   the result of a scientific study. How do they work together and sum
   up the rest of the essay's approach? Explain.
2. What is the writers' claim? Where do they state it most clearly? Is it in
   an effective location? Why or why not?
3. This essay appeared in the *Chronicle of Higher Education*, which has an
   audience of professors and other staff at universities and colleges.
   Why do you think that Rozin and Geier published this essay in that
   venue? Can you tell they are speaking to academics? If so, how? If
   not, why not?
4. The writers are psychologists, but they cite other sciences to help support their argument. How many different scientific disciplines do you
   see influencing their argument? Do they mesh well? Why or why
   not?
5. Are the writers critical of the United States, or do they display caring
   and love? Explain your answer.
6. How effective is the writers' closing? Why do they end with a recapitulation of the claim?

Responding in Writing

1. The writers explain that we evolved to expend the least amount of
   energy to gather as much food as possible, and now we can just go to
   the grocery store. Write a few paragraphs about other aspects of our
   lifestyles in modern America that come into conflict with how *Homo
   sapiens* might have existed before recorded history.
2. Keep close track of everything you eat in a 24-hour period. Then analyze your list. Write an essay relating your experience and what lessons you learned.
3. Write a letter to the board of directors and CEO of your favorite (or
   least favorite) fast-food company, or to the owner of a local restaurant, arguing in specifics how (and why) they might alter their menu,

using Rozin and Geier's suggestions. You may cite their argument in your letter.

SHANNON BROWNLEE
We're Fatter but Not Smarter

Science journalist Shannon Brownlee has written about genetics, cancer research, and public health policy for many publications, including Discover *magazine,* U.S. News & World Report, Time, *the* New York Times, *and the* New Republic. *She is a senior fellow at the New America Foundation. Her book* Overtreated: Why Too Much Medicine Is Making Us Sicker and Poorer *appeared in 2007. In this selection, which appeared in the* Washington Post, *Brownlee takes a look at what many scientists think is the key to the epidemic of obesity in America—out-of-control portion sizes.*

1   It was probably inevitable that one day people would start suing McDonald's for making them fat. That day came last summer, when New York lawyer Samuel Hirsch filed several lawsuits against McDonald's, as well as four other fast-food companies, on the grounds that they had failed to adequately disclose the bad health effects of their menus. One of the suits involves a Bronx teenager who tips the scale at 400 pounds and whose mother, in papers filed in U.S. District Court in Manhattan, said, "I always believed McDonald's food was healthy for my son."

2   Uh-huh. And the tooth fairy really put that dollar under his pillow. But once you've stopped sniggering at our litigious society, remember that it once seemed equally ludicrous that smokers could successfully sue tobacco companies for their addiction to cigarettes. And while nobody is claiming that Big Macs are addictive—at least not yet—the restaurant industry and food packagers have clearly helped give many Americans the roly-poly shape they have today. This is not to say that the folks in the food industry want us to be fat. But make no mistake: When they do well economically, we gain weight.

3   It wasn't always thus. Readers of a certain age can remember a time when a trip to McDonald's seemed like a treat and when a small bag of French fries, a plain burger and a 12-ounce Coke seemed like a full meal. Fast food wasn't any healthier back then; we simply ate a lot less of it.

4   How did today's oversized appetites become the norm? It didn't happen by accident or some inevitable evolutionary process. It was to a large degree the result of consumer manipulation. Fast food's marketing strategies, which make perfect sense from a business perspective, succeed only when they induce a substantial number of us to overeat. To see how this all came about, let's go back to 1983, when John Martin became

CEO of the ailing Taco Bell franchise and met a young marketing whiz named Elliott Bloom.

Using so-called "smart research," a then-new kind of in-depth consumer survey, Bloom had figured out that fast-food franchises were sustained largely by a core group of "heavy users," mostly young, single males, who ate at such restaurants as often as 20 times a month. In fact, 30 percent of Taco Bell's customers accounted for 70 percent of its sales. Through his surveys, Bloom learned what might seem obvious now but wasn't at all clear 20 years ago—these guys ate at fast-food joints because they had absolutely no interest in cooking for themselves and didn't give a rip about the nutritional quality of the food. They didn't even care much about the taste. All that mattered was that it was fast and cheap. Martin figured Taco Bell could capture a bigger share of these hard-core customers by streamlining the food production and pricing main menu items at 49, 59 and 69 cents—well below its competitors.

It worked. Taco Bell saw a dramatic increase in patrons, with no drop in revenue per customer. As Martin told Greg Critser, author of "Fat Land: How Americans Became the Fattest People in the World," when Taco Bell ran a test of its new pricing in Texas, "within seven days of initiating the test, the average check was right back to where it was before—it was just four instead of three items." In other words, cheap food induced people to eat more. Taco Bell's rising sales figures—up 14 percent by 1989 and 12 percent more the next year—forced other fast-food franchises to wake up and smell the burritos. By the late '80s, everybody from Burger King to Wendy's

Brunswick, Maine: Bowdoin College students at dining hall enjoy a meal together.

was cutting prices and seeing an increase in customers—including bargain-seeking Americans who weren't part of that original hardcore group.

7   If the marketing strategy had stopped there, we might not be the nation of fatties that we are today. But the imperatives of the marketplace are growth and rising profits, and once everybody had slashed prices to the bone, the franchises had to look for a new way to satisfy investors.

8   And what they found was . . . super-sizing.

9   Portion sizes had already been creeping upward. As early as 1972, for example, McDonald's introduced its large-size fries (large being a relative term, since at 3.5 ounces the '72 "large" was smaller than a medium serving today). But McDonald's increased portions only reluctantly, because the company's founder, Ray Kroc, didn't like the image of lowbrow, cheap food. If people wanted more French fries, he would say, "they can buy two bags." But price competition had grown so fierce that the only way to keep profits up was to offer bigger and bigger portions. By 1988, McDonald's had introduced a 32-ounce "super size" soda and "super size" fries.

10   The deal with all these enhanced portions is that the customer gets a lot more food for a relatively small increase in price. So just how does that translate into bigger profits? Because the actual food in a fast-food meal is incredibly cheap. For every dollar a quick-service franchiser spends to produce a food item, only 20 cents, on average, goes toward food. The rest is eaten up by expenses such as salaries, packaging, electric bills, insurance and, of course, the ubiquitous advertising that got you in the door or to the drive-through lane in the first place.

11   Here's how it works. Let's say a $1.25 bag of french fries costs $1 to produce. The potatoes, oil and salt account for only 20 cents of the cost. The other 80 cents goes toward all the other expenses. If you add half again as many French fries to the bag and sell it for $1.50, the non-food expenses stay pretty much constant, while the extra food costs the franchise only 10 more pennies. The fast-food joint makes an extra 15 cents in pure profit, and the customer thinks he's getting a good deal. And he would be, if he actually needed the extra food, which he doesn't because the nation is awash in excess calories.

12   That 20 percent rule, by the way, applies to all food products, whether it's a bag of potato chips, the 2,178-calorie mountain of fried seafood at Red Lobster or the 710-calorie slab of dessert at the Cheesecake Factory. Some foods are even less expensive to make. The flakes of your kid's breakfast cereal, for example, account for only 5 percent of the total amount Nabisco or General Mills spent to make and sell them. Soda costs less to produce than any drink except tap water (which nobody seems to drink anymore), thanks to a 1970s invention that cut the expense of making high-fructose corn syrup. There used to be real sugar in Coke; when Coca-Cola and other bottlers switched to high-fructose corn syrup in 1984, they slashed sweetener costs by 20 percent. That's why 7-Eleven can sell the 64-ounce Double Gulp—half a gallon of soda and nearly

600 calories—for only 37 cents more than the 16-ounce, 89-cent regular Gulp. You'd feel ripped off if you bought the smaller size. Who wouldn't?

The final step in the fattening of America was the "upsell," a stroke of genius whose origins are buried somewhere in the annals of marketing. You're already at the counter, you've ordered a cheeseburger value meal for $3.74, and your server says, "Would you like to super-size that for only $4.47?" Such a deal. The chain extracts an extra 73 cents from the customer, and the customer gets an extra 400 calories—bringing the total calorie count to 1,550, more than half the recommended intake for an adult man for an entire day. 13

When confronted with their contribution to America's expanding waistline, restaurateurs and food packagers reply that eating less is a matter of individual responsibility. But that's not how the human stomach works. If you put more food in front of people, they eat more, as studies have consistently shown over the last decade. My personal favorite: The researcher gave moviegoers either a half-gallon or a gallon bucket of popcorn before the show (it was "Payback," with Mel Gibson) and then measured how much they ate when they returned what was left in the containers afterward. Nobody could polish off the entire thing, but subjects ate 44 percent more when given the bigger bucket. 14

The downside, of course, is that 20 years of Big Food has trained us to think that oceanic drinks and gargantuan portions are normal. Indeed, once fast food discovered that big meals meant big profits, everybody from Heineken to Olive Garden to Frito Lay followed suit. Today, says Lisa Young, a nutritionist at New York University, super-sizing has pervaded every segment of the food industry. For her PhD, Young documented the changes in portion sizes for dozens of foods over the past several decades. M&M/Mars, for example, has increased the size of candy bars such as Milky Way and Snickers four times since 1970. Starbucks introduced the 20-ounce "venti" size in 1999 and discontinued its "short" 8-ounce cup. When 22-ounce Heinekens were introduced, Young reported, the company sold 24 million of them the first year, and attributed the sales to the "big-bottle gimmick." Even Lean Cuisine and Weight Watchers now advertise "Hearty Portions" of their diet meals. Everything from plates and muffin tins to restaurant chairs and the cut of our Levi's has expanded to match our growing appetites, and the wonder of it all is not that 60 percent of Americans are overweight or obese, but rather that 40 percent of us are not. 15

Where does it end? Marketers and restaurateurs may scoff at lawsuits like the ones brought this summer against fast-food companies, and they have a point: Adults are ultimately responsible for what they put in their own mouths. But maybe there's hope for us yet, because it looks as if fast-food companies have marketed themselves into a corner. "Omnipresence"—the McDonald's strategy of beating out competitors by opening new stores, sometimes as many as 1,000 a year—"has proved costly and self- 16 cannibalizing," says author Critser. With 13,000 McDonald's units alone, most of America is so saturated with fast food there's practically no place left to put a drive-through lane. Now, fast-food companies are killing each other in a new price war they can't possibly sustain, and McDonald's just suffered its first quarterly loss since the company went public 47 years ago.

17   The obvious direction to go is down, toward what nutritional policy-makers are calling "smart-sizing." Or at least it should be obvious, if food purveyors cared as much about helping Americans slim down as they would have us believe. Instead of urging Americans to "Get Active, Stay Active"—Pepsi Cola's new criticism-deflecting slogan—how about bringing back the 6.5-ounce sodas of the '40s and '50s? Or, imagine, as Critser does, the day when McDonald's advertises Le Petit Mac, made with high-grade beef, a delicious whole-grain bun and hawked by, say, Serena Williams. One way or another, as Americans wake up to the fact that obesity is killing nearly as many citizens as cigarettes are, jumbo burgers and super-size fries will seem like less of a bargain.

Responding to the Essay

1. What is Brownlee's claim? Where is it stated? Is it placed effectively? Why or why not?
2. Analyze Brownlee's use of statistics. Do you find the ones that she chose to be persuasive? Which are most persuasive? Which are the weakest? Defend your answers.
3. Presumably, some of Brownlee's readers are going to be fast-food customers. How does Brownlee make her claim and still ensure that she doesn't make her reader feel bad?
4. Write about Brownlee's use of verbs. How does she use exciting or action verbs to help her argument?
5. What do you think of Brownlee's conclusion and her suggestions for solving the problems she has outlined? Are they sufficient, or do you find yourself hungry for more ideas? Explain.

Responding in Writing

1. In what other areas of business do you see this tendency toward a philosophy of bigger is better? In groups of four or five students, discuss where else in American culture you see this idea spreading. Make an outline for an essay along the lines of "We're Fatter but Not Smarter."
2. Write an essay in which you write a letter to the CEO of a fast-food chain explaining why he or she is singly responsible for the obesity epidemic in the United States and trying to convince him or her to lower portion sizes. Maintain a cordial tone even as you make your accusations.

3. In paragraph 4, Brownlee introduces the idea that the marketing of fast food, even though it causes people to overeat, still makes sense from a business point of view. Write an essay in which you argue that other kinds of marketing and advertising from other industries cause social problems such as obesity.

DAVID ZINCZENKO
Don't Blame the Eater

David Zinczenko, who admits that he was an overweight child, became the editor in chief of Men's Health *at the age of 30. With coauthor Ted Spiker, a faculty member at the University of Florida, Zinczenko wrote* The Abs Diet: 6-Minute Meals for 6-Pack Abs (2006). *In this essay from the* New York Times *in 2002, Zinczenko takes a harsh look at the responsibility that fast-food chains have in adding to the public health crisis of obesity among children.*

If ever there was a newspaper headline custom-made for Jay Leno's   1
monologue, this was it. Kids taking on McDonald's this week, suing the company for making them fat. Isn't that like middle-aged men suing Porsche for making them get speeding tickets? Whatever happened to personal responsibility?

I tend to sympathize with these portly fast-food patrons, though.   2
Maybe that's because I used to be one of them.

I grew up as a typical mid-1980s latchkey kid. My parents were split   3
up, my dad off trying to rebuild his life, my mom working long hours to make the monthly bills. Lunch and dinner, for me, was a daily choice between McDonald's, Taco Bell, Kentucky Fried Chicken or Pizza Hut. Then as now, these were the only available options for an American kid to get an affordable meal. By age 15, I had packed 212 pounds of torpid teenage tallow on my once lanky 5-foot-10 frame.

Then I got lucky. I went to college, joined the Navy Reserves and got   4
involved with a health magazine. I learned how to manage my diet. But most of the teenagers who live, as I once did, on a fast-food diet won't turn their lives around: They've crossed under the golden arches to a likely fate of lifetime obesity. And the problem isn't just theirs—it's all of ours.

Before 1994, diabetes in children was generally caused by a genetic   5
disorder—only about 5 percent of childhood cases were obesity-related, or Type 2, diabetes. Today, according to the National Institutes of Health, Type 2 diabetes accounts for at least 30 percent of all new childhood cases of diabetes in this country.

6   Not surprisingly, money spent to treat diabetes has skyrocketed, too. The Centers for Disease Control and Prevention estimate that diabetes accounted for $2.6 billion in health care costs in 1969. Today's number is an unbelievable $100 billion a year.

7   Shouldn't we know better than to eat two meals a day in fast-food restaurants? That's one argument. But where, exactly, are consumers—particularly teenagers—supposed to find alternatives? Drive down any thoroughfare in America, and I guarantee you'll see one of our country's more than 13,000 McDonald's restaurants. Now, drive back up the block and try to find someplace to buy a grapefruit.

8   Complicating the lack of alternatives is the lack of information about what, exactly, we're consuming. There are no calorie information charts on fast-food packaging, the way there are on grocery items. Advertisements don't carry warning labels the way tobacco ads do. Prepared foods aren't covered under Food and Drug Administration labeling laws. Some fast-food purveyors will provide calorie information on request, but even that can be hard to understand.

9   For example, one company's Web site lists its chicken salad as containing 150 calories; the almonds and noodles that come with it (an additional 190 calories) are listed separately. Add a serving of the 280-calorie dressing, and you've got a healthy lunch alternative that comes in at 620 calories. But that's not all. Read the small print on the back of the dressing packet and you'll realize it actually contains 2.5 servings. If you pour what you've been served, you're suddenly up around 1,040 calories, which is half of the government's recommended daily calorie intake. And that doesn't take into account that 450-calorie super-size Coke.

10   Make fun if you will of these kids launching lawsuits against the fast-food industry, but don't be surprised if you're the next plaintiff. As with the tobacco industry, it may be only a matter of time before state governments begin to see a direct line between the $1 billion that McDonald's and Burger King spend each year on advertising and their own swelling health care costs.

11   And I'd say the industry is vulnerable. Fast-food companies are marketing to children a product with proven health hazards and no warning labels. They would do well to protect themselves, and their customers, by providing the nutrition information people need to make informed choices about their products. Without such warnings, we'll see more sick, obese children and more angry, litigious parents. I say, let the deep-fried chips fall where they may.

Responding to the Essay

1. What is the author's claim? What minor propositions does he offer to back up his claim, and why does he put them in the order he does?

2. What is your opinion of the author's mini-memoir in paragraphs 2 to 4? Do you find it to be an effective way to link the introduction to the rest of the essay? Why or why not?
3. In paragraph 4, the author writes that he "learned to manage my diet." He is arguing, as his title says, not to "blame the eater." Are these two statements contradictory? If not, explain. If so, does he reconcile the statements in the rest of his argument?
4. Analyze the author's conclusion. Is it effective? Why or why not? How well does it wrap up his argument?

Responding in Writing

1. Write an essay called "Don't Blame the . . . ," in which you argue that the responsibility for a problem is not with the actor but with an authority figure. For example, you might write an essay titled "Don't Blame the Downloader" that argues that the fault for people stealing music lies with the music companies.
2. One thing Zinczenko calls for is proper labeling. Do some research about the fight for labeling in this country. Write an essay explaining the history of the present labeling laws and how experts think they have changed how people eat.
3. Divide the class in three groups, and prepare a mock trial. One group will take the side of the defendants, the fast-food companies; one group will take the side of the plaintiffs, the families who are suing the companies; and the last group will act as the jury. The plaintiffs' side should prepare a case against the companies, and the defense should prepare to rebut the arguments they think the plaintiffs will make. The jury should attempt to anticipate both sides' arguments. Your teacher will act as judge. At the end of the trial, the jury will decide the case and, if necessary, award damages.

CAST-A-WAY
Instructions for Stress Diet

There are numerous Internet sites and cable channels dedicated to the funny bone, providing new and old programming designed to make viewers laugh. You can still catch some classic episodes of the naughty cartoon series South Park *if your cable provider offers the channel. And Comedy Central produces a Web site with a number of links to other comedic spots. One excellent site is Cast-a-Way, which offers a joke archive.*

"Instructions for Stress Diet" is a typical selection. How does it provide a humorous sidebar to our problems with weight gain and tantalizing food?

Instructions for Stress Diet

BREAƒKFAST:
- 1/2 grapefruit
- 1 slice whole wheat toast
- 8 oz. skim milk

LUNCH:
- 4 oz. lean broiled chicken breast
- 1 cup steamed spinach
- 1 cup herb tea
- 1 Oreo cookie

MID-AFTERNOON SNACK:
- The rest of Oreos in the package
- 2 pints Rocky Road ice cream nuts, cherries, and whipped cream
- 1 jar hot fudge sauce

DINNER:
- 2 loaves garlic bread
- 4 cans or 1 large pitcher Coke
- 1 large sausage, mushroom, and cheese pizza
- 3 Snickers bars

LATE EVENING NEWS:
- Entire frozen Sara Lee cheesecake (eaten directly from freezer)

RULES FOR THIS DIET:
1. If you eat something and no one sees you eat it, it has no calories.
2. If you drink a diet soda with a candy bar, the calories in the candy bar are canceled out by the diet soda.
3. When you eat with someone else, calories don't count if you do not eat more than they do.
4. Foods used for medicinal purposes NEVER count, such as hot chocolate, brandy, toast, and Sara Lee Cheesecake.
5. If you fatten up everyone else around you, then you look thinner.
6. Movie-related foods do not have additional calories because they are part of the entertainment package and not part of one's personal fuel. (Examples: Milk Duds, buttered popcorn, Junior Mints, Red Hots, and Tootsie Rolls.)
7. Cookie pieces contain no calories. (The process of breaking causes calorie leakage.)
8. Things licked off knives and spoons have no calories if you are in the process of preparing something.
9. Foods that have the same color have the same number of calories. (Examples are: spinach and pistachio ice cream; mushrooms and mashed potatoes.)
10. Chocolate is a universal color and may be substituted for any other food color.
11. Anything consumed while standing has no calories. This is due to gravity and the density of the caloric mass.
12. Anything consumed from someone else's plate has no calories since the calories rightfully belong to the other person and will cling to his/her plate. (We ALL know how calories like to cling!)

Remember, "stressed" spelled backwards is "desserts."

This is a joke, folks!

(www.cast.co.za)

Responding to the Visual Text

1. Explain the assumptions implicit in the presentation of this "diet." What claim or major proposition does this diet present?
2. Where and how does the tone of this text change?
3. How do process analysis and classification bolster the argument?
4. What design elements does the artist use to present this diet?
5. What does the "rules" section of this text contribute to the overall effect?

Responding in Writing

1. In a paragraph or two, analyze the elements that make this text provocative and appealing.
2. Imitate the elements in this visual text and compose your own "Diet for . . ." Aim for a comic effect.

ADAM COHEN

The McNugget of Truth in the Lawsuits Against Fast-Food Restaurants

Adam Cohen is a senior writer for Time, *for which he covers law and politics. He has also written for* Chicago Magazine, Chicago Tribune, *and the* Harvard Law Review, *and is the author of* The Perfect Store: Inside eBay *(2003). He lives in New York. In this editorial, Cohen explores the lawsuits recently being aimed at the fast-food industry and makes some suggestions to the largest of all the chains, McDonald's.*

When McDonald's first rolled out the Chicken McNugget in the 1980's, comedians could always get a laugh by asking, with a leer, just what part of the chicken the McNugget was supposed to be. But thanks to a recent federal court ruling, the composition of the McNugget is no laughing matter.

The Chicken McNugget, a lab experiment of an entree, larded with ingredients like TBHQ, a flavorless "stabilizer," and Dimethylpolysiloxane, an "anti-foaming agent," is Exhibit A in a lawsuit that could transform the fast-food industry. And it is the McNugget's artificiality—the judge labeled it a "McFrankenstein creation"—that is putting McDonald's on the legal defensive.

The showdown over the Chicken McNugget comes in a lawsuit by Ashley Pelman and Jazlyn Bradley, two New York girls who say that McDonald's is to blame for their obesity and health problems. Plaintiffs' lawyers have high hopes. Just as Big Tobacco has been held liable for cancer, they say, Big Food should pay for hypertension, diabetes, and heart disease.

With obesity costing Americans an estimated $117 billion in 2000—and on its way, according to the surgeon general, to causing as much preventable disease and death as cigarettes—the damage awards could be enormous.

4   Critics of the suit call it litigation run amok. The Center for Consumer Freedom, a food and beverage trade group, has taken out ads showing a man with a paunch and the caption: "Did you hear the one about the fat guy suing the restaurants? It's no joke." An industry spokesman has thrown the blame right back on customers, saying that "anyone with an I.Q. higher than room temperature will understand that excessive consumption of food served in fast-food restaurants will lead to weight gain." And the media have largely joined in the skepticism, coining a new word along the way—McScapegoat.

5   Fast-food litigation has been greeted coolly so far because it appears to run up against a core American value: personal responsibility. Judge Robert Sweet, who is hearing the Pelman suit, dismissed it earlier this month for just this reason. If customers know the risks, he held, "they cannot blame McDonald's if they, nonetheless, choose to satiate their appetite with a surfeit of supersized McDonald's products."

6   If Judge Sweet had stopped there, it would have been a happy day in McDonaldland. But the reason Pelman v. McDonald's Corp. may yet be a problem is that the judge went on to explain how the plaintiffs could fix their suit, and gave them time to do it. The key, he said, is to focus on the fact that customers may not have a reasonable chance to learn what they are getting into when they eat at McDonald's.

7   Judge Sweet didn't absolve fast-food customers of the need for self-restraint. Instead, he grounded the case in a basic doctrine of tort law: that certain products may be unreasonably dangerous because they contain items that are "outside the reasonable contemplation of the consuming public." In other words, it is O.K. to sell unhealthy food. But when an item is substantially less healthy than it appears, a seller may be held liable for the resulting harm.

8   Judge Sweet offered up, by way of example, Chicken McNuggets. "Rather than being merely chicken fried in a pan," he wrote, they are "a McFrankenstein creation of various elements not utilized by the home cook." His decision listed 30 or 40 ingredients other than chicken, and noted that although chicken is regarded as healthier than beef, Chicken McNuggets are actually far fattier. "It is at least a question of fact," he held, whether a reasonable consumer would know that a McNugget "contained so many ingredients other than chicken and provided twice the fat of a hamburger."

9   The Pelman plaintiffs may be able to find other, similarly misleading products. McDonald's suffered a legal setback last year when it paid $10 million to settle a class action by Hindus and vegetarians who sued because McDonald's had failed to disclose that even after its widely publicized switch to vegetable oil, it was still using beef in its fries.

Fully understanding McDonald's food can be difficult even with   10
more straightforward items. Consumers who go to the McDonald's Web
site might be confused to find that its "nutrition facts" chart for beverages
contains the calories only for small beverages, a size rarely encountered
in real life. (A downloadable "nutrient card" elsewhere on the site contains more complete data.)

McDonald's argues that the plaintiffs have only themselves to blame,   11
since everyone knows that the highly processed food they serve is less
healthy than normal food. And its Congressional allies are introducing a
bill to insulate fast-food restaurants from suits of this kind.

But the company's stance bucks two key trends in American life—   ·12
healthy eating and corporate transparency. McDonald's would position itself better in the fast-food market if it communicated more
openly with its customers about what they were getting. A good start
would be to listen to consumer advocates and post calorie content on
menu boards.

Better still, McDonald's should ramp up its fitful efforts to make its   13
food more nutritious. The Pelman plaintiffs have plainly identified a
problem. With obesity at epidemic levels—more than 60 percent of adults
are now overweight or obese—McDonald's is doing real harm by promoting "'extra value meals" that contain three-quarters of the calories an
adult needs for a full day.

The news that it could be legally liable could hardly have come at a   14
worse time for the company, which has just suffered the first quarterly
loss in its history. If the McFrankenstein lawsuits start to win, McDonald's may find that it truly has created a monster.

Responding to the Essay

1. Analyze how Cohen uses the Chicken McNugget to lead into his essay. Does he do this successfully? Explain your answer.
2. How does Cohen use syllogistic reasoning in this essay? Trace his argument from the end of his introductory section to his conclusion.
3. Cohen offers surprising facts to his reader to help make his case. Analyze how he does this. Which facts are most surprising? Explain.
4. Does Cohen successfully prepare the reader for his claim? Explain
your answer fully.

Responding in Writing

1. Find some advertisements for fast-food restaurants in a magazine or
newspaper, or watch some on television. Write a description of at
least three different advertisements, and bring them to class. In small
groups, discuss and contrast how the ads represent (or misrepresent)
their products.

2. On the Internet, get the nutritional information for popular meals from two separate fast-food restaurants. Write an essay in which you compare and analyze the nutritional content of the meals. How are they contributing to obesity? (Cohen mentions that accessibility to this information is a crucial part of a possible lawsuit against the companies. As a part of your essay, describe how easy or difficult it was to find the information.)
3. Write an essay in which you compare and contrast Cohen's argument with Brownlee's. What is similar about their arguments? What is different?

GREASE

Food sales depend to a large degree on advertising and on brand recognition, and the fast-food industry regularly places ads and coupons for discounts in daily and weekly periodicals and flyers. McDonald's, the fast-food giant, has an advantage over competitors because it has a familiar "spokesperson," the happy, smiling, clown Ronald McDonald. Of course, not everyone is happy with McDonald's products. The following spoof advertisement, which appears in the Web site adbusters.org., takes a satirical look at Ronald McDonald and the products he promotes.

Responding to the Visual Text

1. If you had to state a proposition that suggests the argument of this spoof ad, what would it be?
2. How does the illustration question the wisdom of consuming any McDonald's product?
3. How does the illustration rely on popular brand recognition to achieve its effect?
4. Advertisements often contain language designed to reinforce the visual impact of the images they present. Why is language (aside from the one word taped over Ronald McDonald's mouth) unnecessary in this ad? Why does this one word sum up the ad's claim?
5. How might this ad contribute, or not contribute, to what a lawsuit against McDonald's—as explained in the essay by Adam Cohen on page 439—alleges as the company's blame for obesity and other health problems of those who buy the company's products? How might Ronald McDonald be perceived as a "McFrankenstein creation," as the judge in the McDonald's lawsuit dubbed Chicken McNuggets?
6. Consider one product that Ronald McDonald promotes—the breakfast sandwich of eggs, cheese, and meat known as "McGriddles." A sausage, egg, and cheese McGriddles contains 450 calories, 270 calories of which come from fat; 30 grams of fat in total, which is 40 percent of the daily value of fat; and 20 mg of cholesterol. (This information appears on the McDonald's Web site, www.mcdonalds.com.) What does this information tell you about the value and attraction of the product? Why doesn't McDonald's print this information in its advertisements?

Responding in Writing

1. In your journal, write your own spoof advertisement for a particular food product, in which you use enticing but satirical language to get people to buy it. You may use a product currently on the market or invent one.
2. Write a letter to junior high school students advising them either to buy or not buy a particular fast-food product. State the proposition clearly enough for your audience to understand, and back up your proposition with appropriate supporting details. You can research many of these products on their Web sites.
3. Write an essay in which you argue that the fast-food industry either is or is not to blame in part for the current high rate of obesity in America.

JONATHAN RAUCH
The Fat Tax: A Modest Proposal

Jonathan Rauch was born in Phoenix, Arizona, in 1960. He attended Yale University before starting his career as a reporter and writer at the Winston-Salem Journal *in North Carolina. Rauch moved to Washington in 1984 for a stint as a staff writer for* National Journal. *He has written freelance for many magazines and newspapers on political and cultural issues, and since 1991 he has worked as an openly gay writer discussing gay issues. He is the author of* The Outnation *(1992),* Kindly Inquisitors *(1993),* Government's End: Why Washington Stopped Working *(1999), and, most recently* Gay Marriage: Why It Is Good for Gays, Good for Straights, and Good for America *(2004). He currently writes a biweekly column for the* National Journal. *In this selection, which appeared in the* Atlantic Monthly, *Rauch proposes— seriously or not?—that the government should levy a tax on fatty food.*

1   In September, McDonald's announced plans to cook its fries in healthier oil. And not a moment too soon. Just a few days later the Centers for Disease Control and Prevention announced that in 2000 (the latest year for which final figures are available) the death rate in America, adjusted for the fact that the population is aging, reached an all-time low. Not only that, but life expectancy reached an all-time high, of about seventy-seven years. Obviously, those numbers can mean only one thing: America is in the grip of a gigantic public-health crisis. To wit—an obesity epidemic!

2   That America is marching fatward seems not to be in doubt. Obesity has risen substantially, in recent years, to 31 percent of adults, according to the most recent data from the National Center for Health Statistics. Soft-drink cups are bigger, restaurant portions are larger, and health campaigns condemning fatty foods have persuaded people, wrongly, that they can eat twice as much bread as before, provided that they cut down on the butter. Also not in doubt is that other things being equal, being blubbery is not good. Still, one cannot help scratching one's head. If Americans are living longer, and if they are dying less (so to speak), and if, as the CDC reports, the proportion rating their own health as excellent or very good has remained at a solid 69 percent for the past five years, what exactly is the problem?

3   Call me oversensitive, but I think I detect a hint of snobbery in the national anti-fat drive. More than occasionally I read things like a recent article from the online *Bully Magazine*, which was headlined "AMERICA: LAND OF THE FAT, DRUNKEN SLOBS." The author, one Ken Wohlrob, writes, "We're quickly becoming a society of sloths who spend their free hours driving around in SUVs and staring at televisions or computer monitors . . . Goddamn, as if we need more fat, bloated people in America." Do I sniff a trace of condescension here? In the September issue of *The*

Atlantic a letter writer named Ken Weiss pointedly (and wrongly) mentioned that "more than 50 percent of our population is obese" amid a list of ways in which America is inferior to Europe, beginning with our shorter vacations, continuing through our lack of a national health plan, and ending, inevitably, with our "polluting SUVs." It's not just that Americans are fat, apparently. It's that Americans are the kind of people who *would* be fat, in the kind of country that would encourage their piggishness.

What is to be done? The letters pages of magazines are often good   4
places to preview the great bad ideas of tomorrow, and recently three letters in *The New Republic* offered a peek. The first, co-signed by the executive director of the Center for Science in the Public Interest and an academic nutritionist, said that the government should "slap small taxes on junk foods like soft drinks" to generate money for public-health campaigns. The next letter, from someone with the Center for the Advancement of Public Health, in Washington, D.C., said, "No one is suggesting the creation of a refrigerator police, but so long as the government is spending $360 billion per year at the federal level on health through Medicare, Medicaid, and the Children's Health Insurance Program, the government's interest in trying to prevent needless illness and death from obesity is kind of simple." The third letter came from a professor of public-interest law who wrote that he had helped to sue McDonald's for "failing to disclose the fat content of its French fries." He warned that more such suits could be on the way. "As with smoking," he wrote, "health advocates may increasingly be forced"—forced?—"to turn to the courts if legislatures continue to do little or nothing about the problem."

If obesity really is such a big crisis, I want to suggest a different approach, because the ones above seem deficient. For one thing, snack taxes that pay for public-health campaigns, and lawsuits against food companies, seem pretty likely to fatten the wallets of the people advocating them—public-health activists and lawyers—without necessarily making anyone any thinner. Besides, most people snack sensibly, so why should they pay to harangue lazy gluttons? And I know of no conclusive evidence that people are fat because food companies fail to disclose that fries and bacon cheeseburgers are fattening.   5

It seems to me that the only honest and effective way to confront this   6
issue is to tax not fattening foods or fattening companies but fat people. It is they, after all, who drive up the government's health-care costs, so it is they who should pay. What I propose, then, is to tax people by the pound.

This needn't be very complicated. Fat-tax rates would be set by a National Avoirdupois Governing System (NAGS). To hit the worst offenders the hardest, the tax could be graduated. People would pay one per-pound rate above the "overweight" threshold, and a stiffer rate above the "obese" threshold. Fat people might not like this tax, but of course they could avoid it by becoming thinner.   7

8   In fact, I might go further. Carrots often work even better than sticks, so I propose a skinny subsidy to complement the fat tax. People who maintain trim, firm physiques should be rewarded for their public-spiritedness with large tax credits—funded, of course, by the fat tax.

9   My plan would address the nation's fat epidemic equitably and efficiently. It would make Americans put their money where their mouths are. And did I mention that I weigh 135 pounds?

Responding to the Essay

1. Analyze Rauch's introduction. How does it use irony to introduce the reader to the essay's rhetorical strategy? Is he successful in this or not? Explain.
2. The subtitle for Rauch's essay is "A Modest Proposal." How does this essay relate to Swift's essay of the same name? How is Rauch's argument similar to Swift's? How is it different?
3. Does Rauch's essay have coherence? Outline his essay, and explain how he uses transitions to move from one minor proposition to the next. Does his argument work? Explain your answer.
4. Does Rauch take too long getting to his "modest proposal"? Why or why not?

Responding in Writing

1. Rauch writes in paragraph 4 that "the letters pages of magazines are often good places to preview the great bad ideas of tomorrow." Look at the letters page of a major political magazine or newspaper, and read the letters about a controversial topic. Is Rauch right? What did you find? Write up your findings in several paragraphs.
2. Write a modest proposal essay in which you ironically argue for a ridiculous solution to a serious problem.
3. Rauch is being ironic about a fat tax, but the government does place taxes on things, and gives tax breaks on other things, in order to influence behavior in a way it thinks is good for the country. In small groups, investigate how the government tries to manipulate the populace through the use of creative taxation.

ROZ CHAST
Trick or Treat

The New Yorker *is perhaps the last bastion among national magazine publishers in its dedication to wry, sophisticated cartoons, usually with an unmistakable urban cast. Each week, in addition to the urbane essays, stories, and sumptuous advertisements that are regular features of the publication,*

readers await the many pen-and-ink drawings by commentators who provide a slightly perverse mirror to human foibles. Roz Chast is one of the New Yorker's *most popular and most frequent contributors to this visual medium. In "Trick or Treat" she implies the grand contrast between expectation and fulfillment as Halloween urchins make their neighborhood visits. In addition, she offers an ironic view of America's eating habits.*

Responding to the Visual Text

1. Who are the characters in the cartoon? Describe them. What familiar American occasion does the cartoon mark?
2. What assumptions does Chast build on here? What major proposition does the cartoon imply?
3. Why are the neighbors offering the children broccoli and lentil salad? What's wrong with this contribution to the trick-or-treaters?

4. What do you think the children expected when they rang the doorbell? How do you think the children feel when they receive their goodies? Why does Chast not show the children's faces? If she did, what expressions do you think they would wear?
5. What is the basic argument that Chast seems to be making here? What assumptions does she build on? What major proposition does the image imply? What warrants does Chast build on?
6. How does the cartoon help explain the success of fast-food outlets like McDonald's, Baskin and Robbins, and Pizza Hut?

Responding in Writing

1. Write a paragraph or two about the relationship between the foods kids crave and the foods that are good for them.
2. Write an essay about trick-or-treating in which you either support it or condemn it. State your major proposition clearly, and provide substantive support for your argument.

Michele Ingrassia
The Body of the Beholder

Michele Ingrassia has been a reporter for the local New York newspapers the Daily News *and* Newsday *and is now a general editor at* Newsweek, *covering family matters. In this selection, which appeared in* Newsweek, *Ingrassia argues, based on a university study, that while white girls seem to be dissatisfied with their bodies, black girls seem to like theirs.*

1   When you're a teenage girl, there's no place to hide. Certainly not in gym class, where the shorts are short, the T shirts revealing and the adolescent critics eager to dissect every flaw. Yet out on the hardwood gym floors at Morgan Park High, a largely African-American school on Chicago's Southwest Side, the girls aren't talking about how bad their bodies are, but how good. Sure, all of them compete to see how many sit-ups they can do—Janet Jackson's washboard stomach is their model. But ask Diane Howard about weight, and the African-American senior, who carries 133 pounds on her 5-foot 7½-inch frame, says she'd happily add 15 pounds—if she could ensure they'd land on her hips. Or La'Taria Stokes, a stoutly built junior who takes it as high praise when boys remark, "Your hips are screaming for twins!" "I know I'm fat," La'Taria says. "I don't care."

2   In a society that worships at the altar of supermodels like Claudia, Christy and Kate, white teenagers are obsessed with staying thin. But there's growing evidence that black and white girls view their bodies in

dramatically different ways. The latest findings come in a study to be published in the journal *Human Organization* this spring by a team of black and white researchers at the University of Arizona. While 90 percent of the white junior-high and high-school girls studied voiced dissatisfaction with their weight, 70 percent of African-American teens were satisfied with their bodies.

In fact, even significantly overweight black teens described themselves as happy. That confidence may not carry over to other areas of black teens' lives, but the study suggests that, at least here, it's a lifelong source of pride. Asked to describe women as they age, two thirds of the black teens said they get more beautiful, and many cited their mothers as examples. White girls responded that their mothers may have been beautiful—back in their youth. Says anthropologist Mimi Nichter, one of the study's coauthors, "In white culture, the window of beauty is so small."

What is beauty? White teens defined perfection as 5 feet 7 and 100 to 110 pounds—superwaif Kate Moss's vital stats. African-American girls described the perfect size in more attainable terms—full hips, thick thighs, the sort of proportions about which Hammer ("Pumps and a Bump") and Sir Mix-Alot ("Baby Got Back") rap poetic. But they said that true beauty—"looking good"—is about more than size. Almost two thirds of the black teens defined beauty as "the right attitude."

The disparity in body images isn't just in kids' heads. It's reflected in fashion magazines, in ads, and it's out there, on TV, every Thursday night. On NBC, the sitcom "Friends" stars Courteney Cox, Jennifer Aniston and Lisa Kudrow, all of them white and twentysomething, classically beautiful and reed thin. Meanwhile, Fox Television's "Living Single," aimed at an African-American audience, projects a less Hollywood ideal—its stars are four twentysomething black women whose bodies are, well, *real.* Especially the big-boned, bronze-haired rapper Queen Latifah, whose size only adds to her magnetism. During a break at the Lite Nites program at the Harlem YMCA, over the squeal of sneakers on the basketball court, Brandy Wood, 14, describes Queen Latifah's appeal: "What I like about her is the way she wears her hair and the color in it and the clothes she wears."

Underlying the beauty gap are 200 years of cultural differences. "In white, middle-class America, part of the great American Dream of making it is to be able to make yourself over," says Nichter. "In the black community, there is the reality that you might not move up the ladder as easily. As one girl put it, you have to be realistic—if you think negatively about yourself, you won't get anywhere." It's no accident that Barbie has long embodied a white-adolescent ideal—in the early days, she came with her own scale (set at 110) and her own diet guide ("How to Lose Weight: Don't Eat"). Even in this postfeminist era, Barbie's tight-is-right message is stronger than ever. Before kindergarten, researchers say, white girls know that Daddy eats and Mommy diets. By high school, many have split the world into physical haves and have-nots, rivals across the beauty line. "It's not that you hate them [perfect girls]," says Sarah Immel, a junior at Evanston Township High School north of Chicago. "It's that you're kind of jealous that they have it so easy, that they're so perfect-looking."

7   In the black community, size isn't debated, it's taken for granted—a sign, some say, that after decades of preaching black-is-beautiful, black parents and educators have gotten across the message of self-respect. Indeed, black teens grow up equating a full figure with health and fertility. Black women's magazines tend to tout NOT TRYING TO BE SIZE 8, not TEN TIPS FOR THIN THIGHS. And even girls who fit the white ideal aren't necessarily comfortable there. Supermodel Tyra Banks recalls how, in high school in Los Angeles, she was the envy of her white girlfriends. "They would tell me, 'Oh, Tyra, you look so good'," says Banks. "But I was like, 'I want a booty and thighs like my black girl-friends'."

8   Men send some of the strongest signals. What's fat? "You got to be *real* fat for me to notice," says Muhammad Latif, a Harlem 15-year-old. White girls follow what they *think* guys want, whether guys want it or not. Sprawled across the well-worn sofas and hard-back chairs of the student lounge, boys at Evanston High scoff at the girls' idealization of Kate Moss. "Sickly," they say, "gross." Sixteen-year-old Trevis Milton, a blond swimmer, has no interest in dating Kate wanna-bes. "I don't want to feel like I'm going to break them." Here, perfection is a hardbody, like Linda Hamilton in "Terminator II." "It's not so much about eating broccoli and water as running," says senior Kevin Mack.

9   And if hardbodies are hot, girls often need to diet to achieve them, too. According to the Arizona study, which was funded by the National Institute of Child Health and Human Development, 62 percent of the white girls reported dieting at least once in the past year. Even those who say they'd rather be fit than thin get caught up. Sarah Martin, 16, a junior at Evanston, confesses she's tried forcing herself to throw up but couldn't. She's still frustrated: "I have a big appetite, and I feel so guilty when I eat."

10   Black teens don't usually go to such extremes. Anorexia and bulimia are relatively minor problems among African-American girls. And though 51 percent of the black teens in the study said they'd dieted in the last year, follow-up interviews showed that far fewer were on sustained weight-and-exercise programs. Indeed, 64 percent of the black girls thought it was better to be "a little" overweight than underweight. And while they agreed that "very overweight" girls should diet, they defined that as someone who "takes up two seats on the bus."

11   The black image of beauty may seem saner, but it's not necessarily healthy. Black women don't obsess on size, but they do worry about other white cultural ideals that black men value. "We look at Heather Locklear and see the long hair and the fair, pure skin," says *Essence* magazine senior editor Pamela Johnson. More troubling, the acceptance

of fat means many girls ignore the real dangers of obesity. Dieting costs money—even if it's not a fancy commercial program; fruits, vegetables and lean meats are pricier than high-fat foods. Exercise? Only one state—Illinois—requires daily physical education for every kid. Anyway, as black teenagers complain, exercise can ruin your hair—and, if you're plunking down $35 a week at the hairdresser, you don't want to sweat out your 'do in the gym. "I don't think we should obsess about weight and fitness, but there is a middle ground," says the well-toned black actress Jada Pinkett. Maybe that's where Queen Latifah meets Kate Moss.

Responding to the Essay

1. Who is Ingrassia's audience, in your opinion? What is her tone, and how does her audience affect the tone? Explain your answers.
2. Analyze how Ingrassia uses contrast analysis to make her argument. Is she successful? Explain.
3. Do you agree with Ingrassia's conclusions? If so, what is the one element that makes her argument so persuasive? If not, what keeps you from agreeing with her?
4. Does Ingrassia end her essay on a satisfying note? Why or why not?

Responding in Writing

1. In groups, listen to the song "Baby Got Back" by Sir Mix-A-Lot, and read along with the lyrics, which you can find on the Internet. Discuss the lyrics as an illustration of what Ingrassia argues for in her essay. How do the lyrics contribute to a healthy body image, and how do they hurt? When you are finished, reconvene as a class and discuss your responses.
2. Write an essay in which you argue that it is not a good thing to be satisfied with a body image that allows young people to be overweight.
3. Write an essay in which you explore the body images of two other classes of people. Instead of black and white girls, what about black and white boys, or men? How do Japanese women feel about their bodies as opposed to Chinese women? Do West Indian women feel different from African-American women?

Jay Walljasper
The Joy of Eating

This selection appeared in the 2002 issue of the Utne Reader, *where Walljasper was the editor at large. He is executive editor at* Ode *magazine and the author of* The Great Neighborhood Book *(2007). In this selection he explores the paradox that being responsible and paying attention to food can take the fun out of eating, but he argues that it doesn't have to be the case.*

1   One of the great joys for my wife, Julie, and me is watching our 7-year-old eat. He approaches a plate of food with something like awe. A smile breaks across his face and questions fly across the kitchen: What's this called? How do you cook that? Why are those potatoes yellow and not brown? If he senses we're not looking, he will surreptitiously grab a handful of vegetables or noodles to explore their texture and temperature.

2   Soren happily chows down with no thought of calories, carcinogens, grocery bills, fat grams, E. coli, or genetically modified ingredients. His only real concerns at the dinner table are that something may be too spicy or, even more tragically, that we might have forgotten dessert.

3   Dining with Soren offers a glimpse of Eden, remembrance of a time when we assumed that everything on our fork was wholesome. This has always been childhood's state of grace, and it was shared by most American adults until sometime in the 1970s. It may have been cyclamates, a carcinogen lurking in every can of diet cola until the FDA banned it. Or the publication of Frances Moore Lappe's Diet for a Small Planet, which indicted meat-eating as a waste of valuable food resources that heightens world hunger. Or maybe it was just our collective belly expanding a little more every year. But over the past three decades, Americans have become ever more wary of what they eat. Now we talk about cheesecake and pork chops in hushed tones once reserved for oral sex and hashish.

4   The simple act of breaking bread has become a complicated matter of personal health, humanitarian concern, political commitment, and public safety. That's one reason it's so much fun to watch Soren eat. For him, food is about tasting good and filling up, not a thrice-daily symposium on medical and moral issues. It's not surprising that many Americans are sick and tired of thinking about everything they put in their mouths. "Damn the tofu and oatmeal and skim milk," they declare, "I'm going to enjoy a double bacon cheeseburger with extra mayo, a supersize order of fries, and a bucket of Coke." Burp!

5   And we can see the results all around us—in rural landscapes overrun by factory farms, in food and water laced with chemicals, in the cardiac unit and cancer ward of a hospital near you.

6   Like it or not, what we eat has consequences for us and for the world. Dinner is not something that just magically appears on our plates. In ordering a burger or making a salad, we are inextricably linked to the land, cycles of rain and sunshine, farmers and farmworkers, compost or chemicals, processing facilities and slaughterhouses, truck drivers and miles of highway, co-ops or corporations, and a whole web of ecological and human activity.

7   "You are what you eat. We all know that old motto," notes Mark Ritchie, a longtime food activist who is president of the Minneapolis-based Institute for Agriculture and Trade Policy. "But now we know that what you eat dramatically affects the well-being of many others—human, animal and otherwise."

The system that delivers food to our table is far different from the   8
days when Farmer Brown trucked his sweet corn, pears, and eggs to
town. It's changed radically over the past 25 years as family farms have
been displaced by huge operations that depend on intensive chemical
use, minimum-wage workers, and industrial facilities such as animal confinement buildings. This same period has also seen the rise of the natural
food business, offering us healthier and more environmentally sustainable alternatives to practically everything in the supermarket aisles.

"Eating is the most intimate relationship we have with the environ-   9
ment," explains Andrew Kimbrell, executive director of the Washington-
based Center for Food Safety, which coordinates the Organic & Beyond
campaign, and the editor of a compelling new book, *Fatal Harvest: The
Tragedy of Industrial Agriculture* (Island Press, 2002). "Three times a day,
it's how we can re-create the world. We can shape a different future for
our children, for farmworkers, the landscape, wildlife, villages around
the world, and genetic diversity."

"We all want to do the responsible thing," Kimbrell continues. "Who   10
wants to be cruel to animals and poison the soil? But what's great is that
being responsible also means better health and better-tasting food you
can enjoy with a greater sense of joy."

The joy of eating! That's what everyone seeks at mealtime. Soren   11
exudes it every time he tears into a a platter of pancakes. Joy is the
much-advertised promise hawked by fast-food chains and frozen dinner
manufacturers. And it's the point of the obligatory picnic scene in almost every foreign movie and food magazine: a long table under a
canopy of trees, laden with fresh-from-the-garden delights and plentiful
wine, surrounded by several generations of smiling people engaged in
robust conversation.

Cooking and eating good food are the cornerstones of human civi-   12
lization, our daily reward for all the hard work and innumerable difficulties of life. I have a favorite story that I've heard quoted numerous times.
There was once an extensive study of National Merit Scholars to find the
common denominator in these bright kids' upbringing. Turns out it
wasn't household income, private schools, parents' educational levels, or
wealthy neighborhoods. It was families who ate their meals together.

Just as the American farm has been transformed in recent years, so   13
has dinnertime. Joy is out of the picture in many (if not most) households,
where time-pressed people wolf down microwaved dinners or swing
through drive-up windows. Breaking bread has become refueling, and
it's often a solitary activity since everyone around the house is ruled by a
hectic schedule. No wonder we cherish movies like Chocolat, Babette's
Feast, and Like Water for Chocolate, and that corporations pour millions
into ads artistically trying to convince us that Velveeta and Kentucky
Fried Chicken are pure, unadulterated fun. The joy of eating has, in many
ways, become a vicarious thrill.

14   That's the real reason—not warnings from killjoy nutritionists and activists—that mealtime now feels unsatisfying to so many of us. Though we're loading up on calories, we are starved for ritual and leisure and pleasure. Thinking too much about what we eat is not what robs us of happy meals, but rather putting too little thought into the important role that food plays in our lives and in the wider world.

15   Don't despair (or head to Taco Bell to drown your sorrows in baja sauce), there's also good news from food's frontlines. In the same way the natural food business sprouted as an alternative to industrialized agriculture and junk food, a new movement has arisen to put the joy back into eating. Beginning with Alice Waters' Chez Panisse restaurant in Berkeley, which, inspired by peasant food traditions around the world, put a premium on fresh, local ingredients, there's been a growing appreciation for authentic, healthy food. The newfound popularity of regional cuisine, the growth of farmers' markets and community-supported agriculture (CSAs), and the happy emergence (or in some cases re-emergence) of microbrew beers, artisan cheeses, traditional breads, all-natural meats, and heirloom fruits and vegetables amount to a culinary revolution.

16   While the quest for tastier food is what drives these trends, they square with most environmental and ethical concerns. Fresh organic produce from local farmers not only improves a meal, it prevents pollution, saves fuel, and boosts your local economy. Dairy and meat from free-ranging animals that have not been force-fed antibiotics are both tastier and healthier. (There is no ethical consensus, however, on using animals for food. Vegetarians and vegans argue that killing animals is cruel no matter how humanely they were raised, while meat eaters note that carnivorism is a fact of nature and that manure from livestock is essential in most methods of organic farming.)

17   The organic label has now become familiar to us, but Jim Slama, president of Sustain, a Chicago-based environmental advocacy organization, says that's just the beginning. Slama envisions a time when you will be able to know the story of what happened to food on its way to your plate. Beyond the organic label ensuring that your food was raised without chemicals, irradiation, genetically modified ingredients, or toxic sludge, a "fair trade" label will certify that the people producing it were treated and paid well, and a "regional" label will let you know where it comes from. Sustain has launched an organic local foods initiative in Chicago. This is also the theme of the Organic & Beyond campaign (www.organic andbeyond.org), a coalition of grassroots groups that includes Sustain.

18   While some folks might view such a project as more reasons to feel guilty over lunch, it actually offers the chance for a richer connection with our food, a way to put meaning back into our meals. Sure, you probably don't want to know the story behind a serving of factory farm meat: an animal stuffed into a tiny cage, living in its own excrement (which is then

flushed into a stream), pumped with antibiotics, slaughtered by a poorly paid worker in a factory notorious for on-the-job injuries, doused in a chemical bath, and then shipped to a faraway supermarket or fast-food joint. Maybe you don't want to know about all this, but it will affect your health, your environment, and the social fabric of your country.

But what if that animal was raised on a farm in your region, perhaps   19 by Farmer Brown's great-granddaughter, and you could see it from the highway grazing in a pasture instead of the ugly confinement buildings that now dot the countryside? And what if your milk and butter came from a small organic co-op, and a lot of your vegetables from the backyard or an old gardener named Tony (or Rosita or Mr. Nguyen), with whom you talk about baseball and the weather every Saturday at the Farmers' Market? Would you feel different cooking it and eating it? Would you mind paying a little more for it, knowing that it was good for you and good for other people too?

Soren remains the joy-of-eating authority around our house. Al-   20 though he doesn't labor over the ethical dimension of every bite he takes (the direct link between the cute piglets he plays with at his cousin Leah's farm and the beloved corn dogs he orders at his favorite neighborhood grill is still hazy for him), he does like to know the story behind his food. We found this out last year when we joined a new CSA run by friends, Don and Joni. Every week all summer we'd get a heaping box of greens, herbs, peppers, and vegetables along with organic eggs Don and Joni brought from one of their country neighbors. On Labor Day, we drove out to the farm to help with the harvest. Julie and I volunteered to weed the tomato patch while Soren was pressed into service picking vegetables. After a while, he ran over dragging a heavy pail. "Mommy, Daddy, look at these cucumbers," he sang, holding one above his head as if it were a championship trophy. "I picked them myself!"

And for the next week, Soren jubilantly ate cucumbers at every meal,   21 including breakfast.

Responding to the Essay

1. What is Walljasper's major proposition in this essay? Where is it located? Is it in an effective place? Why or why not? Why does Walljasper place his major proposition where he does?
2. What is the rhetorical effect of Walljasper's discussion of his son Soren? Is it a strength of the paper or a weakness? Explain your answer.
3. Take a look at the transitions in this paper. Find instances where the transitions are weak. Where are they, and how would you change them?
4. Analyze Walljasper's argument in paragraphs 18 and 19. Do you think it is effective or not? Explain.

5. Do you think Walljasper's essay is realistic, or is he being overly sentimental and idealistic? Defend your answer.

Responding in Writing

1. Read a chapter from Eric Schlosser's book *Fast Food Nation.* Write about how your chosen selection from Schlosser's book illustrates Walljasper's claims.
2. How easy is it to find socially responsible ways of eating in your neighborhood? Are they difficult to find? In groups, answer these questions, and come up with ways to tip the balance in favor of the socially responsible.
3. Write an essay called "The Joy of . . ." Argue for a different point of view of a common activity, such as sleeping or travel.

Weight Loss Guide

The Internet has innumerable sites dedicated to dietary programs and ways to take off weight rapidly through a variety of methods, including food plans, exercise regimens, and diet supplements. This Web site (see the following pages) is one example of the options made available to an American public eager to address the struggle with weight gain that is so much a part of the national obsession with food, calories, diets, and obesity.

Responding to the Visual Text

1. How do you "read" this advertisement? What details hold your attention? How do written and visual texts combine to create the persuasive appeal of this Internet ad?
2. Explain the ways in which this ad touches on people's values, attitudes, fears, and aspirations. What social and cultural codes of meaning underlie the design?
3. What is the effect of including multiple links to other sites in this advertisement?
4. Why does Emma Classen personalize the message? How effective is this strategy, and why?

Responding in Writing

1. Write a complete analysis of this Internet advertisement. Explain how the various details and visual elements create a message that might appeal to a viewer who, after all, is a prospective buyer.
2. Search online for other diet advertisements. Download your favorite ad, and attach it to an essay explaining why you find it effective.

WeightLoss *guide*

Hi! I'm Emma Classen. Over the years I've helped thousands of people just like you lose thousands of unwanted pounds—and keep them off...including many who felt it was utterly impossible. I want to be YOUR Guide...to show you how you too can get that smashing, sexy, new body you envision - without risk to your health. Please read my story

Your Guide - Emma Classen

read my story

The Multi-Purpose Metabolic Marvel

Eat Less - Burn More Fat - Lose Weight - Automatically!

The guiding principle behind weight reduction is for everyone to reduce their caloric intake and do a little exercise. Right? Well, why as a society we're not all thin and perfectly shaped? Because we can't keep our appetites in check. No matter how hard we try we just can't stop eating.

It is this key factor that is most responsible for the growing popularity and phenomenal success of the new "fat-melting pill" that works better than risky prescription drugs to subdue your appetite, invigorate your mind-body-and-spirit, and transform your mood from crappy to happy.

MeltRx 24 Ultra™—It's not magic, it's Science

This smart, ephedra-free, "fast-slimming pill" that achieves remarkable feats without use of caffeine or harmful stimulants is called MeltRx 24 Ultra™. With its special blend of natural herbs formulated in an expensive and exacting procedure it has accomplished the unthinkable. Worried about living without your favorite foods? Don't. Imagine MeltRx 24 Ultra™ as the brakes on your car you need to prevent unwanted mishaps.

When you take MeltRx 24 Ultra™ it literally flips your hunger switch on demand so you feel turned off by food and just don't want to eat. You reduce calories and you slim down automatically. Besides, MeltRx 24 Ultra™ creates a separate afterburner-like effect that fires-up your fat-burning engine causing significant, undeniable weight loss! The result -- you liberate yourself from obsessing over food, you supercharge and prolong your body's natural fat burning capabilities, and you lose weight without dieting or counting calories. What's more, the vast majority of users not only lose weight, but report they look younger, have improved drive and concentration, and become free of stress and anxiety. Don't believe it? Well... published scientific studies don't lie.

Groundbreaking Studies Prove The Phenomenal Success

Results never before seen in the diet supplement industry. In several recent double-blind studies (the only proof accepted by the established scientific community) several MeltRx 24 Ultra™ key ingredients were put to the test. People who took each and every one of the key ingredients in MeltRx Ultra™ lost significant weight. Those who didn't lost absolutely nothing. The primary difference between losing weight and staying fat were the new cutting-edge ingredients in MeltRx 24 Ultra™. What's more, those who continued taking them kept the weight off for more than 12 months with no bounce-back rebound weight gain and no effort. This means, No more guessing! No more wasting your valuable time!

How Does MeltRx 24 Ultra™ Work? (Incredible energy • Fast weight loss • No ephedrine • No caffeine)

While still not entirely clear, researchers say the behavior-controlling chemicals governing appetite, mood and weight loss interact in complex patterns of stimulation and inhibition sometimes leading to discomfort, craving, anxiety and impaired fat burning capability. However, if you ask the thousands upon thousands of overweight men and women who have already used MeltRx 24 Ultra, you get a crystal-clear, straight-forward answer. "Take MeltRx 24 Ultra™ twice daily and you lose weight because you automatically eat less, burn fat, and marshal incredible energy throughout the entire day." It's that simple.

(www.weightlossguide.com)

✓ **Risk-Free, Introductory Offer**

By reading my Newsletter and accepting me as your Guide you've shown that you trust me. And believe me, I take that trust very seriously. Above all, I want the products and supplements I recommend to work for you. But the only way I can be sure you'll try them and discover their benefits is if there is absolutely no risk to you. That's what my "Ultimate Guarantee" is all about: Your 100% satisfaction. Think of it as a contract, a handshake between us that binds my reputation as a Guide to your weight loss success. It's just my way of saying: "I'm sure this product is safe and effective, and that it will help you.

So order new MeltRx 24 Ultra™ fat-melting pills today and take advantage of my risk-free, introductory offer. Simply stated, if you use MeltRx 24 Ultra™ fat-melting pills and do not experience the same fast, significant, effortless weight loss experienced by thousands of delighted users, just return the empty bottle within 30 days for a full, prompt, no-questions-asked refund.

Remember, MeltRx 24 Ultra™ is guaranteed to work for you or it costs you absolutely nothing! Finally, it's your chance to get everything you ever wanted out of a diet pill -- fast reliable weight loss, incredible energy, a blissful contented mood, a lean ultra-firm body, and the magnetic self-confidence you've always wanted. Get fast acting MeltRx 24 Ultra™ "Super Pills" today. You will not be disappointed - I guarantee it.

All the best,

Ellasen

Picture Perfect Proof
Mrs. Holmes lost **104 lbs**
and she looks TERRIFIC.
Click the picture to see
for yourself.

Emma Classen -- Guide & Editor
Weight Loss Guide.Com

P.S. Benefits of MeltRx 24 Ultra (3 in 1) fat burner: appetite suppressant • energizer • mood enhancer •

- Puts you in the driver's seat -- New MeltRx 24 Ultra™ flips your hunger switch on demand so you just don't want to eat. Result - caloric intake is reduced... fat disappears automatically.
- Fires-up your fat-burning engine (without ephedra) causing significant, undeniable weight loss!
- Accomplishes the unthinkable -- burn fat, subdue appetite & alleviate stress all at once!
- Made in America according to strict FDA guidelines
- Gives you incredible energy. Transforms your mood from crappy to happy!

■ Order Online (see below)	■ Call 800.701.4556 to order by phone	■ Order by Mail

New MeltRx™ 24 Ultra 100 Caps
(2X2 caps Daily)

CONTAINS
NO EPHEDRA
Testimonials
Frequently Asked Questions

List price ~~$79.95~~

◉ **Special price $54.00**

○ **Best Value** $39.95 per bottle (3 Pack) Save over 50% off list price

[ADD TO CART]

View Ingredients

*NOTE: MeltRX™ 24 Ultra comes with our full **30-day No-Nonsense** Money-Back Guarantee.

consider this -
The best way to get something done...is to begin!

ELLEN GOODMAN
The Culture of Thin Bites Fiji

Ellen Goodman is a Pulitzer Prize–winning editor and journalist who started out as a researcher at Newsweek. *She has written a column at the* Boston Globe *for many years. She is the author of* Turning Points *(1979) and of several collections of her columns, including* Keeping in Touch *(1985),* Making Sense *(1989), and* Value Judgments *(1993). In this selection from her column, Goodman argues that "going thin" is a cultural phenomenon.*

First of all, imagine a place women greet one another at the market   1
with open arms, loving smiles, and a cheerful exchange of ritual
compliments:

"You look wonderful! You've put on weight!"   2

Does that sound like dialogue from Fat Fantasyland? Or a skit from   3
fat-is-a-feminist-issue satire? Well, this Western fantasy was a South Pa-
cific fact of life. In Fiji, before 1995, big was beautiful and bigger was more
beautiful—and people really did flatter one another with exclamations
about weight gain.

In this island paradise, food was not only love, it was a cultural im-   4
perative. Eating and overeating were rites of mutual hospitality. Everyone worried about losing weight—but not the way we do. "Going thin"
was considered to be a sign of some social problem, a worrisome indication the person wasn't getting enough to eat.

The Fijians were, to be sure, a bit obsessed with food; they prescribed   5
herbs to stimulate the appetite. They were a reverse image of our culture.
And that turns out to be the point.

Something happened in 1995. A Western mirror was shoved into the   6
face of the Fijians. Television came to the island. Suddenly, the girls of rural coastal villages were watching the girls of "Melrose Place" and "Beverly Hills 90210," not to mention "Seinfeld" and "E.R."

Within 38 months, the number of teenagers at risk for eating disorders   7
more than doubled to 29 percent. The number of high school girls who
vomited for weight control went up five times to 15 percent. Worse yet,
74 percent of the Fiji teens in the study said they felt "too big or fat" at least
some of the time and 62 percent said they had dieted in the past month.

This before-and-after television portrait of a body image takeover   8
was drawn by Anne Becker, an anthropologist and psychiatrist who di-
rects research at the Harvard Eating Disorders Center. She presented her
research at the American Psychiatric Association last week with all the
usual caveats. No, you cannot prove a direct causal link between television and eating disorders. Heather Locklear doesn't cause anorexia. Nor
does Tori Spelling cause bulimia.

Calista Flockhart at the Screen Actors Guild
Awards, *Boston Globe.*

9   Fiji is not just a Fat Paradise Lost. It's an economy in transition from subsistence agriculture to tourism and its entry into the global economy has threatened many old values.

10   Nevertheless, you don't get a much better lab experiment than this. In just 38 months, and with only one channel, a television-free culture that defined a fat person as robust has become a television culture that sees robust as, well, repulsive.

11   All that and these islanders didn't even get "Ally McBeal."

12   "Going thin" is no longer a social disease but the perceived requirement for getting a good job, nice clothes, and fancy cars. As Becker says carefully, "The acute and constant bombardment of certain images in the media are apparently quite influential in how teens experience their bodies."

13   Speaking of Fiji teenagers in a way that sounds all-too familiar, she adds, "We have a set of vulnerable teens consuming television. There's a huge disparity between what they see on television and what they look like themselves—that goes not only to clothing, hairstyles, and skin color, but size of bodies."

In short, the sum of Western culture, the big success story of our en-   14
tertainment industry, is our ability to export insecurity: We can make any
woman anywhere feel perfectly rotten about her shape. At this rate, we
owe the islanders at least one year of the ample lawyer Camryn Manheim
in "The Practice" for free.

I'm not surprised by research showing that eating disorders are a cul-   15
tural byproduct. We've watched the female image shrink down to Calista
Flockhart at the same time we've seen eating problems grow. But Hollywood hasn't been exactly eager to acknowledge the connection between
image and illness.

Over the past few weeks since the Columbine High massacre, we've   16
broken through some denial about violence as a teaching tool. It's pretty
clear that boys are literally learning how to hate and harm others.

Maybe we ought to worry a little more about what girls learn: To hate   17
and harm themselves.

Responding to the Essay

1. Do you think Goodman's title matches this essay? Why or why not?
   Think of two alternate titles.
2. How does Goodman use contrast analysis in her essay, and is it effectively done? Explain your answers.
3. Trace Goodman's reasoning throughout the essay? How does she
   build toward the end?
4. Why does Goodman include paragraph 9? What purpose does it
   serve in the argument?
5. What is the rhetorical effect of Goodman's mention of the Columbine
   massacre? Do you see it as a weakness or a strength in her argument?
   Explain.

Responding in Writing

1. Write an essay in which you take issue with Goodman's conclusions,
   arguing that it's a good thing that Fijians are concerned about their
   weight.
2. Find some women's magazines from 1999 (the year this essay was
   published) in the library and some from today. What conclusions can
   you draw about how the image of women has changed in such a
   short time?
3. In small groups, discuss what social problems other than teenage violence and obesity one could blame on the influence of television.
   Write down notes on your discussion, and present your conclusions
   to the class.

DAWN MACKEEN
Waifs on the Web

Dawn Mackeen has been an editor at online magazine Salon, *an on-air reporter for a television station in Madison, Wisconsin, a guidebook writer for* Fodor's/The Berkeley Guides, *and is now a staff writer for Long Island, New York, newspaper* Newsday. *She was a Pew International Journalism Fellow in 2002. In this selection from* Teen People, *Mackeen writes about an online subculture of young women with dangerous eating disorders.*

1   For three days last December, Abbey, 18, subsisted mostly on water. When hunger pangs began to plague her, she simply gulped a little more liquid. Although the 5'6", 115-pound college freshman from Plano, Texas, was achieving her goal—to lose weight as quickly as possible—her body was clearly suffering. On the third day, Abbey (who didn't want her full name used) lay awake in the middle of the night panting uncontrollably, her heart racing. Concerned about what was happening to her, she turned to an online support group. Maybe what she was feeling was normal. This was, after all, the first time she had ever tried starving herself.

2   "I can't see straight, I can't really hear well, and worst of all, I can't catch my breath," she posted on the Pro-Eating Disorder Society's Web site at around midnight. "Has anyone ever experienced these effects, and will they go away?"

3   The response came hours later. "Yeah, I get that sometimes when I've been fasting," wrote someone seemingly well-versed in hunger. "The best thing to do is eat an apple, drink a glass of water and go to sleep. Your body is a little exhausted, that's all." Reassured, Abbey never sought medical attention, nor did she tell anyone else about her scare. "The apple comment made me feel like someone had an answer," she says.

4   What Abbey didn't know is that her body was more than just "a little exhausted." In someone who is fasting, a speeding heart can be a sign of real danger: Severe fasting and dehydration can cause abnormal heart patterns and even cardiac arrest, a condition responsible for many of the anorexia-related deaths each year. Abbey's body was telling her it was in trouble, but her online cheerleaders were telling her she was doing fine—and that's who Abbey believed.

5   It's this dynamic that has eating-disorder experts worried about the recent popularity of secretive, girl-run "thinspirational" Web sites and e-groups with names like Voice of Anorexia, Anorexic Nation and the Pro-Eating Disorder Society. Catering to "Anas" (after America's estimated 8 million who suffer from anorexia and other eating disorders), the sites are havens where girls cybergather to hash out their problems or listen in on discussions about body obsessions and the best ways to avoid prying family members. "What I do to hide it . . . is complain about my teeth being

too sore [because of my braces]," writes Sally The Veggie Stick when asked how she disguises the disease from her mother. "Hi, I'm new to the list," chimes in one participant in the e-group Never Thin Enough. "I am almost 5'10" and I weigh 115. Of course . . . my goal is to weigh around 88."

From there, it's on to discussions of how well laxatives and over-the-counter weight-loss supplements work, sign-ups for group fasts, advice on how to curb hunger (one poster recommends looking at photos of dead, bloody animals) and tips such as eating cotton sprinkled with salt instead of food. In one posting a girl details her exercise schedule for the day—aerobics at 9 A.M., Pilates at 10 A.M. and running in the evening—and urges others to work as hard. Many sites also post something called the Anorexic Creed: ". . . I believe in calorie counters as the inspired word of God and memorize them accordingly. I believe in bathroom scales as an indicator of my daily successes and failures . . ."   6

"With the pro-anorexia sites, you don't feel like people are going to be judging you," says Liz, a high school senior from Oak Park, Ill. "There are people who just want to lose weight, and there are people who want to be underweight. But everyone is supported in reaching their goal." Liz admits she used to frequent anorexia-recovery sites but left because she felt pressured to, well, recover.   7

It's no wonder, then, that therapists, doctors and activists are worried, and some suspect that these sites are increasing the incidence of eating disorders. (Abbey, for example, had never fasted before, but after hearing about the dangers of such sites on *The Oprah Winfrey Show,* she went searching for them. Now she logs on every day and wants to shed 15 pounds to get down to 100.) As a result, after media reports and the National Association of Anorexia Nervosa and Associated Disorders (ANAD) outed the sites last summer, ANAD asked Yahoo to review them. According to a Yahoo spokesman, many of the sites violated the company's online rules of conduct and were removed.   8

More determined than ever to protect their private communities, the Anas responded by going underground, hiding their discussions under headings such as "duct tape" or "allergy" and deleting the word "Ana" from their site descriptions so that search engines cannot easily find them. To weed out curious interlopers, some sites now use entry questionnaires, cherry-picking members who are serious about starvation. Any visitors to the sites who disagree with the Ana philosophy aren't welcome. "Everyone deserves a place where they can feel safe and accepted," wrote a 14-year-old on the Yahoo e-group Anabeauty. "We do not want you ruining what is for many of us the only place we can feel comfortable. This is a sanctuary. Would you go into a church and speak against God? Get the hell out of our place of worship."   9

"[The sites] make me feel pretty helpless," admits Daniel le Grange, Ph.D., director of the University of Chicago's Eating Disorders Program, adding that their covert nature "just reinforces the secretive tendency of   10 anorexics," leaving therapists and doctors at a loss to help patients they can't even find, let alone talk to.

11   Consequently, the burden of spreading the scary truth has fallen to recovering anorexics like Ashley Jaros, 17, who has made it her mission to alert the pro-Anas to the dangers of the disease. "It makes me so furious," says the Redding, Calif., native. "If people try fasting, they will get sucked in. I was never fat to begin with. It was, 'I'll just lose a little weight.' Then I kept going down." At the depths of her illness, Ashley, who is 5'9", weighed just 93 pounds. She stopped menstruating, became suicidal and was hospitalized for a month. Ashley is thankful she didn't know about the sites when she was anorexic—everything she did to lose weight she thought of on her own—and wonders if access to more dangerous diet tricks would have kept her from recovering, or even led to her death. "With anorexia, your everyday life is taken away from you," she says.

12   Abbey in Texas knows that anorexia is taking over her life and that she's on the verge of a serious illness. Unfortunately, knowing that doesn't necessarily mean stopping the behavior. She still turns to the Anas for advice, but unlike others on the sites who chat like old friends, she makes no pretense about the kinds of relationships she is forming there. "I've met some nice girls, but they're not my friends," Abbey says. "These people are helping me starve. I was talking to this one girl and I said something like, 'It's weird that we're basically helping each other starve'. She was like, 'Yeah, I know.' They call it fasting and they use all these PC terms, but it's really starving."

Responding to the Essay

1. What is Mackeen's major proposition? Does she explicitly state it? Why or why not, and how does your answer have to do with Mackeen's projected audience?
2. How does Mackeen use quotes to help her argument? Explain your answer fully.
3. Explain how Mackeen uses shocking facts and images. Does this help or harm her argument? Explain.
4. What is the rhetorical effect of Mackeen's conclusion? How does it achieve that effect?

Responding in Writing

1. Parents used to tell their children who did not want to eat a particular food that they were lucky to have enough to eat because there were children starving elsewhere. Write an essay in the form of an open letter to the users of pro-anorexia Web sites. Argue against them strictly from an ethical standpoint.

2. Why are boys not mentioned at all in this essay? Are they susceptible to anorexia? Why or why not? Do you think that is liable to change? Write several paragraphs on these questions.
3. In groups of four or five classmates, go online and find one of the pro-anorexia Web sites or e-groups. Make a list of disturbing details you did not find in Mackeen's essay, and present them to your class.

Ideas for Writing

These suggestions may help you write an argumentative essay about America's eating habits. Feel free to draw on any of the selections in the casebook to back up your propositions, claims, and warrants. Also, examine the research paper at the end of the appendix to see how one student integrated essential research strategies into an argumentative paper on eating habits.

1. Write an essay in which you argue from one side or the other about the fast-food impact on American society. In other words, do you think that the fast-food industry does more good than bad or more bad than good?
2. Write an argumentative essay about weight-loss programs. Research some of the current popular plans. Then identify what's wrong with many of them, and support a plan that you think makes most sense.
3. Write an essay on how the media is responsible for the contrast between America's eating habits and the way we feel about how we look as a result of our eating habits.
4. Defend or challenge the assumption underlying some of the essays in the casebook—that many eating disorders are "cultural byproducts."
5. Argue for or against the claim made by Brownlee, Cohen, and Zinczenko that fast-food outlets deliberately encourage consumers to buy and eat more, thereby contributing to the obesity and poor health of Americans.
6. Examine Jay Walljasper's argument that there was an Edenic time when "the joy of eating" permeated American culture. Do we still engage in the joy of eating, or is this joy lost to us in our fixation on the unlikely combination of quick meals, snacking, exercise, and weight loss? Is the joy of eating a valuable asset in American life? Write an argumentative essay in which you address some of these points and questions.
7. Overeating has spread from the people in our society to their pets. Do some research on the Internet and in your library, and write an argumentative essay about the way we feed domestic animals and its implications on the weight and health of the pets in our care.

8. Obesity and the struggle to combat it have stimulated a number of radical measures designed to help the seriously overweight to shed pounds. Some of these measures have dubious value (and are downright dangerous), whereas others offer hope and results. Write an argumentative essay about one or several of these extreme measures, and explain the value or dangers inherent in their use. Take a stand on whether radical measures are called for.

9. Very thin people have a reverse problem: they often cannot gain enough weight to sustain good health or good appearance. Write an essay in which you argue about the problems facing the underweight. Do they have real problems? Are their problems serious? How can really thin people address their health needs and their appearance?

10. Do research on societies in which being thin is not valued. Write an argumentative essay to support or challenge cultures that do not revere thinness as an essential goal of good looks and good health.

Part Six

Constructing a Brief
Argumentative Research Paper

USING RESEARCH AND DOCUMENTATION TO SUPPORT YOUR ARGUMENT

A good argument uses compelling factual evidence and emotional appeals to convince readers to take a course of action, to modify their existing opinions, or to consider an alternate point of view. Finding that evidence—and ensuring its accuracy and relevance—is the work of *research.* Researching an issue provides you with the evidence and appeals you need to support your claim. The *research process* will also lead you to different points of view about your claim—either outright opposition, which you will need to address in your rebuttal, or alternate ideas about your issue that might lead you to revise your claim.

A *research paper* is an essay that draws on authoritative *sources* to support and illustrate its thesis. In the case of an *argumentative research paper,* your *claim* is your "thesis," and the sources you consult and *cite* (through quotation, paraphrase, or summary) provide the facts, evidence, and appeals you need to convince your reader of the validity of your claim. All research papers provide documentation of the sources of those facts, evidence, and appeals. *Documentation* is the proper attribution of ideas, facts, anecdotes, illustrations, and other material to the original source. Documentation allows your reader to consult the same sources and authors that you did, to retrace the steps of your argument and pursue your claim further. More important, proper documentation and citation protects you, as a writer, from charges of *plagiarism.*

THE RESEARCH PROCESS

The research process has five key stages:

- *Stage One.* Choosing an *issue*: browsing for ideas and limiting your issue.
- *Stage Two.* Establishing your claim: determining your audience and purpose.
- *Stage Three.* Gathering and organizing evidence: finding facts and expert opinions. Developing a working bibliography, assessing the credibility of sources, taking notes, and constructing an outline. Strategies for avoiding plagiarism.
- *Stage Four.* Writing the paper: drafting, revising, and editing your essay.
- *Stage Five.* Documenting your sources: preparing your final Works Cited page.

Stage One: Choosing an Issue

An *issue* for an argument is debatable and controversial. An issue is *debatable* when there are at least two perfectly reasonable but opposed opinions about it, making debate—that is, informed and civil conversation—possible. "A steady diet of junk food contributes to childhood obesity" is not debatable; no reasonable person would recommend raising a child on Ding-Dongs and Cheetos. However, "To combat childhood obesity, fast-food companies and manufacturers of junk food should be held legally liable for irresponsibly marketing to children" *is* debatable. Parents, pediatricians, lawyers, and, of course, fast-food corporations are all likely to have opposing viewpoints on that specific issue—and even when they are in basic agreement, they are likely to differ on points of strategy. This issue is also *controversial,* in that there is no one clear or obvious solution to the issue, and at least two opinions on the issue are in direct opposition to each other. Even were you to construct an argument supporting the viewpoint of a consumer group pursuing legal action against a snack-food company for marketing to children, you would have to acknowledge that other people—shareholders in that snack-food company, for example—have profound reasons for opposing your viewpoint. Controversial issues are relevant, ongoing, and sometimes insoluble. That's what makes them great topics for argumentation research papers. To determine if a subject that interests you is debatable and controversial, you'll want to begin browsing in the library and online.

Browsing

As you explore an area of general interest, you begin reading and consulting a wide range of sources of information about your general issue. As you browse, remember that you are also beginning to search for knowledgeable, reliable sources to cite in your research paper. Begin your search where you are most likely to find sources appropriate for an academic paper: in the library.

- The library's *reference section* provides both print and online sources of general information, such as encyclopedias, almanacs, maps, dictionaries, bibliographies, and directories. There are many specialized dictionaries and encyclopedias for specific subject areas. Although these general sources should not become primary sources for your argument research paper, they can give you a clearer perspective on your issue and help you begin to determine where the controversy lies.
- The *library catalog* at your campus library probably exists both on paper, in a card catalog, and online. Although it's certainly convenient to access the online catalog from your home or dorm computer, browsing the card catalog can lead to serendipitous discoveries. Card catalogs often contain annotations and corrections by generations of librarians and researchers; much like books on a shelf, they also suggest new ways of thinking about an issue simply through the happy accident of one card bumping up against another. Both a

card catalog and an online catalog will list information by author, title, subject, and key word; you can get a sense of how much material is available on your issue and how much has been written recently. If you haven't already taken advantage of your campus library's orientation programs, now would be a good time to sign up.

- The *stacks* in your library can also provide you with serendipitous browsing material. Books are organized in the stacks (the shelves) by *call number*; books on the same or very similar subject are shelved together. If you notice that many of the books you found in the card or computer catalog share a similar call number, go to that shelf in the library and browse through the books. Books with the most recent publication dates will be your best primary sources of information, but even older books can give you a sense of how a debate or controversy came into being.

  Check the following key items as you browse:
  - Publication date. Recent is best.
  - Table of contents. Do any chapter titles sound similar to your issue?
  - Index. Look up key words and concepts related to your issue. Will there be enough material and information?
  - Bibliography (a good source for additional material).

- The reference section of your library also holds *periodical indexes,* which are alphabetical lists of authors, titles, and subjects in most major newspapers and magazines. These indexes are published annually and will direct you toward specific articles. Your library probably also subscribes to online databases or CD-ROMs, which provide access to a tremendous range of publications. You can search these computerized indexes by subject area or key word. Ask your reference librarian to direct you to periodical indexes and databases for your specific topic area. If your library provides access to such powerful databases as ProQuest or LEXIS-NEXIS, it is to your advantage to learn to use them.

- Although you may be tempted to begin your preliminary research on the Web by typing a few key words into a search engine like Yahoo! or Google, this is actually the *least* efficient way to begin gathering ideas and material for an academic research paper. The search parameter *"obesity* and *children* and *fast food"* in a recent Google search called up nearly 2,900 Web pages! Because the Web is open to anyone, the information posted there may not be reliable, well written, correctly sourced, or even true. In general, a good guideline for Web research is to pay attention to a site's creator, writer, and sponsor. If the site's sponsor is a well-reputed organization or media outlet, the information you gather there is probably substantive enough for your research purposes. For example, the Web site of the Office of the Surgeon General at www.surgeongeneral.gov includes a great deal of information on childhood and adolescent obesity as well as the benefits of physical exercise and nutrition education. Its information is reliable, well sourced, and accurate. On the other hand, a commercial Web page that promises large legal settlements for people willing to participate in a class-action lawsuit against a fast-food chain might have some shock value, but it's not a good source for your academic research paper because it is likely to be biased. If you have questions about information that you find on a Web site, print out the first page and show it to the reference librarian or to your instructor.

Freewriting, Conversation, and Chatting Online

One good test of an issue's controversy is to begin sounding out your friends and your community for their opinions on the issue. Begin by establishing your own beliefs, opinions, and biases. Freewriting can tap in to what you already know—or think you know—about an issue, opening up areas for further exploration and questions for further pursuit. Begin a freewrite—on your computer or in your journal—by writing your issue on the top of the page. Then, for 20 minutes (set a timer!) write down everything your issue makes you think about. What do you already know? Who do you think would disagree with your opinion, and why? How did you come to have this opinion or belief in the first place?

If you and your friends instant-message (IM) each other, find a time when you can post your issue in the form of a question—for instance, "Should parents sue a fast-food restaurant if their child, who eats there frequently, is severely overweight?" In the casual, relatively anonymous world of instant messaging, you'll see a dialogue—or, if you're lucky, an argument!—beginning to take shape.

Many organization Web sites, especially those of academic research centers or government agencies, include a "contact us" button that allows you to e-mail specific questions or concerns to experts in the field. Establishing direct contact with someone involved with your issue can provide you with additional ideas for fieldwork, interviewing, and an immediate perspective.

If you choose to post a query about your issue to a newsgroup or usenet bulletin board, be sure to read the frequently asked questions (FAQ) section of the site to familiarize yourself with the site's etiquette. You should also first browse the site's archives to see if your issue has already been discussed.

Once you have determined the parameters of your issue, you can begin to establish a claim. A claim is your opinion about an issue, which you will defend using well-chosen sources and a carefully organized argument.

Moving from a General Topic to an Issue to a Claim

Broad Topic	General Issue	Specific Claim
Childhood obesity	Junk food marketed to kids	Manufacturers of junk food should not be allowed to market specifically to children.
Kids and physical education	School district cutbacks on physical education programs	Physical education should be mandatory for all school-age children to combat childhood obesity.

Stage Two: Establishing Your Claim

Once you have chosen an issue for your argumentation research paper, you narrow your focus by establishing a claim. (For more on a claim, see p. 479.) Because your claim is a statement that you will support and defend in your argument, you will need to determine the *audience* for your argument as well as your *purpose* in arguing. Are you writing to persuade a hostile audience to consider your viewpoint? Are you arguing for a general audience to move toward your point of view? Or are you arguing for a friendly audience to take a specific course of action? Consider these categories using the example of combating childhood obesity through lawsuits against fast-food and snack-food companies:

> HOSTILE AUDIENCE: Researching the topic, you quickly realize that fast-food and snack-food manufacturers tend to lose a great deal of revenue—and, perhaps, are forced to cut jobs—if lawsuits against them are successfully filed and won. Were you to write for this audience, your purpose would not be to argue that they should stop using cartoon characters and tie-ins to popular kids' movies to promote their food—you already know that your audience is firmly opposed to that idea. Instead, your claim might be that marketing directly to parents by promoting the place snack foods can have in an all-around balanced diet can offset any revenue that is lost when commercials no longer target children. Your research would lead you to sources that focus on what some companies might already be doing to create goodwill among consumers or to promote their products as part of an all-around healthy lifestyle.
>
> GENERAL AUDIENCE: Here you would assume that your audience has no strong opinion about suing fast-food companies for marketing directly to children and contributing to the rise in childhood obesity. Your purpose in arguing for a different ap-

proach to combating childhood obesity would be to educate a general audience and establish their interest and support in your proposed alternatives. In this case, your claim might be that instilling healthy habits, like regular exercise, in young people is more beneficial and cost-effective in the long run than lawsuits. Your research would lead you to sources that address the healthful benefits of exercise to children and adolescents, and how some communities and school districts have managed to maintain physical education programs despite budget cuts (by enlisting the corporate sponsorship of local fast-food franchises, for example).

FRIENDLY AUDIENCE: Perhaps your purpose in writing is to argue for a specific course of action for promoting physical activity in local schools. Your audience might be the readers of a community newspaper or the members of the local school board. Your claim might be that even though the school district has a limited budget, adding more gym classes or sponsoring after-school physical education programs will have long-term beneficial effects for the entire community. Your research would show that children who exercise have greater self-esteem and miss fewer days of school, and it might give examples of communities where local organizations and businesses pitched in to help fund physical education programs.

Remember that your claim, like the working thesis statement of any other research paper, is flexible. As you read more widely and share drafts of your research paper with other readers, you will find additional information and viewpoints that may change the way you phrase your claim.

Having established your claim, you now return to your preliminary browsings and freewritings and begin to gather and organize the evidence (facts, expert opinions, and appeals) that you will need to support that claim.

Stage Three: Gathering and Organizing Evidence

Develop a Working Bibliography

A working bibliography is a list of sources that you consult as you construct your argumentative research paper. It helps you to keep track of where you found information, and in the final stages of drafting your paper it will provide the foundation of your Works Cited page (see p. 483). Your working bibliography provides accurate and complete information about each source that you consult. Because you will rearrange your working bibliography as you find new sources (keeping it in alphabetical order, for example) most researchers keep the working bibliography either on their computer or on index cards. The advantage of index cards, of course, is their portability; you can jot down the information that you need as you browse in the library stacks. A working bibliography on your computer saves time in the later stages of drafting as you finalize your Works Cited page. Whichever method you prefer, you will need to include standard information for each source in your working bibliography:

Working Bibliography: Book Information
Include the following information for each book you consult:

- Author name (or names)
- Complete book title, underlined
- Place of publication
- Publisher's name
- Year of publication
- Call number or location in library

Periodical Information

- Author name (or names)
- Title of article, in quotation marks
- Title of periodical or magazine, underlined
- Volume or issue number
- Publication date
- Page numbers on which article appears
- Call number or location in library

Web Site Information

- Complete site URL
- Date of access

How Much Evidence Do I Need?

Keep your audience and purpose in mind as you do your research and assemble a working bibliography. The evidence (facts, expert opinions, and appeals) you gather should support your purpose in arguing and should provide the kind of information and background that your intended audience will need in order to follow your line of reasoning. Finally, remember that a solid argument includes consideration and rebuttal of opposing viewpoints. Your research should include opposing points of view as well as the necessary evidence on which those viewpoints are based.

Assessing the Credibility of Sources

Your argument will rest on two basic kinds of evidence: facts and expert opinions. *Facts* are generally accepted, irrefutable concepts, ideas, and observations. Paris is the capital of France; diet and exercise are fundamental to good health; seat belts help to save lives—these are all facts. You can assume that your audience will not need the additional support of an expert opinion when you make a statement of fact.

Other evidence you gather to support your claim will come from *expert opinions*. If you are arguing for mandatory physical education in your local school district, you might turn to the opinions of experts in nutrition, pediatrics, child psychology, and education. Your argument would cite the opinions and findings of these experts to support your own claim. But how can you tell if someone is, indeed, an expert? Especially in the age of the Internet, when anyone can publish anything online, it is important to evaluate the reliability and credibility of the sources of evidence.

Here are some general guidelines for assessing the credibility and expertise of the evidence you gather as you research your topic:

Credibility of Print Sources

- How current is the publication date of a book, periodical, or journal? In general, the most recent information is likely to be the most up-to-date and reliable.
- What are the author's own credentials? Turn to the book jacket, or see what information is available on the author in a periodical. Does the author hold an advanced academic degree in the subject? Has the author published other books and articles on this topic?
- What is the source of the publication? Is it a major news media source, a commercial publishing house, or an academic press? In general, the books and print sources you find in your college library have been carefully chosen by library staff. If you aren't sure about the publisher of a book, magazine, or periodical, ask a librarian or your instructor.

Credibility of Online Sources

- Who is the author of the site? Who is the site sponsor? Web sites that are published by major information and media providers, such as sites connected with newspapers, magazines, and television news networks, meet the same standard of reliability and credibility as their print and televised broadcasts.
- Does the site identify its sponsor? Often, a Web site can serve as a political platform or commercial advertisement for a corporation or special-interest group. Be aware of the possible biases in such sites; although they might provide some basic information, they might not give you the whole picture.
- How well designed and maintained is a site? Are links current, or "broken"? A site that does not "work" well might not have been updated for some time.

- Is there information on the site on how to contact the site's authors and sponsors?

Field Research

At this stage of your research, you may wish to bolster your library and online inquiries with research in the real world. *Interviews* with experts on your campus and in your community, *observations* you make of particular phenomena, and informal *surveys* of people can all lend additional perspective and unique insights to your paper. Your browsing of sources and any freewriting may have given you an idea of the kinds of questions you would like to ask an expert. For an interview, contact your subject well in advance of your assignment due date. Arrange a meeting (or phone interview), making your purpose for the conversation clear. Prepare your questions in advance. Although you will want to take notes during your interview, you might also find a small tape or digital recorder to be helpful.

For observations, do a little advance planning to find a place where you know you will observe phenomena that will support your claim. Be sure you can work undisturbed at this location. Take notes or use a digital camera or sound recorder—any technology that will help you gather evidence.

For a survey, keep questions brief and specific, and be sure that your survey sample includes a demographic appropriate to your topic. (For example, if your research paper is on preventing campus binge drinking, your demographic should include mostly people who attend college or live on or near a college campus.)

Taking Notes

Once you have gathered your sources, begin reading more closely for the specific information you will need to support your claim. Taking notes accurately and completely will make drafting your paper, as well as assembling your final Works Cited page, much easier. Index cards might be low-tech, but they are still the most efficient way to take and collect notes on your research. There are three strategies for taking notes: *summary, paraphrase,* and *direct quotation.* Use a new index card for each summary, paraphrase, or direct quotation.

- *Summary* is the best strategy for recording specific facts, summing up general perspectives, and reminding yourself later of what's included in a particular source.
- *Paraphrase* is the recasting of source material in your own words. Rather than copying out a long idea or opinion word for word, you summarize its main points in your own language. However, you still need to provide the correct citation information for a paraphrase; a paraphrase might be in your words, but its idea belongs to someone else, and that original author needs to be properly credited. Para-

phrase is a valuable note-taking strategy, but it's also one area where students and professional writers alike can accidentally plagiarize.

- *Direct quotations* are most useful when the exact words of an expert source or author are the best way of expressing that expert's opinion, idea, or observation. Direct quotations should be concise and clear. *Always* place quotation marks around *any* words you quote directly from another author or source.

Taking Notes on Your Topic

- At the top of each card, write a brief subtopic. Keep a working list of these subtopics, which will help you later as you draft a working outline for your paper.
- On each index card, write the author's name, the book or article title, and the page number. Be sure that you also have an entry for this source in your working bibliography.

The following note cards demonstrate each note-taking strategy:

A. Sample note card: Summary

Subtopic	*Benefits of physical activity for adolescents*
Author/title	*Williamson:* "Study: Crime, lack of PE, recreation programs lead U.S. adolescents to couch-potato status"
Page	(Web site)
Summary	Adolescents who do not have access to physical education programs at school do not develop healthy exercise or eating habits for later in life. The problem is especially severe in communities where adolescents lack access to safe environments.

B. Sample note card: Paraphrase

Subtopic	*Benefits of physical activity for adolescents*
Author/title	*Williamson:* "Study: Crime, lack of PE, recreation programs lead U.S. adolescents to couch-potato status"
Page	(Web site)
Paraphrase	Adolescents who live in high-crime areas are more likely to stay indoors watching television and playing video games than exercise outside. Adolescents from higher-income families tend to get more exercise.

C. Sample note card: Direct quotation

Subtopic	*Benefits of physical activity for adolescents*

Author/title	*Williamson*: "Study: Crime, lack of PE, recreation programs lead U.S. adolescents to couch-potato status"
Page	(Web site)
Direct quotation	"Adolescents from poor families fared ever worse, since high crime rates, low income and less education among mothers reduced vigorous physical activity and increased TV, video, and computer/video game use." Dr. Barry M. Popkin

Organizing Your Notes and Developing a Working Outline

Review the basic structure of an argument. This structure—issue, claim, evidence, and rebuttal—will help to determine the organization of your working outline. Your instructor may have asked you to use a more specific argumentation strategy (induction/deduction, etc.) for your argumentative research paper; be sure that you understand the parameters of your assignment as you begin assembling your outline. A working outline is not the fixed, final version of your argument. Instead, a working outline specifies the order of your main points and the placement of evidence to support those points. As you begin to draft your paper and revisit your notes and sources, you will make some changes in the ordering of your main points and evidence.

Organizing Your Notes

- Print out your list of subtopics. Organize your index cards according to those subtopics. Really large piles of cards might need to be further subdivided into more specific topics; piles of only one or two cards might need to be absorbed into a related subtopic.
- Be sure that all of your index cards include source information and that all of those sources are included in your working bibliography.
- Set aside any index cards that duplicate information, even if they are from different source material. However, do not throw away any index cards yet.
- Within each subtopic, organize your index cards from most important to least important idea, fact, or opinion.

Use the index cards to assemble a working outline. Your instructor may have given you a specific outline structure to follow. If not, a general working outline could look like this:

I. INTRODUCTION. Describe your issue. What is specifically debatable and controversial about the issue?

II. CLAIM. A concise and clear statement of your opinion or position on the issue.
   A. FIRST MAIN POINT THAT SUPPORTS YOUR CLAIM
      1. Evidence (fact or expert opinion)
      2. Another piece of evidence
      3. Still more evidence
   B. SECOND MAIN POINT THAT SUPPORTS YOUR CLAIM
      1. Evidence
      2. Another piece of evidence
      3. Still more evidence
   C. OPPOSING POINT OF VIEW
      1. Summary of viewpoint opposed to your claim
         a. Evidence opposition would cite to support their viewpoint
         b. Additional evidence from opposing side
   D. REBUTTAL
      1. Evidence that refutes, disproves, or calls into question your opposition's viewpoint
   E. CONCLUSION

Stage Four: Writing the Paper

As you begin to synthesize your evidence into a coherent argument, remember that your final essay is more than just a collection of data. In an argumentative research paper, you are taking a clear stand on an issue and supporting that stand with well-chosen evidence. The flow between your ideas and the support provided by other writers and experts should be seamless; the connections between each separate piece of evidence and your overall claim should be absolutely clear.

Drafting

Perhaps the most difficult way to begin drafting a paper is to sit in front of a blank computer screen. Instead, copy your outline into a new computer file. Then, with your index cards handy, begin filling in your outline. Refer to your index cards for summary, paraphrase, and direct quotations as necessary, being sure to include citation information (or, at this early stage, the number of the index card so you can find it later).

As you write, remember that your research paper is not a simple repetition or listing of the data you have accumulated. Keep your claim in mind, and in your own words explain how each piece of evidence supports that claim. Your own ideas, insights, and opinions are key to your argumentative research paper; at the same time, keep your audience and purpose in mind. Is your diction appropriate to your essay's audience? Will the organization of your evidence achieve your purpose?

Your outline is flexible, as is the arrangement of your evidence. As you draft, you might rearrange or even set aside some of your index cards. You might rephrase your claim as you begin to see connections between different pieces of evidence. And you might discover that there are gaps in your evidence, questions that arise as you become more engaged with your subject. Begin a separate document where you jot down these questions. If the answers to those questions aren't in the sources you have already consulted, bring your questions back to the library and do some additional research.

Incorporating Sources

Your skill at interweaving the ideas and direct quotations of other sources with your own opinions will determine the success of your argument. Moving from your own voice to that of a summarized, paraphrased, or directly quoted author or source needs to be clear enough so that your reader can distinguish between "voices," between your point and the evidence you are citing to support that point. At the same time, you want those transitions to be graceful enough that your reader has a consistent sense of just whose argument this is.

Moving from your own voice to information from another source is most easily accomplished by using a transition such as the following:

- Overweight adolescent Jazlyn Bradley *confesses* that . . .
- A McDonald's spokesman *acknowledges* that . . .
- Dr. Barry Popkin *describes the issue* as . . .
- Lawyer John Banzhaf III *argues* that . . .
- John Doyle, cofounder of the Center for Consumer Freedom, *suggests* a comparison between . . .
- In the following examples, the Office of the Surgeon General *notes* that . . .

Revising and Polishing

The drafting process organized your argument, arranging appropriate evidence to support each of your points while acknowledging and rebutting your opposition. Your instructor may ask you to share your "rough draft," during a peer review session in class; you should also consider making an appointment with your instructor or with your campus writing center to review your rough draft. As you review your rough draft, ask yourself (and ask peer reviewers to consider): Is my evidence convincing? Have I provided enough evidence to support my claim? Have I avoided logical fallacies (see pages 65–66)? What was my original purpose for this argument, and will my audience respond in the way I intended? Is it clear where I have incorporated the words and ideas of outside sources, and do I have enough information to correctly document those sources?

Polishing the Final Manuscript

- Does my title accurately describe the content and direction of my argument?
- Do I state my claim clearly in the first paragraph?
- Does each body paragraph include a key piece of evidence to support my claim? Is the link between the evidence and my claim logical?
- Do I incorporate summaries, paraphrases, and quotations accurately and gracefully?
- Have I cross-referenced all of my in-text citations with my Works Cited page?
- Have I fairly and truthfully represented opposing viewpoints?
- Is my diction appropriate for my audience and purpose? Is my grammar correct? Have I read through carefully, without depending on a spell-checking program, to catch any accidental errors?

Before you hand in your paper, check the original assignment one last time to be sure that your paper is formatted and presented exactly as your instructor requested.

Stage Five: Documenting Sources

When you make your research public—by posting it to a Web site, sharing it with a student group, or handing it in to your instructor—you become part of a larger academic conversation. The ongoing creativity and integrity of that conversation depends on each participant's acknowledgement of the work that has come before. The documentation of sources in your paper grants to everyone in your audience the courtesy of being able to follow up on your sources for themselves, should they be intrigued by your argument and wish to learn more. You also extend professional courtesy to those whose ideas, research, and observations support your own claim when you correctly cite them in your paper and on your Works Cited page.

Plagiarism and Academic Honesty

Careful and accurate paraphrase, summary, and quotation, along with the proper documentation of these citations, is the best defense you have against charges of *plagiarism*. In recent years, charges of plagiarism have embarrassed—and led to the demotion or dismissal—of professionals in leading positions in journalism and the academy. Deliberate plagiarism is the theft of another writer's work; it is no more defensible than stealing another's physical property. The Internet makes it extraordinarily easy to reach around the globe for an enormous range of source material. But that same Internet allows a diligent editor—or a savvy instructor—to easily track and catch a plagiarist in the act. You may have already been apprised of your college's policy toward deliberate plagiarism; penalties range from failing the course to expulsion from school. *Don't do it.*

Materials That Require Documentation

- Anything you wrote on an index card: summaries, paraphrases, and quotations.
- Any illustration you incorporate into your paper (cartoons, photographs, charts, etc.).
- Any information that is not common factual knowledge (see p. 474).
- Any interesting expression or turn of phrase (from a song lyric, a poem, a character in a movie, etc.).
- Any line of reasoning or opinion; especially in an argumentative paper, you must distinguish between your own argument and the ways in which other writers have connected similar evidence to similar claims.

Some instances of plagiarism are perfectly obvious: buying a paper from an online service, handing in something that a friend wrote for a similar course, handing in a paper that you yourself already wrote and handed in for another course. But as you learn to incorporate the ideas of other writers and researchers into your own argument, you will have honest questions about where the line between borrowing and plagiarism falls. Be on the safe side. Any time you have a question about plagiarism, ask your instructor or take your draft to your campus writing center. For more information about plagiarism and citing sources appropriately, please refer to the appendix on pages 499–514.

There are two ways of indicating the source of material in your paper: *in-text citations,* where you indicate the author and/or source of an idea or fact right as you present it in your essay, and the *Works Cited list,* your final bibliography.

In-Text Citations

Using in-text citations is one of the smoothest ways of making a transition from your own words and ideas to those of an outside source. An in-text citation ("in" the "text" of your paper, as opposed to the Works Cited list) indicates to your reader that you are introducing evidence to support your claim.

In-Text Citations

- Provide enough information so that a reader can easily find the source on your Works Cited page.
- In MLA style, provide the page number—and the author's name, unless you already clearly state that in your text—in

parentheses placed where the source material appears in your text.
- Double-check the sentence in which you incorporate source material and the citation information to be sure it reads smoothly and correctly.

The following examples demonstrate in-text citations in MLA style.

- Eric Schlosser notes that the "American School Food Service Association estimates that about 30 percent of the public high schools in the United States offer branded fast food" (56). *The author's name is mentioned within the body of the text, so his last name does not need to reappear in the parentheses with the page number.*
- Although the lawsuit was dismissed in 2003, the fast-food industry—and other American food companies, such as Kraft—are beginning to take the threat of legal action seriously (Barboza 3:1). *The in-text citation gives both the author's last name and the page number where this information is found—in this case, the section and page of a newspaper.*

Works Cited List

If you have been keeping a working bibliography on your computer, you can use that same document to build your final Works Cited page. Have all of your index cards handy, and be sure to cross-reference each entry on your Works Cited page with a reference in your paper.

You do not need to include sources on your Works Cited page that you looked at in your preliminary browsing or that appear on an index card you made during your note taking if you do not use those sources in the final draft of your paper.

- Center the words "Works Cited" on top of a new page. Do not underline or italicize these words.
- Double-space every line. Indent everything in each entry (after the first line) by one stroke of the Tab key (about five spaces).
- Paginate your Works Cited page continuously with your entire research paper.
- List your sources alphabetically by author last name. If the source has no named author, list it alphabetically according to the title of the work (ignoring the words *the, an,* or *a*).
- If you use more than one work by the same author, list them alphabetically by title under the first entry for the author's name.
- Book, newspaper, magazine, and journal titles are always underlined; short story and article titles always appear in quotation marks (not underlined).

Book by One Author

McCarthy, Cormac. <u>The Road</u>. New York: Knopf, 2006.

Several Books by One Author

Tannen, Deborah. <u>That's Not What I Meant! How Conversational Style Makes or Breaks Your Relations with Others</u>. New York: Morrow, 1986.

———. <u>You Just Don't Understand: Women and Men in Conversation</u>. New York: Harper Collins, 2007.

Book with Two or Three Authors or Editors

List the names of the authors in the order in which they appear on the book's cover or title page. Begin with the last name of the first author; list the subsequent authors by first and last name.

Bloom, Lynn Z., Donald A. Daiker, and Edward M. White, eds. <u>Composition in the Twenty-First Century: Crisis and Change</u>. Carbondale and Edwardsville: Southern Illinois UP, 1996.

Work with More Than Three Authors or Editors

Use the names of all the authors, or use just the first author listed on the title page followed by the abbreviation *et al.*

Anderson, Lorraine, et al. <u>Literature and the Environment: A Reader on Nature and Culture</u>. New York: Longman, 1999.

Work with Group or Organization as Author

Reader's Digest. <u>Fix-It-Yourself Manual</u>. Pleasantville: Reader's Digest, 1977.

Work without an Author

List the work alphabetically according to the first word (other than *a, an,* or *the*) of its title.

<u>Illustrated Atlas of the World</u>. Chicago: Rand McNally, 2005.

Work in a Collection of Pieces All by the Same Author

Dalrymple, Theodore. "Uncouth Chic." <u>Life at the Bottom: The Worldview That Makes the Underclass</u>. Chicago: Ivan R. Dee, 2001.

Work in an Anthology

Auerbach, Erich. "Odysseus' Scar." 20th Century Literary Criticism: A Reader. Ed. David Lodge. London: Longman, 1972.

Work Translated from Another Language

Sebald, W. G. Austerlitz. Trans. Anthea Bell. New York: Random House, 2001.

New Edition of an Older Book

Beerbohm, Max. The Illustrated Zuleika Dobson. 1911. New Haven and London: Yale University Press, 1985.

Entry from a Reference Book

Specialized reference books are treated like other books (beginning with the author's last name). Familiar, basic references like dictionaries and encyclopedias need only the edition and date. (If the reference work is organized alphabetically, no page numbers are needed.)

"Kaeliinohomoku, Joanh. W. Hula." Encyclopedia Americana. 1998 ed.
"Souter, David H." Who's Who in America. 62nd ed. 2008.

Article in a Weekly or Biweekly Periodical

Basken, Paul. "Student Loan Inquiry Expands to Examine Issues of Race." Chronicle of Higher Education. 22 June 2007: A. 22–23.

Article in a Monthly or Bimonthly Periodical

Fallows, James. "China Makes, the World Takes." Atlantic July/Aug. 2007: 48–72.

Article in a Daily Newspaper

Barboza, David. "If You Pitch It, They Will Eat: Barrage of Food Ads Takes Aim at Young Children." New York Times 3 Aug. 2003, sec. 3:1+.

Article with No Author

"The Subtle Side of Science." New Scientist 13 July 2007: 25.

Editorial in a Newspaper or Periodical

Signed, in a magazine:

Carter, Graydon. "The Phony War." <u>Vanity Fair</u> Aug. 2003: 46.

Unsigned, in a newspaper:

"An Important Human Rights Tool." <u>New York Times</u> 8 Aug. 2003, sec. A: 16.

Letter to the Editor of a Newspaper or Periodical

Bronstone, Adam. Letter. <u>Vanity Fair</u> Aug. 2003: 56.

Article in a Journal with Pagination Continuing Through Each Volume

Susan Peck MacDonald. "The Erasure of Language." <u>College Composition and Communication</u> 58 (2007): 585–625.

Article in a Journal with Pagination Continuing Only through Each Issue

Kogen, Myra. "The Conventions of Expository Writing." <u>Journal of Basic Writing</u>. 5.1 (1986): 24–37.

Film, Video, DVD

<u>Testament of Orpheus</u>. Dir. Jean Cocteau. Videocassette. Janus Films, 1960.

Radio or Television Program

Radio program:

"Is Hip-Hop Today's Civil Rights Movement?" Narr. Scott Simon. <u>Weekend Edition Saturday</u>. Natl. Public Radio. WNYC, New York. 1 Mar. 2003.

Television:

"The Post-It Always Rings Twice." <u>Sex and the City</u>. Dir. Alan Taylor. HBO. 1 Aug. 2003.

CD or Other Recording

For an entire album:

Timberlake, Justin. <u>Futuresex/Lovesounds</u>. Jive, 2006.

To cite a specific song, place the title in quotation marks.

Evora, Cesaria. "Vida tem um so vida." <u>The Very Best of Cesaria Evora</u>. BMG, 2002.

Advertisement

Give the product name, followed by the word *Advertisement* and then the place and date where you saw the ad (for a television program) or the publication date (for an ad in a newspaper or magazine).

McDonald's Dollar Menu. Advertisement. NBC. 21 Apr. 2006.

Personal Interview

Sanderson, Professor Eleanor. Telephone interview. 13 Dec. 2006.

Online Book, Article, or Other Source

Darwin, Charles. The Origin of Species. New York: P. F. Collier & Son Company, 1909–14. Bartleby.com: Great Books Online. Ed. Steven van Leeuwen. 2001. 3 July 2007 <http://bartleby. com/11/>.

Entire Internet Site

Arts and Literature Daily. Ed. Denis Dutton. 2003. Chronicle of Higher Education. 30 July 2007 <http://aldaily.com>.

Magazine Article Available Online

When the URLs for specific articles are too long, or if a site requires payment or registration to see an article, abbreviate the URL to give just enough information so that someone could locate the article in a free archive. After the date of original print publication, include the date that you accessed the electronic version, followed by the URL.

Oppenheimer, Todd. "The Computer Delusion." Atlantic Online July 1997. 13 July 2006 <http://www.theatlantic.com/issues/ 97jul/computer.htm>.

Newspaper Article Available Online

Santora, Marc. "Teenagers' Suit Says McDonald's Made Them Obese." New York Times 21 Nov. 2002. 13 Oct. 2007 <http:// www.nytimes.com/2002/11/21/region>.

Article from an Electronic Journal

Schwarzer, David, Alexia Hayood, and Charla Lorenzen. "Fostering Multiliteracy in a Linguistically Diverse Classroom." Language Arts 80:6 (July 2003): 453–462. 8 Nov. 2006 <http://www.ncte.org/pdfs/subscribers-only/la/0806-july03/LA0806Fostering.pdf>.

Electronic Posting to a Group

A posting to a discussion group hosted by a Web site:

M. E. Cowan. Online posting. 30 Oct. 2001. "News Media 'Discover' Women of Afghanistan." 8 Aug. 2003 <http://tabletalk.salon.com/webx?14@239.0bghaUqZFcQ.5@.eec6c38/0>.

A posting to an academic listserv:

Cook, Janice. "Re: What New Day Is Dawning?" 19 June 1997. Online posting. Alliance for Computers and writing listserv. 4 Feb. 2007 <acw-1@ttacs6.Hu.edu>.

A posting to a Usenet group:

IrishMom. "Re: Spain Will Send Troops to Aid U.S." Online posting. 2 Nov. 2001 <Ireland_list-og@email.rutgers.edu>.

SAMPLE STUDENT RESEARCH PAPER

Rivera 1

Nelson Rivera

Professor Odomsky

Expository Writing 2

November 26, 2007

Combating Childhood Obesity:

Why Can't Johnny Touch His Toes?

1   The headlines at first seemed like a joke from a late-night talk show: overweight people were filing lawsuits against fast-food restaurants, claiming that the restaurants conspired to hide information about the dangers of eating fast food and contributed to their obesity and other health problems. In New York City in 2002, two teenage girls filed suit against McDonald's. One of the girls, 19-year-old Jazlyn Bradley, weighed 270 pounds; 14-year-old Ashley Pelman weighed 170 pounds (Santora). Although the lawsuit was dismissed in 2003, the fast-food industry—and other American food companies, such as Kraft—are beginning to take the threat of legal action seriously (Barboza 3:1). But unlike successful class-action lawsuits against tobacco companies, where a scientifically proven link between the product and catastrophic health consequences as well as proven coverups by the tobacco companies themselves have given a sound basis for legal action, lawsuits against fast-food companies will do nothing to address the problem of childhood obesity. To help overweight

The title of Rivera's paper clearly indicates his topic: childhood obesity. The last sentence of the paragraph establishes the writer's claim.

Rivera 2

children to develop good lifelong eating habits, it is far more beneficial for school systems, parents, and private organizations to promote physical fitness and sports for young people.

2   There is no doubt that American children and adolescents are getting heavier every year. In a report by the Surgeon General's office, 14 percent of adolescents (aged 12 to 19) in the United States were overweight in 1999—a percentage that has tripled since the 1970s (Office). In addition, fewer kids have access to physical education programs in financially strapped school districts, and at home kids are more likely to spend time in front of the computer or television than playing outside. A study at the University of North Carolina at Chapel Hill showed that only 21.3 percent of adolescents had at least one day of physical education during the school week (Williamson). Dr. Barry M. Popkin, professor of nutrition and project principal investigator, took note of an even more disturbing finding. "Adolescents from poor families fared even worse, since high crime rates, low income and less education among mothers reduced vigorous physical activity and increased TV, video and computer/video game use," he reported (Williamson).

3   According to the Surgeon General, the average American child should get at least 60 minutes of "moderate

Rivera cites established authorities to back up his claim that childhood obesity is on the rise. The Surgeon General of the United States and a medical study conducted by a university are credible sources.

In this transitional paragraph, the writer moves from supporting his broad topic (American children are becoming obese) to his specific claim (regular physical exercise is the best way to combat childhood obesity).

Rivera 3

physical activity most days of the week." The Surgeon

General goes on to note that even more exercise is necessary

for children who need to lose weight, while acknowledging

that for many families access to a "safe environment" for

physical activity is an important issue (Office).

4   But an hour of safe, supervised physical activity might

not have been possible for the two New York girls who filed

suit against McDonald's. According to an investigation by the

New York Times in 1999, only 12 percent of New York City

high school students participated in team sports—among the

lowest rates of participation in American cities. In addition,

more than half of 1,500 high school students randomly tested

in the New York City public schools showed elevated risk

factors for heart disease, including obesity and lack of

physical activity (Take the Field; Johnson).

5   McDonald's is burning the candle at both ends. Despite

producing high-fat and high-calorie foods, the company has

established advertising campaigns with well-known sports

figures who endorse McDonald's products. Two of the

greatest African-American female athletes ever, tennis

superstars Venus and Serena Williams, in 2003 began

appearing in a series of commercials promoting McDonald's

new "Dollar Menu" ("Venus and Serena"). That menu

includes not only fries and ice cream sundaes, but also side

salads and "snack size Fruit 'n' Yogurt," which are

> Rivera did some more research to find out more about the lives of his first main illustration, the two girls from New York who tried to sue McDonald's

> The writer's observations of the mass media—even commercials—gives him an interesting perspective on his topic. Notice how Rivera uses quotations from a newspaper interview with one of the teenage girls to prove his own point.

Rivera 4

certainly healthful choices. The message would seem to be that for teenagers who spend their recreation time exercising—as opposed to playing video games, watching TV, or instant-messaging each other—McDonald's can be a reasonable choice for snacks and meals. Jazlyn Bradley, however, wasn't going for the salads and yogurt when she went to McDonald's. By her own admission, "a McMuffin in the morning and the Big Mac meal with an apple pie in the evening was standard operating procedure" (Santora). Apparently no one in Jazlyn's home, nor any health teacher in her school, advised her about making choices between Big Macs and "Fruit 'n' Yogurt."

6   Some school systems are combating student obesity, not by increasing physical education opportunities but by pursuing lawsuits against food-industry giants seeking access to student consumers—this despite apparently deep resentment from the general public against frivolous obesity lawsuits : The Center for Consumer Freedom (CCF) reports that "89% of Americans think obesity lawsuits are ridiculous." ("Trial lawyers").[1] The Seattle School Board took up the issue of Coca-Cola's five-year contract with the school system, which allowed Coke products to be sold on school grounds. The contract brought in about $400,000 to the school system annually (Bach). Pursuing the lawsuit was a Washington, D.C., lawyer named John Banzhaf III,

Here, Rivera considers an opposing viewpoint: that school systems and private citizens can fight childhood obesity through lawsuits.

who had successfully sued tobacco companies and was now taking up obesity issues. He argued that access to Coca-Cola in the Seattle schools made kids fat. Not all school board members agreed. "Obesity and health problems in America have so many different factors, and we are not going to save the world by banning Coke," said one board member. "We need to look at nutrition. Our school lunches are much more to blame" (Bach). Writing about "goods sold in supermarkets or served in restaurants" Rozin and Geier argue that "Reducing the portion sizes of food . . . by an imperceptible amount (say a few percent) would be a good first step" ("Want Fewer Fries," B 16). Certainly, school lunchrooms could heed the advice too.

7   Clearly, the important issue of physical education opportunities for Seattle schoolchildren was not part of the debate. Nor was the issue of health education. John Doyle, cofounder of the Center for Consumer Freedom, notes that "you make choices in the food you want to purchase, and if you make the wrong choices relentlessly and perpetually, you're going to have health consequences" (Fox). Indeed, in the pursuit of legal action against major food corporations, immediate benefits to students—such as nutrition education and sports opportunities—seem to have been left out of the conversation altogether.

Rivera 6

8   While some school systems caught up in budget crunches and tempted to solve problems through lawsuits, others collaborate with fast-food corporations to bring in much-needed revenues. Eric Schlosser notes that the "American School Food Service Association estimates that about 30 percent of the public high schools in the United States offer branded fast food" (56). It's not clear if the revenues provided by fast-food sales on school grounds actually help provide students with "extras"—such as sports programs, music and arts opportunities, and so forth—or if it's just another way to contract out food service that the schools must provide in any case.

9   To address these issues, some private individuals and foundations are exploring other ways to give kids opportunities to exercise safely and learn effective lifelong habits. In New York, the group Take the Field has been renovating and rebuilding abandoned public school gym facilities and playing fields through private donations. As Dr. Penny Gordon-Larsen, an author of the UNC study, pointed out, "School is really the perfect place to start" introducing healthy habits such as exercise. "If we can get schools to provide safe and accessible places for kids to be active, then there's a huge potential to reach a great number of kids. If the schools can't or won't do that,

Rivera goes on to illustrate that fast-food companies do indeed have an influence on the lives of American schoolchildren, even in the students' own classrooms.

After having discussed the opposition, the writer begins a rebuttal with the example of a private group that is working to bring physical education and sports to public school-children.

then community recreation centers can make a big

difference also"("study: crime").

10   Kids and teenagers are always going to prefer potato

chips to carrot sticks and would rather have pizza than salad

for dinner. Rather than wasting time and resources in high-

profile lawsuits against major food companies, it is

demonstrably more productive in the long run to give

children opportunities to develop lifelong healthy habits,

such as getting enough exercise and participating in team

sports. If the Seattle School Board thought about it, that

$400,000 annual revenue from its Coca-Cola contract could

go toward hiring new gym teachers, developing new sports

teams, and eventually producing more Williams sisters

rather than a generation of Jazlyns and Ashleys.

Rivera's conclusion sums up his main points and clearly states why his claim (that physical education, rather than lawsuits, is the best way to combat childhood obesity) should be accepted. Rivera uses his research to argue for a recommendation that would improve children's health.

Rivera 8

Note

1. The Center for Consumer Freedom is supported by restaurants and food companies and opposes compulsory warning labels in food, lawsuits against restaurants that sell fattening foods, and similar activities promoted by "food activists" ("Center"). Despite the CCF's clear anti-regulation stance, the data is hard to dispute.

This note refers to the superscript 1 on page 492 of Rivera's paper. The note adds information that is not essential to the paper but shows readers the depth and honesty of his research. By deflating the credentials of the CCF somewhat, he forestalls critics who might object to the use of the Web site; and he nevertheless affirms the data the site presents.

Rivera 9

Works Cited

"Are Venus and Serena Bad for Tennis?", ESPN Sports
 Business. 3 Feb. 2003. 6 Nov. 2007 <http://www.espn.go.
 com/sportsbusiness/s/2003/0202/1503084.html>.

Bach, Deborah. "Legal Threat Bubbling Beneath School Soda
 Contract." Seattle Post-Intelligencer Reporter 17 July
 2003. 12 Oct. 2007 <http://seattlepi.nwsource.com>.

Barboza, David. "If You Pitch It, They Will Eat: Barrage of Food
 Ads Takes Aim at Young Children." New York Times
 3 Aug. 2003, late ed.: C1+.

"Center for Consumer Freedom." Wikipedia. 25 June 2007. 15
 Nov. 2007 <http://en.wikipedia.org>.

Fox News Channel. "Fat Teens Sue McDonald's." 21 Sept. 2002.
 10 Nov. 2007 <http://www.foxnews.com>.

Johnson, Kirk. "Dropping the Ball: The Decline of School
 Sports; Finding the Middle Ground for Couch Potato
 and Athlete." New York Times 15 Jan. 1999. 20 Oct. 2007
 <http://query.nytimes.com/search/>.

Office of the Surgeon General. "The Surgeon
 General's Call to Action to Prevent and Decrease
 Overweight and Obesity." 11 Jan. 2007. 12 Oct. 2007
 <http://www.surgeongeneral.gov/topics/obesity/
 calltoaction/fact_adolescents.htm>.

Rozin, Paul and Andrew B. Geier. "Want Fewer Fries with
 That?" Chronicle Review 6 Apr. 2007: B16.

Rivera 10

Santora, Marc. "Teenagers' Suit Says McDonald's Made Them
    Obese." New York Times 21 Nov. 2002. 13 Oct. 2007
        <http://www.nytimes.com/2002/11/21/nyregion>.

Schlosser, Eric. Fast Food Nation: The Dark Side of the All-
    American Meal. New York: Perennial/Harper, 2002.

Take the Field. "About Us." 13 Nov. 2007. 27 Nov. 2007
        <http://takethefield.org/aboutus.php>.

"Trial Lawyers: A Timeline of Trial Lawyers and Obesity
    Lawsuits." 14 July 2007. The Center for Consumer
    Freedom. 10 Oct. 2007 <http://www.consumerfreedom
    .com/issuepage.cfm/topic/32>.

Williamson, David. "Study: Crime, Lack of PE, Recreation
    Programs Lead U.S. Adolescents to Couch-Potato
    Lifestyles." University of North Carolina-Chapel
    Hill News Services. 15 Oct. 2007. 27 Nov. 2007
        <http://www.unc.edu/news/>.

Appendix:
A Guide to Avoiding Plagiarism

WHAT IS PLAGIARISM?

Plagiarism is using someone else's work—words, ideas, or illustrations, published or unpublished—without giving the creator of that work sufficient credit. A serious breach of scholarly ethics, plagiarism can have severe consequences. Students risk a failing grade or disciplinary action ranging from suspension to expulsion. A record of such action can adversely affect professional opportunities in the future as well as graduate school admission. Scholars and teachers can face public disgrace and even be forced out of a position. In the business world, plagiarism leads to distrust and can damage careers.

Significance of Intellectual Honesty

Many would argue, in this age of the Internet and music downloads, that information should be "free." However, it's possible to preserve the free flow of information without plagiarizing. In fact, the careful documentation of information sources helps ensure that information remains not only available but reliable.

Others may ask, What's so terrible about copying someone else's work? The issues concerning plagiarism touch two significant points: preserving intellectual honesty and giving credit for work done. The academic community relies on the reciprocal exchange of ideas and information to further knowledge and research. Using material without acknowledging its source violates this expectation and consequently makes it hard for researchers to verify and build on others' results. It also cheats writers and researchers of the credit they deserve for their work and creativity.

Even with the writer's permission, presenting another's work as one's own is equivalent to lying: it's a form of dishonesty. Perhaps most important for students, plagiarizing damages a person's own self-respect and negates the very reasons he or she is in college. A student who hands in a plagiarized paper has missed an opportunity for growth and learning.

Intentional Plagiarism

Suppose you are pressed by a deadline for a paper in your history class and a friend offers you a paper he or she wrote for a similar class the previous year. Handing in that paper as your own is intentional plagiarism. In the same way, buying a paper from an Internet source—or taking one from a sorority or fraternity file—and handing it in, with or without making changes of your own, is plagiarism. Paying someone to write a paper that you then submit as yours is also plagiarism, as is handing in a paper of your own that someone else has rewritten or revised.

Ethical considerations aside, it's hard to get away with plagiarism. Experienced professors can easily tell when a paper is not written in a student's own style or is more professionally prepared than they would expect. In addition, online services now identify plagiarized papers for a fee, and academic institutions are subscribing to such services. The March 2, 2006, online edition of *The New York Sun* reported that in New York City, more and more schools were requiring students to hand in papers through Turnitin.com, "a service that compares students' papers against everything on the Internet and a database of more than 15 million student papers."

Students at these schools will have a hard time getting away with submitting unoriginal papers.

DOCUMENTATION: THE KEY TO AVOIDING UNINTENTIONAL PLAGIARISM

As a student, you may resolve never to be involved in plagiarism. But it can be difficult to tell when you have unintentionally plagiarized something. The legal doctrine of **fair use** allows writers to use a limited amount of another's work in their own papers and books. However, to make sure that they are not plagiarizing that work, writers need to take care that they accurately and clearly credit the source for *every* use.

In the academic and business worlds, documentation is the method writers employ to give credit to the creators of material they use. **Documentation** involves providing essential information about the source of the material—the information that would enable readers to find the material for themselves if they so choose. It tells the reader (1) what ideas are the writer's, (2) what ideas are someone else's, (3) where the writer got the facts and other information, and (4) how reliable the sources are.

Documentation requires two elements: (1) a list of sources used in the paper and (2) citations within the text that refer to items in that list. To use documentation and avoid unintentionally plagiarizing from a source, you need to know:

- How to identify sources and information that must be documented.
- How to document sources in a Works Cited list.

- How to use material gathered from sources—in summary, para-phrase, and quotation.
- How to create in-text references.
- How to use correct grammar and punctuation to blend quotations into a paper.

IDENTIFYING SOURCES AND INFORMATION THAT NEED TO BE DOCUMENTED

Whenever you use information, facts, statistics, opinions, hypotheses, graphics, or ideas from **outside sources**—whenever you use any words or ideas that you have not thought up yourself—you need to identify the source of that material. Major outside sources are:

Virtually all the information you find in outside sources will require documentation. The one major exception is that you do not have to docu-ment common knowledge. **Common knowledge** is the widely known infor-mation about current events, famous people, geographical facts, and familiar history. Asking these questions can help you determine whether a fact is common knowledge:

- Is this information that you know, or that you would expect oth-ers to know, without having to look it up?
- Is the information readily available in many sources without doc-umentation?
- Is the information in a general dictionary?
- Is it a common saying or expression?
- Is this widely known information about authorship or creation?

If you have considered these questions and are still in doubt, the safest strategy is to provide documentation.

DOCUMENTING SOURCES IN A WORKS CITED LIST

You need to choose the documentation style that is dominant in your field or required by your instructor. Take care to use only one documentation style in any one paper and to follow its documentation formats consis-tently. Your documentation needs to be correctly placed within the body of your paper as well as in the list of sources that follows your paper, ac-cording to the documentation style you are using.

Documentation Styles and Their Manuals: MLA, APA, CMS

The most widely used style manuals are those published by the Modern Language Association (MLA), the American Psychological Association (APA), and the University of Chicago Press (CMS). Other, more special-ized style manuals are used in various fields.

- *MLA Handbook for Writers of Research Papers,* **Sixth Edition, by Joseph Gibaldi (New York: Modern Language Association, 2003).** MLA style is used by writers in the fields of English language and literature, as well as by students of foreign languages and some humanities subjects. As writers in these fields can rely on sources from a wide range of time periods, the documentation style puts more emphasis on identifying specific editions of texts.

- *Publication Manual of the American Psychological Association,* **Fifth Edition (Washington, DC: APA, 2001).** APA style is favored by researchers in the fields of psychology and other social sciences. Publication date has a prominent place in the citation formats.

- *The Chicago Manual of Style,* **Fifteenth Edition (Chicago: University of Chicago Press, 2003).** CMS style is favored by researchers in art history, history, philosophy, religion, and other humanities subjects. It is also commonly used in business. A more "traditional" style, CMS style uses raised numbers (with footnotes or end notes) instead of parenthetical references within the text.

Elements Included in a Citation

Remember that the purpose of documentation is to identify others' contributions to your paper and to enable readers to find and evaluate for themselves those source materials. In-text citations identify sources in the text of your paper and direct the reader to the correct entries in your Works Cited (MLA style) list.

Generally speaking, the Works Cited list gives information for the sources you quote, summarize, or paraphrase in your paper. If your instructor asks you to include sources you consulted but did not use in the paper, call the list "Works Consulted."

Certain elements are common to all citation formats in all styles:

- Author or other creative individual or entity
- Title of the work
- Source of the work
- Publisher or distributor
- Relevant identifying numbers or letters
- Relevant dates

Constructing a Works Cited List in MLA Style

As an accompaniment to your English text, this guide explores MLA style. MLA lists are alphabetized by authors' last names. However, an individual item can also be alphabetized by article title (when there is no author), by editor (when, for example, you quote the editor in your paper), or by the sponsoring organization (when no author is given). Computerized programs can format and alphabetize a Works Cited list in a style that you choose using the data that you provide; however, these programs will *not* research the data for you. Understanding how documentation works can help you list and make use of sources more effectively.

The requirements of your topic may make some organizational choices more efficient than others. Whatever element you use to alphabetize an entry, remember to use the same element in the in-text citations. In the first example below, the focus of the paper is on what the editor has to say. As we can see from the Works Cited entry, the writer has used only the introduction to the book. In the second example, the paper has several citations to *Collected Poems* in addition to the citation to the editor's introduction. So the writer included a single Works Cited entry for the book and specified page numbers in each in-text reference.

An MLA in-text citation by editor

Bidart asserts that though Lowell was known as a "confessional" writer, it was his "practice as an artist," rather than simply his outspokenness, that made Lowell one of the twentieth century's great poets (Bidart vii).

Works Cited Entry

Bidart, Frank. Introduction. *Collected Poems*. By Robert Lowell. Ed. Frank Bidart and David Gewanter. New York: Farrar, 2003. vii–xvi.

An MLA in-text citation by author

In his introduction to Lowell's <u>Collected Poems</u>, Frank Bidart asserts that though Lowell was known as a "confessional" writer, it was his "practice as an artist," rather than simply his outspokenness, that made Lowell one of the twentieth century's great poets (Lowell vii).

Works Cited Entry

Lowell, Robert. <u>Collected Poems</u>. Ed. Frank Bidart and David Gewanter. New York: Farrar, 2003.

MLA Style: Sample Formats

In the Works Cited list below, notice how in MLA style you spell out names in full, inverting only the first author's name. Elements are separated with a period. Observe the use of punctuation such as commas, colons, and angle brackets to separate and introduce material within elements. Also, note that MLA style uses underlining, rather than italics, for titles of books, periodicals, and so on.

Books

Chernow, Ron. <u>Alexander Hamilton</u>. New York: Penguin, 2004.

Maupassant, Guy de. "The Necklace." Trans. Marjorie Laurie. <u>An Introduc</u> <u>tion to Fiction</u>. Ed. X. J. Kennedy and Dana Gioia. 7th ed. New York: Longman, 1999. 160–66.

Woodward, Bob, and Carl Bernstein. <u>All the President's Men</u>. 1974. New York: Touchstone-Simon, 1994.

Periodicals

"Living on Borrowed Time." <u>Economist</u> 25 Feb.–3 Mar. 2006: 34–37.

"Restoring the Right to Vote." Editorial. <u>New York Times</u> 10 Jan. 2006, late ed., sec. A: 24.

Ulrich, Lars. "It's Our Property." <u>Newsweek</u> 5 June 2000: 54.

Williams, N. R., M. Davey, and K. Klock-Powell. "Rising from the Ashes: Sto ries of Recovery, Adaptation, and Resiliency in Burn Survivors." <u>So-cial Work Health Care</u> 36.4 (2003): 53–77.

Zobenica, Jon. "You Might As Well Live." Rev. of <u>A Long Way Down</u> by Nick Hornby. <u>Atlantic</u> July–Aug. 2005: 148.

Electronic Sources

Boehlert, Eric. "Artists to Napster: Drop Dead!" <u>Salon.com</u>. 24 Mar. 2000. 17 Oct. 2004 <http://dir. salon. com/ent/feature/2000/03/24/ napster_artists/index. html>.

Glanz, William. "Colleges Offer Students Music Downloads." <u>Washington Times</u>. 25 Aug. 2004. 17 Oct. 2004 <http://washingtontimes.com/ business/20040824-103654-1570r. htm>.

Reporters Without Borders. "Worldwide Press Freedom Index 2005." <u>Re porters Without Borders</u>. 2005. 28 Feb. 2006 <http://www.rsf.org/arti cle.php3?id_article=15331>.

USING MATERIAL GATHERED FROM SOURCES: SUMMARY, PARAPHRASE, QUOTATION

You can integrate material into your paper in three ways: by summarizing, by paraphrasing, and by quoting. Each summary, paraphrase, or quota-tion must be used in a way that accurately conveys the meaning of the source; that is, no material should be taken out of context in a way that distorts the sense of the original.

Summary

A **summary** is a concise restatement in your own words of the source's main ideas. Summary is used to convey the general meaning of the ideas in a source without repeating the specific details or examples that appear in the original. A summary is always much shorter than the work it treats; a sum-mary of an entire book might be just 50 to 100 words long. Some papers require particular types of summaries, such as reviews, plot summaries, annotated bibliography entries, and abstracts. Take care to give the essential information as clearly and succinctly as possible in your own words.

Write a summary when (1) the information is important enough to be included but not important enough to be treated at length; (2) the relevant material is too long to be quoted fully; or (3) you want to give the essence of the material without all the details.

Rules to Remember

1. Write a summary using your own words. If you "borrow" distinctive words or phrases from your source, you must use quotation marks within your summary to enclose that quoted material.
2. Indicate clearly where the summary begins and ends.
3. Use attribution and parenthetical reference to tell the reader where the material came from.
4. Make sure your summary is an accurate and objective restatement of the source's main ideas and that it preserves the source's tone or point of view.
5. See that the summary is clearly separated from your own ideas. One way to do this is to place the parenthetical reference immediately after the summary.

Paraphrase

A **paraphrase** is a restatement, using your own words and your own sentence structure, of specific ideas or information from a source. Paraphrase is useful when you want to capture certain ideas or details from a source but you do not need or want to quote the source's actual words. The chief purpose of a paraphrase is *to maintain your own writing style* throughout your paper. The most effective way to write a paraphrase is to read the original passage, then put the passage aside and compose your own restatement of the material in the passage. If you want to repeat particular words or phrases from the original, put them in quotation marks. A paraphrase can be about as long as the original passage.

Use a paraphrase when (1) you don't want to interrupt the flow of your writing with another person's writing; (2) you want to avoid using a long quotation or a string of quotations; or (3) you want to interpret or explain the material as you present it.

Rules to Remember

1. Use your own words and sentence structure; your paraphrase must not duplicate the source's words or phrases.
2. Use quotation marks within your paraphrase to indicate quoted material.

3. Make sure your readers know where the paraphrase begins and ends.
4. Verify that your paraphrase is an accurate and objective restatement of the source's specific ideas.
5. Conclude your paraphrase with a parenthetical reference indicating the source of the information.

Quotation

A **quotation** reproduces an actual part of a source, word for word. It can be used to support a statement or an idea, to provide an example, to advance an argument, or to add interest or color to a discussion. The length of a quotation can range from a word or phrase to several paragraphs. As a general rule, quote the fewest possible words that will get your point across to the reader. Quoting many long passages from source material can make your paper seem choppy and may give the impression that you have no thoughts of your own.

Use quotations when (1) the original writing is especially powerful, descriptive, clear, or revealing; (2) the original contains language you are analyzing or commenting on; (3) the original provides authenticity or bolsters the credibility of your paper; or (4) the original material is difficult to summarize or paraphrase accurately.

Rules to Remember

1. Copy the material from your source to your paper exactly as it appears in the original. Do not alter the spelling, capitalization, or punctuation of the original. If a quotation contains an obvious error, you may insert [*sic*], the Latin for "so" or "thus," to indicate that the error appears in the original. Use regular type and brackets: "representatives from the 51 [sic] states plus the District of Columbia."
2. Enclose short quotations (four or fewer lines of text) in quotation marks; set off longer quotations as block quotations.
3. Provide clear attribution to your source so that your readers know the origin of the quotation.
4. Immediately follow each quotation with a parenthetical reference that gives the source information required.

CREATING IN-TEXT REFERENCES

Keep in mind that documentation has two parts: (1) a list of works used (the "Works Cited" list in MLA style) and (2) in-text references for all source material. The in-text references need to supply enough information to enable a reader to find the correct source in the Works Cited list. To properly cite a source in the text of your report, you generally need to give some or all of the following information for each use of the source:

- Name of the person or organization that authored the source
- Title of the source (when there is more than one source by the same author)
- Page, paragraph, or even line number. Some sources, such as Shakespeare's plays and the Bible, are customarily referred to by their own internal numbering system. And if more than one version of a work is used, the parenthetical reference must clearly show which version is being referenced in the Works Cited list.

The information above can appear as an attribution in your text ("According to Smith . . .") or in a parenthetical reference immediately following the summary, paraphrase, or quotation. The examples that follow are in MLA style.

Using an Introductory Attribution and a Parenthetical Reference

You can use the author's name, the publication, or a generalized reference to introduce source material. Remaining identifiers (title, page number) can go in the parenthetical reference, as shown in the first sentence of the example below. When a source, such as a Web site, does not have page numbers, it may be possible to put all the information into the in-text attribution, as in the second sentence of the example below.

A parenthetical reference should follow the source material as closely as possible, usually at the end of the sentence. This two-part format—attribution plus parenthetical reference—works well for quotations and is the best practice to follow for a paraphrase because it clearly separates the source material from the writer's own ideas.

MLA in-text citation

Recently The Economist noted that since 2004, "state tax revenues have come roaring back across the country" ("Living" 34). However, McNichol and Lav, writing for the Center on Budget and Policy Priorities, claim that recent gains are not sufficient to make up for the losses suffered.

Works Cited Entries

"Living on Borrowed Time." Economist 25 Feb.–3 Mar. 2006: 34–37.
McNichol, Elizabeth C., and Iris J. Lav. "State Revenues and Services Remain below Pre-Recession Levels." Center on Budget Policy Priorities. 6 Dec. 2005. 10 Mar. 2006 <http://www.cbpp.org/12-6-05sfp2.html>.

Identifying Material by an Author of More Than One Work Used in Your Paper

When you refer to more than one work by a particular author, the attribution and the parenthetical reference combined must provide the title of the work as well as the author and the page number being cited.

> Describing the testing of the first atom bomb, Jennet Conant says, "The test had originally been scheduled for 4:00 A.M. on July 16, when most of the surrounding population would be sound asleep and there would be the least number of witnesses" (<u>109 East Palace</u> 304–05).

Placing All Identifying Information in the Parenthetical Reference

When using a quotation, you can often omit an introductory attribution; the quotation marks may be sufficient to set off the quotation from your own ideas. The page numbers in the in-text reference will guide the reader to the right source of the quotation.

> In its early days, America lacked many of the sophisticated financial mechanisms prevalent in other countries: "The creation of New York's first bank was a formative moment in the city's rise as a world financial center" (Chernow 199–200).

Placing All Identifying Information in the Attribution

In the following example, the writer combines paraphrase and quotation following an attribution that includes all necessary identifying information to locate this Web source on the Works Cited list.

> In its 2005 "Worldwide Press Freedom Index," Reporters Without Borders ranked the United States 44th among 167 countries, a decrease of more than 20 places from the previous year, "mainly because of the imprisonment of *New York Times* reporter Judith Miller and legal moves undermining the privacy of journalistic sources."

Identifying Material That the Source Is Quoting

To use material that is quoted in your cited source, add *qtd. in*, for "quoted in," to the parenthetical reference.

> The weather was worrisome, but procrastination was even more problematic. General Groves was concerned that "every hour of delay would increase the possibility of someone's attempting to sabotage the tests" (qtd. in Conant, <u>109 East Palace</u> 305).

USING CORRECT GRAMMAR AND PUNCTUATION TO BLEND QUOTATIONS INTO A PAPER

Quotations must blend seamlessly into your sentence or paragraph so that the result is neither awkward nor ungrammatical. Verb tenses, pronouns, and other parts of speech within the quotation must work grammatically with the rest of your writing, and punctuation must be handled properly.

Using a Full-Sentence Quotation of Fewer Than Four Lines

A quotation of one or more complete sentences can be enclosed in double quotation marks and introduced with a verb that takes a direct object, such as *says* or *writes*. Note that verbs in attributions are usually in the present tense and are followed by a comma. Omit the period at the end of a quoted sentence before the close-quotation marks (but keep a final question mark or an exclamation point). Then give the parenthetical reference, followed by the period.

> One commentator asks, "What accounts for the government's ineptitude in safeguarding our privacy rights?" (Spinello 9).

> "The test had originally been scheduled for 4:00 A.M. on July 16," Jennet Conant writes, "when most of the surrounding population would be sound asleep and there would be the least number of witnesses" (109 East Palace 304–05).

Introducing a Quotation with a Full Sentence

Use a colon after a full sentence that introduces a quotation.

> Spinello asks an important question: "What accounts for the government's ineptitude in safeguarding our privacy rights?" (9).

Introducing a Quotation with *That*

A single complete sentence can be introduced with a *that* construction. Do not put a comma after the word *that*.

> Chernow suggests that "the creation of New York's first bank was a formative moment in the city's rise as a world financial center" (199–200).

Quoting Part of a Sentence

When you quote only part of a sentence, make sure the quoted material blends grammatically into your own sentence.

> McNichol and Lav assert that "an array of fiscal gimmicks" helped state governments during that period.

> McNichol and Lav assert that during that period, state governments were helped by "an array of fiscal gimmicks."

Using a Quotation That Contains Another Quotation

To indicate a quotation within a quotation, replace the internal double quotation marks with single quotation marks.

> Lowell was "famous as a 'confessional' writer, but he scorned the term," according to Bidart (vii).

Adding Information to a Quotation

Any words added for clarity or any rewording for grammatical reasons should be placed within square brackets.

> Describing how the weather would affect the testing of the first atom bomb, Jennet Conant says, "The test had originally been scheduled for 4:00 A.M. on July 16, [1945,] when most of the surrounding population would be sound asleep" (<u>109 East Palace</u> 304–05).

Omitting Words from the Middle of a Sentence

Indicate an omission from the middle of a sentence with an ellipsis mark (three spaced dots).

> Describing how the weather would affect the testing of the first atom bomb, Jennet Conant says, "The test had originally been scheduled for 4:00 A.M. on July 16, when . . . there would be the least number of witnesses. But the weather was interfering with their plans, and there was talk of a postponement" (304–05).

Omitting Words at the End of a Sentence

When you omit words from the end of a sentence and another sentence follows inside your quotation, insert a period and then an ellipsis mark, with a space after the three dots.

> Describing how the weather would affect the testing of the first atom bomb, Jennet Conant says, "The test had originally been scheduled for 4:00 A.M. on July 16. . . . But the weather was interfering with their plans, and there was talk of a postponement" (304–05).

When your omission at the end of a sentence also comes at the end of the quotation and a parenthetical reference follows, add the three dots with a space before the first one but no space after the third.

> Describing how the weather would affect the testing of the first atom bomb, Jennet Conant says, "The test had originally been scheduled for 4:00 A.M. on July 16 . . ." (304–05).

When your omission at the end of the quotation is not followed by a parenthetical reference, add a period and three dots, with no space after the third dot.

> In their status report, James and Miller say, "An optimal vaccine would have the ability to elicit protective immunity that blocks infection as well as prevents pathology and interrupts transmission of parasites. . . ."

Omitting the End of One Sentence and the Beginning of the Next Sentence

When you omit words from the middle of one sentence to the middle of the next one, use an ellipsis mark but preserve any internal punctuation that makes the quotation work grammatically.

> One expert provides a caution: "Although the stereotypical profile of a hoarder is an older, single female, living alone and known as the neighborhood 'cat lady,' in reality . . . many can lead a double life with a successful professional career . . ." (Patronek).

Omitting Information from the Beginning of a Quoted Sentence

When you omit words at the beginning of a sentence you are quoting, you can integrate the quoted sentence into your text by using brackets to indicate a change in capitalization or, if your instructor permits, simply use proper capitalization without brackets.

> One biographer notes that "the founding of the Bank of New York cast him [Hamilton] in a more conciliatory role" (Chernow 199).

Using a Quotation of More Than Four Lines

Use long quotations only when they are very important for the point you are making and they cannot easily be excerpted. Set off the quotation by indenting it one inch from the left margin. Begin the quotation on a new line, and double-space it throughout. Put the parenthetical reference *after* the period at the end of the quotation. Do not enclose a block quotation in quotation marks.

> Human Rights Watch recently documented the repression of women's rights in Libya:

The government of Libya is arbitrarily detaining women and girls in "social rehabilitation" facilities, . . . locking them up indefinitely without due process. Portrayed as "protective" homes for wayward women and girls, . . . these facilities are de facto prisons . . . [where] the government routinely violates women's and girls' human rights, including those to due process, liberty, freedom of movement, personal dignity, and privacy. (Human)

IS IT PLAGIARISM? TEST YOURSELF ON IN-TEXT REFERENCES

Read the Original Source excerpt and then consider the examples that follow. Can you spot the plagiarism?

Original Source:

To begin with, language is a system of communication. I make this rather obvious point because to some people nowadays it isn't obvious: they see language as above all a means of "self-expression." Of course, language is one way that we express our personal feelings and thoughts—but so, if it comes to that, are dancing, cooking and making music. Language does much more: it enables us to convey to others what we think, feel and want. Language-as-communication is the prime means of organizing the cooperative activities that enable us to accomplish as groups things we could not possibly do as individuals. Some other species also engage in cooperative activities, but these are either quite simple (as among baboons and wolves) or exceedingly stereotyped (as among bees, ants and termites). Not surprisingly, the communicative systems used by these animals are also simple or stereotypes. Language, our uniquely flexible and intricate system of communication, makes possible our equally flexible and intricate ways of coping with the world around us: in a very real sense, it is what makes us human (Claiborne 8).

Works Cited Entry

Claiborne, Robert. <u>Our Marvelous Native Tongue: The Life and Times of the English Language</u>. New York: New York Times, 1983.

Plagiarism Example 1

One commentator makes a distinction between language used as **a means of self-expression** and **language-as-communication**. It is the latter that distinguishes human interaction from that of other species and allows humans to work cooperatively on complex tasks (8).

What's wrong?

The source's name is not given, and there are no quotation marks around words taken directly from the source (the words in **boldface** in the example).

Correction

One commentator makes a distinction between language used as "a means of self-expression" and "language-as-communication." It is the latter that distinguishes human interaction from that of other species and allows humans to work cooperatively on complex tasks (Claiborne 8).

Plagiarism Example 2

Claiborne notes that language "is the prime means of organizing the cooperative activities." Without language, we would, consequently, not have civilization.

What's wrong?

A parenthetical reference—with a page number—should immediately follow material being quoted, paraphrased, or summarized. You may omit a parenthetical reference only if the information you give in your attribution is sufficient to identify the source in your Works Cited list, and no page number is needed.

Correction

Claiborne notes that language "is the prime means of organizing the cooperative activities" (8). Without language, we would, consequently, not have civilization.

Plagiarism Example 3

Robert Claiborne postulates that language makes it possible for human beings to work cooperatively with one another to achieve results that it might be difficult for a single person working alone to achieve.

What's wrong?

No page number reference follows the summary.

Correction

Robert Claiborne postulates that language makes it possible for human beings to work cooperatively with one another to achieve results that it might be difficult for a single person working alone to achieve (8).

Plagiarism Example 4

Other animals also **engage in cooperative activities**. However, these actions are not very complex. Rather they are either the very **simple** activities of, for example, **baboons and wolves** or the **stereotyped** activities of animals such as **bees, ants and termites** (Claiborne 8).

What's wrong?

The wording and the sentence structure follow the source too closely. A paraphrase should capture a specific idea from a source but must not duplicate the writer's phrases and words (the words in **boldface** in the example).

Correction

Other animals are known to work cooperatively. However, these actions are not very complex. Rather they are either the very "simple" activities of, for example, "baboons and wolves" or the "stereotyped" activities of animals such as "bees, ants and termites" (Claiborne 8).

Evaluating Electronic Sources

Because such a wealth of readily available information exists on the Internet, it can be difficult to separate helpful, reliable sources from questionable ones. Consequently, it's important to evaluate critically every source you consult. Ask these questions to help evaluate electronic sources:

- Is the material relevant to your topic?
- Is the source a respected one?
- Is the material accurate?
- Is the information current?
- Is the material from a primary source or a secondary source?

Avoiding Plagiarism: Note-Taking Tips

The only effective approach to avoiding unintentional plagiarism is to keep in mind from the beginning of a writing project the necessity for documenting sources accurately and to follow a systematic method of note taking and writing.

- **Keep copies of your documentation information.** Writers often don't discover that they are missing documentation information until they are finalizing a paper and no longer have access to the original sources. *Tip*: Keep copies of the source material as reference. Photocopy the title and copyright pages of books you use and the pages with quotations you need. Send files of journal articles to your e-mail address or print out copies, making sure the journal title and the page numbers are evident. Highlight the relevant citation information in color. Keep these materials in a folder until you've completed your paper.

- **Quotation or paraphrase?** Writers consulting their notes are often unable to remember whether they recorded direct quotations or paraphrases. *Tip*: Assume that all the material in your notes is direct quotation unless you indicate otherwise. Double-check any paraphrases for quoted phrases and insert the necessary quotation marks. Later you can work on the paraphrase again if you know which portions are really quotations.

- **Create the Works Cited or References list *first*, before you start writing your paper.** It's easy to omit entries from a Works Cited list when, under pressure to finish, you only skim your paper looking for parenthetical references to document. *Tip*: Before you begin writing your paper, start your list as a **working bibliography**, a list of possible sources to which you add source entries as you discover them. As you finalize your list, you can delete the items you decided not to use.

LINDA STERN
PUBLISHING SCHOOL OF CONTINUING AND PROFESSIONAL STUDIES,
NEW YORK UNIVERSITY

Credits

Text Credits

Barone, Michael. "Feeling Safe Isn't Safe," from *U.S. News & World Report*, May 7, 2007. Copyright © 2007, U. S. News & World Report, L.P. Reprinted with permission.

Berry, Wendell. "In Distrust of Movements," from *Citizenship Papers*. Published by arrangement with the publisher, Counterpoint.

Brady, Judy. "I Want a Wife." *Ms. Magazine*, December 1971. Copyright © 1970 by Judy Brady. Reprinted with permission.

Branscomb, Lewis M. "Innovate or Perish." *Los Angeles Times*, January 1, 2006. Reprint by permission of Lewis M. Branscomb.

Brooks, David. "The Triumph of Hope Over Self-Interest." *The New York Times*, January 12, 2003. Copyright © 2003 by The New York Times Co. Reprinted by permission.

Brophy, Beth. "Saturday Night and You're All Alone." *U.S. News & World Report*, February 17, 1997. Copyright © 1997 U.S. News & World Report, L.P. Reprinted with permission.

Brownlee, Shannon. "We're Fatter But Not Smarter," from *The Washington Post National Weekly Edition*, January 6, 2003. Copyright © 2003 by Shannon Brownlee. Reprinted by permission of William Morris Agency, LLC on behalf of the Author.

Carson, Rachel. "The Obligation to Endure," from *Silent Spring*. Copyright © 1962 by Rachel L. Carson, renewed 1990 by Roger Christie. Reproduced by permission of Houghton Mifflin Company. All rights reserved.

CAST-A-WAY Jokes logo from http://www.cast.co.za. Reprinted by permission.

Cohen, Adam. "The McNugget of Truth in Lawsuits Against Fast Food Restaurants." *The New York Times*, February 3, 2003. Copyright © 2003 by The New York Times Co. Reprinted by permission.

Cohen, Jodi S. and Rex Huppke. "How safe are America's campuses?" from *Chicago Tribune*, April 22, 2007. Copyright © April 22, 2007, Chicago Tribune Company. All rights reserved. Used with permission.

Copeland, Libby. "Anyone Need a Friend?" from *The Washington Post*, July 18, 2004. Copyright © 2004, The Washington Post Writer's Group. Reprinted with permission.

Cummings, e.e. "in Just-." Copyright © 1923, 1951, Copyright © 1991 by the Trustees for the e.e. Cummings Trust. Copyright © 1976 by George James Firmage, from *Complete Poems: 1904–1962* by e.e. Cummings, edited by George J. Firmage. Used by permission of Liveright Publishing Corporation.

CyberDating.net home page, http://www.CyberDating.net. Reprinted by permission.

Dargis, Manohla. "Superhero Sandbagged." *The New York Times*, May 4, 2007. Copyright © 2007 by The New York Times Co. Reprinted by permission.

Davis, Bob and John Lyons. "Wealth of Nations." *Wall Street Journal* (Eastern Edition). Copyright © 2007 by Dow Jones & Company, Inc. Reproduced with permission of Dow Jones & Company, Inc. in the format Textbook via Copyright Clearance Center.

Deneau, Daniel P. "Chopin's 'The Story of an Hour.'" *The Explicator*, Summer 2003. Vol. 61, Issue 4. Reprinted with permission of the Helen Dwight Reid Educational Foundation.

Published by Heldref Publications, 1319 Eighteenth St., NW, Washington, DC 20036-1802. Copyright © 2003.

Ecenbarger, William. "We Are the World: American food, music and sports can be found in the unlikeliest places." *New Orleans Times Picayune*, May 12, 2003. Reprinted by permission of the author.

Ehrenreich, Barbara. "Ice T: The Issue is Creative Freedom." *Time*, July 20, 1992. Copyright © Time Inc. Reprinted by permission. Time is a registered trademark of Time Inc. All rights reserved.

Ehrenreich, Barbara. "From Stone Age to Phone Age," *The Progressive*, September 1999. Reprinted by permission of The Progressive.

Fleming, Robert E. "Wallace Stevens' 'The Snow Man' and Hemingway's 'A Clean Bright Place.'" *ANQ*, April 1989. Used by permission of The University Press of Kentucky.

Friedman, Thomas. "Globalization, Alive and Well." *The New York Times*, September 22, 2002. Copyright © 2002 by The New York Times Co. Reprinted by permission.

Gans, Herbert J. "Fitting the Poor Into the Economy." *Technology Review*, October 1995. Used with permission of Technology Review; permission conveyed through Copyright Clearance Center, Inc.

Gelernter, David. "What Do Murderers Deserve?" from *Commentary*, April 1998. Used with permission.

Goldstein, Warren. "Why It's OK to Rat on Other Students." *Chronicle of Higher Education*, May 4, 1997, Vol. 53, Issue 35. Reprinted by permission of the author.

Golway, Terry. "Wrongly Convicted?" *America*, November 13, 2006. Vol. 195, Issue 15. Copyright © 2006. All rights reserved. Reprinted with permission of America Press.

Goodall, Jane. "A Question of Ethics." from *Newsweek International*, May 7, 2001. Copyright © 2001 Newsweek, Inc. All rights reserved. Used by permission and protected by the Copyright Laws of the United States. The printing, copying, redistribution, or retransmission of the Material without express written permission is prohibited.

Goodman, Ellen. "The Culture of Thin Bites Fiji," from *Boston Globe*, May 27, 1999. Copyright © 1999, The Washington Post Writer's Group. Reprinted with permission.

Gopnik, Adam. "Shootings" in "Talk of the Town." *New Yorker*, April 30, 2007. Copyright © 2007 Conde Nast Publications. All rights reserved. Originally published in *The New Yorker*. Reprinted by permission.

Green, Joshua. "YouTube: Maker of Dreams, Destroyer of Lives." *The Pitt News* (University Wire), February 8, 2007. Reprinted by permission of Joshua Green.

Herbert, Bob. "No Margin for Error." *The New York Times*, June 20, 2002. Copyright © 2002 by The New York Times Co. Reprinted by permission.

Hirshman, Linda. "Off to Work She Should Go." *The New York Times*, April 25, 2007. Copyright © 2007 by The New York Times Co. Reprinted by permission.

Hochswender, Woody. "Did My Car Join Al Qaeda?" *The New York Times*, February 16, 2003. Copyright © 2003 by The New York Times Co. Reprinted by permission.

Ingrassia, Michelle. "The Body of the Beholder," from *Newsweek*, May 24, 1995. Copyright © 1995 Newsweek, Inc. All rights reserved. Used by permission and protected by the Copyright Laws of the United States. The printing, copying, redistribution, or retransmission of the Material without express written permission is prohibited.

Jones, Greg. "Rap Fans Desire a More Positive Product." *The Daily Cougar*, August 29, 2002. Reprinted by permission.

Kaminer, Wendy. "Toxic Media," from *The American Prospect*, Volume II, Number 22: October 23, 2000. The American Prospect, 2000 L Street NW, Suite 717, Washington, DC 20036. Reprinted with permission from Wendy Kaminer. All rights reserved.

Kantrowitz, Barbara. "Unmarried, With Children," from *Newsweek*, May 28, 2001. Copyright © 2001 Newsweek, Inc. All rights reserved. Used by permission and protected by the Copyright Laws of the United States. The printing, copying, redistribution, or retransmission of the Material without express written permission is prohibited.

King, Martin Luther Jr. "I Have a Dream." Reprinted by arrangement with The Heirs to the Estate of Martin Luther King Jr., c/o Writers House as agent for the proprietor New York, NY. Copyright © 1963 Martin Luther King Jr., copyright renewed 1991 Coretta Scott King.

Sullivan, Andrew. "Let Gays Marry," from *Newsweek*, June 30, 1996. Copyright © 1996 Newsweek, Inc. All rights reserved. Used by permission and protected by the Copyright Laws of the United States. The printing, copying, redistribution, or retransmission of the Material without express written permission is prohibited.

Takaki, Ronald. "The Harmful Myth of Asian Superiority." *The New York Times*, June 16, 1990. Copyright © 1990 by The New York Times Co. Reprinted by permission.

Traub, James. "All Go Down Together." *The New York Times Magazine*, March 2, 2003. Copyright © 2003 James Traub. Reprinted by permission.

Walljasper, Jay. "The Joy of Eating." *Utne Reader*, May/June 2002. Reprinted by permission of the author.

Weber, Caroline. "Tabloid Princess." *The New York Times Book Review* June 10, 2007. Copyright © 2007 by The New York Times Co. Reprinted by permission.

WeightLoss Guide web page, http://www.weightlossguide.com is reprinted by permission.

Welch, Jack and Suzy. "What's Right about Wal-Mart." *Business Week*, May 1, 2006. Copyright © 2006 The McGraw-Hill Companies. Used with permission.

Woolf, Virginia. "Professions for Women," from *Death of the Moth and Other Essays*. Copyright © 1942 by Harcourt, Inc. and renewed 1970 by Marjorie T. Parsons, Executrix, reprinted by permission of the publisher.

Yaqub, Reshma Memon. "You People Did This," from *Rolling Stone*, October 25, 2001. Copyright © Rolling Stone LLC 2001. All Rights Reserved. Reprinted by Permission.

Zinczenko, David. "Don't Blame the Eater." *The New York Times*, November 23, 2002. Copyright © 2002 by The New York Times Co. Reprinted by permission.

Photo Credits

Index